Evidence and Investigation

FROM THE CRIME SCENE TO THE COURTROOM

Kerry Watkins
Gail Anderson
Vincenzo Rondinelli

with Warren Bulmer

Toronto, Canada
2015

Emond Montgomery Publications Limited
60 Shaftesbury Avenue
Toronto ON M4T 1A3
http://www.emond.ca/highered

Printed in Canada.
Reprinted October 2016.

We acknowledge the financial support of the Government of Canada.
Nous reconnaissons l'appui financier du gouvernement du Canada.   Canada

Acquisitions editor: Bernard Sandler
Developmental editor: Sarah Gleadow
Supervising editor: Jim Lyons
Copy editor & typesetter: Nancy Ennis
Proofreaders: Paula Pike & David Handelsman
Text designer: Tara Wells
Indexer: Paula Pike
Cover image: Janaka Dharmasena

Credits

Figure 8.1: from *The science of fingerprints: Classification and uses* (1957). FBI Identification Division.

Figure 12.1: © 2003 Neil Zielinski, Certified Crime Scene Investigator, Palm Beach, Florida.

Figure 14.1: Leonard Lau, RCMP Forensic Lab Vancouver, Firearms Section.

Figure 14.2: Flickr, Jack Spades' photostream, www.flickr.com/photos/jackofspades.

Library and Archives Canada Cataloguing in Publication

Watkins, Kerry (Kerry G.)
    Evidence and investigation : from the crime scene to the courtroom /
Kerry Watkins, Gail Anderson, Enzo Rondinelli.

Includes index.
ISBN 978-1-55239-377-2

    1. Evidence, Criminal—Textbooks.   2. Criminal investigation—Textbooks.
3. Crime scene searches—Textbooks.   4. Criminal procedure—Textbooks.
I. Anderson, Gail, 1961-   II. Rondinelli, Enzo   III. Title.

HV8073.W37 2012   363.25   C2012-900797-8

Contents

Part I: The Law of Evidence

Chapter 1: Proof
Introductory Concepts

Vincenzo Rondinelli

Chapter 2: Evidence in the Courtroom

Vincenzo Rondinelli

Chapter 3: Principles of Admissibility
Relevance, Materiality, Probative Value, and Prejudicial Effect

Vincenzo Rondinelli

Chapter 4: Exclusionary Rules I
Hearsay and Character Evidence
Vincenzo Rondinelli

Chapter 5: Exclusionary Rules II
Opinion Evidence, Privilege, and Improperly Obtained Evidence
Vincenzo Rondinelli

Part II: Working with Evidence
Chapter 6: Legal Aspects of Search and Seizure
Kerry Watkins

Chapter 7: Crime Scene Investigation and Management

Kerry Watkins

Chapter 8: Pattern Evidence and Collision Reconstruction

Kerry Watkins

Chapter 9: Digital Evidence

Warren Bulmer

Chapter 10: Crime Labs and the Role of Science in Investigations

Gail Anderson

Chapter 11: Death Investigation

Kerry Watkins and Gail Anderson

Chapter 12: Forensic Biology and DNA

Gail Anderson

Chapter 13: Forensic Chemistry and Forensic Toxicology

Gail Anderson

Chapter 14: The Analysis of Tool Marks and Firearms

Gail Anderson

Chapter 15: Questioned Documents

Gail Anderson

Chapter 16: Interviewing Rules

Kerry Watkins

Chapter 17: Interviewing Techniques

Kerry Watkins

Part III: Giving Evidence

Chapter 18: The Duty of Disclosure

Kerry Watkins

Chapter 19: Testifying

Kerry Watkins

Chapter 20: Evidence, Error, and Justice

Kerry Watkins

Preface

Much of what today's novice investigator "knows" about evidence and investigation has been influenced by portrayals of investigative work in popular culture. And while such portrayals—whether of a hard-nosed detective's relentless pursuit of a killer, or a brilliant forensic scientist's ability to identify the one piece of physical evidence that will solve the case—make for great entertainment, they can be misleading. Real investigative and forensic work is almost always less dramatic and less certain and, invariably, involves much more "just plain hard work" than the remarkable, hour-long investigations portrayed on prime-time television.

That said, those who work in the investigative and forensic fields do on occasion experience the exhilaration of figuring out "who done it"—alongside the frustration of spending weeks, months, or even years on other investigations that bear little or no fruit. This text is intended to serve both as a practical guide for those individuals who are just entering the challenging area of investigative work and as a reference for more experienced professionals who wish to refresh their understanding of basic principles or acquaint themselves with some of the new developments in this field.

In *Evidence and Investigation: From the Crime Scene to the Courtroom*, a unique team of authors—consisting of a police investigator, a criminal defence lawyer, and a forensic scientist, all with many years' experience in their respective fields—describe the "real world" of evidence and investigation, explaining the factors that make evidence valuable in the courtroom and pointing to the common pitfalls that can weaken an otherwise promising investigation.

The book is divided into three parts. Part I provides a working knowledge of the law of evidence, explaining the basics of a criminal trial, the types of evidence, and the rules governing admissibility. Part II includes a description of the current law governing search and seizure activities and the requirements for Charter-compliant searches. The importance of continuity and the collection of evidence free of contamination is emphasized, as is the importance of accurate record-keeping. The authors outline the most current information on digital evidence, DNA evidence, crime labs, death investigations, and the forensic sciences. The rules and techniques that apply to conducting interviews with both witnesses and suspects are clearly set out. Part III returns to the courtroom, focusing first on the legal duty of disclosure and the associated obligations on police, and then turning to a detailed discussion of testifying, with a particular focus on cross-examination—an often-gruelling and little-understood stage of a trial for police officers. A wealth of advice is provided on how to function professionally in the witness box and give evidence fully, fairly, and firmly. The text concludes with an exploration of the intimate connection between evidence, error, and justice, and by offering suggested ways in which investigators and other professionals can reduce both the risk of error and the effect of errors that *do* happen.

Kerry Watkins, Gail Anderson,
and Vincenzo Rondinelli
May 2012

Acknowledgments

Although a text is, nominally, the work of the authors, in reality it is the product of those many individuals who had a hand in its preparation. In this regard, recognition is due to both the subject matter experts and editorial staff who contributed their experience and expertise to this project.

Evidence and Investigation: From the Crime Scene to the Courtroom had its genesis in the 1998 Emond Montgomery text *Principles of Evidence for Policing*, written by James Euale, Nora Rock, Dianne Martin, and Jillan Sadek. Many of their contributions are evident in this text—in particular, the contributions of the late Dianne Martin.

Sergeant Steve O'Donovan provided valuable input on the subject of collision investigation and reconstruction. Detective Constable Warren Bulmer—a world-recognized expert in the field of digital evidence and investigation—made a substantial contribution to the text in the form of Chapter 9. Breana Vandebeek undertook legal research with respect to the case law in select chapters, and Pete Thompson (Algonquin College) provided many helpful suggestions in the early stages of this project. Tanya Dare, Reporting Scientist and Local CODIS Administrator, Biology Section, RCMP Forensic Science and Identification Services, Vancouver, provided valuable advice on DNA analysis.

Thanks are also due to the editorial staff at Emond Montgomery Publications, especially Sarah Gleadow, who developed the manuscript, and Nancy Ennis, who copy-edited it. Their eye for detail, organizational ability, and insistence on both clarity and relevance added immeasurably to the readability and value of the text. Thanks are also due to Paula Pike and David Handelsman, who proofread the manuscript.

About the Authors

Kerry G. Watkins holds a bachelor's and a master's degree in Criminology. He has worked for one of Canada's largest law enforcement agencies for more than two decades, investigating crimes from fraud to homicide in a number of specialized units, and has served as a police witness in numerous criminal trials. He has received awards for investigative excellence and holds an Exemplary Service Medal for his continuous public service. Kerry currently works in the area of police education and training. In addition to this text, and *Interviewing and Investigation*, 2nd ed., Kerry has published on investigative topics in *Blue Line Magazine*, *Forensic Evidence in Canada*, 2nd ed., and the *Canadian Journal of Police & Security Services*.

Dr. Gail S. Anderson, BSc Hons. (University of Manchester), MPM, PhD (Simon Fraser University), is a professor and associate director at Simon Fraser University's School of Criminology, and a Board Certified Forensic Entomologist. She has been actively involved in case analyses in homicide, wildlife, and SPCA cases since 1988. She is an instructor at the Canadian Police College, a Fellow of the American Academy of Forensic Sciences and the Canadian Society of Forensic Science, as well as a member of the Canadian Identification Society and the International Association for Identification. Her recognitions include the Derome Award, a Burnaby Mountain Professorship, and a Woman of Distinction Award.

Vincenzo Rondinelli, LLB, LLM (Osgoode Hall Law School), is a criminal defence lawyer in Toronto. He has appeared at all levels of the courts, including the Supreme Court of Canada, and argues appeals regularly before the Ontario Court of Appeal. He joined the adjunct faculty at Osgoode Hall Law School in 2003 and is currently co-director of the Criminal Intensive Program and co-instructor in the Forensic Science & the Law course. He is certified by the Law Society of Upper Canada as a Specialist in Criminal Law.

Warren Bulmer has been a detective constable in the criminal investigations field of one of Canada's largest police services for over two decades. In addition to having been a qualified Computer Forensic Examiner, he has been a member of the Interpol Image Experts Group and the Ontario Attorney General's Victim Identification Task Force. Detective Constable Bulmer has testified in court as an expert in various capacities relating to digital evidence and is actively involved in teaching students and justice professionals about computer-facilitated crime.

PART I

The Law of Evidence

Proof

Introductory Concepts

1

LEARNING OUTCOMES

After completing this chapter, you should be able to:

- Explain the purpose of evidence law.

- Define evidence and identify the sources of evidence law.

- List three types of evidence and distinguish between direct and circumstantial evidence.

- Explain the term "admissibility" and identify reasons why evidence may be inadmissible.

- Explain the roles of the judge, jury, counsel, and witnesses in a criminal trial with respect to evidence.

- Understand the Crown's duty of disclosure.

- Understand the concepts of burden of proof and standard of proof.

INTRODUCTION

trier of fact
the decision-maker(s) charged with determining whether the necessary facts of a case have been proved— the jury in a jury trial, or the judge in a trial by judge alone

In a criminal trial, the critical issue is whether an accused is guilty or not guilty. The rules of evidence were developed to ensure that an accused person has a fair trial and that the **trier of fact** is provided with the most reliable evidence available. The objective of such strict rules is to avoid convicting an innocent person. In trying to prevent such a miscarriage of justice, the rules of evidence seek to control:

1. *what* information the judge or jury will have access to;
2. *how* that information will be presented; and
3. *the use* that can be made of that information.

According to s. 11(d) of the *Canadian Charter of Rights and Freedoms*, anyone charged with an offence has the right "to be presumed innocent until proven guilty according to law in a fair and public hearing by an independent and impartial tribunal." In *R. v. Oakes* (1986, para. 29), the Supreme Court of Canada explained how the presumption of innocence is integral to the protection of life, liberty, and security of the person under s. 7:

> An individual charged with a criminal offence faces grave social and personal consequences, including potential loss of physical liberty, subjection to social stigma and ostracism from the community, as well as other social, psychological and economic harms. In light of the gravity of these consequences, the presumption of innocence is crucial. It ensures that until the State proves an accused's guilt beyond all reasonable doubt, he or she is innocent. This is essential in a society committed to fairness and social justice.

EVIDENCE DEFINED

evidence
any information or physical material relied on in legal proceedings to prove or disprove a fact or legal argument

The term **evidence** is a synonym for "proof" and has come to describe the information presented before the court by the prosecution and the defence in their efforts to prove the facts that will establish the actions and intentions (or lack of either) necessary to prove (or defend against) the offences charged.

In legal cases, "facts" are what a court has decided are the facts, on the basis of the evidence presented. Nothing is a "fact" until a judge or jury has decided that it is. Because our system is adversarial, with both sides presenting evidence, a court will often hear more than one version of an event or interpretation of information.

"THE GOLDEN THREAD"

Our entire criminal justice system is founded on the belief that a person is *innocent until proven guilty.* Implied in this belief is the prosecution's responsibility for proving the accused's guilt. As the House of Lords in the United Kingdom observed in the often-quoted case of *Woolmington v. Director of Public Prosecutions* (1935, p. 481): "Throughout the web of English Criminal Law one golden thread is always to be seen, that is the duty of the prosecution to prove the prisoner's guilt." The same holds true in Canada. The burden of proof *always* lies with the prosecution. The accused is not even required to testify or present evidence, but can sit silently by, hoping that the prosecution will fail to prove its case.

The judge or jury decides which witnesses to believe, and which version or interpretation is preferable.

Evidence in Criminal Investigations

It is worth noting that lawyers and criminal investigators may define "evidence" in different ways. A lawyer may define it as we have above—namely, as anything that has been properly introduced into a legal proceeding, which helps to either prove or disprove a fact in issue. A criminal investigator, on the other hand, may define evidence as anything that can provide information about a case under investigation. For the purposes of this text, both of these definitions are important. Evidence may refer to anything that provides investigators with information on the basis of which they can formulate a tentative idea about what happened (an investigative hypothesis). This idea will help investigators determine what direction their investigation should take, who is likely responsible for the alleged offence, whether or not they should lay a criminal charge, and if so which one(s). Evidence is also the thing that will determine which issue(s) a Crown attorney will be able to successfully prove in court.

TYPES OF EVIDENCE

Evidence may take the following forms:

1. **Oral evidence**, sometimes called ***viva voce*** evidence, is spoken evidence that is given by witnesses when they testify under oath in a courtroom.

2. **Physical evidence** (usually called "real evidence") becomes an "exhibit" once it forms part of the trial record. Examples include an alleged murder weapon, DNA, photographs of a crime scene, and a sample of an illicit substance recovered from a suspect. The collection and preservation of physical evidence is primarily the responsibility of specially trained police officers, while its analysis is often carried out by forensic scientists in crime labs.

3. **Documentary evidence** is evidence contained in written documents such as business or medical records, transcripts of recorded conversations, and affidavits (written records of witness evidence). Like real evidence, it becomes an exhibit or exhibits when introduced in court.

These types of evidence are discussed in more detail in Chapter 2.
Furthermore, evidence is classified as either:

- **direct evidence**, which refers to evidence in the form of testimony from witnesses as to what they personally saw or heard—for example, a witness testifying that he saw that it was raining outside; or

- **circumstantial evidence**, which refers to indirect evidence that could be used to draw an inference (or "logical conclusion")—for example, a witness's testimony that she saw Mr. X enter the restaurant holding a soaking wet umbrella would be circumstantial evidence that it was raining outside.

It is important to note that the law treats both direct and circumstantial evidence equally. One is not "better" than the other. A prosecution typically may involve both types of evidence, but it is able to also proceed entirely on either direct or circumstantial evidence.

oral (*viva voce*) evidence
spoken (verbal) evidence of a witness as given under oath or affirmation in a legal proceeding

physical evidence
evidence that takes the form of actual objects, as opposed to testimony; includes real, demonstrative, and view evidence

documentary evidence
a class of physical/real evidence that consists of documents of any kind, handwritten or mechanically produced

direct evidence
evidence that proves an important fact without the need to speculate

circumstantial evidence
evidence that logically supports a fact, but that is at least partly dependent on speculation

ADMISSIBILITY

The overarching rule of evidence law is that any evidence that is relevant to a material issue should be admitted unless there is a rule of law or policy that requires its exclusion. **Admissibility** is governed by the law of evidence and determined by the trial judge. Among the reasons the judge may have for declining to admit a piece of evidence are the following:

admissibility
process governing which materials (testimony, documents, and physical objects) offered as proof in a legal proceeding can be considered evidence by the trier of fact

1. *Irrelevance.* The evidence is irrelevant or immaterial to the issues to be decided—it does not relate to or does not help to prove any fact that needs to be proved.

2. *Unreliability.* The evidence, by its nature, may be unreliable—for example, it may be **hearsay** (second-hand) evidence. The court will admit hearsay evidence only when the judge is convinced that in the circumstances it is necessary and reliable.

hearsay
evidence that is indirect because it is given by a witness who has heard it from another source; second-hand evidence

3. *Prejudice.* The *prejudicial* quality of the evidence (its tendency to influence decision-makers in a way that is unfair or undeserved) outweighs its *probative value* (its tendency to prove or disprove an important fact).

4. *Unfairness.* The evidence was obtained in a way that was unfair to the **accused** or violated his or her rights under the *Canadian Charter of Rights and Freedoms* or other legislation (which is why extreme care is required in collecting evidence and handling suspects and witnesses).

accused
a suspect who has been charged with a crime

5. *Procedural unfairness.* Because of procedural rules or for other reasons, admitting the evidence would be unfair to the defence or would waste time or confuse the issues. For example, if the prosecution holds back some evidence and attempts to call it only after the defence has finished calling its evidence, this is called "splitting the case" and is not permitted.

SOURCES OF THE LAW OF EVIDENCE

The following three sources provide the rules and principles that govern the admissibility of materials offered as proof in a legal proceeding:

1. *Statutes.* Many rules of evidence are found in statutes such as the *Canada Evidence Act* and the *Criminal Code* of Canada.

2. *The common law.* Also known as "case law" or "precedent," common-law rules of evidence are developed by judges through their decisions.

3. *Canadian Charter of Rights and Freedoms.* Some of the rules of evidence are constitutionally enshrined. For example, s. 11(c) of the Charter provides that any person charged with an offence has the right not to be forced to be a witness in his or her own criminal prosecution.

While the overarching aim of the rules of evidence is to avoid wrongful convictions, the rules also seek to protect the interests of witnesses and complainants. For example, the *Criminal Code* places restrictions on the access to and use of private medical and therapeutic records of witnesses and complainants.

THE PLAYERS IN A CRIMINAL TRIAL

The Judge

The task of deciding whether a piece of evidence will be admitted in court belongs primarily to the judge, who is guided by the rules of evidence. Determining the admissibility of evidence is one of the most important parts of the judge's job, especially when there is a jury, because improper decisions about admissibility can lead to a verdict being overturned (changed) if the losing side successfully appeals. The rules of evidence provide the judge with the flexibility to determine the admissibility of evidence on a case-by-case basis.

In a trial by judge alone, the judge is also the trier of fact. He or she is responsible for applying the law; deciding whether the facts meet the legal requirements (by applying the standard of proof, discussed below); and issuing a verdict based on the evidence.

When there is a jury, the judge is responsible for **charging the jury**. In a statement to the jury at the end of the trial, the judge reviews the legal requirements of the case (as he or she has interpreted them), explains the relevant rules of evidence and the standard of proof, and describes the decision or decisions that the jury must make to come to its verdict.

charging the jury
the judge's instructions to the jury, usually at the end of a trial, in preparation for the jury's deliberations

The Jury

In a trial by judge and jury, the jurors are the triers of fact. They issue a verdict on the basis of the evidence, with help from the judge's charge and his or her instructions throughout the trial. There is never a jury without a judge, because the judge is still needed to interpret the legal requirements.

Counsel

Counsel (lawyers) for the prosecution and for the defence also have a role to play in enforcing the rules of evidence. As the evidence is being presented in court, each lawyer listens carefully to ensure that the judge does not admit any evidence that would be damaging to the lawyer's case and that might be inadmissible. When the other side tries to introduce such evidence and the judge does not intervene to exclude it, counsel will often argue for exclusion by making an **objection**. It is then up to the judge to consider whether the objection is valid, often after hearing **submissions** from the other side.

If the objection is valid, the judge will say that it is *sustained*; if it is invalid, the judge will say that it is *overruled*. Because evidence is not a science and the rules are open to interpretation, knowing when to object and what objections to make are important skills that lawyers develop through experience.

objection
a formal verbal declaration made in a courtroom for the purpose of notifying the judge and opposing counsel of counsel's belief that improper evidence is being adduced (such as hearsay) that should be excluded or that an improper procedure is being employed (such as leading the witness) that should be corrected

submissions
arguments made in court by the parties, either orally or in writing

Witnesses

Witnesses are people who testify in court in response to questions from counsel. They are called to give evidence because they have information about the case or can provide an expert opinion on an issue. Their testimony becomes part of the

witness
in a court case, any person who is called before the court to give evidence under oath or affirmation

trial record
the official written transcript
of a legal proceeding

trial record (the written record of the court proceedings). In some cases, the accused gives evidence, and thus becomes a witness for the defence.

THE DUTY OF DISCLOSURE

According to the Supreme Court in *R. v. Stinchcombe* (1991, p. 2, para. 2):

> The fruits of the investigation which are in its possession are not the property of the Crown for use in securing a conviction but the property of the public to be used to ensure that justice is done.

disclosure
duty requiring the Crown to provide the accused with access to all information in its possession or control that relates to the investigation, provided that there are no legal restrictions on doing so

Along with the presumption of innocence and the requirement for proof beyond a reasonable doubt (discussed below), the right of an accused to **disclosure** is one of the primary safeguards built into the criminal justice system to protect against wrongful convictions. This obligation, described above and guaranteed by s. 7 of the Charter, requires the Crown to provide the accused with access to all information in its possession or control that relates to the investigation, provided that there are no legal restrictions on doing so.

The Crown's duty to disclose the "fruits of the investigation" to the accused places a corollary duty on the police to disclose all material pertaining to its investigation of the accused to the Crown, so that the Crown may in turn disclose it to the accused.

Disclosure is discussed in more detail in Chapter 19, Testifying.

The Duty to Collect and Preserve Evidence

Two additional duties flow from the Crown's duty of disclosure:

1. the duty of police to collect evidence, and
2. the duty of police to preserve evidence.

Where the police have reasonable grounds to believe that a significant offence has been committed, they have an obligation to collect evidence in order to further the investigation of that offence (*R. v. Beaudry*, 2007). Both the police and the Crown must consider whether a particular piece of evidence could be relevant to either the Crown or the defence in a criminal trial. If the possibility exists, the police must take steps to preserve the evidence against loss or destruction. If evidence is lost or destroyed and a court finds that the cause was "unacceptable negligence"—that is, if the appropriate care was not taken to preserve the evidence—then the accused's s. 7 rights will be found to have been breached and the court will order a remedy, such as a new trial or a stay of proceedings.

Collecting and preserving evidence is discussed in detail in Chapter 7, Crime Scene Investigation and Management.

PROVING THE OFFENCE

Evidence law is the law of proof. Once the police charge a suspect with a particular offence (or offences), it is up to the prosecution (the Crown) to *prove* the offence and answer any defences, so that the judge or jury is persuaded of the accused's guilt. The accused can be convicted and sentenced only if the prosecution can successfully prove the offence in court. The aim of this requirement is to avoid convictions of innocent persons.

Elements of the Offence

If an individual is to be found guilty of committing a crime, the prosecutor must prove two things beyond a reasonable doubt:

1. The individual *committed* the prohibited act.
2. The individual *intended* to commit the act.

Together, the acts and intent are known as the **essential elements** of an offence. The prosecution must prove *both* act and intent beyond a reasonable doubt, or the accused must be found not guilty (acquitted).

essential elements
the particular acts and intentions required to prove a specified offence

Acts (Actus Reus)

To prove an offence, the prosecution is required to prove certain acts or actions on which the offence is based. Such action or conduct is commonly known by the Latin term *actus reus*. Many of these acts are described in the wording of the statute that creates the offence. For example, the *Criminal Code* describes the offence of robbery as follows:

Robbery

343. Every one commits robbery who

(a) steals, and for the purpose of extorting whatever is stolen or to prevent or overcome resistance to the stealing, uses violence or threats of violence to a person or property;

(b) steals from any person and, at the time he steals or immediately before or immediately thereafter, wounds, beats, strikes or uses any personal violence to that person;

(c) assaults any person with intent to steal from him; or

(d) steals from any person while armed with an offensive weapon or imitation thereof.

In reading this description of robbery, it becomes clear that there are four ways to commit the offence. For each, it is possible to list the acts that the prosecution will have to prove.

SITUATION (A)

1. Someone *has stolen* something, and
2. in stealing, that person *has used violence* or threats of violence to a person or property.

SITUATION (B)

1. Someone *has stolen* something from another person, and
2. at or very near the time of stealing, the accused *has used "any personal violence"* to the victim.

SITUATION (C)

1. Someone *has assaulted* another person.

    (Note: In this situation, it is not necessary to prove that anything has actually been stolen. The only *act* that needs to be proved is an assault, but the assault must be accompanied by an intent to steal. Intent is discussed below.)

SITUATION (D)

1. Someone *has stolen* something from another person, and
2. while stealing, the alleged robber *was armed* with an offensive weapon or an imitation of one.

Although most of the key acts that the prosecution will need to prove can be found in the words describing the offence, there may be others that cannot. A common and important example is the identity of the accused.

Intent (Mens Rea)

In addition to proving action or conduct, all true crimes require the prosecution to prove certain things about the accused's state of mind at the time of the offence. This aspect of the offence is often referred to as **intent** or *mens rea*. Thus, in the robbery example above, situation (c) depends on proof of a particular intent:

intent
also called *mens rea*; the mental element of an offence that must be proved to secure a conviction

> 343. Every one commits robbery who ...
>   (c) assaults any person with intent to steal from him.

To prove robbery committed in this way, the Crown must prove

1. that the accused *has committed an assault* (an action), and
2. that the accused committed the assault *with intent to steal* from the victim (an intent).

However, in all four robbery situations, the prosecution has to prove that the conduct was intentional (that the accused had a "general" intent, or *mens rea*).

Standard of Proof

The term "standard of proof" refers to the degree to which the judge or jury must be persuaded. In everyday matters we make decisions on the basis of varying degrees of certainty, depending on how important the question is. For example, how certain do you have to be that it will rain before you decide to take an umbrella with you when you go out? What "evidence" persuades you?

standard of proof
the degree of certainty of the truth of a fact required before that fact can be relied on in support of a particular verdict or legal decision

Legal questions are similar. The **standard of proof** is the answer to the question, How convinced does the law require me (or the trier of fact) to be?

There are two recognized standards of proof:

1. proof on a balance of probabilities, and
2. proof beyond a reasonable doubt.

Balance of Probabilities

Proof on a balance of probabilities, sometimes called the civil standard of proof, requires that the evidence be sufficient to convince the trier of fact that the fact at issue is *more likely than not* to be true. In other words, if, after hearing evidence in support of a fact, the jury is 51 percent convinced that the fact is true, the fact has been proved on a balance of probabilities.

In a civil (non-criminal) case, the required standard of proof for the *whole case* is the balance of probabilities. If the plaintiff (the party who started the lawsuit) can prove his or her side of the story (the claim) on a balance of probabilities, he or she wins the case.

proof on a balance of probabilities
proof that leaves the trier of fact at least 51 percent certain of the truth of a fact

Beyond a Reasonable Doubt

Proof beyond a reasonable doubt is the required standard of proof for criminal offences. For an accused to be convicted, the trier of fact must be convinced of his or her guilt beyond a reasonable doubt. This is a much more stringent standard than the one required in civil cases. The reason for this is obvious—a criminal conviction can carry serious penalties (such as incarceration), and the justice system recognizes the need to be very certain of an accused's guilt before subjecting him or her to a deprivation of liberty or other serious sanctions.

proof beyond a reasonable doubt
proof that is convincing and allows a reasonable person to be "sure" that the accused is guilty

WHAT DOES "BEYOND A REASONABLE DOUBT" MEAN?

In *R. v. Lifchus* (1997, para. 39), the Supreme Court of Canada suggested that trial judges use the following explanation of "proof beyond a reasonable doubt" when charging a jury:

> The accused enters these proceedings presumed to be innocent. That presumption of innocence remains throughout the case until such time as the Crown has on the evidence put before you satisfied you beyond a reasonable doubt that the accused is guilty.
>
> What does the expression "beyond a reasonable doubt" mean?
>
> The term "beyond a reasonable doubt" has been used for a very long time and is a part of our history and traditions of justice. It is so engrained in our criminal law that some think it needs no explanation, yet something must be said regarding its meaning.
>
> A reasonable doubt is not an imaginary or frivolous doubt. It must not be based upon sympathy or prejudice. Rather, it is based on reason and common sense. It is logically derived from the evidence or absence of evidence.
>
> Even if you believe the accused is probably guilty or likely guilty, that is not sufficient. In those circumstances you must give the benefit of the doubt to the accused and acquit because the Crown has failed to satisfy you of the guilt of the accused beyond a reasonable doubt.
>
> On the other hand you must remember that it is virtually impossible to prove anything to an absolute certainty and the Crown is not required to do so. Such a standard of proof is impossibly high.
>
> In short if, based upon the evidence before the court, you are sure that the accused committed the offence you should convict since this demonstrates that you are satisfied of his guilt beyond a reasonable doubt.

Burden of Proof

The term **burden of proof** is used to identify which person or party is responsible for proving a particular fact, issue, or case. If a party is responsible for proving something, he or she is said to have the burden of proof (or "onus" of proof). In our adversarial system, the side that makes the allegation (or claim or accusation) has to prove it, while the other side always has the right to answer the accusation, in open court, in front of a fair and impartial judge or judge and jury.

RAISING A DEFENCE

Although an accused has the right *not* to present any evidence in his or her defence, defending the charge may involve asking questions or calling witnesses to raise a reasonable doubt on a material point. Less often, the accused will actually have to prove the defence. Take, for example, an accused charged with murder. The prosecution has the burden of proving that he or she (1) *caused* the death of a human being, and (2) according to the *Criminal Code, meant* to do it:

Murder

229. Culpable homicide is murder
  (a) where the person who causes the death of a human being
    (i) means to cause his death.

The accused can raise a doubt by raising a defence or by calling evidence that will raise a doubt as to any of the elements of the offence. If the defence is that the accused caused the death, but that he or she acted in self-defence, then to be acquitted the accused needs only to raise a reasonable doubt that he or she acted in self-defence. Once the accused has met this burden, the Crown must disprove the excuse or justification beyond a reasonable doubt.

Reverse Onus

While the prosecution must prove the elements of the offence, the *Criminal Code* includes various sections that shift the burden to the defence to disprove a presumption (also known as **reverse onus clauses**). For example:

Possession, etc. of Counterfeit Money

450. Every one who, without lawful justification or excuse, the proof of which lies on him ...
  (b) has in his custody or possession ...
counterfeit money is guilty of an indictable offence and liable to imprisonment for a term not exceeding fourteen years.

Where the offence of possession of counterfeit money is concerned, once the prosecution has proved the fact of possession—that the accused has the money in his or her custody or possession—the offence is successfully proved, unless the accused can prove that he or she had lawful justification or excuse ("the proof ... lies on him"). In general, it is easier *not* to have the burden of proof (and the responsibility for gathering and presenting evidence).

KEY TERMS

accused

admissibility

burden of proof

charging the jury

circumstantial evidence

direct evidence

documentary evidence

essential elements

evidence

hearsay

intent

objection

oral (*viva voce*) evidence

physical evidence

proof beyond a reasonable doubt

proof on a balance of probabilities

reverse onus clause

standard of proof

submissions

trial record

trier of fact

witness

REVIEW QUESTIONS

True or False?

_____ 1. A criminal case can be tried by a judge, a judge and jury, or a jury alone.

_____ 2. "Evidence" can include witness testimony, physical objects, and documents.

_____ 3. The Crown ultimately decides which evidence is admissible in court.

_____ 4. Direct evidence is stronger than circumstantial evidence.

_____ 5. It is up to the accused person to prove that he or she did not commit the offence charged.

_____ 6. Evidence that is irrelevant is not admissible in court.

_____ 7. A criminal offence must be proved beyond a reasonable doubt before a sentence can be imposed.

_____ 8. The *Canada Evidence Act* contains all of the rules of evidence to be followed in a criminal trial.

_____ 9. The standard of proof describes which side is responsible for proving that the offence occurred.

_____ 10. Evidence becomes "fact" only after a trier of fact makes a finding of fact.

Multiple Choice

1. An accused is said to be innocent until proven guilty because
   a. the prosecution has the burden of proof.
   b. the accused cannot be convicted without proof.
   c. the standard of proof must be met before a conviction can be entered.
   d. all of the above.

2. In defending a criminal charge, the accused must
   a. testify on his or her own behalf.
   b. call witnesses.
   c. tender documentary evidence.
   d. none of the above.

3. The following is *not* a reason for excluding evidence:
   a. the evidence is immaterial.
   b. the evidence might cause undue prejudice.
   c. the evidence is circumstantial evidence.
   d. the evidence was collected in violation of the accused's constitutional rights.

4. The criminal standard of proof is "beyond a reasonable doubt" because
   a. the justice system must be very certain of guilt before subjecting an accused to criminal sanctions.
   b. if there is enough reason to arrest an accused, there can be little doubt of the accused's guilt.
   c. before convicting, the trier of fact must be at least 51 percent certain that the accused committed the offence.
   d. in a criminal trial, no amount of doubt is unreasonable.

5. An accused's right to disclosure does not extend to the following:
   a. material in the police possession pertaining to its investigation of the accused.
   b. material in the Crown's possession that has potential relevance to the prosecution of the accused.
   c. material in the Crown's possession that is clearly irrelevant to the prosecution of the accused.
   d. all of the above.

6. Which of the following sources governs the rules of evidence at a trial?
   a. the *Criminal Code*.
   b. judgments from the Supreme Court of Canada.
   c. judgments from the Ontario Court of Appeal.
   d. all of the above.

Short Answer

1. After reading the following section of the *Criminal Code*, list the acts or intentions that the prosecution may have to prove to get a conviction.

   Cheating at Play

   209. Every one who, with intent to defraud any person, cheats while playing a game or in holding the stakes for a game or in betting is guilty of an indictable offence and liable to imprisonment for a term not exceeding two years.

2. List three reasons a judge might have for excluding a piece of evidence sought to be presented in court.

3. Describe the difference between *actus reus* and *mens rea*.

4. Describe a situation in which the burden of proof lies with the defence.

5. Compare the civil "balance of probabilities" and criminal "beyond a reasonable doubt" standards of proof.

Evidence in the Courtroom

2

LEARNING OUTCOMES

After completing this chapter, you should be able to:

- Understand the rules governing who can testify in a criminal trial.

- Describe the order and style of questioning witnesses.

- Understand the doctrines of present memory refreshed and past recollection recorded.

- Explain prior consistent statements and prior inconsistent statements, and the rules that apply to them in a trial.

- Differentiate between real, demonstrative, and view evidence.

- Explain the process by which real evidence is admitted into court.

- Explain the best evidence rule.

INTRODUCTION

exhibit
any piece of evidence
(physical or documentary)
other than oral testimony
that is "entered" in
the trial record

In reaching a verdict in a criminal trial, the trier of fact will consider both the testimony of witnesses and any **exhibits** that were filed at trial. This chapter discusses the three types of evidence—oral, physical/real, and documentary—and the various statutory and common-law rules governing their use in a trial.

ORAL EVIDENCE

In court, witnesses are called by the Crown or the defence to give evidence that will support the story of the side that calls them. Almost anyone can be a witness: the accused, the victim (if there is one), members of the public (often called "lay witnesses"), police officers, and experts. There are rules, however, governing who can testify, what they can testify about, and when they can testify. At the most basic level, witnesses must be both competent and compellable.

Rules Governing Who Can Testify

Competence

competence
being legally permitted
to testify (based on the
absence of factors such
as being a "spouse" or
mental handicap)

For a potential witness to give evidence, he or she must be **competent** to testify. To be competent means that the witness is legally permitted to testify, which in turn means that the witness has four basic capacities:

1. The capacity to perceive (the ability to observe and interpret the event in question).
2. The capacity to remember.
3. The capacity to communicate (the ability to tell the court what he or she saw, heard, or did).
4. The capacity to be sincere (the understanding that he or she has an obligation to tell the truth and that legal consequences may result from lying on the stand).

ADULT WITNESSES

Witnesses over the age of 14 are presumed competent; questions regarding competence usually arise with individuals who have developmental or intellectual disabilities. Section 16(1) of the *Canada Evidence Act* prescribes that where a witness's mental capacity is challenged and the witness is over the age of 14, the court must conduct an inquiry into the witness's competence to testify. This means that the court must determine whether:

1. The witness understands the nature of the oath or solemn affirmation required of him or her (see the discussion below, under "The Mechanics of Testifying").
2. The witness is able to communicate his or her evidence.

Generally speaking, competence is a fairly easy test to pass. A mental disorder, for example, in and of itself will not disqualify a witness from testifying. Even a disposition to lie does not disqualify a witness. Although it may affect the credibility of the witness, it does not affect the assessment of competence.

CHILD WITNESSES

Witnesses under age 14 also are presumed to be competent to testify. If there is a question regarding a child witness's capacity to testify, s. 16.1(5) of the *Canada Evidence Act* prescribes that the court must conduct an inquiry "to determine whether they are able to understand and respond to questions." Child witnesses are not required to take an oath or solemn affirmation; rather, they are permitted to testify on promising to tell the truth.

Unfortunately, young children are most often asked to be witnesses in cases involving abuse, and the accused is often a parent or other adult who is close to them. This can be traumatic for the child, which is why privacy screens and closed-circuit televisions have been permitted in some instances. Sometimes an electronic recording of an interview is permitted to be entered into evidence, so that the child does not have to experience the stress and trauma associated with testifying in court. However, the child witness can still be cross-examined in court on the statement.

COMPETENCE OF SPOUSES

Under s. 4 of the *Canada Evidence Act*, in most circumstances spouses are *not* competent witnesses for the prosecution. This means that even a husband or wife who wishes to testify against a spouse may not do so. (However, if called on by the defence, a husband or wife may testify for the defence.) Spousal privilege is founded on the idea of maintaining marital harmony and protecting the legal construct of marriage. It applies only to legally married husbands and wives. It does not apply to common-law, same-sex, irreconcilably separated, or divorced spouses.

The circumstances under which spouses *may* be compelled to testify are set out in ss. 4(2), 4(3), and 4(5) of the *Canada Evidence Act*. Spousal privilege is discussed further in Chapter 5.

Compellability

In order to testify, witnesses who are found to be competent must also be found **compellable**. This means that they can be legally forced to testify through a **subpoena**. In criminal cases, nearly everyone is a compellable witness. Again, however, there are exceptions:

1. As stated, a person cannot be compelled to testify against his or her spouse, except in the circumstances noted above.

2. Section 11(c) of the *Canadian Charter of Rights and Freedoms* states that the accused is *not* compellable, providing protection against self-incrimination:

    > 11(c) Any person charged with an offence has the right not to be compelled to be a witness in proceedings against that person in respect of the offence.

3. Co-accused charged on the same information cannot be compelled to testify against each other. Because they are "joined" as parties, and therefore tried together, compelling them to testify against each other would amount to forcing them to incriminate themselves, which would violate s. 11(c) of the Charter. The exception does not apply to co-accused charged on separate informations.

compellability
being without legal excuse (such as status as the accused's spouse) for not testifying

subpoena
a written notice, usually hand-delivered, summoning a named person to court on a certain day for the purpose of giving testimony, and stating that if the person refuses to appear, penal consequences may follow

The Mechanics of Testifying

A witness who is served with a subpoena is legally obligated to attend court, and must remain in court until officially excused by the judge. Failure to comply with these obligations may result in arrest and a criminal charge. (No legal repercussions will ensue if a witness is unable to attend court because of illness or for other serious reasons, as long as the court is notified in advance.)

At the start of the trial, the judge may ask all of the witnesses to leave the courtroom. Witnesses are then readmitted to the courtroom one by one as they are called to testify. This is referred to as an "exclusion of witnesses" and its purpose is to prevent the testimony of one witness from influencing the testimony of another.

Once a witness is called to testify, the court clerk will ask the witness to swear an oath or make a solemn affirmation. The **oath** involves swearing on the Bible, while the **solemn affirmation** requires the witness to solemnly agree that the evidence he or she will give shall be "the truth, the whole truth and nothing but the truth" (s. 14(1) of the *Canada Evidence Act*). Witnesses who lie in their testimony can be charged with perjury and sentenced to a maximum of 14 years in prison. In addition, witnesses who are uncooperative or disrespectful to the court may receive an immediate conviction for contempt of court.

oath
a promise to tell the truth that is "sworn" with a hand on the Bible

solemn affirmation
a promise to tell the truth without a hand on the Bible—for the non-religious—as provided for in s. 14 of the *Canada Evidence Act*

Stages of Questioning

Witnesses called by the Crown are referred to as Crown witnesses, and those called by the defence as defence witnesses. The lawyers on both sides are involved in questioning each witness in the following three stages:

1. *Examination-in-chief*

    The witness is questioned first by counsel for his or her side. For example, a Crown witness is questioned first by Crown counsel. On **examination-in-chief**, leading questions are not permitted. A leading question is one that suggests its answer. "You have a drinking problem, don't you?" is a leading question. "How often do you drink?" would be an acceptable alternative. If counsel have properly prepared their witness, the best style of questioning is simply to let the witness tell his or her story in an uninterrupted narrative. Typically, the witness has been called because he or she can provide information helpful to the calling side's argument. However, witnesses sometimes surprise counsel by changing their story. As discussed below, ss. 9(1) and 9(2) of the *Canada Evidence Act* provide ways in which counsel can treat their witnesses as **adverse** and question them in a manner that is more akin to cross-examination.

examination-in-chief
a party's questioning of its own witnesses

adverse witness
a witness called in support of one's own side, but whose evidence turns out to be unfavourable

2. *Cross-examination*

    After the examination-in-chief, opposing counsel have an opportunity to question the witness. Unlike examination-in-chief, leading questions *are* permitted on **cross-examination**, because the lawyer is attempting to elicit information that the witness may be reluctant to recount or does not realize is important. Cross-examination is used to:

    • strengthen the questioner's side by weakening the force of the witness's testimony or using the witness's testimony to corroborate favourable evidence on the questioner's side;

cross-examination
the questioning of a witness by opposing counsel

PURPOSE OF CROSS-EXAMINATION

Cross-examination can be gruelling. Its purpose is to ensure that witnesses are telling the truth and that they are not overstating their evidence or failing to tell the court the whole story. Consider, for example, a witness who is convinced that he or she saw something clearly, and gives evidence to that effect in court. Cross-examination, however, may establish that the witness's view was obstructed or that the witness's eyesight is poor, thus weakening the impact of the original version. It is important to test evidence this way. That is why evidence that has not been subjected to cross-examination (such as hearsay) has less value or weight than evidence that has been. It is important to remember that cross-examination does not always involve an attack. More often, and most effectively, cross-examination brings out new information that did not come out during the examination-in-chief.

- bring out information that supports the questioner's side that was not brought out during examination-in-chief; and/or
- discredit the witness by showing his or her lack of credibility.

Cross-examination is the most difficult stage for police witnesses in a criminal trial. The challenges, and ways in which officers can prepare to meet them, are discussed in detail in Chapter 19, Testifying.

3. *Re-examination*

After opposing counsel have finished their cross-examination, the original examiner has an opportunity to re-examine his or her witness. **Re-examination** (also known as redirection) is limited to questions on issues raised for the first time on cross-examination. Because the questioner is again addressing a witness that belongs to his or her side, leading questions are not permitted. The purpose of re-examination is to rebuild testimony that was disturbed by the cross-examination. Assume, for example, that during examination-in-chief the Crown asked its witness to describe a certain person, and the witness said that that person had "a goatee." On cross-examination, however, opposing counsel pressed the witness into admitting that "it may have been a full beard." On re-examination, the Crown would be wise to ask a question such as, "To the best of your recollection, what kind of facial hair did the man have?" The witness would most likely respond by saying, "A goatee," thus reaffirming his or her original statement.

At the close of a party's case, the opposing party may bring forward **reply** or **rebuttal evidence**, to contradict or qualify any new facts or issues that have been raised.

> **re-examination**
> a party's questioning of its own witness after cross-examination has been completed

> **reply (rebuttal) evidence**
> a party who called the witness may ask him or her further questions relating to new matters brought out in cross-examination of the witness; also called rebuttal evidence

Privilege Against Self-Incrimination

In Canada, unlike in the United States, witnesses have no right to refuse to answer questions that might incriminate them. Barring a claim of privilege or a successful objection (on the issue of relevance, for example), witnesses must answer all questions posed by Crown or defence counsel or by the judge. However, the *Evidence*

privilege against self-incrimination

a privilege exempting the accused from the obligation to give self-incriminating evidence (or any evidence at all)

Act and the Charter both provide **privilege against self-incrimination**, ensuring that the witness's answers cannot be used against him or her in other proceedings. Thus, even if answering a question involves admitting to criminal behaviour, the witness is bound by his or her oath or affirmation to answer the question truthfully. For example, if John was an eyewitness to the disposal of a body at the waterfront, and during cross-examination defence counsel asked, "What exactly were you doing at the waterfront at 3:00 a.m.?" John would have to answer honestly that, for example, he was waiting for a shipment of hashish.

Although s. 5(2) of the *Evidence Act* provides that a witness must answer questions that incriminate him or her, those answers cannot be used in evidence in any criminal trial or other proceeding against the witness. This immunity is also covered by s. 13 of the Charter, which provides that

> a witness who testifies in any proceeding has the right not to have any incriminating evidence so given used to incriminate that witness in any other proceedings, except in a prosecution for perjury or for the giving of contradictory evidence.

The application of this right is automatic and does not require any claim to protection. Thus, even if John does own up to drug smuggling, this statement cannot be used against him at a later date. Police are not barred, however, from using what they now know about John to gather other evidence concerning his actions.

Present Memory Refreshed Versus Past Recollection Recorded

It is typical for witnesses to read notes or statements they made in the past, particularly their statements made to police or their testimony given at a preliminary hearing, before attending court, to assist in refreshing their memories of events that may have occurred months or even years earlier. This is referred to as the doctrine of **present memory refreshed** or present memory revived. Police officers, in particular, who investigate many crimes and testify at many trials, cannot be expected to recall with sufficient detail every investigation in which they took part without the aid of their notebooks, in which they made notes during the course of the investigation.

present memory refreshed

a witness may use a document to refresh his or her memory of past events

The importance of maintaining accurate notes that meet certain standards and specifications—and the consequences of failing to do so for an officer's credibility as a witness in a trial—is covered in detail in Chapter 19, Testifying.

In addition to using their notes or statements in preparation for giving testimony, witnesses, including police, may use these notes *while* testifying to help refresh their memory, as long as they were made by the witness contemporaneously with, or shortly after, the events in question. The stimulus may be in different forms such as an audio recording, a transcript, or a business document. The stimulus itself may be inadmissible because it is hearsay or lacks authentication. However, when a witness refreshes his or her memory from some external source, it is the oral testimony that is given in court that becomes evidence, not the record in which the information was recorded (*R. v. Fliss*, 2002).

Reviewing a record of an event (a written document or an electronic recording), however, will not always help the witness recall the events described in the statement. In such cases, the judge may allow the record to be admitted as evidence as

USE OF POLICE NOTEBOOKS TO REFRESH MEMORY

It is common for police officers to be allowed to use their notebooks while testifying in order to refresh their memory about the details of the investigation in question. However, the Crown will have to seek permission of the judge before a police officer may do so.

The following illustrates how this process typically unfolds:

Officer: *[Takes the witness stand, and swears or affirms to tell the truth.]*

Crown: Officer, I see you have some notes with you today *[a duty notebook, a casebook, or similar materials].*

Officer: Yes.

Crown: What is the purpose of those notes?

Officer: I have brought my notes today for the purpose of refreshing my memory regarding the details of the events of this case.

Crown: Did you make the notes?

Officer: Yes.

Crown: Did you make the notes near the time that the events that are recorded took place, and when your memory of the events was fresh?

Officer: Yes.

Crown: Do the notes accurately reflect your memory of the events at the time you made them?

Officer: Yes.

Crown: Have there have been any additions, deletions, or alterations to those notes since you originally made them?

Officer: No.

Crown: Is there a reason why you require your notes today?

Officer: Only to remind myself of specific details.

Crown: Thank you. Your Honour, may the officer refer to his notes for the purpose of refreshing his memory?

Judge: Are there any objections to the officer using his notes for the purpose of refreshing his memory?

Defence: No objection, Your Honour.

Judge: Officer, you may refer to your notes for the purpose of refreshing your memory.

Officer: Yes, Your Honour.

---

past recollection recorded if the following preconditions are met (see *Wigmore on Evidence*, as adopted in *R. v. Meddoui*, 1990):

1. The past recollection must have been recorded in some reliable way.

2. At the time it was recorded, the recollection must have been sufficiently fresh and vivid to be probably accurate.

3. The witness must be able now to assert that the record accurately represented his or her knowledge and recollection at the time. The usual phrase requires the witness to affirm that he or she "knew it to be true at the time."

4. The original record itself must be used, if it can be obtained.

past recollection recorded
a witness may adopt the events as recorded in a document for which he or she has no present recollection

Prior Statements

Before testifying in court, a witness will typically have recounted his or her evidence to someone else at a time closer to the event in question—for example, by providing a statement to a police officer at the scene of the crime. At trial, sometimes the witness's story remains consistent with that told at a previous occasion. Sometimes it is inconsistent. Various rules must be followed when confronting a witness with prior consistent and inconsistent statements, as discussed below.

Prior Consistent Statements

Generally, witness statements given to the police that are consistent with the version of events the witnesses describe in court are not admissible. This is because such statements usually lack probative value, are self-serving, and constitute hearsay when adduced (presented as evidence) for the truth of their contents (*R. v. Dinardo*, 2008). Consider the example of Sally, a friend of the accused who tells the police that she saw him shortly after the crime was committed and that he was upset and had blood on his shirt. When called to testify at trial, she essentially repeats what she told the police. The prosecution is not permitted to introduce her statement to the police, because that would constitute oath helping, an improper attempt to bolster Sally's credibility as a witness. However, if Sally has trouble remembering what she saw and asks to see her statement while she is on the stand, she may be permitted to see it to help refresh her memory.

prior consistent statement
generally not admissible in court, but, in limited circumstances, an examiner may use such a statement made by the witness to bolster his or her credibility

A **prior consistent statement** may also be admissible in the following circumstances:

1. *To rebut an allegation of recent fabrication.* If the opposing party alleges that a witness has recently concocted his or her story, the prior consistent statement may be admissible to rebut this presumption. Assume, for example, that during a robbery trial, a witness alleges that he remembers the accused's "cold blue eyes." On cross-examination, defence counsel may suggest that the witness, having seen the accused in court for the first time, has decided to spice up his testimony by alluding to the accused's eye colour. The prosecution will be able to rebut this accusation by referring to the witness's initial statement to the police containing a reference to blue eye colour.

2. *To preserve the witness's narrative.* A need to preserve the witness's narrative by including the witness's prior statements arises most often when the witness is also the victim of the crime. In the case of children's complaints or complaints of sexual assault, prior statements often help the judge and jury understand what was going on in the mind of the victim immediately after the act took place.

3. *To establish prior identification of the accused.* Evidence of an out-of-court statement relating to the identification of the accused may be admissible if the witness identifies the accused at trial, or is unable to identify the accused at trial but can state that he or she previously gave an accurate description of the accused (*R. v. Starr*, 2000).

Prior Inconsistent Statements

If a witness in court tells a story different from the one he or she initially told the police, this **prior inconsistent statement** is not immediately admissible. The procedure for dealing with prior inconsistent statements differs depending on which party called the witness to the stand.

prior inconsistent statement
not immediately admissible in court, but an examiner may use such a statement to impeach a witness's credibility

STATEMENTS BY A PARTY'S OWN WITNESS

Under s. 9(1) of the *Evidence Act*, if the court finds that a witness has proven adverse during a trial, counsel may produce evidence to contradict the witness's testimony or, with leave of the court, may prove that the witness previously made a statement that is inconsistent with his or her present testimony. However, before proof is given, the circumstances in which the statement was supposedly made must be mentioned to the witness, and the witness must be asked whether or not he or she made the statement.

Under s. 9(2), where counsel alleges that the witness made a prior statement that is inconsistent with the witness's present testimony, either in writing or reduced to writing, the court may allow counsel to cross-examine the witness regarding the statement *without* proof that the witness is adverse. The court may then consider the cross-examination in determining whether the witness *is* adverse.

The procedure for bringing such an application, once the inconsistent evidence has been given, is as follows:

1. Counsel informs the court that they are bringing a s. 9(1) or s. 9(2) application.
2. The jury is given a recess and a **voir dire** begins.
3. Counsel then pinpoints the areas of inconsistency between the initial statement and the testimony just given.
4. If the judge agrees that inconsistencies exist, it is up to counsel to prove that the prior statement was made by the witness.
5. The witness is asked whether he or she made the statement. If the witness admits to making the statement, the statement is proved; if not, other evidence may be called to prove that it was made (Paciocco & Stuesser, 2008, pp. 516–517).

voir dire
a hearing in the absence of the jury to consider the admissibility of a piece of evidence

For the prior statement to be used for the truth of its contents, it must be found to be reliable. It is one thing to introduce a statement simply to impeach the testimony of a witness and make him or her appear less credible, but a much higher threshold of reliability is needed for the statement to be admitted for the truth of its contents.

STATEMENTS BY THE OTHER PARTY'S WITNESS

Under s. 10(1) of the *Evidence Act*, a witness may be cross-examined on any prior statements relevant to the case of which there is a record. Counsel is not obligated to show the witness the record, but if the evidence is intended to contradict the witness, the witness must be made aware of the parts of the statement that will be used to contradict him or her before proof is given. In addition, at any time during the trial the judge may require that the record be produced, to be used in whatever way the judge sees fit.

Under s. 11 of the *Canada Evidence Act*, if a witness is being cross-examined on a prior statement that contradicts his or her present testimony, and the witness does not admit to making the statement, counsel may provide proof that the witness *did* make the statement. However, before the proof can be given, the witness must be reminded of the circumstances of the statement and asked whether or not he made the statement. If the witness acknowledges having made the statement, the statement can only be used to assess the credibility of the witness. However, if the witness adopts the statement as *true*, the statement becomes part of the trial evidence.

It is important to note that, unlike with s. 9 of the *Canada Evidence Act*, the cross-examination of another party's witness on a prior inconsistent statement does not require permission of the judge.

PHYSICAL EVIDENCE

Unlike testimonial evidence, which "tells" us something, physical evidence "shows" us something. Physical evidence takes the form of actual objects related to a crime—for example, a paint chip, traces of blood or semen, fragments of glass, jewellery, a computer, a hair, an item of clothing, a video recording, a bullet, and so on.

Real Evidence

real evidence
physical objects (including documents in some cases) with a direct link to the crime that are introduced as evidence

Real evidence includes objects directly linked to the occurrence of a crime, such as the counterfeit bills used in a counterfeiting scheme or the gun used in a murder. Such objects are relevant as evidence in a proceeding only if it can be proved they are the *same* objects that were originally collected as evidence. For example, the introduction into evidence of a bloody shirt that connects the accused to a murder is only relevant if it is the *same* shirt that was taken from the murder scene.

In a criminal proceeding, unless the Crown has reached a prior agreement with defence counsel regarding the admissibility of certain proposed exhibits, the Crown will have to go through a process in order to have the evidence admitted. The terms "evidence" and "exhibit" are often used interchangeably, but they do not mean the same thing. An "exhibit" is a tangible piece of evidence (for example, a document, a gun, or a piece of clothing) that has been admitted into a court proceeding according to specific legal rules and that can be shown or "exhibited" to the court.

One of the most important steps is "authenticating" the evidence. This involves a witness testifying that the proposed exhibit is in fact what it is represented to be. For example, if the Crown seeks to enter a piece of clothing that was seized from the suspect by police, it must establish—in this case, through the testimony of a police witness—that the clothing it is seeking to enter is the *same* piece of clothing that was seized by the police. The Crown will usually either show the proposed exhibit to defence counsel or indicate to the court that it has already done so (or state that defence has been given a copy of the proposed exhibit) before showing it to the witness. To authenticate evidence, a witness must be "qualified," meaning that the Crown must show that the witness has the necessary personal knowledge regarding the exhibit to testify about it. This is achieved through a line of questioning, such as the following:

Crown: Officer Smith, do you recognize this piece of clothing?

Officer: Yes.

Crown: Can you tell me how you recognize it?

Officer: Yes. I seized that piece of clothing off of the accused in this case, Mr. Gerald Jones, when I arrested him for an assault that took place at 123 Main Street, on August 7, 2011.

Crown: What did you do with this piece of clothing after you seized it from Mr. Jones?

Officer: I marked it by writing my initials and badge number on the inside of the waistband with a ballpoint pen. I then placed it inside a property bag, sealed it, and submitted it to the forensic laboratory for testing with regard to blood stains that I believed may have come from the victim. When I received the pants back from the laboratory I placed them in an evidence locker, where they have been stored until I was required to bring them with me to court today.

Crown: Officer, how can you be sure that these are the same pants that you seized from Mr. Jones on the day you arrested him?

Officer: Because my initials and badge number are clearly visible inside the waistband, where I wrote them after I seized the pants from the accused.

Crown: Thank you, officer. I have no further questions. [Alternatively, defence counsel may ask the witness questions regarding his or her personal knowledge of the exhibit.]

Once the exhibit has been authenticated, the Crown will normally ask to have it "marked" as an exhibit, which typically involves the clerk of the court assigning an exhibit number to it so that it may be easily identified and referred to later in the trial process. Normally, the exhibit will be marked before the Crown questions the witness about it further.

While there is no single line of questioning that will be followed in all cases to authenticate a proposed exhibit, the general principle is that the witness must be able to swear, on the basis of personal knowledge, that the thing that the Crown (or defence) is seeking to enter as an exhibit *is* the thing that it is held out to be. In the example above, the officer was able to swear on the basis of personal knowledge that the pants were the same ones he seized from the accused, because he was the one who seized them.

Another step involved in having evidence admitted is showing that it is relevant. This is sometimes achieved when the exhibit is authenticated, as in the example above where the police witness stated how he knew the proposed exhibit was authentic and also explained *why* it was relevant (the possible presence of the victim's blood).

Sometimes, the relevance of an exhibit may be more difficult to demonstrate and counsel may need to question a witness further. If, for example, the officer in the example above had authenticated the exhibit by explaining how he knew that the pants were the same ones he had seized but had not explained that he believed the victim's blood was on them (thus providing evidence of the accused and victim having been in contact with one another), the Crown would have had to elicit this in order to show why the pants, which had been shown to be authentic, were also relevant.

Demonstrative Evidence

Demonstrative evidence encompasses items that help explain or illustrate the testimony of a witness. It includes things that are intended to help the court better understand the evidence—for example, photographs, videotapes, maps, diagrams, models, charts, and anatomically correct dolls. Different standards of admissibility apply depending on the type of demonstrative evidence.

Photographs and Videotapes

The admissibility of photographs and videotapes of the crime itself, of the crime scene, or of the crime's aftermath depends on several factors (Paciocco & Stuesser, 2008, p. 459):

- accuracy in representing the facts,
- fairness and absence of any intention to mislead, and
- verification on oath by a person capable of doing so.

The person verifying authenticity does not need to be the camera person. An eyewitness, for example, can also confirm that the photo or video is a fair and accurate reproduction of the scene as it looked at the time of the incident.

The problem with this type of evidence is that it tends to be powerful and may have a sensational effect on the judge or jury. A picture is worth a thousand words, but photos and videos can present a distorted version of reality: the angle of a shot, the lighting, and special effects such as slow motion can create a more sinister impression than is justified and thereby prejudice the accused's case and mislead the court. The issue is not how grotesque or shocking a photo or video is, but its probative value—how accurate it is in portraying what actually happened. That is why photographic and videotape evidence *must* be associated with testimonial evidence if the judge and jury are to draw conclusions from it.

Consider a case where the accused takes no issue with the cause of death of the deceased being a number of stab wounds, but claims that he was too intoxicated to form the intent for murder. Photographs of the deceased's autopsy may be relevant in demonstrating that the accused was capable of performing acts that required a significant level of strength and manual dexterity in order to perform the mutilation of the deceased, thus strengthening the inference that the accused intended to murder (*R. v. Teerhuis-Moar*, 2011).

Maps, Charts, and Visual Aids

These can help witnesses explain, and can help judges and juries understand, concepts and theories referred to in testimony. They can also make it easier to visualize locations. For example, in a case where several accomplices used cellular phones to communicate with one another, and their calls were traced through nearby transmission towers, a witness might find a map of those towers helpful for describing the locations of the co-conspirators. Another example of the use of visual aids is an expert's use of a chart or diagram to explain blood typing or DNA matching.

The only questions that must be answered before visual aids are admitted into the courtroom are:

- Does the visual aid help the witness explain his or her testimony to the judge and jury?
- Does it help the judge and jury understand the witness's testimony?

If these criteria are satisfied, the aid will be admissible.

View Evidence or "Look-Sees"

Having a view or a **look-see** occurs when the entire court visits the crime scene. Because they are costly and time-consuming, and the court's time is precious, look-sees are rare. Only when pictures or a re-creation simply do not do justice to the physical reality of a crime scene, or the parties cannot agree on what constitutes an accurate representation of the scene, may a look-see be permitted. For example, if, in a reckless driving case, an oddity of the street corner in question is best perceived in person, a view may be allowed.

having a view (look-see)
an excursion by the judge or jury to a site outside the courtroom to view evidence that cannot reasonably be presented in court

The rule on what a court is permitted to conclude from a view is set out in an older English case:

> Where the matter for decision is one of ordinary common sense, the judge of fact is entitled to form his own judgement on the real evidence of a view, just as much as on the oral evidence of witnesses.

(Lord Denning in *Buckingham v. Daily News Ltd.*, 1956.)

DOCUMENTARY EVIDENCE

Documentary evidence is a class of physical/real evidence consisting of documents such as business records, financial statements, transcripts of conversations, and graphs. Today, electronically produced documents are increasingly common, and new rules under the *Canada Evidence Act* govern these types of documents.

Best Evidence Rule

The **best evidence rule** requires, whenever possible, that any document of importance to the case be introduced into evidence in its original form. Oral description of the document, or reference to the document in a different document, will generally not suffice. Even photocopies or facsimiles of a document may not satisfy the best evidence rule, because it is possible to produce a document that has been altered in a way that can be almost impossible to detect.

best evidence rule
a legal rule requiring that wherever possible, the original document (the best evidence), rather than a reproduction, should be introduced in evidence

Criminal charges are so serious that the courts have always wanted the best evidence they can get. Over time, the courts have concluded that they should consider only original evidence whenever possible, because originals are the most accurate source of the information they contain. An example of this meticulous tradition is the rule prohibiting hearsay testimony, which is based on the idea that the best evidence is that provided by the person who actually made the statement.

It is often defence counsel who argue that the court should be presented with the original evidence; however, the rule applies equally to the prosecution and the defence.

Section 31.2(a) of the *Canada Evidence Act* states that the best evidence rule in respect of an electronically produced document is satisfied "on proof of the integrity of the electronic documents system by or in which the electronic document was recorded or stored." Therefore, when considering the admission of an electronically produced document, the court will be concerned with the integrity of the electronic system (for example, is the system prone to errors?) rather than with the integrity of the record itself.

Secondary Documentary Evidence

If a party can satisfy the court that the original document is lost, destroyed, or otherwise unobtainable, the best evidence rule may be relaxed to allow the introduction of copies or **secondary documentary evidence**. Some recognized exceptions include the following:

secondary documentary evidence
a piece of documentary evidence that is other than an original, such as a photocopy

1. Someone other than the accused has the original. In this case, the prosecutor will serve the third party with a subpoena. If the person refuses to comply or is outside the jurisdiction, secondary evidence may be admitted.

2. The original cannot be found after due search.

3. Production of the original is impossible, as in the case of an inscription on a tombstone.

4. Statutory provisions allow the introduction of certified copies of government, banking, or business records. Sections 25–30 of the *Canada Evidence Act* contain such provisions. Section 29(1), for example, provides that "a copy of any entry in any book or record kept in any financial institution shall in all legal proceedings be admitted in evidence as proof."

5. The original has been destroyed.

Generally, flexibility is used when applying the best evidence rule, because an overzealous application of the rule succeeds only in hampering the search for the truth.

Authenticating Documentary Evidence

For documents to be tendered as proof of their contents—that is, as direct, not secondary, evidence—they must be shown to be authentic. There are several ways of proving that documents are authentic and thereby introducing them into evidence:

1. The maker of the document can be called to testify that the document is indeed what he or she wrote, and that it represents a true statement of fact.

2. A witness who saw the document signed or who is familiar with the document can be called to testify.

3. Where handwriting is an issue:

   a. A witness who is familiar with the handwriting in question—for example, that of a co-worker or family member—can be called to testify.

   b. The writing in dispute can be compared with writing that the court has already determined is genuine.

   c. Experts who specialize in identifying handwriting can be called to testify.

4. The opposing party can concede that the document is authentic.

5. If a document written by another person is used in the cross-examination of an accused and the accused accepts it as true, the contents of the document become evidence. But if the accused refuses to accept the document as true, its contents cannot be accepted as evidence against him or her. Nevertheless, if the accused has in some way recognized, adopted, or acted on the contents of the document—without having expressly accepted it—the document may be used against the accused.

6. When a document is shown to a witness to refresh his or her memory and, although the witness has no present recollection (does not remember the writing) after seeing it, the witness accepts its validity as past recollection recorded (a record of what he or she remembered at one time), the document can be admitted as direct evidence.

7. According to s. 30(2) of the *Canada Evidence Act*, documents "made in the usual and ordinary course of business" are admissible without the need for testimonial evidence.

8. Documents found in the accused's possession are generally admissible against the accused. However, they must be shown to be relevant to the issues in the trial.

KEY TERMS

adverse witness
best evidence rule
compellability
competence
cross-examination
demonstrative evidence
electronically produced document
examination-in-chief
exhibit
having a view (look-see)
oath
past recollection recorded

present memory refreshed
prior consistent statement
prior inconsistent statement
privilege against self-incrimination
real evidence
re-examination
reply (rebuttal) evidence
secondary documentary evidence
solemn affirmation
subpoena
voir dire

FURTHER READING

Levy, E.J. (2011). *Examination of witnesses in criminal cases* (6th ed.). Toronto: Carswell.

REVIEW QUESTIONS

True or False?

_____ 1. Any witness that is competent is also compellable.

_____ 2. Children under age 14 are incompetent to testify.

_____ 3. The accused does not have to testify at his or her trial.

_____ 4. Leading questions may not be asked of the accused.

_____ 5. Leading questions are not permitted on re-examination.

_____ 6. If co-accused are charged on the same information, they are not compellable witnesses against each other.

_____ 7. Police officers are automatically permitted to refer to their police notebooks to refresh their memories while on the witness stand.

_____ 8. Using prior consistent statements to bolster a witness's credibility is an example of oath helping.

_____ 9. Prior inconsistent statements usually bolster the credibility of a witness.

_____ 10. A witness can refuse to answer a question that raises embarrassing topics.

_____ 11. Documentary evidence includes the testimony of witnesses.

_____ 12. A bloody lampshade would be considered real evidence.

_____ 13. A video of a crime scene is called a view.

_____ 14. A photocopy is acceptable under the best evidence rule.

_____ 15. Only an expert can use handwriting to determine an author's identity.

Multiple Choice

1. Cross-examination may assist in

   a. exposing lies.

   b. bringing out new information to support the examiner's side.

   c. testing the reliability of an eyewitness's evidence.

   d. all of the above.

2. A police officer may refresh his or her memory while testifying

   a. by referring to his or her police notebook.

   b. by referring to his or her partner's police notebook.

   c. by referring to the *Criminal Code*.

   d. all of the above.

3. A witness is competent to testify if he or she
   a. has the capacity to remember.
   b. has the capacity to perceive.
   c. has the capacity to be sincere.
   d. all of the above.

4. Demonstrative evidence can include
   a. maps and charts.
   b. anatomical models.
   c. videotapes and photographs.
   d. all of the above.

5. Continuity always needs to be proved, unless
   a. the documents are lost or stolen.
   b. the opposing party concedes that the exhibit is authentic.
   c. the officers are not available to testify.
   d. the supervisory officer testifies on behalf of all the officers involved.

6. The best evidence rule is important because
   a. the defence often uses stalling tactics to delay the trial, and making the Crown produce originals can be a tedious and lengthy process.
   b. criminal charges are very serious.
   c. it has evolved over time and is necessary for upholding the common-law tradition.
   d. quality, not quantity, is what is important.

Short Answer

1. Most people are compellable to testify at a trial. List three exceptions.
2. Discuss the privilege against self-incrimination.
3. Describe the difference between "present memory refreshed" and "past recollection recorded."
4. Why might photographs of the victim's autopsy be found inadmissible?
5. Explain why business documents are normally admitted into evidence without the need for testimony. Which section of the *Canada Evidence Act* allows this?
6. What questions must be answered before visual aid evidence is permitted?

Principles of Admissibility

Relevance, Materiality, Probative Value, and Prejudicial Effect

3

LEARNING OUTCOMES

After completing this chapter, you should be able to:

- Discuss what would make a piece of evidence more or less likely to be admitted in court.

- Explain the difference between relevant and material evidence.

- Understand the probative value versus the prejudicial effect of evidence.

- Distinguish between the concepts of admissibility and weight.

- Describe factors that would contribute to a piece of evidence being given more or less weight.

INTRODUCTION

As we stated in Chapter 1, it is the trial judge who decides which evidence is admissible and which evidence should be excluded. The burden of proving that the evidence is admissible is on ("lies with") the party—whether prosecution or defence—who presents, or "tenders," the evidence to the court. The standard of proof is usually the civil standard of proof on a balance of probabilities.

In a trial by judge and jury, questions regarding the admissibility of evidence are dealt with in the absence of the jury through a process known as a *voir dire*. During a *voir dire*, the trial itself stops so that the judge can decide an issue of admissibility without the jury being present (the *voir dire* is sometimes called a "trial within the trial"). Once the determination of admissibility is made, the trial resumes. The jury is to hear only admissible evidence and reach a verdict on the basis of that evidence alone.

The principle of admissibility can be boiled down to the following simple rule:

Evidence that is relevant and material is admissible unless:

- there is an exclusionary rule that makes the evidence inadmissible, or
- the probative value of the evidence is outweighed by the prejudicial effect of the evidence.

This chapter explains the concepts of relevance, materiality, probative value, and prejudicial effect. Chapters 4 and 5 discuss the exclusionary rules.

RELEVANCE

relevance
the tendency of a piece of evidence to prove or disprove a proposition

The concepts of relevance and materiality are closely related. **Relevance** is the logical relationship that makes a proposition more or less probable. For example, if the Crown is asserting that Ms. Jones assaulted Ms. Stevens, then a shirt seized from Ms. Jones on her arrest containing blood stains determined to belong to Ms. Stevens would make the proposition that the former had assaulted the latter more probable, by proving that the two had been in contact. In addition, consider the following:

1. An accused is charged with impaired driving. Evidence that the accused's breath smelled of alcohol at the time of arrest is relevant to whether her ability to drive was impaired by alcohol. Evidence that the accused was observed drinking alcohol a week before the arrest is not (Paciocco & Stuesser, 2008, p. 30).

2. An accused is charged with sexual assault, but denies having any sexual interaction with the complainant. Evidence of the accused's DNA in the complainant's vagina is relevant to whether sexual activity occurred. However, if the accused claims that the complainant consented to sexual intercourse, then the presence of his DNA becomes irrelevant to proving whether a sexual assault occurred. The focus of the trial instead will be on whether the complainant consented to the sexual activity.

3. An accused is charged with arson. If the fire was started by gasoline, evidence that the accused had empty jerry cans in his vehicle is relevant to proving his involvement in the offence. If the fire was started by propane gas, the jerry cans would not be relevant.

Relevance is the most important factor in determining which pieces of evidence will be admitted in court. If something is not logically relevant, there is clearly no point in wasting the court's time by having lawyers argue about it during the trial. Thus, by admitting only relevant evidence, the judge streamlines the use of court time and narrows the discussion to exactly what is needed to prove or disprove the propositions made by the prosecution and defence.

MATERIALITY

Materiality refers to matters that one side must prove to win its point or the case. As discussed in Chapter 1, the law defines what must be proved in a particular case or criminal charge (the elements of the offence). In many cases, a point is obvious or not in contention. In those circumstances, the other side can agree that there is no need to call witnesses or present evidence to prove the point—it is admitted. Judges always appreciate counsel who narrow the issues that must be proved to the questions that are truly contentious.

materiality
the degree to which a piece of evidence is necessary in proving a proposition

Material issues are largely defined by:

1. how the parties have defined the case;
2. how the offence is defined in the *Criminal Code*; and
3. how the offence is defined in the **information** or in the **indictment**.

Thus, not all evidence that may be relevant will also be material.

Consider the example of a homicide case where the defence concedes the manner in which a stabbing victim was killed. The autopsy photos would likely not be material evidence, because it would be redundant to introduce photos of a knife wound when the defence has already admitted that the accused stabbed the victim.

information
a form, prepared after the accused person has been arrested, that describes the offence(s) with which the accused is charged

indictment
a form, often prepared after a fuller investigation, that sets out the offence(s) for which the accused person will be tried at trial

EXCLUSIONARY RULES

As we have seen, the preliminary conditions of relevance and materiality must be met before evidence is considered for admission. However, there is one last admissibility hurdle to clear before a trier of fact may consider the evidence in reaching a verdict in a case. Once it is determined that a piece of evidence being tendered by a party is both relevant and material, the trial judge must still ensure that the evidence does not violate any exclusionary rules, such as:

1. Common-law rules that were created to exclude evidence that experience has shown is likely to be unreliable—for example, second-hand hearsay evidence is generally not permitted.
2. Statutory rules that are designed to ensure that only reliable evidence that can be authenticated is admitted at trial—for example, s. 30 of the *Canada Evidence Act* contains a procedure to be followed before business records, such as banking records, can be entered as exhibits.
3. Constitutional limitations such as ss. 8 and 24(2) of the *Canadian Charter of Rights and Freedoms*, which grant the trial judge the discretion to exclude evidence that was illegally seized by the police.

Exclusionary rules are covered in detail in Chapters 4 and 5.

Materiality, however, is not always so easily defined. For example, the prosecutor may argue that even if the cause of death is not a material fact in issue, the violent manner in which the deceased came to die *is*. Thus the autopsy photos showing 40 stab wounds become "relevant" to establishing the "material" issue of intent by showing anger and a guilty mind and should therefore be admissible.

PROBATIVE VALUE

probative value
evidence that logically helps prove a fact or issue

Probative value is a common legal term used to describe evidence that helps prove a fact or issue. In assessing the probative value of the evidence in question—that is, whether the evidence has no, little, or great probative value—the trier of fact will ask the following two questions:

1. *What is the evidence trying to prove?*

   For example, if the perpetrator of a crime is known to ride a yellow bike, and the accused is also known to ride a yellow bike, this is a fact that has some probative value, because it is relevant to identifying the perpetrator. However, a piece of evidence that would have more probative value with respect to identity would be fingerprints left at the scene by the perpetrator that matched the accused's. This evidence would be more helpful—or have a higher probative value—than bike colour in establishing the link between the perpetrator and the accused.

2. *How reliable is the evidence?*

   For example, the Sophonow Inquiry pointed to faulty eyewitness identification as the cause of the majority of wrongful convictions (Cory, 2001). Therefore, while eyewitness evidence may be probative in establishing identification because it is direct evidence, because of its unreliability, triers of fact will exercise caution when relying on it. In contrast, DNA evidence has shown to be a reliable form of evidence in proving identification.

Prejudicial Effect

prejudicial effect
the undesirable "side effects" of a piece of evidence that may be deemed unfair to the accused

In deciding which pieces of evidence should be admitted, the judge must decide whether the benefits of admitting the evidence (probative value) outweigh the costs (**prejudicial effect**). In *R. v. Seaboyer* (1991), the Supreme Court identified four potential prejudicial effects of evidence:

1. *The possibility that the admission of the evidence would cause undue emotional reaction in the trier of fact.*

propensity evidence
evidence that demonstrates that the accused is the type of person who tends to act in a particular manner

   For example, in an impaired driving case, evidence that an accused is a drug dealer has little or no probative value; however, should this fact become known to the judge or jury, it may create a hostile and distorted impression about the accused, because the judge or jury may assume that if someone is a "bad" person, he or she is likely to break the law. This is called **propensity evidence**, and is considered by the Supreme Court to be impermissible reasoning (*R. v. Corbett*, 1988). Judging a case on the basis of the character of the accused is discriminatory and unfairly puts the accused in a position where he or she is being judged for past wrongs instead of being properly tried, in an unbiased manner, on the evidence before the court. Character evidence is discussed further in Chapter 4.

2. *The possibility that the admission of the evidence would create a side issue that would unduly distract the trier of fact from the main issues.*

   Again, this is especially true with bad-character evidence. A trier may become distracted by concentrating on resolving whether the accused committed similar bad acts in the past.

3. *The possibility that the admission of the evidence would create delay or be time-consuming.*

   This is an important consideration when dealing with expert witness testimony. A trial judge may restrict the length of expert evidence to make efficient use of limited court resources.

4. *The possibility that the admission of the evidence would create unfair surprise to the opponent.*

   For example, a new eyewitness emerges during a robbery trial and the Crown wishes to call her as a witness. While the defence may be unprepared to deal with this new witness, the practical remedy in such a case would be an adjournment, not an exclusion of the witness's evidence.

Once the judge has considered these four factors, if the prejudicial effect outweighs the probative value, the trial judge will exclude the evidence in question. The trial judge's discretion to exclude relevant and material evidence as a result of prejudice is centred on ensuring that the accused has a fair trial. In *R. v. Wray* (1970), the Supreme Court of Canada noted:

> [T]he exercise of a discretion by the trial judge arises only if the admission of the evidence would operate unfairly. The allowance of admissible evidence relevant to the issue before the court and of substantial probative value may operate *unfortunately* for the accused, but not *unfairly*. It is only the allowance of evidence *gravely prejudicial* to the accused ... which can be said to operate unfairly. [Emphasis added.]

In *R. v. G. (S.G.)* (1997, para. 99), the Court explained further that the purpose of inquiring into prejudice is to ensure that the accused's rights to make full answer and defence are not compromised:

> The fact that the evidence tendered may be powerful evidence for the prosecution does not lead to a conclusion of prejudice. The inquiry into prejudice focuses not on the effect the evidence may have on the outcome of the trial, but on its effect on the accused's rights to make full answer and defence. *The question is not whether the evidence may tend to convict the accused, but whether it is likely to convict him unjustly.* The just or fair trial is one which gets at the truth, while respecting the fundamental right of the accused to make full answer and defence. [Emphasis added.]

ADMISSIBILITY VERSUS WEIGHT

weight
the probative value/
importance assigned
to a piece of evidence,
based on an assessment
of its reliability

Evidence that is admissible will be given different **weight** depending on how reliable it is and how effectively it establishes a point. A trustworthy piece of evidence—for example, DNA evidence—will be weighted heavily, meaning that the judge will put more emphasis on it and instruct the jury to do the same. Conversely, although another piece of evidence may be admitted, it may be given little weight because it is not deemed as reliable—for example, eyewitness testimony.

This section discusses three important factors that make evidence more persuasive: corroborative evidence, clean evidence, and continuity.

Corroborative Evidence

corroborative evidence
independently sourced
evidence that supports
another piece of evidence

Any independently sourced evidence that supports another piece of evidence or a proposition is called **corroborative evidence**. In a case of alleged sexual assault, for example, semen found on the complainant's underwear that matches the accused's DNA may be evidence that corroborates the complaint. (As noted above, however, this fact may not be *relevant* if the accused advances a defence that the complainant consented to the sexual activity, because, in that case, one would expect to find the accused's DNA on the complainant's underwear.)

Formerly, some kinds of evidence were considered to be particularly unsafe and required corroborative evidence before they could be believed. Judges would warn juries of the dangers of convicting an accused person on the uncorroborated evidence of certain witnesses—namely, children, accomplices to crimes, and complainants alleging a sexual offence (Paciocco & Stuesser, 2008, p. 521). A number of the statutory corroboration requirements relating to these types of witnesses have been repealed. For example, s. 586 of the *Criminal Code* used to provide that "no person shall be convicted of an offence upon the unsworn evidence of a child unless the evidence of the child is corroborated in a material particular by evidence that implicates the accused." The section was repealed in 1988 and the *Criminal Code* currently has no statutory requirements for corroboration of a child's unsworn evidence.

Nevertheless, commonsense assumptions about who is providing the evidence give some evidence less weight. For example, where a friend of the accused was originally charged with robbery of a convenience store but eventually accepts an offer by the Crown for a lenient sentence in exchange for his testimony that it was the accused who committed the robbery, his testimony may be less believable than that of the store owner, who has no obvious motive to lie. Clearly, in this case any independent evidence confirming the friend's version of events would assist in his being believed, but such evidence is not required by the courts.

However, some statutory corroboration rules still apply. For example, s. 133 of the *Criminal Code* provides that no person can be convicted of perjury "on the evidence of only one witness unless the evidence of that witness is corroborated in a material particular by evidence that implicates the accused."

Corroboration generally helps strengthen the evidence given by a witness. Especially when looking at a case from the prosecution's perspective, the case against an accused must be very strong to convince the judge or jury beyond a reasonable doubt. It is unlikely that a judge or jury will be convinced to such a degree without corroborative facts of some kind.

Clean Evidence

The way in which evidence is collected and preserved is extremely important, because improperly obtained and maintained evidence may be excluded in court (see the discussion in Chapter 5, Exclusionary Rules II: Opinion Evidence, Privilege, and Improperly Obtained Evidence). Evidence that is collected and preserved according to proper legal procedures and protocols is referred to as **clean evidence**. The "cleaner" the evidence, the greater the weight a trier of fact will likely give it.

The term "clean evidence" applies to both physical and statement evidence. In relation to physical evidence, it describes evidence obtained by police following correct search and seizure procedures—for example, obtaining a search warrant to search a suspect's computer. It also applies to how the evidence is handled and stored in order to prevent contamination or damage (see the discussion in Chapter 7, Crime Scene Investigation and Management).

In relation to statement evidence, when an individual is detained or arrested, a set of legal requirements with which investigators must comply is triggered. For example, people held in police custody must be informed of the reason for their detention; they must also be informed of their right to counsel and be given a meaningful opportunity to exercise this right. Police failure to provide a suspect with this information and opportunity may jeopardize the admissibility of any statements made following the violation of this right. Where a statement is held to be admissible, it may still raise issues of weight. For example, where issues arise as to the accuracy and completeness of the record, a trial judge may instruct the jury that the police's failure to videotape an accused's statement might affect its reliability and weight (*R. v. Moore-MacFarlane*, 2001). The law governing statements is discussed in detail in Chapter 16, Interviewing Rules.

clean evidence
physical evidence that is free of taint related to mishandling by investigators or prosecutors

Continuity

Another factor that will determine the value of evidence is the Crown's ability to demonstrate its **continuity**, or establish its "provenance" or "history" from the time the evidence was found to the time it is exhibited in court. Continuity is also described as the "chain of continuity" or the "chain of custody." As the term implies, investigators and the Crown must be able to account for each "link" in the chain. This includes establishing:

- who initially collected the evidence;
- who subsequently had contact—or the opportunity to have contact—with the evidence;
- where the evidence was stored, the conditions under which it was stored, and the steps that were taken to ensure that no one was able (either by accident or on purpose) to alter, contaminate, substitute, degrade, or otherwise affect the nature of the evidence.

continuity
in the context of physical evidence, an ability to account for the whereabouts of the evidence (and the identity of those who have had access to it) from the time of its collection to the time it is entered as an exhibit in the trial record

For example, a forensic investigator who collects a piece of bloody clothing from a crime scene should document and package the evidence following correct procedures. If the investigator does not submit the evidence to a forensic testing facility immediately—perhaps because forensic protocol requires that the clothing be allowed to dry before it is submitted or because the investigator has more evidence to collect from the same scene and wants to submit all of the evidence at once—he or she will need to make a note of when and where the evidence was stored before it is submitted. (Continuity could be achieved and demonstrated by storing the item in a secure evidence locker to which only the investigator has access.) Once the investigator is ready to submit the clothing to the forensic facility, he or she will document when it was submitted and to whom. The forensic facility will log the submission into its own evidence management computer system, creating a record of who took custody of the item, when, and from whom, and assign a unique reference number to the item. Following analysis, the investigator will receive a notice of the results and be asked to pick the item up, then will securely store the item in a police facility until it is required for court purposes.

In order to prove that a particular piece of evidence came from the location in question and that it was not tampered with or contaminated, all of the individuals who handled or oversaw the evidence may be required to testify in court. Although proof of continuity goes to the weight that will be given to a piece of evidence as opposed to its admissibility (*R. v. Andrade*, 1985, quoted in *R. v. Singh*, 2008, paras. 31–38), if continuity cannot be demonstrated, then the integrity of the evidence may be called into question and, even if it is admitted, it may be given little or no weight by a court.

Ultimately, the burden of showing that the evidence that is being presented in court is the same evidence that was found at the crime scene and that it is in the same state as it was when it was first gathered is on the party who seeks to introduce the evidence—usually, the Crown. If the state of the evidence has changed, the party must be able to account for any changes. Many changes occur for innocent and acceptable reasons, such as a change in the colour of a piece of paper that has been chemically treated to make fingerprints visible. On the other hand, some changes occur for unacceptable reasons, such as a loss of all or a portion of the evidence, or contamination resulting from improper storage.

Collecting and preserving evidence is covered in detail in Chapter 7, Crime Scene Investigation and Management.

LEGAL IMPLICATIONS OF POLICE FAILURE TO MAINTAIN CONTINUITY

The care taken to ensure sufficient continuity can be the difference between a conviction and an acquittal.

In *R. v. Grunwald* (2008), a large quantity of marijuana was seized from the accused's truck. The officer in charge testified that none of the police officers involved in the case had placed any identifying labels on the Ziploc bags of marijuana that were seized, nor had the Ziploc bags been placed in other marked exhibit bags. Further, the officer in charge testified that he was not even sure how the drugs were stored at the police station. In acquitting the accused of drug charges, the court criticized the police:

> Obviously, the police were very sloppy in their handling of the material seized from Mr. Grunwald. If they had initially marked the Ziploc bags with unique identifiers, or had immediately placed the Ziploc bags and contents into exhibit bags on which they placed unique identifiers, they could very easily have traced the movement of the material.

KEY TERMS

clean evidence

continuity

corroborative evidence

indictment

information

materiality

prejudicial effect

probative value

propensity evidence

relevance

weight

FURTHER READING

Cory, P. (2001). *The inquiry regarding Thomas Sophonow*. The Honourable Peter de C. Cory, Commissioner. ("Sophonow Inquiry"). In particular, see the recommendations for photo pack line-ups. http://www.gov.mb.ca/justice/publications/sophonow/recommendations/english.html#photo.

Technical Working Group on Crime Scene Investigation (2000). *Crime scene investigation: A guide for law enforcement*. Washington, DC: Department of Justice.

REVIEW QUESTIONS

True or False?

_____ 1. If evidence is not relevant, it will never be admitted.

_____ 2. If the prejudicial effect of a piece of evidence outweighs its probative value, it may still be admitted.

_____ 3. If the state of the evidence changes between the time that it is collected at a crime scene and the time it is brought to court, the evidence will always be inadmissible.

_____ 4. A party seeking to tender evidence has the burden of proof in proving its admissibility.

_____ 5. Continuity is disturbed if no one can prove who drove the sample to the lab.

_____ 6. Some *Criminal Code* offences require corroborative evidence.

_____ 7. A trial judge has the discretion to exclude evidence, but only if the judge determines that the police have breached the *Canadian Charter of Rights and Freedoms*.

_____ 8. A child's testimony can never be believed without corroboration.

_____ 9. Evidence that is relevant will also always be material.

_____ 10. Evidence that tends to prove or disprove a proposition is called "propensity evidence."

Multiple Choice

1. Evidence that is both relevant and material may still be determined by the trial judge to be inadmissible if the evidence violates:

   a. an exclusionary rule contained in the *Criminal Code*.

   b. an exclusionary rule contained in the *Canada Evidence Act*.

   c. an exclusionary rule developed by the Supreme Court of Canada.

   d. all of the above.

2. The judge may decide not to admit evidence because

   a. the accused already has a criminal record.

   b. the evidence's prejudicial effect outweighs its probative value.

   c. the evidence lacks corroboration.

   d. the evidence supports only circumstantial facts.

3. Probative value refers to

   a. the degree of directness of the evidence.

   b. how important a piece of evidence is in logically proving a case.

   c. the lack of prejudice attached to a piece of evidence.

   d. whether a generalization can prove a proposition.

4. Prejudicial evidence is usually not admitted because

   a. it does not possess enough probative value.

   b. it may mislead the judge or jury.

   c. it generally reflects impermissible reasoning.

   d. all of the above.

5. "Clean evidence" refers to

   a. evidence that is collected and preserved according to proper legal procedures and protocols.

   b. physical evidence.

   c. statement evidence.

   d. b and c only.

   e. a, b, and c.

6. Which of the following facts relating to continuity is false?

   a. The burden of proving continuity usually rests with the defence.

   b. Continuity is also described as "chain of custody."

   c. Continuity requires the investigators to account for each step of custody that the piece of evidence went through (from the crime scene to the courtroom).

   d. Lack of continuity may call into question the integrity of physical evidence.

Short Answer

1. Explain the difference between relevant and material evidence.

2. List the sources of the exclusionary rules of evidence.

3. In a sentence, describe a crime. Give two examples of evidence that would have great probative value in your scenario, and two examples of evidence that would have little probative value.

4. Explain why it is important that prejudicial evidence not be admitted into court.

5. List factors that make evidence more persuasive, and provide an example of each.

Exclusionary Rules I

Hearsay and Character Evidence

4

LEARNING OUTCOMES

After completing this chapter, you should be able to:

- Define the concept of hearsay and explain the general rule governing hearsay evidence.

- Identify common-law exceptions to the hearsay rule and explain the principled approach.

- Define character evidence.

- Explain the general rules governing character evidence, and exceptions.

INTRODUCTION

As you learned in Chapter 3, the general rule of admissibility of evidence is that relevant evidence is admissible, except where an exclusionary rule applies or where its prejudicial effect outweighs the probative value of the evidence. The exclusionary rules, which prohibit or restrict certain types of evidence, exist to ensure that trials are fair and efficient. This chapter and the following chapter examine these rules and the exceptions to these rules, both of which are important for you to understand.

THE PURPOSE OF EXCLUSIONARY RULES

One of the main factors that renders evidence less likely to be admitted is prejudice to the accused. As discussed in Chapter 3, prejudicial evidence refers to any evidence that is likely to mislead the judge or jury or be unfairly detrimental to the accused—for example, the use of an accused's prior criminal record to suggest guilt with respect to a subsequent offence. Prejudice may arise in a number of ways, and prejudicial evidence generally will not be admitted unless its probative value is high.

The concept of prejudicial evidence is rooted in two of our justice system's fundamental values: (1) accuracy in fact finding, and (2) the importance of the presumption of innocence and the value of a fair trial. It is unlikely that the trier of fact will reach the correct result in a trial if he or she is influenced more by prejudice than by the facts of the case.

HEARSAY

One of the main exclusionary rules of evidence is hearsay. The technical definition of hearsay is testimony or documentary evidence given in court about a statement made outside court, which is offered to prove the truth of what was said outside court. In practice, hearsay arises when a witness relates second-hand information. This is usually a case of person A testifying to what he or she was told by person B, where person B is unavailable or unwilling to testify. Without person B in court, it may be impossible to test that person's perception, memory, narration, or sincerity. The statement itself may not be accurately recorded. Further, mistakes, exaggerations, or deliberate lies may go undetected and lead to unjust verdicts (*R. v. Khelawon*, 2006).

In light of the above, the general rule is that all hearsay statements are presumptively inadmissible in order to preserve the truth-seeking function of the court.

Hearsay evidence is admitted if it either falls within one of the traditional hearsay exceptions established by the common law or meets a principled approach standard. These exceptions are discussed in the following sections.

Traditional Common-Law Exceptions

Many exceptions to the general rule excluding hearsay have evolved over time. They are discussed in the following sections.

Spontaneous Statements

Spontaneous statements, sometimes referred to by the Latin term *res gestae*, are statements made in immediate reaction to a particular event—usually a shocking

---

COMMON-LAW EXCEPTIONS AT A GLANCE

1. spontaneous statements,
2. statements by the accused,
3. declarations against interest,
4. testimony given on a previous occasion,
5. prior inconsistent statements,
6. dying declarations,
7. historical facts and materials relied on by experts, and
8. business records and declarations in the course of duty.

---

one—at the time the person is experiencing the event or condition. Because such statements are spontaneous and contemporaneous (that is, made at the time of the event), it is unlikely that the person who uttered them was concocting a falsehood, and they are therefore considered reliable. For example, if Sally exclaimed, "That guy is going 180 km/h!" just as a car was passing by, and Edward overheard this statement, Edward would be permitted to testify about what Sally said.

Several types of spontaneous statements are covered by this exception to the hearsay rule:

1. *Statements of present physical condition.* Declarations of bodily feelings and conditions are admissible to prove the physical state an individual was experiencing, or its duration. For example, while attempting to pick up a heavy bag at the cement factory where he works, Jim suddenly drops the bag and grabs his back, exclaiming, "Oh! My back!" If Jim is overheard by his co-worker Patrick, Patrick could repeat Jim's exclamation in court, and the evidence would be admissible. However, it would be admissible only to prove that Jim was experiencing the condition at the time, and to establish the duration of the experience (Paciocco & Stuesser, 2008, pp. 174–175).

2. *Statements of present mental or emotional state.* These occur when a person describes his or her present state of mind (emotion, intent, motive, or plan), and are often used to show anger, the presence or absence of goodwill, trust, affection, and so on. For example, if Edweena told George that she was very depressed the night before she was found in a bathtub with her wrists slashed, George would be allowed to repeat that statement in court.

   Naturally, a statement of this kind is admissible only when a person's state of mind is relevant, because mental state is not always material or relevant. This exception further requires that the person whose state of mind is in question be deceased (Paciocco & Stuesser, 2008, pp. 176–178). So, if Edweena had not died, George would not be able to repeat in court what he heard her say, because she would be available to testify herself.

   If the statements are explicit statements relating to a state of mind, as in the example above, they are simply admitted as exceptions to the hearsay rule. If, however, a statement permits one to draw an inference about the speaker's state of mind, it is regarded as original testimonial evidence and admitted as circumstantial evidence from which a state of mind can be inferred. So, if Edweena had told George that she did not want to go to a party that night, an inference may be drawn from her statement, and from evidence that she usually enjoyed parties, that her mental state was not good. Thus, such a statement would be admitted as circumstantial evidence that she may have been depressed.

3. *Excited utterances.* These types of statements relate to a startling event or condition and may be admitted to prove the truth of their contents if they are made while the person making the statement (the **declarant**) is affected by stress or excitement caused by the event or condition. For example, after Rachel's handbag is taken from her in the street, she immediately points at someone and claims, "Hey—he took my handbag!" A passerby, Henry, notices her shouting and pointing. Because Rachel was excited by the immediacy of the event, Henry would be able to relate her words to the court.

> **declarant**
> a person who makes a statement in testimony

For an excited utterance to be admissible, it must generally (1) relate to an occurrence or event sufficiently startling to overcome the normal reflective thought processes of the observer, (2) be a spontaneous reaction to the occurrence, and (3) relate to the occurrence.

4. *Statements of present sense impressions.* These are statements that describe or explain an event or condition made while a person is experiencing an event or condition, or immediately thereafter. These statements are different from excited utterances because the declarant need not be excited by the actual event. For example, if Tom witnesses a big man pummelling a smaller man during a bar fight and says to Ralph, "Boy, that guy should go pick on someone his own size," Ralph will be able to testify to what Tom said. Such statements are considered reliable because they are made during or just after an incident, leaving little time for fabrication or forgetfulness. Moreover, there is often the added safeguard that the declarant is present in court for cross-examination.

Statements by the Accused

> **admissions**
> acts or words of an accused offered as evidence against the accused

Statements by the accused, or **admissions**, are acts or words of the accused offered as evidence against the accused. If the statements or admissions of the accused were made to a person in authority, then separate rules apply in considering the admissibility of a confession. (For a discussion of interviewing rules, see Chapter 16.) Admissions have long been considered an exception to the hearsay rule, because the accused is present at his or her own trial and able to challenge the reliability of the alleged admission. It is important to note that only the Crown is permitted to tender an out-of-court statement of an accused. Once in evidence, however, the statement may be used for or against the accused.

Admissions by the accused may also include admissions by silence and the adoption of statements by others. An example of an admission by silence may be the testimony of a friend of the accused who states, "I asked him if he killed her, and he just looked at me and said nothing." It would be expected that someone in the accused's position on hearing the question would immediately deny the accusation.

An accused can adopt the statement of someone else either expressly or by implication. For example, if Bill and Bob plan to rob a convenience store, and Bob is heard by the store owner to say, "Let's just grab the money and go," this statement may also be admissible against Bill as long as the prosecution can prove that Bill adopted Bob's view. Thus, evidence that Bill nodded or grinned after Bob spoke may constitute implied adoption.

Declarations Against Interest

Declarations against interest are statements made by a declarant that are against his or her best interests. These statements fall into three categories: (1) pecuniary (financial), (2) property, and (3) penal. For example, the statement, "I owe Jonny $6,000," is a statement against the declarant's pecuniary interest. The statement, "I haven't kept up with my car payments for months now," is a statement against property interest. The statement, "They didn't catch me the last time I embezzled from the company," is a statement against penal interest (meaning that if this statement were pursued, penal—that is, punishable—consequences might follow).

declarations against interest
statements made by a person that seem to acknowledge, for example, guilt or a debt—that is, the opposite of self-serving statements

These statements are considered reliable because people generally do not make statements that admit facts contrary to their interests unless those statements are true.

Certain conditions must apply for these statements to be admissible. A statement must involve *the immediate prejudice of the declarant*—that is, as soon as the declarant makes the statement, he or she must feel the gravity of the consequences of such an admission. The declarant must be unavailable to testify and the witness adducing the evidence must have firsthand knowledge of the statement. Also, this exception essentially applies only to non-parties to the proceeding—that is, these statements may not apply against the accused's interests.

The following is an example of how a declaration against interest of a non-party is relevant in a criminal trial. George is on trial for murdering Margaret. There is evidence that Tom confessed to his neighbour, Janet, that he killed Margaret, and George had nothing to do with it. Tom dies before George's trial begins. The neighbour may be able to testify as to Tom's declaration against interest should the trial judge find that it meets the requirements listed above.

Testimony Given on a Previous Occasion

Evidence given by a witness at an earlier judicial proceeding, such as a **preliminary hearing**, is an exception to the hearsay rule; however, it is not technically a *true* exception, because the testimony was given under oath and subject to cross-examination, and thus the hearsay dangers are minimized.

preliminary hearing
a hearing held before the real trial to determine preliminary issues, such as whether there is enough evidence to proceed to trial

The requirements of this hearsay exception are codified in s. 715 of the *Criminal Code*, which provides that a witness's previously recorded evidence may be admitted at trial when any of the following tests are met: (1) the evidence was given at a previous trial on the same charge; (2) the evidence was taken during the investigation of the charge against the accused or at a preliminary inquiry into the charge; (3) the witness refuses to be sworn or to give evidence; or (4) facts are proved on oath from which it can be reasonably inferred that the person is dead, has since become and is insane, is so ill that he or she is unable to travel or testify, or is absent from Canada. Where it is proved that the witness's evidence was taken in the presence of the accused, it may be read as evidence in the proceedings without further proof, unless the accused proves that he or she did not have a full opportunity to cross-examine the witness. In most cases, evidence admitted under this exception is presented by means of **affidavit** sworn by an **affiant** before a witness.

affidavit
a written and witnessed statement of evidence that the maker swears and signs as proof of its truth

affiant
a person who makes and swears an affidavit

Prior Inconsistent Statements

Prior inconsistent statements are statements made before the trial that are inconsistent with the testimony of the witness at trial. For example, if shortly after a crime is committed a witness makes a statement at a police station implicating the accused, but then changes his or her mind and tells the court a completely different story at trial, the original statement made to the police may be admitted for the truth of its contents as long as certain criteria are met. At the very least, it may be admitted to show that the witness is untrustworthy.

This type of statement may be admissible only if it satisfies the tests of necessity and reliability. A statement is made more reliable if it is taken by the police in very particular circumstances:

perjury
lying while under oath or affirmation

1. if the declarant is under oath (or has affirmed) or warned of the possible consequences of **perjury**,
2. if the statement is videotaped, or
3. if there is an opportunity at trial to cross-examine the person who made the statement (*R. v. B. (K.G.)*, 1993).

Dying Declarations

Dying declarations are statements made by someone who has a hopeless expectation of almost immediate death, and are admissible for use by the prosecution or the defence. For example, if Alfred is stabbed by his gardener, found by his mistress, and identifies the killer to her just as he is about to die, Alfred's mistress could relate his words in court. The requirements for dying declarations to be admissible are:

1. that they be about the circumstances of the death (meaning they would have been admissible had the deceased been able to testify), and
2. that the offence in question be the murder, manslaughter, or criminal negligence causing the death of the deceased.

Clearly, in these situations such a hearsay exception is necessary. Imagine how nonsensical it would be if the last words of a murder victim were inadmissible. The justice system's belief in the reliability of these statements is based on the idea that a person who knows that he or she is about to die will normally be truthful.

Historical Facts and Materials Relied on by Experts

It would clearly be impossible to expect experts to account for all of the information, theories, and so forth that they rely on in coming to their conclusions; although technically, it is all second-hand information. Consider the example of an expert accountant who relies on mathematical theories to reach her conclusions, and who is called on to testify in a trial. To avoid the hearsay prohibition, she would have to fill in the chain of evidence that enabled her to reach her conclusions on the matter before the court, and thus have to call all the mathematicians who originally formulated those theories. The courts have decided that this is impractical, and thus the hearsay foundation of expertise is not treated as problematic.

Business Records and Declarations in the Course of Duty

Business records are documentary hearsay evidence in the sense that the people who actually made the records—employees in various capacities—are not present to testify. The exception also covers the statements made in the records (also known as the "course of duty" exception). Thus, the evidence is second-hand. The person who recorded the information is usually not present in court because he or she is unknown and, even if known, he or she would be unlikely to remember having made that exact record and thus could not testify to having done so. Because the person who introduces the business records to the court is not the person who made the documents, business records are second-hand information and are considered hearsay.

Take, for example, the business records of a bank, which include, for example, account forms, loan forms, and credit information about clients. Because many employees have access to the same files, it becomes impossible to determine exactly which employee actually recorded each transaction. Later, a transaction may become important evidence in a criminal investigation, but it would likely be pointless to attempt to ascertain, for example, *who* recorded that a Mr. Edwards withdrew $2,000 on Tuesday, January 3, 2012.

These records should be admissible simply because they are usually reliable. Businesses such as banks, manufacturers, and retail businesses rely on their records being truthful and accurate, and hence should normally have no reason to exaggerate or hide facts. The assumption is that businesses generally have no motive to fabricate. Naturally, if such a motive is found, the records become inadmissible.

Under s. 30 of the *Canada Evidence Act*, business records are to be admitted in evidence as long as they are made in the "usual and ordinary course of business." The courts have developed a similar rule regarding declarations in the course of duty, which include both written and oral declarations in a business setting as long as they are made (1) contemporaneously (made at the time of the event), (2) in the ordinary course of duty, (3) by persons having personal knowledge of the matters in question, (4) by persons who are under a duty to make the record or report, and (5) by persons having no motive to misrepresent the matters. Thus, in court, business records and declarations in the course of duty constitute ***prima facie* evidence** of their contents.

***prima facie* evidence**
evidence that is reliable on first impression, and that is accepted in the absence of any challenge to its validity

WEIGHT TO BE GIVEN TO HEARSAY

If hearsay evidence is ruled admissible by the judge, it may still be given less weight than first-hand evidence. Its weight will depend both on the quality of the hearsay and on the credibility of the witness who relates the hearsay to the court. The jury will usually be told to look to other evidence in the case for corroboration.

The Principled Approach to Hearsay

Despite the many exceptions described above, the current approach to hearsay admissibility is the "principled approach." This involves looking at each piece of hearsay evidence on a case-by-case basis. Hearsay evidence will be admitted if it is (1) necessary, and (2) reliable. That is, if for some legitimate reason the out-of-court speaker is not available to give evidence—and the evidence is necessary—and there are good reasons to accept that the out-of-court speaker's statements are reliable, despite the fact that the evidence is second-hand and cannot be challenged in court, the evidence will be admitted. This avoids some of the more complicated exceptions discussed above.

The principled approach was adopted after the Supreme Court of Canada decided the case of *R. v. Khan* (1990). In that case, a four-year-old girl complained to her mother immediately after leaving the doctor's office that the doctor had put his "birdie" in her mouth. Semen was found on the child's dress, but the child was clearly too young to testify. Despite the fact that this was hearsay evidence and no specific exception applied, the Court allowed the mother to repeat her child's statement as a result of the necessity and reliability of the evidence. The evidence was *necessary* because it was the foundation of the charge, but the child was not available as a witness. It was *reliable* because the circumstances made it trustworthy: the child had told her mother about the event immediately after leaving the office and without prompting; the story involved details that children of that age would usually not know; and the semen stain corroborated the story.

In *R. v. Smith* (1992), the Supreme Court further explained "necessity" as referring to the necessity of the hearsay evidence to prove a fact in issue. It does not mean "necessary to the prosecution's case." Necessity will be established where relevant direct evidence is, for a variety of reasons, not available from another source.

TRADITIONAL EXCEPTIONS AND THE PRINCIPLED APPROACH

In *R. v. Mapara* (2005), the Supreme Court reaffirmed the continuing application of the traditional exceptions to the hearsay rule within the following framework:

1. Hearsay evidence is presumptively inadmissible unless it falls under an exception to the hearsay rule. The traditional exceptions to the hearsay rule remain in place.
2. A hearsay exception can be challenged to determine whether it meets the criteria of necessity and reliability, required by the principled approach. The exception can be modified as necessary to bring it into compliance.
3. In "rare cases," evidence falling within an existing exception may be excluded because the signs of necessity and reliability are lacking in the particular circumstances of the case.
4. If hearsay evidence does not fall under a hearsay exception, it may still be admitted if indications of reliability and necessity are established on a *voir dire*.

SUMMARY: ADMISSIBILITY OF HEARSAY EVIDENCE

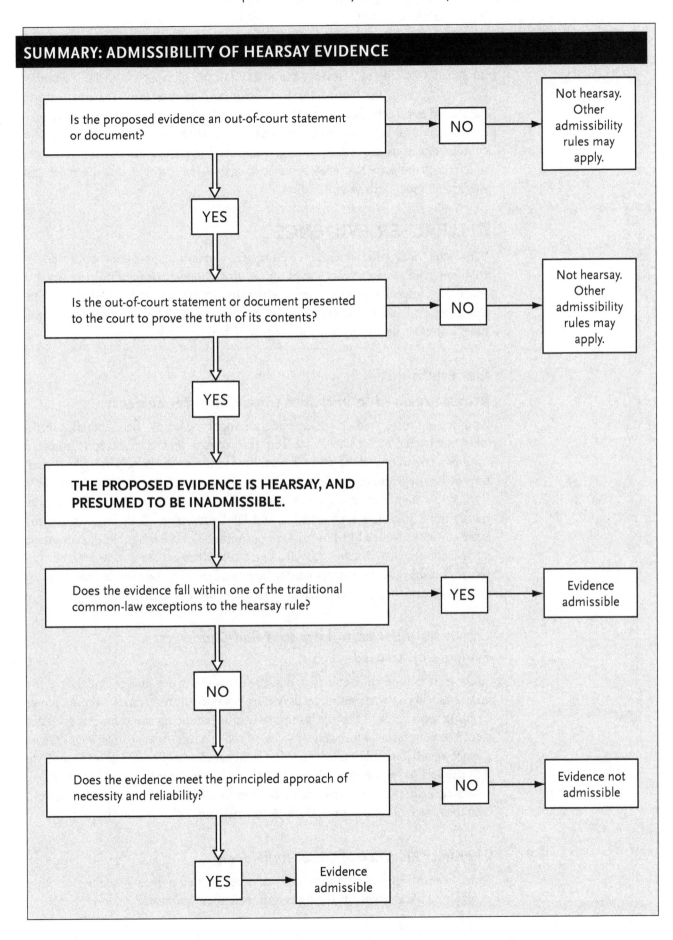

In terms of "reliability," the Supreme Court made it clear in *R. v. Khelawon* (2006) that the trial judge acts as a gatekeeper in making the preliminary assessment of threshold reliability of a hearsay statement and the ultimate determination of its worth is left with the fact finder. In determining admissibility, the court uses a functional approach focused on the particular dangers raised by the hearsay evidence sought to be introduced—for example, that there was no opportunity for contemporaneous cross-examination—and on those attributes or circumstances relied on by the party to overcome those dangers—for example, that the statement was made under oath or affirmation.

CHARACTER EVIDENCE

"Character" is a generalized description of a person's dispositions, or of the dispositions with respect to a general trait such as honesty or peacefulness. In this sense, character is concerned with behavioural traits, and is broader than habit. Character evidence is any evidence that is presented to establish personality, attitude, general capacity, or the propensity to behave in a certain way.

General Rules

Accused Allowed to Introduce Good-Character Evidence

As a general rule, good-character evidence about the accused is generally admissible in criminal trials. This flows from the premise that the accused is innocent until proven guilty, and therefore is permitted to rebut the charges brought against him or her by adducing evidence of his or her good character. This exception is limited to evidence of reputation, excluding specific acts of goodness. Thus, statements from neighbours, co-workers, and family members that, for example, the accused "is really well liked by all," are permitted. On the other hand, statements such as the accused "donates $5,000 a year to the Humane Society" are not permitted. If raised by the defence, good-character evidence can be rebutted by the prosecution by evidence of "bad" character (see the discussion below).

Crown Not Allowed to Introduce Bad-Character Evidence of Accused

In contrast to good-character evidence, the Crown may not adduce evidence of the accused's bad character, either by providing evidence of the accused's reputation or by citing specific acts. This rule is in place because adducing bad-character evidence would be prejudicial to the accused—for example, it might cause the jury to convict the accused based only on the fact that the character evidence seems to indicate that the accused is the kind of person who would commit the crime in question. Character evidence may also be prejudicial in the sense that it wastes time and can lead to tangential issues. Exceptions to this rule are discussed below.

Character Evidence of Other Individuals

Apart from his or her own character, an accused may put the character of other people into issue when advancing certain defences. For example:

- *Third-party suspects.* The defence is permitted to call evidence to show that someone else is more likely than the accused to have committed the crime.

- *Claims of self-defence.* To support a defence such as self-defence, evidence of violence or threats on the part of the victim is admissible.

- *Claims of consent in sexual assault cases.* To support a defence that a complainant consented to the sexual activity with the accused, the defence may seek the trial judge's permission to ask the complainant questions about his or her past sexual conduct. However, ss. 276 and 277 of the *Criminal Code* provide an important limit on evidence about the character of complainants in sexual assault cases, by prohibiting evidence about a complainant's sexual history, except in very rare circumstances.

Expert Evidence Relating to Character

Expert evidence of character is generally not admissible unless the crime could only have been committed by a member of a group with distinctive psychological characteristics. For example, if a murder was clearly committed by a pedophile, and the accused does not have any of the characteristics of that paraphilia (sexual disorder), expert evidence of the accused's sexual character may be permitted. Recently there has been a trend toward not admitting expert evidence of character, because scientific opinion on certain issues is still in flux, and the evidence may be too heavily weighted, without sufficient scientific grounding.

Exceptions to the General Rule Excluding Bad-Character Evidence of the Accused

Although bad-character evidence is in general *not* admissible, there are a number of exceptions. The Crown may adduce bad-character evidence in the following exceptional circumstances:

1. in response to good-character evidence led by the accused,
2. where evidence of character is relevant to an issue at trial, and
3. in the case of similar-fact evidence.

Accused Asserts Good Character

If the accused chooses to put forward evidence of good character or otherwise claims to have a good character, the prosecution is permitted to cross-examine such testimony and put specific examples of bad character to the witness to weaken the force of the witness's evidence. The prosecution is permitted to do so only when the accused first initiates the discussion of his or her character. For example, if the accused's neighbour is asked to testify by the defence and begins to say what a great person the accused is, the prosecution is allowed to rebut this by demonstrating that the accused, for example, has a criminal record (thereby alluding to evidence that would otherwise be too prejudicial to put forward). Therefore, the defence must be careful not to put the accused's character in issue—unless the accused has an absolutely spotless reputation.

Evidence that will *not* put the accused's character in issue includes:

- a denial of the crime (this is not the same thing as testifying to good character);
- an explanation that fleshes out the defence; and
- a description of the accused's background, such as his or her education and employment history (as long as the defence does not stray into philanthropic deeds).

Note that if the accused decides to testify, s. 12 of the *Canada Evidence Act* allows an accused to be cross-examined on his or her criminal record (but not concerning the details of the conduct respecting the conviction). This is subject to the trial judge's discretion to prohibit or limit cross-examination of an accused on his or her criminal record where the potential prejudice of such cross-examination outweighs the potential probative value (*R. v. Corbett*, 1988). In addition, if the accused puts his character in issue during the examination-in-chief, s. 666 of the *Criminal Code* allows for wider cross-examination than under s. 12 of the *Canada Evidence Act*. In such cases, the accused may be questioned about the specific conduct and facts relating to the criminal convictions.

Character Evidence Relevant to Issue

Another situation where the prosecution may raise the issue of an accused's character is in a case where character is directly in issue. For example, John is charged with murdering a drug trafficker, Ricky. The prosecution may be allowed to lead evidence that John was a violent drug dealer and involved in a longstanding "turf war" with Ricky. The evidence would not be admissible to prove that John was the type of bad person more likely to commit the murder; rather, it would be admissible to demonstrate a motive on the part of John to commit the murder.

Similar-Fact Evidence

As stated, evidence that does no more than blacken the character of an accused is inadmissible. However, there may be evidence of an accused's prior misconduct that bears enough similarity to the present charges to suggest that it is not merely a coincidence that the accused is now charged with a similar offence. **Similar-fact evidence** is evidence adduced by the Crown of the accused's past discreditable conduct on other occasions. It is used to infer the disposition of the accused—that is, his or her inherent qualities of mind and character—from which it may be further inferred that the accused acted in conformity with his disposition with respect to the specific issue in dispute.

An example is the famous "brides in the bath" case, which concerned a husband who had a habit of killing his wives. After the murder of wife number three, who was drowned while taking a bath, the prosecution was allowed to bring forward evidence that wives one and two had died in exactly the same fashion.

Similar-fact evidence raises the issue of prejudice, because in certain cases it may resemble propensity evidence. **Propensity evidence** is evidence that would require

similar-fact evidence
evidence that suggests that the accused has acted in the past in a way that is similar to the acts alleged as part of the offence being tried

propensity evidence
evidence that demonstrates that the accused is the type of person who tends to act in a particular manner

a judge or jury to infer that the character of the accused is such that he or she is the kind of person who would commit the offence; this type of reasoning is generally not permissible. Only a *specific* (as opposed to a general) propensity to engage in a particular behaviour may be admitted to help establish that the accused did or did not do the act in question.

Today, the leading case for the admissibility of similar-fact evidence is *R. v. Handy* (2002). The conditions for the admission of such evidence are narrow, and the legal test begins with the view that past discreditable acts are presumptively inadmissible. The prosecution must convince the judge on a balance of probabilities that, in the context of the particular case, the probative value of the evidence in relation to a particular issue outweighs the prejudice it may cause to the accused.

In assessing the probative value of the proposed evidence, an important question to be determined by the trial judge is: "What are the similarities and dissimilarities between the subject matter of the charge and the similar-fact evidence?" The lapse of time between the similar acts, the number of occurrences of the similar acts, and any distinctive features of the conduct will be considered in helping to answer this question.

Factors that are helpful in assessing prejudice include the damaging nature of the similar act, and whether the prosecutor can prove its point with less prejudicial evidence. In addition, the trial judge should remain aware of the potential distraction of the trier of fact from its proper focus on the specific facts charged and the potential time consumption in dealing with this type of evidence.

"PROPENSITY" OR "SIMILAR FACT"?

The following two examples illustrate the difference between evidence that would be considered propensity evidence, and therefore not admitted, and evidence that would be considered similar-fact evidence, and therefore would be more likely to be admitted.

Assume that Julie stands accused of brutally and repeatedly stabbing a stranger. The Crown wishes to adduce evidence that Julie has spent time in a mental institution and suffers from schizophrenia, and thus is more likely to have been the perpetrator of this type of frenzied murder. Clearly, the logical inference identifying Julie as the killer is weak. More than anything else, it proposes that Julie is guilty because she is mentally ill, and thus more likely than the average person to have killed someone. This is propensity evidence, and would not be admitted.

Now assume that Julie stands charged with murdering a stranger, dragging the body into a churchyard, and sewing a cross into the victim's skin. The Crown wishes to adduce evidence that Julie has killed small animals and sewn crosses onto their corpses, and, in the last year, has been charged with cruelty to animals. This presents a situation of strikingly similar facts. The Crown is attempting to infer the identity of the murderer from the similar hallmark of crosses stitched into flesh. Because the Crown is not attempting to say that anyone who does something as bizarre as that is more likely to be a murderer, the evidence will most likely be admitted. In effect, the recent pattern of behaviour is a form of identification evidence.

KEY TERMS

admissions	declarations against interest	propensity evidence
affiant	perjury	similar-fact evidence
affidavit	preliminary hearing	
declarant	*prima facie* evidence	

REVIEW QUESTIONS

True or False?

_____ **1.** Hearsay evidence is presumed to be inadmissible.

_____ **2.** If a witness said on the stand that "Bobby gave me the car," this would be hearsay.

_____ **3.** Spontaneous statements are considered an exception to the hearsay rule because they have a high degree of reliability.

_____ **4.** Hearsay evidence will not be admitted if it does not fit one of the recognized common-law exceptions.

_____ **5.** The "principled approach" refers to a school of thought that prohibits all hearsay from being admitted.

_____ **6.** As an exception to the hearsay rule, dying declarations are only admissible in homicide cases.

_____ **7.** The prosecution has the onus of proving that similar-fact evidence is admissible.

_____ **8.** Good-character evidence is admissible evidence if presented by the accused.

_____ **9.** Bad-character evidence is always admissible against the accused, because convictions would be impossible without it.

_____ **10.** The accused can be cross-examined on his or her criminal record only if the accused raises the issue on examination-in-chief.

Multiple Choice

1. Hearsay evidence is considered unreliable because

    a. people will say anything to get out of a tight spot.

    b. the witness may be prone to misstate what he has heard another person say.

    c. it amounts to oath helping.

    d. there is no way of telling whether the person whose words are allegedly being repeated actually made the statement.

    e. all of the above.

2. Which of the following is an exception to the hearsay rule?

    a. spontaneous statements.

    b. declarations against interest.

    c. the principled approach.

    d. a and b.

    e. a, b, and c.

3. Which of the following is *not* a recognized exception to the hearsay rule?

    a. business record exception.

    b. admission of a party.

    c. similar-fact exception.

    d. dying declaration.

    e. *res gestae.*

4. Which of the following would *not* be covered under a business record exception to the hearsay rule?

    a. medical records.

    b. a photograph of the crime scene taken by police.

    c. bank records.

    d. income tax records.

5. If the Crown is permitted by the judge to introduce detailed information about the accused's prior convictions, the judge has probably based his or her decision on

    a. the issues of necessity and reliability.

    b. the presence of facts strikingly similar to those of the case at hand.

    c. the fact that the Crown requested a special dispensation.

    d. the fact that evidence of the accused's good character was introduced by the defence.

6. The accused may put the character of other people into issue when advancing the defence of

   a. third-party suspect.

   b. self-defence.

   c. consent in sexual assault cases.

   d. a and b.

   e. a, b, and c.

7. Similar-fact evidence is not admissible

   a. where the probative value of the evidence outweighs its prejudicial effect.

   b. to prove a general propensity of the accused to be the kind of person who would commit the offence.

   c. where there are a number of occurrences of similar acts within a short period of time.

   d. where the recent pattern of behaviour is used as a form of identification.

   e. all of the above.

Short Answer

1. In which three exceptional circumstances may the Crown adduce bad-character evidence of the accused?

2. A key witness for the prosecution moved to Cyprus and the police have lost contact with her, although she testified at the preliminary hearing. What can the Crown do?

3. Jim gets hit by a car. As he lays on the road bleeding, he tells a passerby, Scott, "I'm dying. I was on my way to testify in court against Big Bobby. Please tell the court that I saw Big Bobby kill his girlfriend." Jim dies just as he finishes his sentence. The prosecution wishes to call Scott as a witness to testify as to what Jim told him. Defence counsel objects on the ground of hearsay. Is the statement admissible?

4. Define the test for the admissibility of similar-fact evidence.

5. Define the "principled approach" exception to the hearsay rule.

Exclusionary Rules II

Opinion Evidence, Privilege, and Improperly Obtained Evidence

5

LEARNING OUTCOMES

After completing this chapter, you should be able to:

- Understand the difference between fact evidence and opinion evidence.

- Discuss the rules surrounding opinion evidence that apply to lay witnesses and expert witnesses.

- Define privilege, and give examples of recognized class privileges.

- Describe circumstances that may give rise to case-by-case privilege.

- Explain the importance of police informer privilege.

- Understand what constitutes improperly obtained evidence, and why such evidence may be excluded.

INTRODUCTION

In Chapter 4, we discussed the exclusionary rules and exceptions pertaining to hearsay and character evidence. This chapter discusses the rules and exceptions as they pertain to opinion evidence, privilege, and improperly obtained evidence.

OPINION EVIDENCE

The general rule of witness testimony is that witnesses can testify only to facts within their knowledge, observation, and experience. Once a witness has provided this information, it is up to the trier of fact to draw inferences and decide what those facts may mean.

opinion evidence
evidence of what a witness thinks or believes, generally held to be inadmissible

In general, witnesses may not express their opinion—or give **opinion evidence**—on the stand. The statement, "Billy was always a troubled child," is an opinion, whereas "I have seen Billy howl at the moon on many occasions" is simply a statement of fact as observed by the witness. The general rule is that opinion evidence is not admissible. In our judicial system it is up to the judge or jury—not witnesses—to form opinions. The role of the witness is simply to recount facts that he or she has observed (Paciocco & Stuesser, 2008, p. 184).

In the past, any opinion that dealt with a critical issue at trial would not be admissible. It was thought that such opinions would overly influence the court, when an ultimate issue ought to be decided by the judge or jury alone. This rule is no longer considered valid, because it leads to awkward, disjointed, and incomplete testimony. So that the judge or jury can have the most complete picture possible for reaching a conclusion on an ultimate issue, witnesses are allowed to fully describe their observations.

Even though witnesses may express thoughts that touch on the ultimate issue, one thing they may *not* do is express their descriptions or opinions in legal terms. For example, a witness may not testify that a driver was "negligent," because negligence has a specific legal meaning. Instead, the witness should simply describe how the car careened into oncoming traffic and should avoid drawing legal conclusions.

oath helping
when one witness (improperly) expresses an opinion about the credibility of another witness

Witnesses may not express an opinion on the credibility of other witnesses, known as **oath helping**. For example, if an expert witness is called to testify that, in his or her expert opinion, the complainant is telling the truth because a person in such a situation is generally truthful, this evidence will not be admitted, because it is simply evidence that bolsters the idea that the complainant is telling the truth. There is no other merit to that evidence and it does not advance the search for the truth. It is generally believed that this type of evidence may unduly influence the judge or jury without adding to the fact-finding process (Paciocco & Stuesser, 2008, p. 189).

Despite the courts' reluctance to allow opinion evidence, there are exceptions that permit both lay witnesses and expert witnesses to offer opinions.

Lay Witnesses

lay witness
any witness testifying about a subject matter in which he or she is not an expert

Lay witnesses may usually express their opinions in circumstances where the conclusion is one that people of ordinary experience are able to reach. In *Graat v. The Queen* (1982), the Supreme Court of Canada held that non-expert witnesses may give opinion evidence on the following subjects:

- the identification of handwriting, persons, and things;
- apparent age;
- bodily plight and condition, including illness;
- emotional state—for example, depressed, angry, or affectionate;
- the condition of things—for example, new, shabby, or worn;
- some questions of value—for example, an approximate retail price for a commonplace item like a pair of sneakers; and
- estimates of distance and speed.

In addition, because the distinction between opinion and fact is often artificial, and because witness testimony is usually based largely on opinions or a mixture of facts and opinions, a lay witness will be able to give an opinion where the opinion is part and parcel of the witness's narration.

For example, when a witness identifies an accused person in court, he or she is really stating, for example, "This is the person who robbed me," "... who hijacked the plane," or "... whom I saw coming out of the building," which is an opinion, not a fact. Clearly, testimony would become disjointed and awkward if all opinions were weeded out. Accordingly, this rule enables a witness to effectively communicate his or her story, including conclusions, uninterrupted by the rule that forbids opinions. Ultimately, it is up to the judge to decide whether to allow these opinions to be admitted into evidence.

Expert Witnesses

Testimony from **expert witnesses** is also, essentially, opinion evidence. The trial judge will only admit expert evidence that meets the following four criteria (*R. v. Mohan*, 1994):

expert witness
a witness with specialized knowledge in a particular subject that is beyond that of the average lay person

1. *Relevance.* The expert opinion must be related to a relevant fact in issue, making the expert opinion necessary for coming to a correct understanding of the material elements of the case.

2. *Necessity in assisting the trier of fact.* Expert testimony is necessary when ordinary people—such as a judge or the members of a jury—would be unlikely to form a correct judgment about the particular subject of an inquiry without the assistance of individuals with special knowledge of that subject. Consider the example of a woman who is regularly beaten by her spouse. She decides to kill him, fearing that, if she does not, he will kill her. A layperson might ask why she did not go to the police or to a relative for protection. Clearly, being regularly beaten by a spouse is not part of the average person's experience and knowledge. Without an expert to explain the thought processes common among victims of battered wife syndrome, a judge or jury might not understand the defendant's belief that she was acting in self-defence (a defence found in s. 34 of the *Criminal Code*) when she killed her spouse.

3. *Absence of any exclusionary rule.* Expert evidence may not be admitted if it violates one of the other exclusionary rules—for example, the evidence of a

psychiatrist that is relevant only to the disposition of the accused to commit the crime charged would violate the bad-character evidence rule, and therefore be inadmissible.

4. *Properly qualified expert.* An expert is properly qualified during a *voir dire*, where he or she must demonstrate having acquired special knowledge and experience in respect of the matters on which he or she undertakes to testify. It is at this point that the expert must define his or her precise area of expertise. The expert should not be allowed to offer opinion evidence on matters beyond this established expertise.

Police officers are sometimes qualified by the courts to give expert opinion evidence—for example, about the street value of illegal drugs or the behaviour of criminal gangs. In these cases, the court will consider the officer's experience and training (including any special courses taken).

Novel Scientific Evidence

The trial judge must be especially careful when considering the admissibility of expert evidence that advances a novel scientific theory or technique, such as cell-phone tower data used to determine the location of suspects based on their mobile phone usage, or a police dog's signal used to detect accelerants in arson cases. In such cases, the reliability of the body of knowledge on which the expert's testimony is based must be strong. Factors that determine reliability include the extent to which the scientific community accepts the expert's theory or technique, the number and kind of errors the theory or technique can produce, and the care with which the theory or technique has been employed (*R. v. J.-L.J.*, 2000).

EXPERT EVIDENCE: PREJUDICE VERSUS PROBATIVE VALUE

Despite its obvious value in certain situations, because of a number of wrongful convictions in Canada and the United States that have been attributed to faulty expert evidence, expert opinion has come under the spotlight in recent years. In Ontario, for example, a recent review by the Office of the Chief Coroner found that Dr. Charles Smith had made critical errors in at least 20 child autopsies that led to a number of wrongful convictions (Goudge Inquiry, 2008).

In Chapter 3, we discussed that the trial judge has discretion not to admit evidence whose prejudicial effect outweighs its probative value. The judge has the same discretion with respect to opinion evidence. In the case of expert evidence, the risk of prejudice exists because scientific or medical opinion is often impressive and difficult to ignore. There is always a great danger that the judge or jurors will be overwhelmed or overawed by the "glitter" of an expert's experience and knowledge. They may simply accept the expert's opinion and base their judgment solely on the expert's conclusion. The expert's credentials may thus be given exaggerated importance vis-à-vis other evidence (or the absence of evidence) and may lead to faulty conclusions. Another problem may arise where one party does not have the financial resources to hire an expert as impressive as its opponent's to supply a contrary opinion. Finally, experts often have opposing views, and their evidence may succeed only in confusing the judge or jury and clouding the real issues.

PRIVILEGE

Privilege allows certain information to be withheld from the court. For example, with certain exceptions, solicitor–client privilege prevents lawyers from sharing information communicated by their clients.

Privilege is based on the idea that, for individuals in society to benefit from the existence of certain relationships, the confidentiality of such relationships must be respected. Because the normal rules of the court do not apply to information protected by privilege, it may seem that privilege works against the truth-seeking role of evidence. However, the benefits that flow from the confidential nature of such relationships are considered to override the value of disclosing information in certain cases.

Privileged communications are protected either by a recognized class privilege or on a case-by-case basis.

> **privilege**
> a kind of protection (exemption from admissibility) that attaches to evidence produced in special circumstances, such as in the course of certain classes of relationships

Class Privilege

Certain relationships or privacy interests have gained "class privilege" protection from the courts by virtue of the relationship between the parties. Class privilege communications are automatically presumed to be privileged and inadmissible, unless an exception to the privilege can be established. The class privileges recognized by the courts are:

- solicitor–client privilege,
- spousal privilege,
- police informer privilege, and
- Crown or public-interest privilege.

Solicitor–Client Privilege

Solicitor–client privilege protects oral and written communications between lawyer and client. This means that these communications, or knowledge the lawyer has gained about the client through these communications, cannot be disclosed either to the opposing party (which is usually the prosecutor) or to the court. To be considered privileged, and therefore protected, the communications must have been made by a client (1) to a lawyer, (2) confidentially, and (3) for the purpose of obtaining legal advice or preparing for trial.

The privilege is a right of the client (not the lawyer) and, where it exists, only the client may waive it. The privilege also encompasses any third parties who have had access to the communications for the purpose of providing legal services to the client—for example, secretaries, clerks, and experts. There is no privilege for communications that

> **solicitor–client privilege**
> an exemption from disclosure requirements for certain communications between a lawyer and client

1. are made for the purpose of or contribute to the commission of a criminal offence;

2. reveal a clear and imminent threat to public safety;

3. contain information that is necessary for the accused to make full answer and defence;

4. have been overheard by another party—note that this does not include a third party who has access to the communications for the purpose of providing legal services to the client; and

5. are evidenced in documents that have been lost or stolen—that is, that cannot be produced.

Spousal Privilege

spousal privilege
an exemption from disclosure and compellability for the spouse of an accused

As mentioned in Chapter 2, spouses are not required to testify against one another in most circumstances. **Spousal privilege** is founded on the idea of maintaining marital harmony and protecting the legal construct of marriage. As stated in s. 4 of the *Canada Evidence Act*, the privilege does not apply to common-law, same-sex, irreconcilably separated, or divorced spouses.

Sections 4(2), 4(3), and 4(5) of the *Canada Evidence Act* set out the circumstances under which spouses may be compelled to testify—namely, in cases where:

1. The offence involves one spouse against the other spouse, and affects the person, health, or liberty of the victim spouse.

2. The offence involves an indecent act.

3. The offence involves abduction of children.

4. The offence involves criminal neglect of family members.

5. The offence involves an assault against a child under age 14.

In the above circumstances, the need for spouses to be compellable and competent witnesses against each other is clear. If spousal privilege applied, wife batterers and child abusers would be protected by the knowledge that the person most knowledgeable about the crime would be unable to testify against them.

Police Informer Privilege

police informer privilege
a privilege that attaches, in some situations, to the identity of a police informer, such as the provider of a "Crime Stoppers" tip

The police often rely on confidential informants, such as those who contact them through Crime Stoppers, to give them information about crimes. These individuals are protected by **police informer privilege**, which protects not only the name of the informer from being revealed in court, but any information that may implicitly identify him or her.

The Crown or the police may claim privilege on behalf of the confidential informant, but the privilege cannot be waived without the consent of the informant. This privilege is subject to only one exception: the "innocence at stake" exception requires that the identity of the informer be disclosed where it is necessary to demonstrate the innocence of the accused (*R. v. Leipert*, 1997). For example, if the confidential informant is a **material witness** to the crime, then his or her identity must be revealed. This exception is rarely resorted to, however, because the accused will have to demonstrate that factual innocence *is* at stake. Mere speculation that the information *might* assist the defence will not be enough to set aside the privilege.

material witness
a witness who has observed "material" facts, or facts that are relevant to proving the elements of the offence with which an accused is charged

The importance of protecting the identity of police informers must be emphasized. Such protection not only ensures the safety of the informant, but it also encourages others to divulge information about crimes to police; without police informer privilege, people would be less willing to report friends, acquaintances, and others for fear of reprisals. In *R. v. Leipert* (1997, para. 16), the Supreme Court of Canada emphasized the responsibility of courts not to accidentally deprive informants of the privilege the law provides. For example, in the case of an anonymous tip to Crime Stoppers, because the identity and circumstances of the informant are unknown, it can be difficult to know what information might allow the accused to identify the informant. A seemingly small detail, such as the time the call was made, could be enough to allow the accused to identify the informant. Courts must not reveal any information that could identify the informant either (1) directly or (2) indirectly, by disclosing information that narrows the pool of people who share certain characteristics with the informant and allows for identification through a process of elimination.

When police officers are testifying and the issue of informant privilege arises, the phrase commonly used to keep the informant's identity concealed is, "It would not be in the public's interest for me to disclose my source of information."

Crown or Public-Interest Privilege

The **Crown** or **public-interest privilege** is based on the idea that, in certain instances, government documents should remain secret for the protection of the public—for example, the location of a police investigative surveillance post whose disclosure would compromise ongoing investigations. The state may also claim the privilege on the ground that doing so will ensure the highest degree of honesty among its operatives. For example, if operatives believe that they may be called on at any time to disclose the nature of their work, they will be in the position of having to resort to lies to preserve the integrity and secrecy of their projects. (This is not, however, to give credence to the idea that the state is involved in coverups and conspiracies.)

Consider the example of an undercover police officer gathering evidence against a biker gang. If the officer were forced to reveal his or her undercover identity in court, the operation would be jeopardized, as would the officer's safety, the safety of other officers, and the public's interest in catching violent criminals. Claiming Crown or public-interest privilege does not automatically ensure secrecy, because it is still up to the judge to exercise discretion, and he or she may choose to review the evidence and disclose all or part of it.

Case-by-Case Privilege

In addition to the recognized categories of privilege discussed above, the courts will sometimes approve the legal protection of communications made in the course of some other relationships on a case-by-case basis—for example, certain communications between physicians and patients, priests and penitents, and journalists and confidential sources.

Any communication for which privilege is claimed must satisfy the following criteria, known as the **Wigmore test** (*R. v. McClure*, 2001):

1. The communication must have been made in confidence and on the understanding that it would not be disclosed.

Crown or public-interest privilege
a class of privilege protecting information the disclosure of which would threaten the public interest, such as, in some cases, the identity of undercover investigators

Wigmore test
a case-by-case model for establishing privilege

JOURNALIST CONFIDENTIAL SOURCE PRIVILEGE

In *R. v. National Post* (2010), the Supreme Court held that while the common law does not recognize a class privilege between journalists and secret sources, a journalist's claim for protection of secret sources can be assessed using the case-by-case model of privilege established by Wigmore. In the *National Post* case, the Court held that the privilege should not be respected because the document provided by the secret source to the police constituted physical evidence reasonably linked to a serious offence.

2. The confidentiality of the communication must be necessary for maintaining the relationship between the parties.

3. The community must wish to protect the relationship.

4. The injury to the relationship that disclosure would cause must be greater than the benefit to society of exposing the information in the communication.

IMPROPERLY OBTAINED EVIDENCE

Charter rights are fundamental individual rights in a democracy, and underpin all other principles in the Canadian criminal justice system. The legal rights enshrined in the Charter are summarized in the box feature below.

In any investigation, it is critical that police obtain evidence according to proper legal procedures. The rights guaranteed by the Charter are like trump cards, and when a Charter right is violated, the violation often becomes the focus of a case.

For example, consider a case where officers make an unauthorized entry into a private dwelling—that is, they break in without a search warrant—and find a large amount of cocaine. That cocaine might be part of a big trafficking operation, but the evidence might not be admitted, because a break-in without lawful authority is considered an "unreasonable search" that infringes on the s. 8 right to be secure against unreasonable search or seizure.

Similarly, if police fail to observe the legal rights of persons who are detained or arrested, or if they fail to follow proper procedures over the course of an arrest or detention—including during an interview—then any information gained in the resulting encounter will likely be ruled inadmissible. Among the procedures that police must follow are cautioning a suspect or an accused on arrest at the beginning of questioning and at any point where the charges against the suspect or accused change; informing the suspect or accused of his or her right to counsel; and informing the suspect or accused of the reason for his or her detention or arrest. In addition, no statement made by an accused person to a person in authority—for example, a police officer—will be admissible unless the Crown can show beyond a reasonable doubt that the statement was made voluntarily.

Not every Charter violation, however, will cause evidence to be excluded—according to s. 24(2), the violation must be a serious one that brings the administration of justice into disrepute. In determining whether this is the case with respect to a particular violation, the trial judge must consider the seriousness of the police

CHARTER RIGHTS: REVIEW

The following legal rights are enshrined in the Charter:

- The right to life, liberty, and security of the person (s. 7).
- The right to be secure against unreasonable search or seizure (s. 8).
- The right not to be arbitrarily detained or imprisoned (s. 9).
- The right on arrest or detention to be informed promptly of the reasons therefor, to retain and instruct counsel without delay, and to be informed of that right (s. 10).
- Various rights pertaining to proceedings in criminal and penal matters, such as the right to an impartial court (s. 11).
- The right not to be subjected to any cruel and unusual treatment or punishment (s. 12).
- The right against self-incrimination (s. 13).
- The right to an interpreter in a proceeding (s. 14).

misconduct, the impact of the breach on the Charter-protected interests of the accused, and society's interest in the adjudication of the case on its merits (*R. v. Grant*, 2009).

The law governing search and seizure activities is discussed in detail in Chapter 6, Legal Aspects of Search and Seizure. Chapter 16, Interviewing Rules, discusses the legal issues surrounding police interviews of suspects and accused.

KEY TERMS

Crown or public-interest privilege
expert witness
lay witness
material witness
oath helping
opinion evidence

police informer privilege
privilege
solicitor–client privilege
spousal privilege
Wigmore test

FURTHER READING

Goudge, S.T., Commissioner (2008). *Inquiry into pediatric forensic pathology in Ontario*. Toronto: Ministry of the Attorney General.

Grant, R. v. (2009). [2009] 2 S.C.R. 35.

REVIEW QUESTIONS
True or False?

_____ 1. As long as an expert proposes to give relevant evidence, then his or her evidence will be admissible.

_____ 2. Evidence obtained by way of an invalid search warrant will always be excluded.

_____ 3. Reliance on faulty expert evidence has led to wrongful convictions in the past.

_____ 4. "Innocence at stake" is the only exception to the police informer privilege.

_____ 5. Improperly obtained evidence by the police will always be admissible at trial as long as the police officer acted in good faith in seizing the item.

_____ 6. The statement, "I think he was driving at 150 km/h," is opinion evidence and would not be admissible.

_____ 7. In the past, witnesses could not comment on the "ultimate issue" in the trial. This is no longer the case.

_____ 8. "Oath helping" refers to situations where counsel attempt to bolster the credibility of their witnesses.

_____ 9. Spousal privilege does not apply to same-sex couples.

_____ 10. Communications between a patient and a psychiatrist are privileged and presumed to be inadmissible.

Multiple Choice

1. Which of the following are protected by "class privilege"?

   a. doctors and patients.

   b. police informers.

   c. priests and parishioners.

   d. a and c.

2. Spousal privilege does not apply if

   a. the offence involves impaired driving.

   b. the offence involves an assault against a 13-year-old boy.

   c. the offence involves fraud.

   d. all of the above.

3. Opinion evidence may be admissible when

   a. the opinion is related to a fact in issue.

   b. properly qualified experts give testimony.

   c. the opinion is one that the witness is uniquely able to give.

   d. all of the above.

4. A lay witness cannot give opinion evidence relating to

  a. estimates of speed and distance.

  b. the apparent age of a person.

  c. the comparison of fingerprints.

  d. the identification of handwriting.

5. When evidence is improperly obtained

  a. a mistrial is declared and everyone has to start all over again.

  b. it may be excluded from the trial.

  c. the Crown must pay costs to the accused.

  d. the accused's rights are infringed.

  e. b and d.

6. Which of the following forms of forensic analysis is considered to be the most accurate and reliable scientific method?

  a. fingerprinting.

  b. DNA analysis.

  c. handwriting analysis.

  d. toxicology.

  e. all of the above.

7. To be considered solicitor–client privilege, the communication must have been made by a client

  a. to a lawyer.

  b. confidentially.

  c. for the purpose of obtaining legal advice or preparing for trial.

  d. all of the above.

  e. none of the above.

Short Answer

1. Discuss some of the pros and cons of allowing the jury to hear evidence from an expert witness.

2. If a client asks his or her lawyer to hide a gun and a bloody shirt, does solicitor–client privilege protect the lawyer's actions? Explain.

3. The Crown seeks disclosure of communications between a journalist and a confidential source. The defence objects, stating that the communications are privileged. Discuss the test that has to be met in order for the communications to be found to be privileged and, therefore, inadmissible.

4. A witness stated, "I know what I saw. It was a clear case of reckless and impaired driving." Would counsel object to such a statement? If so, why?

5. The Crown wishes to tender evidence from a footprint expert. Define the test for admitting such opinion evidence at trial.

PART II

Working with Evidence

Legal Aspects of Search and Seizure

6

LEARNING OUTCOMES

After completing this chapter, you should be able to:

- Define the legal terms "search" and "seizure."

- Identify the Charter provisions that apply to search and seizure.

- Explain the concept of "a reasonable expectation of privacy," and describe how a person's expectation of privacy affects police search and seizure practices.

- Describe the three areas in which a person has an expectation of privacy.

- Explain the general rule in Canada regarding warrantless searches and seizures, and explain when police can search and seize without a warrant.

- Describe the process for obtaining judicial authorization to search and seize.

- Describe the potential legal consequences where a court finds that a particular search and/or seizure was unreasonable.

INTRODUCTION

Although they are often referred to as two sides of the same coin, search and seizure are in fact (and in law) two distinct concepts (Boucher & Landa, 2005). A **search**, simply put, "is something that infringes one's reasonable expectation of privacy," while a **seizure** involves "the taking of a substance or thing belonging to, or in the care and control of, a person by a public authority" (*R. v. Nairn*, 2011, paras. 38, 39).

One of the defining features of a free and democratic society is the right of individuals to **privacy**, commonly defined as the condition of being free from the unsanctioned intrusion by others. This includes the ability to seclude one's person, property, and information from the rest of society. The right to privacy is a highly valued right that enables individuals to live their lives largely free from the interference of others, including the state.

Despite the enormous value placed on the individual's right to privacy, there are times when society has a valid interest in limiting that right in favour of the greater public interest. As described by the Supreme Court (*R. v. Genest*, 1989, quoting Polyvios G. Polyviou, 1982, p. vii):

> The privacy of a man's home and the security and integrity of his person and property have long been recognized as basic human rights ... . But as much as these rights are valued they cannot be absolute. All legal systems must and do allow official power in various circumstances and on satisfaction of certain conditions to encroach upon the rights of privacy and security in the interests of law enforcement, either to investigate an alleged offence or to apprehend a lawbreaker or to search for and seize evidence of crime ... . The task of balancing these conflicting interests is a matter of great importance and of considerable difficulty.

Under the Charter, law enforcement activities, such as reasonable searches and seizures, are accepted as valid social safety mechanisms; however, despite the social benefits that may flow from police use of such investigative powers, their use must be continually balanced against the right of individuals to expect and enjoy a reasonable degree of privacy in their lives. Investigators who lack an understanding of the central principles of the law of search and seizure—and who fail to gather evidence in accordance with them—jeopardize the admissibility of any evidence they do gather.

GENERAL RULE GOVERNING SEARCHES

Contrary to many popular portrayals of police work, police are not entitled to enter a particular location to search for and seize evidence on the mere belief that a crime has taken place there. Section 8 of the Charter provides that "[e]veryone has the right to be secure against unreasonable search or seizure." According to the Supreme Court of Canada, given that the purpose of s. 8 is to protect individuals' privacy from unjustified state intrusion, it is not sufficient to determine after the fact whether a search or seizure was justified (*Hunter v. Southam Inc.*, 1984). Instead, the Charter requires that unjustified searches *not occur* in the first place, which can only be accomplished by judicial pre-authorization.

search
anything done by the state or its agents that infringes one's reasonable expectation of privacy

seizure
involves taking something belonging to or in the care and control of someone by a public authority

privacy
the condition of being free from the unsanctioned intrusion by others

Judicial pre-authorization, the most familiar form of which is the search **warrant**, involves police obtaining permission from a judicial authority—for example, a justice of the peace or a judge—*before* conducting a search. This mechanism not only provides for judicial review of whether there are reasonable grounds for the state (through the police) to infringe on a person's privacy; it also places restrictions on how, when, and where such a search may be conducted. (Judicial authorization is discussed in detail later in this chapter.)

In *Hunter v. Southam* (1984, p. 146), the court set out the general rule governing searches:

> Prior authorization, where feasible, is a precondition for a valid search and seizure. It follows that warrantless searches are *prima facie* [self-evidently] unreasonable under s. 8. The party seeking to justify a warrantless search bears the onus of rebutting the presumption of unreasonableness.

In simple terms, a search conducted without a warrant is presumed to be unreasonable, and the Crown will face the task of proving that the investigator's search was *not* unreasonable. Note that the words "where feasible" in the quote above do not mean "convenient"; rather, the term implies that an officer who has a reasonable opportunity to obtain judicial authorization before conducting a search or seizure must do so.

Where it appears that an individual may have a reasonable expectation of privacy regarding the place to be searched or the thing to be seized (see the discussion below) and it is feasible for the officer to obtain prior judicial authorization, then the prudent officer will apply for authorization. Failure to do so may result in any evidence obtained being excluded under s. 24(2) of the Charter.

judicial pre-authorization
process in which a police officer obtains permission from a judicial authority to conduct a search or seizure

warrant
a legal order authorizing a police officer or other official to enter and search premises

---

SEARCH AND SEIZURE: RELEVANT CHARTER PROVISIONS

LEGAL RIGHTS

Search or seizure

8. Everyone has the right to be secure against unreasonable search or seizure.

ENFORCEMENT

Enforcement of guaranteed rights and freedoms

24.(1) Anyone whose rights or freedoms, as guaranteed by this Charter, have been infringed or denied may apply to a court of competent jurisdiction to obtain such remedy as the court considers appropriate and just in the circumstances.

Exclusion of evidence bringing administration of justice into disrepute

(2) Where, in proceedings under subsection (1), a court concludes that evidence was obtained in a manner that infringed or denied any rights or freedoms guaranteed by this Charter, the evidence shall be excluded if it is established that, having regard to all the circumstances, the admission of it in the proceedings would bring the administration of justice into disrepute.

GUIDING PRINCIPLE: A REASONABLE EXPECTATION OF PRIVACY

For a search or seizure to be considered "unreasonable"—and thus for the Charter protections to apply if a warrant is not obtained—the subject must be able to demonstrate that he or she had a "reasonable expectation of privacy" in the circumstances, and the circumstances must not be covered by one of the exceptions. This reasonable expectation has been characterized as the pivotal test in determining whether a search or seizure has taken place for the purposes of s. 8 of the Charter (Fontana & Keeshan, 2010, p. 9). Individuals can claim that their rights were violated by a police search or seizure only if they can show that they had a reasonable expectation of privacy in respect of the place that was searched or the thing that was seized, or both (Boucher, 2005, p. 27).

When deciding whether to seek prior judicial authorization, an officer must ask two fundamental questions:

1. Does the individual in relation to whom the search or seizure will be conducted have a reasonable expectation of privacy with regard to the place to be searched, the thing to be seized, or both?

2. Does the proposed search and seizure activity fall under any one of the exceptions (discussed later in this chapter) to the general rule that all warrantless searches are unreasonable?

If the answer to the first question is "yes" and the answer to the second question is "no," then the officer will require prior judicial authorization to conduct a lawful search or seizure.

Determining when, where, and to what extent a reasonable expectation of privacy can be said to exist has become an increasingly important task for Canadian courts. For police, a list of circumstances would greatly simplify the process of determining whether judicial authorization is required for a particular search or seizure; however, determining privacy expectations is not always straightforward. This is because "a reasonable expectation" is *contextual*—that is, it changes as circumstances change—and so a simple list of situations in which police will need judicial authorization to search and seize is not available (Fontana & Keeshan, 2010, p. 22). According to the Supreme Court in *R. v. Tessling*, the "bewildering array" of techniques available to the police with which to conduct searches and seizures, and the many different circumstances in which they could potentially be employed, make the creation of a "catalogue" of situations in which officers require prior judicial authorization unrealistic.

In *R. v. Edwards* (1996), the Supreme Court listed some of the factors that must be considered *in context* to determine whether a reasonable expectation of privacy exists:

1. the individual's presence at the time of the search;
2. the individual's possession or control of the property or place searched;
3. the individual's ownership of the property or place searched;
4. the individual's historical use of the property or item;
5. the individual's ability to regulate access, including the right to admit or exclude others from the place;

6. the individual's subjective expectation of privacy; and

7. the objective reasonableness of the individual's expectation of privacy.

It is worth rephrasing and repeating a definition of search that is consistent with the Charter: a search is *anything* done by the state or its agents that intrudes on a person's reasonable expectation of privacy, in *whatever form* (Boucher & Landa, 2005,

PRIVACY EXPECTATIONS AT A GLANCE

Despite the difficulty in doing so—namely, that reasonableness is contextual—some authorities have attempted to provide investigators with guidance in determining privacy expectations. Hutchison (2003, pp. 14–16), for example, breaks down a number of case law decisions into three categories: those in which a reasonable expectation of privacy exists, those in which a reduced expectation of privacy exists, and those in which no expectation of privacy exists:

Reasonable expectation
- Individual's body
- A person's home
- The area immediately around a person's home (referred to as "curtilage")
- Hotel room
- Passenger in vehicle (with respect to their personal articles)
- Treatment information held by a doctor or a hospital
- Detailed banking information
- An open field without any "no trespassing" signs
- A public washroom (general use area and stalls)

Reduced expectation
- Motor vehicle on a public roadway
- Workplaces
- Border crossings
- Electronic tracking device placed in an individual's vehicle to monitor its location
- Prison cells
- Courthouses
- Public area outside an apartment window

No expectation
- Basic banking information (often referred to as "tombstone data"—for example, name, account number, type, and date opened)
- Cellular phone subscriber information
- Garbage (left at the curb, in a common apartment dumpster, by the roadside)
- Generic hospital information (for example, is a person in the hospital or not?)
- Things that are in plain view of the public
- Surreptitious photographs of people taken in public places
- Information and images obtained by airborne or overhead infrared detection equipment
- Welfare records (where given by welfare agency to police to investigate welfare fraud)
- Stolen vehicles (a thief has no expectation of privacy relative to a vehicle they have stolen)
- Cultivation of marijuana on land where the accused is a trespasser, or cultivation in plain sight on Crown land

p. 6). Thus, while it is obvious that looking through someone's home for evidence of a crime obviously constitutes a search, many other, less obvious scenarios involving police activity would still be defined as "searches"; the broad definitions of the terms "search" and "seizure" mean that a great deal of police investigative activity could be held to involve either one or the other, or both. Add to this the fact that Canadian law clearly states that warrantless searches and seizures are generally unreasonable, and we are left with the fact that a great deal of police investigative activity will require prior judicial authorization in order to be lawful (*Hunter v. Southam*, 1984).

The box feature on privacy expectations at a glance (previous page) outlines common situations where a reasonable, reduced, or no expectation of privacy exists. While the list is helpful, officers must have some understanding of the principles that underlie these categorizations. The following sections examine the application of the "reasonable expectation of privacy" principle in the three key areas identified by the Supreme Court as places where a person can be said to have a privacy interest (*R. v. Dyment*, 1988):

1. personal (a person's body),
2. territorial (a person's places or things), and
3. informational (knowledge or facts about the person).

Personal Privacy

The Supreme Court in *R. v. Tessling* (2004, para. 21) stated:

> Privacy of the person perhaps has the strongest claim to constitutional shelter because it protects bodily integrity, and in particular the right not to have our bodies touched or explored to disclose objects or matters we wish to conceal.

The primary activities covered by the topic of personal privacy are searches of the person and the taking of bodily substances, bodily impressions, and fingerprints and photographs.

Searches of the Person

In contrast to the general rule regarding searches set out above, the search of a person who has been arrested, known as a **search incident to arrest** or "incidental to arrest," is permitted without a warrant. A police officer may, without a warrant, search a person who has been arrested and seize from him or her any property the officer reasonably believes:

search incident to arrest (also search incidental to arrest) search of an arrested person permitted without a warrant

1. is connected with the offence,
2. may be used as evidence against the person arrested, or
3. is a weapon or instrument that might enable the person to commit a violent act against the officer or any other person or facilitate an escape (*Cloutier v. Langlois*, 1990).

Subsequent court decisions have expanded on this common-law power, authorizing warrantless searches of the person for the dual purpose of preserving evidence that might otherwise be destroyed and promptly and effectively discovering and preserving evidence relevant to the guilt or innocence of the person who has been arrested (Fontana & Keeshan, 2010, p. 700). The courts have also recognized that the authority of police to search a *person* incident to arrest extends to searching *the immediate vicinity* in which the individual is arrested and which is under his

STRIP SEARCHES

Are **strip searches**, in which a person's clothing is removed or rearranged to allow visual inspection of the genitals, buttocks, female breasts, or undergarments, as distinct from the less intrusive "frisk" or "pat-down" searches, covered under the common-law authority that permits search incident to arrest? Does a strip search meet the "reasonable" criterion under *R. v. Caslake* required for a search to be lawful?

In *R. v. Golden* (2001, para. 104), the Supreme Court held that, although the common-law search incident to arrest *does* permit strip searches and does not violate s. 8 of the Charter, such searches are so intrusive that they should be carried out only

> where the police establish reasonable and probable grounds [separate from the reasonable and probable grounds for arrest] for a strip search for the purpose of discovering weapons or seizing evidence related to the offence for which the detainee was arrested.

Further, except in exigent circumstances, such searches should be carried out only in a place (such as a police station, and not in public) and "in a manner that interferes with the privacy and dignity of the person being searched as little as possible" (para. 104).

The Court provided the following "framework" of questions that police should consider when deciding how best to conduct a Charter-compliant strip search incident to arrest (para. 101):

1. Can the strip search be conducted at the police station and, if not, why not?

2. Will the strip search be conducted in a manner that ensures the health and safety of all involved?

3. Will the strip search be authorized by a police officer acting in a supervisory capacity?

4. Is there assurance that the police officers carrying out the strip search are of the same gender as the individual being searched?

5. Will the number of police officers involved in the search be no more than is reasonably necessary in the circumstances?

6. What is the minimum of force necessary to conduct the strip search?

7. Will the strip search be carried out in a private area such that no one other than the individuals engaged in the search can observe the search?

8. Will the strip search be conducted as quickly as possible and in a way that ensures that the person is not completely undressed at any one time?

9. Will the strip search involve only a visual inspection of the arrestee's genital and anal area without any physical contact?

10. If the visual inspection reveals the presence of a weapon or evidence in a body cavity (not including the mouth), will the detainee be given the option of removing the object himself or of having the object removed by a trained medical professional?

11. Will a proper record by kept of the reasons for and the manner in which the strip search was conducted?

strip search
search in which a person's clothing is removed or rearranged to allow visual inspection of the genitals, buttocks, breasts, or undergarments

or her control—for example, the search of the interior compartment of a motor vehicle driven by a person who has been arrested (*Canadian Charter of Rights Decisions Digest*, s. 8).

For a search of a person incident to arrest to be lawful:

1. the arrest itself must be lawful;
2 the search must be conducted incidental to arrest; and
3. the search must be conducted in a reasonable manner (*R. v. Caslake*, 1998).

Of these three conditions, the second, perhaps, causes the most confusion. For a search to be conducted incidental to arrest, the police must be trying to achieve some valid objective related to the arrest. For example, in the case of a person arrested for a violation of provincial driving legislation (such as the *Highway Traffic Act*), once the police have conducted a search to ensure their own safety, they will have achieved their valid objective incidental to that particular arrest and they would have no further reason to search. If, however, they continued to search the arrested person's vehicle on a mere hunch that the person might have drugs in there, that search would not be incidental to arrest and would thus be unreasonable.

As Fontana & Keeshan (2010, p. 715) note, "warrantless searches of persons incident to arrest constitute the majority of searches conducted by police."

Bodily Substances

The "constitutional shelter" that protects the privacy of the person, referred to by the court in *Tessling*, means that there are significant restrictions on the ability of the police to search a person's body for the purpose of obtaining bodily substances. The common-law search authority that allows a police officer to conduct a search of a person's body incident to arrest without warrant does not authorize police to take bodily samples—for example, hair, blood, or buccal swabs for DNA analysis.

The Supreme Court has said that "state interference with a person's bodily integrity is a breach of a person's privacy and an affront to human dignity. The invasive nature of body searches demands higher standards of justification" (*R. v. Stillman*, 1997, para. 42). Those higher standards require that bodily samples may be taken from a person only where prior judicial authorization has been obtained. Section 487.05 of the *Criminal Code*, for example, authorizes a provincial court judge who is satisfied of various criteria to issue a warrant authorizing "the taking ... for the purpose of forensic DNA analysis, of any number of samples of one or more bodily substances ... by means of the investigative procedures described in subsection 487.06(1)." The samples themselves are taken by a peace officer following the procedures set out in the Code.

Bodily Impressions

An officer who wishes to obtain bodily impressions—for example, a handprint, fingerprint, footprint, foot impression, or teeth impression—from a person who is not in lawful custody must apply for prior judicial authorization pursuant to s. 487.092 of the *Criminal Code*, which allows a justice to issue a warrant authorizing a peace officer to obtain such impressions.

Fingerprints and Photographs

The *Identification of Criminals Act* (1985) authorizes police to fingerprint or photograph any person who is in lawful custody, charged with or convicted of an indictable offence (subject to a number of conditions, which are specified in s. 2 of the Act). It also allows for fingerprints and photographs to be taken of any person who is in lawful custody pursuant to s. 83.3 of the *Criminal Code*, which relates to terrorist activity, and for a number of other acts mentioned in s. 2 of the *Identification of Criminals Act*. This Act is the authority that police routinely rely on to fingerprint and photograph people who have been arrested.

Territorial Privacy

The Court in *Tessling* also addressed the issue of territorial privacy, recalling its origins in the notion that every person's home was his or her "castle" in which the individual should be free from unwarranted intrusion by the state. This simple notion of privacy, based primarily on private property, subsequently developed into a more sophisticated concept that seeks to protect individual privacy, with the home being the place where the most intimate aspects of one's life normally take place. As the Supreme Court said in *R. v. Silveira* (1995), "[t]here is no place on earth where persons can have a greater expectation of privacy than within their 'dwelling-house.' "

A reasonable expectation of privacy with respect to territory can be considered as a hierarchy, with a person's dwelling house at the pinnacle and other spaces—for example, the space around a dwelling house, commercial spaces, private vehicles, schools, and even prisons—considered less private, but still capable of giving rise to a reasonable expectation of privacy in certain circumstances.

While the central principle of s. 8 of the Charter is the protection of a person's privacy and not of a place per se, the courts will still take the place where a search occurred into account when evaluating whether a person's expectation of privacy, relative to a particular place, was *reasonable* (*R. v. Tessling*, 2004, para. 22). For example, in *R. v. Guiboche* (2004), the accused was arrested without warrant inside his father's dwelling house. He was searched incident to arrest, and police seized some incriminating evidence. The accused argued that, because he was arrested inside a dwelling house without prior judicial authorization and in the absence of exigent circumstances, both his arrest and the subsequent search of his person and seizure of evidence were unlawful.

WHEN IS A SEARCH REASONABLE?

In *R. v. Collins* (1987), the Supreme Court laid out a three-part test to assist the courts in determining whether a particular search is reasonable:

1. The search must be authorized by law—that is, it must either be judicially authorized or fall under one of the warrantless search provisions.
2. The law itself must be reasonable—that is, it must not violate the Charter.
3. The manner in which the search is carried out must be reasonable.

The court found, however, that the accused's father (who had a reasonable expectation of privacy inside the house) had given police consent to enter the dwelling and had told them where his son was hiding; as a result, police were lawfully inside the dwelling. Further, because the police had reasonable grounds on which to arrest the accused, they did not require a warrant, thus making the arrest lawful. With respect to the subsequent search and seizure, the court found that because the accused had not been living at his father's house for a number of years, he had no reasonable expectation of privacy there, and thus s. 8 of the Charter was not applicable. This case is one example of how the principle of a *reasonable expectation of privacy*, while it may be related to a place, is fundamentally concerned with the individual.

Informational Privacy

The question of how much information about themselves and their activities people are entitled to keep private from the state is a difficult one. The challenge lies in determining where exactly to draw the line of "reasonableness" (*R. v. Tessling*, 2004, para. 23). In *R. v. Plant* (1993, p. 293), the Supreme Court stated that s. 8 of the Charter should seek to protect "a biographical core of personal information" that individuals in a free and democratic society would wish to keep private from the state, including information that tends to "reveal intimate details of the lifestyle and personal choices of the individual."

Perhaps the most relevant—and the most contentious—area of informational privacy today is that concerning information stored digitally. The law of search and seizure is constantly evolving, and it is often unclear—even to jurists—exactly how it should be applied in practice. This is especially the case with respect to searches and seizures of information from, for example, computers, smartphones, and other repositories of digital information. It is not surprising, therefore, that even where investigators have obtained judicial authorization prior to searching an individual's personal computer, for example, they may be uncertain about what such an authorization precisely authorizes them to do. This topic is covered in detail in Chapter 9, Digital Evidence.

EXCEPTIONS TO THE GENERAL RULE OF JUDICIAL PRE-AUTHORIZATION

There are a number of exceptions to the general rule requiring judicial pre-authorization for search and seizure activities. These are found (1) at common law, and (2) in statutes. These exceptions are discussed in the following sections.

Incident to Arrest and Investigative Detention

On the basis of common-law authority, an officer may, without a warrant, search a person and the immediate vicinity around that person incident to arrest and seize certain items, as long as the search is conducted in a reasonable manner.

In addition to search incident to arrest, in *R. v. Mann* (2004), the Supreme Court recognized the existence at common law of a related power: search incidental to investigative detention. "Investigative detention" refers to the brief detention by police of an individual who is not a suspect in a crime and who is not under arrest, where police have reasonable grounds to suspect that the person is *connected* to a particular crime and believe that such detention is necessary. In this situation (*R. v. Mann*, para. 45):

> [W]here a police officer has reasonable grounds to believe that his or her safety or that of others is at risk, the officer may engage in a protective pat-down search of the detained individual. Both the detention and the pat-down search must be conducted in a reasonable manner.

The Court was careful to state that search incidental to investigative detention "does not give licence to officers to reap the seeds of a warrantless search without the need to effect a lawful arrest based on reasonable and probable grounds, nor does it erode the obligation to obtain search warrants where possible" (para. 37).

In the companion cases of *R. v. Grant* (2009) and *R. v. Suberu* (2009), the Supreme Court examined investigative detention in more detail and provided additional guidance on the circumstances under which a person could be said to have been detained and what Charter consequences flowed from such a detention. In *Grant*, the Court held that detention

> refers to a suspension of the individual's liberty interest by a significant physical or psychological restraint. Psychological detention is established either where the individual has a legal obligation to comply with a restrictive request or demand, or a reasonable person would conclude by reason of the state conduct that he or she had no choice but to comply. (*Grant*, headnote)

The implications of *Grant* and *Suberu* are discussed in more detail in Chapter 16, Interviewing Rules. The application of the search incident to arrest power with respect to cellphones and digital devices is covered in Chapter 9, Digital Evidence.

Consent and Abandonment

Under common law, an officer has the authority to conduct a warrantless search in a situation where a person who has a reasonable expectation of privacy in relation to the entity to be searched gives them consent to do so. Thus a homeowner whose property has been broken into may give the police permission to search the property for evidence of the crime. A person who is a suspect in a crime might also give police permission to conduct a search in relation to something in which he or she has a reasonable expectation of privacy.

However, as the Ontario Court of Appeal made clear in *R. v. Wills* (1992), there are certain legal requirements for consent to be valid. Where authorities "seek an individual's permission to do something which, without that permission, they are not entitled to do," the individual must "make a voluntary and informed decision to permit the intrusion of the investigative process upon his or her constitutionally protected rights." In practical terms, this means that an individual should only consent to a search following an opportunity to consult with legal counsel. Counsel will, presumably, advise the individual about the potential legal jeopardy that may flow from the decision to consent to the search. The failure to allow an individual to receive legal advice prior to consenting to a police search may result in any evidence that was obtained as a result of the search being excluded pursuant to s. 24(2) of the Charter.

A related warrantless search power exists with regard to property that has been abandoned. In *R. v. Law* (2002), the Supreme Court said that "[w]here an individual abandons his property, he effectively abandons his privacy interest in it." In *R. v. Patrick* (2009), the Court held that a person's right to be free from unreasonable search and seizure is *not* breached where police seize and search bags that have been put out to the garbage, because the individual has abandoned his or her privacy interest in that material. However, certain caveats are attached to this warrantless search power. Unless the garbage is placed "at or within reach of the lot line, the householder retains an element of control over its disposition"—that is, it may not be searched or seized without warrant.

Abandonment is a function of both the *location* in which the property is placed and of an individual's *intent* with regard to it. Thus, property placed on a porch, in a garage, or immediately adjacent to a dwelling would not be considered abandoned.

A related issue is property that has been lost by or stolen from the owner—for example, the contents of a stolen safe—and that is subsequently located by or turned in to the police. In *Law*, the Court said that the warrantless power to search and seize abandoned property does not extend to such situations, because the owners of the property maintain a "residual" expectation of privacy with regard to it.

Plain View

plain view doctrine
a legal principle stating that when a police officer is executing a search warrant in respect of one crime and evidence of another crime comes into "plain view," such evidence may be lawfully seized

The **plain view doctrine** states that when a police or peace officer is executing a warrant or is conducting a lawful search in respect of one crime and evidence of another crime comes into "plain view," such evidence may be lawfully seized. Note that while this doctrine empowers an officer to seize evidence that is *visible*, it does not authorize any search for additional evidence (*R. v. Jones*, 2011, para. 56). Section 489 of the *Criminal Code* also states, in part, that every person who is executing a warrant may, in addition to things mentioned in the warrant, seize anything that the person believes on reasonable grounds has been obtained by, used in the commission of, or affords evidence of a crime. Further, it provides that every peace officer who is lawfully present in a place pursuant to a warrant or otherwise in the execution of his or her duties may, without warrant, seize anything that the officer believes on reasonable grounds has been obtained by the commission of, used in the commission of, or will afford evidence of the commission of a crime under the *Criminal Code* or any other Act of Parliament.

Exigent Circumstances

A search without a warrant may be lawful if the court finds that certain "exigent circumstances" existed at the time of the search that required police to take *immediate* action to ensure their safety or to secure and preserve evidence before obtaining judicial authorization and in which it was not feasible to obtain judicial authorization before executing a search or seizure.

According to the Supreme Court in *R. v. Asante-Mensah* (2003), "[a] certain amount of latitude is permitted to police officers who are under a duty to act and must often react in difficult and exigent circumstances" (para. 73). However, in relation to search and seizure issues, the doctrine of exigent circumstances should not be applied loosely, but only "within very limited perimeters, and with an eye on existing search and seizure legislation" (Fontana & Keeshan, 2007, p. 883). In other words, police may rely on this warrantless search authority only in extraordinary situations.

The following are examples of what the courts have found to be exigent circumstances:

- In *R. v. Winchester* (2010), the accused brought his laptop into a repair shop; a technician discovered child pornography on the computer and called police. Police attended the store and seized the computer without warrant on the ground that it was illegal for the store to possess the pornographic images, and out of concern that if the customer returned for the computer before police could obtain a warrant the evidence would be lost. The court held that the seizure of the computer without warrant was reasonable because of exigent circumstances.

- In *R. v. Blackwood* (2009), the accused was a passenger in a vehicle that was stopped for a traffic infraction. Police escorted the accused to the rear of the vehicle to question him about his identity when he pushed one of the officers. The accused was subdued and searched and police located a loaded handgun on his person. The court held that the search and seizure was lawful because it was conducted under exigent circumstances.

- In *R. v. Ringler* (2004), the accused called the Toronto Humane Society to assist him in caring for a cat that had just given birth. When an officer attended the accused's residence he observed a number of live kittens and a number of mutilated kittens in the house. The officer indicated that it was necessary to take the live kittens to a veterinarian for emergency care, but the accused refused and became aggressive. Police were called to the scene and the accused was arrested for intoxication. The Humane Society officer subsequently seized both the live and dead kittens without warrant. The court held that the search and seizure was reasonable because of exigent circumstances.

- In *R. v. Smyth* (2006), the accused was a resident in a men's hostel when he was investigated for a murder that occurred nearby. Before his arrest, police seized the accused's bedding from the hostel without warrant, because they believed it might contain blood linking the accused to the victim and they were concerned that if they delayed the seizure to obtain a warrant the evidence might be lost. The court held that the search and seizure was reasonable because of exigent circumstances.

Various sections in the *Criminal Code* authorize warrantless searches and seizures in exigent circumstances. For example, under s. 487.11, if exigent circumstances make it impracticable to obtain a warrant, an officer may exercise any of the powers in the common search warrant section (s. 487(1)) or the tracking devices section (s. 492.1(1)) without a warrant. Under s. 529.3, an officer may enter a dwelling house without warrant for the purpose of arresting or apprehending a person if the officer has reasonable grounds to believe that the person is present in the dwelling house and because of exigent circumstances it is impracticable to obtain a warrant; s. 529.3(2) defines "exigent circumstances" as circumstances in which an officer has reasonable grounds to believe that immediate entry to the dwelling house is necessary to prevent imminent bodily harm or death to any person, or to prevent the imminent loss or destruction of evidence related to an indictable offence that is believed to be in the dwelling house.

Sections 117.02(1) and 117.04(2) are two additional sections of the *Criminal Code* authorizing warrantless searches and seizures in exigent circumstances. Section 11(7) of the *Controlled Drugs and Substances Act* (CDSA) also provides for warrantless searches in certain circumstances.

Statute

In addition to the provisions authorizing warrantless searches and seizures under the *Criminal Code* and CDSA, other statutes give officers the authority to conduct warrantless searches where an officer believes, on reasonable and probable grounds, that a violation of an Act has occurred.

For example, s. 32(5) of Ontario's *Liquor Licence Act* (1990) empowers a police officer who has reasonable grounds to believe that liquor is being unlawfully kept in a vehicle or boat to enter and search the vehicle or boat at anytime without warrant, and to search any person found inside.

OBTAINING AUTHORIZATION

Despite the differences among judicial authorizations—for example, the activities they authorize police and others to carry out, the judicial officer who is able to issue the authorization, and the tests that must be met in order for a particular type of authorization to be issued—the process of applying for the various authorizations is essentially the same.

The judicial authorization that is probably used most frequently by police to search for and seize evidence is the conventional search warrant provided for in s. 487 of the *Criminal Code*, known as a "s. 487 warrant."

To apply for a judicial authorization pursuant to s. 487, an **information to obtain (ITO)** must be prepared. An ITO is a document that sets out (in the specific form listed in the relevant section of the Code—for example, a s. 487 warrant is set out in Form 1) specific information, such as:

information to obtain (ITO)
a document used to apply for judicial authorization, setting out, for example, name of individual applying for authorization; offence being investigated; building, receptacle, or place to be searched and things to be searched for; and informant's grounds for believing that the application meets the test for issuance by a justice

- the name of the individual applying for the authorization (the informant);
- the offence being investigated;
- the building, receptacle, or place to be searched and the things to be searched for; and
- the informant's grounds for believing that his or her application meets the test that a justice will apply to determine whether an authorization should be issued.

In the case of a s. 487 warrant, the test requires the informant to provide information, under oath, that there are reasonable grounds to believe that there is, in a building, receptacle, or place:

> 487(1) ...
>
> (a) anything on or in respect of which any offence against [the *Criminal Code*] or any other Act of Parliament has been or is suspected to have been committed,

(b) anything there are reasonable grounds to believe will afford evidence with respect to the commission of an offence, or will reveal the whereabouts of a person who is believed to have committed an offence, against [the *Criminal Code*] or any other Act of Parliament,

(c) anything that there are reasonable grounds to believe is intended to be used for the purpose of committing any offence against the person for which a person may be arrested without warrant, or

(c.1) any offence-related property.

While the law provides little assistance about how the term "reasonable grounds to believe" is defined, practically speaking, it appears to require an informant to set out sufficient, weighable evidence in the ITO to allow a justice to make an independent assessment of that evidence and to determine whether there is a "credibly based probability that all of the preconditions for the issuance of the warrant exist" (Hutchison, 2003, p. 48). In other words, the informant must provide the justice with realistic, assessable evidence in support of his or her belief that the things to be searched for are probably related to the offence being investigated, that they will probably provide evidence of that offence, and that they are probably at the place to be searched.

In order that an ITO and any authorization issued in response to it survive legal scrutiny in subsequent court proceedings, the ITO must:

- be clearly written and free of errors,
- be a "full, frank, and fair" account of what the informant knows about the investigation, and
- provide the justice with the source of the information on which the informant is basing his or her belief.

With respect to the requirement for an ITO to be "full, frank, and fair," the Supreme Court in *R. v. Araujo* (2000, para. 46) stated:

> The legal obligation of anyone seeking an *ex parte* authorization is *full and frank* disclosure of *material facts* ... there is no need for [an ITO] to be as lengthy as [a novel], as lively as [a sex guide], or as detailed as an automotive repair manual. All it must do is set out the facts fully and frankly for the authorizing judge in order that he or she can make an assessment of whether these rise to the standard required in the legal test for the authorization. Ideally, an affidavit should be not only full and frank but also *clear and concise*. It need not include every minute detail of the police investigation over a number of months or even years. [Emphasis in original.]

The Court went on to say that an ITO should never attempt to "trick" the reader, and in this regard strongly counselled against the use of "boilerplate" language— that is, standardized phrasing or stock text that may be customized, in a "cut-and-paste" approach, to meet the requirements of particular applications. Whether done to speed up the drafting process or to make an application sound more "serious" through the use of complex, legal-sounding phrases, boilerplate language in an application is something that the court has said it deplores. Instead, informants should set out the story of their investigation fully and simply and explain in their own words why they believe that their application meets the legal test for the issuance of a judicial authorization.

When setting out their reasons for belief in an ITO, informants must observe the **rule against narrative**, which states that informants may offer conclusions, opinions, and facts in their ITOs—for example, their belief that an offence was committed by a certain person, or that the items they would like to search for and seize are in a particular building, receptacle, or place—but must also provide the court with the source or origin for those beliefs. As Justice Hill explained (*Re Criminal Code*, 1997, para. 8):

> Firstly, and most importantly, any factual assertion by the applicant within the four corners of the affidavit must be sourced to some investigative resource. Otherwise, the applicant breaches what is sometimes referred to as the rule against narrative. It is insufficient for an applicant to simply state conclusions, opinions or facts. The credibility and reliability of the assertions are inextricably linked to the investigative resources themselves.

According to one authority on the law of search and seizure in Canada, the provision of sources of information by the warrant applicant is "the single most important substantive requirement in relation to search warrants," because of the role of the judicial officer in the process—namely, the officer who issues the warrant "is expected to independently assess whether the applicant's belief is a reasonable one. This requires weighing the evidence that gives rise to a police officer's belief" (Hutchison, 2003, p. 42).

COMMON TYPES OF AUTHORIZATIONS

The various investigative activities authorized by the *Criminal Code* are described below. An officer considering whether to make an application for a warrant under one of these sections (or any other section of the Code) should first read the relevant sections in full, especially the portions that set out the grounds for issuance of the judicial authorization.

1. *"Common" warrant to search and seize.* Issued pursuant to s. 487(1) of the *Criminal Code*, and sometimes referred to as a **common** or **conventional warrant**, this is probably the most frequently used of all judicial authorizations. It allows a peace officer to search a building, receptacle, or place for anything that he or she believes (1) will afford evidence of a crime, (2) will reveal the whereabouts of a person who is believed to have committed a crime, or (3) is intended to be used for the purpose of committing any crime against the person for which a person may be arrested without warrant.

2. *General warrant.* Issued pursuant to s. 487.01 and typically referred to as a **general warrant**, this warrant authorizes a peace officer to "use any device or investigative technique or procedure or do any thing described in the warrant that would, if not authorized, constitute an unreasonable search or seizure in respect of a person or a person's property." This section has been used to authorize such investigative activities as covert entry to a

rule against narrative
rule stating that informants may offer conclusions, opinions, and facts in their information to obtain, but must also provide the court with the source or origin for those beliefs

common warrant to search and seize
authorizes search for and seizure of anything that will afford evidence of the specific offence being investigated

general warrant
authorizes a peace officer to use any device, investigative technique, or procedure to do anything described in the warrant with the exception of interfering with a person's bodily integrity

premises and storage locker—to search for, remove, copy, and photograph documents; take samples of controlled substances; fingerprint items; and seize garbage—within the premises (*R. v. Ha*, 2009). It has also been used to authorize surreptitious entries into personal vehicles and residences over an extended period of time (*R. v. Lucas*, 2009).

A significant difference exists between a common warrant and a general warrant in terms of the conditions for issuance. While a common warrant requires the informant to have a reasonable belief that the search "will afford evidence" of the offence, a general warrant requires only that the informant have a reasonable belief that the search will produce "information concerning the offence."

A general warrant (pursuant to s. 487.01(2)) cannot authorize investigative activities that would interfere with a person's bodily integrity.

3. *Warrant to enter a dwelling house.* Issued pursuant to ss. 529 and 529.1 of the *Criminal Code*, the **warrant to enter a dwelling house** (often referred to as a "*Feeney*" warrant, after the *Supreme Court* case of *R. v. Feeney*, 1997) authorizes a peace officer (under certain conditions that are specified in each section) to enter a dwelling house to arrest a person identified by the warrant.

4. *Warrant to obtain bodily impressions.* Issued pursuant to s. 487.092, the **warrant to obtain bodily impressions** authorizes a peace officer to do anything described in the warrant to obtain a handprint, fingerprint, footprint, foot impression, teeth impression—for example, to obtain a "bite" impression from a suspect in an assault investigation in which the victim sustained a bite wound—or other print or impression of the body or any part of the body.

5. *Warrant to obtain blood samples.* Issued pursuant to s. 256, the **warrant to obtain blood samples** authorizes a peace officer (in certain circumstances set out in detail in the section) to require a qualified medical practitioner or technician to take samples of a person's blood for the purpose of testing it to determine the concentration, if any, of alcohol or drugs.

6. *Warrant to obtain bodily substances for forensic DNA analysis.* Issued pursuant to s. 487.05, the **warrant to obtain bodily substances** authorizes (for certain designated offences, and subject to strict conditions) the taking of one or more bodily substances for the purpose of forensic DNA analysis from someone believed to be a party to the offence.

The investigative techniques that may be used to obtain those substances are authorized under separate sections of the *Criminal Code*. For example, s. 487.06(1)(a) authorizes a peace officer or person acting under the direction of a peace officer to take hair samples from a person by plucking individual hairs; s. 487.06(1)(b) authorizes a peace officer or a person acting under the direction of a peace officer to take buccal swabs from a person by swabbing the lips, tongue, and inside cheeks of the mouth to collect epithelial cells; and s. 487.06(1)(c) authorizes a peace officer or a person acting under the direction of a peace officer to take blood from a person by pricking the surface of the skin with a sterile lancet.

warrant to enter a dwelling house to carry out arrests authorizes a peace officer, under certain conditions specified in each section, to enter a dwelling house to arrest a person identified by the warrant

warrant to obtain bodily impressions authorizes a peace officer to do anything described in the warrant to obtain, for example, a handprint, fingerprint, footprint, foot impression, or teeth impression

warrant to obtain blood samples authorizes a peace officer to require a qualified medical practitioner or technician to take samples of a person's blood to test for alcohol or drugs

warrant to obtain bodily substances authorizes the taking of one or more bodily substances for the purpose of forensic DNA analysis from someone believed to be a party to the offence

7. *Warrant to search, seize, and detain proceeds of crime.* Issued pursuant to s. 462.32, the **warrant to search, seize, and detain proceeds of crime** authorizes a peace officer or person named in the warrant to search a building, receptacle, or place for any property and to seize any property in respect of which a proceeds of crime forfeiture order may be made under s. 462.37(1), s. 462.37(2.01), or s. 462.38(2). In essence, s. 462.37 states that where a person is convicted of certain designated offences and the court believes that property exists that was derived from the commission of those offences, the court may order that such property be forfeited to the Crown. Section 462.38 indicates that where a person has been charged with certain designated offences and a judge believes that property was obtained by the commission of those offences and legal proceedings have commenced against the individual who then dies or absconds, a judge may order that such property be forfeited to the Crown.

8. *Warrant to search and seize.* Issued pursuant to s. 117.04, the **warrant to search and seize** allows a peace officer to search a building, receptacle, or place for weapons, prohibited devices, ammunition, prohibited ammunition, or explosive substances, and to seize them.

9. *Authorization to intercept private communications.* Issued pursuant to s. 185, and sometimes referred to as a "Part Six" warrant (referring to Part VI of the *Criminal Code*, which deals with invasion of privacy and includes ss. 183–196), the **authorization to intercept private communications** authorizes listening in on someone's telephone conversations (commonly referred to as "tapping" someone's phone or, alternatively, a "wire"). It also includes the installation of a listening device (commonly referred to as a "bug").

10. *Production order.* Issued pursuant to ss. 487.012 and 487.013, a **production order** is an order from a judge or justice that compels someone other than the person under investigation to produce certain things. It does not authorize a peace officer to carry out a specific investigative activity; however, a peace officer may apply for such an order in the course of an investigation to obtain documents, data, or other information. Such orders are commonly used in the investigation of financial crimes.

    For example, a production order issued under s. 487.012 compels a bank, telephone company, or Internet service provider to produce documents or data or to prepare a document based on existing data. An order issued under s. 487.013 compels a financial institution to produce, in writing, certain basic, or "tombstone," information regarding an account holder, such as their account number.

11. *Tracking warrant.* Issued pursuant to s. 492.1, a **tracking warrant** authorizes a peace officer to install, maintain, and remove a tracking device, electronic or otherwise, in or on anything, to determine someone's or something's location.

12. *Number recorder warrant.* Issued pursuant to s. 492.2, a **number recorder warrant** authorizes a peace officer to install, maintain, monitor, and remove any device used to record or identify the telephone number or

---

warrant to search, seize, and detain proceeds of crime authorizes the searching of a building, receptacle, or place for the seizure of any property under which a proceeds of crime forfeiture order may be made

warrant to search and seize authorizes search for and seizure of weapons, ammunition, and explosives

authorization to intercept private communications authorizes tapping someone's phone by use of a wire and using a "bug"

production order an order by a judge or justice compelling a person or financial institution to produce documents, data, or information for a peace officer

tracking warrant authorizes a peace officer to install, maintain, and remove a tracking device to determine someone's or something's location

number recorder warrant authorizes a peace officer to install, maintain, monitor, and remove any device used to record or identify the telephone number or location from which a telephone call originates or is received

R. v. JONES: A SEARCH FOR LEGAL GUIDANCE

The case of *R. v. Jones* (2011) illustrates how a number of legal issues can flow from a seemingly simple police search, and underscores the need for officers to seek legal advice when they are unsure about whether to obtain judicial authorization for searches, including situations where a search evolves as a result of new information uncovered.

In *Jones*, police obtained a warrant to search an individual's computer for evidence of a fraud and inadvertently discovered images of child pornography. They sought advice from an experienced Crown attorney about whether they could continue to search the computer for additional evidence of child pornography on the strength of the initial warrant, issued for a fraud investigation, and were advised that they could. They subsequently located video files containing additional evidence of child pornography, and charged the individual with possession of the illicit materials.

The trial judge found that police were not authorized to search for child pornography on the basis of the initial warrant; she excluded all of the evidence and acquitted the accused. On appeal, the Court of Appeal considered a number of specific issues:

1. whether the pornographic images that the police stumbled on in their search for evidence of fraud were admissible under the plain view doctrine;
2. whether the police were permitted to continue their search for additional evidence of child pornography under the authority of the first warrant; and
3. whether the purposive search (subsequently found by the Court of Appeal to have been unauthorized) that yielded the additional evidence of child pornography constituted a sufficiently serious breach of Jones's s. 8 Charter rights to justify the exclusion of that evidence.

With regard to the first issue, the court found that the warrant did *not* authorize the search for and seizure of evidence of child pornography; however, the seizure of the image files was justified on the basis of s. 489 of the *Criminal Code* and the common-law plain view doctrine. With regard to the second issue, the court found that the original warrant did *not* authorize a more in-depth search of Jones's computer for additional evidence of child pornography and the police should have obtained a second warrant for that purpose. However, with respect to the third issue, the court found that the police had conducted the additional search of Jones's computer on a "good faith" basis, given the advice they had sought and received from legal counsel. The search did not constitute a sufficiently serious breach of Jones's s. 8 Charter rights to justify the exclusion of the evidence—that is, admitting the evidence would not bring the administration of justice into disrepute—and the trial judge therefore should *not* have excluded the video files containing additional evidence of child pornography pursuant to s. 24(2) of the Charter.

The appeal was allowed, and a new trial was ordered.

location of the telephone from which a telephone call originates, is received, or is intended to be received.

13. *Telewarrant.* Not a warrant per se, a **telewarrant**, issued pursuant to the *Criminal Code* (s. 487.1), is an alternative method of applying for a warrant authorized under another section. Section 487.1 provides that where a peace officer believes an indictable offence has been committed and it would be impracticable to appear personally before a justice to apply for a

telewarrant
an alternative method of applying for a warrant, whether by telephone or by other means of telecommunication

warrant in accordance with s. 256 or s. 487 of the Code, a peace officer may submit an ITO on oath by telephone or other means of telecommunication. Many sections of the *Criminal Code* that authorize the issuance of warrants contain specific subsections providing for a telewarrant application process—for example, ss. 487.05(3) and 487.092(4).

RULES AND RESTRICTIONS IMPOSED BY JUDICIAL AUTHORIZATION

The requirement that police obtain judicial authorization before conducting a search or seizure safeguards individual privacy by allowing only those searches that satisfy certain strict conditions to proceed. Judicial authorization also imposes conditions on how, when, and where a search or seizure may be conducted, and on what an officer must do after a search or seizure has been completed. This provides additional judicial oversight and monitoring of the search and seizure process—for example, was the pre-authorized search actually carried out; was any property seized as a result and, if so, where is the property currently being held?

A warrant issued under s. 487 or 487.1 of the *Criminal Code* will typically contain a specific date or dates on which the warrant may be executed and, unless an officer is able to satisfy a justice otherwise, pursuant to s. 488, the warrant must be executed during the day. A warrant typically allows police only one opportunity to enter and search the property described in the warrant. Once police locate the evidence they were searching for, or conclude that those items are not in the place being searched, their authorization to search pursuant to the warrant ends. If police interrupt their search by leaving the property entirely, whether or not they have located what they are searching for, the authority to search under the original warrant ends. However, it is possible for officers to come and go from a property being searched as long as at least one officer continues to execute the warrant there.

When executing a search warrant at a dwelling house, officers are normally required to follow a "knock and announce" procedure. In other words, before entering the premise officers are required to knock on the door of the house and say, for example, "Police, search warrant." It is possible for police to bypass this requirement where they can show a justice of the peace that announcing their presence beforehand (as opposed to, for example, using a "dynamic entry"—that is, breaking through a door to gain entry) would endanger officer safety or result in the destruction of evidence (Hutchison, 2003, p. 12).

Following the execution of a warrant (or anytime an officer seizes anything without warrant), ss. 489.1 and 490 of the *Criminal Code* provide for judicial supervision of the things that were seized. Section 489.1 requires a peace officer who has seized anything under the authority of a warrant to file a **return**, also referred to as a "report to a justice" (Form 5.2 of the *Criminal Code*), describing the things that were seized and identifying the place where they are being held. Section 490 of the Code and its various subsections provide for what is referred to as an **order of detention**. Section 490(1) provides for detention of the things seized for up to 3 months after the date of seizure if an officer or the Crown shows it is required for investigation, a preliminary inquiry, trial, or other proceeding. Section 490(2) provides for detention of the things seized for 3 to 12 months, and s. 490(3) for a period

return
a document describing things seized and identifying the place where they are being held

order of detention
period of time required for judicial supervision of things seized under s. 490 of the *Criminal Code*

in excess of 12 months. Where charges are laid, the judicial supervision of things seized, under s. 490, no longer applies.

REMEDIES FOR UNREASONABLE SEARCHES AND SEIZURES

Section 24 of the Charter provides the basis on which any person whose Charter rights have been infringed—for example, by an unreasonable police search or seizure—may apply to a court to obtain a legal remedy. Before the Charter, illegally or improperly obtained evidence was admissible as long as it was relevant (*R. v. Wray*, 1970), and the remedies that existed to address illegal searches were largely ineffectual. Such remedies typically included attacking the search warrant itself, if there was one, and the court ordering the return of illegally seized property to its owner (Fontana, 2007, p. 784).

Section 24 requires that, upon the defendant making an application to the court to have evidence excluded on the basis that it was obtained illegally, the court must first make a finding as to whether the applicant's rights were infringed or denied. If the court finds that the applicant's rights were *not* infringed or denied by the search or seizure, the matter proceeds no further. If, however, the court finds that the applicant's rights *were* infringed or denied, the court may decide to exclude the evidence "if it is established that, having regard to all the circumstances, the admission of it in the proceedings would bring the administration of justice into disrepute."

The wording in s. 24(2) means that not *all* evidence obtained by means of an unreasonable search or seizure will be excluded; evidence will be excluded only if a court finds that admitting it would bring the administration of justice into disrepute. Determining what would bring the administration of justice into "disrepute" is a challenging task, in much the same way as determining the "reasonableness" of a search or a seizure. In making a "disrepute" determination, s. 24(2) requires a court to consider "all of the circumstances." The Supreme Court in *R. v. Grant* (2009) stated that the phrase "bring the administration of justice into disrepute" must be understood in the long-term sense of "maintaining the integrity of, and public confidence in, the justice system." The Court emphasized that, although the exclusion of evidence in one particular case resulting in the acquittal of an accused person might be cause for negative public reaction, the purpose of s. 24(2) is to maintain the integrity of the whole justice system *over the long term*, not to focus on individual cases (para. 68).

The Court then set out (para. 71) "three avenues of inquiry" that a court must assess and balance when determining the effect of admitting evidence:

1. *The seriousness of the Charter-infringing state conduct.*

   Admission may send the message that the justice system condones serious state misconduct. The more severe or deliberate the misconduct that led to the Charter violation, the greater the need for a court to dissociate itself from that conduct by excluding evidence that is linked to it.

2. *The impact of the breach on the Charter-protected interests of the accused.*

   Admission may send the message that individual rights are unimportant. The more serious the infringement, the greater the need for a court to dissociate itself from the breach by excluding the evidence linked to it. With respect to search and seizure, the court stated that "[a]n unreasonable search that intrudes on an area in which the individual enjoys a high expectation of privacy, or that demeans his or her dignity, is more serious than one that does not" (para. 78).

3. *Society's interest in the adjudication of the case on its merits.*

   A judgment of a case on its merits is one rendered after argument and investigation, on the basis of the evidence and facts introduced. At the third stage, a court asks whether society's interest in seeking the truth through a criminal trial would be better served by admission of the evidence or by its exclusion, considering factors such as the reliability of the evidence and its importance to the Crown's case.

In other words, a court must weigh *both* the positive and the negative impacts of admitting evidence that was obtained through state actions that breached an individual's Charter rights.

INSTRUCTIVE ERRORS: THE EXCLUSION OF EVIDENCE IN R. v. CÔTÉ

Not long after the *Grant* decision, the Supreme Court was called on to review the case of *R. v. Côté* (2011), in which the police were found to have "violated virtually every Charter right accorded to a suspect in a criminal investigation" (para. 2). While *Côté* may be exceptional in terms of the number and severity of Charter violations involved, it offers the opportunity to see how the courts deal with such violations, and reinforces the importance of following correct procedures in an investigation.

R. v. Côté involved a 911 call in which the accused, Mme Côté, reported that her husband had been injured at their home. Before attending the Côté residence in response to the call, a police officer went to the hospital where he received information from medical personnel that the man who had been transported from the caller's residence had a probable bullet wound to his head. This information was subsequently relayed to two other police officers who actually attended Côté's residence. When the two officers rang the doorbell, Mme Côté answered the door in her pajamas. Police explained that they were there to make sure the premises were safe; they made no mention to Côté of their knowledge that her husband had a bullet wound, and they proceeded to conduct a search of both the interior and exterior of the house and a gazebo on the property. The Supreme Court held that this search was not legally justified, because police had attended the address knowing that a search might possibly yield evidence of the shooting, yet failed to obtain a warrant to search, and there were no exigent circumstances that would have justified a warrantless search. Police also conducted a subsequent "perimeter search" of Côté's property, which was also held to be unjustified.

Following these earlier searches, police applied for warrants to search the premises, but in applying for judicial authorizations the informant "failed to fully and frankly disclose all material facts" in his applications. In particular, the informant failed to mention the earlier illegal searches, and attempted to characterize some of the observations that were made by police during the earlier searches as inadvertent. The search warrants that were obtained by police after their illegal searches were found by the trial court to be invalid because, if the illegally obtained information were removed, there would be insufficient grounds on which to issue the warrants. They were also found to be invalid "on the basis of non-disclosure of relevant information as well as the inclusion of deliberately misleading information" (para. 26). The trial judge excluded the evidence obtained during *both* the unwarranted and the warranted searches of the Côté home, which included a rifle of the same caliber as the bullet found in the victim's skull.

When Mme Côté was detained, a number of serious breaches of her Charter rights occurred in relation to her interrogation by police: the police failed to properly caution her upon detention; they violated her right to silence; and they denigrated the advice given to her by legal counsel. (For a detailed discussion on Charter-compliant interview procedures, see Chapter 16, Interviewing Rules.) As a result of these breaches, in concert with what the trial judge characterized overall as a "systematic violation" of her Charter rights, Côté's statement was excluded from evidence. The trial judge's decisions to exclude the statement evidence and physical evidence obtained in both the warranted and unwarranted searches pursuant to s. 24(2) of the Charter were confirmed by the Supreme Court.

In addition to the Charter problems in *Côté*, the trial judge was also of the opinion that the police officer's testimony was "lacking in frankness and sincerity," with officers attempting to downplay the errors that were made during the investigation. The judge held that the "police witnesses refused to admit obvious facts and offered improbable hypotheses to the court" in an attempt to mislead the court into believing that Mme Côté had not been detained, and thus did not need to be cautioned prior to being questioned (para. 31).

The case of *R. v. Côté* should serve as a cautionary tale to all police investigators. It emphasizes the need to take Charter considerations into account when determining how best to gather evidence, and it illustrates what may happen when this is not done. It also serves to underscore the importance of being comprehensive and forthright when applying for judicial authorization and when giving witness testimony. The courts do not expect perfection from police, and may well excuse errors that are made in good faith while investigating criminal allegations. They will *not*, however, excuse attempts by police to mislead judicial officials in an effort to conceal improper activities.

KEY TERMS

authorization to intercept private communications

common warrant to search and seize

general warrant

information to obtain (ITO)

judicial pre-authorization

number recorder warrant

order of detention

plain view doctrine

privacy

production order

return

rule against narrative

search

search incident to arrest

seizure

strip search

telewarrant

tracking warrant

warrant

warrant to enter a dwelling house

warrant to obtain blood samples

warrant to obtain bodily impressions

warrant to obtain bodily substances

warrant to search and seize

warrant to search, seize, and detain proceeds of crime

FURTHER READING

Boucher, S., & Landa, K. (2005). *Understanding section 8: Search and seizure and the Canadian Constitution*. Toronto: Irwin Law.

Fontana, J., & Keeshan, D. (2010). *The law of search and seizure in Canada* (8th ed.). Markham, ON: LexisNexis Canada.

Hutchison, S. (2005). *Canadian search warrant manual*. Toronto: Thomson Canada.

REVIEW QUESTIONS

True or False?

1. One of the defining features of a free and democratic society is the right of individuals to privacy.

2. A telewarrant, issued pursuant to the *Criminal Code* (s. 487.1), is a special type of judicial authorization that allows police officers to listen in on private telephone conversations.

3. A warrant to enter a dwelling house to arrest a person in that house, issued pursuant to s. 529 of the *Criminal Code*, is also sometimes referred to as a "*Feeney*" warrant after the Supreme Court case of *R. v. Feeney* (1997).

4. The "plain view" doctrine is a legal principle that states that when a police officer is executing a search warrant in respect of one crime and evidence of another crime comes into plain view, such evidence may be lawfully seized.

5. A search without a warrant may be lawful if the court finds that certain "exigent circumstances" existed at the time of the search that made it inconvenient for police to obtain judicial authorization prior to executing a search or seizure.

6. A telewarrant is an alternative method of applying for a warrant where it would be impracticable to appear before a justice.

7. The common-law authority of police to search a person incident to arrest also allows them to take hair samples for the purpose of forensic DNA analysis.

8. A homeowner who places a garbage bag on the curb in front of his residence is considered to have abandoned his or her privacy interest in the bag and its contents, and police may seize it without warrant.

9. The courts have recognized that the authority of police to search a person incident to arrest extends to searching the immediate vicinity in which the individual is arrested.

10. A search is anything done by the state or its agents that intrudes on a person's reasonable expectation of privacy in whatever form.

Multiple Choice

1. Issued pursuant to s. 487 of the *Criminal Code* and sometimes referred to as a common or conventional warrant, this judicial authorization allows police to search:

   a. buildings.

   b. receptacles.

   c. places.

   d. all of the above.

2. Section 24(2) of the Charter states that evidence obtained by means of an unreasonable search or seizure will be excluded:

   a. if the seizure or search violated the accused's Charter rights.

   b. if admitting it would bring the administration of justice into disrepute.

   c. if the search was conducted without prior judicial authorization.

   d. if the affiant who applied for the warrant was not full, frank, and fair.

3. The *Identification of Criminals Act* authorizes police to fingerprint and photograph a person who:

   a. is a criminal.

   b. is in lawful custody, charged with or convicted of an indictable offence.

   c. has previously escaped from lawful custody.

   d. is to be transferred from police custody to a correctional facility.

4. Individuals can claim that their rights were violated by a police search or seizure only if:

   a. they can demonstrate that the police did not have prior judicial authorization to conduct the search or seizure.

   b. they can show that they had a reasonable expectation of privacy in respect of the place that was searched, the thing that was seized, or both.

   c. they can prove that the search or seizure was conducted in an unreasonable manner.

   d. they were charged with a criminal offence as a result of evidence obtained from the search or seizure.

5. The Supreme Court has identified three key areas in which a person can be said to have a privacy interest. They are:

   a. personal, legal, spatial.

   b. personal, territorial, informational.

   c. personal, social, informational.

   d. residential, geographic, informational.

6. A search without a warrant may be lawful if the court finds that certain "exigent circumstances" existed at the time of the search. Exigent circumstances include the necessity to take immediate action to:

   a. ensure police safety.

   b. secure an investigative advantage.

   c. ensure the efficient use of police resources.

   d. ensure that the police search remains confidential.

7. An officer has the authority to conduct a warrantless search where a person who has a reasonable expectation of privacy in relation to the thing to be searched gives them consent to do so; however, there are certain legal requirements for such consent to be valid. What do those requirements include?

   a. allowing the individual to consult with legal counsel before consenting.

   b. ensuring that the individual is of sound mind.

   c. ensuring that the individual provides consent in writing.

   d. allowing the individual a reasonable amount of time in which to decide whether to consent.

8. In *R. v. Collins* (1987), the Supreme Court laid out a three-part test to assist the courts in determining whether a particular search was reasonable. That test requires that:

   a. the search must be authorized by law; the law itself must be reasonable; and the manner in which the search was carried out must be reasonable.

   b. the search must be video recorded in its entirety; the law authorizing the search must be reasonable; and the manner in which the search was carried out must be reasonable.

   c. the search must be carried out under exigent circumstances; the law authorizing the search must be reasonable; and the manner in which the search was carried out must be reasonable.

   d. the search must be carried out for a proper purpose; the law authorizing the search must be reasonable; and the manner in which the search was carried out must be reasonable.

Short Answer

1. Describe the "rule against narrative" as it applies to informants setting out their reasons for belief in an ITO.

2. Describe the essential difference between a production order and a search warrant.

3. Describe a significant difference between a "common" warrant, issued under s. 487 of the *Criminal Code*, and a "general" warrant, issued under s. 487.01 of the *Criminal Code*, in terms of the conditions for issuance.

4. Describe the search power that exists with regard to property—for example, garbage—that has been abandoned.

Case Studies

1. Late one Saturday night, Officer Greene pulled over Randy's vehicle in the entertainment district of the city. The officer had stopped the car because he was suspicious of Randy, who looked too young to be driving an expensive sports car. Officer Greene asked Randy whose car he was driving. Randy replied that the car belonged to his father and he had his permission to drive it. The officer then told Randy that he was going to check his trunk. Randy asked, "Why would you want to check my trunk? It's not my car." Officer Greene replied, "Sounds to me like you don't want me to check back there because you have something to hide. Pop the trunk, now!" Again, Randy explained that it was not his car and he did not know how to open the trunk. The officer stated, "Well, if you won't open it for me, I'll open it myself. You can explain the damage to your father." Officer Greene then grabbed Randy's keys and told him to keep his hands on his head until he returned. The officer retrieved a tire iron from his police cruiser and used it to force the vehicle's trunk open. Under a blanket, Officer Greene discovered 4 loaded handguns and 20 kilograms of cocaine. He exclaimed, "Bingo!" and promptly arrested Randy for possession of prohibited firearms and possession of cocaine for the purpose of trafficking.

   At Randy's trial, his defence counsel brought an application to exclude the evidence of the guns and drugs pursuant to s. 24(2) of the Charter on the grounds that Randy was arbitrarily detained (a violation of s. 9 of the Charter) and subjected to an unreasonable search and seizure (a violation of s. 8 of the Charter).

   You be the judge. Would you exclude the evidence? Why or why not?

2. Jack Brown was arrested by Officers Roberts and Stoddart after communicating with Sandy Lewis for the purposes of securing sexual services. Sandy Lewis was an undercover police officer who had been posing as a prostitute on the corner of First Avenue and Lake Street, an area known to be frequented by sex-trade workers and their customers. Following Mr. Brown's arrest, Officers Roberts and Stoddart searched Mr. Brown's person and seized his car keys and a wallet containing his driver's licence and other identification. Officers Robarts and Stoddart then conducted a cursory search of Mr. Brown's vehicle, looking for items that could form part of a "sexual assault kit," such as duct tape, plastic zip ties, and weapons that could be used to assault or kidnap a sex-trade worker. In the course of conducting their search for these items, Officers Roberts and Stoddart discovered two bags in the area of the driver's seat, both of which contained a large quantity of cash and powdered cocaine. Mr. Brown was subsequently arrested by Officer Roberts on a charge of possession of cocaine for the purpose of trafficking.

   At his trial, Mr. Brown's lawyer argued that the cocaine should be excluded from evidence pursuant to s. 24(2) of the Charter, because Officers Roberts and Stoddart initially arrested his client for communication for the purposes of prostitution and had no legal authority to search Mr. Brown's vehicle for drugs. Defence counsel maintained that the search was unlawful and violated Mr. Brown's s. 8 Charter right to be free from unreasonable search and seizure.

You are the judge in this case. Would you exclude the drugs from evidence? Explain your answer.

Crime Scene Investigation and Management

7

LEARNING OUTCOMES

After completing this chapter, you should be able to:

- Identify some of the myths surrounding crime scene investigation.

- Describe the legal duty of police to collect and preserve evidence.

- Understand the importance of preventing contamination and maintaining continuity in collecting and preserving evidence.

- Explain what a crime scene is, why it needs to be protected, and the legal basis for crime scene security.

- Describe the roles and responsibilities of the various individuals involved in the investigation and management of a crime scene.

- Explain the importance of properly documenting a crime scene.

- Outline measures that can be taken to minimize contamination and ensure continuity of evidence.

INTRODUCTION

The ability of a criminal investigator to determine what happened at a crime scene and the ability of a Crown attorney to accurately re-create that scene through evidence introduced in a courtroom are both affected by the way in which the crime scene is protected and how the physical evidence found there is documented, collected, and preserved. In large part, this is determined by the actions of police officers from the moment they arrive at the scene to the time the first police witness takes the stand to give evidence in court.

This chapter examines some common myths regarding crime scene investigation; the legal obligations of police officers regarding the collection and preservation of physical evidence; what a crime scene is and how to protect it; the various individuals involved in investigating and managing the scene of a crime; and the documentation, collection, and preservation of physical evidence at the scene of a crime.

CRIME SCENE INVESTIGATION: MYTHS AND REALITY

CSI effect
the alleged influence of popular television crime investigation programs on juror behaviour and the broader public's understanding of the criminal investigation process

Portrayals of criminal investigators (detectives)—in particular, crime scene investigators—are a staple of popular entertainment. They figure prominently in television programs and movies. The term **CSI effect** has emerged to describe the alleged influence of popular television crime investigation programs—in particular, the CBS network program *CSI*—on juror behaviour and the broader public's understanding of the criminal investigation process. Such portrayals contribute to an unrealistic view of how crime scene investigators and forensic scientists actually work—for example, on television, both the investigations and the forensic analysis of evidence are typically completed within hours, if not sooner. The real abilities of the professionals involved are often exaggerated or simply made up. Forensic scientists typically present their findings in court with a level of certainty that allows for little or no chance of error; however, this is not how forensic science—or the criminal investigation process—works.

Television programs in this area have motivated a number of young people to consider careers in criminal justice and, in particular, those that deal with some aspect of crime scene investigation (National Academy of Sciences [NAS], 2009, p. 222); within criminal justice programs, many students express a desire to become crime scene investigators, criminal profilers, or forensic scientists (Anderson, Mangels, & Langsam, 2009). Although glamorizing the job of a criminal investigator makes for good entertainment, it unfortunately misinforms people about the realities of the work. Therefore, in the course of their studies and careers, many students need to unlearn what they have been "taught" about crime scene investigation from popular sources. At the very least, students need to realize that forensic work is more tedious—and less certain—than TV leads them to believe.

CSI myths are clustered around the following areas (Durnal, 2010):

- the roles of the various actors involved in the collection and analysis of crime scene evidence;

- the real capabilities of crime scene investigators;
- the nature of the evidence typically found at a crime scene; and
- the time frame in which the collection and analysis of evidence takes place.

The following sections discuss the myths and corresponding realities listed above and paint a more accurate picture.

Roles and Responsibilities of Those Involved in Crime Investigation

No CSI effect is more apparent than the confusion surrounding the respective roles of the various actors involved in crime investigation. On television, the patrol officer, detective, crime scene investigator, and forensic scientist are often rolled into the same character. That character gathers evidence from the crime scene, questions witnesses, analyzes evidence in the laboratory, arrests suspects, and manages the criminal case once it proceeds to court. This is not how real criminal investigations are conducted.

Criminal investigations are typically conducted by a number of individuals, each drawn from a different but related area with its own body of specialized knowledge, training, and expertise. Most criminal investigations start with the arrival of uniformed patrol officers at the crime scene in response to an emergency telephone call. These officers are responsible for conducting an initial search of the scene and surrounding area for suspects, victims, witnesses, and physical evidence; arresting suspects still on the scene; identifying, ensuring the health and safety of, and obtaining preliminary information from victims and witnesses; ensuring the safety of the general public; securing the crime scene; and, in more serious cases, notifying detectives to attend at the location.

The detectives, typically the next to arrive, assume control of and are responsible for managing the investigation. Through the patrol supervisor, they are also responsible for ensuring that the uniformed officers have carried out their responsibilities, including securing the crime scene (see the discussion below) pending the arrival of forensic identification specialists.

In general, forensic scientists become involved only after the above work is complete and the evidence packaged, catalogued, and prepared for submission to a forensic laboratory. Although scientists might occasionally attend at a crime scene—for example, in the case of a buried body, a forensic archaeologist might be called—they typically do not. In the case of large crime scenes or serious investigations (for example, a murder) it could be days or weeks before the evidence is examined by a forensic scientist. Moreover, no "general forensic scientist" performs all manner of testing on all types of evidence. Forensic science is broken down into a series of subspecialties, each of which has its own unique areas of expertise—for example, firearms examiners, biologists who conduct DNA analyses, and chemists who attempt to identify unknown substances. The forensic sciences are discussed in Chapters 10 through 15.

WHO'S WHO IN AN INVESTIGATION?

uniformed police constable
an officer who primarily patrols defined areas to which he or she is assigned and responds to emergency calls for service

uniformed police supervisor
typically, a sergeant responsible for the supervision of uniformed patrol constables who ensures the quality of the uniformed response to calls for service

detective
also referred to as criminal investigator, investigator, or investigative officer; typically, the officer in charge of a criminal investigation

forensic identification specialist
also referred to as an identification (or "ident") officer, an "FIS officer," a "SOCO" (scenes of crime officer), or a "CSI" (crime scene investigator); the person responsible for the physical investigation of the crime scene, including identifying, documenting, collecting, preserving, and analyzing or submitting for analysis the physical evidence obtained from a crime scene

forensic scientist
a civilian, laboratory scientist with analytical expertise in, for example, chemistry, biology, firearms, or questioned documents who analyzes and reports on evidence

- *Uniformed patrol officers.* Typically, **uniformed police constables** are assigned to a defined area, which they patrol. They also respond to emergency calls for service. They are usually the first police officers to arrive at a crime scene, and are responsible for ensuring the safety of the public, arresting any offenders present, and securing the crime scene. The first uniformed patrol officer to arrive at a crime scene assumes control of that scene until relieved of that responsibility by a supervisory officer or a forensic identification specialist.

- *Uniformed police supervisor.* A police supervisor in the uniform branch typically holds the rank of sergeant and is responsible for the supervision of a number of uniformed patrol constables; a police supervisor in the detective branch typically holds the rank of detective or above. **Uniformed police supervisors** are primarily responsible for ensuring the quality of the uniformed response to calls for assistance; they may also supervise a number of detective constables. When uniformed police officers are called to a crime scene, a sergeant is initially responsible for ensuring that sufficient resources are made available to properly protect and manage the scene. The sergeant assumes control of the crime scene until relieved by a criminal investigator or forensic investigation specialist.

- *Detective.* Also referred to as criminal investigator, investigator, or investigative officer, a **detective** is a police officer (who may hold any one of a number of different ranks, such as constable, sergeant, or staff sergeant) whose primary role is the investigation of crimes. Typically the officer in charge of a criminal investigation, a detective's responsibilities include conducting and managing the investigation; laying criminal charges; preparing the criminal case for court; and, as requested, assisting the prosecutor when the case goes to court. There can be multiple detectives in an investigation.

- *Forensic identification specialist.* Sometimes referred to as an identification (or "ident") officer, an "FIS officer," a "SOCO" (scenes of crime officer), or a "CSI" (crime scene investigator), a **forensic identification specialist** is responsible for the physical investigation of the crime scene. In Canada, forensic identification specialists are usually police officers with specialized training and experience in locating, collecting, and preserving evidence from crime scenes. Their responsibilities include identifying, documenting, collecting, preserving, and analyzing or submitting for analysis the physical evidence obtained from a crime scene. While they may sometimes conduct an analysis of the evidence themselves—typically, in the case of fingerprints or boot marks—they are also responsible for ensuring that the physical evidence gathered from a crime scene is properly submitted to other specialists, such as forensic scientists, for analysis. The work of forensic identification specialists is outlined in Chapter 8, Pattern Evidence and Collision Reconstruction.

- *Forensic scientist.* A civilian investigative specialist with scientific training and analytical expertise in a specific area—for example, chemistry, biology, firearms, or questioned documents. Although **forensic scientists** sometimes work in police laboratories—for example, those run by the RCMP—they frequently work in laboratories that are independent of the police—for example, the Centre of Forensic Sciences in Toronto. Forensic scientists are discussed in Chapter 10, Crime Labs and the Role of Science in Investigations. Briefly, forensic scientists are responsible for conducting objective scientific analyses of evidence submitted to them by police and others and for generating a report of their findings. Forensic scientists might give expert opinion evidence about their findings in court during criminal proceedings, but do not generally attend crime scenes except on rare occasions—for example, a forensic archaeologist or anthropologist might assist in the proper recovery of buried or scattered human remains.

- *Forensic pathologist.* A medical doctor with specialized training in forensic pathology, responsible for conducting post-mortem examinations (or autopsies) of people who die suddenly in order to determine the cause of their death. **Forensic pathologists** use their specialized knowledge of medicine, science, and law to explain what may have caused or contributed to such deaths, and offer expert opinions regarding their analyses and finding to a variety of legal bodies, such as criminal courts.

forensic pathologist
a medical doctor with specialized training in forensic pathology who conducts autopsies and determines the manner and cause of death in suspicious circumstances

Databases

The actual capabilities of those involved in crime scene investigation are, in most cases, far more limited than what is presented on television and in the movies. Perhaps one of the most unrealistic portrayals is the existence of an "omniscient database" (Durnal, 2010) that allows investigators to feed samples of anything from a tire print to a soil sample into a computer, which then, typically within seconds, returns a "hit" or a "match." There are, of course, real investigative databases—for example, a fingerprint database (AFIS), a DNA database (NDDB), and a fired bullet and cartridge-case database (IBIS)—that are populated and maintained by law enforcement agencies and that can provide information of tremendous value. However, databases of the sort portrayed in popular entertainment, which allow an investigator to instantaneously match a piece of rope or a hammer, for example, to a particular manufacturer and place of sale in a matter of minutes, simply do not exist.

Presence and Value of Evidence

Often, in popular portrayals, the investigator walks around a crime scene with an intense look on his or her face and soon discovers the key pieces of evidence left behind by the perpetrator. In practice, crime scene investigation is not a simple matter of walking into a scene, sorting through the evidence, and taking only those key pieces that will cinch the case. Instead, it often involves making the most of what little evidence is left behind, and, on occasion, dealing with the frustration of a scene that yields almost nothing of evidentiary value.

Although it is true that investigators have a number of powerful tools to assist them in identifying and collecting evidence from a crime scene, it does not necessarily follow that the typical crime scene contains ample amounts of evidence that investigators need simply to gather up and submit for analysis in order to solve a crime. In theory, a typical crime scene may contain a great deal of evidence; in practice, such evidence may be difficult to locate and use. For example:

- A suspect may have left a fingerprint behind, but it may be on a greasy or rough surface that makes it difficult for the investigator to identify and collect.

- A perpetrator may clean the crime scene after committing the offence, resulting in the destruction of some evidence.

- A suspect may be caught on video surveillance, but he may be wearing a disguise that makes identification exceptionally difficult.

- A perpetrator may wear gloves to cover his or her hands during a break and enter.

- Traces of blood, hair, or skin, flakes of paint, or bits of plastic at an outdoor crime scene may be dispersed or destroyed by a heavy rain before they can be identified and collected.

In addition to limitations on the evidence available at a crime scene, other aspects of the process of investigation and analysis can contribute to only a small subset of evidence "available" at a scene making its way into the courtroom.

Time Frame for Collection and Analysis

Evidence collected from a crime scene by a forensic identification specialist is routinely submitted to an intake officer at a forensic laboratory, typically a civilian employee, who ensures that it is properly packaged, assigns it a tracking number,

MYTHS REGARDING THE SUPERIORITY OF PHYSICAL EVIDENCE

CSI lead forensic investigator Gil Grissom embodies the notion that criminal investigation can be a purely objective, evidence-based process. In one episode of the popular television program, Grissom is challenged by someone who demands to know why the public should believe Grissom's account of a controversial police shooting. Grissom responds by saying that the results of his forensic investigation should be believed because he is a scientist. He identifies, collects, and examines physical evidence from crime scenes to determine who did what to whom and how. According to Grissom, "Physical evidence cannot be wrong. It doesn't lie. It's not influenced by emotion or prejudice. It's not confused by the excitement of the moment." (CBS, 2005, as noted in Ruble, 2009, p. 4.)

In addition to the popular adage "physical evidence does not lie" (in contrast, sometimes, to testimonial evidence), there should be an equally powerful one, "Physical evidence may not *lie*, but it does not simply *speak* for itself." Physical evidence does not "tell" its story independent of human involvement. The "story" of physical evidence is told through an involved process in which people identify, collect, preserve, analyze, and interpret the significance of the evidence, and the potential for error exists at every stage of this process—for example, evidence can be overlooked, lost, or become contaminated; the analysis of physical evidence can be faulty; and the interpretation of that analysis can be flawed. Despite idealistic notions about the inherent superiority of physical evidence, the belief that it can provide us with an objective "certainty" not possible with, for example, eyewitness testimony must be tempered. Physical evidence can and has been negatively affected by the actions, sometimes subjective, of investigators and others involved in the criminal justice process. Therefore, we must be as cautious interpreting the significance of physical evidence as with any other type of evidence.

and logs it into a computer database. The evidence is then assigned to various scientists for analysis, depending on the nature and amount of the evidence and the type of analysis required. The results of those tests might be available to the investigator within days, but more often it takes weeks, or sometimes months. Time frames are dependent on a number of factors, including the nature and complexity of the testing required; the workload of the laboratory; the availability of a particular scientist; and the oversight process in place at the particular forensic facility, which involves the scientist's report being reviewed by his or her supervisor before being approved for release to the investigator.

Sometimes, because of the seriousness of the crime or for public safety issues— that is, when there is a pressing need to identify or link an individual to a particular crime—an investigator can request that the laboratory give priority to certain evidence, but, typically, evidence is submitted to the laboratory, enters the queue, and waits in secure storage until a scientist is available to analyze it. Although the bureaucracy surrounding access to the analysis process can sometimes be negotiated with more or less speed, depending on the nature of the crime, the analytical process itself cannot be rushed. The scientific analysis of evidence takes "as long as it takes"—and it rarely takes as little time in reality as it does on television.

EVIDENCE COLLECTION, PRESERVATION, AND THE CHARTER

Before discussing *how* evidence from a crime scene should be collected and preserved, let's revisit the legal *duty* on the Crown and the police to collect and preserve evidence. As discussed in Chapter 1, Proof, *Stinchcombe* requires that the Crown disclose the "fruits of the investigation" to the accused. This places a corollary duty on the police to collect and preserve all material pertaining to its investigation of the accused, and on the Crown to take steps to preserve evidence that has been gathered. Failure to collect or preserve evidence in accordance with legal requirements might constitute an improper use of police discretion, an abuse of process, an obstruction of justice, or a breach of the accused's Charter rights, all of which carry consequences for the ability of the Crown to prosecute a case. The legal consequences of lost or destroyed evidence are explored further in Chapter 18, The Duty of Disclosure.

Although police officers have a significant amount of discretion in deciding how to carry out their duties—including how and when to collect and preserve evidence—there are limits to this discretion. The Supreme Court case *R. v. Beaudry* (2007) dealt with a police officer who was charged with obstructing justice (*Criminal Code*, 1995, s. 139(2)) for deliberately failing to gather evidence against another police officer who he had reasonable grounds to believe had been operating a motor vehicle while impaired by alcohol. The officer was apprehended while driving at a high rate of speed with a flat tire after going through a stop sign, nearly colliding with a median, and then continuing for some distance even after the pursuing police vehicle's emergency lights had been activated.

The accused officer argued that his decision not to take breath samples from the suspect officer was a proper exercise of his discretion. The court confirmed that, although discretion is an essential part of both police work and the criminal justice system, such discretion is not absolute and its use must be justified. In determining whether a particular exercise of discretion is justified, a court will consider whether the discretion:

1. was proportionate to the seriousness of the offence, and
2. was exercised in the public interest.

In *Beaudry*, the offence was a serious one in which the impaired officer presented a danger to public safety. The court stated that, although in some cases the exercise of police discretion is routine and clearly justified—for example, when giving a young person caught stealing a candy bar a stern warning and contacting his or her parents instead of laying a criminal charge—in other exceptional cases officers will be required to explain their decisions in detail. In *Beaudry*, the accused officer's preferential treatment of the impaired driver because he was a police officer was an improper use of his discretion, and his decision not to obtain breath samples was an obstruction of justice because the officer knew that such evidence was necessary to prove the offence.

PRINCIPLES OF CRIME SCENE INVESTIGATION: PREVENTING CONTAMINATION AND ENSURING CONTINUITY

In any investigation, ensuring the integrity of evidence is key both to *whether* the evidence will be admitted into court and, if so, how much *weight* the court will give the evidence. The integrity of evidence is protected when the individuals who work with evidence follow best practices in the collection, packaging, and analysis of evidence, which help prevent **contamination** and ensure continuity.

contamination
the introduction of material, unrelated to the commission of the crime, into a crime scene after the crime has occurred

Locard's exchange principle
formulation by one of the founding fathers of modern forensic science, Edmond Locard, stating that "every contact leaves a trace"

The 19th-century French criminologist Edmond Locard, regarded by many as one of the founding fathers of modern forensic science, is, perhaps, most famous for formulating what has come to be known as **Locard's exchange principle**, which states that "every contact leaves a trace." In 1953, criminologist Paul Kirk published a highly influential text entitled *Crime Investigation*, in which he described the operation of Locard's principle so vividly that his words are often incorrectly attributed to Locard himself (Kirk, 1953, as quoted in Chisum & Turvey, 2007, p. 30):

> Wherever he steps, whatever he touches, whatever he leaves, even unconsciously, will serve as a silent witness against him. Not only his fingerprints or his footprints, but his hair, the fibres from his clothes, the glass he breaks, the tool mark he leaves, the paint he scratches, the blood or semen he deposits or collects. All of these and more, bear mute witness against him. This is evidence that does not forget. It is not confused by the excitement of the moment. It is not absent because human witnesses are. It is factual evidence. Physical evidence cannot be wrong, it cannot perjure itself, it cannot be wholly absent. Only human failure to find it, study and understand it, can diminish its value.

Although it has a more specific application within forensic science, Locard's principle is central to the issue of crime scene contamination. If "every contact leaves a trace," then anyone who enters a crime scene after a crime has occurred—

such as a police officer—will both leave behind evidence of his or her presence and take away some trace from the scene. (In the case of a police officer, the evidence left behind will be unrelated to the offence, but the evidence taken away *may* be related to it.) This process is one way in which a crime scene can be contaminated or evidence that is potentially related to the crime can be lost.

Cross-contamination is another kind of contamination. For example, a forensic identification specialist wearing protective gloves might pick up a piece of bloody evidence from one part of the crime scene and package it, and, then, while wearing the same pair of gloves, pick up a second piece of evidence. An awareness of the potential for contamination in such circumstances and adherence to proper evidence gathering protocols—for example, placing the pair of gloves used to pick up a particular bloody piece of evidence in the evidence bag along with the evidence and then donning a fresh pair of gloves to continue the evidence-gathering process—is critical not only for preventing contamination but for maintaining the *perception* that evidence was handled correctly.

cross-contamination
the transfer of material from one piece of evidence to another

As Nafte and Dalrymple (2011) point out, a forensic identification specialist does not want to find himself or herself in a situation where an argument can be made in court that the evidence might have been contaminated as a result of how he or she collected it. Even if, for example, the specialist used the same pair of gloves to pick up two separate, clean, dry stones—a scenario where the probability of cross-contamination is extremely low—the possibility of contamination would technically still exist. And it is this possibility or probability battle that a police witness will almost invariably lose. If contamination was a possibility (even if it has not been shown to have actually occurred) and the court perceives that an officer did not do all that he or she could reasonably have done to avoid it, then the value of that particular piece of evidence—and of the forensic investigation as a whole—might be called into question.

While Kirk's vivid description of the importance of physical evidence, above, contains elements of truth, it also serves as the basis for popular portrayals of the nature of physical evidence that are misleading, such as the myth that physical evidence cannot lie. In the world of criminal investigation, contamination of physical evidence is a fact of life, and investigators must be aware of the effects of contamination on the value of the evidence they collect. Contamination causes a change in the original state of the evidence, which may, in turn, affect the interpretation and value of that evidence at subsequent points in the investigative process, such as during forensic testing.

The potential for crime scene contamination exists in the period between when a crime occurs and the police arrive to secure the scene. Some degree of scene contamination will likely occur as a result of police, medical, and other emergency services personnel entering the crime scene to safeguard life or property, search for victims or suspects, and gain some preliminary sense of what has occurred. And when forensic identification specialists and detectives finally arrive at the crime scene and begin to identify and collect evidence, the crime scene is methodically "destroyed" by the very act of moving through it and removing items. As a result, the investigator's task when managing a crime scene is not so much to *prevent* crime scene contamination—although that is the ideal—as it is to ensure that all contamination that has or will necessarily occur is *fully documented*, and then to ensure that *no further unnecessary contamination* takes place. This is achieved primarily by:

1. securing the crime scene and controlling access to it,

2. ensuring that proper evidence collection procedures are followed, and

3. documenting the actions of all involved individuals.

These measures are discussed later in this chapter.

One of the other key principles that guides the collection of evidence during an investigation is ensuring continuity. As discussed in Chapter 3, Principles of Admissibility, one of the factors that determines how much weight is given to a piece of evidence admitted into court is the Crown's ability to demonstrate its continuity—that is, to establish, in conjunction with the police, its "history" from the time it was found to the time it is produced in a courtroom. This includes showing both where the evidence was from the time it was collected at the scene until the time it was brought to court and who had contact with or access to it. The records maintained over the course of an investigation are key to accounting for each link in the chain, through such things as written notes, evidence logs, tamper-proof packages, evidence seals, computer entries, and oral testimony.

Given that evidence can range in size from something as small as a single strand of hair to something as large as an automobile, it is clear that a variety of challenges exist in terms of both collecting and safeguarding evidence as it works its way through the process—from the hands of the forensic identification specialist, to the laboratory of the forensic scientist, to the office of the lead investigator, and then to the courtroom. The best practice when gathering evidence is to allow as few people as possible to have contact with or control over it, because this creates fewer links in the chain of continuity. Although, at times, the continuity of certain pieces of evidence may be conceded, or "admitted," by defence counsel and the Crown will not be required to demonstrate continuity, where continuity is an issue, *all* of the individuals who form part of the chain will likely be called to court as witnesses. The longer the chain, the greater the probability that one of its links will break.

WHAT IS A "CRIME SCENE"?

crime scene
any place in which a crime occurred or in which evidence relating to a possible crime has been located

Although the definition of the term **crime scene** may seem obvious, the novice investigator needs to have a clear understanding of what it means. A simple definition might be that a crime scene is any place in which a crime occurred. A crime scene, however, is not only a place in which a crime occurred; it can also be a place in which evidence relating to a possible crime at some distant location or time has been located.

Consider the following: someone is shot inside a busy nightclub. The gunman runs out of the club and down an alleyway. He discards his jacket in a dumpster and throws a firearm onto the roof of a building. He then emerges from the alleyway, forces the driver of a stopped motor vehicle out of her car, and drives away. The vehicle is found abandoned two days later in a factory parking lot in a nearby town.

In this scenario, the primary crime scene is the nightclub, but there are a number of other crime scenes, all of which are related to and may provide evidence of the original shooting offence or the additional, related offences. Some of these scenes will likely be quickly and easily located and secured, while others may take some time to identify and secure. In other scenarios—for example, where a person is abducted and murdered and their body dumped in a remote location—it could potentially take months or even years before the crime scenes are discovered, secured, and examined.

Clearly, then, a crime scene can take many forms—it can be confined or extensive, located inside or outdoors, the only scene related to the particular offence, or one of many scenes related to the same investigation.

The nature, extent, and number of scenes are all factors that will help determine how quickly the scenes can be identified and secured, which, in turn, will affect the integrity of the evidence contained in those scenes. The longer a scene goes unidentified, the greater the potential for degradation, loss, or contamination of the evidence contained in that scene. An investigator cannot assume that the "known" crime scenes are the only ones that exist. Instead, he or she must make efforts to identify *all* potential scenes related to the offence under investigation in order to ensure that they are secured and preserved, pending proper forensic investigation.

A crime scene is generally regarded as the primary source of physical evidence—that is, evidence that may be used to identify a suspect or link him or her to another person or location. Note that the investigation of a crime scene and the gathering and preservation of evidence can also include, for example, a victim or a suspect who may have received injuries, which will need to be photographed, so that the record of the injuries may later be entered as evidence in court.

Police Authority to Establish and Protect a Crime Scene

The authority of police to establish and protect a crime scene flows from s. 129(a) of the *Criminal Code*, which makes it an offence for anyone to obstruct a peace officer in the lawful execution of his or her duty. Although the section does not specifically mention crime scene security, establishing a crime scene—and protecting its integrity by refusing to allow people access to it—is a legitimate part of police officers' duty to investigate crime.

Temporarily restricting individuals' liberty—for example, by controlling access to a crime scene—is justified if the two criteria in the so-called ***Waterfield*** **test** are met. The test, which was set out in the English case of *Waterfield* (1963) and which is used to determine the common powers of the police, prescribes a way for a court to determine whether the exercise of a power *not* specified in a statute—sometimes called an "ancillary" power, or a power that arises out of a police officer's fundamental duty, such as the duty to investigate crime—was justifiable in a particular circumstance. For a restriction to be justified:

1. interference with an individual's freedom must have occurred in the course of duty, and

2. the police must have exercised their powers in a justifiable manner considering the circumstances.

Waterfield **test**
a legal test that prescribes a way for a court to determine whether the exercise of a power *not* specified in a statute was justifiable

WHAT CONSTITUTES "OBSTRUCTING" AN OFFICER?

In *R. v. Lohidici* (2005), two police officers attended the scene of a motor vehicle collision in which the accused was a passenger in a van that had rear-ended another vehicle. The officers took control of the scene, identified the accused's friend as the probable driver of the vehicle, and took him to their cruiser to commence an impaired driving investigation. Fire and EMS personnel also attended at the scene to deal with a fluid spill and to treat injured parties.

While all this was happening, the accused was running around the scene, yelling at people, and attempting to retrieve property from the van, including alcholic beverages. The officers told the accused to stay away from the van because he was interfering with their investigation. The accused was told that if he continued his attempts to take property from the van he would be arrested for obstructing police. The accused refused to comply with the officers' instructions and, as a result, was arrested, charged, and found guilty of obstruction pursuant to s. 129(a) of the *Criminal Code*. The judge found that the accused was repeatedly warned to stop getting in the way and to stop attempting to remove evidence from the scene, and that, despite being given multiple opportunities to stop, he continued to interfere with the police investigation.

In discussing the law of obstruction, the court pointed out that an individual does not need to completely thwart an officer in the execution of his or her duty to be guilty of the offence; he or she need only "impede," "affect," or make the officer's work "more difficult"; although note that such "obstruction" needs to be something more than merely a "trifling" or "momentary" action to be considered obstruction pursuant to s. 129(a) (*Lohidici*, para. 19).

In some cases, police authority to control access to a crime scene may be complicated by past practices. In *R. v. Amat* (2003), members of the media had historically been granted special access to crime scenes by the Calgary Police Service for the purpose of gathering information and photographs for news stories, but, in one circumstance, a police officer ordered a newspaper photographer out of a crime scene because he believed the possible presence of an armed person made the scene dangerous. The photographer refused to obey the order, and was arrested and charged with obstructing police pursuant to s. 129 of the *Criminal Code*. The court said that because the police had a long-standing policy of giving members of the media special access privileges, they had a corresponding obligation, beyond what they would have toward an ordinary member of the public, to explain to the photographer why they were taking away that privileged status. Because they had not done so, the photographer was found not guilty of obstructing police. In light of this decision, police services and police officers would be wise to consider the potential legal implications of their policies and practices regarding who has access to a crime scene. A prudent approach would be to allow access to only those individuals with a bona fide need to enter a crime scene—for example, police officers and other emergency workers.

CRIME SCENE INVESTIGATION: PRACTICAL AND PROCEDURAL CONSIDERATIONS

A number of practical and procedural issues must be considered to ensure that a crime scene is investigated in a thorough and professional manner. These issues are discussed in the following sections.

Responsibilities of First Officers to Arrive at the Scene

Uniformed officers are typically the first police personnel to arrive at a crime scene. Their primary responsibility is to ensure that the scene is safe both for them and other first responders to enter and for any victims, witnesses, suspects, or members of the general public who may be present. In the case of a violent crime—for example, where an armed suspect is present at the scene and poses an immediate threat to police or others—this may involve some officers setting up a secure perimeter, while other officers directly confront the suspect and attempt to take him or her into custody. In other situations, it may be more appropriate for the first officers to respond to "contain" the scene by setting up a secure cordon of police officers around it, and then call for specialized officers, such as tactical or canine officers to attend the scene and ensure its safety. In still other situations—for example, where an office complex was broken into and a safe was stolen several days before police were called—the same sort of safety concerns may not exist.

Once the first officers to respond to a crime scene and their supervisor—typically, a patrol sergeant—have met their primary responsibilities they will:

- ensure that the crime scene is secured and preserved;
- search the scene itself and the surrounding area for suspects, victims, and witnesses; and
- request the attendance of investigative, forensic, or emergency medical or fire personnel.

The first officers must make careful notes about how they entered the crime scene, what route they took, what they saw, and what they did upon and following arrival. Such notations are part of documenting the crime scene to ensure that both the detectives and forensic identification specialists—and later, a court—can assess the state of the original crime scene and interpret any evidence found there. The first officers must document *all* their relevant activities, even negative ones, because police procedures and codes of conduct require that officers create accurate, honest records of the actions they take while carrying out their official duties.

If, for example, an officer dropped a gum wrapper, turned a light switch on or off, accidentally knocked something over or kicked something out of place, or did anything to potentially alter the crime scene in any way, the detectives and identification officers need this information. While common sense, basic police training, and experience should generally prevent the occurrence of such events, the potential always exists. And although officers might be reluctant to admit that they did something they should not have, whether on purpose or by accident, such information is critical because any such act affects the integrity of the crime scene. Although such errors may ultimately turn out to be of little significance, a failure to record them might result in an officer's integrity being called into question, which could affect the integrity of the entire investigation. Both the officer involved and, later, the investigator must be sure to record any such events in their police notebooks.

Securing and Preserving the Scene

The security and preservation of a crime scene is the responsibility of the first officers to arrive on the scene. The importance of these actions cannot be stressed enough—evidence that is lost or destroyed because a crime scene was not properly secured can rarely be recovered and, even if it is, its integrity may be irreparably damaged.

A crime scene typically consists of (at least) an inner core and an outer perimeter. The inner core is the area in which the actual criminal act took place, while the outer perimeter is, typically, the area that includes the entry and exit routes surrounding the core. One of the mistakes that a novice officer might make in establishing a crime scene is to make it smaller rather than larger. It is far better to err on the side of caution and cordon off a larger area than to cordon off a smaller area only to discover, too late, that the actual crime scene is far more extensive than was first thought. To return to our earlier example of the shooting in the nightclub, the uniformed officers who first arrive at the scene may be inclined to cordon off the nightclub only, when in fact the actual crime scenes—which involved the disposal of evidence, such as the suspect's jacket and firearm—is far more extensive and involves the entire block, encompassing the nearby alleyways and adjacent buildings.

As a general rule, officers should designate as large a crime scene as reasonably necessary based on a worst-case assumption about the severity of the crime and the area involved, and reduce the size only when or if further investigation indicates that it is prudent to do so. A larger perimeter can always be reduced without sacrificing the integrity of the scene and the evidence it contains, but expanding a smaller perimeter *always* involves sacrificing the integrity of that portion of the scene that, for a time at least, was left unprotected. In some circumstances—for example, where information is later received indicating the existence of additional crime scenes—such an expansion, while far from ideal, may become necessary. Using the nightclub shooting example, if police had designated only the building where the shooting occurred as the crime scene, but later learned that the victim had died, and witnesses had reported seeing the gunman discard evidence in a nearby alley as he fled, it would be very difficult to expand what is now a murder crime scene without sacrificing the integrity of the evidence that was found in the areas near the nightclub.

Once police have secured a crime scene, whether inside or outside, large or small, the same principle applies—only those who need to enter the scene for a bona fide purpose related to the investigation or for an emergency should be allowed to do so. Individuals who may enter typically include the investigators assigned to the case; the identification officers responsible for examining and documenting the scene and collecting evidence; and other required officials—for example, the coroner in a death investigation.

Controlling access to a small indoor crime scene—for example, an apartment unit—can be achieved simply by placing a police officer in the doorway and affixing a police seal to the door itself. However, controlling access to a large, outdoor crime scene—for example, the scene of a hit-and-run fatality—can be much more difficult and involve the use of multiple officers to cordon off a large area for several hours while the investigation is under way. Controlling access to such a scene would likely involve street closures, which would restrict both vehicular and pedestrian movement.

Once a crime scene has been secured, a careful record (usually in the form of a crime scene access log) must be kept of all individuals who enter the crime scene, including a record of when, why, and under whose authority they entered (normally, the authority of the officer in charge of the investigation). Again, the importance of controlling access cannot be overstated, because the integrity of the scene affects both the integrity of the evidence and that of the investigation as a whole. The investigator must be able to determine who has entered the scene; how; and exactly what, if anything, they did while there in order to ensure that the scene may be properly interpreted and that any possible contamination is documented.

Responsibilities of Detectives

For the purposes of this discussion, we will assume that the person responsible for conducting the investigation of the crime to which the scene is related is a detective, and not a uniformed officer, as may sometimes be the case with minor crimes. We will also assume that by the time the first detective arrives, the uniformed officers have met their primary responsibility of ensuring their own and others' safety, and that the officers and their supervisors have either completed or are in the process of carrying out the other duties outlined above.

The job of the detective is to manage the investigation, and he or she will take charge upon arriving at the crime scene. The first detective to arrive at a crime scene will typically meet with the senior uniformed police officer or the uniformed supervisory officer on location to ensure that all of the things that should have been done either have been done or are being done and to receive a preliminary briefing regarding the information that has been gathered to that point. Because levels of experience can vary widely among uniformed officers, including uniformed supervisory personnel, detectives cannot simply assume that proper crime scene procedures have been followed. The detective is responsible for ensuring that the crime scene has been and continues to be properly protected and that a preliminary search has been conducted to locate and protect any evidence that may be relevant to the matter under investigation before the arrival of a forensic identification specialist who will search the scene in detail. In smaller police services, the investigator alone might be responsible for gathering physical evidence, in which case he or she will normally have had basic training in the principles of evidence gathering.

Upon arriving at a crime scene, an investigator will typically meet with various individuals in order to obtain and provide certain kinds of information:

- *First officers to arrive at the scene and other first responders.* Before initiating a search of the scene, the investigator should have a preliminary discussion with the officers who were first on scene and with any other first responders—for example, emergency medical or fire personnel—who may be able to provide information regarding what was happening in or around the scene when they first arrived.

Uniformed police officers will be able to advise the investigator about any victims, witnesses, and suspects they have identified; provide an account of what any victims and witnesses have said; and discuss any evidence they may have located. They may require direction with regard to the management of various aspects of the crime scene. The investigator will want to ensure that the officers have made careful notes, as described above, about how they entered the crime scene, what route they took, what they saw, and what they did when they first arrived. Obtaining this information before conducting an initial walk through may be valuable in drawing the investigator's attention to various potentially significant aspects of the scene.

- *Forensic identification specialists.* If present, or upon their arrival, these officers will need to consult with the detective in charge of the investigation before beginning their work.

IMPORTANCE OF MENTAL PREPARATION BEFORE ATTENDING A CRIME SCENE

A veteran homicide investigator once emphasized to a younger detective the importance of "preparing your mind" before attending a crime scene. Although such preparation is especially important in the case of a violent or a large and complicated crime scene—for example, a homicide or a hit-and-run motor vehicle fatality—it is beneficial to the investigation of *any* crime scene.

Crime scenes can be active and intense environments, and detectives may find it helpful to pause and think about how they will manage a scene before they arrive. Once a detective reaches a scene, he or she will need to quickly prioritize the many demands that will be made on them by people seeking information, direction, or assistance, often before they have even exited their vehicle. The veteran homicide detective suggested to his younger colleague that stopping one's vehicle a short distance from a scene and taking a minute to collect your thoughts if you are alone or to have a short conversation with your partner is time well spent before entering a scene.

While dealing with the various demands on him or her, an investigator must remain focused and ensure that the available resources are managed effectively to identify, collect, and preserve the physical evidence present at the crime scene. A detective who fails to take charge and ensure that a serious crime scene is managed properly can cause irreparable damage to an entire investigation.

Uniformed officers may also find it valuable to refresh their minds regarding their priorities before arriving at a crime scene. However, because they need to attend serious crime scenes as quickly as possible, they rarely have the same opportunity as a detective to consider their actions before their arrival. A uniformed officer is well advised to remember that safety comes first—their own and that of the others who may be present at the scene—and that it is only after everyone's safety has been ensured that the officer should begin to take action to protect the scene for the investigation that will follow.

- *Senior police officers.* Senior supervisory officers may attend the scene, especially where a serious crime has occurred—for example, a murder or a child abduction—seeking information to send up through the police chain of command.

- *Media.* In more serious cases, the media will likely be at the scene, seeking information at a time when the investigator himself or herself likely knows relatively little about the event. Upon arrival at the scene of a serious crime, a reasonable approach for an investigator to take with the media, especially if there are multiple members present, is to address them as a group outside the secured crime scene; introduce yourself, and your partner if you have one; advise them that you are the investigator in charge (assuming that you are); explain that you have just arrived and need time to speak to the uniformed officers on scene to obtain updated information; and inform them that, once you have spoken to the officers on scene, you will return at a specified time to make a statement. You must then come back and speak to the media as promised.

  The media can be a valuable resource for investigators in terms of getting requests for information out to the public and generating potential leads. When speaking to the media an investigator should always be truthful, but also careful to limit the amount of information released about the crime under investigation. Releasing information about evidence can potentially damage the investigation at a later stage—for example, if information that only the police and those involved in the crime should know becomes public knowledge, it may contaminate subsequent interviews or interrogations. A safe approach to making an initial statement to the media about a crime you are investigating is to give them basic information about what has occurred and to then describe the general process that police will be following during their investigation. For example:

  > Ladies and gentlemen, my name is Detective Jones and I am the officer in charge of this investigation. Police received a 911 call earlier today and as a result uniformed officers attended 123 Main Street where they located the body of a deceased female inside the residence. The identity of the victim is being withheld pending the notification of next of kin. A post-mortem examination will be held later to determine the cause of death. Police are appealing to the public for their assistance in this investigation; anyone who has information about what may have occurred at 123 Main Street is asked either to call Detective Jones at 647-555-5555 or to provide information anonymously through Crime Stoppers at 1-800-222-TIPS (8477).

Documenting the Scene

Whether one uses a pencil to draw a sketch or a laser to create a three dimensional rendering, the reason for documenting a crime scene is the same—to create a record of the scene that "preserves" the conditions that existed when the crime scene was first identified in order to allow investigators, lawyers, and a court to make informed judgments about the value of evidence.

Documenting a crime scene involves creating a record of:

1. the content (the evidence), and
2. the context (the environment in which the evidence was found, or the relationships that exist between things).

The proper analysis of evidence requires an appreciation of both the nature of a particular piece of evidence and the relationship of that evidence to a specific environment, context, or scene (Houck, 2009). Context is important because it can affect both how the evidence is interpreted and the importance that is attached to it in the overall investigation or prosecution. For example, evidence that links an individual to a particular scene is far more significant if the individual claims never to have been at the scene than if the individual admits to having been there. Similarly, a scene in which an individual is found deceased in his own locked apartment with a ligature tied lightly around his neck, sexual paraphernalia strewn about, and no signs of a struggle may be interpreted differently than a scene in which an individual is found dead with a ligature tied tightly around his neck, in an apartment that shows signs of a forced entry and a fight having taken place. The former may be interpreted, for example, as a case of autoerotic asphyxia, while the latter may be interpreted as a homicide by strangulation.

Historically, much crime scene documentation was accomplished through the creation of police notes, sketches, photographs, and drawings. Although police note taking is still an important aspect of documenting a crime scene and creating a record of the larger investigation, extensive use is now made of both still photography and video recordings. There are many advantages to creating digital records of crime scenes, individual pieces of evidence, and a victim's or suspect's injuries, including ease of creation, storage, searching, retrieval, printing, presentation, and disclosure. (See Nafte & Dalrymple, 2011, chapter 3, for a general reference on this topic.)

In addition to digital recording technologies, other common methods used to document crime scenes include, for example, the Leica or Sokkia "total station"—a surveying device that is used to measure and create maps of crime scenes and to plot the locations at which various pieces of evidence were located (Cheves, 2004)—and laser devices, such as the Faro Laser Scanner Focus 3D, an apparatus that is used to create three-dimensional crime and accident scene reconstructions.

It is especially important, particularly in large investigations where there may be literally hundreds of pieces of evidence, that there be a mechanism to provide a quick overview of the evidence related to the case. The creation and maintenance of a master evidence log serves this purpose. A **master evidence log** is a record of all the individual pieces of physical evidence collected at a particular crime scene and what has been done with them. At a glance, a reader—be it the forensic identification specialist, the detective in charge of the investigation, the Crown attorney, or defence counsel—can answer such questions as whether a particular piece of evidence has been submitted for forensic testing or is being kept in secure storage awaiting court proceedings.

master evidence log
a record of all the individual pieces of physical evidence collected from a particular crime scene and what has been done with them

Because it typically includes information such as evidence descriptions, evidence bag or police seal numbers, the location in which evidence was found, whether evidence was submitted for forensic testing and the results of such tests, an evidence log also serves as a reference in discussions between various parties—for example, the Crown, defence, investigator, and forensic scientist. When conducting a pre-trial, witness-preparation interview with a forensic scientist, for example, a Crown attorney can refer to Exhibit number 87, a pink coat with a bloodstain, collected from the second floor hallway of 345 Main Street and placed in evidence bag #B90785, then submitted to the laboratory with a request from investigators for a scientist to develop a DNA profile in order to compare that profile with one that was developed from a hammer located in the alleyway behind the residence. During the course of the interview, the Crown attorney may ask the forensic scientist to describe what sort of tests were performed on the jacket, what results were obtained, what comparisons were carried out, and what the results of such comparisons were. It would be difficult to have such a discussion, or later discussions in court, without the benefit of a document such as a master evidence log to serve as a reference point.

Searching the Scene and Gathering Evidence

For the purpose of this section, assume that the appropriate judicial authorization to search the crime scene and seize evidence has been obtained (see Chapter 6, Legal Aspects of Search and Seizure) and that a search can now legally begin.

Collecting evidence from a crime scene involves far more than simply picking up items and placing them in bags—a process sometimes derisively referred to as "bagging and tagging." As mentioned, specially trained forensic identification officers are responsible for examining crime scenes in order to document, identify, collect, preserve, and analyze physical evidence.

Before any piece of evidence may be collected, it must first be photographed *in situ*—that is, in the location in which it was originally found. This is in addition to the overall documentation of the crime scene discussed above. A paper or plastic scale (similar to a small ruler) is placed next to the item to be collected, a wide-angle photograph is taken to show the location of the item in the context of the larger crime scene, and then a close-up photograph is taken to show the size and detail of the item itself. The item can then be collected and put into an appropriate evidence container, with the particular kind of container being dictated by the nature of the evidence. Regardless of the kind of container used, it must be properly sealed and labelled to ensure that no contamination, loss, or substitution can occur and that critical information—such as when and where it was gathered and by whom—is recorded on the container.

As discussed in Chapter 2, Evidence in the Courtroom, authenticating evidence, which involves a witness testifying that the item a party is seeking to admit is what it is represented to be, is an important part of getting evidence admitted into court. For example, if the Crown seeks to enter a knife that the police seized from the suspect as an exhibit, they must establish that it is *the same knife* that the police seized. This fact is normally established through the testimony of a witness—for example, the police officer who actually seized the knife—who is able to testify that the exhibit is, in fact, what it is purported to be.

In the case of items that are generic and cannot easily be marked for identification—for example, a small shard of glass—it is critical to ensure that the evidence is placed securely inside a specially prepared evidence container. Specially designed plastic evidence bags, for example, include space on the exterior of the bag where details regarding the evidence—for example, when it was collected—can be recorded. The bags also have individual serial numbers imprinted on them and strong adhesive closures to allow them to be securely sealed. Different kinds of evidence can be placed in different kinds of containers as required—for example, a piece of bloody clothing can be placed inside a paper bag to allow the blood to dry. In such cases, pertinent information can be written on the exterior of these containers and a secure police seal placed over the opening. Police evidence seals have individual serial numbers, with space on which an investigator can write information. The use of an evidence seal allows an officer to say—and to demonstrate—whether the seal is intact and whether a package into which the officer placed evidence has been opened since he or she first placed the evidence inside it. If the seal has been broken (which may be because it was necessary to remove the evidence for testing purposes), then the person who broke the seal will have made a record and returned the evidence to the original or a similarly secure container and affixed a new seal to it. In this way, the investigator can establish continuity of possession, which is a critical component in maintaining the integrity of evidence.

It is also good practice, where possible, to place a marking directly on the actual evidence in addition to on the container. For example, an officer who collects a shoe should carefully write his or her initials and badge number on the shoe itself, taking care not to disturb any evidence that might be attached to it—for example, blood or hair. In court, the officer will be able to say, "Yes, that is the shoe that was collected at the scene; I know that because I collected it, placed an identifying mark on it, and submitted it into evidence." Evidence that is singular in nature—for example, a firearm with a unique serial number—does not necessarily need to be marked in this way (although it could be, for even greater certainty), because the collecting officer can use the unique features to identify the evidence as that he or she collected at the crime scene, where the officer recorded the serial number of the firearm in his or her notebook.

RELEASING THE CRIME SCENE

Determining when a crime scene should be "released"—that is, when the police should relinquish control over it—is a decision usually made by the officer in charge of the investigation (usually, a detective). In investigations involving a death, in which the scene is under the authority of the coroner, practically speaking, the officer in charge of the investigation is still the one to order police to relinquish the crime scene, but *only* after he or she has consulted with the investigating coroner and confirmed that it is appropriate to do so. This typically takes place after the post-mortem examination has been completed, and after the officer in charge of the investigation is satisfied that the scene has been thoroughly documented and all potential evidence has been identified, collected, and preserved for later analysis. This determination will usually be made in consultation with the forensic identification specialist. Death investigations are discussed in detail in Chapter 11, Death Investigation.

Before making a decision about when to release a crime scene, the detective will normally discuss the crime scene with the forensic identification specialist and walk through the scene himself or herself to ensure that nothing more of relevance can be gleaned from it. Although some crime scenes—for example, a simple break and enter—can be examined and released by police in a matter of hours, after photographing the scene and dusting for fingerprints, other, more serious crime scenes—for example, a homicide—might be held by police for days or even weeks. In extreme cases, a crime scene might be held for years. In the investigation of the farm complex belonging to serial killer Robert Pickton, for example, the crime scene was held by police for almost two years, during which time 125 identification officers collected more than 75,000 exhibits (Procunier, 2011).

KEY TERMS

contamination	forensic scientist
crime scene	Locard's exchange principle
cross-contamination	master evidence log
CSI effect	uniformed police constable
detective	uniformed police supervisor
forensic identification specialist	*Waterfield* test
forensic pathologist	

FURTHER READING

Chisum, W.J., & Turvey, B.E. (2007). *Crime reconstruction.* Burlington, MA: Elsevier.

Nafte, M., & Dalrymple, B. (2011). *Crime and measurement: Methods in forensic investigation.* Durham, NC: Carolina Academic Press.

National Academy of Sciences. (2009). *Strengthening forensic science in the United States: A path forward.* Washington, DC: The National Academies Press. See, especially, chap. 4, "The Principles of Science and Interpreting Scientific Data." http://www.nap.edu.

REVIEW QUESTIONS

True or False?

1. The way in which a crime scene is protected by police and the evidence found there is documented, collected, and preserved can affect the ability of a detective to determine what happened there.

2. The decision of when to release a crime scene from police control is made exclusively by the forensic identification specialist.

3. Typically, the gathering of evidence at a serious crime scene is done by the first officers to respond to the scene.

4. A police officer has absolute discretion to determine what evidence he or she will or will not gather from a crime scene.

5. When making a statement to the media it is important for the officer in charge of an investigation to be truthful; however, he or she must also be careful not to divulge details about evidence gathered during the investigation.

6. Forensic scientists routinely attend crime scenes to assist the police in locating and analyzing physical evidence.

Multiple Choice

1. Locard's exchange principle states that "every contact leaves a ...":

   a. mark.

   b. clue.

   c. trace.

   d. residue.

2. Police can use various investigative databases to assist them in identifying different types of evidence. These include:

   a. AFIS, NDDB, IBIS.

   b. AFIS, IBIS, OWDB.

   c. IBIS, OWDB, ADIS.

   d. IBIS, ADIS, NDDB.

3. In court, the Crown and the police seek to demonstrate the "history" of evidence, or its:

   a. authenticity.

   b. validity.

   c. continuity.

   d. objectivity.

4. A crime scene typically consists of (at least):

   a. an inner core and an outer perimeter.

   b. an inner perimeter and an outer core.

   c. an immediate scene and a distant scene.

   d. a private perimeter and a public perimeter.

5. As a general rule, officers should designate as large a crime scene as seems reasonably necessary on the basis of:

   a. information received by the police from the public.

   b. a worst-case assumption about the severity of the crime and the area involved.

   c. the physical evidence that was observed by the first officer to respond to the scene.

   d. the opinion of the most senior officer present at the crime scene.

6. There is perhaps no "CSI effect" more apparent than:

   a. the notion that physical evidence cannot lie.

   b. the idea that there is always ample usable evidence to be located at a crime scene.

   c. the confusion created about the respective roles of the various actors involved in the investigation of crime.

   d. the idea that police have a general database that they can use to "match" a wide variety of items to a manufacturer or place of sale.

7. Documenting a crime scene involves creating a record of both the evidence and the environment in which the evidence was found. Which two terms describe this?

   a. content and context.

   b. continuity and contamination.

   c. inculpatory and exculpatory.

   d. forensic and location.

8. A crime scene is not only a place in which a crime occurred. It can also be a place in which evidence relating to a crime:

   a. is thought to be located.

   b. is now or was previously located.

   c. may be found.

   d. could be hidden.

Short Answer

1. Discuss what authority police have to establish and protect a crime scene, and identify the sources of that authority.

2. Although some people maintain that physical evidence "speaks for itself" and thus cannot "lie," physical evidence is not necessarily superior to testimonial evidence—for example, an eyewitness statement. Discuss why this is the case.

3. An investigator's task when managing a crime scene is not so much to prevent crime scene contamination (although that is of course the ideal) as it is to ensure that all contamination that has or will necessarily occur is fully documented and then to ensure that no further unnecessary contamination takes place. Discuss the primary means by which an investigator can achieve this.

Case Study

You are a uniformed police officer assigned to mobile patrol, and you are working alone. You receive a radio call from your dispatcher to attend an address for an "unknown trouble" call. On arriving at the scene you are met in the lobby of a large apartment building by a woman who tells you that a man kicked in the door of her apartment and threatened to kill her with a hammer if she did not agree to have sex with him. She believes that he may have been either drunk or high on drugs and she reports that one of his hands was "all bloody" because he punched his fist through the wall in her living room. The victim reports that during the sexual assault, which occurred on the couch, the suspect hit her repeatedly on the head and then blacked out, giving her a chance to escape from her apartment to the apartment lobby where she was able to call 911. The victim appears to be in shock and tells you that all she wants you to do is drive her to her sister's house so she can forget about what has happened to her. The superintendent of the building is also in the lobby and he tells you that he thinks the suspect is still in the apartment; he says that he will stay in the lobby with the victim while you go to the victim's apartment to check for the suspect.

Using the information in this scenario, answer the following:

a. Describe the actions you would take immediately after meeting the victim and hearing her account of the assault.

b. You and your partner are dispatched to the scene to back up the first officer to respond. There are no more uniformed patrol officers available to call on for assistance. Describe what actions you and your partner would take upon arriving at the apartment building.

c. You are the forensic identification specialist assigned to assist with the investigation by searching for and collecting physical evidence. You are briefed about the crime by the first officer on scene, and after consultation with the detective in charge of the investigation, you commence an examination of the scene. Describe one of the primary legal concerns you would want to address before beginning your examination; then describe some of the different the types of evidence you would expect to gather in such a scenario.

Pattern Evidence and Collision Reconstruction

8

LEARNING OUTCOMES

After completing this chapter, you should be able to:

- Describe what a forensic identification specialist does.

- Outline the guiding principles of evidence collection.

- Explain the meaning of the term "pattern evidence."

- Describe the information that can be gleaned from the analysis of fingerprints, footwear, tire impressions, and bloodstain patterns.

- Explain what a collision reconstructionist can determine by examining a motor vehicle collision scene.

- Identify areas of potential weakness in the interpretation of physical evidence.

INTRODUCTION

As we saw in Chapter 7, Crime Scene Investigation and Management, television has distorted our perceptions of the role that police crime scene investigators play in the investigation of crime. The work of a forensic identification specialist (FIS) is far more limited than that shown on TV. In Canada, civilian scientists in forensic laboratories conduct most of the analysis of evidence found at a crime scene.

Forensic identification specialists do, however, play an important role at crime scenes—not only in detecting, collecting, and preserving evidence, but also in analyzing certain kinds of evidence. Most commonly, identification officers collect and analyze certain types of **impression evidence**, also called **pattern evidence**—for example, fingerprints, tire marks, boot prints, and bloodstains. Impression evidence and pattern evidence are two distinct types of evidence grouped together because one typically includes the other. For example, a fingerprint is an "impression" (a bloody finger touches a door and leaves an impression), but that impression will include a pattern (an arch, a loop, or a whorl). Similarly, although a tire mark is an impression (for example, a tire impressed into soil), that impression will have a pattern (the tread pattern, plus, for example, any damage, defects, or wear). Identification officers also document crime scenes using digital photography. This work is discussed in the following sections.

Not all police officers may perform the role of an FIS. Although the process through which a police officer becomes an FIS might vary slightly among different police services, typically, an officer must have completed several years of general police service, and then be recommended to receive specialized forensic training. This training involves taking both Scenes of Crime Officer and Forensic Identification Officer courses at the Canadian Police College, which focus on the identification of fingerprint and physical evidence. Officers must then serve a period of apprenticeship before being certified as an FIS. (In the RCMP, the apprenticeship period is four years.) Officers who are fully certified as an FIS must take continuing education courses in their field, and the quality of their work is formally and regularly reviewed to ensure that they continue to meet the established professional standards.

impression evidence
created when two objects come into contact with sufficient force to cause an impression or a mark

pattern evidence
additional evidence typically contained within the mark or impression evidence

EVIDENCE COLLECTION: GUIDING PRINCIPLES

A number of general rules or principles guide forensic identification specialists in collecting evidence from crime scenes. Regardless of a police officer's primary role—for example, uniformed first responder or detective—*all* officers must be aware of and guided by these principles to help ensure the integrity of evidence at a crime scene (Nafte & Dalrymple, 2011). Failure to do so could result in contamination or destruction of evidence, or loss of continuity.

It might be especially important for officers serving in police services with limited resources, such as the RCMP or Ontario Provincial Police (OPP) in small, isolated communities, to be aware of the basic principles of evidence collection, because the "uniformed patrol officer" in such a service may be required to perform the roles of "first responder," "detective," and "identification officer"—at least initially. All officers should be familiar with and apply the following principles as necessary:

- *Conduct a thorough and methodical investigation the first time around.*

  The very process of entering and collecting evidence from a crime scene destroys it, and the scene can never be returned to the state in which it was found. In addition, once a scene is released and the property owner or the public are allowed access to it, a forensic identification specialist will rarely, if ever, have a second chance to gather evidence from the scene. A crime scene is thus a perishable commodity, and identification officers must ensure that they conduct a thorough and methodical investigation the first time around; the first step of which is to thoroughly document the scene.

- *Not all significant evidence can be physically collected and preserved.*

  Certain things that can have an impact on a crime scene and the interpretation of the evidence found there cannot be "gathered" in the same way that one can collect and preserve, for example, a bullet or a blood drop, but they must be carefully documented—for example, the weather, the temperature inside a room, or the presence of animals at a burial site. An FIS must therefore make detailed notes about all such environmental factors because they may potentially become relevant at some later stage in an investigation.

- *Not all evidence is obvious.*

  In the early stages of an investigation, there may be no readily observed relationship between a particular item at a crime scene and the matter under investigation; it may only be after looking at the evidence as a whole or conducting investigative interviews that the relevance of a particular piece of evidence becomes clear. Therefore, forensic identification specialists need to document and collect everything at a crime scene that may possibly relate to the matter under investigation. They need to be guided by the same principle that governs the establishment of a crime scene—that is, it is better to err on the side of caution and protect *too much* evidence than too little. (If applied literally, however, this principle would mean that a forensic identification specialist would have to strip a crime scene bare; while on rare occasions this may be necessary, typically, it is not. Rather, an identification officer's experience, combined with ongoing communication with the detectives in charge of the investigation, will determine what and how much evidence the forensic identification specialist will collect from a particular scene.)

- *Be aware of dangers and minimize risk.*

  Forensic identification specialists often work in hazardous environments that require them to take certain precautions. Crime scenes often contain materials that present either a physical or a biological hazard—for example, shards of glass, weapons, bodily fluids, and unknown chemicals. As a result, identification officers must use safety equipment—for example, gloves, masks, and protective clothing and footwear—that minimizes the chances of their exposure to or injury by dangerous materials. When collecting materials that could pose a danger, forensic officers must ensure that such materials are packaged and labelled in a way that also minimizes the chance of others being injured or exposed.

- *Follow correct protocols.*

    Forensic protocols demand that evidence be gathered, packaged, and submitted according to certain rules. Forensic facilities, such as the Centre of Forensic Sciences in Toronto, publish guides that outline the basic procedures for collecting, preserving, and submitting materials for analysis. If a forensic identification specialist is not familiar with or does not follow such protocols, evidence may either be ruined or contaminated, or the forensic facility may reject the submission.

PATTERN EVIDENCE

Pattern evidence consists of patterns that are created when two or more objects come into contact and one object leaves an impression on the other. Examples of pattern evidence include:

- a fingerprint on a windowsill;
- blood spattered against a wall;
- a boot print in a patch of soil;
- burn marks caused by gasoline poured on the floor of a building and then ignited;
- an automobile tire mark on a snow-covered driveway;
- a bullet with striations on its surface made by the barrel of the pistol from which it is was fired; and
- the impression of the tip of a metal pry bar found on a wooden door jamb at a break and enter scene.

While some types of impression or pattern evidence—for example, ballistic or tool mark evidence—are analyzed by scientists in forensic laboratories or by specialists—for example, investigators from the office of the fire marshal in an arson investigation—others are typically detected, collected, and analyzed by police crime scene investigators. Such evidence includes fingerprints, footwear and tire impressions, and blood spatter.

Fingerprints

Searching for and identifying fingerprint evidence is arguably the type of work most closely associated with police crime scene investigation. Although most identification officers and police use the term "identifying" to refer to the process of matching a fingerprint found at a crime scene to a fingerprint in a police database, and thus to an individual, forensic scientists use the term "individualizing." Both terms refer to the same process.

Fingerprints are one of the oldest and most important categories of evidence in forensic science (Gaensslen & Young, 2003). Typically, specially trained police identification officers or technicians both collect fingerprints in the field and later analyze them.

Fingerprints are composed of a series of friction "ridges" and "furrows" on the skin of the hands and feet, which form three general pattern types that are in turn divided into subgroups (see Figure 8.1). Within each pattern, there are subpatterns and unique variations, referred to as "minutiae," and, as a result, each person's fingerprints are believed to be absolutely unique, even in the case of identical twins. Because fingerprints are believed to be unique to an individual and don't change over a lifespan (unless unusual skin damage has occurred), except to grow, they can be used in various ways, including to identify people, to link an individual to a particular crime, or to put a name to a deceased person who could not be identified through more conventional means.

There are three basic kinds of fingerprints:

- **Patent prints**: Fingerprints readily visible to the naked eye, which may be photographed and, possibly, compared with other prints on file (referred to as "file" or "reference" prints and taken from known individuals) without further processing. Patent prints are composed of substances such as blood, dust, dirt, paint, or grease. They are created through a process similar to that of a person pressing their finger down on an inkpad and then pressing that same finger against a firm object, leaving a clear fingerprint on the object.

- **Latent prints**: Invisible fingerprints that require further processing to make them visible for comparison with file or reference prints. These are the prints we leave on everything we touch—for example, door handles, drinking glasses, furniture, and countertops.

- **Impression prints**: Recognizable fingerprints that have been left behind in a soft material—for example, plasticine, tar, or caulking. Impression prints are sometimes referred to as "plastic" or "indentation" prints, and have a unique three-dimensional character.

patent prints
fingerprints readily visible to the naked eye, which may be photographed and compared with other prints without further processing

latent prints
fingerprints that are not readily apparent, and require further processing to make them visible for comparison with file or reference prints

impression prints
recognizable fingerprints left behind in any soft materials—for example, plasticine, tar, or caulking

FIGURE 8.1   Fingerprint patterns

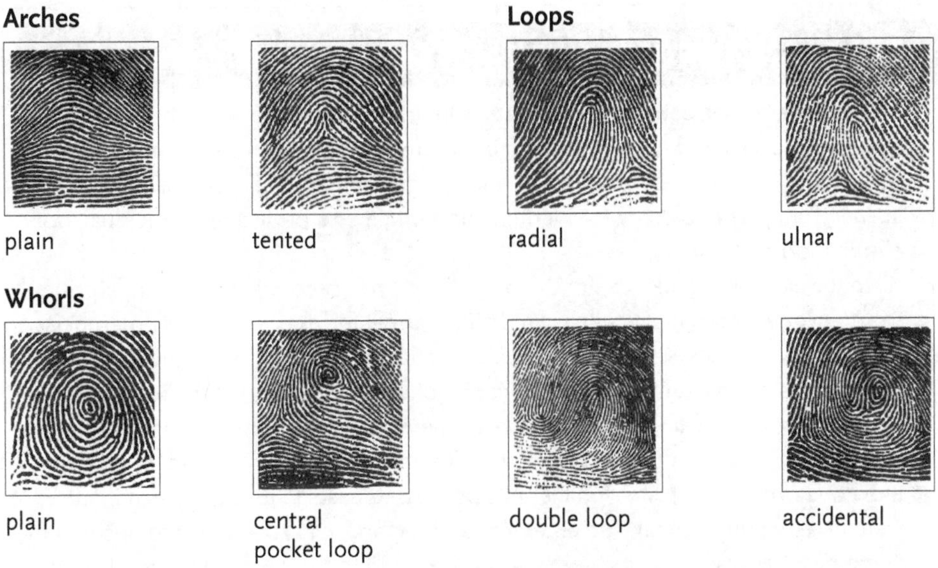

Arches

plain   tented

Loops

radial   ulnar

Whorls

plain   central pocket loop   double loop   accidental

The three groups of fingerprints are (1) arch, (2) loop, and (3) whorl. Arches may be classified as plain or tented; loops as radial or ulnar (depending on the direction in which the loop opens); and whorls as plain, central pocket loop, double loop, or accidental. The most common fingerprint pattern is the loop, found in approximately two-thirds of the population.

People typically associate "dusting" with crime scene investigation as the method of gathering fingerprint evidence. Dusting, technically known as "powder dusting," involves using a special brush to spread a thin layer of a prepared powder over an area—for example, a portion of a wall or a drinking glass—on which fingerprints are either partially visible or, in the case of latent prints, believed to exist. The powder adheres to the sweat residue (most commonly, a type of sweat known as "eccrine," although a second type of latent print residue contains oils produced by sebaceous glands) that forms the latent print, thus making it visible to the eye. Once the latent print is visible, the identification officer photographs it and then "lifts" it.

A fingerprint is "lifted" from a crime scene to preserve it so that it can be taken to a police facility and compared with other prints stored in a computerized fingerprint record comparison system known as AFIS (automated fingerprint identification system). Fingerprints are lifted, essentially, by pressing a piece of specially designed, clear tape over the fingerprint and then peeling, or lifting, the piece of tape off the surface, which results in an impression of the print being captured on the tape. The tape is then placed on a piece of card that contrasts in colour to the type of dusting powder that was used—that is, if black powder was used to dust the print, the lifting tape will be adhered to a white card. The fingerprint, called an "evidentiary print," is then loaded into the AFIS program, which searches for possible matches. If AFIS generates a possible match or matches, an FIS officer or a fingerprint technician (or "examiner") must manually check the possible matches to confirm whether they are indeed a match for the evidentiary print. This is done by comparing a number of unique points on both the evidentiary and reference prints to show that they are, in fact, the same fingerprints. This identification process typically involves a peer review component, in which one expert reviews the work of another to confirm the identification, thus minimizing the possibility of a misidentification.

ELIMINATING FINGERPRINTS AT A CRIME SCENE

Many crime scenes contain fingerprints from individuals other than the victim and the suspect. Depending on the surface where the print was found, fingerprints may last a long time. Consequently, when fingerprints are collected from a crime scene, it may be necessary for identification officers to print other individuals for elimination purposes.

In the case of a residence, for example, the crime scene will contain fingerprints from anyone who has lawfully visited the home—for example, family members, roommates, or guests. Family members or guests, for example, would have their fingerprints taken to allow the identification officer to "eliminate" their prints from the larger group of fingerprints taken at the scene, thus allowing the officer to focus solely on attempting to match the remaining "unknown" prints to a specific individual whose prints are "on file" in a police database. If, for example, the officer were investigating a break and enter into a home and was able to match one of the "unknown" prints to a person who was not known to the homeowner and had no lawful reason to have been in the residence, this person would become a suspect. Further investigation would be required to determine why this person's fingerprints were found inside the victim's residence.

At one time, the standard for matching an evidentiary print found at a crime scene to a known reference print required the examiner to find 16 different matching minutiae points between the two prints, but this standard has now been abandoned. In 1995, the International Association for Identification (IAI) determined that "[n]o scientific basis exists for requiring that a predetermined minimum number of friction ridge features must be present in two impressions in order to establish a positive identification" (Champod & Chamberlain, 2009, p. 73); instead, examiners now take a "holistic," approach, which rests more on an examiner's experience and assessment of the two sets of prints as a whole than on the requirement for a specific number of matching points. Safeguards to this holistic approach involve having two others examiners "confirm" the identification (Champod & Chamberlain, 2009).

THE SCIENTIFIC DEBATE ABOUT UNIQUENESS

Once considered the "gold standard" in forensic science, fingerprinting has come under significant scrutiny by a number of large and influential studies that have raised questions about its reliability. Although fingerprinting remains a persuasive form of evidence, a scientific debate is questioning our ability to say, for example, "all fingerprints are unique," and to make similar statements about the uniqueness of other types of evidence. Given that absolute certainty is unattainable in any science, does this mean that otherwise well-founded opinions are unscientific or inadmissible?

Rather than making absolute statements, it is more accurate for forensic experts to make *probabilistic* statements about certain kinds of evidence. Such statements are legitimate, and are potentially good sources of evidence when combined with other, similar probabilistic statements given in evidence during a legal proceeding. In the case of DNA evidence, for example, it is the statistical frequency of the sample occurring in the population that is expressed, with probabilities ranging from 1 in 1 million to 1 in 100 trillion, and even into the quintillions, depending on the analysis that is carried out. In terms of significance, a forensic expert would not say that a sample *definitely* came from a particular individual, but instead that it would be *extremely unlikely* to find another person with that profile.

For example, in presenting DNA evidence in the 2012 trial of Michael Rafferty for the murder and sexual assault of 8-year-old Woodstock, Ontario schoolgirl Victoria (Tori) Stafford, an expert from the Centre of Forensic Sciences testified that, based on Tori's DNA profile, she "cannot be excluded" as the source of a blood stain found in Rafferty's car. The expert explained further that this phrase means either that the DNA belongs to Tori or that it came from someone with the same DNA profile. The chances of someone else having the same profile were calculated at 1 in 28 billion (CBC News, 2012).

Ultimately, it is up to the trier of fact to determine whether, based on the circumstances, the statistic satisfies them that the person whose profile matches the DNA is in fact the person who left the DNA at the scene of the crime, taking into account any other evidence in support of that conclusion.

In reality, most forensic evidence should be presented in this manner. It is only because the courts have accepted fingerprints to be unique for over one hundred years that specialists are permitted to state that a fingerprint is a direct positive identification rather than providing the *probability* that it matches someone else.

After comparing evidentiary and reference fingerprints, a fingerprint examiner can come to one of three possible conclusions:

1. insufficient detail to make an identification;

2. exclusion—that is, the evidentiary print is *not* the same as the reference print; and

3. identification—that is, the similarities between the evidentiary print and the reference print are such that the examiner can state that both prints come from the same person. (See the box feature on the current scientific debate, below.)

Although powder dusting may be the best-known method for gathering fingerprint evidence, it is not the only method. Other methods include the use of chemicals—for example, iodine, ninhydrin, or cyanoacrylate—that react to biological components of the latent print—for example, amino acids or lipids—causing them to change colour or fluoresce and become visible, sometimes to the naked eye and sometimes with the aid of special lighting. Regardless of the method used to make the print visible, the identification process still involves a technician examining the unknown evidentiary print and comparing it to possible matches among known reference prints (Gaensslen & Young, 2003).

In an age when DNA and other sophisticated forensic technologies are prominently featured in entertainment and news reports, fingerprint identification might seem to be an old-fashioned investigative technique, but it remains a persuasive form of evidence in contemporary criminal proceedings.

Footwear and Tire Impressions

Theoretically, footwear impressions are present at every crime scene that someone has walked through, and tire marks are on every surface that someone has driven over. Practically, however, the real issue is whether such evidence can be found and documented.

For example, footwear impressions can be found:

- on a windowsill that someone has climbed through;
- on a door that someone has kicked; or
- in snow, dirt, or blood that someone has walked through.

As with any other type of physical evidence, the first step is to document the position of the footprint or tire impression, typically by photographing it and also by recording its location in the investigator's notes. However, given that there are typically many footwear impressions at most crime scenes, one of the first things identification officers need to ask themselves is why this particular shoe or boot print is of potential evidentiary value. This question will be easy to answer where, for example, footwear impressions lead through a pool of blood and out the door of a homicide victim's apartment. However, not all scenarios are as obvious as this one. Identification officers must be careful when selecting which footwear impressions to gather and later analyze, because footwear prints from, for example, the victim or emergency services personnel will be of no value to the investigator.

Identification officers must take the time to carefully eliminate prints with no evidentiary value, first, by looking at the footwear patterns of all the innocent parties who had access to the crime scene—for example, the victim, police, fire, ambulance, coroner, or medical examiner. Once the investigator has eliminated irrelevant footwear prints and selected which prints to gather for further analysis, the question becomes how best to collect such pieces of evidence. As with many other forms of evidence, an identification officer will first photograph the larger scene to give some sense of where the print was located relative to the scene as a whole; the officer will then take close-up photographs of the print itself, which will later be enlarged to life size, in an attempt to match the print to a specific type and brand of footwear—for example, footwear recovered from a suspect.

The ideal method of collecting a footwear impression is to take the actual surface on which the print was made to a forensic facility for analysis. This might be possible where the print is located on a door, a windowsill a piece of carpet, a floor tile, or other form of removable material; however, in many cases, a photograph of the footwear mark will be all the investigator has to work with. Other methods of making a print more visible and of creating a record of it for analysis include, for example, electrostatic lifts, dusting the footwear impression with fingerprint powder and lifting it similar to a fingerprint, gelatin film for lifting prints left in dust, special lighting, or chemicals that react and turn colour in the presence of blood to make bloody footwear prints more visible.

In outdoor crime scenes where a footwear impression or a tire track has been left in soil, for example, the investigator may be able to recover the impression by making a plaster cast, which is achieved by pouring a plaster-like substance called "dental stone" into an impression and letting it set, thereby creating a hard, three-dimensional cast of the impression suitable for comparison purposes. Impressions left in snow may be documented by spraying them with a special snow print wax or dusting them with snow print powder, which makes them more visible and easier to photograph; they may also be collected using an impression process.

Once either a footwear impression or a tire mark has been documented and collected, the next steps involve attempting to identify the type or brand of shoe or tire that left the mark, carefully documenting the unique aspects of the print—for example, wear, cuts, or defects—and then attempting to match the print recovered from the scene to a suspect's footwear or vehicle tires. There is no particular magic to this process, but it can take a great deal of time because it involves searching databases in an attempt to determine a brand and model for the footwear or tire impression, or to discover whether a similar impression has been left behind at another crime scene, and then carefully examining the impression with a magnifying glass or a microscope in order to document its unique characteristics, caused by such things as wear, damage, or manufacturing imperfections. Features such as these are critical to the process of matching the impression gathered from the crime scene to a specific piece of footwear or a specific tire belonging to the suspect or suspects. In the case of tire impressions, measurements taken of the different tire marks left at a crime scene can help investigators determine such things as the wheelbase of the vehicle that made the tire marks, thus assisting them in determining, for example, whether the marks were made by a compact passenger vehicle or a large sport utility vehicle.

LINKING A KILLER TO THE CRIME SCENE

Although the collection and analysis of impression evidence produced by footwear and tires may not seem like a particularly sophisticated forensic technique, on occasion it can be quite valuable. For example, in the 2010 case of serial murderer David Russell Williams (formerly known as Colonel Russell Williams), boot impressions and tire treads were key pieces of evidence linking Williams to one of the victims and played a role in Williams's eventual confession.

At the scene of the disappearance of a 27-year-old Belleville woman, Jessica Lloyd, police found distinctive tire track impressions in the snow, and detectives went to work on identifying the type of vehicle that left them. Police subsequently set up a roadside check in the area, looking for possible matches, and Williams passed through in his Nissan Pathfinder. Police photographed his tires and compared them to the impressions left at the crime scene. The impressions were similar, and in the following days OPP officers obtained warrants to search Williams's residences. Police had also found boot prints in the snow behind Lloyd's house, and, when Williams showed up for an interview with OPP Detective Sergeant Jim Smyth approximately a week later, he was wearing the same boots he had worn on the night he broke into Lloyd's home.

During the interview, Smyth asked Williams whether he could help investigators by providing evidence that might clear him as a suspect. Williams agreed to provide a DNA sample, his BlackBerry for analysis, and an impression of his boot tread, which, during the course of the interrogation, officers found matched the prints at Lloyd's home. More than three hours into the interview, Smyth showed Williams a photocopy of the boot prints at the scene and the impressions taken from his boots, which Smyth noted were "identical." In addition to other information revealed by Smyth—for example, the large size of the investigation and the unlimited resources available to investigators; the tire track match; the searches of Williams's residences that were occurring; the search of his vehicle and his office, where further evidence would be found; and the match that would likely be found between Williams's DNA and DNA obtained from the victim's body when the postmortem was complete—the footwear impression evidence helped seal Williams's fate.

Bloodstain Pattern Analysis

Blood is often shed during a violent crime, typically by the victim, but, on occasion, also by the suspect. In some countries—for example, the United Kingdom—bloodstain pattern analysis has traditionally been carried out by forensic scientists, but in North America such work is often done by identification officers. Analysis of the blood itself by a forensic scientist in a laboratory may result in the development of a DNA profile, which can help determine whose blood it is, but documenting the location and analyzing the patterns of blood left at a crime scene is something that can yield a different sort of evidence—evidence about what may have happened to create the bloodstain patterns. Such information can, for example, help either corroborate or disconfirm other evidence, such as statements made by victims, witnesses, or suspects.

Bloodstain pattern analysis—that is, looking at the location, size, shape, and patterns of blood deposited at a crime scene—may allow an investigator to gain information about things such as:

- where an assault happened;
- whether the victim was moved from the location of the original assault;
- what created the bloodstains—that is, the type of object used to deliver the blows, and how much force was involved;
- what direction a blood droplet was travelling when it was deposited on a surface, and where it came from;
- what type of bloodstaining investigators might expect to find on the assailant's clothing;
- the relative positions of the victim and the assailant when the blows were delivered; and
- the sequence in which certain events took place.

(Royal Canadian Mounted Police, 2011; Wain & Linacre, 2009, pp. 229–253.)

The analysis of bloodstain patterns, whether at a crime scene or on objects from a crime scene, is essentially based on the careful observation and measurement of bloodstains, noting their location, size, number, and shape. These observations are then interpreted in light of what specialized branches of science—such as physics, fluid dynamics, and biology—can tell us about how fluids move through space and come to be distributed on various surfaces, and about the composition and behaviour of blood as a specific type of fluid.

Although bloodstain pattern analysis historically did not involve the use of sophisticated equipment, analysts now routinely use specially designed computer software and digital photography to assist them in determining such information as the probable point of origin of a blood source. In the past, such information was determined by "stringing," a method that involved stretching pieces of string through a number of bloodstains, based on a determination of the direction from which they came and the angle at which they landed on the surface where they were deposited. The point at which these multiple pieces of string converged allowed an analyst to determine the probable point of origin of the blood source that created the multiple stains.

A number of problems existed with stringing, not the least of which was the ability of an analyst to place the strings accurately, and although this problem was addressed to some degree through the use of tools such as the laser protractor, stringing is now, essentially, a historical technique. Although the same basic principles of mathematics and physics on which stringing was based remain valid, specialized computer software programs in combination with digital photography allow analysts to apply these principles to bloodstain pattern analysis while taking into account the many variables that affect the movement of blood drops—for example, blood drop volume and air and gravity resistance—with a degree of precision not previously possible (Bevel & Gardner, 2001, p. 184).

Bloodstain patterns can be grouped under various headings on the basis of how they were produced and what they can tell an investigator:

- *Drip patterns:* Bloodstains formed due to blood falling under the force of gravity alone. In reality, such stains are rare because the source of the blood—for example, a person or a weapon—will, in most circumstances, be moving. The size and shape of the bloodstain is determined by factors such as the volume of the drop, the height from which it fell, the angle at which it strikes a surface, and the nature of that surface.

- *Impact spatter:* Bloodstains that are formed as a result of a force that causes blood to break up into small drops and travel through the air. Punching or kicking someone who is bleeding can produce impact spatter, as can striking someone with a bat or shooting them with a bullet. As a general rule, the more force that is involved, the smaller the drops will be, and the smaller the drops are, the less distance they will travel through the air from the point of impact.

- *Cast-off stains:* Bloodstains produced by a bloodstained object—for example, a hammer—being swung through the air, causing blood to be cast off the object; similarly, when a bloodstained object comes to a sudden stop blood can also be cast off from it. Cast-off bloodstains can be produced by anything that has wet blood on it and that is subjected to sufficient force. Thus, a victim or assailant's hand or a victim's hair can all be sources of cast-off staining. Generally speaking, the longer and lighter the object (assuming equal amounts of blood are available), the more cast-off staining will be generated. This is because a longer, lighter object, such as a hockey stick, has to be swung harder and in a larger arc to generate the desired force, than a shorter heavier object, such as a hammer.

- *Expired (or exhaled) blood:* Blood that has entered the respiratory system (for example, the nose, lungs, or trachea) as a result of trauma, which is then expelled from the mouth or nose by force—for example, by coughing, sneezing, spitting, or snorting.

- *Arterial stains:* Bloodstains originating from blood pumped by the heart when the arteries are under pressure as a result of arterial damage, resulting in blood gushing or spurting from the body and forming a characteristic series of "s," "v," or "w" shapes on the surfaces where it lands; these patterns can be affected by the victim's clothing or movement. This pattern of bloodstaining is distinct from that which is left by blood originating from damage to a vein, which typically results in a pooling of blood.

- *Altered bloodstains:* Bloodstains—sometimes referred to as PABS, or physiologically altered bloodstains—that result from blood clotting, often mixed with other bodily fluids (for example, mucus, saliva, or stomach contents), beverages, or cleaning fluids, which alter the normal appearance of clotted blood and produce bloodstains with certain characteristic appearances, depending on what the blood was mixed with. For example, bloodstains that have been mixed with cleaning fluids or water in an effort to remove blood from a scene will often result in dilute blood drops or wipe marks, which may be made more visible using various forensic chemicals or light sources.

- *Contact stains:* Bloodstains that result when two or more items come into contact, at least one of which is wet with blood. Often, this sort of stain consists of blood from one item leaving a smear on the other item, which may allow the analyst to infer relative movement, such as where a victim's bloody shirt leaves a smear against the floor surface. Occasionally, however, a distinctive stain, such as a fingerprint or footwear impression, may be produced through the contact-staining process.

- *Large volume stains:* The average person, weighing 70 kg (154 lbs), has approximately 5 litres of blood in his or her body. On rare occasions, a bloodstain pattern analyst may be asked to assist a pathologist in his or her investigation by offering an estimate of the volume of blood that a victim lost at a crime scene. There are various ways of producing such an estimate—for example, calculating the dry weight or the area of the bloodstain.

- *Complex stains:* Bloodstains composed of a combination of some of the different types of stains mentioned above. For example, where a person's neck is slashed with a knife and their body is then dragged across the room by their assailant, one might expect to see a complex stain composed of arterial staining and contact staining.

A bloodstain pattern analyst should also look for the *absence* of staining where they would normally expect to find staining. If, for example, a large portion of a surface is covered in impact spatter, but a certain area is clean, this may indicate that something, which is also probably covered with impact spatter, has been removed from the scene.

Many bloodstains are obvious, and may require only visual observation, or observation assisted by special lighting or magnification devices. Where bloodstains are not readily visible, there are a number of chemical tests to make blood apparent (see the discussion in Chapter 12, Forensic Biology and DNA).

Despite the fact that certain aspects of bloodstain pattern analysis can be objective—for example, the documenting and measurement of bloodstain patterns—the *interpretation* of these patterns is largely a subjective process; therefore, the results of such an analysis need to be considered carefully, in conjunction with all the other types of evidence gathered during an investigation.

COLLISION RECONSTRUCTION

Traffic collisions exact a high toll on our society. Indeed, inside the traffic division of one of Canada's largest police services, a large plaque is prominently displayed in the room where officers are given their daily assignments. It reads: "Traffic crimes cost society more, devastate more Canadian families, and inflict more physical insult than all other crimes combined."

In Canada, in 2009 (the most recent year for which data are available at the time of writing), there were more than 170,000 motor vehicle collisions in which the occupants of the vehicles involved were injured, and more than 2,200 deaths as a result of motor vehicle collisions (Canadian Motor Vehicle Traffic Collision Statistics, 2009). In any given year, motor vehicle collision deaths far surpass murder figures. And while the investigation of motor vehicle collisions generally does not garner the same sort of attention as the investigation of crimes such as murder, the investigation of traffic fatalities can often be just as complex and is an important aspect of police work. Potential charges that may result from the evidence gathered during an investigation range from disobeying a traffic signal to failing to stop at the scene of an accident, careless or impaired driving, and even criminal negligence causing death. In fact, where a motor vehicle is intentionally used as a weapon to kill someone, a collision investigation can become a murder investigation.

Typically, where a motor vehicle collision has occurred, a specialized collision investigator will detect, collect, and analyze the forensic evidence in an attempt to determine the cause of the collision. These specialists—known as collision reconstructionists or, in police circles, as "recons"—will attempt to "reconstruct" the collision using the available physical evidence, precision measuring devices (such as the Leica or Sokkia "total station"), computer animation software, evidence from the vehicle's event data recorder (black box), statements from witnesses and the drivers, and a knowledge of the laws of physics.

Collision reconstructionists obtain information from things such as the markings on the roadway left by tires, wheel rims, or the vehicle's structure; debris consisting of fluids, glass, plastic, or blood; and other factors such as vehicle damage. Using the various tools at their disposal, they attempt to determine:

- the speed at which the vehicles were travelling at the time of the collision;
- the relative positions of the vehicles on the roadway and the angle at which they collided; and
- the point of impact on the roadway where the vehicles met.

The collision reconstructionist works as a member of a traffic investigative team. As important as the evidence provided by a reconstructionist may be, it typically constitutes only a portion of the total evidence gathered. Other sources of evidence include: victim, witness, and/or suspect interviews conducted by the traffic detective; in the case of a traffic fatality, medical evidence provided by the forensic pathologist; evidence of alcohol impairment provided by a police breathalyzer technician; vehicle fitness evidence provided by the police mechanic; and photographic evidence of the scene provided by a forensic identification officer.

Speeding is a factor in approximately 25 percent of vehicle collision deaths in Canada, which is comparable to the number of victims killed in alcohol-related crashes; the faster a vehicle is travelling, the more energy it has, the more difficult it can be to control, and the longer it takes to slow it down or bring it to a stop (Transport Canada, 2008). Given that excessive speed is one of the most common causes of motor vehicle collisions, vehicle speed is one of the key factors that a reconstructionist will attempt to determine in virtually all collision scenarios. The application of mathematical calculations to physical evidence can tell investigators that, for example, in order to leave a skid mark 28 metres long on a dry asphalt roadway before coming to a stop, the vehicle that left the mark had to be travelling a minimum of 70 km/h. Such a finding can be used to corroborate the statements of witnesses, who might provide different estimates of the vehicle's speed but might all state that it was travelling well above the posted limit of 40 km/h. Information such as this can be valuable in helping the traffic detective determine what factors caused a collision.

An understanding of the laws of physics governing conservation of energy and momentum allow an investigator to use mathematical formulas to determine vehicle speed in a variety of scenarios, including:

- *crush:* where a vehicle strikes a fixed object, such as a bridge support, or is struck by another vehicle, resulting in its structure being crushed or deformed;

- *vault:* where a motor vehicle loses control, leaves a roadway, and travels a distance through the air; and

- *critical curve speed:* where the centrifugal force exerted on a vehicle as it negotiates a curve overcomes the friction of the tires on the roadway, causing the vehicle to slide off the roadway.

If properly qualified, collision reconstructionists can give expert evidence in legal proceedings. The following cases illustrate the role that such evidence has played in various trials and highlight the importance of accurate measurement and documentation:

- *R. v. Kelleher* (2009). A fatal pedestrian collision where the victim was struck by a bus and killed while using a crosswalk. A collision reconstructionist gave expert evidence of the driver's failure to yield to the pedestrian in the crosswalk, and estimated the vehicle's speed, in the absence of skid marks, using "cleaning marks" left by the victim's body on the side of the bus, combined with the distance that it took the bus to stop after the brakes were applied. The accused bus driver was found guilty of failing to yield to the pedestrian.

- *R. v. Hatcher* (2005). A pedestrian fatality collision, where the victim was struck and killed by a truck while walking her dog. Evidence was given by two collision reconstructionists regarding vehicle speed, vehicle path, and position of vehicle occupants, but weaknesses in the reconstruction evidence led to the criminal charge against the accused driver of "failure to stop" (*Criminal Code*, 1995, s. 252) being dismissed.

- *R. v. Smith* (2009). A fatal motor vehicle collision in which the driver of the vehicle lost control on a roadway with a 50 km/h speed limit, skidded, and struck a tree, killing his passenger. Based on a 58-metre-long skid mark on the roadway, a collision reconstructionist calculated the vehicle's speed at 98 km/h. The driver pleaded guilty to dangerous driving causing death (*Criminal Code*, 1995, s. 249(1)).

- *R. v. Singh* (2010). A fatal motor vehicle collision in which the driver of a dump truck, travelling at an excessive speed, failed to stop for a red light at an intersection, collided with a Toyota Camry, and killed the driver of the Camry. The driver of the dump truck was charged with dangerous driving causing death (*Criminal Code*, 1995, s. 249(1)). In contrast to the 60–65 km/h that the accused driver claimed to be travelling, the collision reconstructionist calculated the speed of the dump truck to be approximately 94 km/h at the time of the collision. The judge accepted the reconstructionist's evidence, found that the truck had entered the intersection at 90 km/h against a red light, and convicted the truck driver of dangerous driving causing death. (For a description of how the speed of the truck was calculated, interested readers can refer to para. 61 of the case.)

- *R. v. Brander* (2003). A fatal motor vehicle collision in which an unmarked police car, travelling at a high rate of speed, struck another vehicle at an intersection, killing an occupant in the second car. The police officer was charged with criminal negligence causing death and criminal negligence causing bodily harm (*Criminal Code*, 1995, s. 219(1)). A number of collision reconstructionists gave evidence regarding the likely speed at which the police vehicle was travelling prior to the collision.

PHYSICAL EVIDENCE IN R. v. BRANDER

Brander (2003) is particularly instructive in light of the myth regarding the superiority of physical evidence described in Chapter 7. As objective as physical evidence may be relative to such subjective evidence as, for example, a witness statement, physical evidence does not "speak" for itself; it must be observed and documented by people, and people can make errors in this process that may have a significant impact on the power of physical evidence. In *Brander*, the primary collision reconstructionist took measurements and documented some, but not all, aspects of the skid marks that were left on the roadway by the police vehicle; measured the elevation of the collision scene, but made an error; measured the coefficient of friction of the roadway, but came up with a variety of different values; used incorrect vehicle weights in his initial vehicle speed calculations; and admitted that he had been under pressure to complete his report (*Brander*, paras. 35–40).

The first reconstructionist's evidence was reviewed by a second, and by a professional engineer hired by the Crown. On the basis of the calculations of all three reconstructionists, evidence was produced that the police vehicle was travelling at a minimum speed of between 130 km/h and 142 km/h when it went into a skid before the collision (*Brander*, para. 51). However, the judge questioned the accuracy of the reconstruction evidence,

> not on the basis of their formula or methods, but rather, on the basis of the accuracy of the scene measurements and interpretation of the roadway evidence itself. It is this evidence which is the foundation, the cornerstone, of the reconstructionists calculations. If it is wrong or inaccurate, the opinions of the reconstructionists will be inaccurate. (*Brander*, para. 55)

The judge went on to say that,

> [i]n order to accept the reconstructionists' expert evidence as to the speeds, I must have confidence that the root information that they must depend on—specifically the critical measurements—is accurate. The various errors that were made ... adversely affect my confidence in the accuracy of those critical measurements. (*Brander*, para. 57)

This case is a perfect illustration of the impact that human error in such areas as measuring and documenting physical evidence can have on the weight that physical evidence is given in court. In this case, physical evidence regarding the vehicle's speed was effectively dismissed in favour of the subjective recollection of witnesses, including the accused. In fact, the accused driver's opinion regarding the speed at which he was travelling was given *more* weight than the physical evidence presented by the reconstructionists, despite the fact that the driver admitted that he had not looked at his speedometer, but had simply estimated his speed to have been around 110 km/h. Thus, not everyone—and certainly not the judge in this case—is convinced that they should simply believe an investigator because physical evidence "doesn't lie." All types of evidence, physical and otherwise, will be carefully scrutinized for their strengths and weaknesses.

KEY TERMS

impression evidence
impression prints
latent prints
patent prints
pattern evidence

FURTHER READING

Bevel, T., & Gardner, R.M. (2009). Applying bloodstain pattern analysis to crime scene reconstruction. In *Practical crime scene analysis and reconstruction* (pp. 107–130). Boca Raton, FL: CRC Press.

James, S., Kish, P., & Sutton, T. (2005). *Principles of bloodstain pattern analysis: Theory and practice.* New York: CRC Press.

James, S.H., & Nordby, J.J. (Eds.). (2009). *Forensic science: An introduction to scientific and investigative techniques* (3rd ed.). Boca Raton, FL: CRC Press.

Kaye, D. (2009). Identification, individualization, and uniqueness: What's the difference? *Law, Probability, and Risk, 8*(2), 85–94.

REVIEW QUESTIONS

True or False?

1. Any police officer can gather evidence at a crime scene and perform the role of a forensic identification officer.

2. All police officers, even uniformed first responders, need to be aware of the general principles that guide the work of forensic identification specialists in collecting evidence and be guided by those principles when performing their duties, in order to help ensure the integrity of evidence at a crime scene.

3. The ideal method of collecting a footwear impression is to take a close-up digital photograph of the impression for later analysis by a forensic technologist.

4. The standard for "matching" an evidentiary fingerprint found at a crime scene to a known reference print requires the examiner to find 16 different matching points between the two prints.

5. The analysis of bloodstain patterns, whether at a crime scene or on objects from a crime scene, is essentially based on the careful observation and measurement of bloodstains, noting their location, size, number, and shape.

6. The evidence presented in court by collision reconstructionists is always accepted because it is based on objective measurements, well-established principles of physics, and precise mathematical calculations.

Multiple Choice

1. A collision reconstructionist can often use physical evidence to determine such information as:

   a. the speed a vehicle was travelling before a collision.

   b. the colour of a traffic signal at the time of a collision.

   c. the direction in which the at-fault driver was looking at the time of a collision.

   d. the amount of brake pressure applied by each driver at the time of a collision.

2. A fingerprint examiner can come to one of three possible conclusions as a result of comparing evidentiary and reference fingerprints:

   a. insufficient detail to make an identification; exclusion (the evidentiary print is not the same as the reference print); or identification (the evidentiary print is the same as the reference print).

   b. insufficient detail to make an identification; exception (the evidentiary print is the same as the reference print except for a few minor differences); or identification (the evidentiary print is the same as the reference print).

   c. insufficient number of fingerprints to make an identification; exclusion (the evidentiary print is not the same as the reference print); or identification (the evidentiary print is the same as the reference print).

   d. insufficient detail to make an identification; exclusion (the evidentiary print is not the same as the reference print); or identification (the evidentiary print is identified as a human fingerprint).

3. There are three kinds of fingerprints that identification officers can identify and collect for later analysis:

   a. clear prints, patent prints, and expression prints.

   b. latent prints, patent prints, and impression prints.

   c. latent prints, patent prints, and exclusion prints.

   d. patent prints, latency prints, and impression prints.

4. Bloodstain patterns can be grouped under various headings on the basis of how they were produced and what they can tell an investigator. Some of those headings include:

   a. drip patterns, persistent stains, cast-off stains, and arterial stains.

   b. drip patterns, impact spatter, casting stains, and arterial stains.

   c. drip patterns, impression spatter, cast-off stains, and blood vessel stains.

   d. drip patterns, impact spatter, cast-off stains, and arterial stains.

5. A collision reconstructionist can use different mathematical calculations to determine vehicle speed in a variety of scenarios involving phenomena such as:

   a. cushion, vector, and critical curve speed.

   b. collapse, velocity, and critical pathway.

   c. crush, vault, and critical curve speed.

   d. crumple, vault, and critical velocity.

6. Pattern or impression evidence consists of patterns that are created when two or more objects:

   a. generate an interference pattern that results in an impression being left on one object by the other.

   b. come into contact and an impression consisting of certain patterns is left on one object by the other.

   c. come into contact with a third object, which results in an impression consisting of certain patterns being left on the first two objects.

   d. form a pattern such that impressions consisting of certain identifiable elements are left on one of the objects by the other.

Short Answer

1. Describe some of the general rules or principles that govern the proper collection of evidence from a crime scene.

2. What is pattern evidence? Give some examples.

3. A collision reconstructionist works as part of an investigative team. Explain who else may be involved in a collision investigation and outline the information they may provide.

4. Describe the kind of observations a forensic identification specialist makes in order to analyze bloodstain patterns. Discuss some of the different types of information he or she might derive from an analysis of those patterns.

Digital Evidence

9

LEARNING OUTCOMES

After completing this chapter, you should be able to:

- Define the term "digital evidence" and identify sources of such evidence.

- Understand the value of different kinds of digital analysis in an investigation.

- Understand current Canadian law governing the authority of police to seize and search different kinds of digital evidence.

- Identify challenges in the preservation of digital evidence.

- Outline best practices in the collection of digital evidence.

- Understand the strengths and limitations of digital evidence.

INTRODUCTION

People today lead digitally enhanced lives in which connections to the virtual world are standard in personal and professional contexts. The use of computers to create, store, and transmit information has become routine, and the proliferation of mobile, portable, and compact devices such as smartphones, netbooks, and tablets has created a virtual "epidemic" of data.

technological crime
investigations where digital evidence is paramount, whether in the investigation of a crime or in the commission of the crime itself

The term **technological crime** is used broadly to describe investigations where digital evidence is paramount, whether in the investigation of a crime or in the commission of the crime itself. Today's investigators have access to an unparalleled wealth of potential evidence in digital form and, as technology continues to evolve, this will expand further. However, the *value* of digital evidence will always vary with the nature of the case, the abilities of the individuals involved, and the type of technology used to create the evidence.

Although publicly available Internet-based sources reveal more than any police database ever could, these technologies have raised questions about individuals' privacy and what information is truly "public." As in the collection of any kind of evidence, all police officers must be knowledgeable regarding their legal search authority where digital evidence is involved and aware of the steps they should take to preserve such evidence.

WHAT IS DIGITAL EVIDENCE?

digital evidence
information stored or transmitted in binary form that may be relied on in court—for example, email, pictures, videos, or text messages

Digital evidence is, simply, information stored or transmitted in binary form that may be relied on in court (U.S. Department of Justice, 2004, p. 39). Like other types of evidence used to link particular individuals to a crime, digital evidence may be protected or hidden to evade discovery by police, and it may be inadvertently tainted. More important, however—and, perhaps, more controversial—is the argument surrounding the authenticity of some digital evidence: digital evidence can be manipulated by the very technology used to create it in order to incriminate or exonerate an individual and, as such technology advances, these manipulations will become more difficult to detect.

Case law and the *Criminal Code* describe where or in what format digital evidence might be found and define offences involving computer systems and data. Section 342.1(2) of the Code defines a "computer system" as any device or group of devices that

    (a) contains computer programs or other data, and
    (b) pursuant to computer programs,
       (i) performs logic and control, and
       (ii) may perform any other function.

Thus, a computer system may encompass anything from a toaster, fridge, or dishwasher, to the GPS device in a vehicle or the automatic parking-ticket machine in an underground garage—and, of course, devices such as conventional desktop and laptop computers, tablets, cellphones, and smartphones. The many substantive offences in the Code involving the use of a computer system generally reference the definition in s. 342.1(2).

A computer or a digital device may be involved in a crime in two ways:

1. *As the instrument of the offence.* For example, a computer may be used to send a death threat via an email message. The threat is an offence under s. 264.1 of the Code—that is, the threat of knowingly uttering, conveying, or causing someone to receive a threat of bodily harm or death. Email is simply the vehicle for delivering the threat, which forms the basis of the evidence of the offence.

2. *As the place where digital evidence relating to an offence is stored.* For example, a computer may be used to download child pornography. The contraband is defined in s. 163.1 of the Code. Once police discover the Internet protocol (IP) address of the computer used to access the material, the computer becomes the target of the search for the contraband.

Investigators must consider the potential existence of digital evidence in *every* case and not underestimate the value of such evidence to a criminal investigation. Consider the following examples:

- A photograph collected from Facebook is used to identify the individual responsible for a crime.
- Footage from a surveillance video is isolated, enhanced, and used in a media release seeking the public's help in identifying a suspect. The suspect is identified and the footage becomes a key piece of digital evidence confirming the identity of the suspect at trial.
- Emails, chat logs, and Internet browsing history provide information regarding the planning, facilitation, and execution of an offence.
- Date stamps on a digital photograph provide confirmation of where and when a photograph was taken.
- Text messages extracted from a cellular phone detail communication between co-accused, demonstrating how they conspired to commit the offence.
- Cellular phone-tower dump analysis places a suspect in a geographical area close to the crime scene at the time of the murder.
- Software found on a computer reveals details of user activity, such as what was viewed or searched for, and when.

The above examples of digital evidence may be obtained from a variety of sources, including:

- the public Internet (through search engines, social networks, employer websites, email, blogs, YouTube, and other personal profile sites);
- Internet and cellular providers;
- computers and cellular phones;
- employers' devices, networks, and computers;
- surveillance, security, traffic, and ATM cameras;
- portable storage devices, such as tablets, digital cards, hard drives, and USB flash drives;

> ## DIGITAL EVIDENCE AND THE EVOLUTION OF CASE LAW
>
> As of late spring 2012, the law governing the search and seizure of digital evidence in Canada is still a relatively new and rapidly evolving area. Many of the key decisions come from the lower courts, and the jurisprudence is often inconsistent; there are only a few appellate or Supreme Court decisions. However, many prominent cases are currently pending before the higher courts, and litigation will continue as the law attempts to keep pace with the evolution of technology. In the meantime, the common-law rules are often jurisdictional (for example, officers in Ontario have different binding rules on searching a cellular phone than do officers in British Columbia), and all officers must keep themselves apprised of the rapidly changing rules in order to ensure the evidence they do gather is admissible in court.
>
> Recently, the federal government identified what it believes are certain "gaps" in the existing statutes and is proposing amendments, as well as new authorities, to assist police in searching for and seizing digital evidence. In 2012, the government announced the introduction of the *Investigating and Preventing Criminal Electronics Communications Act*, also known as Bill C-30, which is designed to clarify and establish a protocol in law for the police to obtain personal data of customers from Internet and cellular providers without warrant. The proposed Bill C-30 has met with both scrutiny and backlash from "privacy watchdogs" and the general public, and balancing the rights of individuals—including our ever-evolving expectations of privacy—will be an ongoing challenge.

- cloud computing (online storage of data with services like SkyDrive® from Microsoft®);
- GPS tracking devices and in-car computer systems, such as OnStar® by GM Inc.;
- printers, fax machines, and photocopiers;
- gaming devices such as PlayStation® and Xbox® consoles;
- digital video recorders (DVRs), also known as personal video recorders (PVRs);
- digital video, Blu-ray, and compact discs;
- digital cameras, video, and web cameras; and
- anything capable of storing or transmitting information in binary form.

OBTAINING DIGITAL EVIDENCE

As outlined in Chapter 6, Legal Aspects of Search and Seizure, the foundation of any examination of police search powers is the guarantee in s. 8 of the Charter to be free from "unreasonable search or seizure." In light of this, any search is unreasonable unless:

1. the police have obtained a warrant based on reasonable and probable grounds established under oath; or

2. there is an exception to the warrant requirement (consent, abandonment, search incident to arrest, investigative detention, exigent circumstances, or

plain view; note that only weapons—not digital devices—can be searched for under investigative detention).

Privacy expectations with respect to digital information have been the subject of ongoing discussion and debate both in the legal community and in the courts. In its 2010 decision in *R. v. Morelli*, the Supreme Court said of the search and seizure of a person's computer:

> [2] It is difficult to imagine a search more intrusive, extensive, or invasive of one's privacy than the search and seizure of a personal computer.
>
> [3] First, police officers enter your home, take possession of your computer, and carry it off for examination in a place unknown and inaccessible to you. There, without supervision or constraint, they scour the entire contents of your hard drive: your emails sent and received; accompanying attachments; your personal notes and correspondence; your meetings and appointments; your medical and financial records; and all other saved documents that you have downloaded, copied, scanned, or created. The police scrutinize as well the electronic roadmap of your cybernetic peregrinations, where you have been and what you appear to have seen on the Internet—generally by design, but sometimes by accident.

Digital evidence may be obtained either through a search following informed consent or by a search after a warrant is obtained. The value of digital evidence can be apparent quickly if the lawful authority to carry out the search is consent; it is common for evidence seized and then searched via informed consent to provide a great deal of information about a suspect and his or her activities relating to the offence, because digital evidence on a victim's or witness's computer or device can create a trail of proof about how a crime was committed and by whom.

Consider a situation in which a suspect uses Facebook to criminally harass a victim using messages, posts, and other functions available within Facebook. The best way to determine the value of any potential digital evidence is to take snapshots of all the messages, posts, and other pieces of information visible on the victim's account. That data will provide the content or context of each communication; a date and time for each item; and the identity of the suspect (user name). If required, further information from Facebook Inc. pertaining to the victim's account—such as historical communications, messages, or photographs—could be obtained with his or her consent. A suspect in such cases *cannot* exert an expectation of privacy over information stored on the victim's account. In addition, a production order can be issued (without the suspect's knowledge) to Facebook Inc., seeking the details of the suspect's account information. At this point, the police will likely have enough (digital) evidence and information to arrest and charge the suspect. If the facts indicate that there are grounds to seize the suspect's computer via a warrant, then this would be done at the time of or shortly after the suspect's arrest. The results of the search of the suspect's computer would likely be revealed several months after the arrest.

In the example above, it was imperative to identify the victim's Facebook account as a source of digital evidence: it outlined the details of the offence, identified the suspect, and facilitated the filing of charges in a timely manner. Any evidence subsequently discovered on the suspect's computer would likely only corroborate what was already known.

Evidence obtained through informed consent is generally seized first and analyzed at the outset of the investigation. In contrast, where a warrant is required, the value of the digital evidence will remain unknown for some time. Such evidence generally takes longer to analyze and is sometimes done weeks or even months after the offence.

Search Incident to Arrest

As discussed in Chapter 6, one of the most common search scenarios presented to front-line police officers is that of search incident to arrest. Today, individuals who are arrested often have a cellphone on their person, and officers must understand the current law governing searches of these devices to ensure their actions do not jeopardize potential evidence. A cellular phone or digital device may be returned when a person is released from custody or, if the device is central to the investigation, it might be held as evidence in the offence for which the person was arrested or charged and not returned until the conclusion of the case.

In the past, the police could search a cellular phone without warrant under the search incident to arrest doctrine in certain circumstances—that is, if the phone was found on the person or in the immediate vicinity of the arrest and the search of the phone was related to the offence for which the person was arrested. The BC Supreme Court upheld this application in *Giles* (2007), stating:

> [55] Here, Rempel [the co-accused in the case] was lawfully arrested on grounds that he had just been involved in a very substantial cocaine transaction. The seizure, the examination of the contents of his BlackBerry, and the retrieval of the e-mails was truly incidental to arrest. According to the report of the TCB [technological crime branch] analysis team, the police were looking for evidence of "score sheets" [used to keep track of drug purchases], telephone numbers, e-mail addresses, memos, calendar information, saved digital communications, PIN numbers, bank account numbers and passwords still residing within the device memory. ... All these items, for which the investigators had directed the TCB to search, were clearly reasonably connected to the arrest for a serious drug offence. These are not items which have nothing to do with the offence of large scale drug trafficking.

In the 2009 case of *Polius*, the Ontario Superior Court of Justice took a different view. The judge ruled that personal devices like cellphones are private because of the information they may contain about an individual; although the search incident to arrest doctrine authorizes police to *seize* the phone where they determine evidence exists on the device—for example, through a statement from a witness, victim, or suspect—they must obtain a warrant before carrying out a *search*. In the judge's view:

> [41] [T]he power to SITA [search incident to arrest] includes a power to conduct a cursory inspection of an item to determine whether there is a reasonable basis to believe it may be evidence of the crime for which the arrest was made. However, any examination of an item beyond a cursory examination of it is not within the scope of the power to SITA.

Court decisions following *Polius* held that a "cursory examination" or "cursory search" could refer to attempts to obtain the phone number assigned to a device for the purpose of determining ownership. This may be of value in forming the necessary "reasonable basis to believe" that the item may be evidence of the crime—for example, where a phone is believed to be stolen. An officer cannot, however, conduct a cursory search without a warrant unless the phone is directly related to the offence they are investigating. For example, in a case involving drug trafficking, an undercover officer may receive a text message from the suspect stating the location where the deal will take place. Upon the suspect's arrival, police may arrest him or her. If the suspect is carrying a phone, police may conduct a cursory search to establish that the phone was the same one that sent the text message. Once this is established, the phone will be seized and a warrant obtained to conduct a full search.

There are hundreds of models of phones on the market today, and officers are not typically trained in how to search for a phone number in all the different models. Although some phones require only two or three steps or buttons to be pressed to obtain this information, in others the process is more complicated. In conducting a "cursory search," therefore, officers may inadvertently encounter incriminating evidence. If this happens, the defence will challenge whether the officer was conducting a genuine search or was instead embarking on a "fishing expedition"—that is, pretending not to know how to find the phone number and hoping instead to come across incriminating evidence. In addition to the possibility of the defence misconstruing the honest efforts of police in conducting a cursory search, in the course of such a search, because of the sensitive nature of digital evidence, every push of a button may be altering or destroying important data. For example, the operating system might alter or change the last access date and time of the file—information that is potentially crucial in determining knowledge, control, or possession of the file.

All of the above have forced officers to take a more concerted approach in evaluating whether or not to conduct a cursory search of a phone in complex cases.

Manley (2011) provided more definitive guidance on the issue. The case involved an individual arrested for the robbery of a music store and an outstanding arrest warrant for a break and enter. In the course of conducting a search incident to arrest, police recovered a cellphone on the accused and searched it to determine ownership. Before they found the telephone number, they found a photograph of the accused holding a sawed-off shotgun. The photograph was copied, downloaded, and printed, and a warrant was subsequently obtained to search the contents of the phone.

The trial judge ruled that the search did not breach the accused's s. 8 Charter rights, and the Court of Appeal upheld the ruling. Because police had information from a confidential informant that in the past the appellant had stolen cellphones, they had reason to believe that the phone was stolen and the cursory search to determine ownership was lawful. The fact that the phone's number was found *after* the photograph was key to the decision, which would have been different had the events been reversed. Although the court did not give a detailed explanation of the powers of police to search data in a phone incident to arrest, it did note:

> [39] Cell phones and other similar handheld communication devices in common use have the capacity to store vast amounts of highly sensitive personal, private and confidential information—all manner of private voice, text

and email communications, detailed personal contact lists, agendas, diaries and personal photographs. An open-ended power to search without a Warrant all the stored data in any cell phone found in the possession of any arrested person clearly raises the spectre of a serious and significant invasion of the Charter-protected privacy interests of arrested persons. If the police have reasonable grounds to believe that the search of a cell phone seized upon arrest would yield evidence of the offence, the prudent course is for them to obtain a warrant authorizing the search.

In light of the above, the recommended course of action for police officers is to obtain a warrant before searching any electronic device beyond a cursory search.

The Plain View Doctrine

In many criminal investigations, the police may find themselves lawfully placed to seize a digital device or computer. The plain view doctrine (*Criminal Code*, s. 489) applies to digital evidence—specifically, where the digital evidence is stored on a computer or digital device. These items may be seized under the plain view authority, and a s. 487 search warrant would be required to search the contents of or to view the data contained therein. Failure to obtain a search warrant would likely render any evidence subsequently obtained inadmissible in court. For example, in *R. v. Little* (2009), police obtained a warrant to search Mr. Little's house in the course of investigating the death of his wife. While there, they saw a cellphone stained with blood, which they seized and later searched. The court considered the seizure

---

RISKS OF PREMATURELY SHUTTING DOWN A DEVICE

The recommendation that police obtain a warrant before searching any device beyond a cursory search may at times conflict with the police duty to preserve evidence. This is because, in shutting down a device or a computer until a warrant can be obtained, valuable evidence may be lost. Electronic devices use a type of memory called RAM (random access memory) to work more efficiently. When a device is powered off, data that is currently active or being stored in RAM—for example, data relating to running programs or processes, possibly including passwords—is deleted and cannot be recovered. In addition, powering a device on or off causes the device to write to the data or operating system, which means that things like dates and times at which certain files were accessed may be changed. In some cases, the modification date and time could also change, thereby creating potentially misleading information. Powering off a device may also engage a lock code or other security feature and, because there is currently no enforceable law in Canada that requires a person to provide police with their password or lock code, this may prevent police from examining the device's contents. Although certain techniques can help alleviate this problem, as the technology continues to evolve it will become more difficult; as devices become more advanced, so do the security systems that protect them. These advanced devices also keep more valuable information in RAM while they are powered on, and so there is more at stake when police turn off a device prematurely.

lawful under the plain view doctrine, but said that the search of its contents required a warrant.

Consider, as well, a person who takes his or her computer to a computer repair store. The person authorizes a technician to examine the computer to determine why it is malfunctioning and, in the course of the examination, the technician finds images of a child who appears to be under the age of 18 years depicted in a sexually explicit manner. The technician contacts the police, who attend at the repair store and interview the technician. The technician clearly describes what he saw on the computer, and the police form the grounds that the computer has child pornography on it as defined in s. 163.1 of the *Criminal Code*. In this circumstance, s. 489 authorizes police to seize the computer and place it into custody awaiting a search warrant to conduct a computer forensic examination. This search would be carried out to support the belief that someone was in possession of child pornography and that such an examination would recover this evidence and potentially identify the responsible person.

Search Warrants

As described in Chapter 6, the *Criminal Code* provides police officers with a range of warrants to accomplish various purposes. For example, police may need to obtain data that is stored within a computer, or they may need the actual computer itself. Police must identify what investigative techniques they want to perform and then obtain the appropriate warrant. Because the drafting of the different warrants requires different processes, examinations, and reasons or grounds, depending on what is being searched and on the reason for the search, we examine these separately.

Computers

The *Criminal Code* defines a "computer system" broadly. Here, our discussion focuses specifically on searches of a desktop or laptop computer.

The most common way that police gather digital evidence from a computer system is to seize the original item physically. The hard drive contains the digital evidence sought in addition to any potential evidence of the system and the processes responsible for putting it there. For example, a person who uses a file-sharing program to download contraband may have created an account for the purpose. The analysis conducted on the installation of such a program may indicate the identity of the user or the person who installed the program. A **computer forensic examination**, meaning an examination of a true bit-by-bit copy, requires access to the original medium, which can be obtained through the "common" or "conventional" warrant to search and seize issued pursuant to s. 487(1) of the *Criminal Code*. Recall that such a warrant allows a peace officer to search a building, receptacle, or place for:

computer forensic examination
the analysis of information contained within and created with computer systems, typically for the purpose of determining who accessed the information, how they accessed it, and when they accessed it

    (a) anything on or in respect of which any offence against [the *Criminal Code*] or any other Act of Parliament has been or is suspected to have been committed,

    (b) anything that there are reasonable grounds to believe will afford evidence with respect to the commission of an offence, or will reveal the whereabouts of a person who is believed to have committed an offence, against [the *Criminal Code*] or any other Act of Parliament,

(c) anything that there are reasonable grounds to believe is intended to be used for the purpose of committing any offence against the person for which a person may be arrested without warrant, or
(c.1) any offence-related property,

and to seize any of the above, if found.

There is no point seizing a computer unless it will be searched. However, it is important to note that there is *no* implied authority for police to search a computer just because it is found in the place named in a warrant. This was illustrated in *Vu* (2010), in which police believed that electricity was being stolen in a residence and obtained a warrant. In the residence, they found computers and a cellphone, which they seized and searched, too, even though the warrant did not mention searching computers. The court found that the officers had no authority for the search they carried out.

A properly drafted warrant will set out what police are searching for and why; how they intend to find it; and how it affords evidence of the offence under investigation—that is, what data it is believed to contain. It will also state that the computer, once seized, will be searched for the relevant data, and will outline how the examination will unfold—that is, it will contain the required wordings on the exact investigative technique that will be used by the police.

The courts have challenged police regarding potential over-seizure and abuse of their authority in this area on certain occasions. The Information to Obtain a Search Warrant (ITO) must explain what specific items the police wish to search for—for example, emails sent and received, photos, and videos—and on what grounds. The justice may authorize the warrant with all of the items included or, if the grounds do not support the search and seizure of certain items, the justice may still authorize the warrant, but cross those items off the list. Similarly, at trial, a judge may review the ITO and decide that the police acted outside the provisions of the warrant in conducting their search and exclude all or some of the evidence as a result.

If a warrant does not contain the information described above, a computer or other device may still be seized under the plain view doctrine, but the examination of its contents will require a conventional search warrant. Because computers can contain vast amounts of personal information, the courts have recently held that, for purposes of searches, they could be considered "places" rather than "things," akin to houses. Conceptually, a computer could be a thing to seize or a place to search. The general practice for computers is to obtain a s. 487 warrant, name the location (geographical address) as the "place" to be searched, and name the computer (or other device, and all peripherals) as a "thing to be seized." Once the item has been lawfully seized, a s. 487 warrant is generally the most applicable instrument for obtaining authorization to conduct a forensic examination of the device for data. Failure to obtain such a judicial order will likely render any evidence obtained inadmissible.

In situations where the physical seizure of the computer is not imperative, s. 487(2.1) allows investigators who have obtained a warrant under s. 487(1) to search a computer system for data to take copies of the data, in print form or in another output form, and seize the printout or output. Section 487(2.2) requires the person in charge of the building or place where the search is being carried out to provide any necessary assistance to police in copying the data; this situation often occurs in the case of searches of work computers, where an IT person may be required. Note that the person is not given a choice whether to help, but that the order *requires* their assistance without any agreement.

THE SUPREME COURT ON COMPUTER SEARCHES AND ITOs: R. v. MORELLI

In the 2010 Supreme Court case of *R. v. Morelli*, the Court dealt with and commented on a number of issues, including the requirements of an adequate search warrant and the sensitivity that triers of fact should have to the search and seizure of computers.

In 2005, a computer technician arrived at Mr. Morelli's home and was given access to his computer to install a high-speed Internet connection. The technician saw two apparently pornographic links in the browser's favourites list and a (legal) pornographic image on the computer. In addition, he noticed a webcam pointed toward a young girl who was playing in a room with some toys. When the technician returned the next day to finish his work, he noticed that the toys had been put away, the webcam was now pointed toward the computer, and the computer had been formatted.

The technician spoke to a social service worker, who contacted the RCMP. The technician made a statement to Cst. O., who consulted with a corporal in the RCMP's Technological Crime Unit and with another constable, both of whom provided him with information regarding the behaviours of child sexual exploiters. An ITO to search Mr. Morelli's computer was drafted and issued. Pornographic images of children were found, and at trial Mr. Morelli was found guilty of possession of child pornography. Mr. Morelli challenged the validity of the search warrant under s. 8 of the Charter, but both the trial and appellate courts found the search to be valid. The Supreme Court, however, issued a 4:3 decision in favour of finding that the search was *not* valid. The evidence was excluded and Mr. Morelli was acquitted.

For a search warrant to be issued, there must be "reasonable and probable" grounds to believe that the search will yield evidence of an offence. The majority of the Court found that the way the ITO had been drafted in this case was misleading and presented information out of the context in which it was found. Had all the information been present, the warrant may not have been authorized to begin with. For example, the ITO stated that the technician observed a link on the screen and that when he returned the next day "all the child porn off the computer was gone." This was factually inaccurate. The technician never saw any child pornography on the computer. Just viewing links, or keeping links on hand for easy access to a website would not support a charge of possession. The ITO also failed to note that the links were scattered among a large collection of links to regular adult material, creating a misleading impression that the accused was specifically seeking out or inclined toward child pornography. As well, the description of the webcam, combined with the discussion of the suspicious links, was found to be misleading and left out relevant facts that should have been available to the issuer of the warrant. The ITO described a girl alone in the house with Mr. Morelli, but failed to note that the girl was Mr. Morelli's daughter, that she was fully clothed, that the room seemed to double as a playroom, that there were no signs of abuse, and that Mr. Morelli lived with his wife.

The majority also found that it was inappropriate to rely on opinions regarding stereotyped behaviour of a class of offenders (that is, child pornographers) to support reasonable and probable grounds for a search and seizure. Without the assumption that the behaviour of seeking out child pornography was a habit and that offenders tend to hoard material, it was not reasonable to assume that child pornography would be on a computer four months after it had been formatted, which is when the search was carried out.

The majority did not find that the officer intended to mislead, but did find that the ITO was misleading. They emphasized that an officer must not pick and choose among relevant facts to achieve a particular end. Doing so in this case put the validity of the warrant in doubt and led to a conviction being overturned.

The *Morelli* decision created a maelstrom of revisions to search warrant drafting practices for digital devices. Affiants are held more accountable for their beliefs or opinions held out in their ITO; where they may be qualified to state such beliefs or opinions, their qualifications must be documented. Many officers write an opinion in their ITO, which aids them in forming the basis for their beliefs. The court needs to see that an affiant is *qualified* to state their opinion and why such an opinion is either relevant or factual. If an affiant is not qualified to give an opinion, but requires such an opinion, the affiant must provide a witness who is qualified to provide it and state why that witness is able to do so. For example, an affiant who is a general investigator may not be qualified to state in an affidavit *what* specific evidence a computer forensic examination may uncover. If this information is necessary, the affiant must provide the name of the computer forensic examiner who provided him or her with the information, and the examiner's qualifications must be set out in the ITO.

Cellular Phones

A cellular phone may be seized under the same authorities as any other piece of evidence. This includes cases where police find a cellular phone in the process of searching a dwelling or other "place": if the phone was within the scope of the warrant, then it can be lawfully seized. For example, in a child pornography case, generally, the warrant to search is for any electronic devices capable of storing, transmitting, or creating images and videos. If the phone has a camera, a media card, or a capacity to store images, it may be seized if such a warrant was authorized. As with any item in any search, the police must establish that the item they wish to seize will afford evidence of a criminal offence.

The requirements of a warrant in the case of cellular phones are the same as those for computers, described above. Additional information created by the user of the phone—including but not limited to call records, browsing history, and location (cell tower) information—is stored with the service provider. Such evidence is generally sought through a production order under s. 487.012 of the Code, as described below.

The police may also intercept private communications by targeting a cellular phone; such activities are governed by Part VI of the *Criminal Code*, as explained in Chapter 6. The authorization for an intercept as defined in s. 183 of the *Criminal Code* refers to when the seizure of such evidence is simultaneous or "live" to the communication itself. Sometimes when the police have taken a person into custody and their cellular phone has been seized incident to arrest, the phone will ring. In *Ramsum* (2003), the Court of the Queen's Bench of Alberta considered the question whether the police should "intercept" private communication in the form of cell-phone calls and pagers. In this case, the police did answer the phone, and it was clear that the callers had no expectation of privacy as they were unconcerned whom they were speaking with (para. 28). In this case, the actions of police did not represent "interception" as much as simply answering a ringing phone, notwithstanding that they did impersonate the accused (para. 29). There was no s. 8 violation with respect to the initial seizure of the cellphone and pager, and the court called the subsequent events "nothing more than good police investigative tactics based on a fortuitous set of circumstances" (para. 31).

Nevertheless, as stated, confusion has been created by the various court cases that have considered the issue of the seizure and search of cellphones by police. Sometimes, even where the police did not obtain the "proper" search instrument to examine the contents of a cellular phone, the evidence was not excluded under s. 24(2) of the Charter. The issue of the search of personal electronic devices is extremely volatile, and much litigation of this issue is yet to come. Although inconsistent lower court decisions exist, the Supreme Court has yet to determine whether a handheld personal device, such as a smartphone or cellphone, should be granted the same level of Charter protection as a computer in terms of privacy expectations.

The prudent course for police officers is to seek prior judicial authorization whenever possible before conducting a search of such devices.

Obtaining Data from Third-Party Sources

In a growing number of investigations, often the case starts or is initiated with a requirement of the police to obtain digital evidence from an Internet service provider (ISP) or other third party or entity. For example, in the case of a threatening email, the context of the threat can be read in the body of the email; however, it is likely that the sender will have used an anonymous email address. Police can determine the origin of the email by tracing the originating IP address, which may have been logged by the ISP and be associated with the subscriber of the Internet service.

The data that police will seek to obtain in a case such as the one above consists of customer, name, and address information, known as "basic subscriber information." In the case of a cellular provider, it may also consist of call detail records. This digital evidence is generally owned by and stored with the ISP or cellular provider. The contractual agreements between the ISP and its customers generally disclose that the ISP reserves the right to collect personal information about its customers and share that with the police when presented with a court order or judicial instrument. In certain circumstances, providers may also disclose this information to police following a request without a formal order. These processes are described in the following sections.

Production Orders

A s. 487 warrant is not normally the most appropriate or efficient way to obtain basic subscriber information—police officers do not usually attend the ISP's office and seize servers containing customer databases. Instead, police may obtain a production order, as set out in s. 487.012 of the *Criminal Code*, which compels an organization to produce records if requested by the police when such records afford evidence of a criminal offence. The search for and preparation of the records is conducted by the receiver of the signed order, not by the officer (in contrast to a conventional warrant, in which the search and seizure of evidence is usually carried out by peace officers).

In its current format, s. 487.012 lacks direction on extraterritorial process or execution. A conventional search warrant can be endorsed for execution outside the jurisdiction in which it was issued; a statutory authority for this endorsement is found in s. 487(2) of the *Criminal Code* (Form 28). Unfortunately, s. 487.012 lacks any statutory endorsement for execution of a warrant outside the territorial jurisdiction in which it is signed. There has been some inconsistency among judicial officers in allowing orders to be executed outside their jurisdiction in some cases but not in others. Based on the wording of the section, it has sometimes been inferred that a production order is valid anywhere in Canada.

As of late spring 2012, a federal committee is considering so-called lawful access legislation in the proposed Bill C-30. The Bill would permit law enforcement agencies to access basic subscriber information without a warrant or judicial authorization (usually, a production order). Under the Bill, when an ISP receives such a request from police, it would be required to comply. Currently, compliance is voluntary, and although most ISPs do comply with such requests, some do not.

Law Enforcement Requests

Another option available to police officers seeking basic subscriber information is a "law enforcement request" (LER). Under the *Personal Information Protection and Electronic Documents Act* (PIPEDA), organizations such as ISPs can voluntarily turn over certain personal information such as IP addresses, email addresses, and other subscriber records, in certain limited circumstances, including where "required to comply with a subpoena or warrant issued or an order made by a court, person or body with jurisdiction to compel the production of information, or to comply with rules of court relating to the production of records" (s. 7(3)(c)).

Police can make such requests without warrant as described under s. 487.014(1) of the *Criminal Code*, which states: "[N]o production order is necessary for a peace officer or public officer enforcing or administering this or any other Act of Parliament to ask a person to voluntarily provide to the officer documents, data or information that the person is not prohibited by law from disclosing." An organization may volunteer on that basis to turn over certain records to the police if requested. Template forms are used in submitting the request.

This type of evidence collection generally occurs only when there is an emergency and insufficient time to get a warrant or production order, thereby invoking the exigent circumstances exception. It is also used in child sexual-exploitation cases where an ISP may voluntarily give the police basic subscriber records and IP logs when lawfully requested. It is important to note that not all organizations will cooperate with police in this manner. There may be binding contractual agreements between an organization and its customers about their personal information and how it is disclosed.

Seizure of Data

One of the more controversial issues is the seizure of digital evidence from third-party sources such as websites, social networks, blogs, and web mail service providers.

Although it might seem reasonable to assume that someone who posts information on the Internet cannot have an expectation of privacy over the information and that people ought to know that when they access the Internet they are leaving a digital trail of "bread crumbs" that may lead back to them, this is not, in fact, within the general knowledge of the average computer user.

There are literally tens of thousands of publicly available sources on the Internet where an individual's information is available to others who know which tool to use or where to look, and police or other agents of the state can frequent such places to collect digital evidence in criminal investigations. For example, consider an investigation of a serious hit-and-run fatality on a major street. Witnesses describe seeing two vehicles fleeing the scene, both travelling at a high rate of speed. Through their investigation, police learn who owns one of the vehicles and use the Internet to collect information about the owner from publicly available sources. The registered owner may have a YouTube channel and may have posted and shared videos depicting street racing and stunt driving. The videos would be relevant to the investigation and may become material digital evidence at trial.

Ultimately, the courts will rule on whether the fact that police gathered particular evidence violated an individual's privacy expectation in the situation, considering various factors such as the nature or subject matter of the evidence gathered, the individual's subjective expectation of privacy in the information, and the objective reasonableness of that expectation. Many websites and online sources post privacy policies or terms-of-use policies, either on their site or within their disclaimers, to warn users what may happen with their personal information, and mainstream media campaigns have been launched warning people about putting personal information on the Internet. In the case of social networks—which by their very nature are designed to share information—many of the settings controlling that information are set to "public" and require the individual to opt *in* for privacy, not the other way around.

To date, there have been more cases litigated in the civil courts than in the criminal courts on the issue of what information available on the Internet should be considered "private." In one case, the court addressed the issue of whether an insurance company could access information from the plaintiff's Facebook page in order to show that her injuries were not as serious as she claimed (*Schuster v. Royal*

CRIMINAL BEHAVIOUR AND FACEBOOK PHOTOS

The 2010 criminal case of *R. v. Huxford* involved access to publicly available information captured by the police from a social network. The Ontario Court of Justice dealt with the "public" settings of Christopher Huxford, who had posed in a photo holding a Glock handgun. The photo, which was posted to Mr. Huxford's Facebook page with no privacy settings applied, came to the attention of the police, who used it to confirm his identity and to confirm that he did not have a licence to possess such a firearm. In a subsequent exchange with an undercover detective, Huxford made arrangements to purchase a handgun. A setup was arranged in a mall parking lot, where police arrested Huxford, who pled guilty at trial and was sentenced.

In this case, no privacy interests existed, because Huxford did not have any privacy settings on his Facebook account.

& Sun Alliance Insurance Company of Canada, 2009). The court noted that the plaintiff had set her Facebook settings to "private" and that she restricted its contents to 67 friends—in other words, her profile was not created for purposes of sharing with the general public. According to the court, "unless the defendant establishes a legal entitlement to such information, the Plaintiff's privacy interest in the information in her profile should be respected" (para. 53). The court dismissed the defendant's motion.

The use of personal information collected from publicly available sources such as the Internet as digital evidence in a *criminal* prosecution remains contentious and will be the subject of continual litigation. A Supreme Court judgment on individuals' right to privacy online is only a matter of time.

BEST PRACTICES FOR WORKING WITH DIGITAL EVIDENCE

Digital evidence is extremely volatile. For example, information posted on the Internet can be deleted or changed by someone at any moment. A YouTube video posted last night could be removed today and no longer accessible. Each time a computer is turned on or off, digital evidence is changed forever.

The search for computer-based digital evidence by police during criminal investigations is an area of police forensic work that has expanded significantly in recent years. Although all of the principles of proper evidence gathering apply, because of its nature, digital evidence can be easily altered or even destroyed. In many cases, particularly in the execution of a search warrant where digital evidence is expected to be found, computer forensic examiners will attend at the scene. Members of the Technical Unit (or "tech guys," as they are called) will photograph the scene and meticulously document each item to be seized. They will then dismantle any computer systems and properly package any devices to preserve the evidence on them.

If a tech guy cannot attend, as happens on occasion, it may be necessary for a general investigator, or even a patrol officer, to seize and secure such evidence pending a forensic examination by a computer forensic examiner. In this case, the investigator or officer will often receive direction on the proper methods, protocols, and best practices for seizing and safeguarding each specific piece of digital evidence from a member of the Tech Unit over the telephone. The procedures described in earlier chapters for maintaining continuity and avoiding "contamination" when working with other types of evidence apply equally to digital evidence.

Various agencies and organizations publish "good practice" guides for the investigation of computer-based electronic evidence (see Further Reading), and individual police services will also have their own guidelines. These will likely include a number of basic rules to guide non-specialist officers who may be called on to collect and protect computer-based electronic evidence. For example:

- If there is reason to believe that a computer is involved in a criminal offence, take immediate steps to preserve that evidence.
- Consider your legal grounds for seizing such evidence (do you require a search warrant?).
- *Do not* attempt to access the computer. If it is off, do not turn it on. If it is on, do not search through it.

- Allow any print jobs to finish.
- Do not touch the keyboard or click the mouse.
- If a computer forensic examiner is not available, ensure that the computer is turned off by removing the power cord from the socket on the back of the computer; *do not* pull the plug out of the wall, because this could result in data being written to the computer's hard drive if it is connected to an uninterruptible power supply.
- In the case of a laptop computer, if it continues to operate after the power cord has been disconnected, remove the battery and do not put it back into the computer; however, be aware that in certain circumstances battery removal could result in data loss.
- If you have the technology available (camera, smartphone), and the computer is on, photograph the screen. Also photograph the computer itself and anything that is attached to it. Otherwise, create a written record of the computer set-up before touching or disconnecting anything.
- Document, ideally on video or in a series of photographs, all the steps taken to collect the computer and its components.
- Seize all associated storage media, peripheral devices, manuals, notes, and documentation.
- Look for any potential passwords in the area of the computer. Popular places to secrete such passwords include pieces of paper or labels attached to the underside of the computer keyboard or mouse pad.
- Allow all components to cool down before packaging them securely for transport to the facility where they will be examined.

Procedures will likely also include a number of basic rules to guide the non-specialist officer who may be called on to collect and protect mobile device-based digital evidence, such as that found on smartphones. For example:

- Turn the device off or remove the battery in order to isolate it from the network.
- Photograph the device at the point of seizure.
- Place the device in a protective static-proof bag or container.
- Seize chargers, manuals, packaging, and any other documentation related to the device, if available.
- Deliver the device to the computer forensic examiner immediately.
- For devices with volatile memory, consider charging the device at intervals to ensure that data is not lost.
- Be aware that some devices are always on and cannot be entirely powered off—for example, the iPhone.
- Locate tin foil and wrap several layers of foil around the device to prevent it from receiving a signal.
- Consider the different types of evidence that may potentially be obtained from the device—for example, fingerprints or DNA—and discuss the possible examination sequence with the examiner to ensure that it

optimizes the potential for gathering multiple types of evidence from the device. For example, examining the device for fingerprints first might render the device unusable, which could hamper or make it impossible for the computer analyst to effectively examine the device for digital evidence.

For more detailed information on how to seize, store, and examine mobile devices, refer to Jansen and Ayers, *Guidelines on Cellphone Forensics* (2007), listed in Further Reading.

The Association of Chief Police Officers' (ACPO) *Good Practice Guide for Computer-Based Electronic Evidence* (n.d.) contains four basic principles that officers are well advised to heed, both when seizing and when examining electronic devices:

1. Law enforcement agencies or their agents should take no action that would change data held on a computer or storage media that may subsequently be relied on in court.

2. Law enforcement agents who find it necessary to access original data held on a computer or on storage media must be both competent to do so and able to explain the relevance and implications of their actions.

3. Police must create and preserve an audit trail or other record of all processes applied to computer-based electronic evidence so that an independent third party is able to examine those processes and achieve the same result.

4. It is the responsibility of the officer in charge of the investigation (the case officer) to ensure that the law and the principles of good practice are adhered to.

(Adapted from ACPO, *Good Practice Guide for Computer-Based Electronic Evidence* (n.d.), p. 46.)

An investigative or patrol officer called on to collect and protect electronic evidence pending expert forensic examination must keep one cardinal rule in mind—*consult a computer forensic examiner before touching anything.*

EXAMINING DIGITAL EVIDENCE

Specially trained police officers, civilian analysts, and forensic scientists carry out the actual analysis of digital evidence. A qualified, computer forensic examiner completes several weeks of exhaustive training in how to recover and analyze data from a computer system. This includes the use of specialized software that allows the examiner to make a forensically sound copy of the data from the hard drive in order to perform an analysis without altering the original evidence. Many, but not all, police examiners have a degree or background in computer science or programming. The training is continuous, with examiners required to maintain their certificate by logging hours and taking ongoing courses and certifications.

The most widely used forensic software tool in a computer forensic examination is EnCase®; another is Forensic Toolkit®. These tools allow an examiner to "image" the hard drive of a computer—that is, to create an exact copy—and then search the "imaged" copy in order to locate, collect, preserve, and analyze any evidence that might be present. The tools are used in conjunction with a hardware device known as a "write blocker," which protects data against accidental damage or alteration during the acquisition process by allowing only "read" commands to pass from the one computer to the other, while blocking any "write" commands. This helps ensure the integrity of the original evidence.

Forensic software tools allow examiners to do such things as acquire data from documents, images, web history, emails, chat sessions, backup files, encrypted files, caches, servers, smartphones, and tablets. In *Harris* (2010), a 23-year-old male was charged with "Internet luring" (*Criminal Code*, s. 172.1(2)), an offence in which the male communicated via Facebook with a 14-year-old girl in an attempt to arrange a sexual liaison. The investigator used EnCase and Forensic Toolkit to retrieve emails from the accused's computer that helped establish that he had, in fact, communicated with the female in an attempt to lure her into a sexual relationship. In *Baxter* (2009), an individual was charged with using his computer at work to distribute images of child pornography. The police investigator, an expert in the forensic examination of computers and data recovery, used Forensic Toolkit to establish such things as the accuracy of time stamps on emails sent and received by a particular computer, the fact that a particular computer was used to access Yahoo or MSN accounts on specific dates, and the history of Internet usage of a particular computer on a specific date.

Another valuable function that examiners can perform using forensic software is the recovery of deleted files. A clear distinction must be made, however, between files that have been "marked for deletion" and files or data that have been "wiped" from a computer's hard drive. Although a user cannot restore a file that has been moved to the trash or recycle bin and then "emptied," a forensic examination may still recover the file from the hard drive. What examiners *cannot* do, however, is recover files and data that have been "wiped" from a computer's hard drive by overwriting the existing data—for example, using a commercially available software program. Wiping data can be a time-consuming task; in the case of an average laptop computer, for example, it can take a number of hours.

PRESENTING DIGITAL EVIDENCE IN COURT

Although the process of presenting evidence in court is covered in Chapter 2, it is worth discussing the process briefly with respect to digital evidence in particular.

For any computer record or other digital evidence to be admissible against a defendant, the proponent must show that the offered evidence is authentic. The standard for determining the authenticity of a computer record is no different from that of any other record.

Even in the smallest or simplest of cases, digital evidence is prepared and disclosed in an electronic format. Because the digital evidence itself and any computer forensic examination conducted can be hundreds or even thousands of pages long when placed into a report, it is common for disclosure to be provided by way of a compact or digital videodisc. As technology has evolved, some cases require an entire external hard drive containing gigabytes of data formulating the digital evidence in a single investigation.

In some child pornography cases, the accused has collected hundreds of thousands of images; it is impractical to print all of the evidence, providing both a Crown copy and a copy for the defence. Computer forensic examiners testify in court using their laptops, which are connected to a projector and a screen so that the judge, the jury, and the accused can see the evidence and the examiner's analysis in the original format from the forensic copy. Unlike testimony from officers, the testimony of a computer forensic examiner involves few written notes. The forensic examination and process maintains chronological electronic logs of each step during the analysis, which form part of the disclosure package.

Computer forensic examiners are generally required to provide detailed curriculum vitae outlining their training, experience, and qualifications to the court as a part of the disclosure process. The Crown or defence can seek leave to qualify the examiner as an expert witness, as described in s. 657.3 of the *Criminal Code*. If the Crown is producing the expert witness, it must disclose to the defence within a reasonable period of time before trial a copy of the expert's report or a summary of their opinion and the basis for it (s. 657.3(3)(a)).

Much of the testimony provided by a computer forensic examiner tends to explain technological terms and the forensic examination process, and focuses on what was found on the computer or device. As in the case of certain other evidence, some of it cannot be disputed and the question raised, instead, becomes how the police obtained the computer, device, or evidence. If it was done unlawfully, it may not matter *what* was found.

In conclusion, the strengths and limitations of digital evidence can be both overstated and understated. Too often, police have relied on computer forensics to try and prove a case. The entire criminal investigation is on trial and corroborating police work must accompany the digital evidence to support a *prima facie* case. There are times in a computer forensic examination when the evidence is recovered after deletion, but the person responsible for putting that evidence on the computer remains a mystery. Traditional crime-solving and investigative techniques must be deployed to support the digital evidence, and vice versa. When lawfully positioned, police should always seize electronic devices and search them for the purpose of analyzing the digital data contained on them for evidence. If found, the data can be extremely subjective and incriminating, and the challenge is to establish how it was created and who put it there.

KEY TERMS

computer forensic examination
digital evidence
technological crime

FURTHER READING

Association of Chief Police Officers (ACPO). (n.d.). *Good practice guide for computer-based electronic evidence*. London: 7Safe. http://www.7safe.com/electronic_evidence.

James, S.H., & Nordby, J.J. (Eds.). (2009). *Forensic science: An introduction to scientific and investigative techniques* (3rd ed.). Boca Raton, FL: CRC Press.

Jansen, W., & Ayers, R. (2007). *Guidelines on cell phone forensics: Recommendations of the National Institute of Standards and Technology*. Gaithersburg, MD: Computer Security Division, National Institute of Standards and Technology. http://csrc.nist.gov/publications/nistpubs/800-101/SP800-101.pdf.

U.S. Department of Homeland Security. (n.d.). *Best practices for seizing electronic evidence: A pocket guide for first responders* (3rd ed.). Rockville, MD: National Criminal Justice Reference Service. https://www.ncjrs.gov/app/publications/abstract.aspx?id=239359.

REVIEW QUESTIONS

True or False?

1. Where digital evidence is paramount in a criminal investigation the term that can be used is "technological crime."

2. Digital evidence can only be obtained with a warrant or other judicial authorization.

3. A police officer may in certain circumstances conduct a cursory search of a cellular phone as incident to an arrest.

4. The general advice when seizing a cellular phone is to always turn it off.

5. A production order under the *Criminal Code*, s. 487.012 compels an organization to produce digital evidence such as IP logs.

6. Common-law rules governing the search and seizure of digital evidence are often jurisdictional.

7. Where police have reasonable grounds to believe that a suspect's cellular phone contains evidence of the offence, legislation requires the suspect to disclose his or her pass code.

Multiple Choice

1. Which of the following is true of searches of cellular phones?

   a. Any evidence obtained during a cursory search other than ownership information will be inadmissible in court.

   b. The benefits of determining ownership always outweigh the challenges to police procedures that may arise in court.

   c. The highly sensitive information contained in cellphones makes cursory searches patently unreasonable.

   d. Police should always obtain a warrant to search a phone beyond a cursory search.

2. If a computer is found in a place named in a warrant, which of the following is *not* true?

   a. A s. 487 warrant may be obtained to authorize a forensic examination of the computer.

   b. Police have implied authority to search the computer.

   c. The computer may be seized under the plain view doctrine.

   d. Investigators with a s. 487(1) warrant to search a computer for data may take copies of the data.

3. Though not required by law to do so, an organization may choose to turn over certain records to police in response to:

   a. a law enforcement request.

   b. a production order.

   c. a general search warrant.

   d. an Internet service provider (ISP).

4. Which of the following most accurately describes a basic rule in preserving digital evidence?

   a. Double click on "my computer" and see who the owner is.

   b. Do not attempt to access the computer. If it is off, leave it off; if it is on, do not search through it.

   c. Always pull the power plug from the wall.

   d. Ask the owner to show you the "my documents" folder.

5. Examples of digital evidence could include:

   a. portable storage devices.

   b. ATM cameras.

   c. ISP records.

   d. All of the above.

6. A computer system as defined in s. 342.1(2) of the *Criminal Code* means:

   a. any computer using the Windows operating system.

   b. any device that performs logic and control.

   c. only desktops and laptops.

   d. only computers and cellular phones.

7. Bill C-30 was tabled in the House of Commons to allow police to obtain what kind of information without warrant?

   a. The ability to read emails.

   b. A suspect's Internet browsing history and his or her email address.

   c. Basic subscriber information such as customer name and address.

   d. All of the above.

Short Answer

1. What must police consider when deciding whether to conduct a cursory search of a cellular phone?

2. List the authorities under which a police officer may seize a cellular phone.

3. List three things a computer forensic examination can help determine.

4. Describe the format in which digital evidence is disclosed and the reason for this.

Crime Labs and the Role of Science in Investigations

10

LEARNING OUTCOMES

After completing this chapter, you should be able to:

- Understand the role and value of science and crime labs in an investigation.

- Identify the sections of a crime lab and understand how evidence is handled at the lab.

- Know which scientists and specialists outside the crime lab are available to investigators.

- Understand the difference between class and individual characteristics of evidence and the significance of these characteristics to investigators.

INTRODUCTION

forensic science
the application of
science to law

Simply stated, **forensic science** is the application of science to law. Science plays an extremely important role in police investigations, answering myriad questions, linking a suspect to a crime scene or victim, and exonerating innocent people. In the past, convictions were often obtained on the basis of subjective evidence—for example, that of an eyewitness. While eyewitnesses may be accurate, they can also be misled, deceitful, or simply mistaken. Today, the use of scientific evidence allows police investigations and criminal trials to be more objective than they were in the past.

Science is neutral. Crime labs exist to assist in criminal investigations, not, as is sometimes assumed, to support the police case. Forensic scientists who work in crime labs—even those affiliated with a police agency such as the RCMP—do not work for the police. Rather, they are impartial specialists whose job is to analyze and interpret evidence and report their findings. Their results may support or refute the police case, but they have no stake in the overall outcome. However, no police investigator wants to follow the wrong investigative path and convict an innocent person, missing the correct offender who remains free to reoffend. Therefore, whether science supports the original police theory or not, it is always valuable, pointing the investigation in the right direction.

THE IMPORTANCE OF FORENSIC SCIENCE

In everyday life, we are constantly touching things. Throughout our normal, daily routine, we leave traces of ourselves behind and pick up traces of the environment and other people. These traces include such things as, for example, hair, fibres, drywall, glue, paint fragments, skin fragments, and fingerprints. There is a constant exchange of this material occurring in the course of everyday life.

Crimes occur as people go about their routines, in places such as bedrooms, kitchens, parking lots, offices, and bars. In all crimes, therefore, offenders take something from the environment and the victim, leaving their own traces behind. These traces become physical or **trace evidence**. (See the discussion of Locard's

trace evidence
physical evidence left
behind at a crime scene
or exchanged between
an offender and victim

IMPARTIALITY

Scientists in a crime lab are unbiased. For example, a DNA specialist can tell an investigator that the sample in Exhibit A matches that of Exhibit B, but not Exhibit C. The scientist does not care, nor usually even know, whether Exhibits A, B, and C come from the suspect, the victim, the couch, or the best friend. That information is known to the investigator who, when the lab report comes back, can move forward with the investigation. If, for example, Exhibit A is from the vaginal swab of a rape victim, Exhibit B is DNA from the roommate, and Exhibit C is DNA from a suspected neighbour, the investigator now knows that the neighbour can be eliminated (avoiding hours of wasted time), but the roommate warrants further investigation. Such a report from the lab will greatly speed up and focus the investigation, avoiding time wasted on irrelevant suspects. Such evidence, when competently presented in court, is probative.

exchange principle in Chapter 7, Crime Scene Investigation and Management.) Although such evidence transfer is greatest in interpersonal crimes such as assault, rape, and murder, a simple break and enter can still involve trace evidence—for example, fingerprints, sweat, paint, and drywall chips. This evidence can be analyzed to link the victim with a suspect and a scene and to help identify or eliminate a suspect.

Although forensic science is extremely important in a police investigation, it does not solve crimes on its own. Good police investigators do, by using forensic science to understand what has transpired and allow the truth to be proved in a court of law.

THE CRIME LABORATORY

Television shows have given many people an inaccurate picture of forensic scientists, suggesting that they process crime scenes, analyze the evidence in the crime lab, interrogate witnesses, chase the bad guys, shoot people, and arrest them, all in less than an hour. In reality, this is the work of a number of people, with different backgrounds, training, and many different types of jobs.

Crime or forensic lab scientists are bench scientists—that is, they spend their days in a laboratory, analyzing specimens. With some rare exceptions, they do not attend crime scenes. They are not sworn police officers, but civilians with strong scientific backgrounds. Although they frequently attend court to testify as expert witnesses, they do not have a direct role in the police investigation—they simply analyze the evidence that police officers collect at the crime scene and prepare a report that will assist the police in their investigations. As well, each section of the lab employs scientists specialized in just one area of science. Training for any position takes years, and no one person could be a master of all.

As outlined in Chapter 7, at a crime scene, sworn forensic identification specialists collect evidence, which is then taken to the crime lab. Most crime labs in Canada include the following sections or units:

- *Case receipt unit (CRU).* Evidence collected at a crime scene is next taken to the crime laboratory, where it enters the case receipt unit. Every single exhibit is tagged with a computer code that allows its movements through the various units of the laboratory to be monitored at all times. Exhibits are frequently examined by several sections, so this allows the exhibit to be tracked. Thus, when an investigator contacts the lab to see what progress is being made, the CRU personnel can immediately find out exactly who has the evidence at the moment and how far the analysis has progressed. Often, a small portion of the exhibit is destroyed under analysis, and this is also recorded.

- *Evidence recovery unit (ERU).* Once tagged, the exhibit will go to the ERU, where scientists will examine it, looking for forensically significant trace evidence. ERU technologists will search, locate, and collect all forensically important material and submit it to the appropriate unit. For example, in the case of a seized bed sheet, ERU technologists may cut out areas where they can detect body fluids such as semen, blood, or saliva. These will be submitted to the forensic biology unit for analysis.

- *Forensic biology unit.* Forensic biologists deal with all body fluids that might relate to a crime scene—for example, blood and semen as well as tissue and hair. Their purpose is to identify who the substances came from. This section used to be called the serology section, but, with the advent of DNA analysis, it is now called the biology unit.

- *Forensic toxicology unit.* Forensic toxicologists quantify toxins—primarily drugs and alcohol, but also poisons—in body fluids and needles, pills, and drug paraphernalia that may relate to a crime. As well, they also determine the physiological effects of such toxins. Their analysis will determine, for example, whether the dose of a particular drug found in a body would kill or cause memory loss or impairment.

- *Trace evidence unit.* This section used to be called the forensic chemistry unit. Forensic chemists analyze any non-biological substance found at a scene—for example, paint, fibre, glue, drywall, gasoline, and bomb components. They are the main scientists involved in hit-and-run, break and enter, arson, and terrorist crimes. In the United States, this unit is sometimes referred to as the physical science unit.

- *Firearms and tool marks unit.* Firearms specialists analyze tool marks and firearms to determine whether a tool made a certain mark—for example, whether a chisel was used to break open a door or whether a gun fired a specific bullet.

- *Questioned documents unit.* Questioned document examiners look primarily at handwriting to determine whether a person wrote a suspect document. They also look at documents to see whether they have been altered, and at machines—for example, fax machines and printers—that produce writing.

Each of the units described above employs a number of forensic scientists, as well as technicians who assist them and run part or all of the scientific analyses. However, the scientists oversee the work, perform the interpretations, write the reports, and, perhaps, testify in court.

In many cases, some individual exhibits may be examined by a number of sections, involving all or several of the above-mentioned sciences in the analysis of the crime-scene exhibits. For example, the firearms and tool mark unit might examine a gun to determine whether it fired the bullet and cartridge recovered from the victim and the scene; the biology unit might be involved to determine whether there is any blood from the victim that has back splashed onto the weapon, and whether sweat left on the gun can be used to identify the shooter. As well, fingerprint specialists will attempt to determine whether there are any fingerprints present that can be individualized (see the box below, "The Anthrax Letters in the United States"). The lab and the scientists all work together to provide the investigator with the best and most up-to-date information about an exhibit.

The individual sciences are described in detail in Chapters 12 to 15. Other areas of analysis include pattern analysis—for example, fingerprint, boot print, and tire track evidence—as well as bloodstain pattern analysis; as described in Chapter 8, Pattern Evidence and Collision Reconstruction, these are usually performed by sworn police members in the identification section. Photography, crime scene

THE ANTHRAX LETTERS IN THE UNITED STATES

Most crime scene investigations involve several sections of the laboratory. A classic example of the number of sciences and lab sections involved in the analysis of a single crime or piece of evidence is that of the anthrax letters that were mailed in the United States immediately after the terror attacks of September 11, 2001 (9/11). These letters underwent ten separate forensic analyses, several by the questioned documents unit, but also by the biology unit, the trace evidence unit, the firearms and tool marks unit, and the identification unit. The questioned documents unit analyzed the indented marks left by the handwriting; the handwriting itself; and the photocopier toner, the paper, and the ink used. The biology unit analyzed the DNA from the envelopes and stamps, and the trace evidence unit analyzed hairs and fibres found on the paper; both the trace evidence and the firearms and tool marks units examined associated cellophane tape, while the identification unit examined everything for fingerprints. Other evidence included the barcodes placed on the envelopes as they travelled across the United States via the U.S. mail service (Saferstein, 2011). This example provides a sense of the types of evidence and the sections of the lab, as well as the work by the identification section, that all go together to analyze what at first just seems to be a single piece of evidence.

investigation, and latent print analysis also fall under the concerns of the identification section, and so most labs in Canada do not have specific sections for these.

OVERVIEW OF THE MAIN CANADIAN CRIME LABS

Canada has a number of crime labs, including six RCMP labs across the country (in Vancouver, Edmonton, Regina, Winnipeg, Ottawa, and Halifax) under Forensic Science and Identification Services. (However, the RCMP announced in mid-2012 that the Regina, Winnipeg, and Halifax labs would be closed shortly and their files transferred to the remaining labs in Vancouver, Edmonton, and Ottawa.) The other crime labs are the Centre of Forensic Sciences in Toronto and Sault Ste. Marie in Ontario, and the Laboratoire de sciences judiciaires et de médecine légale in Montreal. The Laboratoire in Montreal, established in 1914, was the first forensic laboratory established in North America.

Each lab group deals with a different range of agencies. The RCMP labs deal only with criminal cases for all official investigative agencies. The Centre of Forensic Sciences deals with cases for investigative agencies and defence counsel; in some circumstances, it will also deal with civil cases. The Laboratoire in Montreal is available to any organization in Quebec requiring its services—in particular, the police, corrections, Coroner's office, Department of Natural Resources and Wildlife, Commission of Health and Safety at Work, and departments of Liquor, Gaming, and Racing—giving it the broadest mandate of all.

Recently, there has been a move to amalgamate certain sections in RCMP laboratories so that each of the major crime labs has a main specialty. For example, instead of having questioned document specialists in every RCMP lab, all questioned documents from RCMP cases across Canada are now processed only in Ottawa. The idea is to increase efficiency and reduce duplication of services. Also, much of the equipment is now so expensive that it is not possible to supply all the labs. This is particularly true of DNA evidence, which is now processed only in Vancouver, Edmonton, and Ottawa.

The Laboratoire in Montreal has sections in biology, toxicology, chemistry, tool marks and firearms, questioned documents and gaming machines, explosives, and photography. The Centre of Forensic Sciences has sections in biology, chemistry, documents and photo-analysis, electronics, firearms and tool marks, and toxicology.

Science, and consequently forensic science, has made giant leaps in just a few short years. Concerns about maintaining and improving quality led the U.S. National Academy of Sciences (NAS) to study and report on the state of forensic science in that country (NAS, 2009). The long, detailed report resulted in 13 major recommendations, including setting up an independent body, the National Institute of Forensic Sciences (NIFS), to establish best practices, standards, and mandatory certification; promote top quality research; develop standard terminology; receive and distribute funds for research into many areas, including human observer bias and error—"accuracy, reliability and error" (NAS, 2009, p. 22); and establish a code of ethics. All these are excellent ideas, and it will be a big step forward if funding is established to fulfill the recommendations. Although some of the report's elements relate specifically to the U.S. arena, forensic science crosses all geographical boundaries and the report is relevant to Canada too. Addressing its findings will, we hope, result in greater efforts in research and more support from governments, both in the United States and worldwide.

A few of the report's recommendations, if Canada decides to follow them, would have major impact here. These include replacing coroners systems with medical examiners systems, making forensic laboratories independent of police or prosecutorial agencies, and ensuring that all forensic scientists be professionally certified.

In Canada, many of our provinces have coroners systems rather than medical examiners systems. Both coroners and medical examiners investigate unexplained deaths, but they have different backgrounds and powers. Except in Ontario, coroners do not have to be medical doctors, and they come from a variety of backgrounds. They have quasi-judicial powers, so they can preside over coroners inquests. Medical examiners are doctors, but not necessarily forensic pathologists, and they do not hold any judicial powers. RCMP laboratories are, of course, affiliated with the RCMP, although they function independently of the investigation. The certification of all scientists will be an issue in both Canada and the United States because many sciences have not yet established certification bodies, and some of those that exist have a minimum qualification of a Ph.D., which many practising scientists do not possess.

FORENSIC SPECIALTIES OUTSIDE THE FORENSIC LAB

Although the forensic lab covers the main sciences that most crime scenes warrant, many other forensic specialists can assist in a criminal investigation. Most of these scientists have non-forensic jobs, usually as university professors, but their research and specialized training can be invaluable in certain types of investigations. It is important that investigators understand which specialists are out there, what they do, and when they would be valuable in an investigation. Many of these highly trained specialists are little used in investigations, and much valuable forensic evidence is wasted because investigators are unaware of the treasure trove of information such people can provide. Police services often contact local universities to see which specialists are available. The following paragraphs briefly describe some of the scientists useful to police investigators.

Forensic Archaeologist

Archaeologists are professionals dedicated to the study of the evolution of ancient and past peoples and their remains. One of the central techniques archaeologists use is excavation—for example, the meticulous documentation of ancient graves, middens (scrap heaps), and long-buried villages. Their excavation techniques are also of essential use in other endeavours—for example, criminal and forensic investigations. Their methodologies for documentation and evidence collection are invaluable in the careful and exacting reconstruction of a crime scene, particularly when the remains are buried.

It is, therefore, important to have a forensic archaeologist attend and actively assist in the excavation of scenes involving clandestine graves. These types of graves may have difficult structures that need to be carefully excavated—for example, buried human remains may be commingled, disturbed, incomplete, or dispersed over a broad area. In cases of mass burial, determining the number of individuals buried, joining their body parts, and isolating their belongings and clothing within the space of the grave are essential for further investigation into the event—namely, defining the manner of death, identifying the dead, and prosecuting the culprits.

Forensic Anthropologist

Forensic, or physical, anthropologists study the human skeleton, and are thus extremely important in investigations involving skeletal remains. They are expert in developing a biological profile of a victim. First, they can determine whether a found bone belongs to a human or an animal. It is common for a helpful member of the public to find a bone and believe it to be human. Involving a forensic anthropologist at this stage can forestall a large forensic expedition to investigate a potential homicide victim, when the bones come from an animal. It is therefore helpful to have a forensic anthropologist assist in the recovery of remains at a crime scene.

Depending on the completeness of the skeleton, a forensic anthropologist can determine sex, age range, ancestry, and height range of the deceased. He or she can also assess pre- (before) and peri-mortem (at time of death) trauma, as opposed to post-mortem (after death) damage to the skeleton and, if a weapon was used, may be able to determine which type.

Forensic Entomologist

Entomologists study insects, so forensic—or, more correctly, medico-legal—entomologists primarily study the insects associated with a human body to estimate elapsed time since death. Insects are attracted to remains immediately after death and develop at a predictable rate. As well, different insects are attracted at different stages of decomposition, so a forensic entomologist can analyze the insects on human remains and estimate how long they have been associated with the body. For example, the entomologist might determine that the oldest insects were laid as eggs on the body seven days before its discovery, which means that the victim's death predated this. It is thus valuable to invite a forensic entomologist to a crime scene to assist in the investigation by collecting insect evidence.

In some cases, forensic entomologists can also determine whether a body has been moved or disturbed after death, as well as the position and presence of wounds that may no longer be visible to the naked eye.

Forensic Dentist

Dentists or odontologists are experts in all aspects of dentition—the condition of the teeth—and are frequently called in to determine the identification of human remains by comparing the dentition of the remains with known pre-mortem records. Human dentition patterns are believed to be unique to an individual, so are considered a method of positive identification. If the victim is unknown, the dentist will chart the dentistry, which will then be entered into the **Canadian Police Information Centre (CPIC)**, a national police computer database containing information about many aspects of police investigations, including the known details about any missing persons. When someone is reported missing, his or her details are entered on CPIC, including, for example, dental records, fingerprints (if on record), what they were wearing when they went missing, their biological description, any distinguishing marks, and anything else that might help identify them. When the remains of an unknown person are found, he or she is assessed and compared with the missing persons on file in the CPIC to see whether there is a match. The details of a found body are entered with the hope that someone will eventually come forward to report that person missing, allowing their details to be added, and a match to be made.

Some forensic odontologists also specialize in bite mark analysis. Bite marks are frequently left behind in sexual assault and homicide cases. Each person's bite pattern is believed to be unique, although this is a more controversial area than simple identification by dentition.

Canadian Police Information Centre (CPIC) a national law enforcement computer database maintained by the RCMP, containing data on aspects of police investigations, such as stolen property, people in conflict with the law, surveillance, and missing persons

Forensic Botanist

Plants and plant parts, seeds, and especially pollen are common forms of trace evidence. A forensic botanist can use plants or pollen to link a suspect or a vehicle to a scene or an area. Plants and pollen vary among regions, so a forensic botanist who examines an exhibit, a suspect vehicle, or a deceased victim can shed light on where, for example, the victim has been. Or, if a suspect were to say that he had only been driving in the Lower Mainland of British Columbia over the past few months, an examination of the pollen in the car's air filter might instead tell an investigator that the vehicle had spent some time in the more northern parts of the province.

Plants grow at a predictable rate. Plant growth over evidence at a crime scene can tell a forensic botanist how long that evidence has been there. For example, plant growth through the skull of a murder victim can show how long the victim has been at the scene. Or, even years after a crime has taken place, the accumulated mulch of fallen leaves can be analyzed to indicate how many years ago the victim was placed there. Thus it is often helpful to invite a forensic botanist to a crime scene to interpret the botanical evidence.

Forensic Geologist

Geologists study rocks and minerals, which often includes an understanding of soil and soil type. Soil, like pollen evidence, contains ubiquitous trace evidence, which is often overlooked. Like plant material, soils can be specific to certain areas. A forensic geologist can analyze soil found on a tire or boot, or left behind in a footprint, and potentially link it to an area in question.

CHARACTERISTICS OF EVIDENCE

Evidence can have class characteristics, individual characteristics, or both.

Evidence that has **class characteristics** can be associated with a group, but not with a single source (Saferstein, 2011). For example, a chip of paint found on the victim of a hit-and-run fatality can be analyzed by a forensic chemist and found to have come from a yellow car. There are, of course, many yellow cars out there, but the yellow used by Toyota is different, both chemically and visually, from the yellow used by Honda—in fact, a yellow Honda Civic is different from a yellow Honda CR-V. Car colours also change over the years as market research suggests that a new variety is more popular than the previous one. Crime labs have databases of all car paints from all manufacturers, models, and years, which are regularly updated. Therefore, a forensic chemist can narrow a paint chip down to a particular make, model, and year of car. The chemist will be able to state that the yellow paint chip comes from a yellow Honda Civic manufactured between 1999 and 2005. This is extremely valuable because it eliminates all vehicles with the exception of yellow Honda Civics from those years. It has therefore associated the evidence, the paint chip, with a group—yellow Honda Civics from 1999 to 2005—but it cannot indicate which yellow Honda Civic was involved. The colour of the paint chip is a class characteristic. Its significance will be either high or low depending on the number of yellow Honda Civics from those years in existence. All yellow Honda Civics registered for those years, no matter how many, will need to be examined. On the other hand, it would be helpful if the chemist found that the paint chip belonged to a much rarer vehicle—for example, a 2009 yellow Boxster Porsche. Records might indicate that only two such vehicles are registered locally, making the evidence much more significant.

In addition to class characteristics, which most evidence has, evidence can also have **individual characteristics**, also referred to as "accidental" characteristics. These are characteristics that can be identified with just one source with a high degree of accuracy (Saferstein, 2011); in other words, the evidence came from one particular car or person and no other. In the above car example, even though the yellow Porsche is much rarer than the Honda Civic, there are still more than one. Therefore, the evidence still has only class characteristics, albeit highly significant. However, what if, on further examination, the paint chip can be seen to have a certain shape, like a unique jigsaw puzzle piece, which shattered off the car during the impact with the victim? If the car responsible is located before it has been repaired, it may

class characteristics
characteristics that link an object to a group of objects, eliminating all other groups

individual characteristics
characteristics that can be linked to a single source, belonging to a particular object and no other

be possible to fit that chip back into the paint work it came from. This would be an exact match. Even if 3,500 yellow Honda Civics from those years are located, and, of those, 100 have front end damage, only one—the vehicle of interest—will be an exact match for the chip. The pattern of the paint chip would exhibit individual characteristics, linking the paint chip—and hence the victim and the accident—to that one vehicle. Further investigation will then be required to determine the driver at the time of the accident, but the vehicle has been positively identified. Common forms of evidence that possess individual characteristics include fingerprints, DNA, and dentition.

Evidence with only class characteristics is of little value if you don't know the probability of, for example, another person or car sharing the same class characteristics. To determine probability, the examiner must determine how many other such items are available. In the case of cars, which must be legally registered, the parent population—that is, the total number of cars that fit the description—is known. However, because so much material is mass-produced, it is impossible to know, for example, how many white, cotton T-shirts there are. Anything mass-produced is difficult to investigate. But if data are available on a product, significance can be determined. In most cases, several types of evidence are found relating to a suspect. These can be added together to increase their significance. For example, if the suspect is found with a sweater whose fibres are similar to fibres found at the scene, glass chips on his shoes similar to those from the broken window at the scene, and other fibres similar to those from the blanket on which the victim was raped, the value of the pieces of evidence is compounded. Even if all the items together possess only class characteristics, and thus do not link only the suspect to the scene, how many people would be likely to have the combination of all three? If probabilities can be obtained for each item, they can be multiplied to determine the probability that anyone else might have this evidence on them.

FAMOUS CASES IN WHICH CLASS CHARACTERISTICS BECAME ALMOST INDIVIDUALIZING

There are several well-known cases where so much evidence was recovered, and probabilities for each piece could be calculated, that the class characteristics became almost as significant as individual characteristics.

In the early 1980s, many children and young men were found murdered in Atlanta, Georgia. In many of the cases, a large amount of fibre evidence was recovered from the victims. Wayne Williams was identified as a suspect when his vehicle was seen near a river at the same time as one of the victims was heard to be dumped into the water. This was before such individualizing evidence as DNA was understood. During the investigation, the crime lab determined that the fibres were a match for carpets in Williams's home and car. However, a match simply states they are the same. A white cotton fibre may be a match for the cotton fibre in a suspect's T-shirt, but it will also be a match for every other white cotton T-shirt in the room, the city, and the province. Therefore, it would have very low significance. In order for the fibre evidence to be of value in the Williams case, investigators had to determine the "parent population" for each of the fibres—that is, the total number of carpets with the identical characteristics that were sold and were still in existence in that region—the significance of each, and the overall significance of finding them all together. In each case, the source and manufacturer were identified, then the number of carpets that had been made and then sold in the Atlanta area was calculated to determine the parent population, which indicated the chance of such a fibre being found randomly. In all, 28 different types of fibres linked Williams and his environment to the victims. The court accepted that the chance of anyone else having all of these same fibres in their home was realistically zero, and Williams was convicted (Saferstein, 2011).

In the case of the murders of Nicole Brown Simpson and Ronald Goldman, very clear bloody shoe prints found at the crime scene were identified as having been made from size-12 Bruno Magli shoes. These are very expensive shoes, and the particular style was available for only a short time. It was determined that only 299 were sold in the United States. Further information narrowed the number to just 29 pairs that could have made that print. O.J. Simpson called the shoe style ugly and denied ever having worn a pair; however, photographs of him wearing this exact style of shoe were taken just a few months before the murders. This should have been extremely probative in the criminal trial, but, unfortunately, the photographs proving that Simpson owned such a shoe were not discovered until shortly after the criminal trial where he was found not guilty was over. This evidence was, however, extremely valuable in the subsequent civil trial in which O.J. was held liable for the murders (Saferstein, 2011).

KEY TERMS

Canadian Police Information Centre (CPIC)
class characteristics
forensic science
individual characteristics
trace evidence

FURTHER READING

Byers, S.N. (2010). *Introduction to forensic anthropology*. Upper Saddle River, NJ: Prentice Hall, Pearson.

Centre of Forensic Sciences. Ontario Ministry of Community Safety and Correctional Services. http://www.mcscs.jus.gov.on.ca/english/default.html.

Forensic Entomology. http://www.forensicentomology.com.

Forensic Science and Identification Services. Royal Canadian Mounted Police. http://www.rcmp-grc.gc.ca/fsis-ssji/index-eng.htm.

Haglund, W.D., & Sorg, M.H. (Eds.). (1997). *Forensic taphonomy: The postmortem fate of human remains*. Boca Raton, FL: CRC Press.

James, S.H., & Nordby, J.J. (Eds.). (2009). *Forensic science: An introduction to scientific and investigative techniques* (3rd ed.). Boca Raton, FL: CRC Press.

Laboratoire de sciences judiciaires et de médecine légale. Sécurité publique Québec. http://www.securitepublique.gouv.qc.ca/lsjml.html.

Murray, R.C. (2004). *Evidence from the earth: Forensic geology and criminal investigation*. Missoula, MT: Mountain Press Publishing Company.

REVIEW QUESTIONS

True or False?

1. Crime or forensic laboratory scientists regularly attend crime scenes.

2. Crime laboratory scientists are usually not sworn police officers.

3. Exhibits are examined for forensically significant trace evidence in the case receipt unit.

4. Forensic toxicologists can determine the physiological effects of a drug or toxin on a person.

5. The main forensic scientists involved in an arson crime are forensic chemists who work in the trace evidence unit.

6. The RCMP laboratories deal only with criminal cases for investigative agencies.

7. The Laboratoire de sciences judiciaires et de médecine legale in Montreal deals only with criminal cases for investigative agencies.

8. The Centre of Forensic Sciences in Ontario deals only with criminal cases for investigative agencies.

9. A forensic anthropologist is of assistance only when remains are found outdoors.

10. Individual evidence cannot identify a specific person.

Multiple Choice

1. Evidence with body fluids on it will be taken *first* to the:

   a. forensic toxicology unit.

   b. forensic biology unit.

   c. evidence recovery unit.

   d. case receipt unit.

   e. trace evidence unit.

2. The first forensic laboratory in North America was:

   a. the Centre of Forensic Sciences in Toronto.

   b. the RCMP lab in Ottawa.

   c. the Centre of Forensic Sciences in Sault Ste. Marie, Ontario.

   d. the Laboratoire de sciences judiciaires et de médecine légale in Montreal.

   e. the New York State Crime Lab.

3. Which of the following forensic laboratories deals with defence cases?

    a. the Centre of Forensic Sciences in Ontario.

    b. the RCMP lab in Ottawa.

    c. the Laboratoire de sciences judiciaires et de médecine légale in Montreal.

    d. the RCMP lab in Vancouver.

    e. both a and c.

4. Which of the following forensic scientists would be valuable at a crime scene?

    a. forensic archaeologist.

    b. forensic anthropologist.

    c. forensic entomologist.

    d. forensic botanist.

    e. all of the above.

5. Which of the following scientists would you not expect to see working in a forensic crime lab?

    a. forensic biologist.

    b. forensic toxicologist.

    c. forensic entomologist.

    d. firearms specialist.

    e. forensic chemist.

Short Answer

1. Are forensic scientists on the side of the police? Explain.

2. What is Locard's exchange principle? Give an example.

3. Why doesn't every RCMP lab include all sections or units?

4. Give a clear example of evidence that exhibits class characteristics.

5. Give a clear example of evidence that exhibits individual characteristics.

6. What is a piece of evidence with low significance? What is a piece of evidence with high significance? Explain why each example has high or low significance.

7. What is the main problem when trying to determine the significance of evidence possessing only class characteristics?

Death Investigation

11

LEARNING OUTCOMES

After completing this chapter, you should be able to:

- Understand the role of the coroner or medical examiner in death investigations.

- Explain the circumstances in which a coroner will investigate a death.

- Understand when police officers may assume and pronounce death.

- Know the five questions—who, how, when, where, and by what means—that death investigations seek to answer.

- Understand the role of both the forensic pathologist and an autopsy in a death investigation.

- Understand the kind of information that forensic science can provide in a death investigation.

INTRODUCTION

In Canada, the investigation of a death, whether by homicide, accident, suicide, or natural causes, is conducted through a working partnership between provincial medical authorities and police, each with their own areas of responsibility and each bringing their own unique resources to the task.

Although police attend the scene of many sudden, unexpected deaths, the investigation of such deaths, and the scenes in which they occur, falls under the primary authority of provincial medical authorities—that is, the coroner or the chief medical examiner. Coroners or medical examiners (MEs) are responsible for overseeing the investigation into a sudden death under criteria that are defined under each province's *Coroners Act* or medical examiners Act (*Fatality Inquiries Act*). Both coroners and MEs investigate unexplained deaths; however, a coroner is not required to be a medical doctor, whereas a medical examiner must hold a medical degree. In Ontario, coroners are medical doctors, but this is not the case in all provinces. In British Columbia, for example, coroners require legal, medical, or investigative experience, and some are ex-police officers. Coroners hold quasi-judicial powers, allowing them to conduct inquests, whereas medical examiners do not hold such powers and rely on another body to conduct inquests.

coroner
a provincial medical authority responsible for determining the cause of sudden, unnatural deaths

Canada's death investigation system stems from the British coroner system, which dates to 900 C.E. The term **coroner** comes from the word "crowner," because, historically, all such investigators were appointed by the Crown. In those days, the coroner's responsibilities encompassed the roles of today's police officers and investigators in the larger justice system. Coroners examined the bodies of the deceased, held inquests, and arrested the person or persons they found responsible for causing the deaths.

Today, Canada has a mix of medical examiner and coroner systems for death investigations. Ontario has a chief coroner, as do British Columbia, Saskatchewan, Quebec, New Brunswick, Yukon, Nunavut, and the Northwest Territories. Medical examiners lead death investigations in Alberta, Manitoba, Nova Scotia, and Newfoundland and Labrador.

WHEN WILL A CORONER INVESTIGATE?

In Ontario, s. 10(1) of the *Coroners Act* (1990) requires that deaths falling into any of the following categories be reported to the coroner:

- deaths occurring as a result of violence, misadventure, negligence, misconduct, or malpractice;
- deaths occurring by unfair means;
- deaths occurring during or following pregnancy and that might be due to complications;
- sudden and unexpected deaths;
- deaths as a result of disease or sickness *not* being treated by a legally qualified medical practitioner;
- deaths resulting from any cause other than disease; and
- deaths occurring under other circumstances that may require investigation.

In addition, s. 10(2) requires the following to be reported:

- deaths of inpatients of designated institutions such as children's residences designated under the *Child and Family Services Act* (1990), supported group-living residences for persons with developmental disabilities, or psychiatric facilities designated under the *Mental Health Act* (1990), or deaths of patients in hospitals to which they were transferred from one of these facilities;

- deaths of individuals in long-term care homes;

- deaths of individuals on the premises of a detention facility or lockup, in a place of temporary detention, in a correctional institution, or in a place of secure custody;

- any death during detention by or in custody of a peace officer;

- deaths occurring while a person is restrained in a psychiatric facility, hospital, or secure treatment program; and

- work-related accidents at construction or mining areas.

Similar provisions exist in the legislation of other provinces and territories.

Under s. 15(1) of the *Coroners Act*, the coroner is required to investigate deaths in any of the above circumstances. Under s. 9, the police force in the coroner's jurisdiction must make police officers available to facilitate the coroner in carrying out the duties of his or her office.

Powers of the Coroner

Section 16 of the *Coroners Act* grants significant powers to enable coroners to carry out death investigations. Under s. 16(1) of the Act, a coroner may:

> (a) examine or take possession of any dead body, or both; and
>
> (b) enter and inspect any place where a dead body is and any place from which the coroner has reasonable grounds for believing the body was removed.

Under s. 16(2), a coroner who believes on reasonable and probable grounds that to do so is necessary for the purposes of the investigation may,

> (a) inspect any place in which the deceased person was, or in which the coroner has reasonable grounds to believe the deceased person was, prior to his death;
>
> (b) inspect and extract information from any records or writings relating to the deceased or his or her circumstances and reproduce such copies therefrom as the coroner believes necessary;
>
> (c) seize anything that the coroner has reasonable grounds to believe is material to the purposes of the investigation.

And pursuant to s. 16(3), a coroner may delegate any or all of his or her powers to a qualified medical practitioner or a police officer.

STAGES IN A DEATH INVESTIGATION

In Ontario, death investigations proceed in five basic stages (Sossin, 2008):

1. A death is reported to the coroner, and the coroner decides whether to investigate the death. If the decision is made to investigate, the coroner attends the scene to conduct a preliminary examination of the body.

forensic pathologist
a medical doctor with specialized training in forensic pathology who conducts autopsies and determines the manner and cause of death in suspicious circumstances

2. The coroner decides whether an autopsy is necessary. If it is, a **forensic pathologist** will examine the body and conduct any necessary tests. The forensic pathologist will consider information given to him or her by the coroner and the police regarding the circumstances of the person's death.

3. The forensic pathologist will advise the coroner (and, the police, if appropriate) about the results of their investigation.

4. The coroner will consider the pathologist report, together with other information obtained in the investigation of the person's death—for example, that provided by a police investigation—to determine how and why the death occurred. The coroner's determination as to the cause of death will be indicated on the medical certificate of death.

coroner's inquest
typically conducted after an accident or unnatural death, provides recommendations in an attempt to prevent further deaths in similar, future circumstances

5. The regional coroner will decide whether the case should be reviewed or whether a **coroner's inquest** should be held. In Ontario, for example, a chief coroner and chief forensic pathologist co-manage the death investigation system for the province. The chief coroner is responsible for all the coroners and the chief forensic pathologist is responsible for all the forensic pathologists. In Ontario, there are four regions (Central, East, North, and West), each of which has a regional supervising coroner who supervises the coroners in his or her region.

Inquests do not usually relate to a criminal occurrence. They are typically conducted after an accident or unnatural death, and provide recommendations in an attempt to prevent further deaths in similar circumstances in the future. (See the box feature on the inquest into the death of Junior Alexander Manon.)

RESPONSIBILITIES OF POLICE WHERE A DEATH HAS OCCURRED

Although police officers are involved in many death investigations, note that such deaths are rarely the result of homicide. In Ontario, for example, there are close to 90,000 deaths each year, but only about 200 are determined to be the result of homicide. The vast majority of deaths in Ontario, as elsewhere in Canada, are of a non-suspicious nature—the result of natural causes, accident, or suicide (Statistics Canada, 2011a and 2011b). However, where foul play is either obvious or suspected, the police are responsible for directing the criminal investigation into the death, with the advice and support of the coroner's office through the various specialists in its employ. The body itself is always under the jurisdiction of the coroner.

When police arrive at a scene where someone is supposed to have died, they must assume that the person is alive, provide first aid or procure emergency medical assistance, and ensure that the person is transported to hospital. While legislation—for example, Ontario's *Vital Statistics Act* (1990), ss. 35(2) and (3)—specifies who

SAMPLE INQUEST FINDINGS: JUNIOR ALEXANDER MANON

In May 2010, two Toronto police officers pulled over 18-year-old Junior Manon at a traffic stop. When they tried to arrest him, he fled, and they pursued him on foot. A struggle ensued, during which Manon died. When paramedics arrived, it was too late for them to use a defibrillator to restore the teen's heartbeat, and he was pronounced dead at a nearby hospital.

Two years later, in May 2012, a coroner's jury struck by the Office of the Chief Coroner of Ontario ruled that Manon's death was an accident but that the actions of the two officers had contributed to his death. The jury had to consider the testimony of the officers—who claimed they had not restrained Manon in a way that could have caused his death—in addition to eyewitness accounts stating that the officers had put their weight on Manon's back as he was lying prone (face down) on the ground. The inquest determined the cause of death to be "restraint asphyxia, following a struggle and exertion," implying that the officers had restrained the teen improperly, in a way that impaired his breathing.

The jury made a number of recommendations to the Toronto Police Service, St. John Ambulance, the Ontario Police College, and the Special Investigations Unit. Among the recommendations were the following:

TO THE TORONTO POLICE SERVICE

[1.] [Procedures] should be revised in order to separate the discussion regarding the risks of prone positioning from the discussion of the management of excited delirium [and] should reinforce current understanding and knowledge regarding the risks of prone positioning.

2. Consider equipping all primary response vehicles and supervisor vehicles with automated external defibrillators (AEDs) and bag-valve-mask ventilation devices, and training road officers in their use.

3. Implement mandatory advanced first aid training every two years.

...

TO THE ONTARIO POLICE COLLEGE

1. Training of all police officers in use of force should include best practices for apprehension techniques in confrontations involving two police officers vs. one subject.

2. Training should include apprehension techniques that do not involve placing the subject on his or her stomach when the subject is exerted.

3. Implement simulation training for all new recruits that incorporates positional asphyxia.

TO THE SPECIAL INVESTIGATIONS UNIT

1. The SIU should ensure that subject officers are interviewed within 48 hours of an incident.

is qualified to *certify* death, such legislation, at least in Ontario, does not specify who can *pronounce*—or officially declare—a death.

Typically, a physician has the authority to certify death by signing the medical certificate of death, though in some cases a registered nurse may have this authority. The only person who typically has the authority to pronounce a death is a qualified medical practitioner. There are exceptions, however, which allow other professionals—for example, police, nurses, and paramedics—to do so in certain circumstances. These are set out in the procedures of individual police services, and officers should ensure that they are familiar with them.

In the field, police officers may *assume* that someone is dead where a person has been pronounced dead by a hospital physician in consultation with a paramedic at the scene. Police may *pronounce* that a person is, in fact, dead where the person is "obviously dead." In Ontario, the term "obviously dead" means that any of the following "gross signs of death" are apparent (Ontario, Ministry of Health, 2010, p. 11):

- decapitation,
- transection,
- visible decomposition,
- putrefaction,
- gross rigor mortis,
- gross outpouring of cranial or visceral contents, or
- a grossly charred body.

When police assume that someone is dead in circumstances other than those noted in the list above but the person is still alive, this may result in the person failing to receive timely medical attention, and also in a loss of public confidence in the professional capabilities of the police.

When police are notified or become aware of a death that has occurred in any of the circumstances set out in s. 10 of the Ontario *Coroners Act*, they must immediately notify the coroner and describe the circumstances. Where the police will need to conduct a criminal investigation—for example, where a death is either obviously the result of violence or negligence or where police suspect that such factors led to the person's death—they must secure the scene and leave the body

DEAD OR ALIVE?

Although it may be difficult to imagine a situation in which police might mistake a live person for a dead one, such errors do occur. In one such case, police arrived at a motel room to discover a woman who appeared to be dead, in circumstances that strongly suggested foul play. The responding officers immediately sealed off the scene denying access to everyone, including paramedics, and a criminal investigation was commenced. However, a few hours later, a forensics officer who had been documenting the condition of the victim with a video-camera noticed her twitch. Paramedics were called back to the scene and determined that the apparent homicide victim was, in fact, alive. The victim was subsequently transported to hospital, where she was treated and released a short time later. An internal investigation of the matter was subsequently conducted by police, who determined that their policies regarding when officers may pronounce death were not followed. The chief of the police service involved characterized the event as "an eye-opening experience" that presented "an excellent learning opportunity" (*Guelph Mercury*, March 4, 2011).

In other examples, police appear to have been overly cautious when pronouncing death. In one case in the United Kingdom, police called the medical examiner to pronounce the death of a headless, decomposed corpse found floating in a river (*London Evening Standard*, April 26, 2011).

where it was found. They must then await the arrival of the coroner before proceeding with their investigation of the scene.

Once the coroner arrives, he or she will examine the body and the circumstances in which it was found, speak to police about any information they may have regarding the death, and issue a coroner's warrant authorizing the body to be removed. Also, if the coroner determines that an autopsy is necessary, which will always be the case where the police intend to carry out an investigation, the coroner will issue a warrant to a forensic pathologist authorizing a post-mortem examination of the body.

When a body is removed from a crime scene, it is typically placed inside a body bag. To ensure continuity, a police seal is affixed over the zipper and a police officer is assigned to accompany the body to the morgue. In the case of a police investigation where a victim is transported to hospital by ambulance, a police officer typically accompanies the victim to the hospital, either in the ambulance or by police vehicle. If a victim dies in hospital, a similar process takes place to that described above— that is, the coroner is notified and attends the hospital, after which the deceased's body is transported to the morgue, accompanied by police. Police confirm with the morgue personnel that the body that has arrived at their facility is the same body that was removed from a particular scene. They then work with the personnel at the coroner's office to arrange to have someone come to the morgue to identify the deceased person, which must typically be done before an autopsy is conducted.

In cases of sudden or unexpected death—for example, where foul play is obvious or suspected, in traffic fatalities, or in suspicious deaths—it is customary for police investigators to attend the post-mortem examination to

- provide information regarding the circumstances of the death to the forensic pathologist;
- witness and make notes of the injuries sustained by the victim;
- obtain a cause of death from the forensic pathologist, who may be able to offer a definitive cause at the conclusion of the post mortem—for example, massive cerebral hemorrhage caused by a gunshot wound to the head—or may advise that an official cause of death will have to wait until further testing has been completed—for example, toxicological or neuropathological testing; and
- gather evidence from the body and to photograph the autopsy process, which is handled by the identification officer.

If efforts to identify the body are unsuccessful, the identification officer may take fingerprints in an attempt to identify the person through police fingerprint records.

THE FIVE QUESTIONS IN A DEATH INVESTIGATION

The role of coroners and medical examiners in investigating deaths is not to determine legal responsibility. Rather, they seek to answer five main questions:

1. Who died? (identification)
2. How did the deceased die? (the medical cause of death—for example, by asphyxiation due to strangulation by a rope)

3. When did he or she die? (the date of death)

4. Where did the deceased die?

5. By what means did the deceased die? (the category of death—for example, by homicide, suicide, or accident)

The following sections explore how answers to each of these questions are uncovered.

Who Died?

When investigating a death, a great deal of forensic evidence may be present. The successful collection of this evidence, together with its analysis, can be extremely valuable in determining whether or not a death was the result of a criminal act. If it appears that it was, forensic evidence can help police apprehend the perpetrator of the crime.

Although it is always important to identify the deceased, in a homicide it is essential. Unless the killing was a "smoking gun" case—that is, where the perpetrator is found with the victim with the gun (or other weapon) still in his or her hands and ready to give a confession—if you can't identify the victim, you have almost no chance of identifying the killer.

Much of forensic science is based on matching a piece of evidence—for example, a fibre or hair—with a known sample. When the victim is identified, samples can be taken from the victim's residence, clothes, and known associates in order to eliminate suspects and narrow the search for the murderer. Many people are killed by people they know, and, when the victim has been identified, investigators can attempt to determine such things as who they were last seen with, where they were going, whether they had any problems with anyone, whether they had reported to friends that they felt as if they were being followed, whether they normally carried large quantities of cash or drugs on their person, and any other factors that might help to determine their movements just prior to death.

There are two levels of identification. In a tentative identification, investigators believe that the deceased is a certain person, but are not yet positive. In a positive identification, investigators are certain of the identity of the victim.

Tentative Identification

A tentative identification tells the police investigators who the decedent—that is, the deceased person—*might* be and allows them to then use positive identification methods to confirm this. These methods are discussed in the next section.

There are two main ways to develop a tentative identification: (1) by using information found at the death scene or on the victim, and (2) by using information from the physical body itself—for example, by developing a biological profile of the victim to compare with missing persons in the Canadian Police Information Centre (CPIC).

FROM EVIDENCE ON THE VICTIM OR AT THE SCENE

In a natural death, when a person is found, for example, dead in a hotel bed, unless he or she registered using a false ID, the deceased is probably the person registered at the hotel. In a car accident, unless the driver's licence and car were stolen, the driver's licence and the vehicle registration will most likely identify the victim. However, as far-fetched as they seem, cases of mistaken identity happen. In a plane crash in the United States, a man was identified on the basis of the driver's licence in his wallet. His face was undamaged and the picture on the licence looked just like him. This was considered a good enough identification, and the remains were released to his family, who buried him. Shortly afterward, the identified man turned up alive and well. The deceased was his younger brother who had lost his driver's licence and had borrowed his brother's to travel.

In a homicide, it is even more likely that evidence at a scene may have been stolen, planted, or in some way manipulated or tampered with. Thus, although evidence found at the scene is valuable for giving investigators a first step toward identifying the victim, such evidence must be confirmed by using a positive method of identification.

FROM THE REMAINS

When an intact and undamaged body is found without any associated information, the police may be able to get a tentative identification by matching the victim to a reported missing person with a simple physical description. It may be possible to visually assess that the victim is a male Asian in his mid-twenties, 180 cm tall, of slight build, with long black hair and no facial hair. This description can be entered on CPIC to discover whether there are any matches and, if not, can be released to the public to see whether anyone comes forward with information. In some countries it is common for photographs of the dead to be shown to the public on television and in newspapers to assist in identification. In North America, a police artist may be asked to make a drawing of the person for release. If the deceased has injuries in the facial region or the body has begun to decompose, a good artist can account for these changes and still make a reasonable drawing of the person as they would have looked in life.

Today, such drawings can be made electronically, but these are often not as successful as a simple sketch. When people see an image that looks like a photograph, they believe it to be an exact image and, if it does not look exactly like their relative or friend, they will say that it is not him or her. However, people looking at a simple sketch are more inclined to think, "Well, yes, it does look a bit like him; the expression is wrong, but, yes, it could be," and come forward. For this reason, although computerized drawings are still used, police tend to generate a sketch as opposed to a more realistic looking image.

When human remains are found highly decomposed or skeletal, investigators typically call in a **forensic anthropologist** to assist. A forensic anthropologist is usually an external consultant to the police. Forensic anthropologists need a minimum of a master's degree in physical anthropology, but typically have a Ph.D. Most have academic positions at universities or museums and act as consultants to the police when needed.

Forensic anthropologists help the coroner and police to recover the remains, if skeletal, and then analyze the bones to develop a biological profile of the decedent (described below). In many cases, the skeleton is not complete, with tissue and bones often removed by scavengers such as bears, coyotes, dogs, rodents, and birds. Most people are unable to recognize individual bones as bones, let alone as human

forensic anthropologist
an expert who specializes in human identification using the human skeleton in a medico-legal context

bones, when the skeleton is disarticulated, so it is extremely valuable to invite a forensic anthropologist to attend the crime scene to lend his or her expertise to the recovery and *in situ* examination of the body.

Forensic anthropologists also understand the **taphonomy** of the death. Taphonomy includes decomposition, interaction with the environment (for example, meteorological conditions, soil type, and elevation of the grave), and the effects of insects and vertebrate scavengers. Taphonomy is particularly important in outdoor scenes.

In some cases, investigators may request a facial reconstruction, which is usually performed by forensic artists or forensic anthropologists with specialized training. Several techniques are involved in such a reconstruction, the most common of which entails placing clay markers on prominent bony ridges of the skull to approximate skin thickness. The size of each marker is exact and based on normative standards of tissue depths, sex, and ancestry. A person's face is unique, primarily because of the underlying bone structure. Skin thickness, however, is fairly uniform, so when wax is used to link the clay markers and molded to the skull, the unique features of the skull should become apparent. A photograph of the clay face will then be released to the media. It can be augmented by any known features about the skull, such as the teeth or length and colour of hair. A photograph of the reconstruction is then publicized with the hope that someone will recognize the person.

Building a Biological Profile

In building a biological profile, a forensic anthropologist will attempt to estimate the decedent's sex, age, ancestry, and stature.

1. *Sex.* Sex is an important criterion to determine, because it is an *absolute*, as opposed to a *graded* factor (for example, height or weight, where a range must be given). It also eliminates many potential missing people.

    It is easier to determine sex in an adult than in an immature person, because sex is not expressed in the skeleton until puberty. Most of the differences we see between the skeletons of men and women relate to sexual maturity. In an adult, the forensic anthropologist can determine biological sex from a number of bones, including the pelvis and the skull. An adult female's pelvis is designed for childbirth, which makes it different from that of an adult male. In addition, scarring on the pubic bone can indicate whether a woman has given birth naturally. With respect to the skulls of males and females, there are differences in the shape of many bones, including those of the orbits and forehead (Bass, 1987).

2. *Age.* Age is always given as a range, rather than as an absolute. Several features are important in estimating age, including tooth and bone formation, as well as skeletal changes resulting from wear and tear, degeneration, and disease.

    In children, tooth formation and skeletal ossification are valuable as markers of age. Teeth begin to form in a baby several months before it is born, and tooth formation and eruption continues into adolescence. Dental eruption and formation charts can be helpful in estimating the age of a child, even though only a range can be given—for example, "5 to 6 years

taphonomy
the study of everything that happens to a body from the moment of death to the time the body is discovered

old." Until a person reaches their mid-20s, bones are still undergoing a process of gradually fusing together. Because the bones complete this process at different times, forensic anthropologists can use the levels of fusion to give an age range for a skeleton. However, this is fraught with variables because timing varies with many factors—for example, sex, different populations, and level of nutrition (Sorg, 2005).

It is much harder to estimate an adult's age, because dramatic changes are no longer occurring in the skeleton. However, certain markers can give some indication of age. These include bone density (our bone density decreases as we age, which in extreme cases leads to osteoporosis); suture lines in the skull (these are apparent in youth, but close up over time); and skeletal wear and tear and arthritis (both of which appear over the course of a person's life). Such changes are used to give a relative age for a person, but this is often expressed as a large range—for example, 45 to 55 years old. In addition, just as someone can appear younger or older in life than they actually are, so too a person's skeleton can suggest that he or she is younger or older than that person's chronological age. For example, someone who has worked physically very hard since childhood is likely to have a skeleton that shows more wear and tear and arthritic and degenerative changes than someone of the same age who has led a much more sedentary life.

3. *Ancestry.* Ancestry, commonly referred to as "race," is a broad term that is usually divided into three major groups: Caucasoid (European descent), Negroid (African descent), and Mongoloid (Asian descent). These 19th-century terms, associated with outdated notions of racial types, are now considered offensive, but may be of value forensically. In addition to differences *within* the three groups, broad differences exist *between* them. These can be identified on the skeleton—primarily, the skull—and include the shape of the forehead, the width of the nasal opening, the prominence of the nasal bone, and the width of the face (Bass, 1987).

   Many people are of mixed ancestry but may only have identified with a single ancestry in their life; others may have been unaware of a mixed ancestry. For this reason, although friends and family may describe a person in terms of a particular ancestry, the bones—and thus the biological profile—may indicate something different.

4. *Stature.* In general, a person's body is in proportion—that is, tall people have longer legs and arms than short people. Stature or height estimates are based on the relationship between the length of one of the long bones and the rest of the skeleton; the long bone is measured and then compared with a set of normative standards to determine the original stature of the victim. For example, if the femur, or thigh bone, is X cm long, the stature of the person is Y. These standards are based on many skeletal measurements taken from a known population—that is, the femur or thigh bone has been measured in a large number of people of a particular sex and ancestry whose stature is known to generate normative standards for that ancestry and sex. Problems occur when normative standards are not available for the population to which the victim belonged.

Stature, even in adults, is not static, because people tend to shrink as they age, and a small shrinkage occurs from morning to night. Also, records of stature—for example, those on a driver's licence—are often not accurately reported. Many people exaggerate their height on official records, which are rarely checked (Sorg, 2005).

The forensic anthropologist will develop a biological profile based on the bones recovered and will add any unusual features, such as healed fractures, injuries, or birth defects. For example, the anthropologist may report that the victim was a Caucasian female, approximately 25 to 35 years old, approximately 160 to 170 cm tall, with a broken right arm that healed in childhood. This profile is then entered on CPIC for possible matches. With luck, it will generate a single profile, giving a tentative identification. However, this ID must still be confirmed using a positive method, because many women might fit that biological profile.

Positive Identification

Once investigators have a tentative identification, they will follow up with one of several methods for positively identifying a person. A positive identification is *individualizing*—that is, it states that someone is a specific person who could not possibly be anyone else. Most methods of positive identification require a pre-mortem record—that is, a record made in life, such as fingerprint or dental records. The following methods of positive identification are listed in order of how easy they are to obtain and analyze.

VISUAL IDENTIFICATION

Surprisingly, the most common method of positively identifying a person is the simplest and least scientific, and the one most often portrayed on television—that is, a simple visual identification. This method relies on someone's visual memory and is only possible when the remains are fresh and the face relatively undamaged. Once a tentative identification has been made, the police will contact family members or close friends and ask them to come to the morgue to identify the deceased.

FINGERPRINTS

Fingerprints can be an excellent means of positive identification, as they do not change over a person's life except to grow, and are even distinct in the case of identical twins. However, fingerprints are only of value if they are on record, which limits their value to people with criminal records or those belonging to certain professions.

If a tentatively identified victim has no pre-mortem record, it may be possible to collect latent prints from his or her home, as described in Chapter 8, Pattern Evidence and Collision Reconstruction. The best fingerprints for a positive identification would come from such personal items as a toothbrush or hair brush, something that only the owner was likely to have touched. However, this is not an easy method of obtaining an identification, because most personal items do not easily pick up a print.

Even when a body is decomposed, it might still be possible to obtain fingerprints. In decomposition, initially, the skin wrinkles and shrinks. In such cases, the fingers can be chemically rehydrated and then fingerprinted. As decomposition progresses, the skin of the hand slips or is sloughed off in layers, much like a glove, with the fingerprints still on the skin. Prints are also on the lower layer of skin, which is still on the hand, although not as deep or clear. The best fingerprints come from the outermost layer of skin. In such a situation, a police officer—typically, the identification officer—would put on a latex glove, then put the human "glove" on his or her hand to obtain a print.

DENTAL RECORDS

Even though we all begin life with the same number and type of teeth, forensic dentists consider each human mouth to be unique. Each of us has slight differences in the shape of our teeth, the position of the roots, the teeth's rotation, and their history—for example, fillings, extractions, and wear and tear. All of these contribute to dental individuality, a fact that has been recognized for hundreds of years. In the past, many people could not write their name, but they still needed to sign contracts. In such cases, people might make their mark by biting the paper or sealing wax on the document to leave the impression of their teeth, their unique mark. In fact, this is where the terms "indenture" and "indentured servant" come from.

When a person goes to a dentist, the dentist indicates on a chart where, for example, there are fillings, what type of filling, how much of the tooth is filled, the material used, any missing teeth, bridges, and crowns. Dentists indicate cavities and areas where work will be required, and technicians take X-rays. These charts and X-rays are excellent tools for positive identification; however, no centralized database of all dental records exists. Therefore, investigators need a tentative identification to determine who the decedent consulted as a dentist. Once they have identified the dentist and retrieved the decedent's dental records, a forensic dentist can compare the dentition of the victim at the morgue with that of the pre-mortem dental records. It's possible that differences exist between the decedent's dentition and that of their most recent records—for example, they may have developed more caries, lost a tooth, or had dental work done elsewhere since the last visit to their regular dentist. However, if the pre-mortem records show, for example, a lost tooth that is present in the decedent's dentition, this is obviously not a match because adults do not grow more teeth.

When someone is reported missing, his or her dental records, together with other information, will have been collected and entered on CPIC. When an unknown body is found, the forensic dentist will chart and X-ray the decedent and this information will be entered on CPIC to search for a match. Enamel is much harder than bone, so teeth preserve well. Teeth are often found many years after death, and are thus tremendously valuable in a death investigation.

MEDICAL RECORDS: X-RAYS AND CLINICAL REPORTS

Medical records should be able to confirm any healed injuries to the skeleton shown in the biological profile of the decedent, as X-rays should be on record for the original trauma and the site can be compared with the healed fracture in the decedent.

Such X-rays may also reflect arthritic changes or other degeneration, which can also be compared. The decedent may also have implanted medical devices—for example, a pace maker or artificial joint. Such devices have serial numbers that link the device to the manufacturer, the hospital, the surgeon, and the patient, and are thus helpful.

Facial X-rays are rare, but if they exist they are useful because they show the sinuses. The shape of the sinuses is unique, so sinuses can be compared with post-mortem X-rays. Written medical records may also be helpful, documenting surgeries that might account for scars, any medical conditions, or injuries that may not have been X-rayed. Of course, medical information is of value only if it is on record and can be obtained.

IDENTIFICATION IN PRACTICE

The cases below illustrate the uses of the positive identification techniques discussed in this chapter.

Case 1: The skeletonized remains of a young male were recovered. Although the hands were mostly skeletonized, one finger had been protected by its position and investigators obtained a usable fingerprint. The print was run through the fingerprint databases, but no match was found and it was assumed that the decedent did not have a criminal record. A photograph of a facial reconstruction was subsequently printed in newspapers. Because the man's dentition was distinctive, he was shown smiling to reveal his teeth, and almost immediately his parole officer identified him; he did have a criminal record. However, when his fingerprints had been taken, that particular finger had been slightly smudged and thus was not considered a match. Once the man was tentatively identified, he was positively identified on the basis of his dental records.

Case 2: A man was murdered in Australia. To dispose of the body, the killers cut up his remains and threw them into the ocean. One of the man's hands was eaten by a small shark, which was in turn eaten by a larger shark. Unfortunately for the killers, the larger shark was caught in a trawler's net by a fisherman. The shark was recognized as a fairly unusual specimen, and so was donated to the local aquarium where it was put on display. For three weeks, it swam around in a somewhat sickly manner, then vomited up a human hand. The shark had been in shock after capture, so his digestion had slowed; when it resumed, the shark digested the small shark but not the hand. The hand, which was in excellent condition, was fingerprinted and the victim identified.

Case 3: Well-known forensic anthropologist Dr. Bill Haglund was investigating a mass grave when he recovered a skeleton with an extremely unusual repair of a fractured femur. The jagged ends of the fracture were not in alignment, but had been placed side by side and the two broken pieces bound together with what appeared to be wire used to make fences. Amazingly, the leg had healed and the bone had knitted somewhat with the wire. In life, this person must have had a severe scar, one leg considerably shorter than the other, and a decided limp. Such an injury and repair are unique and individualizing, but because no pre-mortem record was available, this person remains unidentified.

DNA

DNA contains the genetic material that is the blueprint of life. It is considered the gold standard for positive identification because, except in identical twins, it is unique to an individual. Nonetheless, analyzing a DNA sample takes a few days, so more immediate methods—for example, comparing dentition or fingerprints with known records—are often used first.

DNA is discussed in detail in the next chapter, Chapter 12, Forensic Biology and DNA.

CIRCUMSTANTIAL EVIDENCE

In rare circumstances, where the above methods are not available, a person may be identified by circumstantial evidence. In some situations, this may be valid. If an elderly woman is found dead in bed in an apartment, and is biologically identified as a female Caucasian between the ages of 75 and 90 years old and 140 to 150 cm tall, and the person who rents the apartment is a woman who fits the description and was known to have a heart condition, then that identification is probably valid. However, it would not be acceptable in a homicide.

Once a victim has been positively identified, investigators will use this information to learn about the victim's life, plot his or her timeline before death, and talk to people linked to the victim.

How Did They Die?

This question, which relates to the medical cause of death, is determined by a forensic pathologist. Forensic pathologists are medical doctors who have specialized in pathology, then further specialized in **forensic pathology**. Forensic pathologists perform autopsies to determine cause, mechanism (mode of death), and manner of death. They also have expertise in injury interpretation so can help the investigator understand what type of weapon was used and, perhaps just as useful, what type of weapon was *not* used. For example, they may be able to determine the size of the knife blade used, whether it had one edge or two, and whether it was serrated. They may be able to tell whether a person in a motor vehicle accident was the driver or a passenger at the time of impact, whether the decedent had a preexisting medical condition that could have caused or contributed to his or her death, whether certain injuries were survivable for a period of time, and many other factors relating to the death. The forensic pathologist will also consider the history of the victim, including medical records, police records, lifestyle, information from family members, as well as any scene information that the police, coroner, or medical examiner collected.

The autopsy, or post mortem, includes an examination of the clothing the victim was wearing; an external examination of the remains, which might reveal injuries, scars, tattoos, or needle marks; and an internal examination of the entire body, including organs, any injuries, or diseases. A full autopsy includes photographs, X-rays, swabs for DNA, toxicological samples, and possible cultures. In a murder investigation, the autopsy is usually attended by the coroner or medical examiner as well as the investigating police officers.

forensic pathology
the application of pathology in law through autopsies to determine manner and cause of death

The autopsy will determine the *medical cause* of death and the *mechanism* of death. If a person was shot and bled to death, the cause of death will be exsanguination, or bleeding out, and the mechanism will be gunshot wound and bullet.

Forensic pathologists often testify in court as expert witnesses.

When Did They Die?

One of the most important questions in a death investigation concerns time of death. This provides police with a time frame and allows them to investigate the timeline prior to death. In all deaths, family members want to know "when," but this is of paramount importance in a homicide. Knowing *when* death took place can make or break an alibi. For example, if a man reports finding his wife dead upon his return from work, the first question the investigators are going to want answered is whether she died before or after her husband left for work.

It is always assumed that a forensic pathologist or other specialist can determine an *exact* time of death, but this is not true. Unless a death is witnessed by a trained observer—for example, a police officer or a medical person—all given times of death are estimates. Time of death is usually given as a range, which can be a short range when a victim is fresh—for example, four to six hours—or a much longer range in an older body—for example, eight to twelve months.

Estimating time of death can be broken into two major time frames: (1) the early post-mortem interval in the first 24 to 48 hours, and (2) the later post-mortem interval.

Estimating Elapsed Time Since Death in the Early Post-Mortem Interval (24 to 48 Hours After Death)

Several medical and biological changes take place in the body in the first day or two after death, which a forensic pathologist can assess to estimate an elapsed time since death. These include algor mortis; rigor mortis; livor mortis; eye or ocular changes; and, in some cases, digestion. A forensic pathologist must first assess as many of the above as possible before he or she can comment about time of death. In many cases, so many variables affect these estimates that time of death is presented as a guide only.

1. *Algor mortis.* Algor mortis (Latin, meaning "coldness of death") is the cooling of the body after death. Humans are mammals, which means that they maintain an optimum, precise body temperature. When a person dies, the body's temperature begins to drop to the temperature in the surrounding environment, known as the ambient temperature. This drop occurs at a predictable, documented rate. If the body temperature is taken when the remains are discovered, it can be compared against a chart indicating the drop in temperature over time. All people have a relatively consistent, normal body temperature, so if the temperature of the body is, for example, 5°C below normal, and the average drop in body temperature is known, the time of death can be estimated. This technique is of value only until the body has cooled to the temperature in the surrounding environment. It is also affected by many variables, such as the size of the body and whether the person had a fever or had been drinking or fighting just before death.

2. *Rigor mortis.* Rigor mortis (Latin, meaning "stiffness of death") is the stiffening of the body that occurs after death as chemical changes take place in the muscles. These chemical changes occur at a predictable rate, and can thus serve as a guide to time of death. The effects of rigor are first visible in the small muscles, so time of death is estimated based on the timing and amount of rigor seen in various muscle types. In most cases, rigor can start to be seen a few hours after death, with full rigidity occurring approximately 6 to 12 hours after death, and passing about 24 to 50 hours after death. The formation of rigor is affected by many variables—for example, ambient temperature; amount of muscle mass (very young or very old people have very little muscle mass); type of muscle; presence of certain drugs such as cocaine; and whether the person was exerting himself or herself before death, which will increase internal temperature and affect the chemical content of the muscles, speeding up the formation of rigor.

   Cadaveric spasm is a rare condition that results in a false rigor that gives the appearance of an instant rigor at the moment of death. It only occurs when the individual is extremely stressed at the point of death. Cadaveric spasm is most commonly seen in war casualties or drowning deaths. It may also occur when someone shoots himself (the hand may be found tightly clutching the gun, with the trigger finger locked in an apparent rigor on the trigger despite the fact that witnesses heard the shot just seconds before), and in the presence of certain drugs, including an overdose of Aspirin. It is not true rigor because the normal chemical changes have not had time to take place. Its origin is still unknown, but its presence can be misleading if not understood.

3. *Livor mortis.* Livor mortis (Latin, meaning "bluish colour of death") is the coloration seen in certain areas of the body a few hours after death. After death, because of gravity, blood sinks to the lowest parts of the body and, after a few hours, it "sets." These areas demonstrate "lividity," appearing dark red or puce coloured, while the areas that are supporting weight remain white or blanched. For example, if a person is found dead and lying on their back, their weight is borne on the backs of the shoulders and buttocks as well as the backs of the legs and head. Therefore, lividity will appear on every back area except these pressure points, which remain white. Whether lividity has started to form, is still movable if pressed, or has set can all be used as indicators of how much time has elapsed since death. As well, the marks of lividity can indicate the position the body was in during the hours after death and can thus show whether a body has been moved after death.

4. *Eye changes.* In most deaths, the human eye does not close. In the hours after death, as the cornea becomes dry, a thin film forms, making the eyes look cloudy. If the eyes are closed at death, this can take up to 24 hours. This film can give an indication of elapsed time since death.

   As well, the eye is considered to be sealed from the rest of the body; although many changes take place in the body as it decomposes, the eye is less affected. This is one of the reasons that the eye is considered an excellent organ for toxicological analysis.

5. *Digestion.* In some cases, the rate of digestion of the stomach contents can be used to give a broad approximation of the time of death. The rate of digestion of different foodstuffs is known, so, hypothetically, if the time and contents of the last meal are known, the amount of food that has been digested can provide an idea of how long after the meal the person died. This method is, however, loaded with variables, many of which are unknown. These include whether the person exerted himself or herself (either by exercise or by resistance, which halts digestion), the person's age, and the presence of alcohol. At best, digestion gives only a very broad range (see the box about Steven Truscott, below).

Estimating Elapsed Time Since Death in the Later Post-Mortem Interval (More Than 48 Hours After Death)

As the body begins to decompose, other medical and biological parameters can be assessed. These include the autocatalysis or autolysis of the body, caused by the body's natural enzymes breaking down its tissue, and putrefaction, the breakdown of the body by naturally occurring bacteria. As gases are released from bacterial

---

STEVEN TRUSCOTT CASE

In 1959, in Ontario, 14-year-old Steven Truscott was charged, tried, convicted, and sentenced to death by hanging for the murder of his 12-year-old schoolmate Lynne Harper. His conviction was based almost entirely on the time of death provided by the pathologist who examined Lynne Harper's body. The pathologist based his testimony on the level of digestion of the food found in Lynne Harper's stomach. The pathologist's testimony put her time of death to within a 30-minute period during which Truscott was seen giving her a ride on his bicycle. This was the only time frame, in the almost two days before her body was found, for which Truscott had no alibi. Although several pathologists testified that examining digestive contents of the stomach for level of digestion was not an exact science and could not predict such a specific time frame, the court believed the original pathologist and Truscott was sentenced to die. A re-examination of the case in the 1960s upheld the original verdict. Truscott's sentence was eventually commuted to life, and he served ten years before being released into the community, where he has lived an exemplary life. This case was in no small part responsible for the elimination of the death penalty in Canada because the public was horrified that a young boy very nearly lost his life to hanging.

In the early 2000s, interest in the Truscott case was revived by a CBC television program and a subsequent book that suggested that significant evidence had been ignored or not allowed in testimony at the original trials. In 2006, Truscott's conviction was brought before the Court of Appeal for Ontario, where a forensic pathologist reiterated that, even today, we cannot use digestion to give such a precise time of death and, given the many variables involved, it should not have been used at all. Forensic entomology was actually able to show that death could have occurred any time up until the next morning, including many more potential suspects. In 2007, Steven Truscott was acquitted of all charges and received an apology on behalf of the provincial government for this terrible miscarriage of justice.

decomposition, the body bloats and, as the degraded blood seeps out of blood vessels, marbling becomes visible. Skin begins to slough and blister and, as the bloat collapses, gases are released. As time passes, the entire body breaks down. Although a specific time of death cannot be given on the basis of decomposition alone, a forensic pathologist might be able to give an indication of time of death in general terms.

In very dry environments, the body or extremities may mummify; natural mummies from hundreds of years ago have been found in very dry environments. In warm, wet, anaerobic situations, the tissues *saponify*—literally, turn to soap, as adipose (fatty) tissue turns into adipocere (waxy) tissue. Both mummification and saponification may preserve a body well for long periods of time.

USE OF INSECTS

In the later post-mortem stage, a much more accurate estimate of time of death can often be derived from the insects that feed on the remains or from plant material growing on and through the remains. Entomology is the study of insects. Forensic or medico-legal entomology is the study of the insects associated with a dead body, primarily to estimate a minimum time since death but also to determine things such as whether the body was moved or disturbed after death, the position or presence of wounds, and whether the victim used drugs. A forensic entomologist typically has a B.Sc. in biology and an M.Sc. in entomology, and usually a Ph.D. in entomology. Most forensic entomologists work as university professors or at natural history museums.

Insects are attracted to a dead body, whether human or animal, within minutes of death. They are used in two main ways to estimate elapsed time since death:

1. Up to 30 days after death, depending on the area, maggot age and development are analyzed.

2. Up to a year or more after death, the presence of other insects is analyzed.

Maggots are the larvae or immature stages of Diptera, or two-winged flies. These include blow flies, the big metallic flies we see near food in summer. They are immediately attracted after death to a wound site or the natural orifices. This is why insects can sometimes be used to indicate wound pattern—they are primarily attracted to wounds, and colonization patterns can often still be seen when decomposition has obscured a wound.

Blow flies lay eggs on the remains, which hatch into maggots and develop in a predictable manner, depending primarily on temperature and species. As temperature increases, they develop faster, and as it decreases, they develop more slowly; this relationship is relatively linear. Consequently, the age of the insects and, therefore, their tenure on the remains can be determined by a careful analysis of the insect species, insect stage, ambient temperature records, and known developmental rates. If the oldest insects on the body are determined to be, for example, seven days old, then the victim has been dead for at least seven days.

As an illustration of this method of determining time since death, in central Canada, the remains of a young girl were found on the 17th of the month. She had suffered head trauma and early third instar—that is, third-stage larvae—were found in the wounds. The insects were a common rural blow fly or green bottle fly, *Lucilia illustris*

(Meigen, 1826). The local weather station showed that temperatures over the previous few days ranged from 17°C to 22°C (Anderson & Cervenka, 2001). A portable data-logger was placed at the crime scene to determine whether the weather station was a reliable indicator of the temperature there. Regression analysis showed that there was a good correlation between the weather station and the crime scene and that the scene was slightly warmer than the weather station. The temperature data, the species of insect, the stage of insect, and known developmental data for that species were used to indicate that the insects had colonized the remains no later than noon on the 14th of the month, and the eggs could have been laid earlier. Blow flies do not normally lay eggs at night (Baldridge, Wallace, & Kirkpatrick, 2006), so it is possible that the victim died during the night of the 13th, but must have been dead before noon on the 14th. The victim was last seen alive on the 13th (Anderson & Cervenka, 2001).

The second method used to estimate time since death is based on the fact that as the body decomposes, it goes through many chemical, physical, and biological changes, and each change attracts different groups of insects. For example, a fresh body attracts blow flies, but a body dead for a few weeks starts to attract other species of flies and beetles. As decomposition proceeds, these species lose interest in the remains, and other species arrive. The sequence of insects that colonize the remains differs by geographical region, habitat, and season, and depends on whether the body is exposed to the sun or is in the shade, and on whether it is buried or not, but within these parameters is predictable. Scientists can estimate, therefore, that a victim has been dead, for instance, for at least 75 days, based on the species present.

USE OF PLANTS

Long after a person has died, a forensic botanist may be able to use plants at the crime scene to estimate the number of years that a person has been dead. For example, an analysis of the layers of leaf litter covering the remains can indicate the probable year of death, and any woody plant material that has grown through the skeleton can be aged by tree rings.

Forensic botanists can also use pollen to determine the season of death. Pollen is released by plants when they flower, and we inhale it when we breathe. Different species of plants release pollen in different months, and pollen counts are taken regularly; this information is available in the form of pollen charts, which can be compared with the levels and types of pollen found in the nasal cavities of human remains.

In 1994 the skeletal remains of 32 men were found in a clandestine grave in an area of Germany controlled by the Gestapo until 1945, when it was taken over by Soviet troops. It was thought that the victims were either anti-Nazi agents, murdered by the Gestapo in the spring of 1945 at the end of the Second World War, or Soviet soldiers, killed by the Soviet secret police in the summer of 1953, allegedly, for refusing to assist in stopping the revolt by the German Democratic Republic (Szibor et al., 1998). Forensic botanists collected pollen, which the deceased would have breathed in just prior to death, from the nasal cavities of 21 of the skulls and compared the samples with pollen charts for that region. The types of pollen and their relative amounts matched pollen charts for the summer, not the spring—indicating that the decedents were probably Soviets killed by the Soviet secret police in the summer of 1953 (Szibor et al., 1998).

Where Did They Die?

In natural deaths, in most accidents, and in suicides, the body is typically found where the person died. In a homicide, however, the body is often removed from the original scene and dumped at another site in an effort to hide the death and confuse the police. When remains are found in the bush, for example, it is probable that death did not occur there and that a primary crime scene exists somewhere else. Investigators hope that an identification of the victim will help lead them to the original crime scene, which probably contains more evidence.

The fact that a body has been dumped does not necessarily indicate a homicide. It is not uncommon for a person who has died of an overdose of drugs to be removed from the death scene and dumped elsewhere by "friends" to disguise the death and the use of drugs. In one case, a wrapped body was found at the bottom of an embankment. It was assumed to be a homicide, but autopsy and pathology findings showed that death was a result of a drug overdose. It turned out that the victim had been partying with friends in a hotel, and overdosed. The friends did not want to spoil the party, so they wrapped the body and placed the deceased in a closet. After a few days of continued partying, the friends noticed an odour, so took the body to a rural area and dumped it. The crime was tampering with a dead body.

By What Means Did They Die?

The final part of a death investigation is determining the classification or *manner* of death. There are five classifications:

1. **Homicide** is the death of one person at the hands of another person. It is the result of the *intentional* infliction of injury on another person in order to cause death, and it includes first- and second-degree murder and manslaughter. Homicide charges typically imply intent, but the term is considered neutral in the coroner system, which does not determine blame. This is the role of the court.

   homicide
   death, directly or indirectly, of one person at the hands of another

2. **Suicide** is the *intentional* taking of one's own life. Some deaths that initially look like suicide turn out to have been accidental. For example, in autoerotic deaths, people who intend to partially asphyxiate themselves to achieve sexual gratification may end up accidentally strangling themselves. This is an accident, because there was no intent to commit suicide.

   suicide
   the intentional taking of one's own life

3. An **accidental death** is caused by unexpected or unintentional injury. It includes deaths that are a result of earlier injuries—for example, a death following injuries received in a car accident. Accidental deaths include drug overdoses, motor vehicle crashes, falls, and anything that might relate to these—for example, pneumonia in an elderly person secondary to a fall.

   accidental death
   death caused by unexpected or unintentional injury

4. A **natural death** is caused by a disease and is not a result of an injury or any abnormal environmental factors. Most deaths are natural, but if a person has not recently seen a doctor and is not known to have had a life-threatening condition, it is necessary to conduct an investigation, which typically includes an autopsy, to determine whether the death was natural.

   natural death
   caused by disease and not attributable to injury or abnormal environmental factors

5. A death is classified as **undetermined** when there is no obvious reason why the person should not still be alive and there is not enough evidence to list

   undetermined death
   death that cannot be determined to be natural, accidental, suicide, or homicide

the death as homicide, suicide, accident, or natural. It is most often the outcome when highly decomposed or skeletal remains are discovered, but it may occur when a young, seemingly healthy person dies from no apparent cause. It is arguably the most difficult of all classifications for a family to come to terms with, and, unfortunately, it is not uncommon.

PUTTING IT ALL TOGETHER: THE SHAFIA CASE

The police investigation into the deaths of sisters Zainab, Sahar, and Geeti Shafia, and Rona Amir, their father's first wife, was a massive undertaking on the part of police and involved the collection and analysis of a wide variety of evidence. The investigation began after the bodies were recovered from the locks near Kingston, Ontario, on June 30, 2009. The trial of the girls' father, Mohammad Shafia, his second wife, Tooba Yahya, and the girls' 18-year-old brother Hamed lasted for three months. It involved 58 witnesses and 160 exhibits, and revolved around a significant amount of circumstantial evidence. In January 2012, the three were found guilty of four counts each of first-degree murder.

When police first heard about the Nissan submerged in the locks, they thought it might be a prank or a stolen vehicle scenario. Around midday, before the bodies were recovered, Mohammad, Tooba Yahya, and Hamed attended at the police station to report the deceased as missing. According to the family, the eldest daughter, Zainab, had taken the keys the night before; the result, they suggested, must have been the tragic outcome of a joyride. But by the end of the first day, investigators had their suspicions. A number of findings did not support the family's theory:

- The small space through which the vehicle had to pass in order to reach the water suggested that it must have been driven there deliberately.
- The driver's window was open, the car's ignition was off, the front seats were reclined completely, and none of the victims was wearing a seatbelt.
- Although the car seemed to have entered the canal during the night, the lights were off.

In the ensuing sudden death investigation, police recovered key physical evidence in the form of broken bits of plastic (the source of which was initially unknown) and obtained information through interviews with Mohammad, Tooba Yahya, and Hamed. The three reported that the family had been in Kingston for the night, travelling back to Montreal after a trip to Niagara Falls; later, police discovered that although the Shafias had stated that all ten members of their family were at the motel, only six had checked in. Hamed told police that he did not spend the night in the motel with the rest of his family but instead returned to Montreal, on business. Curiously, he failed to mention an early morning collision between the family's Lexus SUV and a parking barrier in a near-empty Montreal parking lot, which he had reported to police with a request that the minor damage be repaired immediately. Police suspicions were raised when they learned of the report, and the following day they obtained consent to search the Lexus.

In what became the turning point in the investigation, investigators discovered that the bits of plastic from the crime scene came from the broken headlight of the Lexus, which Hamed had claimed was damaged in Montreal and which the family initially asserted had not been at the crime scene (though they later changed their story). On July 4, the investigation became a homicide investigation, with the Lexus functioning, in the words of one investigator, as the "murder weapon."

According to the version of events put forth by the Crown, the "accident" was staged by the accused, with the women already dead (or at least incapacitated) by the time the car hit the water. This theory was supported both by the appearance that no one had attempted to escape through the open window and by autopsy evidence showing that three of the women had minor bruises on their heads; while a forensic expert did testify that the cause of death was drowning, it was not possible to determine where the women had drowned.

With the car in neutral, the Crown suggested, the Nissan was manoeuvred to the edge of the lock. Someone then reached in through the window and shifted it into first gear, hoping it would go into the canal on its own. Instead, the car became stuck on the ledge, at which time someone reached in through the window and turned off the ignition. The car was then pushed in by the Lexus, explaining both the damage to the back of the Nissan and to the headlight of the Lexus. Police had also learned that the Nissan was bought the day before the family left for their trip, used, for $5,000, and the Crown suggested that it was purchased both because it was cheaper than the family's other van and because the van would not have fit under the small space it had to pass through to get into the water.

Additional evidence included the following:

- Cellphone records showing that on June 27, Hamed's cellphone was pinging off a Kingston-area tower and that someone using his phone drove from Niagara Falls to Kingston and back the same day. (The Crown argued that Mohammad and Hamed went to check out the scene they had chosen for the murder.)
- Wiretap conversations recorded by police between the three accused in the family's minivan. Police said that they had found a camera at the lock and that they hoped it would provide footage of the Nissan entering the water. This was a lie, told in the hope that the family would begin to talk about the events of the night—which they did. In taped conversations, Shafia describes the darkness of the night and the fact that there was no electricity; he asks his wife if she remembers, and she says yes. In addition to this, the wiretap caught Shafia cursing his daughters and making numerous references to "honour," which was ultimately put forth as the motive for the murders. (Zainab and Sahar had secret boyfriends, and Geeti was acting out at school. Mohammad Shafia testified that the girls were "treacherous" to their family, but denied killing them.)
- A diary belonging to Rona Amir, found by police in the course of executing a search warrant, which alleged mistreatment from Shafia and Yahya.
- Conversations the girls had had with social workers, school officials, and police officers, which provided a sense of the dysfunctional life in the Shafia household.
- Forensic computer searches on a family laptop used primarily by Hamed, which uncovered attempts to find out whether a prisoner could retain control of his real estate; "facts and documentaries" about murder; a large number of searches and access to photos of bodies of water (including a map time-stamped June 15, centred on a road next to the locks); searches about Montreal jails; and, most notably, ten days before the deaths, a search for "where to commit a murder."

In commenting on the verdict, the judge called it "clearly supported by the evidence" presented at the trial.

KEY TERMS

accidental death   forensic pathologist   suicide
coroner   forensic pathology   taphonomy
coroner's inquest   homicide   undetermined death
forensic anthropologist   natural death

REVIEW QUESTIONS

True or False?

1. When police arrive at a scene where someone is supposed to have died, they must assume that the person is alive.

2. In cases where foul play is suspected, it is customary for police investigators to attend the post-mortem examination.

3. The role of coroners and medical examiners in investigating deaths is to determine legal responsibility.

4. Coroners do not necessarily suggest an autopsy where the police intend to carry out an investigation.

5. Coroners do not investigate homicides.

6. The coroner or medical examiner has legal jurisdiction over the body.

7. Forensic anthropologists are of no value at the crime scene.

8. An anthropologist can tell if a woman has given birth naturally by studying the pelvis.

9. Investigators who know the sex of the victim can get a tentative identification.

10. Identical twins have identical fingerprints.

Multiple Choice

1. In Ontario, by law, the following categories of death must be reported to the coroner:

    a. deaths of individuals in long-term care homes.

    b. deaths occurring as a result of malpractice.

    c. any death during detention by or in custody of a peace officer.

    d. sudden and unexpected deaths.

    e. all of the above.

2. In Ontario, police officers may pronounce death where a body exhibits any of the following signs *except*:

    a. gross rigor mortis.

    b. visible putrefaction.

    c. transection.

    d. absence of pulse.

    e. decapitation.

3. When investigating a death, which of the questions below do coroners *not* seek to answer?

   a. Who died?

   b. Who was responsible for their death?

   c. How did the deceased die?

   d. When did the deceased die?

   e. Was the death an accident?

4. Which of the following can provide a positive identification of a dead body?

   a. driver's licence.

   b. prescription medicine.

   c. viewing by family member.

   d. passport.

   e. engraved wedding ring.

5. Which of the following does a forensic anthropologist attempt to estimate in developing a biological profile of a victim?

   a. age.

   b. ancestry.

   c. sex.

   d. height.

   e. all of the above.

6. Which is the *best* set of bones from which to determine sex?

   a. pelvis.

   b. skull.

   c. ribs.

   d. long bones.

   e. spinal column.

7. Which of the following is *not* true of time of death?

   a. Forensic pathologists can usually only provide a range.

   b. It is important in confirming suspects' alibis in a homicide.

   c. It is often possible to determine the exact time at which a person died.

   d. Plants can provide useful information regarding the time frame.

   e. Time of death is one of the most important questions in a death investigation.

Short Answer

1. Describe the five stages of a death investigation.

2. List the five questions that a coroner or medical examiner seeks to answer in a death investigation.

3. Describe the actions police must take when they become aware of a death that has occurred in one of the circumstances listed under s. 10 of the *Coroners Act*.

4. Give two examples of things at a crime scene that might give the police a tentative identification and explain why they are tentative, not positive.

5. Explain the one situation where circumstantial evidence may be considered enough to positively identify a dead person.

6. When is circumstantial evidence *not* acceptable as a means of identification?

7. Give two methods of positively identifying a person and explain why they are positive.

8. Explain what causes rigor mortis and name two variables that can affect it.

9. How can insects be used to provide an estimated time since death?

Forensic Biology and DNA

12

LEARNING OUTCOMES

After completing this chapter, you should be able to:

- Identify the two types of DNA and the value of each in an investigation.

- Identify the main types of biological evidence found at a crime scene.

- Understand the value of the analysis of biological evidence.

- Understand the difference between presumptive and confirmatory tests, and when these tests are used.

- Explain some of the concerns with DNA evidence.

INTRODUCTION

The biology unit is one of the largest sections in the forensic laboratory. Forensic biologists analyze any biological materials recovered from a crime scene or collected from a suspect or victim, such as blood, semen, and other body fluids. Forensic biologists are concerned primarily with determining whether a sample is human and, if so, who it comes from. Until the mid-1980s, biological analyses could not individualize a sample—that is, point to a single person as the "donor"—but could only indicate a strong *possibility* that the sample came from a particular person.

That changed with the development of **DNA typing** or DNA "fingerprinting" in 1985. In 1987, in England, Colin Pitchfork became the first person in the United Kingdom to be convicted using DNA evidence; in the same year, DNA evidence was first used in the United States in the conviction of a Florida rapist. One year later, Timothy Spencer was sentenced to death in Virginia on DNA evidence for several rapes and murders and David Vasquez, who had been wrongfully convicted for one of Spencer's earlier crimes, was the first person exonerated based on DNA evidence. In 1991, serial killer Allan Legere became the first Canadian to be convicted using the new technology. These early convictions and exonerations were the first in a trickle and then a flood of similar cases. Unfortunately, some of these exonerations are posthumous—that is, after the person was executed or died in prison.

Since it was first introduced, DNA analysis has become the biggest tool in forensic science. Today, DNA evidence can be used:

- to specifically identify a single person as the donor of a sample or, more correctly, to eliminate almost all other people in the world from possibly having contributed the sample (see the box feature on determining donor probability);
- to rule out a suspect as the donor of DNA;
- to link the same perpetrator to multiple offences, regardless of whether the crimes were committed in the same city or in another part of the world; and
- to identify the victim of a crime by using DNA from close relatives.

DNA typing
also called DNA fingerprinting and DNA profiling, a technique used by forensic biologists to individualize a person using their genetic profile

---

DETERMINING DONOR PROBABILITY: THE CASE OF PRESIDENT CLINTON

In the impeachment trial of then-president Bill Clinton, White House intern Monica Lewinsky stated that she possessed a dress that was stained with Clinton's semen, proving that she had had sexual relations with him.

When DNA results are presented, the biologist does not say that the sample came from X or, in this case, President Clinton; rather, biologists say that the chance of the sample coming from anyone else is so small that it is virtually impossible it could be anyone but the suspect.

In Clinton's case, the FBI biologist was able to analyze the DNA and state that the chance that the semen sample came from anyone other than Clinton was almost 1 in 8,000,000,000,000—that is, 1 in 8 trillion (Saferstein, 2011). Because there are approximately only 7 billion people in the world, clearly no one else could have contributed this sample.

THE FORENSIC BIOLOGIST

Forensic biologists are civilian scientists, not police officers, even though they are considered civilian members in RCMP labs. Even so, they are entirely independent of the investigation.

Forensic biologists enter the laboratory with a minimum of an honours degree in biology or biochemistry and, preferably, molecular biology, although many also have graduate degrees. Once in the laboratory, forensic biologists receive extensive further training. In the RCMP labs, after basic training, they start in either the Evidence Recovery Unit (ERU) (where, for example, a stain on a bed sheet is isolated from the rest of the sheet) or the Biology Analytical Unit (where DNA is extracted and analyzed), before moving on to the Biology Reporting Unit (where DNA profiling software is used to determine the significance of the evidence—that is, the probability of someone else having a particular genetic profile). The Centre of Forensic Sciences in Toronto and the Montreal lab have slightly different structures.

After a scientist has gained experience in the ERU, followed by further training, understudy work, exams, and mock trials, he or she may become a DNA analyst in the Biology Analytical Unit. After further training and understudy work, the biologist can become a specialist in the Reporting Unit, analyzing results, writing reports, and testifying in court.

DNA

The human body is composed of trillions of cells. Inside almost every one is a nucleus that contains structures called chromosomes. Nucleated cells have 46 chromosomes in 23 matching pairs; in each pair, one chromosome is from our mother and the other is from our father. One pair of chromosomes, the sex chromosomes, determines whether we are male or female. Males have an X and a Y chromosome, while females have two Xs (thus, female parents can donate only an X chromosome to their offspring, while male parents can donate either an X or a Y and, in so doing, determine their offspring's sex).

Our chromosomes contain deoxyribonucleic acid—our **DNA**. Every cell in our body contains the same DNA (except in those people who have had a bone marrow transplant, where the DNA in their blood will be different from that in their tissue). The only cells that do *not* contain DNA are red blood cells; however, white blood cells contain DNA, which is why blood is still a major source of DNA in a forensic investigation.

DNA consists of repetitions of four basic units called nucleotides. The sequence of these nucleotides provides the genetic code of life, telling our bodies how to develop and function. In fact, DNA is sometimes referred to as the "blueprint of life." In humans, DNA is organized into approximately 20,000 to 25,000 units called genes, which determine our qualities and characteristics—for example, our hair colour, height, eye colour, liver function, skin structure, heart function, and all our biological features and functions.

However, not all DNA is found in the nucleus of cells. A different type of DNA is found within other structures called mitochondria. Thus, there are two kinds of DNA:

1. nuclear DNA, and
2. mitochondrial DNA.

DNA
deoxyribonucleic acid, the genetic material found in the nucleus of cells, unique to every human except identical twins and used to individualize biological samples in an investigation

mitochondrial DNA
genetic material found in the mitochondria of cells, shared by all individuals in a particular maternal line and thus of more limited use in an investigation than (nuclear) DNA

Nuclear DNA is what we refer to when we simply say "DNA." Because nuclear DNA is unique to each person, it is the most valuable kind of DNA in an investigation and is thus the most widely used. **Mitochondrial DNA** (mtDNA), often referred to as "the other DNA," is *not* unique to each person. It is passed on directly from the mother and is shared by all individuals in a particular maternal line, and thus its uses in an investigation are more limited. The following chart provides a summary of each type of DNA.

(Nuclear) DNA	mtDNA
• Found only in the nucleus of cells	• Found only in the mitochondria of cells
• One copy per cell	• Many copies per cell
• Unique to the individual	• Identical in entire maternal line
• Both parents contribute equally, but different from parents' DNA	• Only mother contributes

Although every human's nuclear DNA (hereinafter "DNA") is unique, the majority of each person's DNA—99 percent—is identical to that of every other person; in addition, we share more than 96 percent of our DNA with chimpanzees. However, in a forensic context, we are not concerned with this part of DNA.

The application of DNA to forensic science began in 1985, when Sir Alec Jeffreys and his team in Leicester, England discovered that certain regions of our nuclear DNA contain repeating units of a short DNA sequence, called "short tandem repeats" (STRs). At certain places on certain chromosomes, these are extremely variable between any two people, and thus these regions can be used to differentiate between any two people *except* identical twins. (Because identical twins are *genetically* identical, they share the exact DNA, making this the only situation in which DNA cannot individualize people.)

Despite its great evidentiary value, DNA is still only a tool. It does not tell us who committed a crime, only that a person was present at the crime scene. When someone goes missing and their DNA is found, it does not prove that the person is dead, only that he or she was in a particular place. Similarly, when a suspect's DNA is found, it indicates that the suspect was at the crime scene, but not necessarily that the suspect committed the crime. However, there must be an explanation for the presence of the suspect's DNA at the scene—for example, if the accused is a friend of the deceased, it is quite probable that his or her DNA will be in the victim's car or home. If the recovered DNA is in the form of semen and was found in the vagina of a sexual assault victim, it is more suspicious, but it does not necessarily prove guilt. (The suspect may be the boyfriend or husband of the victim and may claim to have had consensual intercourse with her before she was attacked by a rapist wearing a condom.) In a case where the suspect claims never to have seen the victim before, explaining the presence of his or her DNA at the scene will be more difficult.

THE FIRST DNA CONVICTION

Colin Pitchfork was the first murderer worldwide to be caught on the basis of DNA evidence. In 1983, in England, a teenage girl was raped and murdered. Semen was recovered, but DNA typing was not yet available, so the best the forensic lab could say was that the person who contributed the semen had a blood and enzyme profile seen in only 10 percent of men.

In 1986, a similar crime occurred, and the semen profile fit the previous sample. However, by this time, Sir Alec Jeffreys and colleagues had just published their seminal work on "fingerprints" in human DNA (Jeffreys et al., 1985). A suspect was identified in the second killing, but DNA analysis showed that, although both girls were murdered by the same man, the suspect was not the killer. He was the first person to be eliminated as a suspect by DNA.

In a precedent-setting investigation, the police asked all adult men in the area to voluntarily provide a DNA sample for elimination purposes. Over 5,000 men came forward and were excluded, including a man calling himself Colin Pitchfork. Many months later, a man was overheard boasting that he had earned a quick £200 for pretending to be his buddy, Pitchfork, and giving his DNA as Pitchfork's. Pitchfork was arrested, tested, and identified. He confessed to the crimes and was sentenced to life in prison.

Mitochondrial DNA

When a sperm and egg fuse to make a zygote, the genetic material in the nucleus comes equally from both parents. However, while the sperm provides the entire male contribution of chromosomes, it is too small to carry anything more. The egg, whose volume is 195,000 times that of the sperm, provides not only chromosomes but the rest of the material the zygote will need for life. This includes the first mitochondria, which produce energy to maintain cell function.

Mitochondria have a distinct and unique DNA. Because a person's mitochondrial DNA is identical to his or her mother's mitochondria, a person's mtDNA is passed down *unchanged* through the generations. (Thus, you have the same mtDNA as your mother, grandmother, great-grandmother et al., maternal aunts and uncles, and siblings.) Both sons and daughters inherit mtDNA, but only daughters can pass it on. Technically speaking, barring small mutations that occur over time, a person's mtDNA is exactly the same as that of their great-, great-, great-grandmother et al., going back 20, 200, or even 2,000 generations.

Although mtDNA is class rather than individual evidence, it is helpful in that it restricts the evidence to a family line. It is usually used to identify a victim, by matching him or her with known maternal relatives. For example, in a plane crash, mtDNA from a mother or sibling can be used to positively identify a person, assuming that this closed population—that is, the victims of the crash—contained only one maternal relative of the family. In some cases, mtDNA is also used to identify a suspect, and has been used to determine whether living people are related.

MtDNA has several advantages over nuclear DNA:

- There are large quantities of mtDNA in every cell.
- It is found in certain samples where nuclear DNA is not present—for example, in the hair shaft, which often persists much longer than other samples.

- It is less susceptible to damage resulting from environmental conditions, and thus can easily be recovered from very old remains.

As well, a mtDNA[1] match is possible between a sample and a living relative regardless of the number of maternal generations separating the two. For example, not long ago in Britain, mtDNA was used to determine whether an ancient skeleton (Cheddar Man) still had living descendants in the area. A local schoolteacher was found with matching mtDNA, indicating that his maternal line had been in that region for over 12,000 years. It was also used to identify the remains of U.S. outlaw Jesse James, based on a comparison between mtDNA from his remains with that of his sister's great-granddaughter's son.

Because mtDNA is much more difficult, costly, and time-consuming to analyze than nuclear DNA, and because it is not individualizing, it is rarely used in criminal investigations unless it is the only evidence found. In Canada, its use is so rare that the equipment to type it is not available in forensic labs, and police rely on examiners in Britain and the United States to carry out this analysis when required. However, even in the United States, mtDNA is rarely used.

ANALYSIS OF BIOLOGICAL EVIDENCE

There are many different types of biological evidence, but the primary samples are blood and semen. Other samples include saliva, hair, vomitus, feces, and tissue. As with most forensic evidence, analysis is all about matching one sample to another—for example, matching semen found on the victim to a suspect. Forensic biologists are not concerned with foreign substances that might be in the blood, such as alcohol or drugs. These fall under the auspices of the forensic toxicologist (discussed in Chapter 13, Forensic Chemistry and Forensic Toxicology).

Samples may be found at the scene of a crime or taken directly from a victim or a suspect, as described in Chapter 6, Legal Aspects of Search and Seizure. Where samples are taken from a suspect—for example, a blood sample or **buccal swab**— the sample is known to be a biological sample. However, when a sample is collected from a crime scene, this is not necessarily the case (a dark stain on a carpet at the scene of a crime, for example, could be blood, but it could also be any number of other perfectly innocent materials, such as oil). Therefore, before a sample from a crime scene is subjected to DNA analysis, several steps must be taken.

buccal swab
sample of tissue taken from the inside of the mouth to obtain skin cells; less invasive than taking blood, with the advantage of obtaining tissue cells rather than blood

Presumptive tests, for example, are screening tests that will tell the investigator whether a sample *might* be a certain substance (for example, blood). Presumptive tests can also tell investigators that a substance is definitely *not* a certain substance. They are performed either at the crime scene by identification officers or at the crime lab by evidence recovery technicians. They are usually fairly quick, easy, and inexpensive and can thus cover a large area, such as a wall, to show investigators if the area warrants further investigation.

Presumptive tests are helpful in eliminating suspicious-looking stains, but, before an investigator can be sure that the sample is a particular substance, a confirmatory test must be done following a positive reaction. This is because presumptive tests,

---

1   "mtDNA" is usually pronounced as "mitochondrial DNA."

NOTABLE CASES INVOLVING mtDNA

The Boston Strangler

In the early 1960s, a number of women were strangled in Boston. Albert DeSalvo confessed to the murders, and was convicted and sentenced to life imprisonment. DeSalvo was murdered in prison and his killer was never identified. At the time of DeSalvo's conviction, the absence of physical evidence linking him to the crimes, and inconsistencies between known facts and his confession, cast doubt on whether he was indeed responsible for all of the crimes he claimed he had committed.

In 2000, a semen sample was found during the re-examination of the remains of Mary Sullivan, who was purported to be the Strangler's last victim. Although nuclear DNA was no longer recoverable, mtDNA was extracted and compared with that of Richard DeSalvo, Albert's living brother. The profiles did not match, proving that Albert was not the donor (Starrs, 2005), and putting the entire investigation and conviction in doubt.

The Romanov Family

In July 1918, the entire Russian royal family—Tsar Nicholas II, Tsarina Alexandra, and their five children—was brutally murdered. In 1991, a mass grave was officially uncovered, containing all the bodies but two of the children and fuelling existing rumours that the two had survived. Various people claimed to be Anastasia, who U.S. experts believed was the missing daughter. The most famous was a woman named Anna Anderson, whose claim was disproved by comparing her mtDNA with that of a known living maternal relative of Tsarina Alexandra, Prince Philip of England. (Because the tsarina was the granddaughter of Queen Victoria and Prince Philip is the son of one of Queen Victoria's great-granddaughters, his mtDNA is the same as that of the tsarina and her children.)

In 2007, another grave was uncovered near the first. MtDNA analysis of bone fragments indicated that the samples were maternally related to Tsarina Alexandra (the new samples also matched the mtDNA of Prince Philip). These results make it virtually certain that the missing children were in this grave and, hence, none of the children survived.

The "Disappeared" of Argentina

In the late 1970s, political liberals were "disappeared"—that is, imprisoned, tortured, and killed in extra-judicial executions by the military rulers of Argentina. During their imprisonment, some of the young women gave birth, and their babies were either sold or given to high-ranking families who supported the regime. Following the overthrow of the regime in 1983, forensic anthropologist Clyde Snow worked to identify the victims' remains and document the crimes. Many families had heard rumours that, although their children had died, their grandchildren had lived and been adopted. They approached Dr. Snow for assistance in finding their grandchildren. Based on a comparison of the grandmothers' mtDNA with that of their grandchildren, Dr. Snow was able to help reunite many families. For others, the search continues.

Although this was a tremendous victory for forensic science, by the time the children were identified they were ten or more years old. They had no idea that they had been stolen, that the people they knew as their "parents" were not their biological parents, or that these "parents" had been involved with the regime responsible for their true parents' deaths; the transition must have been extremely traumatic. In a recent case, one of the alleged grandchildren, now a grown woman, refused DNA testing because it might be used in a war crimes trial against the man she believes to be, and loves as, her father.

in addition to producing a positive reaction in the presence of the fluid they are designed to react to, can also give false positives to other substances. For example, the substance luminol (used in a presumptive test for blood) gives a false positive to any substance containing iron.

Confirmatory tests are performed by biologists in the laboratory. They often take longer and are more expensive, but they are specific. They will indicate that the substance is definitely blood, for example, and could not be any other substance; however, they cannot indicate that the sample is human. Further tests, called precipitin tests, are next used to determine which animal species the blood comes from. Once tests have determined whether the sample is human, further tests are done to individualize the sample.

The various stages described above make it clear why such analyses cannot be performed in less than an hour, minus commercial breaks, as commonly seen on television.

Blood

Suspected blood at a crime scene can be collected using a sterile swab if the blood is wet, or with a sterile swab dampened with sterile water if the blood is dry. If blood is on clothing or bedding, this might be seized and tested in the laboratory. If on a wall or carpet, it might be tested *in situ*—that is, in position. Wet blood on clothes or items such as weapons can also be swabbed, but care must be taken not to destroy evidence, such as a bloody fingerprint.

Paper evidence bags are always used to collect biological evidence, because plastic allows the evidence to mould and, although DNA is fairly robust, mould quickly destroys it. In the lab, each sample is placed in a secure, separate drying cabinet to allow the blood to dry and thereby preserve it for further analysis.

Presumptive Tests

Blood at a crime may be obvious. However, if there has been an attempt to clean the scene or if only a small amount of blood was spilled, it may not be visible. A police officer can determine whether blood is present using light sources that sometimes illuminate blood and other body fluids. Even when the crime scene has been cleaned and the blood is diluted, it can still be detected by certain presumptive chemicals:

- *Luminol.* Luminol is a substance that is sprayed onto an area then viewed in complete darkness under special light sources. In the presence of blood or any other substance with iron, it will fluoresce (see Figure 12.1). Luminol can detect blood that has been diluted up to 100,000 times (Saferstein, 2011) and years after the blood was shed. In one case, a person was murdered and dismembered in a bathtub of a residential rental house. The room was cleaned, and appeared so to the naked eye, and then rented to a couple who used the bathroom in a typical way and regularly cleaned it. Following information that the death and dismemberment had occurred in this house, police obtained a warrant and examined the bathroom. When sprayed with luminol, the whole room lit up, and one could even see swipe marks in the blood where it was originally cleaned up.

FIGURE 12.1   Application of luminol to blood residue in bathtub

Application of luminol to blood residue in a staged crime scene, using real blood, after the tub was washed with water and bleach. In the dark, luminol causes traces of blood invisible to the naked eye to glow blue–green. Blood particles can remain on surfaces for years.

Because luminol reacts to the iron, or heme, in the blood, it gives false positive reactions to any other substances containing iron. Unlike some other substances, the use of luminol has not been shown to destroy DNA so does not interfere with subsequent DNA testing (Gross, Harris, & Kaldun, 1999).

- *Hemastix.* Hemastix gives a positive reaction in the presence of blood, but gives false positives with rust, bleach, and certain vegetable extracts. Hemastix used to be swabbed directly over the stain, but, unlike luminol, it has been found to interfere with later DNA analysis. Therefore, the stain is swabbed and then the swab tested, so that the hemastix does not touch the stain directly.

- *Kastle-Meyer.* The Kastle-Meyer, or phenolphthalein, test is another presumptive test for blood, which also reacts to horseradish and potatoes (Saferstein, 2011). Because these are not usually a major part of a crime scene, a positive reaction probably indicates blood, but a confirmatory test must still be done.

- *Bluestar.* Bluestar is a newer presumptive test and is taking over from luminol in some areas because it does not need complete darkness to fluoresce under certain light sources. The use of Bluestar does not affect later DNA testing (Saferstein, 2011).

Confirmatory and Individualizing Tests

A common confirmatory test for blood is the hemochromagen chemical test, which has no false positives; other tests include the Teichmann and Takayama tests. Once the substance has been confirmed to be blood, precipitin tests are performed to determine whether it is human or animal blood. If the blood is human, further tests are conducted to individualize the sample.

In the past, scientists would have determined the blood type, which would provide class evidence whose significance was based on how rare or common the blood type was in the general population. For example, a blood type present in only 5 percent

THE DINGO BABY CASE AND THE MISUSE OF A PRESUMPTIVE TEST

In Australia, in 1980, the Chamberlain family made sad headlines worldwide when they claimed that a dingo had taken their newborn baby from their tent while the family was camping at Uluru (Ayers Rock). However, when no remains were recovered, Lindy Chamberlain was eventually arrested for murder. In what became one of the most controversial cases in Australian history, Lindy Chamberlain was tried and convicted of the murder of her baby, and her husband Michael was convicted as an accessory.

Forensic mistakes were made on both sides, but one made by the prosecution's side involved luminol. The police believed that the baby had been murdered in her parents' car. They sprayed the interior of the car with luminol and it fluoresced. The pattern that appeared looked like arterial spurting, suggesting that someone's throat had been cut in the floor area of the passenger seat. However, no confirmatory tests were done following the presumptive test. Because the chemical constituency of neonatal, or newborn, blood is different from blood at any other stage in a person's life, the prosecution further stated that the blood was that of a neonate or baby. Luminol cannot prove that a substance is definitively blood, or even human blood, and it certainly cannot show that it is neonatal blood.

It was later shown that any other car manufactured at the same factory would have fluoresced in the same manner, because the luminol was reacting to the protective coating sprayed on the underside of the car when it was made, which had spurted up under the engine and into the car interior. The luminol reacted to the iron coating, not to iron in hemoglobin. After serving several years in prison, and giving birth to her fourth child while there, Lindy Chamberlain was exonerated and her conviction was overturned.

On June 12, 2012 an Australian coroner released the findings of the fourth inquest into the case. Based on the evidence, the coroner concluded that after Mrs. Chamberlain placed her baby in the tent, a dingo or dingoes entered the tent, took the baby, and dragged her away.

of the population would be much more significant than a blood type found in 50 percent of the population. However, conclusively identifying a donor was not possible with this method. With the advent of DNA typing, classifying blood based on blood type is no longer of value and the method is no longer used.

Semen

The lab may receive clothing, bed sheets, or something else thought to have semen on it—for example, a mattress or a part of one. Semen stains may be obvious, but they are often difficult to locate. Therefore, a careful and minute examination must be made of any material submitted to the lab. This, again, is the duty of the evidence recovery technologist. DNA has been recovered from clothing that has been completely laundered, so such stains would not be visible to the naked eye (Jobin & De Gouffe, 2003). Troublingly, semen on clothing has been shown to be transferred to previously clean clothing during laundry (Kafarowski, Lyon, & Sloan, 1996).

Presumptive Tests

As with blood, presumptive tests are first used to determine whether the stain is possibly semen. The best presumptive test is commonly called a "fast blue test," although its correct name is an "acid phosphatase colour test." Acid phosphatase is an enzyme secreted by the prostate gland into the seminal fluid. Its concentration in seminal fluid is up to 400 times greater than its concentration in other body fluids (Saferstein, 2011), and its presence can be detected easily with a solution of sodium alphnapththylphosphate and fast blue B dye. A rapid positive result means that the stain is indicative of semen. Because it tests for enzymes in the semen, not sperm, semen from a male who has had a vasectomy can still be identified.

The examiner will moisten a piece of filter paper with sterile water and lightly run it over any suspect area. If semen is present, the paper will pick up the acid phosphatase, which can then be tested with the dye. A purple colouration indicates the probable presence of semen. This allows an examiner to search large areas, such as a bed or sheet, quite quickly. Again, this is a presumptive test because other substances such as fungi and contraceptive creams can also show positive reactions. Unlike the vegetable false positives seen with some presumptive tests for blood, fungi and contraceptive creams are likely to be associated with the same exhibit. In most situations, a true positive result will be shown within 30 seconds, and a slightly later colour change would suggest a false positive. However, because the fast blue test does react to other substances, a confirmatory test must be used. Acid phosphatase is also found in other body fluids, such as vaginal fluids.

Confirmatory and Individualizing Tests

The only true confirmatory test for semen is a microscopic examination for spermatozoa. The stain is immersed in sterile water, the water is agitated, and a sample is placed under a microscope. Live spermatozoa are motile and have long tails, but even after they die and the tails drop off, the sperm are still identifiable. Because every millilitre of semen contains approximately 100 million or more spermatozoa and a single ejaculation releases between 2.5 and 6 millilitres of semen, a considerable number of spermatozoa are usually present in a stain.

Until recently, PSA (prostate-specific antigen) was believed to be found *only* in semen, and so it was thought that the prostate-specific antigen (p30), or PSA, test could function as a confirmatory test for semen in vasectomized males. However, PSA has been recovered in small amounts in other body materials, including in breast milk and amniotic fluid, prompting Canadian laboratories to stop using the PSA test. In reality, however, a high PSA value is most probably indicative of semen.

The next step is to individualize the evidence. In the past, this was done in a manner similar to that used in blood typing. Approximately 80 percent of the human population are considered "secretors"—that is, they secrete their blood type into other body fluids such as semen and saliva. But this could still only provide class evidence. Sperm is the most obvious source of DNA in semen, and today DNA typing is used to individualize a sample.

Although vasectomized men do not ejaculate sperm, they can still be individualized from their semen. Skin, or epithelial, cells are constantly shed and replaced by our bodies. Friction produces the most shedding—for example, if you rub your arm with your hand, you will shed millions of cells. Both partners shed cells during intercourse, and vasectomized men can be identified using DNA from their skin cells, which are almost always commingled with semen during intercourse. In this case, an eliminating sample must be taken from the victim as well.

Other Body Materials

Although blood and semen are probably the most commonly analyzed substances, other materials can also be analyzed to individualize a sample. These include saliva, hair, feces, vomitus, sweat, and tissue.

Saliva

Saliva can be individualized to a single person. In the past, blood type would have been determined, and, in the case of a person who was a secretor, blood type would provide class evidence. Today, DNA is of much more interest. It is not the saliva itself that is typed, but the skin cells present within it. Every time you run your tongue along the inside of your mouth, you slough off skin cells. These cells can be recovered from the back of a stamp, a cigarette butt, or a sealed envelope, as well as from, for example, bite marks.

It is impossible to bite someone without leaving traces of saliva on the skin, and saliva remains on the skin for quite some time. Therefore, any suspected bite wounds will be swabbed with a sterile, water-dampened swab, followed by a dry swab to collect saliva (Sweet, Lorente, Lorente, Valenzuela, & Valenzuela, 1997). DNA evidence from skin cells in saliva has been instrumental in many convictions. In one case, DNA from a piece of cheese that a burglar had bitten into during a break and enter was used to identify a suspect. The bite mark was swabbed for DNA and examined by a forensic odontologist. The evidence was compared with both the suspect's dentition and DNA in order to identify him as the cheese-biter (Sweet & Hildebrand, 1999). In another case, in which a murder victim's body was thrown into a canal where it remained for several hours before it was recovered, the murderer's DNA was extracted from saliva in a bite mark on the victim's body, despite the prolonged submergence. This evidence was crucial in his conviction (Sweet & Shutler, 1999).

When we speak, we spray a fine mist of saliva. (Put your hand over your mouth as you speak, and you will feel a mist.) It has been shown that we contaminate the area in front of us with our own DNA within minutes of beginning to speak. This is yet another reason why police officers should wear head to toe, including facial, protection when working at a crime scene.

Hair

Hair is one of the most common pieces of trace evidence recovered from a crime scene. We constantly shed our head hair, on average about 200 hairs per day. Hair is also commonly transferred between people and scenes.

Two kinds of analysis can be done involving hair. The first, known as a morphological analysis, is conducted on the hair shaft itself. In this analysis, examiners study features of the hair, such as the diameter, cross-section, pigment granule size and distribution, length, and presence of enhancements such as dye. Because the physical features of hair are class characteristics, a morphological analysis can usually tell examiners only whether a particular sample is consistent with a comparison sample. However, this information can provide valuable corroborative evidence where other evidence linking a suspect to a crime scene exists. Morphological analysis can also reveal whether a hair was forcibly removed or simply shed (which can be useful in the understanding of a fight or in child abuse) and whether a hair came from a human or other species of animal. In the case of human hairs, the analysis can reveal where on the body the hair came from.

Because morphological examination of hair can be used to give only a presumptive identification, it is not commonly used today. The second, more valuable kind of analysis involving hair is of the follicle at the end of the hair. (The follicle is the tiny globular ball you see at the end of a hair if you pluck one out of your head.) Because the follicle contains nuclear DNA, the hair can be individualized. If only the hair shaft is available, mtDNA can tell investigators whether a person comes from a particular maternal line.

Sweat, Vomitus, Feces, and Other Tissues

Other materials that may contain skin cells include sweat, vomitus, and feces; tissue is examined, because the cells contain DNA. Vomitus and feces contain skin cells sloughed off during excretion or expulsion, and sweat contains skin cells sloughed from the skin. Although urine does not usually contain DNA, the urine of someone with a urinary infection contains white blood cells.

In a case that briefly closed the U.S.–Mexico border in 1985, U.S. Drug Enforcement Agency (DEA) agent Kiki Camarena was kidnapped near the Guadalajara Airport, brutally tortured, murdered, and his body hidden. The torture was carried out in a shower stall in an effort to make cleanup easy. Camarena was so savagely beaten that not only blood but also fat droplets were spattered onto the walls and ceiling of the stall. The killers assumed the stall could be easily wiped down, but they did not look up and so did not clean the ceiling of the unit; many weeks later, Camarena's blood and tissue were still identifiable. Because this was before DNA typing, identification was based on blood type.

DNA ANALYSIS

Techniques for analyzing nuclear DNA have improved vastly over the years. The original techniques were expensive, took six to eight weeks to complete, and worked only on high-quality DNA. This meant that degraded, older stains and samples could not be analyzed. In addition, the specimen had to be about the size of a dime, so single drops of blood, bloody fingerprints, and traces of semen could not be analyzed. Finally, enough of the sample had to be reserved for the defence to reanalyze, if they so wished, which presented problems if the sample was not large enough to analyze more than once.

Today, a relatively inexpensive technique known as polymerase chain reaction (PCR) is used to create as many copies of DNA as necessary from even a small sample—18 cells, at the time of writing (Saferstein, 2011), which will no doubt drop as techniques improve. PCR works well even on degraded DNA, and is so sensitive that it can recover viable DNA from a sheet that has been laundered several times (Jobin & De Gouffe, 2003). At the time of writing, PCR can be completed and a profile developed in under two days.

The discovery of PCR has allowed many cold cases to be reanalyzed, resulting in both convictions where none could previously be made and the exonerations of many innocent people. In Canada, for example, the advent of PCR was instrumental in the high-profile exonerations of David Milgaard and Guy Paul Morin, both of whom were sentenced to life in prison for crimes they did not commit.

DNA typing looks at certain STRs (9, in Canada) found to be extremely variable among people. During the analysis, a profile is produced for each region. Each individual STR has a particular frequency of occurrence in the population, and biologists and statisticians have compiled databases of the occurrence of STR combinations in several populations. (Different databases exist for different ethnic populations because some profiles are found to be more or less common within particular ancestral groups.) For example, in a particular analysis, the profile identified in the first region may be found in 5 percent of the population. When the frequency of each individual STR is known, the chances of all the profiles occurring together *in the same individual* can be calculated and the statistical significance determined—a scientist could say, for example, that the chance of the entire DNA profile occurring in the population is 1 in 50 billion. This is referred to as the "random match probability." In Canada, where a fully matched profile consists of 9 locations on the DNA, a common range is from 1 in 1 million to 1 in 100 trillion. In the United States, where 13 locations or loci are typed, the random match probability becomes even more rare and can be in the quadrillions or quintillions.

Note that the frequency of the sample occurring in the population does *not* express the probability of guilt or tell investigators that the DNA *definitely* came from the suspect. However, it *does* say that the probability that it came from someone other than the suspect is extremely low—in the example above, in reality, with only approximately 7 billion people in the world, it is extremely unlikely that the DNA could have come from anyone other than the suspect. Regardless of the odds, they are always phrased as a probability, not a certainty. In court, the specialist will state the random match probability to indicate how unlikely it is that someone else would have the same profile, because the data are based on statistical estimates.

The DNA profile is entered into the Combined DNA Index System (CODIS), a software program developed by the FBI and U.S. Department of Justice. The profile will be compared with the victim for elimination purposes and with any possible suspects. The profile is then entered into the local investigative index (LII), which is a database for that local jurisdiction. There are four RCMP laboratory sites that have local investigative indices: Ottawa (which serves the eastern provinces and Nunavut), Regina (which serves Saskatchewan and Manitoba), Edmonton (which serves Alberta and the Northwest Territories), and Vancouver (which serves British Columbia and Yukon Territory). The Centre of Forensic Sciences in Toronto and the Laboratoire de sciences judiciaires et de médecine légale in Montreal also maintain LIIs. The profile is then entered into the Crime Scene Index (CSI) in the DNA databank. This allows the analyst to determine whether the DNA can be matched to anyone already convicted of certain offences.

If there is no match, the profile will be maintained in the CSI. If the offender commits future crimes and his or her DNA is recovered, links can be made between offences and offenders, even if the offender is unidentified. There is no automatic comparison between a Canadian profile and international databanks. If it is thought that the offender may not be from Canada or may have committed crimes in other countries, then a request is sent from the local Canadian CODIS administrator through the NDDB to Interpol, who will then direct the request to the partner

THE NATIONAL DNA DATA BANK

Today, Canada maintains a National DNA Data Bank (NDDB), which includes several thousand DNA samples collected from across the country. These are divided into two indices:

1. *The Convicted Offender Index (COI)*. An electronic index developed from DNA profiles collected from offenders convicted of the offences identified in s. 487.04 of the *Criminal Code*.

2. *The Crime Scene Index (CSI)*. An electronic index containing DNA profiles obtained from crime scene investigations of the offences listed in s. 487.04 of the *Criminal Code*.

Offences for which DNA may be collected include those of a violent or sexual nature; other serious offences, such as hijacking, using explosives, endangering the safety of an aircraft, and participating in terrorist activities; indictable offences under the *Criminal Code*, for which the maximum sentence is five years or more; indictable offences under ss. 5, 6, and 7 of the *Controlled Drugs and Substances Act*, for which the maximum sentence is five years or more; and other offences including escaping from custody, assault, arson, criminal harassment, and uttering threats. The NDDB helps law enforcement agencies:

- link crimes together where there are no suspects,
- eliminate and identify suspects, and
- determine whether a serial offender is involved.

country, assuming there is an information-sharing partnership agreement between Canada and the other country. Although information-sharing agreements exist between many countries and Canada—for example, the United States— many countries still do not have DNA databanks, and there are other countries with which we have no partnerships.

Major advancements are made in the field of DNA analysis every day. As is often the case, rapid medical and scientific breakthroughs often arise out of tragedy or war. This has been true of DNA. The laboratory techniques described here—that is, the physical parts of the analysis—were originally performed by hand. However, with the 18-month search of the properties of Robert Pickton following his 2002 arrest for the murder of many women from Vancouver's downtown eastside, faster analytical techniques were needed. Pickton's farm and another site Pickton previously owned were laboriously searched in an investigation that covered an area larger than the World Trade Center, known as "Ground Zero" after the terrorist attacks of September 11, 2001. Because almost all of the evidence involved very small pieces of tissue or bone from the missing women, DNA became the major science required. It was estimated that performing the DNA analyses on all the exhibits would completely bog down all of our forensic labs and take approximately 12½ years to complete. Therefore, a new robotic or automated system was developed, which allows many samples to be processed simultaneously and continuously, speeding up the analysis of all the DNA evidence to approximately 18 months. This system is now used in Ottawa for our DNA databank.

CONCERNS WITH DNA

As discussed throughout this text, contamination of evidence is a concern in every case and with every sample, and nowhere is this of more concern than in handling DNA evidence. Although the chances of contamination were slim with the earlier analytical methods, the microscopic samples used today can be contaminated by just a few skin cells. The contaminating DNA might come from the forensic biologist; the police officer who collected it; or, more worryingly, from an item collected from the suspect. To help guard against contamination, there have been manifold increases in lab security and sterility. DNA profiles are obtained from the collecting officer and the forensic biologist for elimination purposes and, in addition, all the specimens from the suspect are handled and analyzed in an entirely different part of the laboratory from that in which the victim's specimens are examined. The specimens from suspect and victim are also handled by different scientists.

For the same reason, where multiple crime scenes are linked to a crime—for example, a house and a vehicle—two separate police identification teams are sent out and each examines only one scene. To ensure that DNA evidence is not transmitted from one scene to the other, even the officer in charge will not enter both scenes. This ensures that if the suspect's DNA is found at both scenes there will be no questions regarding whether it was taken from one scene to another by a police officer or contaminated at the lab. Finally, laboratory protocol and procedures are regularly checked to ensure that they conform to the highest standards and labs must receive accreditation before they can handle DNA evidence.

Although extremely unlikely, one concern with DNA, which received considerable media coverage, is the possibility that DNA might be planted. For example, in one case that began as sexual stalking, a woman became obsessed with a married man. When he continuously rejected her, she searched his garbage regularly and eventually retrieved his used condom. She placed the semen on the inside of her underwear and then told the police that he had raped her. The DNA evidence was there to support her case. Eventually it was shown that he was innocent, but the presumption of guilt must have had a terrible effect.

Another concern, again extremely unlikely, is that DNA may be manufactured, as shown by recent research from Israel. Scientists manufactured DNA, removed the original DNA from the exhibit (for example, from saliva or blood), and then replaced it with the new DNA (Frumkin et al., 2010). The researchers also proved that DNA can be manufactured in the absence of an actual sample, using only information in a DNA profile. However, tests can distinguish between manufactured DNA and the real thing, although, at the time of writing, forensic labs have not announced whether or not they are using this new test. DNA fabrication of this type is highly unlikely to be involved in the vast majority of cases, because most cases involve simple opportunistic crimes and are not so carefully planned and premeditated.

KEY TERMS

buccal swab
DNA
DNA typing
mitochondrial DNA

FURTHER READING

James, S.H., & Nordby, J.J. (Eds.). (2009). *Forensic science: An introduction to scientific and investigative techniques* (3rd ed.). Boca Raton, FL: CRC Press.

Wyatt, S. (2001). *Forensic DNA evidence: Investigative procedures for law enforcement.* Victoria, BC: Queen's Printer.

REVIEW QUESTIONS

True or False?

1. Forensic biologists look at foreign substances in the blood such as drugs.

2. The main concern of a forensic biologist is to individualize the evidence.

3. DNA cannot distinguish between fraternal twins.

4. Confirmatory tests are performed at the crime scene.

5. If luminol is used on a blood sample, the sample can no longer be used for DNA analysis.

6. If Bluestar is used on a blood sample, the sample can be used for DNA analysis.

7. Semen from a man who has had a vasectomy can still be individualized.

8. Saliva cannot be individualized using DNA.

9. Mitochondrial DNA can individualize a person.

10. The same scientist will analyze the DNA from both victim and suspect.

Multiple Choice

1. Which of the following does *not* contain nuclear DNA?

   a. muscle tissue.

   b. white blood cells.

   c. red blood cells.

   d. skin cells.

   e. mouth swab.

2. Which of the following are good samples for DNA?

   a. blood.

   b. semen.

   c. saliva.

   d. tissue.

   e. all of the above.

3. Luminol has false positives in the presence of
   a. iron.
   b. horseradish.
   c. potatoes.
   d. bleach.
   e. vegetable extracts.

4. What is the only confirmatory test for semen?
   a. PSA or p30 test.
   b. hemastix.
   c. presence of spermatozoa.
   d. fast blue.
   e. Kastel-Meyer.

5. A man's mitochondrial DNA is *not* identical to which of the following?
   a. his mother.
   b. his mother's sister.
   c. his sister.
   d. his daughter.
   e. none of the above.

6. Mitochondrial DNA is *not* found in which of the following?
   a. hair shaft.
   b. hair follicle.
   c. blood.
   d. semen.
   e. none of the above.

Short Answer

1. Explain what forensic biologists do and what they attempt to determine.
2. List four uses of DNA evidence.
3. Give and explain the two parts of the National DNA Data Bank.
4. Explain the difference between presumptive and confirmatory tests and the value of each.
5. What sort of bags should be used to collect biological evidence and why?
6. Explain why contamination is a real concern with more recent DNA analysis techniques.

Forensic Chemistry and Forensic Toxicology

13

LEARNING OUTCOMES

After completing this chapter, you should be able to:

- Discuss the significance of trace evidence.

- Understand the types of materials considered to be trace evidence.

- Understand, generally, the methods used to analyze trace evidence.

- Understand the role of forensic chemistry in arson and bombing investigations and the evidentiary value of the remaining material.

- Understand both the analytical and interpretive roles of a toxicologist.

- Discuss the different types of substances used as toxicological specimens and the advantages and disadvantages of each.

INTRODUCTION

Forensic chemistry and forensic toxicology are often confused. Both subjects deal with chemistry, but they occupy very different areas of the lab. Forensic chemists, also known as trace evidence specialists, analyze non-biological trace evidence. Forensic toxicologists analyze toxins, including drugs, alcohol, and poisons in body fluids, as well as exhibits such as drug paraphernalia.

FORENSIC CHEMISTRY OR TRACE EVIDENCE

Forensic chemists examine the myriad materials that people come into contact with every day, and which can provide various kinds of information about a crime—for example, how it was committed, by whom, and under what circumstances. Almost anything transferred during the commission of a crime can be considered trace evidence. Your own house, car, and workplace contain any number of things that could become trace evidence if a crime were to be committed there. The evidence analyzed by forensic chemists are classical examples of Locard's exchange principle. (See the discussion of Locard's exchange principle in Chapter 7, Crime Scene Investigation and Management.)

Forensic chemists analyze evidence ranging from fragments of broken glass and drywall to packing material, soil, gunshot residue, clothing fibres, rope, and paint chips. Many of the common materials forensic chemists analyze are part of a crime scene because many crimes occur between ordinary people in ordinary places; however, these common items may be specifically related to the crime—for example, the duct tape used to tie up a victim, the glass chips from the headlight of a car in a hit and run, or materials used to construct a bomb in a terrorist attack. Forensic scientists must therefore determine—and make it extremely clear in their reports and court testimony—the *significance* of the evidence they analyze, or the lack thereof.

Forensic chemists analyze evidence in crimes ranging from common break and enters to terrorist attacks. They are the primary scientists involved in arson investigations, and determine such things as what type of accelerant was used and how, where the fire started, and whether a timer was used. They are also the frontline scientists involved in bombings, such as the London Underground bombings and the bombing of Air India Flight 182. They determine the type of bomb used, the type of explosive, how the bomb was constructed, and whether it can be linked to equipment or materials found in a suspect's residence.

Different laboratory systems have different names for this unit of the forensic laboratory. At both the Centre of Forensic Sciences in Ontario and the Laboratoire de sciences judiciaires et de médecine légale in Montreal, the section is called forensic chemistry, but the RCMP labs now refer to it as the Trace Evidence Unit; in the United States it is often referred to as the Physical Science Unit. The RCMP labs in Edmonton and Ottawa now handle all trace evidence for RCMP cases across the country.

Scope of Work and Training

The preliminary qualification required to train as a trace evidence specialist in a forensic lab is an honours B.Sc. in chemistry or a branch of chemistry; however, the majority of forensic chemists have graduate degrees. Although today forensic chemists are often called "trace evidence specialists," the discipline is still forensic chemistry, which requires a strong, core chemistry background, and candidates must be familiar with common analytical techniques. Trace evidence specialists, like all lab scientists, are civilians. In most laboratories, new trace evidence specialists are trained under a mentor for 12 to 18 months, following the mentor's cases and undergoing further training, exercises, examinations, and, eventually, a mock trial based on a real case they have analyzed themselves. After candidates successfully complete the understudy period, they take on their own caseloads, analyzing cases and testifying in court.

Analyzing Substances and Determining Their Significance

When working with trace evidence collected from a crime scene, the trace evidence specialist must first determine *what* the particular substance is. A substance is identified through various chemical tests that determine and analyze its components. Common techniques include chromatography and spectrometry, which together separate a substance into its component parts and allow it to be specifically identified.

The techniques used to analyze forensic evidence are the same as those used in other—that is, non-forensic—chemical laboratories throughout the world. The difference is, simply, that once a forensic chemist analyzes materials involved in a crime, he or she must then determine their *significance*. The first tests determine, through a *qualitative* analysis, what the substance is in general—for example, gasoline or engine oil. Further tests determine, through *quantitative* analysis of the substance's chemical constituents or elements, the percentage of each component. Using the example of petroleum oil, these findings could link the substance to a distributor—for example, Esso, whose oil might differ slightly in its composition from Shell's—and also to a particular batch of oil and where that batch was sold— for example, the particular gas station that sold the gasoline to a consumer.

Once a substance has been identified, the significance of the evidence must be determined. It is at this point that the job of a trace evidence specialist, or forensic chemist, differs from that of other chemists. The evidence a forensic chemist examines is almost entirely evidence bearing class characteristics—that is, it can be linked to a *group*, but never to a *single source*. Evidence exhibiting class characteristics can have either low or high significance, depending on the circumstances. For example, a suspect is identified and brought to the police wearing a T-shirt with identical cotton fibres to those found at the crime scene. However, because cotton T-shirts are extremely common, there is no realistic method of determining the size of the parent population—that is, how many T-shirts with cotton fibres identical to those found at the crime scene might exist in the particular area. (See the discussion in Chapter 10, Crime Labs and the Role of Science in Investigations, "Characteristics of Evidence.") So, the significance of that evidence is very low. If, however, the fibre is rare—for example, from an unusual animal or an uncommon synthetic fibre—then its significance increases, but *only if* the examiner can determine how common the fibre is in the local population. Even then, it would not be unique, and it's significance would still be limited. (See the discussion of O.J. Simpson's shoes in Chapter 10, and the box on the following page.)

DETERMINING LEVELS OF SIGNIFICANCE

Someone enters a house by breaking a window, robs the house, and leaves. A suspect is soon apprehended near the house. When the suspect's clothing is examined at the lab, many minute fragments of glass are found on it. Does this imply guilt?

The forensic examiner will first examine the glass found on the suspect's clothes to determine its physical properties—for example, its density and refractive index. These are class characteristics that can be compared with the glass from the house. If these basic physical properties do not match, then the glass on the suspect did not come from the broken window. If the basic properties are the same—that is, if they share the same class characteristics—it means that the suspect glass came from a similar window, perhaps the window in question. Class evidence can eliminate a suspect piece of evidence completely, but it cannot individualize that evidence.

For the information—that the glass from the suspect's clothes and the glass from the broken window match in all physical properties—to be of value, the forensic examiner must determine how common the glass is. Could the suspect have picked up the glass fragments elsewhere? Because there is so much glass in our society, unless it is rare—for example, old stained glass—the glass is likely to be common, and its significance low. The forensic examiner could state in court that the suspect had glass fragments on his clothing consistent with the window that was broken at the scene; however, the defence would immediately point out that the suspect could have picked up consistent glass fragments just about anywhere, and the examiner's testimony is unlikely to have much weight.

However, because the suspect *did* have glass fragments on his clothing, research is required to determine how common it is for people to have glass fragments on their clothing. In many types of cases, such research is conducted by trace evidence specialists. In a case just like our break-in scenario, chemists at the Vancouver RCMP laboratory went to various settings—for example, schools, malls, parks, and city streets—and asked people to shake their clothing onto a sheet of paper—that is, the chemists brushed them down. Their shoes were also brushed to pick up any fragments. Scientists then analyzed the fragments to determine how many people had glass fragments on their clothing. The result of the Vancouver experiment showed that about a third of people have glass on their shoes, but less than 2 percent have glass on their clothing.

These data show that, although glass itself is common, having glass *on clothing* is rare. So the presence of glass on the suspect's clothing is now significant. Add to this the fact that in its physical properties the glass matches the window glass exactly, the evidence has now achieved some level of significance. It is still not individualizing, but it is relatively significant when combined with other evidence. Glass on the suspect's shoes alone would have had much less significance. But even where the glass was on the shoe might matter—for example, was it on the top of the shoe or on the sole? Further research would be required to determine whether there was a difference in significance based on where the glass was found.

Factors that relate directly to each case must also be considered. The next question would be how likely is it that this particular suspect would naturally have this type of evidence on him? This brings into question the validity of the database in relation to the crime under investigation. For example, it has been established that, in the average population, it is relatively rare to have glass fragments on clothing; the people tested to generate the database were average people with a range of occupations. What would happen if the suspect was a glazier by profession, a person who works with and installs glass every day? Is the database still relevant? The evidence has significance only if the suspect is a typical member of society with an occupation that is unlikely to increase the chances of having glass on his or her clothing.

Class evidence increases in significance when it is *cumulative*. Once the significance of an individual piece of evidence is determined, together with its probability of occurrence, the probabilities of all the pieces of class evidence can be added. Although a piece of class evidence may have little significance on its own, when added to numerous other pieces of class evidence found at the scene, the chances that any one person will have all the pieces are decreased. (See the discussion of Wayne Williams in Chapter 10.)

Consider a hit and run crime, where the victim was wearing a fuzzy black sweater. The sweater is not particularly rare—that is, the parent population is relatively large—but pieces of fibre matching the victim's sweater are found stuck to the broken glass of a suspect's car. While the fibre itself is not rare, the chances of it becoming stuck to the front of a car in any other way—for example, by hitting another car or a wall—seem unlikely. It is still class evidence and, therefore, circumstantial, but what if fragments of glass from a car headlight are also found on the victim? The glass, too, is class evidence, but adding the two pieces of evidence together makes them more significant.

Once the parent population has been identified, and the significance of the evidence is determined, the actual scenario must be examined. For example, manure, a high source of nitrates, is a common ingredient in homemade bombs (the bomb used in the Oklahoma City bombing was derived from manure). In a bombing, police search the suspect's residence for evidence that the suspect made the bomb. If the suspect lives in a high-rise apartment, finding manure there would have great significance; but, if the suspect lives on an active dairy farm, the presence of manure would have little significance. Even here, significance depends on where the manure is found. If it is in a shed or garage, it probably has little significance. If it is in a bedroom, the significance increases because manure is not commonly found in bedrooms. Defence counsel could argue that it came in quite innocently on the suspect's boots, which would fit if the manure were found on the floor, but it's presence is still more significant than if it were found in the barn. However, if the manure were found on top of a kitchen table, or on a counter in the bedroom, it would have considerably more significance.

As an impartial witness, it is the duty of the forensic examiner to clearly explain the evidence, both in court testimony and in reports, in terms of its significance. Otherwise, the judge or jury may be misled. In the above example of the T-shirt, simply stating that the fibre from the victim's T-shirt exactly matches the fibres from the suspect's T-shirt is not enough. As stated above, to determine the significance of any one piece of evidence, the size of the parent population must be known. Forensic examiners develop and maintain databases to allow them to determine the likelihood that a particular piece of evidence could come from a source other than a suspected source. In fact, Canadian forensic labs are world leaders in this area.

Types of Trace Evidence

As previously stated, almost anything used in the commission of a crime can be a source of trace evidence. For example, duct tape is commonly found in sexual assaults, and there are many types of duct tape available, including different tapes, different sizes, shapes, weaves, and type of glue. Duct tape is usually cut or torn, and if the perpetrator is still carrying the roll of duct tape, the most recent tear can be matched. Garbage bags are manufactured by a machine that makes tiny marks on the stream of bags as they are produced, which can be matched back to the roll. Drywall or wood fibres might be involved in a break and enter, and glue and similar materials are frequently involved in bomb making.

Some of the more common types of evidence that trace evidence specialists examine are described in the following sections.

Fibres

Fibres can be divided into natural and synthetic, or man-made, fibres. Natural fibres are those that come from animals or plants—for example, wool or cotton. Man-made fibres are synthetic, and are usually formed of polymers—that is, substances made up of many atoms. Polymers, which are now common, are also used to make plastics, adhesives, and paints.

Trace evidence specialists will examine many of the fibre's features—for example, colour, striations on the fibres, and cross-sectional shape—to help narrow down the fibre to a group. Once identified, the *significance* of the fibre evidence depends on the circumstances, as explained above.

Glass

Many features of glass can be assessed, including its composition and density. After the glass itself is analyzed, as in most forensic examinations, it is compared with a sample from a suspect or scene. The examiner can determine whether the two specimens are the same with respect to certain key characteristics. This can eliminate many possible sources, but, remember, even if the specimens are exactly the same, this is still class evidence, and there are probably many sources of the exact glass.

Paint

Paint is a common type of trace evidence because so many things have paint on them, including potentially lethal weapons such as motor vehicles. This is particularly important in motor vehicle accidents and hit-and-run scenarios because paint frequently transfers from a vehicle to whatever it hits, including a wall, another vehicle, or a person. Forensic labs have access to large paint databases and car manufacturers must update these databases every time they develop a new colour. There are countless variants, which can be used to identify a vehicle make, model, and year. A 1993 blue Toyota Camry, for example, is a different colour of blue from a 1993 blue Honda Civic, a 2003 blue Camry, or even a 1993 blue Toyota Corolla. Car paint has many layers, including electrocoat primer, primer surfacer, basecoat (colour), and clearcoat, so any new car has at least four layers of paint (Saferstein, 2011). These can be compared with the database to determine, for example, that the vehicle involved was a 1999 yellow Chevy Cavalier. There may be many of these vehicles in town—that is, the parent population may be large—but at least the possible vehicle has been narrowed down and many others eliminated. A benefit of some of this type of evidence is that it breaks, or fractures. In some situations it is possible to match a paint chip to a suspect car much like one matches a piece in a jigsaw puzzle.

If the car has been repainted, the paint chip will include the basic four layers, but it will also have the new layers on top, so the significance of the paint chip increases. How many 1999 yellow Chevy Cavaliers have been painted blue? It will be harder to locate such a car, however, because it might still be registered as yellow.

Chemists can also determine whether a light was on or off when it was broken. This factor is useful in car accidents because it can be used to determine whether a brake light was being applied when the car struck the person. Chemists look for the presence of oxides on the light filament. If present, they indicate that the filament was hot when it was exposed to air, so it must have been on at impact. In other words, the driver attempted to stop the car.

Common Applications of Forensic Chemistry

Although almost every crime can involve trace evidence that will require the lab services of forensic chemists, today, forensic chemists are involved in two particularly pertinent crimes—arson and terrorist acts involving bombs.

Fire and Arson

In most jurisdictions, any fire scene will be examined by specially trained fire investigators, most of whom have a firefighting background. These are very differently trained people from forensic identification specialists. To the average person, the aftermath of a fire looks completely disorganized, but a firefighter can interpret how the fire has been handled and put out. However, as with any crime scene, the evidence will be taken back to the laboratory to be examined by the trace evidence unit.

The fire may be a direct result of **arson**, the deliberate setting of a fire, whether, for example, by vandalism, for "fun," to collect insurance, or to disguise another crime, such as homicide. The human body is almost entirely made up of water and is thus difficult to burn. Even in a professional crematorium, which reaches temperatures in excess of 1000°C, the body is not completely broken down to ashes. Ashes are ground down after cremation to allow the family to spread them. It is almost impossible to achieve such temperatures normally. Cases have involved people returning to the body over several days to keep stoking the fire, and yet they still have not destroyed the body completely (see the box on the following page).

The first question concerning a fire is whether it was deliberately set—that is, was the fire arson? Investigators will study the burn patterns to determine where the fire began and will search for any possible accelerant. There are many types of accelerant, ranging from the simple—for example, gasoline or a pile of newspapers—to the complex—for example, chemical mixtures. As with other types of evidence, the examiner must determine the *significance* of the finding. If the fire is a car burning in a garage, then the presence of traces of gasoline under the car is not significant, but traces on the backseat or in several different areas of the car are more significant. It is important that the investigator also collects a control sample or substrate control. For example, a stain on a piece of carpet may look suspicious. When it is collected and analyzed, it is found to contain a chemical that could be an accelerant. Defence counsel might argue that the substance was naturally found

arson
the deliberate setting of a fire

THE CASE OF THE INCINERATED VICTIM

Dr. David Sweet, a Board-certified forensic odontologist and the head of the Bureau of Legal Dentistry (BOLD) at the University of British Columbia, was involved in a rare case in which the killer threw his victim into a garbage dumpster, added a fire **accelerant** (in this case, gasoline), and set fire to the remains. Quite accidentally, he achieved temperatures almost as high as a crematorium because the lid was up on one half of the dumpster and down on the other half, creating a draft that fed the flames and incinerated the body. A man who had been seen leaving a bar with the victim, who it was known owed the suspect money, was soon identified. Human blood was found in the suspect's vehicle and on a tire iron suspected to be the murder weapon. The suspect claimed that the blood came from a hitchhiker who had cut herself when she had helped the suspect change a tire a few days earlier (the hitchhiker, of course, could not be traced). Because no DNA was on record for the victim and no relatives were identified, it could not be proven that the DNA belonged to the victim. The body was too badly burned to retrieve DNA by conventional means, but, when Dr. Sweet learned that DNA was required, he pointed out that the victim had impacted wisdom teeth, which were still deeply encased in the jaw bone. Because they were protected by the bone and tongue, they might still have usable DNA. Dr. Sweet extracted the DNA from the teeth and was able to identify the victim's DNA, which was identical to that found on the weapon. Even in this extreme case, the body was still identifiable, and the suspect was convicted (Sweet & Sweet, 1995).

in the carpet, because many carpet cleaners could be used as accelerants; however, if a non-stained, control sample did not have the same chemicals present, then the substance was not a carpet cleaner.

It is amazing how much evidence is left behind in a fire. In experiments conducted to determine whether forensic entomological evidence can still be recovered, I arranged the setting of a number of house fires with decomposing animal carcasses inside. After each fire, enough evidence remained to still use the insects to estimate elapsed time since death, despite the fact that the final fire involved the entire house and burned it to the ground (Anderson, 2005).

Bombs and Terrorism

Forensic chemists also investigate some aspects of terrorism—in particular, those involving a variety of bombs. As in a fire, it is surprising how much is actually left behind for investigators to recover. A forensic chemist can frequently determine how the bomb was constructed, what it was made from, and what the explosive was. Complex bombs and military explosives are sometimes used, but most bombs in North America are homemade by single individuals. The investigator needs to find and identify the explosive chemicals recovered from the crime scene as well as to identify the detonating mechanisms.

An explosion is produced by combustion and accompanied by the creation of gases and heat; it is similar to fire, except for the incredible speed with which it happens. When an explosion is confined to something small and rigid, like a metal pipe—the typical pipe bomb—the gases expand with the heat given off by the explosion. This results in immense pressure, which stretches and then explodes the rigid pipe, producing sharp, deadly fragments, or shrapnel. As the gases are released from the pipe and move out from the blast, they expand and compress layers of surrounding air. The blast can move as fast as 11,000 km/h, creating a gale that can knock over walls, collapse buildings, and kill people. In large explosions, it is this action, rather than the shrapnel, that causes the most damage (Saferstein, 2011).

Explosives are classified as low or high explosives on the basis of the speed at which they decompose or break down. In *low explosives*, this speed is the speed of deflagration or burning speed, and it is characterized by a rapid oxidation producing heat, light, and a *subsonic* pressure wave. In *high explosives*, this speed is called the speed of detonation, which refers to the creation of a *supersonic* shock wave

THE FIRST NON-MILITARY BOMBING OF A PLANE

When someone mentions bombing attacks and planes, we immediately think of the 1985 bombing of Air India Flight 182, which resulted in the largest mass murder in Canadian history, with 329 people dead. Or we think of September 11, 2001, known as 9/11, when planes were used as weapons. But, sadly, Canada holds the record for the first passenger plane to be brought down by a bomb.

In 1949, in Quebec, a small Canadian Pacific Airlines plane with 23 people on board exploded shortly after takeoff. Chemists from the Laboratoire de sciences judiciaires et de médecine legale in Montreal examined the plane's debris and identified bomb materials and a dry-cell battery. A journalist reported that, just before takeoff, a mysterious woman had sent a parcel on the plane. Police identified her as Marguerite Ruest-Pitre. She stated that a watchmaker, Joseph-Albert Guay, who was her brother Généreux Ruest's employer, had given her the parcel to mail by air freight (Pelchat, 2006).

As the victims were identified, it was found that one, a young woman called Rita Morel Guay, was the wife of Joseph-Albert Guay. Just days before the crash, Guay had purchased his wife's ticket and taken out a substantial insurance policy on her life. He was found to be having several affairs, and was also in extreme financial difficulties. As well, he was known to have purchased the same type of battery as that recovered from the time bomb. It was believed that, with the assistance of Généreux Ruest, he had made a timing device to explode in the air. Tests of the watchmaker's work area showed the presence of blasting cap material (Pelchat, 2006).

Even in 1949, the bombers knew about forensic evidence and that some material might be left to incriminate them, so they timed the bomb to go off when the plane was over the St. Lawrence River, making recovery and analysis difficult. However, takeoff was delayed by five minutes and the plane went down over land.

Guay was convicted of murdering his wife and 22 other people, and executed in 1951. Ruest was executed in 1952 and Marguerite Ruest-Pitre in 1953, the last woman to be hanged in Canada. Since then, a book and a film of the case have suggested that Ruest and Ruest-Pitre were not aware of what the bomb material was actually for; Ruest claimed that he thought it was either to clear stumps in a field or for fishing, although this does not explain why a timing device was needed. Ruest-Pitre proclaimed her innocence all along, but the jury remained unconvinced (Pelchat, 2006).

within the explosive charge. This shock wave leads to an instantaneous build-up of heat and gases. An example of a low explosive is black powder, which, unconfined, simply burns. Black powder is often used in fuses because it burns slowly, allowing a person to get away. However, when confined to a rigid structure like a pipe, black powder can become lethal. High explosives can also be subdivided into primary and secondary explosives. Primary explosives are supersensitive to shock or friction and detonate violently. They are not usually considered safe to use as a main explosive, but are often used in small amounts to detonate other explosives—for example, in the form of blasting caps. Secondary explosives are relatively insensitive to shock and are usually detonated with an initial explosion. Examples include most commercial and military explosives such as dynamite, TNT, PETN, and RDX (Saferstein, 2011).

Many of the older explosives—for example, dynamite—have been replaced commercially with ammonium-nitrate–based explosives, such as water gels, emulsions, and ANFO explosives. Ammonium nitrate, which is simply manure, is available anywhere, so it's presence at a scene has low significance. It is also easily washed away by fire hoses or water sprinklers. The increase in the use of such explosives is therefore a concern to forensic investigators.

In addition to the explosive, a bomb contains many parts, including timers, detonators, fuses, batteries, and something to hold it all together—for example, duct tape. A lot of this material will survive and can be used to identify the bomber. Although duct tape is common, there are many kinds with different types of adhesives. Although all this evidence exhibits only class characteristics, together, the many materials that formed the bomb can be significant (see the box on the previous page).

FORENSIC TOXICOLOGY

Forensic toxicologists analyze toxins—usually, drugs, alcohol, or poisons— to determine the presence and amount of toxins in a body, and then interpret these findings to indicate whether the toxins could have caused death or a certain level of intoxicated behaviour.

In a death investigation, the main goal of a forensic toxicologist is to establish the cause of death where the autopsy examination is inconclusive. When there is no obvious cause of death, samples from the body are sent to the toxicology section of the lab. Toxicologists will undertake tests to discover whether drugs were present and, if so, what type of drugs they were, the quantity found, and how much remains of the original drug and its metabolites. Their findings will allow them to determine the original dose and establish whether it was high enough to kill or, perhaps, whether it might have exacerbated an existing medical condition.

Forensic toxicologists also provide information about intoxicated behaviour— that is, they determine whether someone was drunk at a particular time and, if so, how drunk. This is important because intoxication can be used as a defence in certain situations.

They also try to provide clues to the clinical history of someone either unwilling or unable to do so—that is, someone who is unconscious or dead. This information can give police an idea of how long someone had been using a drug or whether the drug was used only once. Some drugs—for example, marijuana—remain in the system for a long time, whereas the body rapidly processes a drug like heroin. Drug metabolites are often deposited in hair, so, depending on hair length, a person's drug history can be determined for the past months or even years. Finally, forensic toxicologists assist in establishing the truth of a suspect's statements—for example, "I was really high so I don't remember whether I killed her or not." Some drugs cause memory loss, but many do not.

Scope of Work and Training

The preliminary qualification required to train as a forensic toxicologist is a minimum of an honours B.Sc. in biochemistry, pharmacology, physiology, or chemistry, but many toxicologists have advanced degrees. Suitable candidates must have strong, core biochemistry backgrounds and knowledge of the effects of toxins on people; therefore, a background in pharmacology is useful. Once accepted into the forensic lab, trainee toxicologists understudy with a qualified and experienced toxicologist for up to two years, taking courses and doing exercises, mock cases, and mock trials before taking on their own cases. The toxicologist's expertise is primarily in analytical chemistry and pharmacology, but it also borrows from the fields of pathology, physiology, and biochemistry.

In the RCMP labs, toxicology units are found in Vancouver, Winnipeg, and Halifax, with some work also done in Edmonton (although, as noted in Chapter 10, the RCMP announced in mid-2012 that the Winnipeg and Halifax labs would be closed). Toxicology labs are also found at the Centre of Forensic Sciences in Toronto and Sault Ste. Marie as well as in Montreal at the Laboratoire de sciences judiciaires et de médecine légale. Provincial toxicology labs may also exist to assist in coroners' or medical examiners' cases. Health Canada, which includes the Bureau of Dangerous Drugs, looks at violation of the *Controlled Drugs and Substances Act* (1996). Private labs may be involved in employee drug screening.

Analysis of Evidence

A forensic toxicology investigation has two main parts: an analytical phase and an interpretive phase. The analytical component involves, first, choosing the best specimen for analysis—for example, blood or urine; second, extracting the chemical compounds using chemical procedures and separating their component parts, and, last, *identifying* the substances.

Unless it is instantly fatal, when someone ingests a drug, the body immediately begins to process, or metabolize, the substance—that is, it breaks the drug down into other substances called metabolites. The parent or original drug can be identified either by its actual presence or by the presence of its known metabolites. Even when a person has taken only one drug, there will be many metabolites of the drug present. These metabolites break down further into their own metabolites. For example, one of the breakdown products of heroin is morphine. Heroin breaks down into morphine so quickly that heroin itself is never detected in a person, only morphine and other metabolites.

Once the drug is identified, the toxicologist must *interpret* the results to address such questions as when was the last dose taken; was the dose acute or chronic; and how was it taken—for example, by intravenous injection, orally, snorted, or smoked? The number of metabolites present determine how much of the drug was originally taken. Also, because drugs break down at predictable rates, the toxicologist can usually determine when the drug was taken. This information allows the toxicologist to determine the drug level at an earlier time—for example, at the time an assault took place. The toxicologist can also determine which symptoms this level of drug is likely to produce.

Choosing the Best Toxicological Specimens

The specimens that a toxicologist chooses to analyze vary with the situation. Blood and urine are most common, but many others are also used.

Blood

Blood is one of the major specimens used for several reasons. First, it is usually easy to get a sample of blood. Second, blood is considered a primary specimen in drug screening as well as for both confirmatory tests and quantification—that is, determining how much of the drug is or was present. Blood is also a primary index for drug or poison effects, and is thus used for drug and alcohol testing.

However, there are several problems with blood as a toxicological specimen. It is considered a "dirty" specimen because it has lots of other materials in it—for example, proteins, which must be removed before it can be analyzed. In addition, the drug levels present in blood are low. Obtaining blood is invasive if the person is alive and blood may not be available if the person is dead and decomposed. Also, sometimes the level of a substance in the blood is not truly reflective of the effects of that substance. For example, the levels of THC, the active ingredient in cannabis, in the blood is not a good representation of the behaviour induced. Fortunately, the level of alcohol in the blood of a living person has been shown to be directly proportional to the level in the brain, which means that a blood sample can give an accurate representation of the level of impairment.

Even in a recently dead body, obtaining blood can be a problem. In an autopsy, the easiest place to collect blood is from the heart. However, after death, drugs and alcohol are redistributed in the body. Therefore, a drug level taken only from the blood in the heart may not be representative of the level in other areas of the body. Bacterial decomposition (putrefaction) actually produces alcohol in the body after death. As a result, if a person is tested for alcohol at autopsy, the alcohol detected may come from bacterial action and not reflect the actual consumption of alcohol in life. In order to get an accurate postmortem alcohol level, the pathologist needs to compare blood from several sites. If the alcohol levels from different areas of the body are the same, it is likely that the alcohol was consumed as opposed to being the result of post-mortem decomposition, but if the levels are different in different areas of the body, it may be an artifact of decomposition.

Urine

After blood, urine is the most popular body fluid for toxicological analysis. It is easily available, and its collection is much less invasive than collecting blood. Urine is the primary fluid used in screening and confirmation, but it is not so useful for quantification. By the time drugs reach the urine they have travelled all over the body and have been broken down to their excretory products. Their presence in the urine indicates that the person took drugs, but the amount is hard to determine. After death, urine can still be extracted from the bladder. Once it has entered the bladder, it can no longer be contaminated by the rest of the body. Urine is much less subject to post-mortem alcohol production, and is thus a good specimen for alcohol at an autopsy. It is a clean specimen because it is almost all water, so it is easy to work with, but, in a living person, because people are rarely watched when they give a urine sample, there is always the possibility that it may have been tampered with.

Hair

Toxins in the body are stored in the hair, which makes hair an interesting drug specimen. Most specimens show only recent drug use, but hair reveals a person's drug history for as long as the hair has been growing. Someone with hair to their waist, for example, carries their drug history for the past several years, whereas someone with a buzz cut reveals a history of a day or two at most. Hair collection is not invasive because analysis requires only a few strands. Hair, and to a lesser extent, fingernails, not only reveals length of drug use, it also shows drug-free periods (see the box below).

THE STRANGE FATE OF NAPOLEON

After his defeat by Wellington, at the Battle of Waterloo in 1815, the former French Emperor Napoleon Bonaparte was exiled to St. Helena, a small island in the South Atlantic Ocean, with his alleged mistress, the wife of his valet, and about 20 servants. It was originally believed that Napoleon died from a cancerous stomach ulcer. However, in the 1950s, when his valet's diaries were published, it was postulated that Napoleon had been poisoned. Fortunately, a number of his staff had kept some of his hair as a souvenir and scientists were able to retrieve the hair samples from their descendants. Napoleon's hair was tested and found to contain arsenic, which had been consumed over the months leading up to his death (Leslie & Smith, 1978). This suggested that Napoleon had been murdered. Members of his staff came under suspicion (Weider & Harry, 1999), but it has also been suggested that the British government had him killed.

Later investigations showed that some wallpaper used at that time was found to contain arsenic (Jones & Ledingham, 1982). Apparently, a popular green wallpaper of the day used a green dye called "Scheele's Green," which contained copper arsenite. A piece of the wallpaper used in Napoleon's quarters was located and it contained this green in the pattern. Normally, this fact would not have posed a problem, but it was found that if the paper became mouldy, the mould could result in the arsenic being released into the air and breathed in. Later investigation showed that members of Napoleon's staff also became ill and one had died. It is now thought that the arsenic aggravated his stomach ulcer, resulting in death, although the conspiracy theory still lingers.

A few years ago, hair analysis provoked a controversy. When blood or urine tests positive for a substance, there can be no arguing that the person actually took the drug (willingly or not). However, in early cases, drug evidence from hair was sometimes found to be *on* the hair, not *in* it. As a result, people could claim that they did not take drugs themselves, but were at a party where others were smoking pot, which adhered to their hair. Techniques have now been developed that carefully wash the hair samples so that any drugs detected must have actually been in the hair. In Canada, hair testing is done in criminal cases only, but in the United States hair is tested in both criminal cases and in employee tests. Employee drug screening is rare in Canada.

Other Toxicological Specimens

Many other body fluids and tissues can be analyzed—for example, the liver, kidney, gastric or stomach contents, bile, brain, lungs, injection sites, cerebrospinal fluid, bone marrow, maggots feeding on the body, vitreous humour (jelly-like substance in the eye), synovial fluid, stains, saliva, fingernails, and meconium (the first feces a baby produces). The vitreous humour is a particularly good specimen for alcohol testing because the eye is sealed and thus protected, so post-mortem production of alcohol does not affect it. The obvious problem with most of these specimens is that they can only be collected postmortem.

Non-biological exhibits are also analyzed—for example, drug paraphernalia, syringes, spoons, and pipes, which can include residues such as powders, stains, food, or medicines. For example, pills in a prescription drug bottle might be seized from a crime scene to determine whether they are actually the pills listed on the label.

Analysis and Interpretation

Specimens presented to a toxicologist for analysis could be one of thousands of different drugs or toxins. A few that are most common, as well as evidence from the scene—for example, drug paraphernalia or prescription bottles—may give some clues as to where to start, but a myriad of substances could be present.

Unlike television, where a scientist simply plugs a sample into one end of a machine, which, after some interesting noises, spits out the identification (and usually the name of the killer as well), there is no single test or scheme that can identify everything. This is why many tests have to be done when poison is suspected. Often, when a specimen from the morgue is sent for toxicological analysis, the toxicologist has no idea what might be present. If no specific drug or poison is suspected, a general set of tests are done. If they do not reveal a cause of death, further tests are performed. Forensic toxicologists use a repertoire of tests that they modify depending on the case, the type of specimen they receive, and how much of the specimen they have. The tests can exclude or indicate the presence of a drug, poison, or a class of compounds.

As in forensic biology, there are presumptive or screening tests, which, if positive, must be followed up with a confirmatory chemical test. Presumptive tests are quick and fairly sensitive, but they are not specific. They do not determine exactly what a substance is, but they can point to a class of drugs. Presumptive tests are particularly useful for excluding a drug or a class of drugs. Confirmatory tests are done after presumptive tests, and they are sensitive and specific to a single drug or metabolite.

The final determination of what the drug was comes after all the information is put together—that is, how much was taken; what are the symptoms of taking that sort of dose; and, overall, what would the person's behaviour be like at a given time after the substance was ingested? For example, in a case in which two men were sharing drugs, one man was beaten to death, allegedly by the other. The survivor claimed that he had used so much of the drug that he had completely lost control, killing his friend. However, toxicological analysis of the blood of both men showed that, in actual fact, very little of the drug had been consumed, so the drug was not responsible for the murder.

Clandestine Laboratories

In general, crime scenes are attended and processed by sworn police officers and some specialists—for example, forensic archaeologists—while lab scientists do all their work in the laboratory. One exception is when a possible clandestine drug lab is discovered. In such cases, a forensic toxicologist may attend the scene with the police. There are several reasons for this. First, clandestine drug labs use a variety of substances and methods that can be highly dangerous if mishandled or not properly identified and understood. For example, one stage in the production of crystal methamphetamine requires refrigeration of some extremely volatile and explosive materials. There have been cases where uninformed investigators have opened a refrigerator door without first disconnecting the refrigerator and a simple spark from the light has caused the entire area to blow up. Some chemicals and equipment used in drug manufacture are extremely unstable and may explode on contact or exposure to air. The toxicologist can identify such substances as dangerous and can also specify which specimens they need for analysis.

WHAT REALLY HAPPENED TO THE FRANKLIN EXPEDITION?

In 1845, famed British sea captain Sir John Franklin led a voyage to find the Northwest Passage. This passage would have allowed ships to travel to the Pacific without sailing the long way around Cape Horn, South America. A passage through the top of Canada would be safer, quicker, and less expensive. Franklin's voyage was well planned; it consisted of two ships, the Erebus and the Terror, which were well equipped for their time. Although the voyage was supposed to last a year and a half, the ships had provisions for three years. Besides their provisions, the crew had a vast library to read from, musicians to entertain them, and teachers to impart knowledge. Both ships were designed to withstand ice-locked conditions. Canning was a new invention, and Franklin's ships were the first to carry canned food. Food no longer needed to be preserved with salt, and live animals did not need to be brought on the journey to be slaughtered later. One could bring as many cans as the cupboards would hold and the food would last a long time.

The ships set sail, to much fanfare, on the morning of May 19, 1845. They stopped at the Whalefish Islands, on the west coast of Greenland, to meet a supply ship and send letters home. The letters described the crew's confidence in the voyage. Then the ships set sail once more, never to be seen again. They were last sighted by two whaling ships near Baffin Island (Beattie & Geiger, 1998).

Two years passed before it became obvious that the ships were lost. Franklin's voyage had been so well planned and the ships so well equipped that failure had been unthinkable, and no plan of action was in place. Sir John's young wife kept her husband's name before the British government and in the press. Consequently, rescue missions were organized to find the Franklin expedition. At one point, three ships attempted Franklin's passage from three different routes. All failed to locate the ships or any member of the crew. Because everyone knew the ships were well equipped to survive for many months, even years, people were not overly concerned. Then, in 1850, a reward was offered.

The ships were never found, but, in 1850, remains from the voyage were discovered, including cairns made of tin cans, scraps of old clothing, and, ultimately, three carefully dug graves on Beechy Island, dated 1846 (Beattie & Geiger, 1998). Interest in the lost expedition remained high. Lady Franklin funded many other ships to solve the mystery of how and why the Franklin expedition failed.

Sailors on the rescue missions spoke to local Inuit, who described the deaths of many white men by starvation, also describing tales of insanity. They reported that the white men had become violent, irrational in their behaviour, and so near starvation that they had resorted to cannibalism. These stories were not believed because no one could accept that British sailors could ever act in this manner.

The solution to the mystery appeared in the 1980s, when Dr. Owen Beattie, a forensic anthropologist, exhumed and examined the three well-preserved bodies buried on Beechy Island. Many tests were conducted, and it was discovered that the three men had extremely high levels of lead in their bodies (Beattie & Geiger, 1998).

Beattie and his team examined some of the tin can cairns. In 1845, canning was in its infancy, and the government had accepted the cheapest bid for the making of the cans. The solder used to seal the tins was, of course, lead. When a can is soldered, its two ends should overlap. In the case of these cans, they did not. They met and were then soldered, which meant that lead was in contact with the food inside the can. Two things next occurred: first, because many of the cans were not sealed properly, the food rotted and the cans burst; second, those cans that stayed sealed were heavily laden with toxic lead.

Beattie discovered some of these damaged and poorly soldered cans on Beechy Island. As the Inuit had reported, the men were starving because the food in tins, meant as supplies, was inedible. There were empty cans in the cairn as well, which proved that lead-contaminated food had been ingested.

It is now believed that the men of the Franklin expedition died as a result of a combination of starvation and lead poisoning. Today, we know that lead is a major neurotoxin, and even low levels have been shown to affect cognitive behaviour and aggression (Needleman et al., 1996), so the behaviours reported by the Inuit are understandable.

KEY TERMS

accelerant

arson

FURTHER READING

Christian, D.R. (2004). *Forensic investigation of clandestine laboratories.* Boca Raton, FL: CRC Press.

James, S.H., & Nordby, J.J. (Eds.). (2009). *Forensic science: An introduction to scientific and investigative techniques* (3rd ed.). Boca Raton, FL: CRC Press.

O'Connor, J.J., & Redsicker, D.R. (1996). *Practical fire and arson investigation* (2nd ed.). Boca Raton, FL: CRC Press.

Saferstein, R. (2011). *Criminalistics: An introduction to forensic science* (10th ed.). Upper Saddle River, NJ: Prentice Hall.

REVIEW QUESTIONS

True or False?

1. Trace evidence specialists, or forensic chemists, are the primary scientists involved in arson investigations.

2. Identifying trace evidence is of little value without also determining its significance.

3. Most cars have at least four layers of paint.

4. Newspapers can be considered a fire accelerant.

5. Low explosives produce a supersonic shock wave.

6. From an analysis of the metabolites in a blood sample, forensic toxicologists can determine the amount of each metabolite, how much of the parent drug was taken, and when.

7. From an analysis of the metabolites in a urine sample, forensic toxicologists can determine the amount of each metabolite, how much of the parent drug was taken, and when.

8. Blood is an excellent toxicological specimen for quantification.

9. Urine is an excellent toxicological specimen for quantification.

10. Urine is an excellent toxicological specimen for screening.

Multiple Choice

1. Which of the following would not be considered trace evidence by a forensic chemist?

   a. blood.

   b. drywall.

   c. fibres.

   d. cosmetics.

   e. paint.

2. In a house fire that is a suspected case of arson, which of the following findings would be most significant?

   a. gasoline in the garage.

   b. gasoline in the kitchen.

   c. gasoline on the bedroom floor.

   d. gasoline on top of the bed and other furniture.

   e. none of the above.

3. Which of the following facts are *not* true of low explosives?

   a. The term "low explosive" refers to the speed of deflagration.

   b. A low explosive produces a subsonic pressure wave.

   c. A low explosive simply burns if unconfined.

   d. An example of a low explosive is dynamite.

   e. A low explosive is often used in pipe bombs.

4. Which of the following is best for post-mortem alcohol quantification?

   a. blood.

   b. hair.

   c. vitreous humour.

   d. liver.

   e. kidney.

5. Which of the following is a drawback when using blood as a toxicological specimen?

   a. Taking blood is invasive.

   b. Blood is "dirty."

   c. Drug and alcohol levels in blood are redistributed post-mortem.

   d. The drug level in a blood specimen may not be reflective of the effects of that drug.

   e. All of the above.

6. Which of the following is best for determining long-term drug use?

a. blood.

b. hair.

c. vitreous humour.

d. liver.

e. kidney.

7. Which of the following can be used as a toxicological specimen?

a. gastric contents.

b. meconium.

c. bone marrow.

d. maggots.

e. all of the above.

8. Forensic laboratory scientists rarely attend crime scenes. Which of the following investigations might prove the exception?

a. clandestine drug labs.

b. arson fires.

c. terrorist attacks.

d. break and enter.

e. sexual assault.

Short Answer

1. Explain how a forensic chemist determines the significance of a piece of trace evidence.

2. A glass door has been kicked in during a break in, and a suspect is found nearby with glass shards on the top of his shoes. What must the forensic chemist do to determine the evidentiary value of the glass?

3. Explain two major forensic problems with ammonium nitrate explosives.

4. Explain how evidence possessing only class characteristics can be used cumulatively to make it more significant than any one piece of evidence on its own.

5. Explain the problem with taking a single blood sample from the heart at an autopsy to determine alcohol levels. What should be done to get a correct reading from blood at an autopsy?

6. Explain the two major roles of a forensic toxicologist.

The Analysis of Tool Marks and Firearms

14

LEARNING OUTCOMES

After completing this chapter, you should be able to:

- Understand the broad definition of a tool.

- Explain the class and individual characteristics created by the manufacture and use of a tool, including a firearm.

- Define the two different methods that make a tool mark unique.

- Understand the parts of a gun cartridge, how the projectile is fired, and which parts of the gun make marks on the projectile.

- Explain how an examiner makes a physical match between a bullet and a suspect gun.

- Understand the value of examining gunshot residue on a target and on a suspected shooter, and the limitations involved in these assessments.

INTRODUCTION

When we think of a tool mark, the first thing that comes to mind is the impression that a chisel or a hammer makes, but tools in a forensic context are much broader. A **tool** is any hard object that can make a mark on a softer object. Although this definition includes the types of tools we are generally familiar with, a **tool mark** can also include a boot mark on skin or a tire impression in mud. A tool can even be something as large as a backhoe. Firearms examinations are extensions of tool-mark examinations, and, in the forensic laboratory, the same unit performs both types of examinations.

Note that firearms examinations in the crime lab are not the same as **ballistics**, which is the study of the path or trajectory of ordnance, usually studied in the military. Firearm examiners in the forensic lab try to determine whether a particular weapon fired a suspect bullet, cartridge, or other ammunition component.

tool
any hard object that can make a mark on a softer object

tool mark
the impression made by any tool

ballistics
the study of the path or trajectory of ordnance

SCOPE OF WORK AND TRAINING

The work of tool-mark and firearms examiners primarily comprises examining any sort of tool mark, tool, firearm, and ammunition and physically matching the tool to a suspect mark. Tool-mark and firearms examiners thus mainly compare one piece of evidence with another. For example, they might match a bullet to a possible gun, a screwdriver or chisel to a window frame that has been broken into, or a knife to a cut in a bone. They also perform a number of other tasks, including restoring serial numbers that have been ground down to obliterate them or matching broken fragments to an object.

An examiner looking at a firearm does not just do physical matching; he or she also assesses the mechanical condition and safety of the weapon, determines whether it is legal, develops reference tables for firearms, and maintains the Canadian Integrated Ballistics Identification Network (CIBIN). In some situations, examiners might attend autopsies to assist in determining bullet path and to help recover projectiles. In collaboration with the forensic pathologist and identification officers, examiners determine the distance a target was from the shooter, look at gunshot residue on hands and target, and reconstruct shooting incidents to determine the veracity of witness or suspect statements.

The preliminary qualifications required to train to be a firearms examiner in the forensic lab are, typically, a minimum of an honours bachelor of science (B.Sc.) in engineering or physics, although training in other sciences might be accepted. Some background in chemistry is also preferred. In particular, applicants must have strong mechanical aptitude and logical, analytical minds; most have extensive experience with firearms. In most labs, candidates undergo a two-year period under a senior tool-mark and firearms examiner, which includes assisting in cases, undergoing examinations, and participating in mock trials.

An exception to the general rule of civilian scientists, in the firearms unit, firearms and tool-marks examiners are sometimes serving police officers, although most are civilians. Also, most forensic lab sections are found only in the forensic labs themselves, but city and other police sometimes have their own firearms section, even though they use forensic labs for all other evidence analysis. The Centre of Forensic Sciences in Ontario and the Laboratoire de sciences judiciaires et de médecine légale in Quebec have tool-marks and firearms sections and, at the time of writing, the RCMP have laboratories with tool-marks and firearms sections in Vancouver, Regina, and Halifax.

TOOL MARKS

Class and Individual Characteristics

When a tool leaves a mark on a softer object, the mark will possess both class and individual characteristics.

In the context of tool marks, class characteristics link a mark to a group of tools and eliminate all other groups, whereas individual characteristics indicate that the mark was made by this particular tool and no other. The marks left behind by a tool can be classified as impressed or striated. *Impressed tool marks* are made when the tool is simply pressed into the softer object, such as with a blow. *Striated tool marks* involve movement, so the tool is impressed then moved. Any one tool can make a variety of different types of marks depending on how the tool makes contact with the object and what part of the tool makes contact. Think of a screwdriver. The marks it makes will differ depending on whether the tip or the entire surface is used. Also, a tool mark is not one-dimensional—it has both depth and dimension. Think of pushing a chisel into a piece of wood to pry open a door. The chisel will make a 3-dimensional mark, so there are many areas to look at. The tool mark might not include the entire width of the tool because only a part might have made the mark. For example, a 20-cm-long knife blade might only be inserted into a wound for 10 cm.

Class characteristics—for example, the width, shape, and size of a knife blade or screwdriver—can indicate the class or group of tools from which the suspect tool came. These characteristics are helpful in eliminating many other groups of tools and will give investigators an idea of what sort of tool to look for when they are searching a suspect or a scene.

TOOL MARKS IN DEATH INVESTIGATIONS

Although we typically think of tool marks as small marks caused by a tool, remember that a tool is any hard object making a mark on a softer object. A spade or shovel will often leave a mark in soil. This is particularly important in the investigation of clandestine graves. When a hole is dug in undisturbed soil, the edges and sides of the grave may be marked by the back of the spade. When a grave is exhumed, identification officers take special care to preserve the original sides of the grave. In some cases, clear impressions of the tool that was used to dig the grave can be seen and casts can be made of these marks. Although a killer is likely to get rid of a murder weapon such as a gun or knife, he or she is unlikely to think of getting rid of the spade used to dig the grave. What is more innocent than a spade resting in a garden shed? When a suspect's property is searched, the spade used to dig the grave might be identified. On a larger scale, where mass graves have been dug using heavy equipment, tool marks on the edge of the mass grave have been linked to the backhoe that was used to dig the grave.

Individual characteristics, formed by accidental or unplanned events, can restrict, or individualize, a tool mark to a specific tool. Tools acquire individual marks in two different ways:

1. *Manufacture.* One might assume that mass-produced tools are identical. However, although the manufacturing process primarily produces class characteristics, it can produce individual marks as well. During manufacture, the machinery producing the tool picks up tiny bits of metal, grease, and dust, which may mark an individual tool as it is being made. The manufacturing instrument thus changes slightly, so that each knife or chisel has slightly different marks on it. Lab scientists regularly test this fact. They purchase new items directly from the assembly line, manufactured immediately one after the other, and compare them. In every case, the marks are individual.

2. *Use.* Many individual characteristics are formed during use. Any object will become scuffed, scratched, and chipped as it is used, and these marks are individualizing—for example, a shoe sole worn with use (see the box below). Also, a tool is often sharpened or cleaned, which may change its surface. Use can create many individual marks as it continues. Earlier marks will be obliterated by new marks if the tool remains in use so the characteristics will be dynamic. This can be a problem if a tool is used in the commission of a crime and then continues to be used, changing the individual marks.

A concern in any forensic comparison is the possibility of a false match. Chances of a false match decrease with the number of individualizing marks found. Usually, seven to eight matches are considered identifying, but, in most cases, there are many more matches, perhaps hundreds. Therefore, as long as enough individualizing points are examined, there should be no false matches. The chance of a false match is likely to be a problem only when a fraction of a tool mark is recovered from a scene. In such a case, the examiner might say that the marks are consistent

---

THE INDIVIDUALIZING OF A BOOT PRINT

Although we know that manufacture can produce individual marks on a tool, and that use or wear will add further individual marks while obliterating others, one might think that the same types of tools used in the same manner would not be readily distinguishable. To assess this, RCMP examiners studied a group of new RCMP recruits at the Regina depot. All were assigned uniforms that included the same type of boots. The recruits went through the same basic training, which included the same exercises on the same paths and routes. These recruits, although wearing different sizes of footwear, were of a similar level of fitness and walked and ran in the same areas. The boots were worn only at the depot, never off the grounds.

Each boot was examined before being first worn, halfway through training, and at the end of training. The boots were found to have individual marks from manufacture and, despite being used on the same surfaces for weeks, they were each individually marked at all stages of the experiment.

with the suspect weapon, but that not enough marks exist for comparison to allow the weapon to be individualized. Even when only part of a tool is found, however, it often has enough points to individualize it (see the box below).

It has always been accepted that a tool mark, like a fingerprint, can be individualized because the markings created by manufacture and use are believed to be unique. However, the National Academies of Science (NAS) report on forensic science (NAS, 2009) was scathing about all types of pattern evidence, stating that uniqueness has never been proven. This is true, but, like fingerprints, tool-mark matching and all other aspects of pattern analysis were judged to be unique decades ago and have been accepted as such without further question. This is why a tool-mark or fingerprint specialist is allowed to testify that, for example, this specific tool and no other made this mark, or this fingerprint belongs to Joe Brown and no one else; however, newer sciences such as DNA fingerprinting are not allowed to be presented in this manner. A DNA specialist has to quantify his or her results and can state only that, for example, the chance of the DNA coming from anyone other than the suspect is 10 billion to 1. Realistically, such a statement means that the DNA can only be the suspect's, but the specialist cannot state for the court that it *is* his, as a fingerprint specialist can.

Since the NAS report, there has been an upsurge of research in many areas of forensic science in response to the criticisms. One paper (Bachrach, Jain, Jung, & Koons, 2010) showed that the premise of uniqueness is valid and that such analyses *can* be quantified.

Physical Matching

When an examiner considers whether a suspect tool made a specific mark, he or she cannot directly compare the tool to the mark. The suspect tool must *never* be placed into the tool mark because this would contaminate the evidence. Defence counsel could claim that the investigator may have changed the tool mark by applying the tool. Therefore, the examiner makes an impression (a cast) of the suspect

THE KNIFE AND THE BEAR

The highly decomposed remains of a murdered person were found weeks after death in a rural area. The remains had been scavenged by a bear. An observant coroner noticed bear scat around the deceased and suggested that it be collected in case the bear had eaten and passed any parts of the victim. Together with the remains, the scat was taken to the morgue and X-rayed. The X-ray showed a tiny piece of metal, so the scat was hand-searched. It was found to contain hair from the victim (useful to determine length and colour for a facial reconstruction and, possibly, for DNA) as well as a small piece of rib bone, which the bear had eaten when scavenging the remains. Lodged in the bone fragment was a minute piece of metal that was later identified as a chip from a knife blade. When the suspect was apprehended, he still had the knife, and the tiny chip was matched back to it. The chip break pattern matched the pattern on the knife, and the individualizing striations were consistent.

Source: Adapted from Mendel (2008). Reproduced by permission.

tool, in a soft substance, which can then be directly compared with the suspect mark. Often, many marks are made because angle is important. If the tool does not make an impression on the soft material, harder materials are gradually tried.

In the case of foot prints or tire tracks, photographs and then a cast are taken. In some cases, various chemicals will be used to visualize the impression. There are a variety of techniques used to cast a print, and the technique used depends on the material the impression is in—for example, blood, mud, or snow.

like with like
the comparison of two objects, side by side—for example, a tool mark with a cast of the suspect tool

The examiner then compares **like with like** under a comparison, or compound, microscope, which is two microscopes joined together (see Figure 14.1). A comparison microscope allows the examiner to compare objects under two independent objective lenses, side by side, in the same ocular field. When the examiner looks through the comparison microscope, he or she sees one image that is made up of two images, one from each microscope. This sounds confusing, but it isn't. Basically, the examiner sees one image, with a line down the centre (see Figure 14.2). One half of the image is the tool mark, the other the cast of the suspect tool. This means that the examiner can precisely compare every millimetre of each image.

1. *Class characteristics.* First, the examiner looks to determine whether the two marks have the same class characteristics. If they don't, the tool is immediately eliminated. If the characteristics are the same, then it means that the tool that made the known mark and the tool that made the crime-scene mark belong to the same class. Examples include such characteristics as the width and size of the tip of a chisel.

2. *Individual characteristics.* The examiner next looks at the individual characteristics. In every case and for each point, to avoid bias, the examiner first looks at the unknown, then the known. This holds true for any pattern evidence. If the examiner were to look at the known first, find

FIGURE 14.1 Comparison microscope

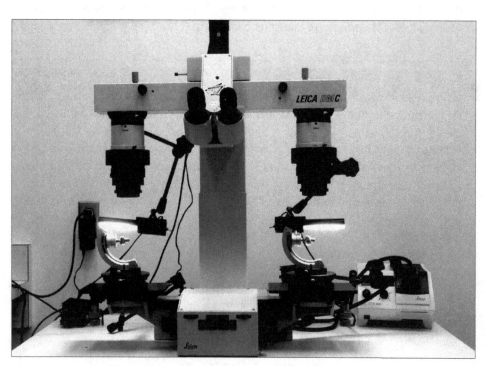

FIGURE 14.2 Comparison of the scuff marks on the primer of an unknown cartridge found at a crime scene with an exemplar fired from a suspect weapon. Scuff marks are caused by individual marks on the firearm created during manufacture, which transfer to the cartridge during firing. The marks are a match.

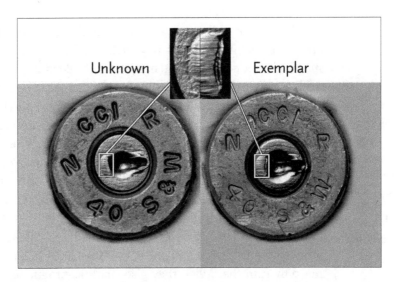

a mark, and then look at the unknown to see whether the mark is also there, the examiner would be actively trying to find the matching mark in the unknown, which could result in bias. As discussed above, at least seven to eight matches are necessary for a positive match, but usually there are many more.

In order to establish conclusively that a specific tool caused a specific mark, the examiner must find that both class *and* individual characteristics match. There must be no unexplained differences—for example, a mark found on a tool used after the suspect tool mark was made. If a burglar is caught after performing a series of break and enters in one night, the chisel used to pry open the window might be matched to the last house entered as well as to the houses entered just before, but there will probably be changed individual characteristics between the marks made 24 robberies earlier and the tool. Class characteristics will be unchanged, but some individual marks may have been obliterated and new ones created. If the sequence from first to last burglary can be shown, but with changing marks, these marks are considered to be explained differences.

FIREARMS

Firearm identification aims to determine whether a bullet, cartridge case, or other ammunition component was fired by a particular firearm. Firearm identification is therefore a specialized form of tool-mark identification in that the barrel of the firearm acts as a tool, producing marks on the bullet and the breech face; and the firing pin, chamber, extractor, and ejector of the firearm act as tools producing marks on a cartridge.

The Making of a Gun

A gun barrel is produced from a solid bar of steel whose centre is then drilled out. The drill is made of extremely hard metal in order to cut through the solid steel bar. As the drill removes the centre, it leaves microscopic marks on the inside of the barrel. As it drills one barrel after another in a continuous process, it picks up and leaves behind fine bits of metal, iron filing, dirt, and so on. These tiny bits make unique, random scratches on the inside of the gun barrel. Even two barrels drilled immediately after one another are unique. The barrel of the gun is a harder substance than the bullet, so it acts as a tool, marking the projectile.

Once the drill has made a single smooth hole through the metal bar to create a hollow pipe, the barrel is drilled again to produce **rifling**, a series of spiral grooves. This drill is called a broach cutter. The broach cuts grooves into the inside of the barrel, simultaneously rotating as it does so. A bullet fired from a straight barrel would tumble and not fly in a straight line. A bullet is useless as a projectile if it does not fly straight, so a spin must be placed on it as it leaves the barrel. This is the job of the spiral grooves. As the bullet travels along the barrel, it engages the grooves and is spun out of the end of the barrel in a straight line. These grooves not only spin the bullet, they also mark it, producing both class and accidental characteristics. The grooves are the deeper cuts and the original drilled areas are called the lands.

rifling
a series of spiral grooves made in the barrel of a gun to ensure that the bullet flies in a straight line and providing class characteristics

There are several ways of creating rifling in a gun barrel, and various gun manufacturers use different techniques. Some use the broach drill; others use the button process, which involves forcing a metal plug though the barrel; still others use a mandrel or hummer (Saferstein, 2011). As well, the number of grooves that are cut, the width between them, and whether they spin the bullet clockwise or counterclockwise vary between manufacturers and between guns. This is why all Colt 45s have the same number of grooves and lands, with the same distance between them, and each spins the bullet the same way, whereas a Smith and Wesson 45 has a different number of lands and grooves; thus the rifling provides class characteristics. The diameter of the original barrel, before the rifling was added, determines the **calibre** of the gun, which is another class characteristic. Calibre is measured between the lands.

calibre
the diameter of the barrel of a gun, before rifling is added, measured from lands to lands, and providing class characteristics

If you closely examine the inside of a gun barrel, you can see minute scratches along the length of the grooves and lands. These are the individual characteristics made during manufacture and the subsequent use of the gun, and they make it possible to match a bullet to a specific gun.

Ammunition

A firearm fires a projectile from its muzzle. The cartridge loaded in a gun has many parts. It consists of the metal case that contains the propellants, or gunpowder, as well as the bullet itself. Gunpowder needs a small charge to set it off. The base of the cartridge usually contains a primer that will ignite the smokeless powder and eject the bullet when it is struck. Gunpowder is not actually a powder; it is made up of tiny granules. Some cartridges do not have separate primers; instead, the primer powder is stored in the rim of the cartridge. These are referred to as rim fire cartridges and are common in .22 calibre rifles. In these, the cartridge is discharged by striking the rim.

Examiners in the crime lab try to determine whether a particular weapon fired a suspect bullet, cartridge, or other ammunition component. The "bullet" itself is the actual projectile or "slug," and it is the part of the cartridge that injures or kills.

It is the piece of the cartridge that is shot out; the cartridge case will stay in the gun or be ejected close by, depending on the type of gun. The lead bullet may have a full metal jacket, which prevents it from fragmenting, or it may have a hollow point, which makes it mushroom.

The actual bullet is quite small; the bulk of the space in the cartridge is taken up by the gunpowder, which burns rapidly and releases gases that propel the bullet forward. A shotgun cartridge has a quantity of lead shot, rather than a bullet; however, the basic principles are the same.

When the hammer is cocked, the gun is ready to be fired. Cocking the gun moves the hammer back toward the webbing between the shooter's thumb and forefinger. The trigger releases the hammer, which falls rapidly, striking the primer (or rim, in a rim-fire cartridge). The bullet travels at great speed along a hard barrel. Because the bullet is the softer object, the barrel acts as a tool, leaving both class and individual characteristics on the bullet.

Physical Matching

As in any other tool-mark examination, examiners must compare like with like. They cannot simply look at a bullet and then up the barrel of the gun. When a suspect gun is brought in, a test bullet is fired into something soft so the bullet is not deformed. Before it is fired, the examiner must first ensure that the gun is harmless. It is not cleaned before firing a test bullet because cleaning might damage or scratch the inside of the barrel, changing it from when it may have fired the suspect bullet. Most labs fire test bullets into a large water tank because water slows a bullet rapidly. The test bullet will be as perfect as the gun can make it, but the suspect bullet will have been retrieved from something it was fired into—for example, a wall or a body—and will probably be deformed, especially if it struck a hard substance.

The test bullet is next compared directly with the suspect bullet, using a bullet holder underneath one objective lens of a comparison microscope. This method allows the examiner to rotate the bullet very carefully and precisely. The other bullet is placed in a similar holder under the other objective lens of the comparison microscope.

The examiner looks at both bullets—that is, at number of grooves, width, and direction of the lands and grooves, as well as the calibre of the bullets—to determine whether they have the same class characteristics. Calibre is measured in inches—for example, .22, .38, or .45—or in millimetres—for example, 9 mm. In an unrifled shotgun, the width of the barrel is called the **gauge**.

gauge
the width of the barrel in an unrifled shotgun

The examiner turns the two bullets until they are both in the same position, with a well-defined land or groove in view. Then the bullets are rotated together to compare the class and individual marks, just as in any tool-mark examination. As always, the unknown is examined first to find a mark, then the known is examined in an attempt to locate the same mark.

Although the bullet usually contains the bulk of the class and individualizing characteristics, individual marks may also be found on other parts of the cartridge. When the gun is fired, the primer is struck by the hammer or firing pin of the gun. The hammer is also a tool, or hard object, which leaves a mark on the softer object, the primer. This mark can have both class and individual characteristics. This may prove useful, especially when the bullet is not recovered, but the cartridge remains in the gun to be ejected later or is ejected by an ejector mechanism, which may also leave marks on the cartridge. Cartridges are often found at the scene, especially if the gun has an automatic ejector mechanism. Shooters are unlikely to recover all the cartridges even when they try to do so.

When the hammer strikes the primer, two forces occur simultaneously. The first is the force of the hammer descending; the second and opposing force is created by the primer igniting and then igniting the powder in the cartridge. The bullet is forced back, but it can go no further, so it is forced forward out of the barrel. For a split second, the hammer comes down and the back of the cartridge goes back, hard, into the breech face of the gun. The breech face or breech block is the bit of the inside of the barrel that you would see if you viewed the gun by looking up the barrel, but *never* do this. If the bullet is a rim fire, similar hammer markings will be seen around the edge of the cartridge rim.

Shotguns do not have rifling, but some things can still be determined. The weight and diameter of the shot gives the examiner an idea of the its size and, if the wad—the piece of material that pushes the shot out—is recovered, it indicates the gauge of the shotgun and, thus, perhaps, the manufacturer.

When a gun is collected, it must be carefully labelled and identified. A gun should *not* be collected as is often seen on television—that is, by putting a pencil up the barrel, because doing so will clearly damage the inside of the barrel, removing old and creating new individual characteristics. A gun or bullet retrieved from water should not be removed, because it will quickly rust, again changing internal characteristics. Instead, it should be picked up in gloved hands and placed in a tub with enough of the same water covering it so that it can be taken to the lab to be handled by the experts (Saferstein, 2011).

Firearms Databases

Several computer systems, maintained by different countries, store automated databases of bullets and firearms. Digitized images of the bullet and cartridge surfaces can be created and kept in a similar manner to fingerprints, and are therefore within reach of law enforcement agencies anywhere in the world. Several systems have been introduced since computer imaging became common in the 1990s. In the United States, the FBI developed a system called DRUGFIRE, which, primarily, takes images of spent cartridge cases, but also bullets (Saferstein, 2011). At the same time, the Bureau of Alcohol, Tobacco, Firearms and Explosives developed the Integrated Ballistic Identification System (IBIS), based on two software systems— "Brasscatcher," which analyzed cartridge cases, and "Bulletproof," which analyzed bullets. Finally, DRUGFIRE and IBIS combined to produce the National Integrated Ballistics Information Network (NIBIN), which is used in the United States today. Images of bullets and cartridges from crimes are input into the database and a search is conducted to find matches to other crimes and to known weapons (Saferstein, 2011). However, as with fingerprint databases, the matches made by the computer are for screening purposes only—that is, presumptive tests. The confirmatory test is done by a human examiner using the comparison microscope.

Canada uses the Canadian Integrated Ballistics Identification Network (CIBIN). This database is a partnership between the major forensic labs—the RCMP Forensic Science and Identification Services, the Centre of Forensic Sciences in Ontario, and the Quebec Laboratoire de sciences judiciaires et de médecine légale. CIBIN is a network of special instruments called "Integrated Ballistics Identification Systems" (IBIS), which are used to input images of firearms evidence in a similar manner to the NIBIN system. At the time of writing, these instruments are found in forensic laboratories in Vancouver, Regina, Ottawa, Toronto, Montreal, and Halifax; as with NIBIN, once data are entered into the database, there is an automatic check across the nation. At present, many cold cases are being entered into CIBIN.

In addition to the above, the FBI maintains the General Rifling Characteristics (GRC) file, which has a record of all the different types of rifling performed by different gun manufacturers in different guns. Some rifling processes are quite unusual—for example, the microgrooving used on Marlin rifles (Saferstein, 2011). Canada maintains and expands a similar record.

Gunshot and Primer Residue

When a gun is fired, it leaves gunpowder residue behind. Some gunpowder flashes back at the shooter, but most goes forward toward the target. Gunshot residue analysis can be helpful in determining how the shooting took place—for example, how far the shooter was from the target, who fired the shot, and the position of the protagonists. It can also be useful for evaluating statement evidence. For example, someone might admit to killing another person with a gun, but claim it was in self-defence because he was being attacked. To prove self-defence, it is necessary to determine the distance the protagonists were from each other. Gunshot residue might indicate that the shooter was only 60 cm from the victim, or it might indicate that the two were more than 3 to 4 metres apart. Also, in a case of suspected suicide, it is important to be able to show that the gun was fired at close range because few people succeed in shooting themselves over a long distance.

When a gun is fired, the gunpowder in the bullet is ignited, which results in the creation of gases that push the bullet out of the barrel. Theoretically, this burns up all the powder, but, in practice, not all the powder is burned. This means that a mixture of burned, partly burned, and unburned powder, as well as soot, is shot out of the barrel together with the bullet. The bullet is fired a long distance, but this discharge of powder will only hit a target that is close by (Saferstein, 2011). The amount, type, and pattern of gunshot residue can be used to determine the distance the gun was from the target when it was fired; however, the residue itself might not be visible to the naked eye and magnification may be needed.

To make any assessment about distance, the examiner must have the suspect weapon and the suspect ammunition, or the same type of ammunition. Different weapons firing the same ammunition or the same weapon firing different types of ammunition each produce different patterns of residue. The test ammunition should be fired into the same type of material from which the original suspect residue was collected, because the type of material the residue strikes affects the way the residue pattern forms. Tests must be fired at a number of distances to determine which one fits the target pattern.

In a contact shot—that is, when the muzzle of the gun is in contact with the target—nearly all the unburned powder is forced directly into the wound and may not be externally visible. As a result of the tremendous pressure from the gases released as they enter the wound, the skin around the bullet wound tears in a star shape, or stellate pattern. The impression of the gun may even be seen on the skin.

When the shot is fired from a close distance, but the gun is not actually in contact with the target—for example, less than 2.4 cm (1 inch) away—the bullet wound will have a rim made up of a heavy concentration of smoke-like, vaporous lead. Loose fibres from clothing around the hole may be scorched or melted. Much of the unburned powder will have been driven into the wound.

When the gun is about 30 to 45 cm (12 to 18 inches) from the target, soot and powder together are deposited around the bullet hole. At this distance, there is a halo of vaporous lead smoke around the hole, as well as some unburned powder particles.

At a further distance—that is, about 60 cm (24 inches)—only soot is deposited on the target, and when the distance is 63 to 100 cm (25 to 36 inches), scattered specks of unburned and partially burned gunpowder grains will be found, but no soot or blackening or vaporous lead. Unburned grains can create a stippling, which will be visible on skin and, if the victim survives, the stippling may be permanent because of the presence of gunpowder granules under the skin.

When the gun is discharged more than 1 metre away from the target, there is usually no residue on the target. The only visual sign showing that the hole was made by a bullet is the bullet wipe around the perimeter of the wound. This is a dark ring consisting of, for example, lubricant, primer residue, and lead, which was wiped off the bullet when it passed through the target (Saferstein, 2011).

It is always important to know the type of ammunition, the type of gun, and whether the gun was altered or used with a silencer. If the suspect weapon and ammunition are not available, the examiner can determine only class characteristics of the weapon; the examiner will therefore be able to draw only general conclusions, which are never as precise as those he or she could make with the actual weapon and ammunition.

Matching a bullet to a suspect weapon can be precise, leaving little room for argument, but many more variables are involved when trying to determine the distance of the shooter from the target using gunshot residue. In addition to the variables already discussed, the gun may have been fired through a pillow, a curtain, or any other material, which would clearly affect the residue.

The primer is the part of the bullet that is ignited when struck by the hammer. It is either in the centre of the bullet or the rim in rim-fire cartridges. The primer ignites the gunpowder, which propels the bullet down the barrel. When a gun is fired, this primer residue blows backward onto the hand that fired the gun, particularly into the webbing between the thumb and forefinger. Also, even though the majority of gunpowder is blown forward when a bullet is fired, some is blown back.

Because the powder contains nitrates, in the past, the hands of a suspected shooter were tested for nitrates using a test called the dermal—that is, skin—nitrate test. This involved putting warm wax on the suspect's hands and then testing the wax for nitrates. However, this was merely a presumptive test, because nitrates are in many things—for example, fertilizers, feces, urine, tobacco, and cosmetics, to name a few—so it was easy to get a false positive reaction (Saferstein, 2011). A result strongest on the webbing between thumb and forefinger was more probative, but could still be easily argued against in court. Powder is also easily washed off or transferred to someone else—for example, by shaking hands.

Today, a more specific or confirmatory test is used looking specifically for the constituents of primer, including lead styphnate, barium nitrate, and antimony sulfide (Saferstein, 2011). This mixture is found only in gun primers, so there are no false positives. Two techniques are used. The simplest involves using a cotton swab dipped in 5 percent nitric acid on the skin and testing the swab with a variety of chemicals. A better technique involves adhesive tape on the hands, which is then examined with a scanning electron microscope (Tillman, 1987; Saferstein, 2011).

Nonetheless, problems still remain with primer residue; firing a gun leaves residue on the web of the hand, but so does handling a gun shortly after it has been fired. Also, substances can be deposited on people near the weapon at the time of discharge, or on anyone who handled the weapon before it was cleaned. Determining whether a person was the shooter or just nearby can be estimated by looking at the *amount* of residue on the hands. However, as with the dermal nitrate test, primer residue does not stay on hands for long, and may be gone in a couple of hours from simple movement and contact with other objects. Also, some rim-fire ammunition does not contain the same constituents as normal primer (Saferstein, 2011).

KEY TERMS

ballistics
calibre
gauge
like with like
rifling
tool
tool mark

FURTHER READING

An introduction to forensic firearm identification. FirearmsID.com.
    http://www.firearmsid.com.
James, S.H., & Nordby, J.J. (Eds.). (2009). *Forensic science: An introduction to scientific and investigative techniques* (3rd ed.). Boca Raton, FL: CRC Press.

Latham, T.H. (2012). *Analyzing ballistic evidence: On-scene by the investigator.*
    Self-published. http://www.amazon.com.

REVIEW QUESTIONS

True or False?

1. Ballistics is the matching of a bullet to a gun.

2. When making a physical comparison, a tool-marks and firearms examiner always needs to examine like with like.

3. When comparing a suspect tool with a mark, a tool-mark examiner first looks at the known, then the unknown.

4. A firearms specialist is never allowed to say in court, "This gun fired this bullet." He or she must instead give probabilities—for example, "The chance that a different gun fired this bullet is 100 to 1."

5. Calibre of a gun is measured between the lands of the barrel.

6. Rifling can be clockwise or counterclockwise.

7. A test-fire bullet is fired into the same sort of material as the suspect bullet in order to be able to directly compare the bullets.

8. A comparison, or compound, microscope is simply two microscopes joined together with a bridge.

9. The National Integrated Ballistics Information Network is an amalgamation of DRUGFIRE and IBIS.

10. To determine the distance from the shooter using gunshot residue, an examiner must have both the suspect weapon and the suspect ammunition.

Multiple Choice

1. The dermal nitrate test has false positives with:
   a. cosmetics.
   b. urine.
   c. tobacco.
   d. feces.
   e. all of the above.

2. The following are individual characteristics:
   a. rifling.
   b. striations in the gun barrel.
   c. calibre.
   d. gauge.
   e. none of the above.

3. Which of the following is used to produce rifling in a gun barrel?
   a. broach.
   b. button.
   c. mandrel.
   d. hummer.
   e. all of the above.

4. Which of the following does not make individual markings on a cartridge?
   a. gun barrel.
   b. breech face.
   c. hammer.
   d. trigger.
   e. all of the above.

5. A gunshot wound shot from less than 2.5 cm will not show which of the following?
   a. stellate tearing.
   b. bullet wipe.
   c. rim of vaporous lead.
   d. unburned powder in wound.
   e. scorched clothing.

Short Answer

1. Explain what causes individual characteristics in a tool. Give examples.
2. Give an example of both class and individual characteristics in a gun. Explain your answer.
3. Explain why a tool-mark examiner looks at the unknown first before the known mark. Explain your answer.
4. Why must an examiner never place a suspected tool into the tool mark?
5. Discuss what would be acceptable as "explainable differences" between a tool mark and the tool the examiner says caused the mark.
6. Explain the purpose of rifling a gun barrel and describe its importance from a forensic point of view.
7. Explain what the dermal nitrate test was and discuss two problems with it.

Questioned Documents

15

LEARNING OUTCOMES

After completing this chapter, you should be able to:

- Understand the types of analyses that a questioned document examiner performs.

- Explain class characteristics in handwriting.

- Explain what makes handwriting unique.

- Understand the advantages and disadvantages of collected and requested handwriting exemplars.

- Describe some of the extrinsic influences on handwriting.

- Describe the difference between "class" and "innate characteristics" in a machine.

- Understand how a questioned document examiner can discover alterations made in documents.

INTRODUCTION

questioned document
anything that contains letters, numbers, or any type of symbol that could express a meaning to another person and whose authorship is in doubt

A **questioned document** is anything that contains letters, numbers, or any type of symbol that could express a meaning to another person and whose authorship is in doubt. It might be as obvious as a letter written in ink, or it could be symbols written in blood; it can be visible or invisible. Most of a document examiner's work involves comparing handwriting or hand printing samples; but examiners also analyze the many different methods for creating a document, from the type of writing material, such as ink, to the machines that can make a document, such as a computer printer, and to the materials used in a document, such as paper. As well, examiners might analyze documents after they have been altered or damaged in some way—for example, when someone changes the amount of money written on a cheque or when a document is burned.

As was the case with other forensic sciences, all forensic laboratories in Canada used to have their own questioned document sections. Now the only RCMP Questioned Document Examination Unit is part of the National Anti-Counterfeiting Bureau (NACB), which is in the Ottawa forensic laboratory. The Centre of Forensic Sciences (CFS) and the Quebec Laboratoire de sciences judiciaires et de médecine légale also handle questioned document examinations. Other agencies outside law enforcement also have questioned document sections.

THE QUESTIONED DOCUMENT EXAMINER

A few years ago, a person entering the questioned document unit of a forensic lab required a baccalaureate degree, but not necessarily in science. Some examiners practising today have arts degrees. Of all the sciences at the lab, perhaps questioned document examination has been considered the least scientific, which has caused some problems in court. Much of questioned document examination has been considered more art than science, and much of it is based on the individual skills and experience of the examiner. More recently, a baccalaureate degree in science, preferably chemistry, is required, because more current kinds of analysis require chemical and general scientific knowledge, as well as a working knowledge of a range of optical, electrical, and chemical instruments, and the field has generally become much more dependent on scientific analyses.

In addition to meeting educational requirements, before being accepted into the lab for training, qualified applicants must pass several basic word blindness and dexterity tests. These include looking at a piece of paper covered in words for 60 seconds and being able to pick out several specific words immediately. The tests determine whether a person suffers from word blindness or is trainable in this field. As with other forensic lab scientists, questioned document examiners are civilians. In fact, people recruited into the questioned document unit from the regular police ranks must resign their police positions. This requirement helps to ensure that the lab is impartial. Once accepted into the lab, new members undergo a long understudy period—up to two and a half years. They train under qualified examiners and undergo course work, exercises, re-analyses of materials already analyzed, and a mock trial before being able to take on their own caseload. Questioned document examiners can be board certified under the American Board of Forensic Document Examiners (ASQDE).

It is important to understand that **questioned document examination** is not the same as graphology—the study of handwriting to determine a person's personality. Questioned document examination is the *scientific* comparison and analysis of a document. Graphology, on the other hand, looks at a person's handwriting with the intention of determining a person's personality. It has no scientific basis and is akin to palm reading. However, courts in the United States have often made mistakes, allowing graphologists to testify as experts on handwriting. Technically, graphologists probably know more than the average person about this subject, and so they would fit the broad definition of an expert witness, but they have no training in true scientific questioned document examination and should not be used in this context.

questioned document examination
the scientific comparison and analysis of a document

THE EXAMINATION OF HANDWRITING AND HAND PRINTING

Handwriting is considered to be unique to a person, much like a fingerprint, as long as the writing has been written freely and fluently, and the examiner has a large enough exemplar or sample with which to compare.

Handwriting has both class and individual characteristics. When children first learn to write, regardless of the language or script, they do so by copying someone else. They carefully form letters from a book designed for the purpose or from those written down for them by their teacher. Children try to adhere strictly to the example, repeating the formation of each letter very carefully. Once they have mastered the alphabet, children attempt whole words and then sentences. Eventually, as they keep repeating this exercise, their focus moves from just copying the letters, words, and sentences to thinking about the actual contents of the material. Once this shift occurs and children concentrate more and more on the thoughts they are writing down, the act of writing itself is forgotten and it becomes a semiconscious habit. By adulthood, we tend to think only of the contents of the text. Once they are developed, such handwriting habits become extremely difficult to change. This is why disguising our own writing is always difficult to begin with and extremely difficult to maintain. If a lengthy forged document is studied, it is often obvious that forgers begin to relapse into their own handwriting style quite quickly.

If you study children's first writing books, you notice that all the letters in the different books are similar. In fact, most such copybooks show an identical writing style across North America. This means that most children learn to write from the same style of copybook. In North America, the same basic writing style is a class characteristic. As well, teachers instruct many children over their careers. All the students of a given teacher will have some of the same class characteristics. Class characteristics vary from one country to another, but they will still be a class within that nation. In other words, there may be differences between the copybook type of class characteristics seen in North America and those seen, for example, in Africa, but they are still class characteristics. Most class characteristics are established early, but some relate to a profession, such as architecture, which requires a specific style. Teenage girls often use bubble writing, which is a class characteristic of that age group (and also probably only found in North America in a certain time period). People who are visually challenged also display certain class characteristics in their writing style.

Handwriting also contains individual characteristics that can be used to identify a single writer. Individual characteristics in handwriting occur even among those who learned to write from the same teacher for four major reasons. First, every person has an individual perception of different images—that is, people see things differently. Second, we all have different and individual physical makeups, which affect our dexterity. Third, all children make errors, which vary from person to person. If these are not corrected in the early stages of learning to write, they become habits and form part of that person's normal writing. Finally, children learning to write incorporate specific features of writing style from significant people in their lives, such as their parents or siblings (Greg Smith, RCMP Ottawa, personal communication).

In combination, these individual features produce writing that is unique. Competent examiners can identify the writing of one person to the exclusion of all others. Their findings are based on a specific analysis of all the features of the writing together with the examiner's experience. As well as the variation between different people's writing, each person's writing also contains **natural variation**. We do not write exactly the same way all the time, so there are always normal and natural deviations that occur in a person's normal writing. This is one of the reasons that an examiner needs a large sample of writing from a suspected writer to be able to compare the questioned document to the writer's normal writing. If only a small sample is available, the differences may just relate to natural variation.

It is not only a person's writing that is unique, but factors such as spacing and size of margins, as well as punctuation and spelling—just as errors in forming letters and words become habit if not corrected when we are children, the same is true for spelling and punctuation errors. In addition, people favour different styles. Indentations of paragraphs and placement of date and address, although not unique, add to the overall analysis.

natural variation
differences in an individual's normal writing

Handwriting Analysis

An examiner cannot simply look at a questioned document and analyze it on its own. The questioned document alone tells nothing about the writer. As in much of forensic science analysis, the basis of handwriting examination is founded on a comparison of an unknown to a known—that is, the questioned document compared to an example of a suspect's handwriting. In order for a questioned

NATURAL VARIATION

Our handwriting is unique to us, but even within our own writing there are differences between one piece of writing and another. This is called natural variation. We all have natural variation in our writing, and the range of variation is unique to each person. A person's signature is a classic example. Take a piece of paper and write your signature as you normally would 20 times. Now look at the writing. There are differences between these supposedly identical signatures that you can see yourself. These differences are the natural variation in your own writing. No two signatures are ever identical. If they are, then one is a forgery, copied from an original. This is usually accomplished by either tracing over an original or scanning it and inserting it into a document.

document examiner to determine anything about a document, he or she must have the questioned document itself and a comparable sample from a suspect.

Comparison samples are referred to as **exemplars**, which can be obtained by either collection or request. Collected exemplars were written during the normal course of someone's day-to-day activities. Such exemplars include, for example, old cheques, notes, letters, shopping lists, diaries, and school notes. **Requested exemplars** are obtained under warrant—that is, a police officer requests that a person produce writing samples at the police station under the watch of an officer. Both methods have advantages and disadvantages and, ideally, a mixture is best.

There are several advantages to collecting specimens of handwriting from normal day-to-day activities. Because the writer was unaware at the time that they would come under scrutiny, they are likely to be naturally written and undisguised in any way. Because they come from a number of sources, they are likely to include a broad range of natural variation. As we age, our writing changes. This is true throughout our life. Look at some samples of your own handwriting when you were a young adult and compare it to your writing now; or look at old letters written by your parents through the years—you will see that their writing has changed. If a questioned document is not from present times, but was written when the suspect was much younger, it might be possible to collect handwriting exemplars from the same time frame to eliminate changes caused over the years. For example, the writing style of a questioned document such as an execution order in a Second World War crimes investigation, written when the suspect was 25, will not be representative of the writing style that is now typical of the suspect at 90 years of age. If possible, it would be best to collect samples of the suspect's writing known to be written when he was a young man. One of the downsides of collected exemplars is that it is often difficult to prove that the suspect actually wrote the document unless someone can swear that they saw the person doing so. For a court's purpose, the authorship of text can be determined in several ways. The writer might admit that he or she wrote the text, someone might have witnessed the person writing the text, or the text might be identified by someone who is familiar with the person's writing. The court can use any means it deems acceptable (Greg Smith, RCMP Ottawa, personal communication). Another disadvantage is that, as with other forensic sciences, the examiner must examine "like to like," which means that the best comparison exemplars involve the same writing and phrases, which are unlikely to be duplicated in the collected samples.

Some of these problems are ameliorated if the police collect the sample under a warrant. One of the main advantages of requesting writing samples at a police station is that authorship is not in doubt because a police officer can confirm the identification of the person when the warrant was executed and witness the writing in a controlled environment. As well, the police officer can request that the person write anything—for example, specific sentences on specific writing material, using a specific style of pen or pencil. The writing style can also be controlled—for example, standing and writing on a hard surface, as in a bank, or in a small writing area such as a signature on a cheque.

There are, however, disadvantages with requested exemplars, the most obvious being that people under warrant are clearly aware that they are under suspicion and, if guilty may attempt to disguise their writing in some manner or, if not guilty,

exemplar

a sample of someone's handwriting, which can be either collected or requested, for comparison with a questioned document

requested exemplar

a sample of someone's handwriting requested by warrant and written under observation so that authorship is not in doubt may be nervous, which could distort their writing. Also, because the writing is taking place at one time in a restricted situation it is unlikely to exhibit the full range of natural variation and, depending on when the questioned document was written, the exemplar may not be contemporary. Although these are obvious problems with requested samples, a police officer can mitigate some of them (see, for example, Huber & Headrick, 1999; Saferstein, 2011).

In most cases, it is undesirable for the suspect to know the actual contents of a questioned document. However, the investigator needs all the words and numbers used in that document repeated in the exemplar. Certain standards were therefore used to develop a set piece of text, originally referred to as "the London letter" (Huber & Headrick, 1999). The London letter was a stock letter that included dates, names, places, upper- and lowercase letters, and all letters and numbers in the English alphabet. A later modification was referred to as "the Idaho letter." However, both the London and Idaho letters were old-fashioned, formal, difficult to follow unless the writer was highly intelligent and well-educated, and almost impossible for many immigrants to understand (Huber & Headrick). As well, the phrases used appear to be more in keeping with Second World War spy novels than everyday life. Therefore, the RCMP developed a new letter that included information more familiar to Canadians and more easily understood by the average person. This is now referred to as "the Canada letter" (reprinted in full in Huber & Headrick, p. 254), which is basically a formal letter with a return address, the address of the addressee, and a body of text describing a vacation, which mentions old friends and places. It contains all the letters and numbers in the alphabet. A similar letter is also available in French. Other such generalized texts are available, but the beauty of these letters is that they can be adapted to the case at hand. For example, the questioned document might be a blackmail note to a person named Victoria Dawson in Prince George, demanding $1,000. The Canada letter can be adapted so that the address is Prince Rupert and says something like, "Dear John, we just got back from a lovely visit to Victoria. We met up with an old friend from Dawson's Creek and we stayed with him at (here you could add or adapt an address) and the whole trip cost less than $1,000." In this way, the contents of the actual document are kept secret, but the words and phrases are repeated.

If necessary, an examination can be done with copies, but originals are always preferred. Photocopies, carbon copies, and photographs do not include some of the features examiners need, such as pen pressure, fine detail, and the sequence of strokes.

Examiners first determine whether the class characteristics are the same before considering individual characteristics. As in any forensic examination, if the class characteristics do not match, the writer can be eliminated. Examiners perform a minute comparison of the questioned document and the collected and requested exemplars. They look at the slope and angularity of each letter, the proportions of the letters—for example, how much of a letter is above or below the line—the speed of the writing, the pen pressure at different points in a letter, which letters are joined and which are not, pen stops (or lifts), pen gooping, word spacing, relative dimensions of letters, ratios, connections between letters, pen movement, writing skill, and finger dexterity. They also consider size of margins, spacing, crowding, spelling, and punctuation. The examiner is trying to determine whether the questioned document was written by the known writer and whether there was an attempt at disguise. There is no set number of points that must match before the examiner can positively identify a writer, but if just one clear difference between the two exists, the questioned document must have been written by someone other than the suspect.

As with all other comparisons, the questioned document and the exemplar must be of the same type. For example, if the questioned document is printed, the exemplar must be printed; lowercase can only be compared with lowercase, and signatures with signatures. An examiner cannot compare printing with writing, or uppercase with lowercase. Just as in a fingerprint examination or a tool mark examination, the analysis is a comparison from unknown to known.

A questioned document examiner can analyze handwriting in any language or script and does not need to be able to speak, read, or understand the writing in order to be able to make a comparison.

Factors That Can Affect Handwriting

There are many things that can affect a person's handwriting (Huber & Headrick, 1999). Some of these are under a person's control, while others are not—for example, transient factors, such as the use of drugs or alcohol, or illness, which may be long-lasting. Below are some of the factors that can influence handwriting.

Handwriting changes through a person's lifetime. Dramatic changes are seen throughout childhood and adolescence and, as a person ages, their dexterity and, consequently, their writing changes. This important fact emphasizes why a questioned document must be compared with exemplars that are *contemporary in time*. It is difficult to compare a questioned historical document with present day writing, which may result in the examiner being able to give only a qualified opinion. This is particularly important in such things as wills that are signed close to the time of death. Effects of terminal illness may vary in the same person over short periods of time, and writing may become illegible close to death (Huber & Headrick).

Illicit or therapeutic drugs as well as alcohol can affect handwriting, including extending the range of natural variation. A great many studies on the impacts of a variety of drugs and particularly alcohol have been conducted (see Huber & Headrick). There are many arguments about the actual effects of different drugs on handwriting in the literature, but it is clear that drugs can have an impact, which is important to understand because drugs, in particular alcohol, are frequently involved in a questioned document examination—for example, someone may claim not to have been aware of what they signed because they had consumed excessive amounts of alcohol.

Stress or high emotion, including fear, anxiety, or excitement, can also affect handwriting, causing extensive variation as well as tremor and poor line quality. Again, these may be common in a questioned document because many documents are written in a heightened state of anxiety. A writer who deliberately forges a document may be stressed, fearful, or even excited; a person writing a suicide note or a kidnap victim forced to write a letter is also likely to be extremely anxious or fearful. Physical stress or exhaustion can also affect writing.

Illness or physical challenge can affect handwriting. For example, dyslexia, Alzheimer's disease, amyotropic lateral sclerosis (ALS), arthritis, cerebral palsy, diabetes mellitis, Parkinson's disease, multiple sclerosis, and other degenerative diseases can produce specific changes or alterations as the diseases progress, although the effects would be class characteristics for people suffering from each particular disease (Huber & Headrick).

Visual impairment affects writing, most commonly resulting in overwriting margins or lines; each line may be badly aligned and the writing may go close to or even off the edge of the page. In some cases, a person may use a writing aid to prevent these errors and this would also affect the writing. Again, these would be class characteristics for the visually impaired.

Other factors that can influence handwriting include extrinsic factors under the control of the writer—for example, writing position (sitting comfortably at a desk, standing at a counter, or sitting on a stool, which affects freedom of movement). The writing surface, such as a single sheet of paper on a hard surface or a pad of paper, affects a person's writing as does the writing implement, whether ballpoint pen, ink pen, gel pen, or pencil. This is why it is important to duplicate the writing position and means and media when getting a requested exemplar.

Deliberate and Fraudulent Alteration of Handwriting

Questioned document examiners not only match writing from an unknown questioned document to a known exemplar, but, understandably in criminal investigations, frequently examine documents in which writing has been simulated to mimic another person's writing or disguised as in a blackmail note.

Because writing is a semiconscious habit, it is difficult for people to disguise their normal writing, and most disguises are fairly simple—for example, changing the slope of the writing. Someone who normally slopes their letters to the left might try sloping them to the right. The simplest way to attempt to disguise writing is to use the unaccustomed hand—that is, for a right-handed person to write with the left hand or vice versa. Disguise is typically simple, and people quickly revert to their normal writing style, which is why a requested writing exemplar is several paragraphs long. It would be difficult for a suspect trying to disguise his or her writing to maintain the disguise for that length of writing time. This is especially true if the dictation is fast, not allowing the added time needed to disguise the writing. Also, those features of the writer's style that he or she is unaware of—for example, punctuation and spelling errors as well as margins, spacing, and parts of the actual writing—are rarely disguised, and a competent examiner will be able to detect disguised writing.

Someone may pretend to be another writer by copying or simulating the other person's style. However, the quality of the simulation is often poorer than the original because the simulator is writing carefully and slowly, resulting in gooping; heavy pen pressure; and the misinterpretation of letters, proportions, and ratios. Simulators may also include touch-ups in an attempt to improve the writing. A person might try to simulate another's writing by tracing over an original. As with a signature, no two pieces of writing are identical because of natural variation, so, if the original is available, it should be obvious that the two pieces are identical.

HANDWRITING EXERCISES

Get a few people together and give each a pen and pad of paper. Get each one, including yourself, to write a paragraph, but attempt to disguise your writing. Look at your own attempts and those of others to see the different techniques people used and how long they were able to maintain the "disguise."

Get a partner to write a sentence. Attempt to simulate the sentence. Examine the original and your simulation and see how easy or difficult it is to spot the simulation. Try tracing it. Does that look better? Is it obvious from the indentations on the original that it has been traced?

Place a single piece of paper on the top of a pad of paper and write a short sentence. Then move the single sheet of paper to the top of a hard surface such as a desk and repeat the same sentence. Repeat the exercise using different surfaces and different types of pen, such as a ballpoint or a rollerball, and even a pencil. Note how the surface you write on and the implement you use affects your writing. Note the minute details of the pen stroke, the lines, the spaces, the striations in the ink, and the hesitations.

Concerns and New Directions for Handwriting Examinations

The field of questioned document examination received a wake-up call in the landmark U.S. decision *Daubert v. Merrell Dow Pharmaceutical* (1993). In this case, questioned document examination was deemed to lack scientific rigour because no statistical analyses were involved, no error rates were known, and much reliance was placed on the individual examiner's experience. The ruling raised major concerns at the time, but the community of questioned document examiners rallied to the challenge, some 16 years before the release of the National Academy of Sciences (NAS) report (2009).

Since *Daubert*, there has been a concerted effort in questioned document examinations to include a more systematic and scientific analysis. Although most examinations are still performed by an experienced examiner, new techniques involving computer analysis have been developed. It is now possible to use a computer to break every single letter into thousands of tiny pieces and then measure, for example, the slope, pressure, and width of every piece. Each point is then compared between questioned document and exemplar.

Another computerized technique used by the post office was developed to generally recognize such words as the name of a province, state, city, and street for sorting purposes. This little-known technique came to prominence shortly after the terrorist attacks of September 11, 2001, when the technique was used to identify potentially dangerous letters thought to contain anthrax from suspect areas.

Research has validated existing methods in handwriting examination, developing both error rates for techniques and examiners and likelihood ratios. The research has been encouraging, supporting the previously established methods and inherent understanding of the uniqueness of handwriting.

Scientific research into the motor control processes and neuroscience of normal handwriting has led to a better understanding of the cognitive control of writing, which in turn has led to a more scientific understanding of normal handwriting compared with disguise and simulation as well as the effects of disease, alcohol, drugs, medication, and aging on hand movement and writing.

More recently other technology has evolved, which is automating more handwriting examinations. As well, new and exciting scientific methods of examining handwriting are being developed, such as the use of infrared microscopy techniques to look at crossed lines to determine the chronological sequence of deposition, the use of hyperspectral imaging, chromatography, ramen and laser induced breakdown spectroscopy to discriminate between different types of inks, chemical analyses of adhesives used in different types of paper, and techniques to determine the software used to print a document (see the most recent issues of the Proceedings of the American Academy of Forensic Sciences Annual Meeting).

MATERIALS, METHODS, AND MEDIA USED IN CREATING DOCUMENTS

It is not only handwriting that is the questioned part of a questioned document; it can also be printing and typing. Examinations of machines include typeface, ink used, and paper. Today, most of our documents are produced on computers. So examinations include such machines as computer printers, photocopiers, fax machines, rubber stamps, and graphic arts used to make, for example, currency and lotto tickets. The questioned document examiner can determine the make and model of a machine used to create a document—that is, the class characteristics—and then, using individual characteristics, identify a particular machine as being responsible for producing that document.

In addition to class and individual characteristics, many machines possess a third category, called "innate characteristics" (Greg Smith, RCMP Ottawa, personal communication). A class characteristic for a machine would be the font size, font design, pitch, shape, and so on. All of these would be common to a group of the same machines. An individual characteristic for such a machine would be something that was unique and identifying to that machine, which could include damage that has occurred through manufacture, use, and misuse. An **innate characteristic** is a characteristic that is common to a group, but does not apply to all objects in the group—for example, dirt in the mould of a letter that was not detected for a portion of the production run and so affected just ten machines.

innate characteristic
a characteristic common to a group that does not apply to all objects in the group

Photocopies of a document can be examined to determine the make and model of the machine that produced the photocopy. Once a number of machines are located, the machines can be examined and the machine responsible identified by the tiny trash or dirt marks that it makes on a page, dirt or damage to the lens or platen, and picker marks and marks left by the mechanism used to move the paper through the machine.

Newer machines actually place an invisible identification mark on the paper that can be traced back to the machine. The examiner can also determine the generation of a photocopy—that is, how many copies have been made since the original was duplicated. Canadian photocopiers are designed to detect currency: if someone attempts to photocopy money, the copier will immediately shut down when money is placed on it. Photocopiers connected to the Internet can even phone the police.

In addition to the machines and the writing itself, the questioned document examiner will analyze the ink and paper used. There are myriad types of ink available and the chemical constituents of these inks have changed over the decades and centuries. It is a common mistake in art forgery that a painting claimed to be by da Vinci is painted with paints not yet available in the 15th century. In the same way, documents are often proven fraudulent when they are shown to be written with an ink that was not available at the time of the supposed writing. The material that the message is written on can also be important (see the box below).

The need to perform many chemical analyses on papers and inks has required today's questioned document examiner to have a strong background in chemistry as well as in other sciences.

DOCUMENT ALTERATION

Questioned documents may be deliberately damaged, altered, or destroyed, and a questioned document examiner is often asked to restore these documents. It is important for an investigator at a crime scene to understand that even paper so badly burned that it is black or totally soaked paper should not be discounted as evidence because it can still be examined by a questioned document examiner.

Documents that have been water-soaked can often be restored if they are carefully air dried or freeze dried. If found wet at a scene, they should be frozen for transportation to the laboratory. Charred documents may look completely blackened, but reflected light, contact photography, or infrared or ultraviolet light may reveal the text. Surprisingly, burning the document further in a muffle furnace may also reveal the writing. The document is superheated and then allowed to cool before it is examined.

If a person has altered a document by adding something to a number—for example, changing a 3 to 80—it is often possible to separate the original writing from the newer writing because the inks, although visually appearing the same, may have different chemical constituents. The different pen strokes and ink can often be separated by applying infrared reflectance or luminescence or ultraviolet light to the document. Even though the inks are the same colour, they are probably of a

HITLER FORGERY UNCOVERED

The purported third volume of Hitler's *Mein Kampf* and his 27-volume diary were exposed as frauds on the basis of the chemical constituents of the paper on which they were written, rather than on the handwriting (Saferstein, 2011). At first, the volume and the diaries were considered genuine because several experts agreed that the handwriting matched known exemplars of Hitler's handwriting. However, later analysis showed that the whitener used in the paper was not developed until nine years after Hitler's death and the threads in the paper were made with substances not available until long after the war. The questioned document examiners were, however, proven to be correct; the questioned volume, diaries, and exemplar were all written by the same person—it just wasn't Hitler, because the exemplar was found also to be a forgery.

different type and vintage so the chemical constituents will be slightly different and can be separated by the light. The added portion can then be clearly seen.

In some cases, investigators may want to read a document that has had something erased or crossed out. Again, various forensic light sources can be used to separate the erasure marks from the original if the ink sources are different. If the same type of ink has been used to cross out something, the original can be restored by first digitizing it, next enhancing it with various software programs, and then carefully computer erasing the added lines.

Many documents have latent impressions of writing on them from documents that were written on top of them—for example, the blank sheet below a questioned document on a pad of paper. Latent impressions might help determine the sequence of events leading up to the production or signing of a document or might even identify the writer.

Writing, whether by hand or from a computer, is still a major part of modern life. Many scenes and crimes thus include documents that might come under question. It is important that the investigator recognizes the importance of not just the content, but the value of the piece of writing itself to link a suspect to a scene or a crime, or even to identify the crime itself.

MISTAKES OF A WOULD-BE KIDNAPPER

In a Vancouver case, a letter was sent to a prominent and wealthy businessman, threatening to kidnap his child if he did not produce a certain sum of money. At the time, the letter was taken to the questioned document section of the Vancouver RCMP Lab. Normally, it is impossible to determine anything without comparison material, but in this case the examiner noticed that there were indentations on the paper from the writing of a previous letter on the sheet of paper above the questioned document. Such latent impressions can be detected using oblique light (light shined at the document from different angles) or an electrostatic detection apparatus (ESDA), which detects invisible marks. In this case, a simple light revealed the writing underneath. The text was a lengthy letter of complaint sent to the would-be extortionist's MLA (member of the legislative assembly), giving his full name and address. The examiner was able to tell the police investigators who the suspect was and exactly where he lived (Greg Smith, RCMP Ottawa, personal communication).

KEY TERMS

exemplar
innate characteristic
natural variation
questioned document
questioned document examination
requested exemplar

FURTHER READING

James, S.H., & Nordby, J.J. (Eds.). (2009). *Forensic science: An introduction to scientific and investigative techniques* (3rd ed.). Boca Raton, FL: CRC Press.

REVIEW QUESTIONS

True or False?

1. A word written in blood on the skin of a homicide victim is a questioned document.

2. A questioned document examiner must understand the words before he or she can analyze a questioned document.

3. A questioned document can be in invisible writing.

4. If two signatures are identical, one is a forgery.

5. The Canada letter is the letter used to obtain a warrant to request a handwriting sample.

6. A writing exemplar should be contemporary with the questioned document.

7. Most people trying to disguise their writing will use a simple form of disguise.

8. A questioned document examiner can determine which photocopier made a particular copy and how many copies ago it was produced.

Multiple Choice

1. A graphologist is
   a. a palm reader.
   b. a questioned document examiner.
   c. a person who claims to determine personality traits from handwriting.
   d. a person who identifies the machines used to produce a document.
   e. a person who restores charred documents.

2. Handwriting is considered to be unique because
   a. every person has an individual perception of different images.
   b. every person has different and individual physical makeup.
   c. errors not corrected in childhood become habits.
   d. children incorporate writing features from people they admire.
   e. all of the above.

3. All signatures are different because of
   a. innate characteristics.
   b. natural variation.
   c. individual characteristics.
   d. class characteristics.
   e. all of the above.

4. An advantage of collecting exemplars of handwriting is that
   a. authorship is known.
   b. all letters in the alphabet are present.
   c. only a very limited amount of natural variation would be present.
   d. they can be expected to be naturally written.
   e. none of the above.

5. An advantage of requesting exemplars of handwriting under a warrant is that
   a. the writing will be contemporary with the questioned document.
   b. they can be expected to be naturally written.
   c. they are unlikely to be disguised.
   d. have a broad range of natural variation.
   e. authorship is known.

6. An innate characteristic is
   a. a class characteristic.
   b. a characteristic that belongs to the class of a particular country.
   c. an individual characteristic in a machine.
   d. a characteristic that is common to a group but not all objects in that group.
   e. a characteristic innate to a specific person.

7. Which of the following is likely to affect a person's handwriting?
   a. anger.
   b. fear.
   c. drugs.
   d. alcohol.
   e. all of the above.

Short Answer

1. Explain why handwriting can have class characteristics.
2. What makes handwriting unique?
3. What is natural variation?
4. Explain the problem with requesting a handwriting sample for comparison with a blackmail note written in 1970.
5. Give two disadvantages of collecting handwriting specimens from a person's day-to-day life.
6. Give two advantages of collecting handwriting specimens from a person's day-to-day life.
7. Give three disadvantages to requesting handwriting specimens under warrant.

8. List three advantages of requesting handwriting specimens under warrant.

9. Why might certain emotional states be important in questioned document examinations?

10. Explain what a questioned document examiner looks for to identify a photocopied sheet with an individual photocopier.

11. When a document has been changed by adding writing in ink that looks the same as the original, the two layers can often be separated. Explain how this is done and the scientific principle behind it.

Interviewing Rules

16

LEARNING OUTCOMES

After completing this chapter, you should be able to:

- Distinguish between investigative interaction, investigative detention, and arrest.

- Understand what a person's legal rights are upon arrest or detention under the *Canadian Charter of Rights and Freedoms*, the *Criminal Code*, and case law, and the steps that officers must take to ensure that these rights are respected.

- Understand the reasons for a primary and secondary caution, and the information that each of these cautions should convey.

- Identify the circumstances under which a suspect or an accused should be re-cautioned.

- Understand the restrictions that the *Youth Criminal Justice Act* (YCJA) places on police when interviewing young persons, and the procedures that investigators must follow.

- Explain the connection between the voluntariness of a statement and its admissibility.

- Explain the kinds of false confessions and the reasons why individuals give them.

- Identify factors the courts will consider in determining the admissibility of a statement made by an accused.

INTRODUCTION

Gathering information from people through the structured conversation process known as the **interview** is one of the most important ways in which investigators interact with witnesses and victims, on the one hand, and with **suspects** and accused persons, on the other. Ontario Superior Court Justice O'Connor emphasized the importance of interviewing to the investigative process when he said that "questioning suspects and witnesses to a crime is an essential and often the most effective investigative tool the police possess" (*R. v. L.F.*, 2006, para. 10). This is true even with the advances that have been made in forensic science over the last few decades.

The interview process is of central importance to all investigations because, despite popular portrayals of criminal investigations and the importance of physical evidence, more crimes are solved as a result of information gathered from witnesses and suspects than as a result of physical evidence (Eck, 2009, p. x).

This chapter discusses the legal rules governing interviews with suspects. Although most police investigators will conduct more interviews with witnesses than with suspects over the course of an average career, the way in which investigators interact with an individual prior to and during an interview will ultimately determine whether and how any information gained will be used in court. Specifically, s. 24(2) of the *Canadian Charter of Rights and Freedoms* (the Charter) states that any evidence obtained in a manner that infringes or denies a suspect's rights or freedoms under the Charter will be excluded if admitting it in the proceedings would bring the administration of justice into disrepute.

This chapter begins by outlining the legal context of police interactions with individuals who are detained or arrested, including the enhanced rights of young persons. We then discuss statements made by accused persons, and the connection between the admissibility of a statement in court and the circumstances under which it was obtained. Best practices for suspect interviews are summarized in the box on page 304. The next chapter discusses how to prepare for and conduct successful interviews with suspects and witnesses.

LEGAL RIGHTS OF PERSONS WHO ARE DETAINED OR ARRESTED

When an individual is detained or arrested, a set of legal requirements are triggered with which all investigators must comply. These requirements are set out in the Charter, the *Youth Criminal Justice Act* (YCJA), the *Criminal Code*, and Canadian case law. Investigators must understand and respect these requirements. Failure to do so will likely result in any information gained in a subsequent interview with the individual being ruled inadmissible in court, which in turn will hamper the ability of lawyers to prove or disprove aspects of the case against the accused.

Definitions

In the course of investigating a crime, police may interact with individuals in various ways. The nature of the interaction will determine the legal rights of the person in the particular situation.

RIGHTS AT A GLANCE

Section 10 of the Charter outlines the rights guaranteed to any individual who is detained or arrested:

> 10. Everyone has the right on arrest or detention
>   (a) to be informed promptly of the reasons therefor;
>   (b) to retain and instruct counsel without delay and to be informed of that right; and
>   (c) to have the validity of the detention determined by way of *habeas corpus* and to be released if the detention is not lawful.

Section 29(2)(b) of the *Criminal Code* also requires an individual to be informed promptly of the reason for his or her arrest. Additional rights are the right to silence and the special rights of young persons under the *Youth Criminal Justice Act*. Sections 7 and 11(c) of the Charter, and case law, require the use of police cautions (discussed below).

Note that under the Charter the defence bears the burden of proving any allegation that a Charter right has been violated on a balance of probabilities.

The three distinct scenarios that must be distinguished for purposes of this discussion are:

1. investigative interaction,
2. investigative detention, and
3. arrest.

In the aftermath of a crime or in the course of an investigation, police may speak with members of the public for the purpose of conducting general investigative inquiries. In so doing, they may briefly delay or keep individuals waiting. Although the liberty of these individuals is restrained, as long as the interaction does not involve significant physical or psychological restraint, the courts have held that **investigative interaction** does *not* constitute a detention for the purposes of the Charter and thus does not activate a person's Charter rights related to arrest or detention.

In contrast to the interaction described above, when police have a reasonable suspicion that an individual who is not a suspect in a crime and is not under arrest nonetheless has some connection to the crime under investigation, they can detain that person to determine what he or she knows and what, if any, involvement he or she has in that crime. The term **investigative detention** (or simply "detention") is used to describe such a situation. *Detention* for the purposes of ss. 9 and 10 of the Charter refers to a suspension of an individual's liberty interest by a "significant physical or psychological restraint" (*R. v. Grant*, 2009, para. 29). Physical detention is relatively straightforward and includes situations where a person is handcuffed, locked in a police cruiser, or held in a detention facility. Psychological restraint can be more difficult to determine. It occurs when an individual has a legal obligation to comply with a restrictive demand by an agent of the state (for example, a police officer) or where a "reasonable person" would conclude that they had no choice but to comply (*R. v. Grant*, 2009, para. 44).

investigative interaction
interaction between the police and a member of the public who may be kept waiting by police conducting a general investigative inquiry; as long as it does not involve significant physical or psychological restraint, it does not activate a person's Charter rights related to detention or arrest

investigative detention
brief detention by police of a person who is not a suspect in a crime, involving significant physical or psychological restraint, where police have reasonable grounds to suspect that the person is connected to the crime; activates a person's Charter rights related to detention or arrest

To exercise the common-law power of investigative detention, police must have reasonable grounds to suspect that a person is connected to a particular crime and must be able to articulate how the circumstances caused them to form this suspicion. Unlike an investigative interaction, investigative detention *is* considered detention for purposes of the Charter, and therefore activates a person's Charter rights.

A source of confusion in attempting to understand the difference between investigative interaction and investigative detention is that an investigative interaction is sometimes referred to as a "detention." However, for purposes of the Charter, it is important to understand that police do not "detain" every person whom they delay or keep waiting.

Often, it is the courts that determine whether an individual was "detained" for purposes of the Charter in particular circumstances—particularly where there was no physical restraint or legal obligation involved. In deciding whether a reasonable person would conclude they had no choice but to comply with a directive in a particular situation, the courts will examine the entire interaction and the context and consider, among other things:

1. the circumstances as perceived by the individual (consideration of whether the police were making general inquiries or singling the individual out for focused investigation);

2. the nature of the police conduct (the use of language, use of physical contact, presence of others, duration, and location); and

3. characteristics relevant to the individual's particular situation (for example, age, physical stature, and minority status).

(*R. v. Grant*, 2009, para. 44.)

arrest

the actual seizure or touching of an individual by an officer with the intent of taking physical control of that person for the purpose of detention; or an announcement by an officer of his or her intent to arrest a person accompanied by an attempt to take physical control of that person

Finally, **arrest** is defined as the actual seizure or touching of an individual with a view to depriving them of their liberty under legal authority. An arrest may also take place where an officer announces his or her intention to arrest and *attempts* to take physical control of a person or where the person acquiesces to the officer (Watts, 2007).

Note that the legal standard for arrest is higher than that for detention, as shown by s. 495(1) of the *Criminal Code*:

495(1) A peace officer may arrest without warrant

(a) a person who has committed an indictable offence or who, *on reasonable grounds, he believes* has committed or is about to commit an indictable offence;

(b) a person whom he finds committing a criminal offence; or

(c) a person in respect of whom *he has reasonable grounds to believe* that a warrant of arrest or committal, in any form set out in Part XXVIII in relation thereto, is in force within the territorial jurisdiction in which the person is found. [Italics added.]

The Right to Be Informed of Reasons and Rights

When someone is detained or arrested, police must inform the person of both the reason for their detention and the fact that they have the right to retain and instruct legal counsel without delay (including the right to consult duty counsel and the right to legal aid). Two Supreme Court cases, *R. v. Black* (1989) and *R. v. Borden* (1994), established a link between ss. 10(a) and (b) of the Charter, holding that a violation of an accused's s. 10(a) right to be informed promptly of the reasons for their arrest or detention can affect the accused's decision whether or not to exercise their s. 10(b) right to retain and instruct counsel. The Court stated that people can only exercise their right to counsel in a meaningful way if they know the extent of the jeopardy in which they have been placed—that is, the risk or consequence they are facing.

The Right to Counsel

The **right to counsel** is designed to allow individuals to consult with a legal expert in order to be able to make an informed choice about whether to participate in the state's investigation of them. Under s. 10(b) of the Charter, police officers have three duties:

right to counsel
the right of a person to consult with a lawyer upon arrest or detention, as guaranteed by s. 10(b) of the Charter

1. Officers must inform all detainees of their right to retain counsel "without delay" and of the existence and availability of legal aid and duty counsel.

2. Where the detainee has indicated a wish to exercise this right, officers must provide the detainee with a reasonable opportunity to do so (see below).

3. Investigators must refrain from attempting to elicit incriminating evidence from the detainee until the detainee has had a reasonable opportunity to exercise their right to counsel, unless the matter is so urgent that they must proceed with the questioning (*R. v. Manninen*, 1987; *R. v. Bartle*, 1994).

To continue questioning a detainee otherwise is a serious breach of Charter rights, and any subsequent responses or voluntary statements will typically *not* be admitted into court unless the court finds that the accused was intent on speaking to police.

Section 10(b) includes the phrase "without delay" in describing the right of arrested or detained persons to retain and instruct counsel and to be informed of this right. The Supreme Court has held that the phrase "without delay" means that *the moment* an interaction becomes a detention or an arrest, police are required to inform an individual of his or her s. 10(b) rights *immediately* (*R. v. Suberu*, 2009). Failure to do so, in the absence of an exception to this rule (for example, officer or public safety concerns), will almost certainly render any statement that a suspect may subsequently provide inadmissible, and will leave the investigator and the investigation open to criticism by a court.

As can be seen from the list of police obligations above, the right to counsel consists of both an *information* component and an *opportunity* component. To satisfy the information component, investigators must tell any persons whom they detain or arrest:

1. that they have the right to consult with a lawyer without delay; and

2. how they can exercise their right to counsel.

As part of the information above, investigators must inform *all* suspects that, if they wish, they can immediately speak with a free lawyer (known as duty counsel) and that, if they cannot afford to pay for a lawyer on their own, they can retain a lawyer at a later time who will be paid by the government through legal aid (*R. v. Brydges*, 1990). For example:

A legal aid duty lawyer is available to you without charge. They will provide you with free legal advice and can explain the legal aid plan to you. If you wish to contact a legal aid duty lawyer, I can provide you with a telephone number. The number is 1-800-XXX-XXXX. Do you understand? Do you want to call a lawyer now?

To satisfy the opportunity component of the right to counsel, investigators must ensure that the person has a "reasonable opportunity" to exercise their right. This includes providing them with a telephone and a telephone number they can call to speak to duty counsel, and telling them that they can speak to counsel in private. What constitutes a "reasonable opportunity" depends on the circumstances, including the availability of duty counsel in the jurisdiction in question (*R. v. Prosper*, 1994). Police are only required to allow a person to speak with a lawyer *once* prior to questioning. During questioning, if the person's jeopardy changes, they must be informed of this and given another opportunity to consult counsel (see the box feature on page 296).

A number of court cases have considered the question what constitutes a "reasonable opportunity" to retain and instruct counsel and the scope of an individual's right to contact his or her counsel of choice. In *R. v. McCrimmon* (2010), the appellant was arrested and advised of his right to counsel. He asked to speak to a particular lawyer, whom police were not able to contact, and subsequently agreed to speak to legal aid duty counsel instead. Following a conversation between the appellant and duty counsel, police interrogated the appellant, who made incriminatory statements. The appellant stated several times during the interrogation that he wished to speak to a lawyer again and have a lawyer present during questioning. Police refused these requests. The Court stated that the actions of police did not constitute a s. 10(b) violation: the appellant had exercised his right to counsel before the interrogation began, had indicated that he was satisfied with duty counsel's advice, and had indicated at the outset of the interrogation that he understood his rights. In this case, the police had no obligation to delay questioning until the appellant was able to speak to his counsel of choice.

In another case, *R. v. Ross* (1989), the appellants were arrested and charged with break and enter. They were advised of their right to counsel and, although they attempted to contact their counsel of choice—at approximately 2:00 a.m.—they were unsuccessful. One of the appellants stated that he did not wish to contact a lawyer other than the one he had originally attempted to contact, and was placed in a cell. Shortly thereafter, the appellants were told to participate in a lineup, in which evidence against them was obtained. The Court held that, while the police initially complied with s. 10(b) in advising the accused of their right to retain and instruct counsel, the accused did not receive a "real opportunity" to do so prior to the lineup. In this case, the admission of the lineup evidence into the proceedings would have brought the administration of justice into disrepute, and the evidence was therefore excluded.

Finally, in *R. v. Willier* (2010), the appellant was arrested for murder, informed of his right to counsel, and given a brief opportunity to speak to duty counsel. The following day, he was given another opportunity to speak to counsel; his attempt to contact a specific lawyer was unsuccessful. Police advised him that because it was the weekend, the lawyer was unlikely to call back until Monday, and they reminded him of the availability of duty counsel. The appellant chose to speak to duty counsel a second time, and said he was satisfied with the advice he received. Police advised him that they were going to interview him and that he would be free at any time during the interview to stop and call a lawyer. The appellant did not attempt to contact his lawyer again and subsequently provided police with a statement. Later, the appellant argued that his statement should be excluded under s. 10(b) of the Charter because he had been denied a reasonable opportunity to consult with counsel of his choice before the interview and because his two conversations with duty counsel were too short to allow him to meaningfully exercise his right to instruct counsel. The Court held that the appellant's s. 10(b) right was not violated: the police did not interfere with his right to a reasonable opportunity to consult with his counsel of choice by reminding him of the availability of duty counsel when he was unable to contact a particular lawyer. The Court stated that, "unless a detainee indicates, diligently and reasonably, that the advice he or she received is inadequate, the police may assume that the detainee is satisfied with the exercised right to counsel and are entitled to commence an investigative interview" (para. 42).

The courts require diligence—that is, an earnest effort—on the part of the accused in the exercise of the right to counsel. If a detainee is not being reasonably diligent in the exercise of this right, the related duties imposed on the police in a situation where the detainee has requested the assistance of counsel are suspended and are not a barrier to the police continuing their investigation (*R. v. Tremblay*, 1987).

In *R. v. Eakin* (2000), the appellant was informed of his right to counsel and indicated his wish to speak to a particular lawyer. He was provided with a telephone book, which he appeared "to thumb through randomly" without locating the lawyer's number. A detective tried unsuccessfully to find the number in the telephone book and went to look for a lawyers' directory, but was unable to locate one. The police requested duty counsel and ceased questioning; the appellant spoke to duty counsel a short while later and made no objection to this, nor did he make further requests to speak to the lawyer he had wished to consult initially. The appellant subsequently provided hair, saliva, and blood samples. At trial, he argued that he had not been provided with the proper information to allow him to contact his lawyer of choice. The Court found that the appellant was both properly informed of his rights and given a reasonable opportunity to exercise those rights; in addition, he appeared to accept duty counsel as an alternative to the lawyer he originally requested. While the police could have made greater efforts to help the appellant locate his preferred lawyer, the appellant himself made "no earnest attempt" to locate his lawyer and did not pursue his request, showing a lack of diligence.

In another case (*R. v. Richfield*, 2003), the appellant was arrested for impaired driving at 1:00 a.m. and advised of his right to counsel. The appellant stated that he wished to speak with a particular lawyer. At 1:42 a.m., the arresting officer placed a call to the lawyer the appellant had requested and left a message with a person who was staffing the answering service. At 2:44 a.m.—one hour and 45 minutes after the time of the arrest—the officer's call had not been returned, and he asked the appellant if he wished to speak to duty counsel. The appellant said no, maintaining that he wished to speak only to counsel of his choice; the appellant disregarded further information regarding the purpose of duty counsel and the officer's advice that the appellant make use of this service in the circumstances. Aware of the two-hour period within which a breath sample had to be taken for the prosecution for the evidence to meet the requirements in s. 258(1)(d) of the *Criminal Code,* the officer delivered the appellant to a breath technician, who obtained a sample with the appellant's consent. The appellant argued that the evidence should be excluded, because his right to counsel of his choice was breached. However, the Court stated that the appellant was not reasonably diligent in exercising his right to counsel in the circumstances—when informed that his chosen lawyer had not called back, he did not ask to make a further call to his counsel of choice or to another counsel, or choose to consult with duty counsel.

Finally, in *R. v. Smith* (1989), the accused was arrested around 7:00 p.m. and instructed on his right to retain counsel. He said several times that he did wish to speak with counsel, but when he arrived at the police station at 9:00 p.m. and was given a phone book and a phone, he refused to call his lawyer, claiming it was too late at night. The police suggested that he attempt a call in case there was a machine with an alternative number, but he refused. The Court said that because the accused was not making a sincere attempt to exercise his right, the police were justified in continuing to question the accused, and the statements they obtained were admissible.

As the discussion above illustrates, accused persons do not have unlimited rights under s. 10(b), and cannot use the s. 10(b) right to delay a police investigation.

The right to retain and instruct counsel is not necessarily violated the moment the police refuse an accused's request to contact counsel; police officers making arrests in potentially volatile situations may be justified in briefly delaying the exercise of an accused's rights until the situation is under control. For example, in *R. v. Strachan* (1988), an RCMP officer arrested the accused in his home. The officer knew that there were weapons, as well as two unknown individuals, in the house. Although the accused requested to speak to a lawyer right away, the officer delayed the exercise of the accused's right, telling him he could not use the telephone until he had "matters under control." The Court said that because of the volatile situation, the officer was justified in delaying granting the accused his rights until the police had taken care of the unknown variables. However, the Court noted that it was not until the accused arrived at the police station that he was allowed to telephone his lawyer, one hour and 40 minutes after the search began. Once the accused was arrested, the other individuals had left, and the guns had been found, *then* the accused should have been given his right to counsel.

The Supreme Court has described three instances in which an accused's s. 10 rights *will* be found to have been violated (*R. v. Burlingham,* 1995):

1. The police continue to question an accused despite the repeated protests that he or she will say nothing without consulting a lawyer.

2. The police belittle the accused's lawyer in an attempt to undermine the accused's confidence in counsel.

3. The police pressure the accused to accept a deal without first affording the accused an opportunity to consult his or her lawyer.

Accused Who Waive the Right to Counsel

A person may waive (give up) their right to speak to a lawyer, but they must do so voluntarily. In addition, for such a **waiver** to be valid, the person must understand the consequences of giving up their right to counsel. If the waiver leads to the police obtaining an incriminating statement or full **confession**, proving that the waiver was unequivocal becomes key to the admissibility of the statement or confession. The standard of proof is very high. In *R. v. Bartle* (1994), the Supreme Court established guidelines for accepting a waiver. An effective waiver under s. 10(b) requires that the accused be fully apprised of the information he or she has the right to receive. The mere fact that an accused indicates that he or she does not wish to receive the information does not, in itself, constitute a valid waiver. A waiver is valid only when it is clear that the accused fully understands his or her rights under s. 10(b) and fully understands the means by which those rights may be exercised. *R. v. Smith* (1991) established that a trial judge must be satisfied that the accused understood the jeopardy he or she faced when making the decision to dispense with counsel.

An accused's understanding of the jeopardy he or she faces in this context has been the subject of much recent research, most of which focuses on people's ability to comprehend police cautions (Eastwood, Snook, & Chaulk, 2010; Eastwood & Snook, 2010; Moore & Gagnier, 2008; Rogers, Harrison, Hazelwood, & Sewell, 2007; Rogers, Hazelwood, Sewell, Harrison, & Shuman, 2008). It turns out that many people—including, but not limited to, youth; people with developmental disabilities; and people for whom English (or French, in Canada) is not their first language—do not fully comprehend some of the words and some of the concepts when their rights are delivered by police. Perhaps more important, it is possible that many people *comprehend* their rights, in terms of what the words mean, but don't fully appreciate *why* those rights exist (Basarke, Stanley, & Turtle, 2011). In fact, Saul Kassin's (2005) article on this point is subtitled, "Does innocence put innocents at risk?" in reference to the finding that most people assume that they don't need a lawyer if *they* know that they didn't do anything wrong. But, of course, innocent people are the *only* ones who are in jeopardy of being wrongfully convicted, so they are the ones who should perhaps be *most likely* to take advantage of their rights. The only jeopardy facing a guilty person in this context is the potential for self-incrimination.

Current research on this issue concerns innocent people's understanding of the risks they face (as small as they might be) if the circumstances in a case conspire to make them a likely suspect, such as being a recent ex-partner of a murder victim or being a person who matches the description of an offender and is apprehended in the vicinity of a recently committed crime. It is in these situations that the investigation might mistakenly conclude that an innocent person is guilty if, for example, they don't have a good alibi, some physical evidence coincidentally points to them as the culprit, or they exhibit signs of nervousness that are interpreted as indicators of deception. Yet "lawyering up" is often perceived as a sign of guilt, or at least suspicion, so innocent people might assume that they're making things worse for themselves by invoking their rights. It remains to be seen whether further research and thinking on this issue translate into changes in the way police cautions are delivered.

waiver
a decision, communicated clearly by words or actions, to decline the exercise of a particular right

confession
an admission to all of the elements of an offence, including the mental element

The Right to Silence

Even before the Charter was enacted in 1982, Canadian courts and common-law courts around the world recognized the impropriety of convicting accused persons on the basis of coerced, self-incriminating statements. Today, protection against self-incrimination is considered by the courts to fall within s. 7 of the Charter, which reads:

> 7. Everyone has the right to life, liberty and security of the person and the right not to be deprived thereof except in accordance with the principles of fundamental justice.

The right against self-incrimination is also protected by s. 11(c), which provides that any person charged with an offence has the right "not to be compelled to be a witness in proceedings against that person in respect of the offence."

right to silence
the right of an individual not to be compelled to be a witness against himself or herself and to freely choose whether or not to speak to agents of the state, such as police officers

Unlike the right to counsel, the **right to silence** has no information component. This means that there is no legal requirement for police to tell a person about their right to silence (*R. v. Singh*, 2007), although most standard police cautions do so (see below). The right to silence means that individuals are free to choose whether or not to speak to agents of the state, and the police (as agents of the state) are not allowed to subvert the choice of a person who has been arrested or detained to remain silent. This means, for example, that police cannot place an undercover officer in the cell of a person who has specifically said that they do not wish to speak to police in order to actively elicit information from that person (*R. v. Hebert*, 1990).

In Canada, the right to silence is not absolute. While the Supreme Court has acknowledged that a person has the right to remain silent in the face of questioning by police, it has also stated that this right does *not* mean that investigators must stop questioning people who assert their right to silence. In the somewhat controversial decision of *R. v. Singh* (2007), the majority of the Court (5:4) said that if a statement is found to be voluntary, there is no s. 7 breach, because a voluntariness inquiry includes consideration of whether the accused was denied his or her right to silence. In *Singh*, the accused asserted his right to silence 18 times, but the police continued to question him. Because his statement was made voluntarily, the majority held that the police questioning did not violate s. 7.

Effect of Counsel's Advice on Investigators' Duty to Investigate

Some investigators are reluctant to attempt to question a suspect after he or she has consulted a lawyer (and has presumably been advised to exercise his or her right to silence). *This is a mistake*, and results in a wasted opportunity to obtain further information if the accused has decided not to follow the lawyer's advice to remain silent. The Supreme Court case *R. v. Sinclair* (2010) confirmed that once the accused has been informed of his or her right to counsel and has been given a reasonable opportunity to exercise this right, police officers are free to question the accused. Section 10(b) of the Charter does not afford the accused the opportunity to re-consult with counsel during an interview (except as a result of a change in jeopardy), nor does it require an officer to cease questioning an accused if they ask to re-consult with counsel. Further, s. 10(b) does not mandate the continued presence of defence counsel during the custodial interview.

ENHANCED RIGHTS OF YOUNG PERSONS

Persons 12 years of age or older but *less than* 18 years of age who come into contact with the police have all of the same legal rights as individuals 18 and older, but because of their unique status in the criminal justice system their rights are enhanced. Section 25 of the YCJA states that a young person has the right to retain and instruct counsel at *any* stage in their interaction with the criminal justice system (in contrast to adults, for whom that right exists only upon arrest or detention), while s. 146 provides a number of special rules that govern the admissibility of any statements made by a young person to a police officer or person in authority. In order for a young person's statement to be admissible:

1. it must be voluntary, and
2. the person to whom the statement was made must have explained to the young person in age-appropriate language, before they made the statement, that
   - they are not obliged to make a statement,
   - any statement they do give may be used as evidence against them, and
   - they have the right to consult with counsel and a parent or other person.

Before making the statement, the young person must have, in fact, been given a reasonable opportunity to consult with counsel, a parent, or an adult relative (or other appropriate adult) chosen by the young person.

A young person may waive their right to counsel, but such a waiver must either be recorded or be in writing, and must contain a statement signed by the young person that says that they have been informed of their right to counsel and they are choosing to waive it. Section 146(8) of the YCJA holds that in situations where a young person represents themselves to be 18 years of age or older when they make a statement or waiver, or where the person to whom the statement or waiver was made took reasonable steps to determine the age of the young person and believed that they were 18 years of age or older, the court may rule the young person's statement or waiver admissible. A special form (Form 9.1, Statement of a Young Person) is provided under the YCJA, and includes the steps that police must follow when taking a statement from a young person.

Officers who are required to take a statement from a young person are advised to prepare themselves by reading the applicable sections of the YCJA and by consulting the Department of Justice Canada website (http://www.justice.gc.ca) section entitled YCJA Explained, which contains copies of the related forms and checklists of the key sections related to the rights and statements of young persons. On the Department of Justice Canada homepage, click the Programs and Initiatives link, then click the Youth Justice Renewal link under Criminal Justice, and then click the Youth Criminal Justice Act link. Officers would also be well advised to read the case of *R. v. L.T.H.* (2008), which includes a detailed discussion of s. 146(2) of the YCJA and the requirements that must be met in order for a statement from a young person to be admissible.

That said, officers must keep in mind that the accused always has the right to remain silent and that all statements must be voluntary. Thus, officers are advised to always proceed with caution and to be careful to record everything that is said (see the discussion in Chapter 17, Interviewing Techniques). There must be no evidence to suggest that the evidence provided was coerced in any way.

A related point concerns instructions from counsel to police, either in person or over the phone, asking police not to question the suspect any further. The law places *no requirement* on investigators to follow such requests. Again, there are no disadvantages to attempting to obtain a statement from an accused, even if the statement is composed entirely of lies; in fact, lies that can be shown to be lies can be helpful to the Crown's case. In the case of a statement that the Crown does not feel will strengthen its case, the Crown does not have to seek to have it admitted in evidence (Sherriff, 2003).

Investigators must not automatically assume that because a suspect has spoken to a lawyer, the suspect will decline to make a statement. Although the suspect's lawyer will typically advise him or her not to speak to police, the decision ultimately rests with the suspect. Because investigators have a duty to investigate criminal allegations, there is no excuse for not attempting to obtain a statement from a suspect, within the limits discussed here.

CAUTIONING SUSPECTS

One of the most important police procedures related to interviewing suspects and accused persons is the administration of a caution upon arrest, at the beginning of questioning or at any point where the charges against the accused have changed. The cautioning process is designed to allow police to discharge the obligations imposed on them by case law and legislation such as the Charter. Even if a suspect has not been formally arrested or detained, the courts have advised that an investigator should provide a caution where there are reasonable grounds to believe that the person being interviewed has committed an offence (*R. v. Singh*, 2007).

Primary Caution

primary caution
a warning given by an investigator to a suspect informing him or her that an officer is conducting an investigation into a criminal allegation; that they are a suspect in that investigation; that they do not have to speak to the police, but if they choose to do so the police will make a record of it that may be used against them in court if they are charged with a criminal offence

Because the exact content of a caution will vary, specific wording is not provided here. However, it is clear that a legally sufficient **primary caution** should inform the suspect

1. that the officer is conducting an investigation into a specific criminal allegation (and what that allegation is), and the person is a suspect in that investigation;

2. of the nature of each offence that is being investigated, or with which the accused is being charged;

3. that the suspect or accused has the right to retain counsel before making any statement, and free legal advice (including legal aid) is available;

4. that the suspect or accused does not have to speak to the police if he or she does not want to; if he or she decides to speak to the police, the police will make a record of whatever is said to them (remember, however, that there is no *duty* to inform suspects of their right to silence); and

5. that if the suspect is later charged with a criminal offence, whatever the suspect tells the police can be used against him or her in court.

Police recruits can expect to receive instruction from their police service on the appropriate forms of caution, and should be alert to legal developments that suggest improvements to the cautioning procedure.

In administering the caution, the investigator must not only provide the requisite information, but also ensure to the best of his or her ability that the suspect has understood the information (as described below and, where language may be an issue, by arranging for an interpreter) and has been given an opportunity to exercise the right to counsel. In fulfilling these responsibilities, the police must provide privacy and access to a telephone so that the accused can call a lawyer. After an investigator has given the primary caution (or the secondary caution, discussed below), it is good practice to have suspects restate the cautions in their own words, in order to confirm that they have understood them. As with any police or suspect interaction, it is strongly advised that the giving of the caution and the suspect's restatement of it be recorded to prove that the caution was read to—and understood by—the suspect.

Secondary Caution

Where the investigator is not the first police officer to have contact with the suspect, there is a danger that the past behaviour of less scrupulous officers or other persons in authority will affect the admissibility of any further statements that the accused chooses to make. For this reason, where an accused has had previous contact with other persons in authority, a **secondary caution** should be given in addition to the primary caution, advising the suspect that, if he or she has had any previous contact with police officers with regard to the matter under investigation, the suspect should not be influenced by anything that was said or done during that contact (in particular, any threats or promises), and that the suspect remains free to decide whether to speak to investigators. For example:

> I wish to give you the following warning: you must clearly understand that anything said to you previously should not influence you or make you feel compelled to say anything at this time. Whatever you may have felt influenced or compelled to say earlier you are not now obliged to repeat, nor are you obliged to say anything further, but whatever you do say may be given in evidence. Do you understand?

In the absence of a secondary caution, it may be difficult for the Crown to prove that the statement was made voluntarily (see the discussion below on the admissibility of statement evidence).

secondary caution
a warning given by an investigator to a suspect where the investigator is not the first police officer to have contact with the suspect, advising the suspect that if he or she has had any previous contact with the police regarding the matter under investigation the suspect should not be influenced by anything said or done during that contact, and that he or she remains free to decide whether to speak to the investigator

The Need to Re-caution

Accused persons who consult counsel after being informed of a particular charge have not necessarily exhausted their s. 10 rights, according to the Supreme Court in *R. v. Black* (1989) and *R. v. Borden* (1994). If the police alter the charge or add a new charge, the accused must be granted another opportunity to consult counsel. These cases suggest that if an investigating officer begins to suspect that a person has committed additional offences beyond those for which he or she has already been charged, the person should immediately be re-cautioned and given a new opportunity to obtain counsel. If, for example, an officer visits a residence to investigate a report of stolen property and cautions a suspect on the premises with respect to that offence, but a few minutes later notices what appear to be marijuana plants growing under a heat lamp, the officer should caution the suspect again, this time with respect to the marijuana offence.

CHANGES TO A SUSPECT'S JEOPARDY

If during the course of an interview with a suspect an investigator becomes aware that the suspect's jeopardy has changed, the investigator must take certain steps. *Which* steps will depend on the particular situation, but the ability of the investigating officer to choose the correct course of action is critically important to the outcome of an investigation and requires good judgment and a full understanding of the law.

The following examples illustrate changes in a suspect's jeopardy and the actions that the investigator should take in each situation:

- An investigator is conducting an interview with a person who was not previously a suspect in a crime (for example, a witness); in the course of the interview, the investigator receives new information or the person says something that causes the investigator to believe that the person is now a suspect in the crime under investigation or in another crime. For example, suppose the witness admits to being present at the scene of a shooting and to carrying a firearm, but denies firing a shot. In this case, the investigator must stop the interview, advise the person of their new status as a suspect, advise them of their legal rights pursuant to the Charter, allow them to consult with legal counsel, and caution them before continuing the interview.
- The police are interviewing a suspect with respect to one or a series of offences and it becomes apparent as a result of an admission by that person that he or she is now a suspect for a different offence or series of offences. Again, in this case the suspect must be informed of the change in status and be given his or her rights once more before questioning continues.
- While questioning an individual regarding an assault, the investigator is notified of the fact that the victim of the assault has died. As in the examples above, because of this change in circumstances, the investigator must inform the suspect of the nature of the new investigation and explain the suspect's rights to him or her again.

Where an investigator must caution a suspect or advise the suspect of his or her rights again during an interview, this should be done before the suspect has an opportunity to volunteer *any* additional information.

ADMISSIBILITY OF STATEMENT EVIDENCE

inculpatory
that which establishes or tends to establish a person's guilt

exculpatory
that which clears or tends to clear a person of guilt

If an accused chooses to waive the right to silence and make a statement (whether **inculpatory** or **exculpatory**), no matter how incriminating or valuable to the prosecution an accused's statement may be, if it is shown to have been obtained involuntarily or through some other violation of the accused's legal rights, it may be ruled inadmissible. A ruling of inadmissibility is usually the product of carelessness by investigators and is, in most cases, preventable.

For an accused's statement to be admissible, the Crown must demonstrate that the accused:

- was aware of why he or she was being spoken to by the authorities and the potential jeopardy associated with that;
- had been advised of and understood his or her constitutional rights and had a meaningful opportunity to exercise those rights; and
- still chose freely to speak to authorities.

The voluntariness of a statement is normally established by a *voir dire*, or a trial within a trial. Although an electronic record is the most effective way to prove the voluntariness of a statement, the court may also require that *all* officers who had contact with the accused prior to the taking of the statement—that is, not only the investigators who were present with the suspect in the interview room—be available to testify, in order to determine whether or not they had any conversation with the suspect that may have influenced his or her decision to speak to the police. This is the reason why the secondary caution, discussed above, is so important.

Statements Made to Persons in Authority

Statements made to a person *not* in authority (for example, a friend or a doctor of an accused) are admissible without consideration of their voluntariness. However, the **confession rule** holds that a statement, an admission, or a confession made by an accused person to a **person in authority** is admissible against them *only if* the Crown can prove, beyond a reasonable doubt, that the statement was given voluntarily. This rule is embodied in current Canadian case law in decisions such as *Oickle* (2000) and *Spencer* (2007).

The test to determine who is a "person in authority" is partially subjective—for example, a parent, a doctor, a teacher, or an employer may be found to be a person in authority in certain circumstances, depending on the accused's belief as to the ability of the person to influence the prosecution or investigation of the crime with which they are charged—and partially objective, and was articulated by the Supreme Court in *R. v. Hodgson* (1998). In that case, the Court held that a person in authority is a person *who the accused believes on reasonable grounds* (1) is acting on behalf of the state or (2) has influence or control over the proceedings. The subjective component is the accused's *perception* that the statement was given to a person in authority, and the objective component is the requirement that the accused's belief be *reasonable*.

The question who is a person in authority has produced a great deal of case law, most of which is concerned with what constitutes reasonable grounds. A person's occupation is an important consideration in an accused's perceptions of who is a person in authority. Police officers, Crown attorneys, corrections personnel, and any others involved in the arrest, prosecution, or incarceration of an accused may reasonably be found to be persons in authority, because their ability to influence the prosecution is obvious.

A child's parents or guardians may be persons in authority when the child is a victim of crime. At times, social agency employees such as family counsellors and social workers qualify as persons in authority. The proprietor of a business may be found to be a person in authority in cases involving theft, fraud, or embezzlement within the business, by virtue of the fact that the proprietor may be the one who decides whether the police are notified of the crime.

Persons acting on behalf of a federal, provincial, or municipal branch of government may be found by the courts to be agents of a specific department and thus persons in authority. Threats, coercion, or **inducements** directed at an accused in the presence of the police by someone who is not a police officer can make that person a person in authority if he or she is found to have acted on behalf of the police or if his or her conduct was such that the accused could have reasonably inferred that the threats, coercion, or inducements received police consent or acquiescence.

confession rule
a long-established doctrine of common law that holds that no statement made by an accused person to a person in authority is admissible against them unless the Crown can show beyond a reasonable doubt that the statement was given voluntarily

person in authority
typically refers to persons who are formally engaged in the arrest, detention, examination, or prosecution of the accused—for example, police officers, prison guards, and Crown attorneys

inducement
a promise, favour, threat, or representation made to an accused that can be perceived as an effort to coerce the accused into making a confession

A medical doctor who in his or her professional capacity examines an accused or treats an accused's injury or other physical condition is *not*, according to the courts, a person in authority, and statements made to such a person may therefore be admissible. However, statements made to a psychiatrist during a court-ordered assessment are considered to be induced statements and are therefore, generally, inadmissible.

Whether a statement made to an undercover police officer will be admissible will depend on the actions of the officer in a particular situation. See the discussion in the box feature below.

UNDERCOVER OFFICERS

The question whether an undercover police officer is a person in authority is an interesting one, given that a suspect who is unaware of the true identity of an undercover officer might volunteer information that he or she would never disclose to a known police officer. The issue was considered in the 1981 case of *Rothman v. The Queen*. In that case, an accused being questioned by the police refused to make a statement and was placed in the cells. The police then sent an undercover officer into the cells with the accused. Although the accused was suspicious of the undercover officer, the officer was able to convince the accused that he was not a police officer. The accused made inculpatory statements involving narcotics charges to the officer. The Court ruled that a *voir dire* was not necessary to judge the voluntariness of the statements, because the accused believed that the undercover officer was not a police officer (and thus not a person in authority). The Court also ruled that the undercover officer's deception did not constitute a situation in which the administration of justice had been brought into disrepute. The accused's statements were admitted into evidence against him.

After the passage of the Charter in 1982, a similar set of facts arose in *Hebert* (1990). In *Hebert*, the Court's conclusion about the significance of the Charter protection of the right to silence effectively changed the result in *Rothman*, with the Court finding that it is improper for the police to use an undercover agent to elicit a statement that an accused has previously refused to give the police. *Hebert* did not, however, specifically reject the *Rothman* finding that an undercover agent may be a person not in authority vis-à-vis the accused. Recently, in *R. v. Grandinetti* (2005), the Supreme Court held that a confession made to an undercover officer was admissible, because the accused did not view the officer as a person in authority, although, in other situations, the Court has focused on whether the statement was given *voluntarily*. In *R. v. Liew* (1999), the Court held that an accused's confession to an undercover officer did not violate the accused's right to silence because the officer did not actively elicit the information in violation of the accused's right to remain silent.

Thus, because of *Hebert*, if the police use undercover officers to subvert the right to silence, then the Charter will operate to exclude any statements. However, where undercover officers obtain information from an accused in a voluntary manner without attempting to breach the accused's right to remain silent, such statements may be admissible.

Confession Evidence

Despite many people's intuitive belief that no one would confess to a crime they didn't commit, the problem of false confessions is real. One recent study documented 125 cases of proven, interrogation-induced false confessions, 81 percent of which occurred in murder cases (Drizin & Leo, 2004). Consistent with this finding, other research has found that in about 25 percent of all DNA exonerations in the United States, innocent people made incriminating statements, gave outright confessions, or pleaded guilty to crimes they did not commit (Kassin, 2008; Innocence Project, 2010; Uphoff, 2006).

In Canada, the issue of false confessions has been the subject of television documentaries (CBC, Disclosure, 2003), and false confessions (such as that of Simon Marshall, a mentally handicapped man who falsely confessed to crimes he did not commit in the late 1990s; he spent five years in jail after being wrongfully convicted, but was subsequently cleared by DNA and awarded $2.3 million by the government of Quebec in 2006) have played an important role in wrongful convictions in this country (Seguin, 2006; *Marshall c. R.*, 2005).

The leading Canadian case on the admissibility of confession evidence in Canada is the Supreme Court case *R. v. Oickle* (2000). In *Oickle*, the Court identified five kinds of false confessions and the interrogation scenarios most likely to produce them:

1. **Coerced–compliant** This is the most common type of false confession. Individuals give this type of confession knowingly, in response to threats or promises. Being told, for example, that it would be better to confess to a lesser charge than to be found guilty of a more serious one could cause an innocent person to make a coerced–compliant false confession.

2. **Stress–compliant** Individuals give this type of false confession knowingly, to escape from what they perceive to be an intolerably intense, punishing interrogation experience or in a situation in which they have been convinced that it is futile to protest their innocence.

3. **Non-coerced–persuaded** Individuals give this type of false confession because, as a result of the use of certain police interrogation tactics, they have become confused, have come to doubt their own memory, and have been temporarily persuaded of their own guilt.

4. **Coerced–persuaded** This type of false confession shares the characteristics of the non-coerced–persuaded confession, but, in addition, threats or promises have been used.

5. **Voluntary** In this type of confession, a person who did not commit the crime confesses without any prompting from the police. This often occurs in high-profile cases, for a variety of reasons ranging from mental illness to a desire for attention. For example, in the JonBenet Ramsey case, John Mark Karr confessed, and was arrested and charged, but the charges against him were dropped when DNA evidence excluded him as a suspect.

Only the first four types of false confessions are relevant to police interrogations, because the fifth is the result of a person coming forward, falsely confessing of his or her own free will, and is not the product of police questioning methods.

coerced–compliant false confession
the most common type of false confession identified in *R. v. Oickle* (2000), it is given knowingly by an individual in response to threats or promises

stress–compliant false confession
a false confession given knowingly in order to escape from what the person perceives to be an intolerably intense, punishing interrogation, and/or a situation in which someone has been convinced that it is futile to protest his or her innocence

non-coerced–persuaded false confession
a false confession given as a result of certain police interrogation tactics that have confused a person or caused them to doubt their own memory, and which have temporarily persuaded them of their own guilt

coerced–persuaded false confession
a false confession that shares the same characteristics as the non-coerced–persuaded false confession, but in which threats and promises have also been used

voluntary false confession
a false confession given voluntarily for a variety of reasons, including mental illness or a desire for attention, and not as a result of the use of police interrogation techniques

Determining Voluntariness

Today, the admissibility of confessions by accused persons is determined according to the approach set out by the Supreme Court in *Oickle*. In *Oickle*, the Court noted that false confessions are "rarely the product of proper police techniques" (para. 45) and stated that, if a confession is produced in certain situations or under certain circumstances, the voluntariness of the confession is difficult to determine. Judges must look carefully at *all* of the circumstances surrounding a confession and how it was obtained and consider the degree to which the following four factors were present:

1. threats or promises,
2. an atmosphere of oppression,
3. an operating mind, and
4. police trickery.

The first three factors are connected with the voluntariness of a statement; depending on the context in which the statement was made, the presence of just one of these three factors to a sufficient degree, or a combination of all three, may be enough to render the statement involuntary. The presence of the fourth factor to a sufficient degree may be enough to exclude a statement on the basis of the fact that the actions of the police reflect negatively on the justice system and have the potential to bring the administration of justice into disrepute.

The four factors are discussed immediately below.

Threats or Promises

The Court in *Oickle* stated that false confessions are likely if the police employ threats or promises before the suspect confesses. Threats or promises, also known as inducements, in the form of words or gestures by a person in authority will make the statements or confession of the accused inadmissible if, whether standing alone or in combination with other factors (such as an atmosphere of oppression or lack of operating mind, discussed below), they are strong enough to overbear the will of the accused. This is based on the notion that the statement or confession must be a product of the accused's free will and not the result of the police having convinced the suspect that making the statement will put him or her in a better position.

Not every police technique to get an accused to confess will be considered an inducement; the courts will look for a quid pro quo (which means "something for something") offer by interrogators. If a confession is given in exchange for, or because of, something else (that is, to obtain a benefit or avoid a negative consequence, as opposed to for its own sake), it is more likely to be false—and therefore likely to be inadmissible.

Investigators who employ threats or promises cause a suspect to perceive the "fear of prejudice" or the "hope of advantage." An example of the hope of advantage would be a promise of preferential treatment, where a police officer suggests to a suspect that, in exchange for his confession, the officer will make efforts to see that the suspect faces a lesser charge or receives a more lenient sentence. Similarly, if a police officer offers an accused bail in return for a statement, that offer will likely render the statement inadmissible. An example of the fear of prejudice would be where a police officer threatens to carry out an act (such as hitting the suspect) unless the suspect provides a confession, *and the officer has the capacity to carry out the threat.* Any act of physical violence or torture will always render a statement inadmissible. The threat or suggestion of violence to prompt an accused to give a statement may on its own render a statement involuntary.

Threats or promises do not have to be directed at the suspect alone to be considered coercive—the Court has held that threats or promises regarding another person may constitute an improper inducement. For example, a mother who is told that her daughter will not be charged with shoplifting if she confesses to a similar offence is being offered the hope of advantage.

Commenting on the position of an accused before the courts is *not* considered an inducement as long as the police officer states only the facts and does not include an opinion on sentence or release from custody. The courts have held that a police officer who tells an accused person that he or she does not believe what the person is telling them is not engaging in conduct sufficient to make any subsequent statement that the accused person may make to the officer inadmissible unless the accusations of lying are prolonged.

The way in which police phrase questions or statements directed toward an accused may cause the statements to be considered inducements. Comments that hint at the possibility of prejudice (or advantage), such as "it would be better if you told the truth," are problematic. Although such comments may not automatically render a statement inadmissible, they *will* attract the court's scrutiny, because of the possibility that the suspect perceived them as either a subtle threat or an inducement. By contrast, moral or spiritual promises or appeals to a person's conscience— for example, promising a suspect that they will "feel better" or gain a "clear conscience" if they confess—are not problematic, because the things that are being promised are not under the control of the police.

Atmosphere of Oppression

Any police interrogation approach that creates an "atmosphere of oppression" increases the likelihood of a false confession because it effectively removes the ability of the suspect to make a meaningful choice about whether or not to speak to the authorities. Actions that contribute to an atmosphere of oppression include the following:

- *Prolonged interrogations.* The courts have held that prolonged interrogations can create an atmosphere of oppression. In this case, the concern is that an oppressive atmosphere may lead to a false confession— that is, an accused may confess in order to escape the horrible conditions rather than confess voluntarily. Although case law has not laid down a precise time limit, interrogations lasting as little as three hours have been called "excessive" by the courts and held to affect the voluntariness of a statement. What constitutes excessive varies from case to case, but when there has not been any apparent adverse treatment or lack of respect for the accused's rights, the courts have been generous in allowing statements gathered during prolonged interrogations into evidence. On the other hand, statements obtained as a result of subjecting the suspect to excessively aggressive questioning over an extended period of time have been ruled inadmissible.

- *Disregard for the dignity and well-being of the accused.* Interview circumstances that jeopardize the dignity and well-being of the accused have been viewed negatively by the courts. Where an accused has made a statement to a police officer after being denied food, water, sleep, use of the washroom, or medical attention, the courts have treated this as a serious violation of basic human dignity and have rejected assertions that the statement was voluntary. Denying clothing to an accused during an interrogation also causes statements to be ruled inadmissible.

  In addition, a harsh custodial or interview environment—that is, one that strips the accused of his or her dignity—can contribute to the creation of an atmosphere of oppression. Basements, locker rooms, and the like can fit into this category.

- *Excessive number of interviewers.* The courts have also considered the presence of an excessive number of police officers during the taking of a statement as a possible ground for a ruling of inadmissibility. Generally speaking, the courts consider two officers an appropriate complement, although the presence of other people essential to the statement-taking process (for example, translators) has been permitted. The number of officers and others interacting with the accused should be kept to a minimum because all of them may be asked to testify about their interactions in order for the Crown to prove that none of them used threats or inducements (see the discussion of *voir dire*, above).

- *Fabricated evidence.* The courts have generally held that confronting a suspect with "entirely fabricated evidence" (for example, suggesting that the crime was caught on camera when it was not) can contribute to the production of a false confession. This action will not automatically result in a statement being ruled inadmissible, but it will be one of the things that the court considers, because of its potential—especially in combination with other factors—to persuade a vulnerable suspect (for example, a person with a developmental disability or a psychological disorder) that he committed the crime, or at least to persuade him that there is no point in claiming that he is innocent.

No Operating Mind

This criterion applies to the cognitive abilities of the suspect rather than to police questioning practices. Even if police investigators proceed properly with respect to all other circumstances, a suspect's statement may not be considered voluntary if it is not the product of an "operating mind." An operating mind means that, at the time the statement was made, the accused had the cognitive ability to understand what was being said to him or her, what he or she was saying, and that it was being said to the police, who could use it to his or her detriment. The determination of the presence or absence of an operating mind is made by the trial judge during a *voir dire*. Shock, acute mental illness, or intoxication by drugs or alcohol may make a person incapable of understanding the consequences of his or her actions, the nature of a police caution, or the right to counsel. Individuals who are functioning at a reduced mental capacity (for example, at that of a young child) may also be said not to possess an operating mind.

In cases of intoxication, the accused's coherence on being questioned by the police is the criterion on which the judge bases his or her decision. That an accused was intoxicated at the time of questioning does not necessarily exclude a confession or statement made to the police. The judge must determine whether the intoxication was such that the accused was incoherent when the confession or statement was made. Determining admissibility is therefore predicated not on the presence or absence of intoxication, but on the severity of the effects of that intoxication. A confession or statement made by an accused who is so intoxicated as to be incoherent will probably be ruled inadmissible.

Police Deceit or Trickery

This criterion is aimed at maintaining the integrity of the criminal justice system. While the Supreme Court clearly says that deceit and trickery are acceptable tools that the police can use when questioning suspects, it is equally clear when it says that in a society governed by the rule of law there must be limits on the use of such techniques. Those limits are determined by what is referred to as the "community shock test." Quite simply, any use of deceit or trickery by the police to obtain a confession that would shock the community—for example, an officer pretending to be a chaplain or a legal aid lawyer, or an officer injecting truth serum into a diabetic suspect while telling him it was insulin—will likely result in a confession being ruled inadmissible.

SUMMARY: INTERVIEWING SUSPECTS

1. Upon detaining or arresting individuals

Immediately inform them:

- of the reason for their arrest or detention;
- of their right to retain and instruct legal counsel without delay, including free legal counsel;
- of the ways in which they can exercise their right to counsel, which includes giving them the telephone number for duty counsel and telling them that they can speak to counsel in private; and
- of the fact that they are not legally required to answer questions posed by the police.

NOTE: Do *not* attempt to obtain incriminatory evidence from a person who has been arrested or detained until you have provided the individual with the above information and the individual has understood the information you have provided. Before you proceed, the individual must have had a reasonable opportunity to consult with a lawyer or must have chosen *not* to consult with a lawyer.

---

2. Before conducting an interview with a suspect

Read the suspect the following:

- A primary caution, informing them (1) that the police are investigating a criminal allegation (specify) and that they are a suspect; (2) of the nature of each offence or charge; (3) of their right to obtain and instruct counsel (including duty counsel or legal aid); (4) that their statements may be used against them in court; and (5) that they may choose whether or not to speak to police.
- A secondary caution, informing them that, regardless of whom they may have spoken to previously, the decision whether or not to speak to police is theirs alone.

NOTE: Do *not* conduct an interview or an interrogation until you have read suspects these cautions and checked that the suspect has understood them. You should be aware that this may require an interpreter.

---

3. Before taking a statement from a person over the age of 12 but under the age of 18:

- Obtain a copy of Form 9.1 under the YCJA; and
- Ensure that you are familiar with the key sections related to the rights and statements of young persons, and that you give the necessary cautions and receive the necessary responses required to properly take a statement from a young person.

NOTE: Interviews of young persons are different from interviews with adults and are best conducted by officers who have received special training in both the psychological and legal issues involved.

---

4. During an interview with a suspect

If a suspect makes an inculpatory statement about an offence other than the one being investigated or if you receive information that changes the jeopardy faced by the suspect:

- explain the suspect's legal rights to him or her again,
- give the suspect another opportunity to consult counsel, and
- caution the suspect again before continuing the interview.

KEY TERMS

arrest
coerced–compliant false confession
coerced–persuaded false confession
confession
confession rule
exculpatory
inculpatory
inducement

interview
investigative detention
investigative interaction
non-coerced–persuaded
   false confession
person in authority
primary caution
right to counsel

right to silence
secondary caution
stress–compliant false confession
suspect
voluntary false confession
waiver

FURTHER READING

Canadian Charter of Rights and Freedoms. (1982). Part I of the *Constitution Act, 1982*, R.S.C. 1985, app. II, no. 44. Department of Justice Canada. http://laws.justice.gc.ca/en/charter.

Eastwood, J., Snook, B., & Chaulk, S. (2010). Measuring reading complexity and listening comprehension of Canadian police cautions. In *Criminal Justice and Behavior, 37*(4), 453–471.

Smith, S., Stinson, V., & Patry, M. (2010, August 12). Confession evidence in Canada: Psychological issues and legal landscapes. *Psychology, Crime & Law, 16*, 1–17.

Watkins, K., Turtle, J., & Euale, J. (2011). *Interviewing and investigation* (2nd ed.). Toronto: Emond Montgomery.

Youth Criminal Justice Act. (2002). S.C. 2002, c. 1. Department of Justice Canada. http://laws.justice.gc.ca/en/Y-1.5/index.html.

REVIEW QUESTIONS

True or False?

1. When asking a suspect who is not under arrest to attend a police station for questioning, the investigator must disclose the offence being investigated.

2. Detention and arrest amount to the same thing as they pertain to a person's rights under s. 10 of the Charter.

3. The confession rule squarely places the onus on the Crown to prove that a confession made by an accused to a person in authority was a voluntary act on the part of the accused and that the accused was aware of his rights under ss. 7 and 10 of the Charter. The defence bears some responsibility to prove to a lesser degree that the accused's rights were violated.

4. When the police inform a suspect or an accused of his or her right to counsel, they need not advise the accused of his or her right to legal aid if the accused appears to be financially stable and able to pay for the services of a lawyer.

5. A person who is only under investigative detention need not be informed of his or her right to counsel or legal aid.

6. Under certain circumstances, a "person in authority" may include a suspect's employer.

7. Police must cease their questioning of a suspect if they receive verbal or written instruction to do so from the suspect's lawyer.

8. There is no exception to an officer's obligation to immediately inform a suspect, upon detention or arrest, of the suspect's right to retain and instruct counsel.

Multiple Choice

1. A coerced–persuaded false confession can result when
   a. as a result of the use of certain police interrogation tactics, a person becomes confused, comes to doubt their own memory, and is temporarily persuaded of their own guilt.
   b. threats or promises have been used.
   c. an innocent person wishes to protect a loved one who he or she knows is the guilty party.
   d. both a and b.

2. Which of the following are police *not* required to tell a suspect as part of the primary caution?
   a. the nature of the offence(s) under investigation.
   b. that the person has the right to retain counsel before making a statement.
   c. that the Charter protects the person from self-incrimination.
   d. that the person is a suspect in the investigation.

3. In Canada, the right to silence:
   a. is absolute.
   b. forms part of most standard police cautions.
   c. has an information component.
   d. may be subverted by police to effect their lawful purpose.

4. The leading case on the admissibility of confession evidence in Canada is:
   a. *R. v. Stinchcombe*
   b. *R. v. Oickle*
   c. *Ibrahim v. The King*
   d. *R. v. Singh*

5. The purpose of a secondary caution is:
   a. to make sure the suspect is aware that whatever he or she tells police can be used against him or her in any subsequent legal proceedings that may arise.
   b. to advise the suspect that any previous contact he or she has had with police regarding the investigation should not influence the current contact.
   c. to ensure that the suspect has properly understood all of the protections guaranteed by the Charter.
   d. to advise the suspect that the police will make a complete record of anything the suspect chooses to say to them.

6. Which of the following is true of young persons under the YCJA?

   a. A young person may only be detained following notification of their legal guardian.

   b. Unlike adults, young persons are *not* permitted to waive their right to counsel.

   c. In certain circumstances, a young person may make an application to have the police cease their questioning.

   d. Unlike adults, young persons may retain and instruct counsel at any stage of the proceedings against them.

7. A ruling of inadmissibility on a statement made by an accused to police is usually:

   a. because the accused did not understand that the statement would be used against him or her in court.

   b. a result of carelessness on the part of investigators.

   c. not due to the actions of investigators at the time the accused gave the statement.

   d. related to the problem of false confessions.

Short Answer

1. A 16-year-old boy admits to his mother at dinner that he stole a vehicle from a neighbour. Would the boy's mother be considered a "person in authority" pursuant to the confession rule and, if so, what effect would this have on the admissibility of the boy's statement?

2. Two adult male suspects are arrested on charges of breaking and entering. They are advised of their rights pursuant to ss. 10(a) and (b) of the Charter. They are also given both primary and secondary cautions. On being cautioned, they advise police that, on instructions from their lawyers, they do not wish to make a statement. The two men are then placed in a police station cell, unaware that an undercover police officer is in the cell next to them, pretending to be asleep. The undercover officer overhears a conversation between the two men in which they make several incriminating statements. Would the officer be considered a "person in authority"? Would it be necessary to hold a *voir dire*? Is the officer's evidence regarding what he overheard likely to be admissible?

3. The police arrest a man on a charge of sexual assault. He is informed of his rights under s. 10 of the Charter, which includes the right to counsel, and is given both a primary and secondary police caution. The man asks to speak to a lawyer and, after having done so, advises the police that his lawyer has instructed him to say nothing more to the police. However, the police continue to question the man, who says, at least five times, that he has the right to remain silent; however, after approximately an hour of questioning, the man makes an inculpatory statement concerning the sexual assault. Is the man's statement to police likely to be admissible? Provide a case law reference in support of your answer.

4. Police arrest a man on a charge of aggravated assault and inform him of his rights under s. 10 of the Charter, including the availability of free legal advice and a telephone number for legal-aid duty counsel. The man is then given a primary and secondary police caution. The police inform the man that they intend to question him regarding the assault and ask him if he wishes to speak with a lawyer. The man indicates that he understands his right to consult counsel, but does not ask to speak to a lawyer. He subsequently provides police with a full, signed confession. At trial, defence counsel argues that the confession should be excluded because police should not have questioned the accused until he had consulted a lawyer. Will the confession be admissible? Provide a case law reference in support of your answer.

5. A 40-year-old woman is arrested for fraud. She is advised of her Charter rights and transported to a police station where she is given the opportunity to speak to a lawyer. An investigator then begins to question her about the offence for which she has been arrested. She subsequently makes a confession to the officer. Would the woman's confession be admissible, given that the officer advised her of her legal rights and allowed her to speak to a lawyer, but did not caution her prior to taking her statement? Provide a case law reference for your answer.

6. A 27-year-old man is arrested for the knifepoint robbery of an elderly man. The accused is informed of his Charter rights, allowed to speak to a lawyer, and given both a primary and secondary police caution before being questioned by police. During questioning the accused is reluctant to speak to the investigator. In an attempt to elicit a confession from the accused, the investigator tells him that, because he didn't hurt the elderly man, if he confesses, the investigator will only charge him with theft of the man's wallet and not with robbery. The accused subsequently confesses to the robbery. Will his confession be admissible? Provide a case law reference.

7. A 17-year-old male is arrested as a suspect for a break and enter at a local high school in which a number of laptop computers were stolen and extensive damage was done to the school building. The young person is advised of his rights under s. 10 of the Charter and is given both a primary and secondary caution. The investigator then proceeds to question the young man, saying, "Listen, kid, it would be better for all concerned if you just come clean and admit what you did." The suspect subsequently makes an inculpatory statement to the officer. Would the young person's statement likely be admissible? Provide both a legislative and a case law reference for your answer.

Interviewing Techniques

17

LEARNING OUTCOMES

After completing this chapter, you should be able to:

• Outline the steps and considerations in preparing for interviews with witnesses and suspects.

• Describe the steps of the enhanced cognitive interview.

• Explain the difference between an interview and an interrogation.

• Describe the stages and techniques that comprise the Reid method of interviewing and interrogation.

• Describe the PEACE model of interviewing.

• Understand what research suggests about the effectiveness of the Reid and PEACE methods, and the criticisms that have been made of these methods.

INTRODUCTION

Among an investigator's most important skills is the ability to gather information from victims, witnesses, and suspects. In the past, many believed that common sense and the ability to ask questions were the only requirements of a good interviewer. However, years of attention from the law enforcement and legal communities, and a considerable body of scientific research, have shown that the interview process is considerably more complex than was first thought.

One of the most relevant observations to emerge from the field of interview research is that many investigators believe their interviewing skills to be significantly better than they really are, which limits their prospects for improvement (Walsh & Bull, 2010). Acknowledging one's limitations, educating oneself about developments in the field, and doing the necessary preparatory work before entering the interview room will help investigators meet the challenge.

The ability to conduct an effective interview requires training, planning, patience, problem solving, and lots of practice. This chapter provides an introduction to the key considerations and techniques used in interviewing witnesses and suspects. Note that the discussion assumes that the interviews are being conducted with average adult subjects. Interviews with individuals belonging to certain groups—for example, children, elderly persons, individuals with special needs, and individuals who may have difficulty speaking or understanding English—almost always require special consideration, further training, and additional planning. Interviews with young persons are best conducted by officers who have received special training in both the psychological and legal issues involved.

INTERVIEWING WITNESSES

Obtaining information from apparently cooperative witnesses and victims of crime has often been regarded as a process that does not require much more than asking a series of questions and accurately recording the responses. However, certain elements *are* necessary, including good communication skills on the part of the interviewer and a substantial effort by the interviewee to recall what happened.

This section of the chapter focuses on interviews with observer witnesses, non-traumatized victims, and people who may end up as suspects after more information is gathered. The distinction between interviewing a witness or victim versus interviewing a potential suspect is not always clear-cut; similar techniques are often useful and necessary in both cases (although special strategies are sometimes required for victims). Furthermore, in the early stages of an investigation, it is sometimes difficult to determine who is a victim, who is a witness, and who is a suspect until information from all involved parties and evidence from other sources are obtained.

tunnel vision
the single-minded and overly narrow focus on a particular investigative or prosecutorial theory that unreasonably colours the evaluation of information received and one's conduct in response to that information

At least initially, police interviewers should treat everyone with the same reasonable degree of politeness and respect—little is to be gained from adopting a confrontational attitude at the outset toward a person from whom one needs to elicit information. Establishing rapport and treating a person with respect have been shown to reliably open the lines of communication (St-Yves, 2006) and, by treating all witnesses equally, investigators reduce the risk of displaying bias or acquiring **tunnel vision**.

Witnesses and potential witnesses are typically briefly interviewed at the crime scene (assuming they are present and have been identified by the first officer or investigating officer), which often serves merely to identify the witness and where he or she may be located at a later time. During the on-scene interview, a witness's bare-bones observations may be recorded to assist in a future determination of the evidentiary value of the witness's testimony. In addition, a rough description of an offender provided by an on-scene witness can be useful in trying to locate the offender in the area soon after the event. Witnesses should be advised that they may be contacted again soon by the interviewing officer or other officers to make a formal statement.

Preparation

Although there is no sure-fire way to conduct a successful interview every time, preparation is essential. An investigator should begin by learning as much as reasonably possible about the case, which includes becoming familiar with:

- information from previous interviews with other witnesses;
- evidence collected through other aspects of the investigation—for example, physical evidence collected at the crime scene or video surveillance evidence; and
- any special characteristics of the witness—for example, the witness's age, state of mind, and relationship to the suspect or suspects.

Creating a plan around which to structure the interview is essential. Flexibility is important, but no one can conduct a good interview by "winging it." The investigator should keep a rough outline at hand in case he or she is at a loss for words at certain times or wants to remember key points to address later. The headings used to describe the steps in the enhanced cognitive interview (discussed below) can be used to structure the outline.

In selecting a location for the main interview, several factors should be considered, including the witness's age, the type of crime that he or she witnessed, the time that has elapsed since the crime was committed, and the witness's work or school schedules. As a rule, police officers must be flexible in choosing a location and make the best of what is available. A formal witness statement can be successfully taken at a witness's home, place of employment, or in any setting that provides privacy and comfort. The location should allow the witness to concentrate without interruption and to reflect on his or her observations. Although a controlled setting such as a police station may provide geographical and psychological distance from, for example, the scene of a traumatizing domestic dispute or an act of workplace violence, conducting an interview at the scene of the crime can have significant advantages with respect to memory recall.

If the statement is to be taken at the witness's residence, the officer should consider taking it at a time when the witness will not be interrupted. Distractions lead to poor concentration, which in turn may produce a less than optimal interview. Privacy must also be considered if the witness suggests that the police drop by his or her office or other place of employment. Any location chosen should offer a physical layout that allows the officer to conduct the interview and take notes in a professional manner.

If it is impractical for a witness to meet with an investigator in person, it may be necessary to interview a witness over the phone. Although this is not ideal, it is a reasonable option, especially when the alternative is not obtaining a statement at all.

Before the interview, the necessary materials and equipment must be prepared. Recording equipment should be checked and double-checked, and related supplies, such as DVDs and fresh batteries for digital audio recorders, should be on hand. Beverages, pens, and paper should be available in the interview room in sufficient quantities.

"Packaging" the Statement

Today, most, if not all, statements taken during the course of any significant criminal investigation are recorded in their entirety. Although there is no statutory requirement for police to record interviews, the courts have expressed a clear preference for recorded—and preferably video-recorded—statements of both suspects and witnesses (*R. v. Oickle*, 2000; *R. v. Moore-McFarlane*, 2001; *R. v. Roks*, 2007; *R. v. Ahmed*, 2002). A copy (on DVD, for example) of all witness statements, and sometimes also a summary or transcript of the statement, is included in the Crown brief and is also disclosed to the defence, regardless of whether the Crown intends to call a particular witness to testify at trial.

Although there is no one single format, or template, for "packaging" a statement, investigators should begin all statements with a "preamble," or introduction, providing such basic information as:

- the investigator's name and position and the name of the investigator's partner, if more than one investigator is present;
- the name of the witness being interviewed;
- the date, time, and location of the interview; and
- the fact that the interview is being recorded (if it is) and that the witness is aware of this fact and consents to being recorded.

KGB caution
a prepared statement read to an interviewee by the police before an interview, informing the interviewee that the interview will be electronically recorded and that the interviewee will be swearing an oath to tell the truth and will face potential criminal consequences if he or she lies to or deliberately misleads police during the interview

The introductory phase of the interview process, before the witness gives his or her account, is also the appropriate time to read the **KGB caution** (see the box feature, KGB Caution, on the next page) and to explain for the record how the witness came to be sitting in the interview room. This can be accomplished by simply running through the chronology of events that led up to the interview. For example:

> Mr. Smith, you are here today because on Tuesday, after the robbery occurred at the National Bank, you told the first officer who arrived at the scene, Officer Jones, that you had seen what had happened, and you gave Officer Jones your name and phone number. I then took over the investigation of the robbery, and on Wednesday I called you to make arrangements to have you come in today for an interview. And other than that, we have had no other contact or communication regarding this case. Is that correct?

The witness will normally confirm the account, if it is indeed accurate, and then the investigator can begin his or her questioning. At the end of the interview, before turning off the recording equipment, the investigator should state the end time of the interview.

KGB CAUTION

An officer who is conducting an interview must identify himself or herself to the witness, not only as a matter of courtesy and professionalism but as a legal precaution. Occasionally, witnesses may lie to or deliberately mislead the police during an interview. Such witnesses may be charged with a criminal offence such as public mischief or obstruction of justice, but, in order for the court to find the witness guilty, it must be proven that the witness was aware at the time of deliberately making the false statement that he or she was talking to the police.

A witness may also claim in a later proceeding—for example, a criminal trial—that what the witness told the police in his or her original statement was false and that his or her story has since changed. Many investigators deal with this potential legal issue during the introductory phase of the interview by reading the witness a so-called KGB caution—named for the Supreme Court case *R. v. B. (K.G.)* (1993), commonly referred to as the "*KGB* case." This caution informs witnesses that their statement will be taken under oath or affirmation; that they are agreeing to tell the truth; and that they could face potential criminal consequences if they knowingly give false information to or attempt to mislead the police during the course of their investigation, which of course includes the interview.

The reading of the KGB caution and the taking of the witness's statement under oath can have an impact on the admissibility of the witness's statement at a trial if the witness later "recants" his or her statement or claims it to be false. In a situation where a witness changes his or her story at trial and their original statement was voluntary, sworn, and videotaped (the essential ingredients of a KGB statement), the Crown can apply to have the original statement admitted for the truth of its contents.

If an investigator or a uniformed police officer has to take a full statement from a witness in the field—for example, because the witness refuses to attend a police facility—and the officer does not have access to recording equipment, the officer should record the person's full name, date of birth, and contact information on paper; make a note of why it was necessary to take the statement in the field instead of at a location where recording equipment was available; record the starting time of the interview and the location; record the witness's statement in writing as close to verbatim as possible; and record any of the follow-up questions asked and any answers given. When the interview is complete, have the witness read through your notes and make any necessary corrections (by putting a line through the entry and writing above it). Ask the witness to initial each page and then place the witness's signature and the date at the end of the statement. The investigator should also place his or her signature and the date at the end of the statement following the witness's entry.

Development of Police Interviewing Techniques

The primary objective of interviews with witnesses is to elicit the maximum amount of reliable information from a person's memory of an event, while minimizing both errors in the person's recall and any potential contamination that might be introduced by the interviewer. Studies conducted on police interviewing techniques in the 1980s (for example, Fisher, Geiselman, & Raymond, 1987) noted that police interviewers varied widely in their styles and techniques, were largely unaware of the limitations of their interviewing practices, and had little logic or reasoning underlying the ways in which they interviewed witnesses. Many interviews were, quite simply, haphazard.

It seemed clear that police required a method for investigative interviewing that was reliable and based on what had been learned about memory through empirical research. In response, in 1992, American psychologists Ron Fisher and Ed Geiselman published *Memory-Enhancing Techniques for Investigative Interviewing: The Cognitive Interview.* The cognitive interview (CI) was designed to improve the quality of police interviews with witnesses. Rather than an "interview," the CI was actually a group of four techniques to be used *during* an interview, either on their own or in combination, to assist cooperative witnesses in recalling events or knowledge from memory and to motivate them to make the effort necessary to effectively search their memories (Milne & Bull, 1999; Schollum, 2005). Fisher and Geiselman subsequently developed what has come to be called the **enhanced cognitive interview (ECI)**, which, in addition to the four techniques of the CI, includes additional techniques and outlines the sequence in which the components should be used to maximize their effect.

While research on the original CI had indicated that it was about 30 percent more effective than a standard police interview (Geiselman, Fisher, MacKinnon, & Holland, 1985), research on the ECI indicated that it resulted in approximately 45 percent more correct details being produced by witnesses than the original CI (Fisher, Geiselman, Raymond, Jurkevich, & Warhaftig, 1987). It was thus concluded that the ECI elicited *almost 90 percent more correct details* from witnesses compared to the standard police interview.

The effectiveness of the ECI has been demonstrated in both laboratory and real world conditions. North American studies have proven its effectiveness in significantly increasing the amount of information detectives are able to elicit from witnesses (Dando & Milne, 2009), and similarly positive results have been found in developing countries (Stein & Memon, 2006). Research has consistently shown that the CI or ECI enhances the *quantity* of information that witnesses are able to recall without decreasing its *quality*. These effects have been demonstrated in a number of countries (the United Kingdom, Canada, Spain, and Germany) and among a number of different witness populations (children, individuals with special needs such as learning disabilities, and the elderly) (Dando & Milne, 2009).

enhanced cognitive interview (ECI)
an interview that uses the four original CI techniques, but attempts to maximize their effectiveness by placing them in an appropriate structure and providing interviewers with instructions on how best to use them to minimize the tendency of police interviewers to engage in counterproductive behaviours such as interrupting or using short-answer questions

The Enhanced Cognitive Interview: Step by Step

The ECI consists of seven steps and various techniques that cover the entire interview process. These are discussed in the following sections and are summarized in Figure 17.1 on page 321.

Step One: Greet, Personalize, and Establish Rapport

The aim of the first step is to defuse any unnecessary anxiety the witness might be experiencing about being interviewed. Investigators need to remember that, although they might conduct hundreds or thousands of interviews over the course of their careers, for many witnesses, an interview—especially an interview with the police—is a rare event.

Just as the police officer will use the interview to evaluate the witness's sincerity, reliability, and credibility, the witness will be evaluating the police officer's credibility and professionalism. The interviewer must therefore present himself or herself in the best possible manner. Be sincere, be interested, and value your witnesses. Witnesses speak more freely when a relationship of trust exists between them and the police, and when they believe that the police will value what they have to say and will give them fair opportunity to tell their story.

An investigator can begin establishing a working bond with a witness by simply interacting on a personal level. This will help strike a balance between the investigator's "official" persona and his or her "human side." For example, the investigator might ask whether the witness had any trouble finding the office or a parking spot, or ask if the witness would like to use the washroom before beginning. The witness should be asked to turn off any electronic devices for the duration of the interview in order to minimize distractions.

Next, the witness should be informed about the procedures that must be followed at the outset of all witness interviews: the recording device must be started to ensure that everything discussed is "on the record" and an accurate record of the interview is created; introductory information such as date, time, and location of the interview must be read; and any legal cautions must be read. Once these are complete, the investigator might acknowledge that some people find it stressful to be a witness to a crime and explain that, if the witness wishes, after the interview is over the investigator can put the witness in touch with someone who can help him or her through the process—for example, someone from the Victim/Witness Assistance Program.

There is no mandatory script or time limit for establishing rapport, and the investigator should judge the point at which the witness seems comfortable enough to start the interview. Once rapport has been established, it must be maintained. Witnesses will notice if you seem to have lost interest and are just "going through the motions." The following advice comes from a veteran investigator: "It takes far less time to arrange and properly prepare for an effective interview—including the time necessary to establish and maintain rapport—than it does to have to conduct a second interview because you did a poor job on the first one." Also, you might not always have a second opportunity to interview a particular witness.

The rapport-establishment phase allows the investigator to gauge the witness's language abilities and his or her mental state, and to modify the interview process as necessary. The investigator should also attempt to gather additional insight into any issues that may have had an effect on the witness's ability to observe and recall events. Witnesses should be asked if they usually wear glasses or contacts and, if so, whether they were wearing them when they witnessed the event; in some cases, witnesses should also be asked whether they consumed any drugs or alcohol before witnessing the event, because this can become relevant if the witness is cross-examined in court. This question should be asked in a non-judgmental manner, to avoid sending the witness signals before the interview has even begun that you believe his or her account may not be accurate or reliable. Rapport can be lost just as easily as it was established.

Step Two: Explain the Aims of the Interview

For a witness to perform well during an investigative interview, you must explain the purpose of the interview and what you expect from the witness. This includes:

- *Focused retrieval.* Encourage witnesses to make focused retrieval efforts by telling them that, to use their memory effectively, they must focus and concentrate. During the interview, give them as much time as is reasonably necessary to allow them to make those efforts.

- *Report everything.* Tell witnesses to report everything they can remember about the event, and to leave nothing out because they think it's unimportant. Mention that in the early stages it's impossible to tell what information may end up being significant later in the investigation.

- *Don't guess.* Tell witnesses not to guess or "fill in the gaps" while recalling events, but to say only what they actually remember—for example, "If there are some things you don't recall, don't worry about it, no one has a perfect memory. Just do your best, tell me what you remember, and please do not guess. If you are not sure of something, just say so."

- *Transfer control.* Make it clear to witnesses that you are transferring control of the interview to them, that you expect them to do most of the talking, and that they can do so at their own pace—for example, "Of course, I wasn't in the bank when the robbery occurred, so I'm relying on you to tell me as much as possible about what happened. Take as much time as you need." Make it clear to witnesses that you are likely to ask some follow-up questions later in the interview, but that you will not do so until they have given their account of the event—for example, "I might need you to clarify some of your remarks, and I might have some questions for you, but I'll try and hold my questions until after you have told your story."

Step Three: Initiate a Free Narrative Account

When conducting witness interviews, it is important to allow the witness to provide an uninterrupted recollection of events (also called a "free narrative" or "free recall" account). For this to be of maximum value, the witness should be instructed to begin the account at a point preceding the event in question, because this can be helpful in recalling details. For example, if the interview concerns a bank robbery that occurred a week ago, the interviewer might ask the witness to cast her mind back to what she was doing earlier that day, and then to what was on her mind while she was waiting in line at the bank. Once the witness has done so, ask the witness to begin the free-recall account, taking as much time as necessary to relate everything she can remember in her own words. Once the witness has begun the free-recall account of the events, *be quiet.* According to Fisher and Geiselman (1992), *the single most important skill an interviewer can learn is not to interrupt witnesses* during their free-recall account. Instead, pay attention; listen carefully; and take some brief, point-form notes to assist you in the questioning stage that will follow.

Witnesses may pause to think about certain details during their recall and, although it can be tempting to jump in, *do not fill a pause.* Instead, convey the impression that you are willing to wait for the witness to continue (within reason, of course) by using non-specific encouraging expressions such as nodding, saying "Mmmm," or raising your eyebrows slightly. You need to be non-specific so that you don't provide any clues about which information you consider correct or useful. Saying, "Yes, yes, that's what we heard from the other witnesses," can "contaminate" the current witness's statement and must be avoided. The strategic use of silence, which requires conscious effort on the investigator's part, ensures that the witness is given the best opportunity to provide the most complete and accurate recollection of the event.

During the witness's free recall, you need to take notes to provide a basis for follow-up questions. This involves looking for "markers" to which you'll want to return later. An extreme lack or abundance of detail is a good indicator of an area to probe in the next phase of the interview. Consider the following example:

> So I was standing in line in the bank ... oh, it must have been about 5:45 or 5:50 because they were locking the doors so no more customers would come in before closing at 6. I remember the guy in front of me was dressed very poorly, and he was very nervous. He kept looking back at me and at the guards at the door ... then all of a sudden he pulled a gun, grabbed some money, and ran out.

This passage includes examples of both extremes of detail. On the one hand, the investigator should note that the witness had a good opportunity to view the offender, so there is likely much more information regarding the offender's appearance stored in the witness's memory. On the other hand, the minimal detail devoted to the climax of the event suggests that this area needs to be explored further. The investigator also needs to record any apparent inconsistencies so that they might be reconciled in the next phase.

NOTE TAKING DURING AN INTERVIEW

Devoting too much attention to taking notes during an interview takes away from the attention that you should be devoting to your witness in order to sustain rapport; witnesses do not feel encouraged to tell their stories if they are forced to stare at the top of your head while you scribble away trying to write down their every word. Taking notes can also limit your ability to observe witnesses while they speak. Further, taking extensive notes during particular parts of an interview risks "educating" your witness about what you feel are the most, or the least, important aspects of the witness's account. Remember, the interview is being recorded (or it certainly should be), so the purpose of taking notes is not to create a record of the interview, but to serve as a guide during the questioning phase.

One good note-taking strategy is to draw a line down the centre of a page of lined paper, dividing it into two equal halves. As the witness expresses certain points or touches on certain areas of interest, note these "markers" on the left side of the page; a phrase or a single sentence will usually suffice. The right side of the page will be used later during the questioning phase to record the witness's comments in response to your questions. Once you have made a quick note on the left side of the page, turn your attention back to your witness. This approach allows you to balance the requirement to pay attention to your witness with the suggested practice of taking notes to assist you in asking relevant questions during the latter stages of the interview.

Always remember that the rough, point-form notes you take during an interview, and any other notes that you take during the course of an investigation, will be disclosed to the defence if criminal charges are laid as a result of the investigation.

Step Four: Questioning

In this phase, the investigator follows up on the markers recorded during the free-recall phase. Before beginning, remind witnesses to *report everything* and not edit details they think are insignificant out of their answers. Explain that recalling additional details from memory is a task that requires *concentration*. Tell witnesses that, in response to any of your questions, it is okay to say, "I don't understand," and that you will take the time to repeat and clarify the question, and remind them once again that when they answer your questions they are *not to guess*; if they can't remember something, it is okay for them to say, "I don't know."

Before beginning, consider how to phrase the questions you intend to ask, because this will have a significant effect on the information you receive. Use open-ended questions at the beginning of questioning. You will use closed questions later to clarify ambiguous information or elicit specific details, but closed questions are not appropriate in the early stages.

When phrasing questions, interviewers should avoid

- compound questions (a large question composed of a number of smaller questions);
- grammatically complex questions (the simpler the language, the better); and
- police jargon or technical language—for example, instead of asking witnesses to tell you what happened "pursuant to the commission of the indictable offence," simply ask them to tell you what happened "after the man ran out of the bank."

With these points in mind, a good strategy for posing questions to a witness is to use the witness's own words to draw their memory back to a specific point. For example:

> You said before that the offender appeared very nervous and that he kept looking back at you and the guards at the door. I'd like you to concentrate on that point in time for a moment [*focused retrieval*] so that we can get some more detail about what he looked like. Put yourself back into that lineup in the bank and try to imagine him standing in front of you in that line. Close your eyes if you think that will help. Now, is there anything else about his appearance that you can remember?

If you doubt the value of having people close their eyes and pause to remember details, just consider your behaviour when you try to recall something. Most people engage in some or all of these behaviours: closing their eyes, looking at the ceiling, pursing their lips, covering their mouth with the front tips of their fingers, or talking quietly to themselves. Letting the witness know that it's normal to behave like this will work to your advantage.

When posing questions, try to use "witness-compatible questions." This simply means questions that are compatible with witnesses' personal strengths and their mental images of the event as they describe them to you. For example, an interviewer might reasonably expect to elicit more detailed information about any automobiles involved in an event from a witness who is an automobile enthusiast than from someone who has no such special interest. As to questions that are compatible with a witness's mental images of the event, in order to elicit the maximum amount of information from the witness, the interviewer should initially ask the witness questions based on the witness's perspective of the event, using the words that the witness used in the free-recall phase. For example, in the bank robbery scenario, "You told me that you were waiting behind the guy in the bank lineup, he was sloppily dressed, looked nervous, and turned to look at you; what else can you tell me about him?" This questioning approach is distinct from what often occurs in police interviews, where the witness is simply asked a series of standardized questions about the suspect—for example, gender, complexion, age, height, and weight—with no effort being made to activate or probe the mental images that the witness has of the event.

Step Five: Varied and Extensive Retrieval

If witnesses appear to be having difficulty recalling information about some particular aspect of the event they are describing, ask them to make a "varied retrieval" attempt—that is, to try to recall the details of the event in a different order or from a different perspective. Recalling details in a different order can be an advantage for a witness who has told the story many times and remembers it only in a familiar order. Recalling the event out of sequence can shake out details that might otherwise be hidden. For example, the investigator might suggest that the witness start from the end of the crime and work back to the beginning, or begin at a particular point in the narrative and work back from there to the beginning and then move forward to the end.

Another way to elicit additional information from witnesses is to encourage them to "activate" all their senses when describing an event. When asked to describe something they have experienced, most people focus on what they saw and, to a lesser extent, heard, but do not normally include much detail about what they experienced through their sense of smell, touch, or taste. An interviewer may be able to elicit additional information from an assault victim, for example, by asking him to think about the sensation he experienced when the suspect grabbed him around the neck. The victim may then recall that the suspect had very rough skin on his hands, long ragged fingernails, and smelled strongly of alcohol.

Having the witness recall the event from a different perspective can be especially helpful if the witness appears fixated on a particular aspect of the event—for example, "All I remember is looking at that big silver gun." Asking the witness to adopt, for example, the perspective of one of the bank tellers looking at the suspect from behind the counter might help to elicit additional details as the witness concentrates on the scene and probes his or her memory. As we mentioned earlier, however, the investigator must be careful to ensure that the witness does not misinterpret such instructions and guess about what he or she thinks the teller "might have seen"; the witness is simply to think about the event from another perspective in order to jog his or her memory and report only those things that he or she actually witnessed.

These strategies can have the added benefit of assisting an investigator to determine the strength and reliability of a witness's statement. For example, it is difficult for witnesses who are manufacturing some or all of their stories to ostensibly recall a fabricated version of an event from a different perspective or in an order other than the one they followed the first time they recounted the event.

Step Six: Summary and Review

In the summary phase, the investigator, using his or her notes as a guide, summarizes and reviews all the relevant information that the witness has provided. This will satisfy the interviewer that his or her understanding of the witness's statement is complete and correct, and give witnesses a final opportunity to review their memory to ensure that they have told the investigator everything they can recall.

Investigators should go through this stage slowly in order to give the witness time to listen, think, and respond. Witnesses should be told that, if they remember something new or if the investigator's summary is not accurate, they should interrupt and tell the investigator so. A witness who offers additional pieces of information should be allowed to freely recall them, after which the witness should be probed in the same manner as that described in the earlier stages of the ECI process.

When the summary and review process is complete, but before the investigator moves on to the final stage of the interview, the investigator should ask the witness whether he or she can think of *any* other information that may be relevant and that might assist the investigator. If the witness replies with a comment like, "No, that's about it" or some similar phrase, the investigator must use his or her judgment to determine whether there is actually anything more that the witness can reasonably add or whether the witness is simply using a common expression to conclude a conversation. What is most important is to give witnesses the opportunity to tell the investigator everything that they can about the event and to allow them to clarify anything that they might have said. This ensures that the information they have provided is as complete and as accurate as possible; it also gives witnesses the opportunity to "adopt" their statements—that is, to confirm that their statements are what they said, that they are satisfied with the contents of the statement, and that they believe the statement represents an accurate account of the event as they recall it. Such an approach makes the interview fair in both practice and appearance, and prevents witnesses from claiming later that what they said was not what they *meant* to say or that the investigator misinterpreted what they said during the interview.

Step Seven: Closure

After their review of hundreds of police interviews, Fisher, Geiselman, and Raymond (1987) found that investigators simply stopped their interviews after they ran out of questions, with little thought given to the effect that this might have on the witness. The closure stage of the interview is an opportunity to leave a positive final impression with the witness; it is also the investigator's last opportunity to gather information that may not be directly relevant to the interview contents—for example, is the witness going away; how is the witness coping; does the witness know how to get in touch should he or she recall anything new?

Investigators should ensure that they have all of the witness's personal and business contact information, and should leave witnesses with their business card.

FIGURE 17.1   STEPS AND TECHNIQUES IN THE ENHANCED COGNITIVE INTERVIEW

Step	Techniques
Step 1: Greet, personalize, and establish rapport	• interact on a personal level • put witness at ease • establish working bond • explain procedures • be sincere and interested • assess special needs of witness and adapt
Step 2: Explain the aims of the interview	Focused retrieval: • tell witness to report everything • transfer control to witness • tell witness not to guess • explain need to concentrate hard
Step 3: Initiate a free narrative account	Context reinstatement: • pause • do not interrupt • use non-verbal behaviour
Step 4: Questioning	• tell witness to report everything, concentrate hard, not to guess, okay to say "I don't know" and "I don't understand" • use open-ended and closed questions • use witness-compatible questions • activate and probe an image
Step 5: Varied and extensive retrieval	• change the order in which events are recalled • change perspective • focus on all senses
Step 6: Summary and review	• summarize relevant information • go slowly • incorporate witness corrections • request any other relevant information
Step 7: Closure	• exchange contact information • indicate interest in hearing from witness with new information • leave a positive impression

Source: Adapted from Milne & Bull (1999).

They may want to ask witnesses whether they have any holidays or business trips coming up or whether they will be available in the coming weeks or months should any investigative follow-up be required. Investigators should tell witnesses that, if they recall anything further in the coming days, they should feel free to contact them; this is far more likely to happen if the investigator states it explicitly and indicates a genuine interest in hearing from the witness should he or she recall anything new. The investigator should always thank the witness for their participation and ensure that they are coping well. Some witnesses can be profoundly affected as a result of witnessing a criminal act, and the investigator should ensure that such witnesses are given appropriate referrals to victim/witness assistance programs or similar social agencies. Remember, the interview may be over, but the criminal justice process is just beginning. A witness who believes that he or she was given the best opportunity to recall the event and was treated with interest and respect is more likely to agree to further participation in the case if required, and more likely to be an effective witness if the matter proceeds to trial.

Follow-up Interviews

Conducting a follow-up interview at a later date is one way to elicit new information from a witness. Psychological data and theory suggest that people are likely to remember at least a few new details about an event by repeatedly engaging in the recall process (Turtle & Yuille, 1994). Take, for example, a witness who is still shaken when giving an initial statement; in this case, it makes sense to elicit only the basic facts and arrange for a more in-depth interview at a later time. Even in less dramatic circumstances, however, conducting another interview can be beneficial. A different setting, a different interviewer, or different instructions or strategies might lead to the recollection of new details. If specifics regarding, for example, the offender's appearance, a vehicle, or a weapon are important to the case, it is possible that the relevant details can be elicited the second or third time around.

If more than one interview is conducted with a witness, subsequent statements can (and probably will) differ in some respects from the original statement—a fact that defence counsel will almost certainly attempt to emphasize in order to make the witness appear less reliable. For example, the defence may note: "Mr. Smith, in your initial statement to Detective Jones you said the offender was a white male, about 20 years old, with a scruffy beard. But in your second interview, you described him as a white male, 20 years old, with sandy-coloured hair, and you didn't mention a beard at all. Which one of these descriptions is correct?"

Investigators who decide to conduct a second or subsequent interview with a witness must become thoroughly familiar with the witness's original statement so they are able to recognize any differences or inconsistencies that might arise and be prepared to address them. In the example above, the investigator could simply read the witness's first description of the suspect to him after he finished giving his second description, and ask him to reconcile the differences. The witness may confirm that, "yes," the suspect did, in fact, have a beard, but he simply forgot to mention it in his second description. If the matter subsequently progresses to trial, the court would have to determine what, if any, effect such a difference would have on the evidentiary value of the witness's description.

INTERVIEWING SUSPECTS

Because they occur far less frequently than witness and victim interviews, suspect interviews are an area in which the typical investigator tends to be the least experienced and the most anxious. This section begins with a discussion of how to prepare for an interview with a suspect. We then discuss two significantly different approaches to conducting suspect interviews or interrogations: the Reid technique and the PEACE model.

Preparation

Because suspect interviews occur less frequently, careful preparation is especially important. The most important thing an investigator can do to prepare for a suspect interview is research. As when interviewing a witness or victim, taking the time to become thoroughly familiar with the case and all its existing evidence (both statement and physical) and learning as much as possible about the individuals involved are key. In addition, before going into an interview, investigators should develop a rudimentary plan that outlines the areas that must be covered, the critical questions that must be asked, and the order in which they can be asked most effectively.

Questions an investigator should attempt to answer (though the time that is typically available will likely not permit answering them all) include:

- Does the suspect have a criminal record or any convictions for offences similar to the one under investigation?

- Does the suspect's name come up in any other police reports or records of police contact and, if so, under what circumstances? Have you spoken to investigators who may have dealt with the suspect previously to learn as much as you can about the suspect?

INTERVIEW VERSUS INTERROGATION

The two basic processes that investigators use to obtain information from suspects are interviews and interrogations. Although some experts hesitate to draw a clear line between the two approaches, there are important strategic and philosophical differences between them:

- An interview is a structured conversation between an individual and an investigator, in which the investigator asks a series of questions to elicit information from the individual about something that he or she observed, experienced, or did or about which he or she has knowledge. An interview is a *non-accusatory, fact-finding* process. The PEACE method is an example of an interview approach to gathering information during an investigation.
- In contrast to an interview, an **interrogation** is an *accusatory* process, the primary purpose of which is to elicit a confession from a suspect who is believed to be responsible for the offence under investigation. The Reid method contains an interrogation stage, designed to obtain a confession, which is preceded by an integral interview component.

interrogation
an accusatory process, the primary purpose of which is to elicit a confession from a suspect who is believed to be responsible for the offence under investigation

- Is there any evidence linking the suspect in any way to the scene of the crime? For example, shortly after the robbery you are investigating occurred, was the suspect stopped for speeding while driving his car a block away from the scene? Or did the suspect's car receive a parking ticket near the park where the sexual assault took place? Was the suspect captured on video surveillance leaving the apartment building where the murder occurred? Did the suspect leave anything behind (fingerprints or DNA) that could link him to the crime scene?

Investigators must also review the evidence that has already been collected in the course of the investigation, including photographs, video, seized property, and victim and witness statements. If the investigator conducting the interview is not the officer who arrested the suspect, the investigator should speak with the arresting officer(s) to learn as much as possible about the suspect. What conversations did the officers at the scene have with the suspect before he was brought into the police station? Did the suspect make any statements upon arrest? How did the suspect behave when he was arrested; what was his attitude and demeanour? Is there any other relevant information available to the investigator that was not included in the arrest reports?

A solid knowledge of the existing evidence is critical to an investigator's ability to put the suspect's statement into context and determine whether it is consistent with what is already known and which areas of the statement need to be further explored. Nothing causes an investigator to lose credibility faster in a suspect interview than not being familiar with the evidence.

As mentioned above in the context of witness interviews, Canadian courts have expressed a clear preference for recorded—and preferably video-recorded—statements. In the case of suspects, video-recorded statements allow the decision-maker to observe with his or her own eyes the context in which the statement was made and thus make more accurate determinations regarding inducements, atmosphere of oppression, and operating mind. As noted by one court, it is difficult for the Crown to prove voluntariness beyond a reasonable doubt where proper recording procedures are *not* followed (*R. v. Moore-McFarlane*, 2001). And, where recording facilities are readily available, but the police interrogate a suspect in custody *without* attempting to make a reliable record, the resulting interrogation will inevitably be deemed "suspect" (*R. v. Khan*, 2010).

In the unlikely event that an investigator *cannot* record a suspect interview despite efforts to do so—for example, where the equipment fails or the subject refuses to be recorded—the investigator would need to take extensive contemporaneous notes to account for both the content of the statement and the circumstances in which it was taken. Even with this documentation, however, in the light of existing Canadian case law, such a statement would likely face a substantial legal challenge.

Whether or not a suspect is in custody will affect where—and whether—an interview is conducted. Wherever possible, interviews should be conducted in a quiet environment free of distractions or where distractions are kept to a minimum. A suspect who is already in custody can simply be escorted to a police interview room. A suspect who is *not* in custody, however, has the same right to refuse to attend a police station or to be interviewed as does any other person.

When asking a suspect to attend a police station voluntarily, the investigator should both specify that he or she wants to conduct an interview and indicate the offence about which the suspect is to be questioned. Failure to ensure that a person is aware of his or her status as a criminal suspect and the associated legal rights will leave the prosecution open to claims that the suspect's statement was involuntary.

While many officers prefer to conduct interviews by themselves, there are advantages to having *two* investigators present—for one thing, there are two opportunities to establish a bond with the suspect, thus increasing the chances of obtaining a statement. Once it has been determined which investigator has the stronger connection to the suspect, he or she should become the primary questioner, with the other assuming the secondary role, carefully observing the suspect and taking notes in preparation for following up on anything the first investigator may have missed or that may have been discussed but requires further clarification.

Where two investigators are involved, the following issues seldom work themselves out *during* an interview and should be resolved before the interview begins:

- who is going to start the questioning;
- when and how will the two officers transition between the primary and secondary roles;

REQUESTS FOR OTHERS TO BE PRESENT DURING THE INTERVIEW

Some suspects may request the presence of a friend or relative during an interview. Except in the case of a youth (where the request to have a lawyer or adult present *must* be honoured), it is generally not advisable to comply with such a request. The presence of another person can create a significant distraction, questions put to a suspect to clarify a statement may provoke interaction between the suspect and the other person, and the other person may interject and interrupt the flow of the interview. This is conducive neither to eliciting information from the suspect nor to the creation of an atmosphere of privacy in which a suspect may decide to confess. The presence of another person in the interview room will also complicate any subsequent *voir dire* proceedings.

Of course, if you have no other choice (for example, because the suspect refuses to speak unless another person is present), the presence of another person is preferable to no interview at all—provided that the investigator has ensured that the person is in no way involved in the offence under investigation. Some suspects may request that a lawyer be present during questioning. Investigators are not obligated to honour such a request (*R. v. McCrimmon*, 2010; *R. v. Sinclair*, 2010), though some experts believe that counsel's presence during an interview should be *encouraged*, for the reason that if the suspect makes a statement in such circumstances, it is likely to be admissible. In the relatively rare situation where counsel is present, the investigator should insist that the suspect—not counsel—answer the questions. If counsel nevertheless persists in answering questions on the client's behalf, any statements made may be offered as evidence against the accused *only if* the accused adopts the statements. Thus, a wise investigator will occasionally ask the suspect if he or she agrees with what his lawyer is saying.

- will the suspect be shown any evidence such as photographs and, if so, who will show them;
- who will ensure that the recording devices are operating properly;
- how will the two officers communicate information to one another during the interview; and
- how will the interview be concluded?

During the Interview

The goal of a suspect interview is to elicit information from the suspect. To achieve this objective, the interview must be managed to ensure that the suspect—not the investigator—does most of the talking. Actively listening to what a suspect is saying is at least as important as asking questions. If you talk too much or fail to listen carefully, the suspect may not provide the information you are looking for or you may fail to recognize the significance of the information the suspect *does* provide.

Police officers are taught to take control of situations, and often equate control in an interview context with talking. You do *not* need to be talking to be in control of an interview. The deliberate use of silence after a suspect has offered a few words, for example, can often result in suspects offering more than they would have if you had immediately resumed your questioning. The use of verbal "encouragers" (neutral phrases such as "aha," "uh hum," "go on") and non-verbal encouragers (eye contact and head nods) can have a similar effect. Resist the urge to talk too much in the early stages of a suspect interview; the more the suspect speaks, the more material you will have to explore later in the interview. And the more carefully you listen to what is said, the better equipped you will be to do so.

Remember that any notes that you make during the interview process, whether you consider them to be "rough notes" or otherwise, must be submitted to the Crown attorney as part of the disclosure process. As in the cognitive interview for witnesses, the notes taken during a suspect interview are designed to highlight significant issues that will inform your questions during the follow-up phase of the interview. Do *not* use your notes to create a verbatim record of the interview, because it will be recorded.

It is important to be prepared for the ways in which a suspect may respond to questions during an interview. Most responses are likely to fall (in no particular order) into one of the following categories:

- the suspect will refuse to say anything at all;
- the suspect will deny responsibility and provide a false alibi;
- the suspect will deny responsibility and provide a full and honest exculpatory account;
- the suspect will deny responsibility, but provide one or more true admissions;
- the suspect will make a full and honest confession; or
- the suspect will make a false confession.

A suspect who chooses to respond to police questioning is said to be making a "statement." In his or her statement:

1. A suspect may deny any knowledge of or involvement in the matter under investigation; this is called a *denial*, and it can include the offering of an **alibi**, or excuse, which typically takes the form of a claim that the person was somewhere else when the crime was committed. Of course, a suspect's exculpatory statement may be honest or dishonest, which the investigation will ultimately seek to establish.

2. A suspect may deny responsibility, but make an *admission*, which is defined as a statement that concedes *at least one* fact that, if true, is relevant to proving the suspect's guilt (Skinnider, 2005). Although this does not necessarily mean that the subject is guilty of the crime, admissions by a suspect regarding *any* element of the crime are a boon to the investigator and should lead to new lines of questioning. Any admission that links the suspect to the crime (revealing, for example, that the suspect has knowledge of the victim, crime scene location, or location of the proceeds of the crime, or that the suspect possesses a skill or physical ability necessary for committing the crime) is extremely important to the case, as are any admissions regarding motive (for example, drug addiction, financial difficulties, revenge, infatuation with the victim).

3. A suspect may make a confession—whether honest or false—which at its simplest is defined as an admission to *all* of the elements of an offence, including the mental element, or *mens rea* (Skinnider, 2005). Among all of the possible responses, a confession is regarded as a "uniquely potent" form of evidence, followed closely by eyewitness testimony (Kassin & Neumann, 1997). When a person confesses, they acknowledge that they are guilty of the offence, they provide details of the offence, and they describe the role they played in it.

    A confession can become the central piece of evidence in a criminal case, or it can corroborate other evidence. It also provides reasonable grounds for laying a criminal information (the form in which a criminal charge is specified), making an arrest, having an arrest warrant issued for a co-accused or accomplice, or obtaining a search warrant. Even if a confession is eventually excluded at trial, it can still provide reasonable grounds for pre-trial investigative purposes. Because of its powerful effect, police investigators strive to obtain a confession from suspects where possible. There is no criminal case so strong that it cannot be strengthened by an admissible confession. Moreover, a confession may lead to evidence concerning other ongoing cases.

alibi
an excuse, which typically takes the form of a claim that a person was somewhere else when the crime was committed

As discussed in Chapter 16, Interviewing Rules, remember that if during the course of an interview with a suspect an investigator becomes aware that the suspect's jeopardy has changed, the investigator must take certain steps depending on the particular situation—for example, stopping the interview, advising the interviewee of his or her new status (for example, as a suspect), advising the person of his or her rights under the Charter, permitting the suspect to consult with counsel, re-cautioning the suspect, and so on. Investigators must fully understand their legal obligations in *all* situations.

The Reid Method of Interviewing and Interrogation

In the 1990s, when formal training in suspect interview techniques became more widely available in Canada, the most common approach taught to police officers was the **Reid technique**, offered by a private company, Reid and Associates, based in Chicago. The technique originated in the 1940s and '50s, based largely on the work of university law professor Fred Inbau, who had spent decades developing and teaching interrogation techniques in an attempt to move them away from a crude, physical approach to a more "psychological" approach that included the use of isolation, trickery, and displays of interrogator confidence.

In 1962, Inbau published *Criminal Interrogation and Confessions*—now the most well-known and influential interrogation text in North America—with John Reid, a former polygraph student of his. By the time the third edition was published in 1986, Inbau, Reid, and a third co-author, Joseph Buckley (now the president of Reid and Associates), had transformed the formerly haphazard approach to interrogation into a nine-step, mostly psychological approach.

Reid technique
an approach to questioning criminal suspects that consists of three principal elements: a non-accusatory fact-finding interview; a behavioural analysis interview designed to detect deception; and an accusatory, persuasive interrogation designed to obtain a confession

The Interview

Reid and Associates have traditionally characterized their process as involving two stages—interview and interrogation. For clarity's sake, we have broken the interview stage into two parts—the fact-finding interview and the behavioural analysis interview (BAI). Although you would begin with the fact-finding interview, you would always conduct *both* the fact-finding interview and the BAI as part of the interview, or first stage, to determine a suspect's "probable guilt." Then, *if* as a result of the interview, you determined that the person was "probably guilty," you would proceed to the interrogation.

THE FACT-FINDING INTERVIEW

The first part of the interview stage of the Reid method involves a non-accusatory, fact-finding interview. The purpose of this stage is to establish rapport with the subject and gather some basic investigative information regarding the subject's possible motive, opportunity, or means to commit the crime. Subjects are more likely to volunteer this kind of information if asked about it in a non-accusatory manner. Another important purpose served by this stage is that it allows the investigator to get a feel for the subject's "normal"—also referred to as "baseline"—behavioural responses to non-accusatory interview questions, including body language and verbal responses. These observations can be important during the subsequent behavioural analysis stage, because a person's deviation from their baseline behaviour may indicate deception.

THE BAI

In the second part of the interview stage, the investigator uses a behavioural analysis interview (BAI) to determine whether, in the investigator's opinion, the suspect is "definitely" guilty of the offence being investigated or whether the investigator can be "reasonably certain" of the suspect's guilt. It is important to note that the "guilt" referred to here is not *legal* guilt, but guilt *in the opinion of the investigator* (Buckley, 2006).

In addition to a consideration of the facts gathered during the fact-finding interview, Reid recommends three methods for determining guilt during the BAI stage:

1. *Observation and evaluation of the suspect's verbal and non-verbal behaviour for indicators of truth or deception.* This includes a subject's non-verbal body movements and position changes, gestures, facial expressions, and eye contact, as well as the way in which he or she responds to questions, including the words or phrases used. For example, a lack of eye contact, slouching or leaning back in a chair, and using phrases such as "as far as I know" and "I swear to God" are all considered by Reid to indicate deception.

2. *Behaviour-provoking questions.* The BAI is based on asking a suspect "behaviour-provoking" questions designed to evoke behavioural responses. From these responses, Reid says that the investigator can determine whether the suspect is being truthful or not. There are 15 questions in total, and particular responses to each one are believed to be indicative of guilt.

    For example, if the interviewer asks the subject, "Do you know why you are here?" and the subject responds in a vague or evasive manner, Reid suggests that this response should be viewed with suspicion. On the other hand, a clear, blunt response is thought to be more characteristic of innocence. Or the interviewer might ask: "John, why do you think someone would do this to Jane?" If John hesitates, repeats the question, or offers an explanation such as, "Well, I never thought about it," in conjunction with one or a number of the non-verbal behaviours described in method 1, this is believed to be characteristic of guilt. Conversely, if John says without hesitation, "I have no idea why anyone would do this" while maintaining eye contact and leaning forward, this is thought to be more consistent with innocence.

3. *Use of baiting questions and dealing with an alibi.* Baiting questions are to be used only after the suspect has made a specific denial. Their purpose is to induce a deceptive suspect to change, or at least to think about changing, a previous denial of guilt.

    Baiting questions are non-accusatory questions suggesting that evidence exists that implicates the suspect in the offence under investigation. For example, an interviewer might say: "John, is there any reason that you can think of why your car was seen at the same plaza as the bank that was robbed?" Before John can answer the question, the investigator is advised to interject by saying something like, "Look, I am not actually accusing you of anything; maybe you just stopped by at the variety store in the plaza to buy some cigarettes?" If John is innocent and was not there when the bank was robbed, it is believed that he will emphatically deny that his car was anywhere near the plaza. If, on the other hand, John is guilty, it is believed that he will hesitate to answer while he thinks about the possibility that someone could have seen his car near the bank and, if that is possible, he will have to decide whether to offer an explanation or devise a lie.

    Although Reid maintains that the best way to deal with an alibi is through investigation, it also states that there are times when this is not feasible or possible. In those cases, the investigator must rely on interrogation methods alone (Inbau, Reid, & Buckley, 1986, p. 73).

The Interrogation

If, based on the BAI, an investigator is reasonably certain of the suspect's guilt, he or she can proceed to the interrogation phase. The interrogation is an accusatory process that uses active persuasion in an attempt to undo deception and elicit a confession from the suspect. It consists of nine steps designed to raise a suspect's anxiety level while simultaneously decreasing the perceived consequences of confessing (Inbau, Reid, & Buckley, 1986, p. 332; Leo, 2008, p. 113). The steps are:

1. *Direct positive confrontation.* The interrogator states that the subject is believed to be the person who is responsible for the offence under investigation and observes that suspect's verbal and non-verbal responses. For example: "John, there is no doubt in my mind that you are responsible for the robbery of the Lucky Gas Mart." Regardless of the suspect's response, the interrogator will then offer a reason why it's important for the suspect to tell the truth. This is referred to as a transition statement, which will introduce the interrogation theme.

2. *Theme development.* The interrogator offers a possible reason, or excuse, for the commission of the crime; this involves shifting the blame to another person or circumstance. For example: "John, I know you recently lost your job, and I know how hard it is to provide for a family these days. Is that why you robbed the Lucky Gas Mart? You didn't do it for yourself, John, did you? You did it for your family, didn't you? I am a father, I understand that." If the suspect appears to listen to or be considering the suggested theme, this is believed to be indicative of guilt. A rejection of the suggestion is thought to be more indicative of innocence.

3. *Handling denials.* Virtually all suspects will offer denials during the theme-development phase, but should be discouraged from repeating or elaborating on them and instead directed back to the moral excuse theme offered in step 2. For example: "John (*interrogator raises his hand, palm outward, in a "stop" gesture toward the suspect*), we are not going to go there. It is not a question of *if* you did it. I know you robbed the Lucky Gas Mart; that has already been established. What I am trying to figure out now is *why* it happened."

    Suspects who react strongly to the interrogator's attempts to prevent them from voicing their denials and who attempt to take control of the interrogation to repeat them are thought to be innocent. In contrast, a guilty person will normally stop repeating the denial, or their denial will become progressively less forceful as the interrogator directs them back to the earlier theme.

4. *Overcoming objections.* After the denial phase, the suspect may offer reasons—often moral, economic, or religious—why he or she "would not" or "could not" have committed the offence. For example: "Officer, I am a churchgoing, family man. I am not the kind of guy that would steal anything, let alone rob a gas mart. I just couldn't do that sort of thing." It is thought that, typically, only a guilty person offers these sorts of excuses, especially when they follow the denial phase. As in step 3, the interrogator

should return to the theme established earlier. For example: "John, I don't want to hear any excuses about why you could not have robbed the gas mart. You did it, and we both know you did it. Now, let's get back to figuring out why you did it."

5. *Procurement and retention of suspect's attention.* After the interrogator has successfully dealt with any denials or excuses offered by the suspect and returned him or her to the theme of the interrogation, the suspect may attempt to "mentally withdraw" from, or "tune out," the interrogator. An interrogator who allows this to happen risks losing control of the process and failing to achieve his or her purpose. Useful strategies for getting and keeping a suspect's attention include moving physically closer to the suspect; touching the suspect's arm or hand; calling the suspect by his or her first name; changing voice tone; and maintaining eye contact. For example: "John, are you listening to me? Do you understand what I am saying? John, look at me. It is important that we deal with this matter here and now. It is important for you to listen to me when I am talking to you, John, so that we can work our way through this."

6. *Handling a suspect's passive mood.* By now, the suspect is considering the possible benefits of telling the truth, which may be reflected in non-verbal behaviour (slumped in the chair, looking at the floor, looking depressed, perhaps crying). The interrogator must concentrate on the interrogation theme and preparing the suspect for the possible alternatives that will be presented to him or her in the next step. In step 2, the interrogator offered a general reason and excuse to John for robbing the gas mart; now, the interrogator must focus on the key reason for the robbery. For example: "John, in this economy it's hard to pay your bills and put food on the table. The money at the gas mart was just sitting there in an open cash drawer. The cashier was lazy; he didn't put the money in the safe where it should have been. You could see the money and you couldn't ignore it. The money seemed to be the solution to your problems, John. You were in a very difficult position. You had to do something, John. You had to feed your kids. You told the cashier that you had a weapon, and you told him to give you all the money from the cash drawer because it seemed to be the only solution to a terrible situation."

   The interrogator must continue to monitor the suspect's behaviour during this step and display sympathy and understanding while continually urging the suspect to tell the truth for his or her own good and for the sake of everyone concerned. The interrogator must be careful to speak only in generalities and not to make any threats or offer any inducements.

7. *Presenting an alternative question.* The alternative question technique requires that the suspect choose between two scenarios, one of which is presented as being more "acceptable" than the other, but both of which are inculpatory. This offers the suspect a way of saving face and begins to "smooth the way" toward the suspect telling the interrogator the truth. For example: "John, did you plan the robbery? Or did it just happen when you saw the money sitting there in the open?" When the suspect chooses one

of the two alternative questions, he has, in effect, made an admission, thus incriminating himself, which is a critical step toward obtaining a full confession.

8. *Having the suspect orally relate various details of the offence.* This step aims to develop the admission made in the previous step. As soon as the suspect has chosen one of the alternative questions, the interrogator must immediately reinforce the suspect's choice (for example, "Good, John, that's what I thought"), and then have the suspect commit himself to his choice by discussing the details of the crime ("Now tell me what happened next"). The interrogator must encourage the suspect to describe the details of the offence, which will ultimately be required to establish legal guilt. Such details can include exactly what John did with the money, if he actually had a weapon during the robbery, and, if so, what kind of weapon it was and what he did with it.

9. *Converting an oral confession into a written confession.* The suspect's "oral confession" from the previous step is converted into a written confession.

Research and Criticisms

Researchers have conducted various studies into the effectiveness of the Reid method and some of the specific techniques on which it relies. Although some have come out in support of the method, others have cast doubt on its claims. Reid itself claims that an experienced investigator using its method can achieve a success rate as high as 80 percent in obtaining confessions (Inbau et al., 2001, p. 364), and cites studies that point to the superior ability of Reid employees to detect deception (for example, Horvath & Jayne, 1994) as well as others that show high rates of success in detecting deception among a group of individuals trained by a Reid instructor (for example, Blair & McCamey, 2002). Critics, on the other hand, claim that many of the studies on which Reid relies to support its position were not conducted properly and therefore the seemingly favourable results do not present an accurate picture (for example, Vrij, 2008).

Some critics of Reid have pointed to the fact that some aspects of the technique are consistent with risk factors for false confessions. The most common strategies for obtaining a confession fall into two categories: minimization techniques and maximization techniques (Kassin & McNall, 1991). *Minimization strategies* seek to minimize the seriousness of the offence and the perceived consequences of confessing; according to some (for example, Leo et al., 2006), the use of interrogation techniques that imply a promise of leniency in exchange for a confession is the primary cause of false confessions. Minimization techniques involve gaining the suspect's trust by appearing sympathetic and understanding and offering the suspect face-saving excuses (Russano et al., 2005). The investigator might suggest that "Anyone else in the same circumstances might have done the same thing," or that "Everyone makes mistakes." In the example above of John robbing the gas mart, the investigator suggested that John committed the crime for his family, to put food on the table. Whatever excuse the investigator uses, the effect is to suggest to the suspect that his or her actions are somehow less morally blameworthy than they really are because they were the result of some external factor—for example, peer pressure, an accomplice, an accident, spontaneity, or hard times—and thus "not really" the suspect's fault.

Maximization strategies are essentially scare tactics intended to intimidate suspects by confronting them with unequivocal accusations of their guilt, refusing to listen to denials of responsibility or claims of innocence, presenting fabricated evidence to support the investigator's claim of the suspect's guilt, and exaggerating the seriousness of the offence and the possible consequences of a conviction (Russano et al., 2005). Minimization and maximization techniques are designed to work together to alter a suspect's perception of his or her crime and of the consequences of confessing. Examples of minimization and maximization strategies are found in several of Reid's nine steps of interrogation, including step 1 (direct positive confrontation), step 3 (handling denials), and step 4 (overcoming objections). They may be more or less prominent depending on how investigators are applying the Reid method.

Because minimization and maximization techniques are designed to get suspects to confess, they are useful when interrogating suspects who are in fact guilty; however, they can be dangerous in cases where innocent suspects are being interrogated. Although one of Reid's presumptions is that, as a result of the BAI, only guilty suspects will be interrogated, investigators do not always correctly determine guilt as a result of using the BAI. The effects of emotionally charged, suggestive questioning can be devastating on innocent suspects, as the inquiry into the high-profile wrongful conviction case of Thomas Sophonow demonstrates. The inquiry revealed that the interviewers employed techniques designed to break Sophonow's will so that he would confess, and Sophonow himself testified that the interviewers succeeded in taking his will from him (Sophonow Inquiry, 2001).

The validity of the BAI as a tool for determining guilt has also been questioned. Although Reid points to studies that indicate the ability of those using the BAI to detect deception at high rates (for example, Horvath & Jayne, 1994; Blair & McCamey, 2002), critics maintain that the BAI is a tool of questionable validity and point to other studies that support *their* position. The indicators of deception used in the BAI are based on the idea that liars experience more stress than truth tellers, which exhibits itself in easily recognizable indicators of deception. Deception research, however, indicates that the phenomenon of lying is far more complex than this theory suggests. With respect to a suspect's non-verbal behaviour, Reid maintains that liars are more likely (among other things) to look away, shift in their chairs, cross their legs, and make grooming gestures, but recent empirical research suggests that this is simply *not* true. As a result of his own studies and analyses of studies conducted by others, Vrij (2008) has concluded that liars tend to move *less* than truth tellers and that eye contact is simply *not* related to deception. Other studies have found the success rate of officers who used the BAI criteria to determine whether videotaped suspects were telling the truth or lying to be 51 percent—essentially equivalent to chance (Vrij et al., 2007)—and that observers who were trained to look for the cues of discomfort that Reid maintains are indicative of deceit were less accurate than observers who had received no training at all in the detection of deception (Kassin & Fong, 1999).

CANADIAN COURTS ON THE USE OF REID

In Canadian court cases since *Oickle*, the courts are clearly arrayed along a spectrum with respect to their opinions on the use of Reid and its impact on the admissibility of confession evidence. In *R. v. L.F.* (2006), for example, the Ontario Superior Court stated that Reid "is not inherently objectionable" and that "the police must be afforded the necessary latitude to perform their responsibilities to society," whereas in *R. v. Brinsmead* (2006) the Court said that "while the use of [Reid] is not objectionable per se, a Court must be extremely vigilant in evaluating the statements that result from the use of these techniques."

In one case, the Court ruled that Reid was used to psychologically manipulate the suspect, break his will to resist manipulative suggestions, and cause him to doubt his own memory of the events; the suspect's statement was ruled inadmissible as a result (*R. v. M.J.S.*, 2000). In another case, the court found that the use of deceit, moral and spiritual inducements, and minimization techniques, coupled with the absence of food or refreshment for a number of hours, "created an atmosphere in which the accused had to trade admissions in order to extract himself from the more serious consequences of a murder charge" (*R. v. Minde*, 2003). In *R. v. Barges* (2005), although the Court did not identify Reid by name, it said that "[t]he technique as used in this case is objectionable in that where anything is said by the accused, he is often not allowed to finish it, as it appears to be the police perception that he is going to deny, or where he does say something, it is difficult to say what, if any, parts of the preceding monologue he is responding to." Finally, in *R. v. Amos* (2009), the court had little criticism of some of the questioning techniques used by the investigator (including positive confrontation, minimization, alternative questions, and deceit), saying only that "police must be permitted to outsmart criminals" and the community would not be shocked by this.

The PEACE Model

PEACE model
a best practice approach to interviewing victims, witnesses, and suspects developed by police, academics, and lawyers in the United Kingdom during the 1990s that focuses on eliciting the maximum amount of information from a subject and, in the case of a suspect, using that information to challenge inconsistencies between the suspect's account of events and the totality of the evidence

Whereas Reid uses deception detection and persuasion processes in an attempt to identify guilty suspects and elicit a confession from them, the **PEACE model** seeks to elicit the maximum amount of information from the suspect in order to use it, along with all of the other information gathered during the investigation, to challenge the suspect to explain any inconsistencies that may exist between his or her account of events and the account based on the totality of the evidence. The name "PEACE" is a mnemonic device whose letters stand for the four stages of the model: (1) preparation and planning, (2) engage and explain, (3) account, and (4) closure and evaluation. Although the primary goal of PEACE is not to elicit confessions and admissions from suspects, by following this process, investigators are often successful in doing so. Proponents of the model point to research indicating that it reduces the chances of false confessions and wrongful convictions while being no less effective at eliciting confessions than more persuasive suspect questioning approaches (Snook et al., 2010). In addition, because PEACE does not involve persuasive questioning techniques, false confessions are less likely and the statements produced are therefore more likely to be ruled admissible.

The PEACE model originated in Britain in 1992, following a review, in the 1970s and '80s, of police investigative practices and an examination of the interviewing techniques used by police to elicit confessions. The review found that police questioning approaches involved highly persuasive, manipulative techniques that contributed to wrongful convictions (Milne & Bull, 1999). Following a decade of collaboration between police, academics, and lawyers, the PEACE model emerged. Today, PEACE has been widely adopted in the United Kingdom as a best-practice model for conducting interviews with suspects, victims, and witnesses and is also used in Norway and New Zealand. In 2010, the Royal Newfoundland Constabulary began delivering a training program in the PEACE model to its officers, becoming the first police force to adopt the system for use in North America.

Stages

The following description of the four stages is adapted from Shepherd (2007) and Snook et al. (2010).

1. *Preparation and Planning.* In the first stage, the interviewer considers how the information obtained from an interview will contribute to the larger, ongoing investigation. The investigator prepares by learning about the interview subject, making a list of investigative objectives, and making the practical arrangements necessary for conducting the interview. Time is spent developing a timeline of events related to the offence under investigation; preparing a questioning plan on the basis of a review of the existing evidence; creating an outline of how the interview should proceed; and planning for different interview contingencies, such as a suspect who invokes their right to silence and refuses to participate in an interview.

2. *Engage and Explain.* In this two-part stage, the interviewer first engages the subject in conversation, establishing rapport by being personable and professional, and then explains what will happen during the interview. The interviewer ensures that the subject understands the purpose of the interview, gives any requisite police cautions in a manner that ensures the subject understands his or her legal rights, and identifies any exhibits that may be referred to in the interview. The interviewer also explains how the interview is expected to progress and outlines any expectations and ground rules that will be followed. In the case of a witness, this involves telling the witness that they have information that the interviewer requires and will therefore play a central role in the interview; in the case of a suspect, it involves telling the suspect that you, the interviewer, have an open mind, are trying to build a complete and truthful account of the event, and are willing to listen objectively to what the suspect has to say.

3. *Account.* In obtaining the subject's account of an event, the particular technique used will depend on whether the subject is cooperative. Regardless of the technique, the interviewer will employ the same general "account" framework, which consists of three substages. First, open-ended questions are posed, giving the subject an opportunity to provide an *uninterrupted account* (also referred to as a "free narrative" account) of the event. In this substage, the interviewer should (1) encourage and allow the subject to do most of the talking and ask for as much detail as possible;

(2) listen carefully and pay attention; (3) give the subject time to listen to, understand, and respond to each question; and (4) help the subject remember by suggesting, for example, "take your mind back to ..." and then giving the subject time to search his or her memory. The interviewer should *not* interrupt, rush to fill silences, or talk too much. From the information gathered, points of interest to be explored further for accuracy and reliability are identified.

The next substage involves *clarification* of the uninterrupted account. This is achieved systematically by asking more open-ended questions (using phrases like "tell me more about ... ," "explain how ... ," "describe what ... ," and so on), in order to explore the accuracy and reliability of the points that were raised during the uninterrupted account.

Finally, in the *challenge* stage, the interviewer asks probing questions (using the familiar who, what, when, where, and how format), then summarizes all the information that has been gathered from the interview on a particular topic. If the subject gives an account of an event that is itself inconsistent, or is inconsistent with the evidence or information known to the interviewer, then the subject's account is "challenged" and the subject is requested to explain the inconsistencies. Rather than challenging in an aggressive fashion, the investigator presents the challenge as an opportunity for the suspect to explain and clarify the discrepancy.

This process is repeated until all the topics that were identified in the subject's free narrative account have been thoroughly examined. The interviewer uses the same three-substage process to question the interviewee about topics that formed part of the interview plan prepared beforehand, but which the subject did not touch on during the initial narrative account. In the case of a suspect, the investigator must be sure to ask whether they committed the crime. If the suspect confesses, his or her confession should be explored for its consistency, accuracy, and reliability in the same manner as any other account a suspect might give.

4. *Closure and Evaluation.* The interview is drawn to a close in a professional and courteous manner. The interviewer ensures that the interview objectives have been met, summarizes the main points of the subject's statement, provides the subject with the opportunity to correct or add to his or her statement, and explains to the subject what will happen after the interview. The interviewer then considers how the information obtained in the interview fits with the information gathered in the rest of the investigation and considers the effect of any new information on the investigation overall. Interviewers are encouraged to reflect on their interview performance, and investigative supervisors give investigators feedback on their interview skills as part of their routine performance review.

Research and Criticisms

One of the most general criticisms of the PEACE model is that it does not involve making overt attempts to persuade suspects who the interviewer believes are guilty to confess. However, such criticisms represent more of a difference in investigative philosophy than they do a criticism of the PEACE model per se. While it is true that PEACE is focused on information gathering and information challenging and not on overt attempts to elicit confessions, research indicates that the number one reason that people confess is their perception of the strength of the evidence against them (Gudjonsson, 2007). Given the rough similarity in confession rates between countries that use the Reid technique and countries that use the PEACE model (see below), it appears that people's perception of the strength of the evidence against them can be influenced as effectively by using a PEACE challenge approach as by using a Reid interrogation approach.

Another criticism of the PEACE model suggests that it limits the investigator's ability to solve cases in contrast to methods like Reid. For such an assertion to be true, the solution to most cases would have to turn on an investigator's ability to successfully interrogate and secure a confession from a suspect, which it does not. In fact, research suggests that, of those things that are under police control, the factors that most influence the solution of cases include the timeliness and thoroughness of the detective response, the number of detectives initially assigned to a case, thorough computer checks of all involved parties, and the number of witnesses who are located at the primary scene (Wellford & Cronin, 2000; McEwen, 2009). Moreover, if the fact that PEACE does not include an interrogation component severely limited an investigator's ability to solve cases (that is, by obtaining confessions), a significant *drop* in confession rates in Britain after PEACE was introduced might have been expected, but this did not take place; the confession rate in Britain has remained essentially unchanged since PEACE was implemented (Gudjonsson, 2007), and that rate (60 percent) does not differ greatly from the rate in countries where the Reid approach is widely used (50 percent) (King & Snook, 2009; Gudjonsson, 2007). (Because of possible variability in the way key terms are defined, direct statistical comparisons should be approached cautiously; however, it appears that they don't vary much between PEACE and non-PEACE countries and periods.)

In addition, there are no significant differences in crime clearance rates in Britain compared to the United States or Canada—another difference that might be expected. In 2006, Britain's clearance rate was 28 percent, compared to 36 percent in Canada and 32 percent in the United States (Statistics Canada, 2007; Home Office, 2008; U.S. Department of Justice, 2006). With regard to the U.S. Department of Justice statistics, because no overall clearance rate was provided in the publication, a simple (that is, non-weighted) average was determined (31.9 percent) from the seven clearance rates that were provided.

ANALYSIS OF AN INTERROGATION: DAVID RUSSELL WILLIAMS

On February 7, 2010, Detective Sergeant Jim Smyth of the Ontario Provincial Police, Behavioural Sciences Unit, interrogated David Russell Williams (formerly known as Colonel Russell Williams) as part of an investigation into the disappearance of a 27-year-old Belleville woman, Jessica Lloyd. Portions of the interview, which lasted for approximately ten hours, were shown at Williams's sentencing hearing and have been released for public viewing. As the opportunity to see videotaped confessions of serial murderers is extremely rare, it is recommended that you view the excerpts as part of your study of the material in this chapter; the excerpts may be accessed by searching for "Russell Williams confession" on YouTube (http://www.youtube.com).

One of the first observations a viewer might make regarding the Williams interview is its "gentle" nature. Unlike interrogation scenes portrayed on television and in movies, which are often characterized by intense confrontation and overt attempts at persuasion, this interrogation more closely resembles a psychotherapy session. Smyth speaks quietly to Williams, never raising his voice; he asks Williams how he can help him deal with the issues he is facing; and he remains silent over long periods, allowing Williams to consider the information that has been presented to him and to decide what, if anything, to say in response. The changes in Williams's body language, evident from the beginning of the interview (upright torso, with arms folded across his chest chewing gum, casual demeanour) to the end (torso bent forward, arms on thighs, long gaps in his response times, and so on), are worth noting. Through the process, Williams slowly folds—physically and mentally—before confessing.

While a detailed analysis of the interview footage is beyond the scope of this text—an entire book could be written on the subject—we explore several areas here because they serve as an excellent illustration of the techniques described in this chapter. Of course, not all interrogations will go as well as this, but students and investigators would do well to study the "textbook" examples of Smyth's use of the various techniques:

1. *Preparation.* It is evident from Smyth's knowledge of Williams and his background, the details of the offences, the evidence that has been gathered in the investigation to the present time, and the ongoing investigative activity that Smyth had done a great deal of preparation prior to the interrogation. It is also evident that effective communication had taken place—and continued to take place—between members of the investigative team.

2. *Legal rights.* With respect to his legal rights, Williams
   - is told that he is not under arrest;
   - is told that the door to the interview room is not locked and he can leave at any time;
   - is told that he can call a lawyer at any time;
   - is told that if he wants to call a lawyer he will be taken to a private room where he may consult with a lawyer;
   - is told that everything is being recorded;
   - is told that if he does not have his own lawyer, free legal advice is available to him;

- is asked if he wants to call a lawyer (Williams responds that he does not want to exercise this right);
- is told what the investigation is about and informed that the criminal offences being investigated range from first-degree murder to forcible confinement, sexual assault, and break and enter; and
- is told that it is important that he understand that he does not have to talk to the police and is given both a primary and a secondary caution.

3. *Rapport building.* During the first few minutes of the interrogation, Smyth

- asks Williams to have a seat;
- asks whether Williams has ever been interviewed by police before;
- explains that everything that is discussed will be recorded;
- explains what is going to happen in the interrogation, that the interrogation will be detailed, and that it will take some time;
- offers to get Williams a coffee;
- politely asks Williams to take his gum out of his mouth and thanks him for doing so;
- talks about him giving Williams respect and expecting it in return; and
- talks about the events under investigation being featured in the news and people being widely aware of them.

During the interview, Smyth

a. gently regains Williams's attention when it seems to wander: "Russell, listen to me for a second" (18:08:23);

b. asks Williams, after explaining the evidence against him: "What are *we* going to do?" (18:22:50); and

c. maintains a low-key approach, at some points asking Williams how he can help him: "Russ, maybe this would help—can you tell me what the issue is that you are struggling with?" (18:25:33); "Russ, is there anything you want from me, anything missing, anything I can shed some light on for you?" (19:11:07).

4. *Use of silence.* Smyth's use of silence is one of the best examples in any publicly available interrogation footage. During the interrogation, there are numerous periods of silence, some in excess of a minute in length. Especially interesting is the two-minute period from 19:40 to 19:42 immediately preceding Williams's confession, which takes place approximately four and a half hours after the interrogation begins. Smyth speaks for approximately 18 seconds in total, and there is more than 100 seconds of silence.

During the two-minute period immediately before Williams's confession:

a. Smyth advises Williams of the unlimited resources available to the investigation. This is followed by *31 seconds* of silence (19:40:01 to 19:40:32).

b. Smyth advises Williams that he has done the best he can to help him understand what is going on in the investigation and its impact. This is followed by *18 seconds* of silence (19:40:52 to 19:41:10).

c. Smyth asks Williams if the two of them can talk. Williams responds by saying that he wants to minimize the impact of what has happened on his wife, and Smyth says he would like to do the same thing. Williams asks how this can be achieved, and Smyth responds by advising Williams to tell the truth. This is followed by *29 seconds* of silence (19:41:31 to 19:42:00), after which Williams says "Okay," indicating he is going to reveal what happened.

d. Smyth asks Williams where Jessica Lloyd's body is. This is followed by *23 seconds* of silence (19:42:03 to 19:42:26), after which Williams asks, "Got a map?" indicating that he is going to reveal the location of the body.

5. *Shaping of the subject's perception of the strength of the case against him.* During the interrogation, Smyth revealed evidence gathered during the investigation, discussed evidence that was still likely to be found, and talked about the unlimited resources behind the investigation in order to effectively shape Williams's perception of the strength of the case against him. The information he revealed included the following:

- In terms of the investigation, the fact that there were 60 to 70 people working on the investigation, including technical experts; that every request for investigative resources would be granted; that the investigation is costing at least $10 million; and that it is ongoing.

- In terms of the evidence that had been gathered up to that point, that there was a geographical connection between Williams and the crimes; that there was a tire track match between Williams's vehicle and one found at one of the crime scenes; and that during the interrogation Williams's boot print was compared to a boot print found at one of the crime scenes and was a match.

- In terms of the evidence that was likely to be found in the ongoing investigation, during the interrogation Smyth revealed that police were searching Williams's cottage, his vehicle, his office, and his wife's house. He emphasized that further evidence would likely be found in those locations and, additionally, that once the post-mortem examination of the victim's body was complete there would likely be a DNA match with Williams.

KEY TERMS

alibi

enhanced cognitive interview (ECI)

interrogation

KGB caution

PEACE model

Reid technique

tunnel vision

FURTHER READING

Bull, R., Valentine, T., & Williamson, T. (Eds.). (2009). *Handbook of psychology of investigative interviewing: Current developments and future directions.* West Sussex, UK: Wiley.

Gudjonsson, G. (2007). Investigative interviewing. In T. Newburn, T. Williamson, & A. Wright (Eds.), *Handbook of criminal investigation* (pp. 466–492). Cullompton, UK: Willan Publishing.

Inbau, F., Reid, J., Buckley, J., & Jayne, B. (2001). *Criminal interrogation and confessions* (4th ed.). Gaithersburg, MD: Aspen Publishers.

Kassin, S. (2006). A critical appraisal of modern police interrogations. In T. Williamson (Ed.), *Investigative interviewing: Rights, research, regulation* (pp. 207–228). Cullompton, UK: Willan Publishing.

King, L., & Snook, B. (2009). Peering inside a Canadian interrogation room: An examination of the Reid model of interrogation, influence tactics, and coercive strategies. *Criminal Justice and Behaviour, 36*, 674–694.

Snook, B., Eastwood, J., Stinson, M., Tedeschini, J., & House, J. (2010). Reforming investigative interviewing in Canada. *Canadian Journal of Criminology and Criminal Justice, 52*(2), 215–229.

Snook, B., & Keating, K. (2011). A field study of adult witness interviewing practices in a Canadian police organization. In *Legal and Criminological Psychology, 16*(1), 160–172.

Watkins, K., Turtle, J., & Euale, J. (2011). *Interviewing and investigation* (2nd ed.). Toronto: Emond Montgomery.

REVIEW QUESTIONS

True or False?

1. Asking leading questions is an excellent technique for witness interviews.

2. The Crown is obligated to give the defence copies of all statements obtained through its witness interviews.

3. Today, most if not all statements taken during the course of any significant criminal investigation are recorded in their entirety, preferably on both video and audio.

4. Preparation on the part of investigators can enhance the quality of a witness interview.

5. Police should not encourage a witness to recall events out of sequence or from a different perspective because it tends to limit the witness's ability to recall events accurately.

6. If a witness statement is recorded (video and audio), it is not necessary for the police officer to make any notes of the interview.

7. Like any other witness, a suspect should be encouraged to provide a free-recall account of the events in question.

8. A behavioural analysis interview includes drawing a conclusion of the truthfulness of the statement made by an accused based on the language used in that statement.

9. Suggesting that any reasonable person might have acted in the same manner as did the accused is an example of a minimization interrogation strategy.

10. The indicators of deception used in the BAI are based on the idea that liars experience more stress than truth tellers.

11. The police in Canada are mandated by law to videotape and record all interrogations conducted with an accused.

Multiple Choice

1. Treating all witnesses, including potential suspects, with equal respect is important because
   a. who is and who is not a suspect may not be clear at the beginning of an investigation.
   b. intimidation by investigators may lead to a suggestion that the witness's testimony was not voluntary.
   c. establishing a respectful rapport with the witness has been shown to inspire fuller communication.
   d. all of the above.

2. Allowing the witness to relate his or her memories in a free-recall manner is important because
   a. it reduces the likelihood that the investigator's views on the incident will influence the witness's account.
   b. it encourages the witness to reinstate the event context in his or her own mind.
   c. it allows the witness to volunteer details that might not come up in response to specific questions.
   d. all of the above.

3. Some critics of the Reid method have pointed to the fact that some aspects of the technique are consistent with risk factors for false confessions. The most common strategies for obtaining a confession fall into two categories:
   a. expansion and explanation.
   b. context reinstatement and suspect-compatible questioning.
   c. minimization and maximization.
   d. closure and evaluation.

4. The PEACE model seeks to
   a. elicit the maximum amount of information from a suspect.
   b. use deception detection and persuasion processes.
   c. calm the suspect so they will explain their side of the story.
   d. introduce a British investigative technique to North America.

5. One of the most general criticisms of the PEACE model is that

   a. it will not work in a North American context.

   b. it does not involve making overt attempts to persuade suspects who the interviewer believes are guilty to confess.

   c. the model's emphasis on closure and evaluation can contribute to false confession.

   d. it is not as effective as the Reid technique at detecting deception.

6. The essential elements of a "KGB caution" are that the statement is:

   a. voluntary, sworn, and videotaped.

   b. sworn, audio-recorded, and truthful.

   c. voluntary, videotaped, and false.

   d. truthful, sworn, and voluntary.

7. Research has shown that the CI/ECI:

   a. is not an effective method for use with witnesses with special needs.

   b. results in witnesses recalling more information but recalling it less accurately.

   c. is most valuable when used in conjunction with interrogation methods.

   d. enhances the quantity of information witnesses recall without decreasing its quality.

Short Answer

1. It is important for an interviewer not to "jump in" during pauses in a witness's free recall of events, but to encourage the witness to resume their account. Explain why this is important, and describe some techniques that an investigator could use in such a situation.

2. Explain how asking a witness a "closed" question can contaminate the testimony of that witness at trial.

3. Explain the meaning and significance of "witness compatible" questions.

4. How do the purposes of an "interview" and an "interrogation" differ?

5. How do the ultimate goals of the PEACE model and Reid technique differ?

6. In a 2010 article published on its website, Reid made the following comments with regard to the PEACE model:

   > Essentially the PEACE Model is the initial step in The Reid Technique—a non-accusatory fact finding interview. The difference thereafter is that in the PEACE model they are not allowed to engage in the interrogation process in which the investigator attempts to persuade the suspect to tell the truth about what they did.
   >
   > As a result the PEACE model severely limits the investigator's ability to solve cases.

   Do you agree or disagree with this criticism of the PEACE model? Explain your answer.

Case Study

You are investigating the shooting of a known drug dealer. A suspect who was seen running from the scene of the shooting along with two other unknown males was arrested by uniformed officers and brought into the police station. The two other males escaped. When the suspect was arrested, he was searched at the scene and found to be in possession of a handgun. The suspect is 27 years old, appears to understand his legal rights, does not wish to consult legal counsel, and seems willing to talk to investigators.

1. Choose either the Reid method or the PEACE model as your questioning approach toward the suspect. Explain the ultimate goal of whichever questioning approach you choose.

2. Outline the major stages involved in the questioning approach you choose to interview the suspect.

PART III

Giving Evidence

The Duty of Disclosure

18

LEARNING OUTCOMES

After completing this chapter, you should be able to:

- Explain the purpose and importance of the duty of disclosure.

- Describe the Crown's duty of disclosure, including the limits on that duty.

- Describe the police duty of disclosure and its connection to the Crown's duty.

- Understand the legal consequences of lost or destroyed evidence.

- Identify the disclosure requirements set out in *Stinchcombe*, *O'Connor*, *Mills*, and *McNeil*.

- Explain third-party records and how an accused can gain access to them.

INTRODUCTION

As discussed in Chapter 1, disclosure is the process through which the Crown discloses or provides access to all information related to the investigation of the accused that it has in its possession or control, regardless of whether that information is inculpatory or exculpatory. The duty of disclosure serves both the interests of the accused and the broader interests of justice, and is guaranteed by s. 7 of the Charter.

Along with the presumption of innocence and the requirement for proof beyond a reasonable doubt, the duty of disclosure ranks among the key protections within the criminal justice system against wrongful convictions. In the past, disclosure was often viewed "as an act of goodwill and cooperation on the part of the Crown" rather than a duty (*R. v. Taillefer; R. v. Duguay*, 2003, para. 1), but this informal approach played a significant role historically in wrongful convictions—for example, the case of Donald Marshall Jr. (1989), who spent 11 years in jail for a crime he did not commit. One of the key factors leading to Marshall's conviction was the failure on the part of the Crown to disclose "all the relevant evidence" (*R. v. Taillefer; R. v. Duguay*, 2003, para. 1).

A 2008 report that examined the role of disclosure in more serious criminal cases concluded that because the failure to provide adequate disclosure is linked to miscarriages of justice, the duty is "one of the most important obligations in the criminal justice system" (*Lesage Code Report*, 2008, c. 3, p. 21). Disclosure has also been called a "means to an end"—that is, it aims to ensure that the verdict is reliable (*R. v. Horan*, 2008, para. 26).

In *R. v. Stinchcombe* (1991), long recognized as the leading case dealing with the issue of disclosure, the late Supreme Court Justice John Sopinka outlined disclosure's two fundamental purposes:

1. To ensure that the element of surprise is eliminated from the trial process and that both parties are prepared to address the issues having the benefit of all relevant information available in the case.

2. To ensure that the accused has the ability to make "full answer and defence" to the charges against him or her, which is considered "one of the pillars of criminal justice" (*Stinchcombe*, section 2).

In the following sections we explore the primary duty of disclosure that falls on the Crown and the corollary duty falling on the police. In addition, we discuss access to third-party records.

THE CROWN'S DUTY OF DISCLOSURE

As we have seen, the Crown's duty to disclose its case to the accused has evolved over time. Although the duty was acknowledged long ago in common law, in practice it was sometimes regarded as an act of goodwill and cooperation on the part of the Crown. The nature of disclosure as a "duty," as distinct from a procedural nicety, has been strengthened and formalized gradually as a result of the Charter and various case-law decisions. In *R. v. Stinchcombe*, the Supreme Court enshrined the duty "among the fundamental rules of Canadian criminal procedure" (*R. v. Taillefer; R. v. Duguay*, 2003, para. 1), noting:

> The fruits of the investigation which are in the possession of counsel for the Crown are not the property of the Crown for use in securing a conviction but the property of the public to be used to ensure that justice is done. [*R. v. Stinchcombe*, section 2.]

The Crown's duty of disclosure flows from the Crown attorney's role as an officer of the court, whose function is not, as is often mistakenly assumed, to obtain a conviction, but to serve the public by laying before a trier of fact what it considers to be *credible* and *relevant* evidence in relation to a criminal allegation. The duty of the Crown is thus not to win a trial, but to see that justice is served. For this to happen, an accused must be able to make "full answer and defence" to the charges against him or her—a nececessary precondition to which is "full and fair disclosure" by the Crown of its case (*R. v. Taillefer; R. v. Duguay*, 2003, paras. 68–70).

The Crown's duty of disclosure is triggered when a request for disclosure is made by the accused or their counsel. Once this happens, the Crown must disclose *all* information in its possession or control to the accused, unless:

1. the information is clearly irrelevant,
2. the information is privileged, or
3. access to the information is regulated by statute—for example, the treatment records of victims in sexual offences, as set out in *R. v. Mills* (1999).

Note that the Crown's duty is dynamic—that is, the Crown must continue to provide new evidence to the accused as it is gathered.

In general, there is no corresponding duty on the defence to disclose any information in its possession to the Crown. (Notable exceptions include the requirement that the defence notify the Crown if it intends to call an expert at trial; the common practice of disclosing alibi information to the Crown before trial; and the obligation to turn over to authorities any incriminating evidence provided by the accused to his or her counsel.)

When the Supreme Court set out the general principles of disclosure in *Stinchcombe*, it acknowledged that the details of their application would have to be worked out in the years to come. Since then, a number of cases have refined and even expanded those principles. The 2009 Supreme Court case *R. v. McNeil* placed greater disclosure obligations on the Crown as well as on police. With regard to the Crown's obligations, for the first time in Canadian common law, the court held that these obligations extended to information *not* under the Crown's control. Specifically, where the Crown or police are aware that another Crown agency or department was involved in the investigation and are put on notice of the existence of relevant information, unless the notice appears unfounded, the Crown has a duty to inquire and obtain the information if it is reasonably feasible to do so (*McNeil*, 2009). Again emphasizing the role of the Crown, the court said (para. 49):

> The Crown is not an ordinary litigant. As a minister of justice, the Crown's *undivided loyalty* is to the administration of justice. [Emphasis added.]

The above duty set out in *McNeil* does not compel the Crown to hand over information that it does not control, but it does oblige the Crown (when put on notice) to inquire about and attempt to obtain relevant information that may be of benefit to the accused (Paciocco, 2009, p. 30). Where the Crown inquires about but is unable to obtain the information, it must report this to the defence. This obligation on the Crown to "inquire and obtain" has been characterized as a new era in disclosure. To obtain information held by a Crown agency or department, the accused need only put the Crown "on notice" regarding the existence of the information, and the Crown must then act. If the Crown is not able to obtain the information, the accused may pursue the information through an *O'Connor* application (discussed below; Paciocco, 2009, pp. 31–32).

Criminal law in Canada has matured considerably since *Stinchcombe*, and accused now have better access to every aspect of the Crown's case against them (Kaiser, 2009, p. 46). Yet even with such access, disputes regarding the proper application of the principles of disclosure are bound to continue.

THE POLICE DUTY OF DISCLOSURE

The police duty of disclosure is connected to that of the Crown. Traditionally, under *Stinchcombe*, police were obligated to provide the Crown only with the information they had gathered during their investigation of the accused ("the fruits of the investigation"); all other records had to be obtained by an accused through an *O'Connor* application.

In expanding the Crown's disclosure obligations, *McNeil* similarly widened the scope of the records that police must provide to the Crown. The court held:

> The necessary corollary of the Crown's disclosure duty under *Stinchcombe* is the obligation of police to disclose to the Crown *all material pertaining to its investigation of the accused*. For the purposes of fulfilling this corollary obligation, the investigating police force ... is not a third party. Rather, it acts on the same first party footing as the Crown. [*R. v. McNeil*, 2009, para. 14; emphasis added.]

As a result of the *McNeil* court's holding, the Crown, and thus the police, must now disclose records of the discipline or misconduct of officers involved in the investigation of an accused where either

1. the misconduct is related to the investigation—for example, where an officer falsified information to obtain a search warrant; or
2. the findings of misconduct could reasonably affect the case against the accused—for example, where an investigating officer has engaged in criminal conduct that calls his credibility as a witness into question (*McNeil*, 2009, section 3).

The above requirements go further than *Stinchcombe* toward ensuring that the accused has access to *all* of the information that could possibly be relevant to the case against him or her. In the case of *McNeil*, for example, the arresting officer was convicted of a drug-related offence. Given that the officer was the main witness against the accused, the officer's conviction would have raised questions about the officer's credibility as a witness; because the credibility of a witness is potentially relevant to the accused's case, the accused has the right to this information.

Records that may be covered by the above criteria include, for example, police reports related to the investigation of the accused—for example, a notice of hearing

---

DISCLOSING MISCONDUCT: "THE FERGUSON FIVE"

The court in *McNeil* identified the *Ferguson Report* (2003), which dealt with various aspects of police misconduct, as a good reference for determining what kinds of misconduct the police are under a duty to disclose to the Crown. With respect to officers involved in the investigation of an accused, Justice Ferguson recommended that police should automatically disclose acts of misconduct that fall into any of the following categories, often referred to as "the Ferguson Five":

1. Any conviction or finding of guilt under the *Criminal Code* or the *Controlled Drugs and Substances Act* (CDSA) for which a pardon has not been granted.
2. Any outstanding charges under the *Criminal Code* or the CDSA.
3. Any conviction or finding of guilt under any other federal or provincial statute.
4. Any finding of guilt for misconduct after a hearing under the relevant police legislation related to police officer misconduct.
5. Any current charges of misconduct under the police disciplinary legislation for which a notice of hearing has been issued.

---

under the *Police Services Act*, where an officer is accused of misconduct arising out of the particular investigation—as well as records *not* generated by the particular investigation, but that involve officers involved in the arrest or investigation of the accused. Police disciplinary records and criminal investigation files that do *not* meet the above criteria are considered third-party records, and must be applied for through an *O'Connor* application.

Since *McNeil*, Canadian police services have implemented procedures to ensure that records in the above categories are included in their basic disclosure package to the Crown. It has been suggested that, when determining their duty of disclosure, the police should apply the standard that any information in their records regarding misconduct by a police officer involved in the investigation should be provided to the Crown, unless it is clearly irrelevant. Not all information provided by police, however, will necessarily be disclosed to the defence; the Crown will still act as a "gatekeeper," reviewing the material submitted by police to decide what it, in turn, will ultimately disclose (Paciocco, 2009, pp. 28–29).

LIMITS ON THE ACCUSED'S RIGHT TO DISCLOSURE

Although *Stinchcombe* says that the Crown has a duty to disclose *all* relevant material in its possession to the accused, it also states that the "obligation to disclose is not absolute." There are some exceptions to what must be disclosed, in what manner, and when, and the Crown retains the discretion necessary to make such determinations. The most significant exceptions to the general rule of disclosure relate to:

1. the withholding of information by the Crown, primarily on the basis of issues of privilege and relevancy; and
2. the timing and manner of disclosure.

Although the Crown retains considerable discretion with respect to determining what must ultimately be disclosed and when, that discretion is reviewable by a trial judge. In the event that a disclosure issue arises during a trial and defence initiates such a review, the judge will be guided by the general principle that *all* relevant information should be disclosed in a timely manner. The Crown will be required to justify witholding or delaying the disclosure of relevant information by demonstrating why it falls under an exception to the general rule.

Privilege

The Crown has a duty to protect those who have legal privilege—for example, confidential informants—and it is not required to disclose information that might reveal their identity. The Crown may address issues of confidential informant privilege by witholding some documents entirely or by editing out certain pieces of information that would tend to identify the informant. The Crown may also withold information out of concern for the safety or privacy of witnesses or others who have given information during the investigation of the accused. This is routinely done by editing personal identifiers—for example, address, date of birth, telephone number—out of the documents to be disclosed.

Relevancy

The Crown has discretion to determine what material it believes is relevant to an accused's case and what material is not. It is not obligated to disclose information that is clearly irrelevant. For example, an officer's notes detailing his or her attendance at a radio call that was not related to the arrest or investigation of the accused is not relevant and would thus not normally be disclosed.

Timing

With respect to the timing of disclosure, *Stinchcombe* held that "initial disclosure"— that is, of the material gathered to date at the time that charges are laid and shortly thereafter—should be made before the accused elects the mode of trial or enters a plea. These are crucial steps in the process that have a significant impact on the accused's rights, and knowing the strengths and weaknesses of the Crown's case before making such decisions is of significant value to an accused. The Crown also retains some discretion to delay disclosure if early disclosure would impede the completion of an investigation; however, the court in *Stinchcombe* was clear that this sort of delay should occur only in rare circumstances.

LOST OR DESTROYED EVIDENCE

In a situation where the Crown (or the police) has lost or destroyed evidence, the Crown must disclose this fact to the defence and explain what happened to the evidence. If the evidence was lost or destroyed due to "unacceptable negligence" (see the box feature on page 354), then the Crown will have failed in its duty of disclosure. In considering the Crown's explanation for lost or destroyed evidence, the court will consider the circumstances surrounding the loss/destruction—in particular, whether or not reasonable steps were taken to preserve the evidence. The more relevant the evidence is, the greater the duty of care on the Crown and police to ensure that it is preserved properly.

The following is a summary of the law governing lost or destroyed evidence (*R. v. B. (F.C.)*, 2000, para. 10):

1. The Crown has an obligation to disclose all relevant information in its possession. This duty gives rise to a duty to preserve relevant evidence.

2. There is no absolute right to have originals of documents produced. However, if the Crown no longer has the original documents, it must explain their absence to the court.

3. In determining whether the Crown's explanation is satisfactory, the court should consider the circumstances surrounding the loss/destruction of the evidence, including whether it was perceived to be relevant at the time it was lost/destroyed and whether the police acted reasonably in attempting to preserve it. The more relevant the evidence, the greater the care that should be taken to preserve it.

4. The duty to disclose is not breached in all cases where evidence is lost or destroyed. However, if the loss or destruction resulted from "unacceptable negligence," the accused's s. 7 Charter rights have been breached.

5. A failure to produce evidence may also represent an abuse of process—for example, if the evidence was destroyed deliberately for the purpose of defeating the disclosure obligation.

6. A stay is the appropriate remedy for a s. 7 breach or an abuse of process only if it is one of those rare cases that meets the criteria set out in *O'Connor*. Those criteria specify that it "is only appropriate 'in the clearest of cases,' where the prejudice to the accused's right to make full answer and defence cannot be remedied or where irreparable prejudice would be caused to the integrity of the justice system if the prosecution were continued" (*R. v. O'Connor*, 1995, para. 82).

7. Even if the Crown has shown that there was no unacceptable negligence, in some cases there may still be a s. 7 breach if the loss can be shown to be *so prejudicial to the right to make a full answer and defence* that it impairs the right to a fair trial. In this case, a stay may be an appropriate remedy.

The case of *R. v. Banford* (2010) involved an accused who was arrested and charged with impaired driving. The Crown's initial disclosure package did not include a surveillance video from the police station, and by the time the defence made another request for the tapes, the police had destroyed them in accordance with their video retention policy. During the period of the initial and subsequent disclosure requests, the Crown took no steps to preserve, copy, or disclose the videos.

The court found that police appeared to be following a policy that resulted in the routine destruction of highly probative evidence, which represented a systemic disregard for the Crown's disclosure obligations. The Crown's failure to preserve and disclose the video offended the Charter, and as a result the case was stayed.

In its decision, the court remarked that in any instance of non-disclosure there is a "threshold question"—namely, whether the evidence that was lost or destroyed was relevant. The threshold for relevance is low, with the accused being entitled to

CASES INVOLVING LOST OR DESTROYED EVIDENCE

The issue of lost or destroyed evidence arises frequently in criminal cases:

- *R. v. Buyck* (2007): An in-car camera recording of an encounter between a police officer and an accused was taped over. The court found the officer's failure to preserve the evidence to be "unacceptably and inexcusably negligent," violating the defendant's right to disclosure under s. 7 of the Charter. The trial judged stayed the proceedings, but on appeal a new trial was ordered.
- *R. v. Scott* (2002): "Unacceptable negligence" on the part of police resulted in the loss of a videotaped eyewitness statement. Because the evidence was clearly relevant, and therefore disclosable pursuant to *Stinchcombe*, the accused's s. 7 Charter rights were breached. The trial judge stayed the proceedings, but on appeal a new trial was ordered.
- *R. v. Dulude* (2004): A police station security videotape that collected one-second clips from multiple video cameras throughout the police station was not disclosed to the defence and was later erased. Although the videotape was of minimal relevance in the case, the court found that the Crown had not met its obligation to explain why the tape was not disclosed before it was erased and was not satisfied that the tape had *not* been lost due to unacceptable negligence. The trial judge stayed the proceedings, but on appeal a new trial was ordered.
- *R. v. Bero* (2000): The accused was convicted of impaired driving causing bodily harm and driving with a blood alcohol level over the legal limit. He appealed on the grounds that the Crown had failed to maintain possession of his vehicle, thus denying him the opportunity to conduct an independent forensic examination. The court held that the failure to preserve the vehicle was the result of either ignorance of or indifference to the duty on the Crown and the police to preserve the fruits of their investigation, and was sufficiently serious to constitute an abuse of process. The appellate court overturned the original conviction and ordered a new trial.
- *R. v. Ranger* (2010): As a result of an absence of proper procedures, police notebooks belonging to a retired officer who had been involved in the investigation of a sexual assault complaint were lost. This constituted "unacceptable negligence" by police, and, combined with the loss of other documentary materials related to the investigation, resulted in a breach of the defendant's Charter rights. The accused applied for a stay of proceedings prior to commencement of his trial, but his application was denied. The judge stated that "a judicial stay of proceedings short circuits the trial process and should be used sparingly" (para. 35). Accordingly, the accused's trial was allowed to proceed.

"material which may have *only marginal* value to the ultimate issues at trial" (para. 13, emphasis added). The lesson, then, is that both police and the Crown must give some thought to whether or not a particular piece of evidence might possibly be relevant to *either* the Crown or the defence. If the answer is yes, then steps must be taken to preserve it.

DISCLOSURE IN PRACTICE

Traditionally, the process of disclosure involved the officer in charge of an investigation making two photocopies—one for the Crown and one for the defence—of all documents, reports, officers' notes, and written statements; making copies of photographs, audiotapes, videotapes, and similar forms of evidence; and then physically delivering the material to the Crown's office. Before an officer could deliver the material, however, it had to be "edited" (also referred to as "vetted," or "redacted") to remove certain information—for example, personal identifiers of witnesses, secret police investigative techniques, or any information that might identify a confidential informant.

Although developments in technology and methods—for example, electronic documents, digital photography, and electronic disclosure protocols—have simplified the disclosure process, even "routine" cases such as theft or assault can still be time-consuming; in larger, more complex cases—for example, homicides, corporate fraud, organized crime, or acts of terrorism—the demands are considerably more onerous. Some senior police officials have characterized the disclosure obligations flowing from *Stinchcombe* as a "huge challenge" that has added significantly to the cost of police investigations in terms of the time, personnel, and equipment necessary to reproduce and edit the "fruits of an investigation" prior to disclosing them. In the face of such concerns, it is worth remembering that the current disclosure regime is in large part a product of the lessons learned from past miscarriages of justice, in which it became painfully apparent that the disclosure practices existing at the time were insufficient to maintain the integrity of the criminal justice system (Leblanc, 2011).

In their comprehensive review of large and complex criminal cases in Ontario (*Lesage Code Report*, 2008), former Chief Justice of the Ontario Superior Court Patrick Lesage and Ontario Superior Court Judge Michael Code examined various aspects of the disclosure process and the role that disclosure plays in more serious criminal cases. They found that disclosure is an ongoing source of dispute causing delay and inefficiency. On the Crown/police side of the issue, they attributed the problem to the absence of a standard "best practices" approach to disclosure in terms of form, content, and timeliness (*Lesage Code Report*, p. 21). On the defence side, they concluded that most problems arise primarily in relation to requests for materials that (1) are not part of the investigation, (2) are "marginally relevant," or (3) give rise to third-party privacy issues, thus causing further delay.

Since the *Lesage Code Report*, two developments in particular have begun to address the difficulties highlighted by the authors:

1. *Closer collaboration between the police and the Crown before charges are laid.*
    Consultation regarding the size and focus of a case results in a more manageable case for prosecution. For the police to conduct an expansive investigation and charge a large number of individuals, for example, would be of little value if it resulted in a case that would be practically impossible for the Crown to prosecute because of insurmountable logistical and disclosure issues.

    Consultation before charges are laid also allows the construction of the disclosure brief (the "package" of evidence gathered by police to be given to the defence) to begin at the earliest stages of the investigation, which results in disclosure being ready in a more timely manner once charges are laid. The quicker disclosure is made to the accused, the quicker the accused can assess the strengths and weaknesses of the Crown's case, enabling the accused to make important decisions about how to proceed with the case—for example, whether to request a date for a trial or to enter a guilty plea.

Finally, consultation at an earlier stage allows for a discussion of such issues as vetting, the transcription of interviews and wiretap intercepts, and who is paying for what costs to occur early in the process, thus minimizing some of the factors that commonly contribute to a delay in making disclosure once charges are laid.

2. *The use of electronic disclosure in the standardized major case management (MCM) format.*

The use of an electronic disclosure brief containing a series of standardized, searchable "folders" provides a model—derived from the Ontario *Major Case Management Manual* (2004), which is designed to assist investigators in managing information in serious criminal cases such as homicides, sexual assaults, and abductions—to be followed in different cases and in different jurisdictions. The model helps ensure that the initial disclosure "product" is more comprehensive, consistent, and thus of a higher quality. The Toronto Police Service, for example, recently began an electronic disclosure pilot project, which has resulted in significant savings in terms of both time and paper, and which allows defence lawyers to conduct efficient electronic searches of the materials disclosed to them. By helping to ensure that all or most of the materials relevant to the investigation are disclosed in the "first round" of disclosure, this practice should serve to minimize defence follow-up requests for additional materials, and the resulting time delays.

DISCLOSURE: CHALLENGES AND CHANGES

The primarily paper-based, more casual disclosure practices that existed in Canada prior to *Stinchcombe* are gradually becoming a thing of the past as full, timely, electronic disclosure becomes the benchmark for contemporary disclosure practices. However, disclosure, far from becoming less difficult for police services, is likely to remain a constant, if not a growing, challenge. This is shown by the common-law trend, in cases such as *McNeil*, toward expanding the range of material that the Crown (and, by extension, the police) is responsible for disclosing.

Some police services in Canada have responded to this challenge by creating dedicated "disclosure teams." For example, the Calgary Police Service's (CPS) Court and Disclosure Unit in the Investigative Support Section consists of four teams: the Court Team, the Criminal History Team, the Joint Disclosure Team, and the Crown Transcription Team. The teams work with members of the CPS and Crown prosecutors to provide the most complete and accessible evidence package. Police services are also looking for increasingly innovative disclosure strategies centred on the use of electronic and web-based technologies. The Toronto Police Service, for example, is using Adobe PDF electronic documents, electronic document transfer protocols, and flash drive technology to deliver disclosure to the Crown and defence (McKeirnan, 2011).

The use of electronic media, such as DVDs or, in large cases, computer hard drives, allows for quicker vetting of material by police and the Crown prior to disclosure, and permits the inclusion of diverse kinds of material—for example, scanned documents, audio or video recordings, and photographs—in a single package. It also enables both the Crown and the defence to use the efficient search capabilities inherent in the electronic format.

REMEDIES FOR "FAILURES" OF DISCLOSURE

As stressed throughout this chapter, disclosure is much more than the bureaucratic exercise of collecting, copying, editing, and handing over materials collected during an investigation; it is a critical precondition of an accused's ability to exercise his or her Charter right of full answer and defence. As a result, courts have a variety of remedies available for situations in which the Crown (or police) fails to meet its disclosure obligations.

In *R. v. Dixon* (1998, p. 3, para. 1), the Supreme Court said that if an accused shows that there is a "reasonable possibility" that any undisclosed information could have been used to meet the case for the Crown, then the accused's s. 7 Charter right to disclosure has been impaired. Once this impairment has been established, the question becomes: How can it be remedied? In *R. v. Horan* (2008, para. 30), the court stated that trial judges may apply such remedies as staying the proceedings,

LATE DISCLOSURE

In *R. v. Bjelland* (2009), the Supreme Court addressed the issue of late disclosure, in which evidence that was to be used at trial was disclosed to the accused after his preliminary hearing had concluded. The accused moved to have the proceedings against him stayed or, alternatively, to have the evidence that was disclosed late excluded, arguing that his right to full answer and defence had been impaired. The Court found that the exclusion of evidence that was disclosed late should occur only in exceptional cases, either:

- where late disclosure results in the trial process being unfair, and such unfairness cannot be remedied through an adjournment and disclosure order—for example, where evidence is disclosed in a trial after "important and irrevocable decisions" about the accused's defence have been made or where an accused is being held in custody—or
- where the exclusion is necessary to maintain the integrity of the justice system—for example, where the Crown has engaged in misconduct by deliberately withholding evidence.

In coming to its decision, the Court referred to the earlier case of *O'Connor* (1995), in which it held that where late or insufficient disclosure leads to a breach of the accused's s. 7 Charter rights, the remedy will typically be a disclosure order and adjournment, and only in "extreme cases where the prejudice to the accused's ability to make full answer and defence or to the integrity of the justice system is irremediable" will a stay of proceedings be appropriate (para. 25).

ordering disclosure and subsidiary remedies—for example, costs against the prosecution—and excluding the undisclosed evidence.

Section 24(1) of the Charter requires that any remedy must be "appropriate and just in the circumstances." The court in *Horan* held that, in most cases, the appropriate remedy for the failure of the Crown to meet its disclosure obligations would be an order of disclosure accompanied by an adjournment, if necessary, to give the accused an opportunity to carry out any additional investigation or preparation that may arise from the newly disclosed information. However, in some cases, an adjournment may not be an appropriate remedy—for example, if it delays the trial of an accused who is being held in custody. In such a situation, a more appropriate remedy may be the exclusion of the evidence that was not properly disclosed.

OBTAINING THIRD-PARTY RECORDS

For an accused to exercise his or her right to make full answer and defence, it might be necessary to gain access to records that may be relevant to his or her case but that

1. are not in the possession or control of the Crown, or
2. do not form part of the "first-party" *Stinchcombe* disclosure obligations of the police.

third-party records
records not created as a result of a police investigation, but that contain information about "third parties" to a criminal proceeding—for example, a witness or a complainant

O'Connor application
procedure through which an accused can gain access to third-party records outside the first-party disclosure duty of the Crown as set out in *Stinchcombe*

production
the process by which an accused gains the right, through an *O'Connor* application, to third-party records—for example, medical or psychiatric records

Mills regime
supersedes *O'Connor* as the procedure that governs the production of third-party records in sexual assault cases only

Third-party records are records that do not deal directly with the investigation of the accused's case but that may contain information *relevant to* it—for example, certain records held by psychiatrists or doctors, which would normally be subject to a reasonable expectation of privacy; an officer's disciplinary records that do not fall under first-party disclosure obligations; personal financial records; or business records. Access to such records must be sought by way of a special application known as an **O'Connor application**, named for the Supreme Court case *R. v. O'Connor* (1995).

In *O'Connor*, the court considered whether the accused had the right to gain access to the medical and treatment records of the victim in a sexual assault case. The court held that an accused has the "right to **production**" of any relevant information that is not in the possession or control of the Crown prosecuting the case—for example, therapeutic records of a victim or a witness held by a hospital—if the positive consequences of producing those records outweigh the negative effects (Ives, 2009, p. 226). Unlike material that is "disclosed" under the *Stinchcombe* regime, third-party records obtained under *O'Connor* are said to be "produced."

Following the *O'Connor* decision, the 1997 passage of Bill C-46 resulted in the addition of a number of new subsections to the *Criminal Code* (ss. 278.1–278.91) that modified the *O'Connor* production process in sexual assault prosecutions. The constitutionality of the new subsections was questioned, but it was upheld in the 1999 Supreme Court case of *R. v. Mills*, in which the court considered the issue of an accused's right to production of the medical and psychiatric records of a victim in a sexual assault case. Today, the procedure, known as the **Mills regime**, governs the production of third-party records in sexual assault cases only.

The different processes for acquiring records described in this chapter—that is, disclosure and production—are the result of an attempt to balance the privacy right of the individuals to whom the records pertain with the right of accused persons to make full answer and defence through the use of those records.

KEY DISCLOSURE CASES: REVIEW

Case	Rules
R. v. Stinchcombe (1991)	• The Crown has a legal duty to provide the defence with all relevant evidence in its possession or control, regardless of whether it is inculpatory or exculpatory, or whether the Crown intends to use the evidence at trial. • Police have a corresponding obligation to disclose all relevant material in their possession pertaining to the investigation of an accused to the Crown.
R. v. O'Connor (1995)	• A judge can order third-party records to be disclosed to an accused if the accused establishes that the records are likely to be relevant to their case and, if upon review by a judge, the judge believes that ordering production of the records strikes a proper balance between the victim's right to privacy and the accused's right to make full answer and defence. • An *O'Connor* application is the procedure through which an accused person can gain access to third-party records that do not fall under the first-party disclosure duty of the Crown as set out in *Stinchcombe*.
R. v. Mills (1999)	• The *Mills* regime supersedes *O'Connor* as the procedure for obtaining third-party records in sexual assault cases only (*Criminal Code*, ss. 278.1–278.91).
R. v. McNeil (2009)	• Although an accused does not have the automatic right to receive records relating to a police officer's employment history or to disciplinary records that have no relationship to the charges against them, where such information is relevant to the case against the accused, such records should form part of the Crown's first-party disclosure obligation. • Police must disclose more than just investigative materials to the Crown—they must disclose all material pertaining to the investigation of the accused, including information that may affect the credibility of police witnesses. • Upon notice, the Crown must inquire about and attempt to obtain records that are not in its control, but are in the control of other state agencies or departments and that may be relevant to an accused's case.

KEY TERMS

Mills regime
O'Connor application
production
third-party records

FURTHER READING

Ives, D.E. (2009). R. v. McNeil: Narrowing the gap between disclosure and production. *International Journal of Evidence and Proof, 13*(3), 225–231.

Kaiser, H.A. (2009). McNeil: A welcome clarification and extension of the disclosure principles: "The adversary system has lingered on." *Criminal Reports, 62* (6th), 36–46.

McNeil, R. v. (2009). 2009 SCC 3, [2009] 1 S.C.R. 66.

Paciocco, D. (2009). Stinchcombe on steroids: The surprising legacy of McNeil. *Criminal Reports, 62* (6th), 26–35.

Stinchcombe, R. v. (1991). [1991] 3 S.C.R. 326.

REVIEW QUESTIONS

True or False?

1. The three fundamental purposes of disclosure are to eliminate the element of surprise from the trial process; to ensure the accused has the ability to make full answer and defence; and to ensure that the media have full access to public court documents.

2. The Supreme Court case of *R. v. Stinchcombe* (1991) sets out the general principles of disclosure and clearly defines the Crown's disclosure obligations.

3. The duty of the Crown attorney is to prosecute and convict accused persons.

4. The accused's right to disclosure of materials in the possession of the prosecuting Crown is absolute—all relevant material must be disclosed without exception.

5. The court will only impose legal consequences where evidence is lost if the evidence would have played an important role in the outcome of the trial.

6. The right of an accused person to make "full answer and defence" to charges against him or her is protected by the fundamental justice provisions of the *Canada Evidence Act*.

7. The *Mills* regime refers to the process that governs disclosure of all third-party documents.

8. The court in *Horan* held that, in most cases, the appropriate remedy for the failure of the Crown to meet its disclosure obligations would be a stay of proceedings.

9. The "Ferguson Five" refers to the five key issues that must be considered by the Crown when deciding which materials must be disclosed pursuant to an *O'Connor* application.

Multiple Choice

1. Where the Crown fails to meet its duty of disclosure the court has a number of remedies available. These include:

   a. an adjournment accompanied by an order of disclosure.

   b. acquitting the accused of all charges.

   c. the exclusion of evidence that was not properly disclosed.

   d. citing the Crown for professional misconduct.

   e. both a and c.

2. An accused can attempt to gain access to third-party records by making what is referred to as

   a. a *Stinchcombe* application.

   b. an *O'Connor* application.

   c. a *McNeil* application.

   d. a *Mills* application.

3. The term "the fruits of the investigation" refers to

   a. information gathered during the police investigation of an accused.

   b. evidence that grew out of a tip provided by an anonymous informant.

   c. evidence that is tainted as a result of having been obtained illegally.

   d. information that, given its nature, is ripe for scrutiny by the defence.

4. The *Ferguson Report* (2003) reviewed and made recommendations regarding

   a. the adequacy of police disclosure practices.

   b. the disclosure practices of the Crown in large, complex cases.

   c. various aspects of police misconduct.

   d. the ability of an accused person to obtain disclosure of third-party records.

5. Canadian criminal law has matured considerably over the past two decades, especially with regard to disclosure issues. Accused now have dependably better access to

   a. competent legal representation.

   b. every aspect of the Crown's case against them.

   c. the *Canadian Charter of Rights and Freedoms*.

   d. the Supreme Court in order to appeal convictions they believe to be unjust.

6. The *Lesage Code Report* (2008) reviewed large complex criminal cases in Ontario. It found that disclosure is

   a. an ongoing source of dispute causing delay and inefficiency.

   b. a simple bureaucratic process that is easily complied with.

   c. an optional process much of which is informal in nature.

   d. an ongoing process that starts the moment an arrest is made.

7. The Crown must disclose all information in its possession or control to the accused unless

   a. the information could possibly be irrelevant.

   b. the information is privileged.

   c. access to the information is regulated by tradition.

   d. the Crown feels it would be a disadvantage to disclose it.

8. The necessary corollary of the Crown's disclosure duty under *Stinchcombe* is the obligation of police to disclose to the Crown all material pertaining to:

   a. its investigation of the accused.

   b. its investigation of the accused at the sentencing stage of a criminal proceeding.

   c. third parties who may have an interest in the investigation of the accused.

   d. the service records of the officers involved in the investigation of the accused.

Short Answer

1. Explain the purpose of disclosure and why it is regarded as one of the most important obligations in the criminal justice system.

2. Compare and contrast the disclosure and production processes.

Testifying

19

LEARNING OUTCOMES

After completing this chapter, you should be able to:

- Understand the basic structure of a criminal trial.

- Understand the proper role of a witness in a criminal trial.

- Understand the different stages in which witnesses give evidence.

- Appreciate the complex nature of the cross-examination process.

- Appreciate some of the difficulties police experience when giving evidence.

- Understand the importance of police officers' notes.

- Understand what is required to be an effective witness.

INTRODUCTION

Part of a police officer's job includes testifying, or giving evidence in a court of law—typically, in relation to allegations that people have committed municipal, provincial, or federal (criminal) offences. Sometimes such testimony is given before a justice of the peace, which typically occurs in the case of traffic or bylaw offences; at other times, such testimony is given before a judge, or a judge and a jury, during a criminal trial.

This chapter focuses on police witnesses giving evidence in the context of criminal trials. We review:

- the structure of a criminal trial,
- the role of witnesses in a criminal trial,
- the different stages during which a court hears evidence,
- what an officer can expect during these stages (with particular attention to cross-examination of police witnesses by defence counsel), and
- the purpose and importance of police officers' notes.

Throughout the chapter, we suggest ways that police officers can be most effective in their role as professional witnesses.

STRUCTURE OF A CRIMINAL TRIAL

One of the challenges facing a novice police officer trying to gain an understanding of the structure of a criminal trial, and how and where police officers fit into that process as witnesses, is the fact that this structure isn't written down in either the *Criminal Code* or any other statute. Rather, various parts of the process are described in different sections of the Code, and in language that is not readily accessible to those without legal training.

The best way to learn about the trial process is by participating in it as a witness, as an officer in charge of a case, or simply by sitting in court and observing a trial. However, it is beneficial to have a broad sense of the process before becoming involved in it, and new officers can benefit from some excellent sources of information about the structure of criminal trials. Stuesser (2005), in his primer for novice lawyers, provides an instructive, general summary of the steps in which a criminal trial unfolds (adapted from pp. 132–183):

1. *Crown and defence counsel introduce themselves to the court.* After the judge has entered the court, taken his or her seat, and is ready to begin, the judge will look toward counsel, who will then introduce themselves to the court. Crown counsel will typically say, "Your Honour, my name is Mark Jones, and I appear on behalf of the Crown." Defence counsel will then typically say, "Your Honour, my name is Sheila Smith, I act for Mr. Phelps, and we are ready to proceed."

2. *The court deals with preliminary matters.* Before any evidence is called, the court may deal with a variety of preliminary matters—for example, where the accused will sit (with counsel, if out of custody, or in the prisoner's

box, if in custody); whether witnesses will be excluded from the courtroom until required to give evidence (to prevent the testimony of one witness from influencing the testimony of another); whether any pre-trial motions or amendments are necessary to the charge documents—that is, the **criminal information.**

criminal information
a sworn document in which the charges against an individual are set out

3. *Crown counsel makes their opening statement.* Traditionally, Crown counsel opens the trial by making a statement outlining the Crown's case for the judge. This statement highlights the legal issues that the Crown anticipates will be important and the evidence that will be heard.

4. *Defence counsel may make admissions.* An accused person may, if he or she wishes, admit to certain facts so that the Crown is not required to prove them at trial. The advantage of making such admissions is that it helps to expedite the trial process and can focus the trial on what the defence feels are the key legal issues. The Crown must agree to any such admissions, which is normally done in the form of an "agreed statement of facts," a document that is signed by both Crown and defence counsel.

5. *Crown counsel calls evidence.* Evidence is called by the Crown as follows:

   a. the witness takes the stand,

   b. Crown counsel conducts the examination-in-chief of its witness,

   c. defence counsel cross-examines the witness,

   d. Crown counsel re-examines the witness,

   e. judge may question the witness, and

   f. the next witness is called.

   Note that if the cross-examination of a witness is interrupted by either a recess or an adjournment, neither the defence nor Crown counsel may communicate with the witness, whether directly or indirectly, until cross-examination of the witness is complete (Bryant, Lederman, & Fuerst, 2009, p. 1142).

6. *Crown counsel closes its case.* The Crown must put forth all the relevant evidence it has and then close its case—that is, the Crown cannot withhold aspects of its case until the defence has called evidence, and then introduce more evidence in an effort to strengthen the case. The accused has the right to know exactly what the Crown's case is based on before responding to it.

7. *Defence counsel may make "a motion of no evidence" to stop the trial.* After the Crown closes its case, defence counsel may make a motion to have the trial stopped and the accused acquitted. This is called "a motion of no evidence" (or, in a jury trial, a "directed verdict of acquittal"). In a motion of no evidence, defence is asking the court to decide "whether there is sufficient evidence to permit a properly instructed jury to reasonably convict" (Stuesser, 2005, p. 144). Defence is entitled to have the court rule on the motion before deciding whether to call evidence.

   If the judge decides that there *is* sufficient evidence, the motion is denied and the trial continues. If the judge decides that there is *not* sufficient evidence, the motion will be allowed and the case against the accused will be dismissed. (The process in a judge-alone trial is slightly different. For a detailed discussion, see Stuesser, 2005, p. 144.)

8. *Defence counsel opens its case with a statement.* Although the defence does not have to make an opening statement, and often does not in judge-alone trials, the right of the defence to make an opening statement is provided for in the *Criminal Code*. The opening statement provides an opportunity for defence to tell the judge about its case.

9. *Defence counsel calls evidence.* The defence uses the same procedure that the Crown does (see step 5, above) to call its witnesses, with the roles being reversed—that is, the defence conducts the examination-in-chief and the Crown then cross-examines the witness.

   The accused has the right to decide whether or not to testify. If the accused chooses to testify, defence counsel will decide where in the sequence of defence witnesses he or she will be called.

10. *Defence counsel closes its case.* Once the defence has finished calling evidence, it closes its case.

11. *Crown counsel may seek to call further evidence.* Once the defence has closed its case, the Crown may seek either to call further evidence "in reply" (or in rebuttal) or to "reopen" its case. The Crown is limited in reply to calling evidence in response to new facts adduced by the defence that the Crown has not had an opportunity to deal with or that it could not have reasonably anticipated. The Crown will only be allowed by the judge to reopen its case (to introduce evidence that it failed to introduce earlier) in exceptional circumstances, where doing so will not prejudice the accused.

12. *Defence and Crown counsel make closing submissions.* Generally speaking, where the defence calls evidence in a case, it makes its closing submissions first, followed by the Crown, and where the defence has not called evidence in a case, the Crown makes its closing submission first, followed by the defence.

13. *The judge makes a decision.* After hearing all the evidence and submissions, the judge may either render judgment immediately or reserve his or her decision for a future date.

14. *The accused is dealt with by the court.* Where the judge finds an accused guilty, the court may immediately sentence the accused, after hearing submissions from both the Crown and the defence on sentence. The court may also put the matter over to a future date to allow counsel to prepare for a hearing on sentence. Where the court finds the accused not guilty, the trial process is complete and the accused is free to go. Where a judge is sitting alone, as, for example, is the case in the Ontario *Court of Justice*, which deals with the majority of criminal charges in Ontario, "the court" is synonymous with "the judge." Continuing to use Ontario as an example, in the *Superior Court of Justice*, which deals with more serious criminal charges, "the court" may refer to a judge sitting alone, or to a judge and a jury.

THE CRIMINAL TRIAL AT A GLANCE

1. Counsel introduce themselves to the court.
2. The court deals with preliminary matters.
3. The Crown makes its opening statement.
4. The defence makes any admissions.
5. The Crown calls evidence.
6. The Crown closes its case.
7. The defence may make a motion of no evidence to stop the trial.
8. Opening statement by the defence.
9. The defence calls evidence (although it is not required to call any evidence).
10. The defence closes its case.
11. Crown counsel may seek to call further evidence.
12. Defence and Crown counsel make closing submissions.
13. The judge makes a decision.
14. The court deals with the accused.

ROLE OF POLICE WITNESSES IN A CRIMINAL TRIAL

To perform effectively as a professional witness, police officers must have a clear understanding of the role that witnesses play in criminal proceedings. Despite misconceptions, it is not true that much of the evidence adduced at trial "speaks for itself." As Justice Dickson of the Supreme Court of Canada pointed out, "[o]ne of the hallmarks of the common law of evidence is that it relies on witnesses as the means by which evidence is produced in Court" (*R. v. Schwartz*, 1988, para. 59). The calling of witnesses forms the basis of our trial system (Paciocco & Stuesser, 2008, p. 399), and witnesses' oral testimony is "the lifeblood of the trial process" (Sankoff, 2006, p. 3).

Contrary to what some people might think, a police witness's role does not differ significantly from that of any other witness. In particular, it does *not* include trying to help the Crown convict the accused. As we saw in Chapter 18, The Duty of Disclosure, the Crown attorney's role as an officer of the court is not to obtain a conviction, but to serve the public by laying before a trier of fact what it considers to be credible, relevant evidence in relation to a criminal allegation. Although legal proof of the facts must be presented "firmly," it must also be done "fairly," without attaching any notion of winning or losing to it (*R. v. Boucher*, 1954, p. 24).

Similarly, although police officers must be prepared to give their evidence firmly, their job is not to assist the Crown attorney. Nonetheless, some police officers appear to believe that their role *as a witness* includes trying to help the Crown win its case. Because of such beliefs, some defence counsel believe that police officers often skew their testimony in favour of the Crown. For example, in his influential text the *Examination of Witnesses in Criminal Cases*, Earl Levy advises defence counsel to "always keep in mind that police officers generally are biased in favour of the prosecution and some may suffer from the human tendency to shade the truth in favour of the prosecution" (Levy, 2004, p. 396).

Although at one time police officers were presumed to be highly credible witnesses whose word was rarely questioned, experienced investigators will acknowledge that such credibility is no longer taken for granted by either the public or the courts. As a result, police officers must work harder to establish and maintain their trustworthiness as professional witnesses; to establish such trust, they must have a clear understanding of their proper role as witnesses in the criminal process. During evidence-in-chief, their role is to give an accurate and objective account of what they did or observed in the course of an investigation. During cross-examination, it is to respond truthfully and fairly to the questions put to them by defence counsel.

To function effectively as a witness in a criminal proceeding, officers must appreciate the distinction between the various aspects of their role that *do* involve trying to prove who is responsible for committing a crime—for example, their duty to investigate alleged offences, gather evidence, arrest alleged offenders, lay charges, and participate in prosecutions—and their duty as a witness. From the moment a police officer steps into the witness box, he or she has only *one* duty—that is, to tell the truth. This does not mean that officers must become passive witnesses who allow themselves to be manipulated and intimidated by defence counsel. On the contrary, officers should be prepared to give their evidence fully, fairly, and firmly, and may properly oppose defence efforts to mischaracterize what they believe, on the basis of their own actions or observations, to be true and accurate aspects of their evidence.

Despite the fact that officers routinely testify in court, relatively little research has been conducted on how they *experience* this process. The research that does exist suggests that, although officers have relatively little difficulty testifying during evidence-in-chief, cross-examination poses a number of significant challenges that can negatively affect an officer's ability to give credible evidence (Kebbell & O'Kelly, 2007, pp. 8–9). Therefore, in the discussion, immediately below, of the three stages in which evidence is heard during a criminal proceeding—examination-in-chief, cross-examination, and re-examination—we focus primarily on the cross-examination process.

EXAMINATION-IN-CHIEF

examination-in-chief
a party's questioning of its own witnesses

The first stage in which evidence is heard in a criminal trial is referred to as **examination-in-chief** (sometimes called evidence-in-chief or direct examination). During examination-in-chief, the witness is questioned by the party (Crown or defence) that called them. In the case of police officers, that party is, typically, the Crown attorney (Paciocco & Stuesser, 2008, p. 413).

Exclusion of Witnesses

Before the Crown calls its first witness (and, ideally, before the Crown makes any opening submissions), counsel will typically ask the judge to make an order excluding witnesses from the courtroom until such time as they are actually required to give their evidence; although the judge is not compelled to make such an order, he or she will usually do so. Such orders exclude both prosecution and defence witnesses, but not the accused. The Crown will often ask the judge to make an exemption for the officer in charge of the investigation, so that the officer may be allowed to remain in the courtroom to assist the prosecution.

An order excluding witnesses serves a number of related purposes:

- it helps prevent the testimony of earlier witnesses from contaminating the testimony of witnesses who testify later;

- it helps to prevent witnesses intentionally colluding with one another to "fix" their stories while the trial is progressing;

- it can help to reveal similarities in the evidence of different witnesses, which may indicate earlier attempts to "get their stories straight" before trial; and

- it prevents witnesses from listening to all the evidence, which might assist them in anticipating what sorts of questions they may be asked during cross-examination.

(Bryant, Lederman, & Fuerst, 2009, p. 1099.)

Manner of Questioning

During examination-in-chief, a witness does not just step into the witness box and begin to give evidence; rather, evidence is elicited from witnesses in the form of answers given to questions put to them by the party who called them. The question and answer format serves a number of purposes:

1. it structures the way in which evidence is presented;

2. it helps ensure that only relevant, admissible evidence is given by the witness; and

3. it serves a strategic function by allowing the party who called the witness to selectively elicit evidence from "their" witness.

(Paciocco & Stuesser, 2008, p. 413.)

During evidence-in-chief, the party who called the witness is generally limited to asking open-ended questions to elicit evidence from that witness. Open-ended questions are preferable because they minimize the influence of the questioner on the evidence of the witness—an important consideration, because the court wants to hear the witness's evidence in the purest form possible, not the witness's evidence as influenced by what the lawyer wants the witness to say.

Open-ended questions of the kind a witness might be asked in evidence-in-chief include, but are not limited to, the classic, "who," "what," "why," "when" and "where," sorts of questions—for example, "Where were you when it happened?" "Who, if anyone, was with you?" "Why did you do that?" "What, if anything, did you do next?" Evidence can also be elicited from the witness in response to statements such as "Tell me more about that" and "Describe the vehicle that you just mentioned." When eliciting evidence from a witness during evidence-in-chief, the key requirement is to allow witnesses to tell their own story with as little input as possible from the party who called them (Paciocco & Stuesser, 2008, p. 414). As a police witness, if the Crown asks you a question, and the defence lawyer makes an objection, be quiet until the matter is resolved and the Crown either rephrases the question or the judge instructs you to answer the question.

Although leading questions are a standard technique employed by defence counsel in cross-examination (described below), only certain types of leading questions are

open-ended question
a question that gives the person to whom it is directed the opportunity to give a full and detailed response—for example, "Tell me about Mr. Smith."

OBJECTIONS

Judges have a great deal of discretion when it comes to enforcing the rules of evidence. Both Crown and defence counsel can make objections while a witness is giving evidence. The primary reason for making an objection is to draw the court's attention to what is believed, by the party making the objection, to be improper evidence in an attempt to have the judge rule that the evidence is inadmissible (Stuesser, 2005, p. 311). An objection thereby serves to highlight a potentially problematic piece of evidence and requires the court to rule on its admissibility.

Given that the law of evidence tends toward allowing, as opposed to excluding, evidence that is probative, judges may overrule counsel's objection and allow a particular piece of information to be admitted into evidence; the issue then becomes what is the proper weight to attach to that piece of evidence. Although it is ultimately up to the court to make that determination, counsel, by making an objection and calling a particular piece of evidence into question, may succeed in causing the court to attach less weight to the evidence than it might otherwise have done had no objection been made.

As a rule, when making a proper objection, counsel must be specific about what they are objecting to. For example, a police witness may be giving evidence during examination-in-chief, and defence counsel may rise and object that Crown counsel is leading the witness. If defence counsel makes an objection while an officer is giving evidence, the officer should simply stop talking. This allows the judge either to sustain the objection and require that the Crown rephrase its question or elicit the evidence in some other way or to overrule the objection and instruct the witness to continue and answer the question.

While a police witness is giving evidence during examination-in-chief, defence counsel may object that Crown counsel is:

- suggesting answers to the witness (leading questions);
- asking the witness to tell the court about what someone else has said (hearsay);
- asking the witness about things that have nothing to do with the issues being dealt with at trial (relevancy); or
- asking the witness to express an opinion that the witness is not qualified to give (opinion evidence).

Although there are a number of potential grounds on which defence counsel can object, in contrast to popular portrayals of trials in movies and on television where counsel frequently and dramatically object, in practice counsel tend to be selective and will likely object only to more serious issues. If defence counsel objects too frequently and to too many issues, they risk irritating the judge, calling their own credibility into question, and highlighting the very evidence that they are seeking to have excluded (Stuesser, 2005, chap. 15).

leading question
a question that suggests an answer to the person to whom it is directed, and limits their opportunity to respond to either a "yes" or "no" response, or to a short response—for example, "Was Mr. Smith a nice man?"

considered appropriate during evidence-in-chief, and the use of leading questions at this stage may negatively affect the weight given to the witness's evidence. Leading questions are often described as questions that ask for a "yes" or a "no" response, but, more accurately, a **leading question** is one that, in the context in which it is asked, suggests the answer. Determining whether a question is a leading question—or leading to the degree that it should be objected to—is often a matter of judging the *degree* to which it suggests the answer rather than whether it simply *is* suggestive of an answer (Paciocco & Stuesser 2008, p. 417; Bryant et al., 2009, p. 1107).

There are two types of leading questions:

1. those that directly or indirectly suggest the answer to the witness; and

2. those that presuppose the existence of a fact that has not been testified to by the witness.

Examples of the first type of leading question—that is, questions that suggest an answer—include: "How fast was the red car going before it hit the blue car?" (suggesting that the red car was speeding before the collision); and "Did you stop at the red light before entering the intersection?" (indirectly suggesting that stopping at a red light is a good thing to do, thus influencing the witness's answer). A more appropriate way to elicit information from the witness in the first scenario is for counsel simply to ask what, if anything, the witness can say about the red car before the collision, and, in the second scenario, what if anything did the witness do before entering the intersection (Paciocco & Stuesser, 2008, p. 414). The use of this kind of leading question may be appropriate, even preferred, in certain circumstances—for example, where:

- the question refers to matters that are undisputed or introductory in nature—for example, "I understand that you are a police detective?"

- the question is used to identify persons or things—for example, "Have you ever seen this shoe before?"

- the question is used to contradict statements made by another person—for example, "Would it be correct to state that John Smith said you punched him in the face?"

- the question is used to help explain complicated, or technical issues—for example, "I understand that fingerprints have to be "lifted" on a piece of plastic before they can be fed into the AFIS computer for analysis?"

- the witness is having difficulty answering the question, whether because of language, age, or cognitive abilities, and the court has given permission to lead the witness—for example, "Did John tell you not to tell anyone else about what happened while you were at his cottage?"

- the question will help refresh the witness's memory and the court has given permission to lead the witness—for example, where a witness previously mentioned the name of a person that he or she met, but is temporarily unable to recall the person's name—"Did you also meet Jim Peterson?"

- regardless of circumstance, in the interests of justice, the court has given permission to lead the witness.

(Paciocco & Stuesser, 2008, pp. 416–417.)

The second type of leading question is *not* appropriate for use during either evidence-in-chief or cross-examination. This type of question presupposes the existence of a fact that the witness has not testified to (unless there is no controversy about the presupposed fact)—for example, "What did you do after you stopped at the red light?" would be an inappropriate question unless the witness had testified earlier to having stopped at the red light. These kinds of leading questions are inappropriate for three reasons—they may

1. lead the trier of fact to believe that a fact has been testified to when it has not;
2. cause a witness to respond to the question itself without challenging what is implicit in the question—that is, that the witness did in fact stop at the red light; and
3. suggest to the witness that the implied fact actually occurred.

To the extent that this type of "question" does not call for comment on the presupposed fact, it is not really a question at all (Paciocco & Stuesser, 2008, pp. 415–416).

During examination-in-chief, if a witness omits certain details in his or her answer, counsel may pose follow-up questions to seek the desired information. For example:

Crown: Officer, did you observe any animals at the scene?

Officer: I saw a dog.

Crown: Officer, can you describe the dog?

Officer: He was brown.

Crown: Officer, did you make any other observations about the dog?

Officer: He appeared to have a red substance on his muzzle, his coat was covered in something dark, and he appeared wet. When I first saw him, he was chewing on something.

Crown: Thank you, officer.

CROSS-EXAMINATION

Cross-examination can be an anxiety-producing experience for even the most experienced professional witnesses. Witnesses who have a clear understanding of their role and of the purpose of cross-examination will be well equipped to give their evidence fairly and accurately to the court. However, witnesses who fear cross-examination or who adopt a combative attitude toward defence counsel rarely fare well.

Although cross-examination is used by both Crown and defence counsel, our focus in this chapter is on the cross-examination of police witnesses by defence counsel.

Purpose of Cross-Examination

The right of an accused to cross-examine prosecution witnesses "without significant and unwarranted constraint" is an essential element of the right to make a full answer and defence (*Lyttle*, 2004, para. 41) and is protected by ss. 7 and 11(d) of the Charter.

cross-examination
the questioning of a witness
by opposing counsel

Cross-examination has been called "the greatest legal engine ever invented for the discovery of truth" (Wigmore, as cited in *Innisfil Township v. Bespra Township*, 1981, p. 167); although this may overstate the power of cross-examination (or any legal process) to determine what really took place during a historical event such as a crime, cross-examination *is* a central feature of the criminal trial process.

Determining which side is telling the truth is often a difficult task for the trier of fact, because evidence is not as trustworthy as is commonly believed (Wellman, 1997, p. 27). This is not primarily because people lie when giving evidence (although, on occasion, some do), but rather because of witnesses' honest but mistaken beliefs about the accuracy of their evidence. Although the most "dramatic" quality of cross-examination is its power to detect deliberately false testimony, its greater value is in exposing "errors of perception, defects of memory and deficiencies of narration" (Morgan, 1927, quoted in Bryant et al., 2009, p. 1148). These can stem from any or all of cognitive biases, prejudice, partiality, and a limited capacity or ability to make accurate observations of events in the first instance.

Because errors can result from the direct examination of even honest witnesses, to prevent erroneous testimony from being received by the court, evidence should be tested in "the fire of cross-examination" (Morgan, 1927, quoted in Bryant et al., 2009, p. 1148). This process can expose falsehood, correct error and distortion, and uncover vital information that would not otherwise be brought to light (*R. v. Lyttle*, 2004, para. 1). Cross-examination is therefore the primary tool used to test:

1. the credibility of a witness, and

2. the reliability of the evidence a witness gives to a court.

The importance of cross-examination to the defence cannot be overstated. Trial lawyers believed a hundred years ago, and still believe today, that cross-examination is an important factor in determining their success at trial. As some have said, "[t]he advocate is not a scientific and disinterested truth-seeker, [but] ... first and foremost *a seller of a story*. The advocate's job at trial is to fashion and present ... a version of the truth—the client's version of reality" (Underwood, 1997, p. 121, emphasis added).

For defence counsel, therefore, cross-examination provides the opportunity to:

1. weaken the Crown's case, strengthen their own case, or both; and

2. create a reasonable doubt as to the guilt of their client in the mind of the court.

Defence counsel do not automatically cross-examine *all* prosecution witnesses. Instead, they ask themselves questions to determine whether it is necessary to cross-examine a particular prosecution witness (Salhany, 2006, p. 48). These may include whether the witness has testified to anything that runs counter to the defence

IN THE WORDS OF THE COURT

There can be no question of the importance of cross-examination. It is of essential importance in determining whether a witness is credible. Even with the most honest witness cross-examination can provide the means to explore the frailties of the testimony. For example, it can demonstrate a witness's weakness of sight or hearing. It can establish that the existing weather conditions may have limited the ability of a witness to observe, or that medication taken by the witness would have distorted vision or hearing. Its importance cannot be denied. It is the ultimate means of demonstrating truth and of testing veracity. Cross-examination must be permitted so that an accused can make full answer and defence. The opportunity to cross-examine witnesses is fundamental to providing a fair trial to an accused. This is an old and well established principle that is closely linked to the presumption of innocence.

Source: Justice Cory, in *R. v. Osolin* (1993, section IIIA(1)).

theory of the case; whether the witness has given testimony that is damaging to the defence case; whether the witness made an impression on the trier of fact that is damaging to the defence case; and whether it would be possible to elicit something favourable to the defence case from the witness.

In cross-examining a witness, defence counsel seek to achieve several specific goals. These include (Salhany, 2006, p. 48; Stuesser, 2005, p. 245; Underwood, 1997, p. 119; Bryant et al., 2009, p. 1133):

- to discredit testimony that a witness gave during evidence-in-chief that is harmful to the defence;
- to discredit the unfavourable testimony of another, opposing witness;
- to corroborate the testimony of another, favourable witness;
- to bring out evidence that is favourable to the defence, but which was not elicited from a witness during evidence-in-chief; and
- to show that the witness is unworthy of belief and weaken the effect of his or her testimony.

However the goals are set out, "the overall objective of cross-examination for the defence is to create reasonable doubt" regarding the Crown's case, while promoting its own theory of the case (Levy, 2004, p. 103).

The "Ten Commandments" of Cross-Examination

Cross-examination is a source of anxiety not only for police witnesses; it can have the same effect on defence counsel, especially novice lawyers. Cross-examination is the stage of a criminal trial at which defence counsel are most vulnerable, yet it is also the stage at which they are expected to perform most effectively—engaging witnesses in an intellectual battle, exposing the weaknesses in their testimony, and scoring dramatic points on behalf of their clients.

The source of anxiety for defence counsel in cross-examination is fear of the unknown. Defence counsel often do not know the witnesses they are cross-examining or what they might say during cross-examination. Therefore, counsel are advised to learn as much as they can about the witnesses—through evidence witnesses have given during a preliminary inquiry and from material included in Crown disclosure—before cross-examining them. Counsel are also advised to carefully structure their cross-examination to maximize the opportunity for eliciting information favourable to their case while minimizing the opportunity for the witness to talk about anything that might damage the defence position. Learning about the witnesses before questioning them and carefully designing both the overall questioning strategy and the individual questions counsel ask is designed to allow defence counsel to create that one element that is essential to the successful cross-examination of any witness—control (Stuesser, 2005, pp. 243–245; see also the discussion in the next section).

Being aware of the number of rules that are likely to guide defence counsel in cross-examining a Crown witness provides a witness with a better understanding of the cross-examination process. These rules have been expressed in various forms over the years, but the form that is perhaps most often reproduced is referred to as "the ten commandments" of cross-examination (Younger, 1976):

1. Be brief.

2. Use plain words and short questions.

3. Ask only leading questions.

4. Be prepared—that is, don't ask a question to which you don't know the answer.

5. Listen to the witness's answers.

6. Don't quarrel with the witness.

7. Don't allow the witness to repeat his direct testimony.

8. Don't permit the witness to explain his answers.

9. Limit questioning—that is, don't ask the "one question too many."

10. Save the main point of your cross for summation.

Creating Control

In the words of one authority, if there were *one* commandment for cross-examination, it should be: "Thou shalt control the witness" (Levy, 2004, p. 181). Defence counsel use various techniques, including "the ten commandments," to establish and maintain control over Crown witnesses. These techniques, along with recommended responses to them, are summarized in the chart on pages 378–379.

One of the finest cross-examiners in Canada, John Rosen, has the following as his first rule of cross-examination: "[N]ever ask questions that allow you to lose control" (quoted in Small, 2009). Experienced Canadian defence lawyer John Struthers has said, similarly, that "cross-examination is about what the lawyer has to say, not what the witness has to say" (Small, 2009). Thus, another critical element to conducting a successful cross-examination is controlling the witness's answers to the questions that witnesses *are* asked. The witness must not be permitted to steer the examination "into areas where he or she wishes to go thereby giving answers which could be potentially detrimental to the questioner's position" (Levy, 2004, p. 181). Given this emphasis on control, what kinds of questions can a police witness expect to be asked during cross-examination?

As a result of television and movie portrayals of the trial process, some witnesses and some inexperienced counsel may believe that one of the best ways to control a witness's response to a question is to demand that the witness give either "yes" or "no" answers. Such a tactic is intended to prevent witnesses from explaining their answers or supplying the necessary detail and context to make them fully intelligible. Despite the fact that defence counsel are given a great deal of latitude to cross-examine Crown witnesses in Canadian courts, a judge is unlikely to allow counsel to engage in this sort of yes-or-no demand as a blanket approach to questioning.

Witnesses are "entitled to give a full and complete answer" in response to the questions put to them (Salhany, 2006, p. 76; see also Brauti, 1997, p. 103). Nonetheless, if defence counsel asks a question that *can* reasonably be answered with either a "yes" or a "no," the witness should answer accordingly; to do otherwise would be unnecessarily difficult, which will detract from the witness's effectiveness. However, if defence counsel demands a yes or no answer to a question that cannot reasonably be answered in this way, witnesses might respond by stating that they are not able to accurately answer the question with either a yes or a no response and then proceed to answer in their own words. Alternatively, witnesses might say that their answer is composed of a number of parts, and then proceed to address each as they answer the question.

If defence counsel interrupts and continues to demand that the witness answer with either a "yes" or a "no," the witness should pause. A pause will give Crown counsel the opportunity to object; it may also prompt the judge to intercede and permit the witness to complete the answer in his or her own words (Sherriff, 2003, p. 419). Be advised, however, that permission from the court to answer a question in your own words is not licence to make a speech or to evade the question; witnesses must respond to the questions they are asked.

If, as a general rule, defence counsel are not allowed to insist that a witness give only a yes or no response to their questions during a cross-examination, how can they maintain that all-important element of control? There are two common approaches to this issue: the first involves the use of leading questions, and the second involves the use of questions framed as statements of fact or suggestions. Police witnesses can expect to be asked both kinds of questions.

Leading Questions

Asking open-ended questions such as: "Why do you say that?" "What do you mean?" or "What happened next?" is one of the easiest ways for defence counsel to lose control, because it allows a witness to "explain" his or her answer, thus violating one of the ten commandments of cross-examination (Younger, 1976; Stuesser, 2005, pp. 259–260; Bogoroch, 2005, p. 6). To try and prevent witnesses from explaining their answers, defence counsel are advised to "lead" the witness—in fact, they are told to, in effect, "tell the witness what to say." This is achieved through the use of "closed" or "leading" questions.

Although the use of leading questions is generally forbidden during evidence-in-chief, it is permissible during cross-examination; as a result, police witnesses can reasonably expect that the majority of the questions they will be asked during a typical cross-examination will be leading. In fact, witnesses can expect that defence counsel will attempt to phrase such questions so as to ideally, but not always, elicit a series of yes or no responses from the witness (Levy, 2004, p. 181). For example:

> Q: Officer Jones, you identified my client as one of the men you saw running out of the bank that night, didn't you?
>
> A: Yes.
>
> Q: You had never seen my client before the day of the bank robbery, had you?
>
> A: No.
>
> Q: How can you be sure that my client was one of the men you saw running out of the bank?
>
> A: Because he ran out of the bank with the two other guys, we chased all three of them and caught them a short distance away, and he was one of those guys.
>
> Q: So you saw all three men run out of the bank at the same time?
>
> A: Yes.
>
> Q: The three men were running quite quickly, weren't they?
>
> A: Yes.
>
> Q: You had only a fraction of a second to look at the faces of all three men, from a distance, in the dark, before they fled, didn't you?

A: Yes.

Q: You didn't have the opportunity to study all three of their faces closely before they ran away, did you?

A: No.

Q: All three men were wearing dark-coloured clothing when they were arrested that night, weren't they?

A: Yes.

Q: Isn't it true that it was your partner, Officer Smith, who was the first one to see the three men run out of the bank?

A: Yes.

Q: In fact, you were driving the police car that night, and you only looked toward the bank after Officer Smith said that he saw three men running out through the bank door, isn't that right?

A: Yes.

The effect of this series of leading questions is clear: defence counsel is able to control the witness by constraining his possible responses. The officer is thus forced to give a series of mostly yes or no replies to the questions he is asked. In this particular example, defence counsel is able to use leading questions to make two important points: first, Officer Jones did not have a good opportunity to see the accused, and, second, Officer Jones's identification of the accused as one of the three men seen running out of the bank was not entirely independent of, and may have been influenced by, what Officer Smith said he saw.

Witnesses might reasonably respond to leading questions by focusing on the facts as they know and understand them, and basing their response to the questions on that knowledge and understanding, rather than on the premises inherent in the question. For example, if a witness were asked the question, "How tall was the bearded man who entered the store," but the witness knew from having reviewed surveillance video that the man who entered the store was approximately 6 feet tall and clean shaven, the witness might respond by saying, "The man who entered the store was clean shaven, and was approximately 6 feet in height."

Questions Framed as Statements of Fact or Suggestions

Another questioning technique that defence counsel commonly use to control a witness is asking questions framed as statements of fact or suggestions. These types of questions often start with phrases such as, "Wouldn't it be fair to say," or, "I suggest to you that"—for example, "Wouldn't it be fair to say that my client was a hard-working man who devoted a great deal of his time to the company?" or "I suggest to you that my client was a hard-working man who devoted a great deal of his time to the company." Of course, it's possible that a witness could answer "no," but this would likely be less damaging to the defence than an answer given in response to an open-ended question such as, "What kind of man would you say my client is?" When faced with an open-ended question of this kind, a witness has more latitude to expand on their answer, with greater potential for damage to the defence case. Although there is no guarantee that defence counsel will elicit a favourable response to questions framed as statements of fact or suggestions, such questions give them more control and restrict the opportunity for a witness to give an expansive, negative response (Salhany, 2006, p. 76).

Defence Tactics for Controlling a Witness

In addition to methods intended to attack their credibility and questions designed to control their responses, witnesses should be prepared for other tactics that may be used to further manipulate them and render them less-effective. Recognizing that such tactics exist—and understanding why they are used—can help you react appropriately when faced with them.

Tactic	Defence Actions	Reasonable Response
Condescending approach	Counsel might treat the witness in a condescending manner to give the court the impression that the witness is insecure, incompetent, and unreliable.	Focus on the questions you are being asked, not on counsel's attitude. Give firm, decisive answers.
Friendly approach	Counsel might smile at the witness, asking questions in a polite, low-key fashion to decrease the witness's anxiety and increase his or her sense of well-being. Counsel thereby hopes the witness will respond with answers favourable to the defence case. Remember, defence counsel has two objectives during the cross-examination: to diminish the impact of the witness's evidence or to diminish the witness's credibility. Neither of these involves making a new friend.	Focus on the content of the question while trying not to be influenced by the manner in which it is asked.
Nasty approach	Counsel might raise his or her voice, stare at the witness, or ask questions quickly and repetitively, demanding that the witness answer immediately, hoping to evoke an emotional response from the witness—either fear or anger—thus making the witness appear less objective and rational.	Do not allow yourself to be drawn in by these tactics. Pause, remind yourself why counsel is behaving in this way, collect your thoughts, then answer the question in a calm and controlled manner.
Alternative or "trick" question	Counsel might ask the witness whether he or she has discussed the case with anyone else. This question is designed to make witnesses feel they have done something wrong by doing so, in the hope that the witness will deny it, or to make it appear that, as a result of having such discussions, the witness's evidence has been tainted.	A police witness most likely *will* have discussed the case with other involved officers and with the Crown prosecutor. Do not hesitate to admit to having such discussions, if you did. Do not concern yourself with the potential consequences of giving truthful, candid responses, but *do* be on guard against any tendency to give evasive responses out of a misplaced sense of fear.
Repeat question	Counsel might ask a witness the same question repeatedly, sometimes in a slightly different form, to elicit inconsistent or conflicting answers. The Supreme Court has ruled that repetition of questions that have already been answered is improper (*R. v. Fanjoy*, 1985).	Listen carefully to the questions you are asked. If you have already been asked and have answered a particular question, politely indicate this ("I have already answered that question"), then sit quietly and wait for the next question.

Tactic	Defence Actions	Reasonable Response
Skipping approach	Counsel might skip from one subject to another during cross-examination, attempting to keep the witness off balance, making it more difficult for the witness to keep his or her story straight, and exposing the untruthful witness (Underwood, 1997, p. 120).	Take the time you need to ensure that you understand the question and think carefully about your answer before responding. There is no limit to how much time you can take to answer a question. The court expects you to be prepared and knowledgeable about the case, but does not expect perfection from you; if you need additional time to ensure that your answer is accurate, you will generally be allowed it. If you have been truthful in giving your evidence, you do not need to worry about the use of the skipping approach to expose untruthful testimony.
Stare down	Counsel might continue to stare at a witness who has answered a question to make the witness feel that he or she should expand on the answer.	Once you have answered the question, break eye contact and wait patiently for the next question.
"Other witness said"	Counsel might attempt to shake a witness's confidence in his or her answer by suggesting that it is inconsistent with something that another witness has said—for example, "Mr. Smith just told us that *he* saw the car drive through the intersection of Main and First at 11:00 p.m., and now *you* are telling us that the car went through that intersection at 11:15 p.m., is that right?"	If you are certain that you observed something at a specific time, stand firm and don't be shaken by the suggestion that another witness saw things differently. On the other hand, if you have only an approximate idea of the time you observed something, say so. In either case, focus on what you know and how you know it, and do not concern yourself with the testimony of other witnesses.
Deliberate error	Counsel might deliberately address a police witness by a higher rank—for example, refer to a constable as a detective or to a detective as an inspector. If counsel is able to do this several times without the witness correcting them, counsel may choose to "correct" the situation later, thereby embarrassing the witness by suggesting that he or she allowed the error to go uncorrected for the purpose of trying to look better by, for example, inflating his or her rank or status.	Correct such "errors" as soon as you notice them—for example, "My rank is constable, Sir, not detective."
Anti-defence reflex	Counsel might try to capitalize on the almost reflexive tendency of some police witnesses to disagree with any defence suggestion simply because the suggestion was made by the defence. (For example, defence counsel might say, "I suggest to you that my client was the first person you suspected of this crime.") Doing so might result in a police witness looking foolish, by attempting to deny or downplay things that are obvious or are of minimal consequence, and such behaviour can destroy credibility.	If the suggestion is true, then simply say so. Professional witnesses are most effective when they focus on the question they are being asked and answer it fully, fairly, and firmly, instead of focusing on who is asking the question.

Source: Adapted from Sherriff (2003, pp. 418–420); Underwood (1997, p. 120).

Common Methods of Discrediting a Witness

During cross-examination, witnesses can expect to encounter attempts to challenge or discredit their testimony. In this section we consider four methods commonly employed for this purpose that focus on demonstrating how a witness's testimony is:

- based on limited witness abilities,
- inconsistent with other witnesses or evidence,
- inconsistent with common sense, or
- inconsistent with prior statements made by the witness.

Browne v. Dunn rule
a rule of fairness stating that if counsel is going to challenge the credibility of a witness by calling contradictory evidence, the witness must be given an opportunity to address the contradictory evidence

Counsel who intend to discredit a witness on a specific point must, according to the **Browne v. Dunn rule**, cross-examine that witness on that specific point. This ensures that the witness has the opportunity to explain or clarify evidence that defence counsel will ask the court to disbelieve. Fairness dictates that such an exercise should not take place after a witness has left the witness box, in an "after the fact" attack on the witness's credibility. However, counsel are neither expected nor required to give witnesses multiple opportunities to explain or clarify potential inconsistencies in their evidence. Asking the witness a few questions that raise inconsistencies between the witness's evidence and the defence position is generally sufficient (Brauti, 1997, p. 96).

Evidence Based on Limited Abilities

There are at least three areas of witness ability that can be attacked by defence counsel during cross-examination:

- *Observation.* Defence counsel may ask questions designed to show that the witness was not able to accurately observe the event they have described because of a number of factors, including physical impairments (for example, poor eyesight); environmental conditions (for example, heavy rain, darkness, obstacles); or location (for example, the witness was not in a position to be able to perceive accurately). Questions of this kind are designed to illustrate that the witness did not have a good opportunity to observe the event in the first instance.

- *Memory.* Defence counsel may ask questions designed to show that the witness's memory is limited or has been contaminated, and is affecting the quality of his or her evidence—for example, that too much time has passed since the witness first observed the event:

    Q: Officer, the event you are describing, in which you say you observed my client jumping over a fence with a knife in his hand, occurred over a year ago, is that correct?

    A: Yes.

    Q: Officer, did you make detailed notes of those observations?

    A: Well, I noted that I saw a guy in a blue jacket with white sneakers jump over the fence with a knife in his hand, yes.

    Q: Officer, is that all that you wrote down?

    A: Yes.

Q: Officer, do you have any recollection of whether any of the other men arrested along with my client were also wearing a blue jacket and white sneakers?

A: I don't remember anyone else was wearing the same clothing, no.

Q: But, Officer, you have no notation of the clothing worn by the other men, is that correct?

A: That's correct.

Q: And would you not agree with me, Officer, that, generally speaking, our memories do not improve with time?

A: I would agree, yes.

Q: So, Officer, it's possible that one of the other men may have been wearing the same type of clothing and you just don't remember.

A: Well, I don't think anyone else was wearing the same clothing, but it's possible, I guess.

Q: So, Officer, you cannot be certain, on the basis of your memory from more than a year ago, that my client was the only one dressed in a blue jacket and white sneakers, can you?

A: Well, I think he was the only one; he was the only one I remember, but I can't say for sure, no.

Q: Thank you, Officer, I have no more questions.

The passage of time between when an event is observed and later described in a courtroom can distort a witness's recollection of the event, either as a result of imperfect recollection or through contamination from other sources of information about the event—for example, other witnesses or media reports.

- *Articulation.* Counsel might also attack the witness's ability to articulate what he or she observed—in other words, the witness's ability to accurately translate his or her experience into words. This ability, or lack thereof, can have a significant impact on the accuracy of a witness's evidence. Defence counsel can be expected, therefore, to ask questions designed to show that the witness has, for example, confused observations with assumptions— that is, the witness is assuming that something took place on the basis of the circumstances surrounding the event, rather than because the witness actually observed it:

A: Well, when my partner and I pulled into the alleyway we saw a guy lying in a pool of blood, and then we saw two guys run out from behind a dumpster with hoodies pulled up over their heads. So my partner and I chased them down and arrested them for the assault.

Q: Officer, you did not see these two men actually assault the victim, did you?

A: Well, no but they were the only people around, and they took off running when they saw us pull into the alleyway, and when we arrested them they both had blood on their sweatshirts.

Q: Well, Officer, would you be surprised if I told you that these two men were actually trying to help the victim, who, when they found him in the alley, had already been beaten up?

A: I don't think that is what happened.

Q: Officer, the victim couldn't tell you who assaulted him because all he remembers is getting hit on the back of the head, is that correct?

A: Yes, that's right.

Q: So, Officer, it is possible that these men were telling you the truth when they said they had nothing to do with the assault, isn't it?

A: Well, it's possible, I guess, but I don't think so.

Q: But, Officer, is it not true that neither you nor your partner saw these two men assault the victim, and you were not able to locate any witnesses, isn't that correct?

A: Yes.

Q: So, Officer, is it fair to say that you made an assumption that my clients assaulted the victim, based on the circumstances you observed that night?

A: Well, they were the only ones around.

Q: But neither you nor anyone else actually witnessed the assault, isn't that correct?

A: Well, I guess so; when you put it that way, that's true, yes.

Defence can also be expected to ask questions designed to show that although the witness might accurately have observed something, the witness's description has left a distorted impression with the court (Bryant et al., 2009, pp. 1147–1148).

Inconsistent with Other Witnesses or Evidence

Despite the fact that the credibility of police officers today is no longer taken for granted to the degree it once was, many defence counsel still regard the cross-examination of a police witness as a challenging task, and believe that attacking an officer's credibility head-on (in the absence of any evidence indicating that the officer is lying) is unlikely to be successful (Salhany, 2006, p. 108; Levy, 2004, p. 395). Experienced police officers often develop a style of giving evidence that causes them to be perceived as honest and confident, and police officers, in general, still enjoy a good level of trust among the public at large. As a result, some counsel believe that the best way to impeach a police witness is to demonstrate that his or her testimony during evidence-in-chief is inconsistent with the evidence given by another credible witness—ideally, another police officer (Salhany, 2006, pp. 108–109; Levy, 2006, chap. 17). Defence may also attempt to highlight inconsistencies between the officer's testimony and other evidence—for example, documents.

Inconsistent with Common Sense

The evidence of a police witness may sometimes be discredited simply by highlighting how it is inconsistent with common sense and shared experience. For example, a witness who claims to have the extraordinary ability to recall details of events that occurred months or even years before without reference to any notes or other records may find their evidence discredited because we all "know" that it is difficult to accurately recall details of past events unaided; our own experience tells us that our memories for such details do not generally improve with the passage of time. Similarly, an eyewitness who claims to have accurately observed some specific detail—for example, a tattoo on a suspect's neck—from 50 feet away on a dark, rainy night is likely to find that evidence discredited because shared experience tells us that the chance of anyone being able to make such an observation accurately under such conditions is slight.

Inconsistent with Prior Statements

Any witness, including a police witness, may be cross-examined on an earlier statement for the purpose of showing inconsistencies between that statement and what the witness is saying at trial. A prior statement is considered to be any account of something made by the witness either:

1. in writing—for example, in police notes;

2. reduced to writing—for example, a court transcript; or

3. recorded electronically—for example, comments made during a news conference.

The law allows witnesses to be cross-examined on a "prior inconsistent statement" for the purpose of either proving a fact in issue or attacking the witness's credibility. Defence counsel might attempt to show that the witness has made inconsistent statements to demonstrate that the witness is, for any number of reasons, including bias, poor observation skills, poor ability to recollect, or a willingness to lie, capable of making errors in his or her evidence. Highlighting in court the witness's capacity for making errors places that witness's overall credibility in doubt.

Restrictions on Cross-Examination

Defence counsel are given a great deal of latitude when cross-examining witnesses. Essentially, any question that is relevant to the issues at trial or to a witness's credibility is fair game (Bryant et al., 2009, p. 1134). The Supreme Court has said that an accused has the right to cross-examine prosecution witnesses without "significant and unwarranted constraint" (*Lyttle*, 2004, para. 41), but there are limits to what defence can do during a cross-examination. However, the limitations placed on counsel affect the Crown more than they do the defence (Brauti, 1997, p. 71).

The limits on defence fall into two broad categories: general conduct and questioning.

General Conduct

As "officers of the court," counsel are bound by a code of professional conduct that prohibits them from being unnecessarily abusive toward a witness. Counsel are also prohibited from threatening a witness during cross-examination. It is also improper for counsel to attempt to intimidate a witness during cross-examination by, for example, repeatedly reminding them while they are testifying that they are still under oath (Brauti, 1997, p. 93).

CROSS-EXAMINING A WITNESS REGARDING A PRIOR INCONSISTENT STATEMENT

Counsel are recommended to take a number of steps when cross-examining an opposing witness on a prior inconsistent statement (Stuesser, 2005, pp. 292–297):

1. *Confirm.* Counsel will seek to have the witness confirm his or her present testimony to ensure that it is clear and to prevent the witness from being able to explain away any inconsistencies by claiming, for example, that counsel has misunderstood the witness's answer, that the witness did not understand counsel's question, or that the witness did not say what he or she meant to say. Defence counsel are advised to highlight the part of the witness's testimony that is inconsistent so that the inconsistency is perfectly obvious later in the process when it is contrasted with the witness's earlier evidence. For example: "Officer Jones, during your evidence-in-chief at this trial, you were asked by the Crown attorney, 'What was the accused doing when you first arrived at the accident scene?' and in response you said, 'She was walking around the scene with some difficulty, like she was unsteady on her feet.' Is that correct?" The officer will presumably confirm the evidence, given that it is contained in the court record. Defence counsel will later seek to contrast this statement with one given during the earlier preliminary inquiry.

2. *Confront.* During this step, counsel may seek to emphasize the circumstances in which the witness made the prior statement. In our example, Officer Jones made the prior statement during the preliminary inquiry, six months before the trial in which he later testified. Counsel may have Officer Jones confirm that when the earlier statement was made the events were fresher in his mind; he knew that it was important to try and be as accurate as possible when giving his evidence, and he tried to do so; and, when he gave his testimony at the preliminary inquiry, he was under oath and gave his evidence truthfully.

3. *Contradict.* Next, counsel may put the prior inconsistent statement to the witness. Some defence counsel refer to the actual transcript of the earlier proceeding during this process, because it allows them to put the exact question to the witness that was put to them in the earlier proceeding and to show the witness exactly what was said in the earlier proceeding in the event that the witness says that he or she didn't make or can't remember making the statement. For example, defence counsel might say: "Officer Jones, during the preliminary inquiry you were asked by the Crown attorney, 'What was the accused doing when you first arrived at the accident scene?' and you responded, 'The accused was walking around the accident scene speaking to various emergency services personnel and bystanders.' Is that correct?" The officer will presumably answer "yes," because the words are right there. A significant inconsistency has thus been established between the officer's evidence at trial (the accused was having difficulty walking and appeared unsteady) and the officer's evidence at the preliminary inquiry (the accused was walking around talking to people, with no mention of unsteadiness or difficulty).

4. *Commit.* At this point, counsel may have the witness commit to the prior statement by asking the officer: "When you gave that answer during the preliminary inquiry, your answer was truthful wasn't it?" When the officer answers, "Yes," he or she has now committed to the prior inconsistent statement. Once this stage has been reached, defence counsel are advised not to give the witness the opportunity to explain the inconsistency, but rather to provide counsel's explanation for the inconsistency during their closing argument. The witness can reasonably expect counsel to suggest that the officer is an incompetent witness who is unable to make consistent observations of important issues and thus cannot be relied on or that the officer has purposely changed his or her story at trial to make the accused look worse, and is thus not a fair and impartial witness who can be trusted.

For additional information on the issue of cross-examining opposing witnesses on prior inconsistent statements, see the *Canada Evidence Act*, ss. 10 and 11.

Defence counsel are restricted from giving evidence themselves during cross-examination. For example:

Q: Officer, would you agree that the roadway at the accident scene is 12 metres wide?

A: I believe it is actually 16 metres wide.

Q: I have been to the collision scene myself, and I measured the width of the road. It is only 12 metres wide. Is your evidence still that the road is 16 metres wide?

A: That is what I have recorded in my notes, yes.

Defence counsel would not be permitted to give evidence as to the width of the road—only witnesses who have sworn to tell the truth may give evidence. If defence counsel wants to provide evidence that contradicts a witness, they must do so through another witness. It is also improper for counsel to give evidence because the court, perhaps assuming that lawyers have special knowledge in the context of legal proceedings, may give it undue weight.

Questioning

Perhaps the first general rule of cross-examination is that counsel must ask relevant questions—that is, questions that bear on or are in someway related to the matters at issue.

A second general rule is that counsel must not ask questions whose prejudicial effect is stronger than their probative value—that is, questions that are more likely to create a negative impression of or lead to a negative inference about a witness than they are to assist the court in discovering the truth.

A third general restriction on cross-examination limits counsel to asking questions or making suggestions to a witness on what is called a "good faith basis." Simply put, this means that counsel must have a reasonable basis for believing that something is true before they can suggest it to a witness or ask a question about it. It follows, of course, that counsel cannot suggest things to a witness or ask questions about something that counsel *knows* to be false (Stuesser, 2005, pp. 287–288; Brauti, 1997; Bryant et al., 2009, p. 1135).

Under what is referred to as the "prior consistent statements" rule, counsel are not allowed to question a witness on a previous statement the witness made out of court that is consistent with a statement the witness is currently making in court (although there are some exceptions, such as circumstances in which a witness is alleged to have fabricated parts of his or her testimony: see *R. v. Stirling*, 2008). Prior consistent statements are generally inadmissible because they are seen as lacking in probative value—that is, they don't prove anything—and as self-serving (*R. v. Stirling*, 2008, para. 5).

Although this rule is perhaps most frequently applied when a witness is giving evidence during evidence-in-chief and is asked about a previous consistent statement, defence counsel may attempt to elicit such evidence from a police witness during cross-examination. For example, counsel may ask, "Officer, isn't it true that as soon as you arrested my client he told you that he knew nothing about the killing?" In some circumstances, this question may be allowed: the trial judge may admit spontaneous out-of-court statements made by an accused upon arrest or when first confronted with an accusation as evidence of the reaction of the accused to the accusation and as proof of consistency, as long as the accused takes the stand and allows himself or herself to be cross-examined. The statement will not provide evidence of the truth of what was said, but will provide evidence of the reaction of the accused, which is relevant to his or her credibility and as circumstantial evidence (*R. v. Edgar*, 2010, para. 72).

It is improper for counsel to ask a witness a question that calls for a legal conclusion. Commenting on the law is the job of the court, not the witness (Brauti, 1997, p. 100).

Counsel may not ask a witness questions during cross-examination unless the questions are relevant to an issue at trial or to the credibility of a witness. The primary reason for this rule is that irrelevant questions may distract the trier of fact from the issues the court is required to determine. For example, questions about a witness's sexual behaviour during a trial for fraud would be impermissible (Brauti, 1997).

It is not proper for counsel to ask a witness questions prefaced with phrases such as, "Do you honestly expect this court to believe that"; or "Are you honestly asking the jury to accept that evidence." The purpose of such questions is to belittle the witness and emphasize the fact that counsel does not believe the witness's evidence, not to elicit an answer to the question (Brauti, 1997, p. 101). Similarly, counsel may not ask questions that are intended solely to provoke an argument. A rhetorical question, such as "I suppose you are going to tell us next that the gun just went off?" invites the witness to engage in an argument rather than answer a question, and that is not the witness's role (Brauti, 1997, p. 102).

RE-EXAMINATION

re-examination
a party's questioning of its own witness after cross-examination has been completed

The purpose of **re-examination** is to ensure that a witness's evidence receives a fair hearing by allowing a witness to address significant issues that were raised during cross-examination, but which may have become confused or made less clear during that process. The witness is not allowed to augment the evidence given during examination-in-chief by introducing new material during re-examination; rather, the witness is generally confined to clarifying or explaining issues that arose out of cross-examination. Counsel can use re-examination as an opportunity to re-establish the credibility of a witness damaged during cross-examination by allowing the witness to explain any inconsistencies in the evidence pointed out during cross-examination.

In rare circumstances, a judge may allow counsel to re-examine a witness on issues that were not raised in cross-examination—namely, issues that counsel may simply have forgotten to raise during examination-in-chief. In such circumstances, opposing counsel will be given the opportunity to cross-examine the witness on any new issues that are addressed (Bryant et al., 2009, p. 1164; Stuesser, 2005, p. 212).

POLICE OFFICERS' NOTES

Responsible note taking has been called "part and parcel of a police officer's duty, and both an ethical and legal obligation of the police" (*R. v. B.(M.)*, 2006); nowhere is it more important than in the course of investigating an alleged crime.

As described in Chapter 2, Evidence in the Courtroom, officers may use their notes to help them give evidence in the prosecution of offences (see *R. v. Schertzer*, 2007, para. 16). Such testimony may take place months—or even years—after an event, and although an officer may have an independent recollection of certain aspects of the event, depending solely on memory as the basis for such testimony is inadequate. For these reasons, the careful preparation of comprehensive notes by officers documenting their activities, interactions, and observations related to an event, either at the time of the event or shortly thereafter, is an important professional practice.

The law with respect to police officers' notes has evolved over time. At one time, such notes were considered primarily an aid—a tool to help officers refresh their memory while or before giving testimony in court—and defence counsel were not allowed to view an officer's notes unless the officer referred to them while testifying. This is no longer the case. Since *Stinchcombe* (1991), officers are required to disclose all notes made in the course of an investigation, whether or not they refer to them or use them to refresh their memory while testifying.

In recent years, officers' notes have acquired an increased importance as evidentiary documents, playing a significant role in courts' assessments of an officer's evidence in a case. In particular, the quality of an officer's notes—that is, their accuracy and completeness—can have a major impact on an officer's perceived credibility as a witness. In addition to serving as a memory aid, an officer's notes can suggest that the officer considered an action or event important enough to record it; lend credence to an officer's testimony regarding observations and actions (if the notes were recorded at the time that or shortly after the events took place); and confirm that the officer did, in fact, say or do something that he or she claims to remember saying or doing (see *R. v. B.(M.)*, 2006, on the adequacy of police note-taking in the investigation, paras. 2 and 3). Where an officer fails to make a note or makes inadequate notes about an obviously significant event or observation, his or her credibility as a witness can suffer serious damage. In addition, a court may be reluctant to give much weight to an officer's verbal testimony in the absence of notes that corroborate what the officer claims to have observed or experienced (*R. v. Odgers*, 2009, para. 16).

Defence lawyers are well aware of how the quality of a police officer's notes can affect the officer's overall credibility. In *Examination of Witnesses in Criminal Cases*, Levy (2004) says that a police officer's notebook is "a common area of attack" for defence (p. 397). In *Cross-Examination: The Art of the Advocate*, Salhany (2006) expands on this, saying that because the foundation of officers' evidence is the accuracy of their notes, "what the cross-examiner must do is concentrate the attack upon the witness's notes" (p. 128).

Qualification of Notes

Before officers can use their notes to refresh their memory for the purpose of giving testimony in court, those notes must be "qualified" (described below). This is done to determine the reason why the witness seeks to use them. As described in Chapter 2, Evidence in the Courtroom, testimonial aids, such as police officer's notes, may be used either:

1. to provide a record of a past recollection where the witness has no present memory of the events (referred to as the past recollection recorded doctrine), or

2. to refresh a witness's present memory of (past) events (referred to as the present memory refreshed doctrine).

For a more detailed discussion of the legal concepts of past recollection recorded and present recollection revived, see Paciocco and Stuesser (2005, pp. 378–385) or *R. v. Biondo* (2009, especially, paras. 15–21), which draws on the Paciocco and Stuesser text in its analysis and has a detailed discussion of this issue.

During the process of qualifying an officer's notes, the Crown asks the officer questions to determine, for example, whether the officer is the one who made the notes; when the officer made the notes; whether the notes reflect the officer's memory of the events at the time the officer made the notes; and whether there have been any changes to the notes since they were made. (A sample series of questions and answers is provided in Chapter 2, Evidence in the Courtroom, p. 23.)

One of the questions commonly asked of an officer in the course of qualifying his or her notes is, "Do you have an independent recollection of the event?" Although this question means a recollection without reference to the notes, and although most officers typically respond that yes, they do, some legal authorities feel that this question, and any answer that might be given, is unnecessary for determining whether a witness is entitled to refresh his or her memory from notes. This is because no witness is "obliged, to have a recollection in existence prior to referring to something that jogs his memory" (Paciocco & Stuesser, 2nd ed., quoted in *R. v. Colangelo*, 2007, para. 35).

Defence counsel who object to officers using their notes to refresh their memories may ask the officer questions to satisfy any concerns they might have. However, defence counsel are advised that they should rarely object to police officers referring to their notes, because it is one way for counsel to physically examine what the officer has written down. Although defence counsel will typically have been provided with copies of the officer's notes (either in paper form or electronically) through the normal disclosure process, if the officer refers to his or her notes while giving evidence, defence counsel has the opportunity to physically examine those notes in their original form. Defence counsel are also cautioned to be wary of any situation in which an officer does *not* ask to refer to his or her notes, because this may signal that there is an issue or an entry in the notes that the officer does not want defence to explore (Levy, 2004, p. 397).

Once an officer's notes have been properly qualified, the officer is free to review the notes while giving evidence. However, the notes are meant only to serve as an aid; officers are thus not allowed to read from them as though they were a script, because this would constitute something more or different than simply using the notes to refresh the officer's memory.

Factors Affecting Reliability and Credibility

Three common aspects of police officers' note taking are commonly attacked by defence counsel in an effort to call the officer's credibility into question:

1. delay in creating the notes,
2. collaborating with other officers to create the notes, and
3. omissions in the notes.

Delay

The reason police officers need to prepare their notes in a timely manner is obvious: the more time that elapses between an event and the time that event is recorded, the more memory fades and the greater the probability that the record that is eventually prepared will contain inaccuracies. At one time police officers were not allowed to use their notes to refresh their memories at all, unless they were made at the time of the event or shortly afterward. However, this restriction has since been relaxed, and any delay between an event and the preparation of notes documenting that event now goes to determining the *weight* to be given to an officer's testimony (Salhany, 2006, p. 129).

The weight given to the testimony of officers who depend on notes prepared long after an event has taken place may be negatively affected by such delays. Some courts have characterized delayed note taking as a "shoddy" police practice (*R. v. Mita*, 2005); others have noted that, where officers fail to make contemporaneous notes of their actions and observations, the "precise reconstruction of events, times, and comings and goings is sacrificed to reliance on human memory" (*R. v. Cook*, 2010). Some courts have felt strongly enough about this issue to address it in considerable detail. In *R. v. Peglar* (2006), for example, Justice Feldman said, "I would strongly encourage the making of contemporaneous notes of material facts upon which an investigating officer relies in refreshing his or her memory. A significant gap in time in the making of notes and possible reliance on the memory of colleagues can affect the weight given an officer's evidence on important issues of fact. The perception of reliability and independence accorded a witness's testimony may be diminished" (*R. v. Peglar*, 2006, para. 13).

The opportunity to diminish the reliability of a police officer's testimony in the eyes of the court, thereby diminishing the weight of his or her evidence, is one reason that defence counsel regard delays in note taking as "[o]ne of the first areas of attack" in cross-examination (Salhany, 2005, p. 129).

Collaboration

Defence counsel can be counted on to fully explore any situation in which they believe that two or more officers discussed their observations of or actions during an event prior to preparing their individual notes documenting that event. Various terms are used to describe this practice; officers may variously be said to have "conferred," "collaborated," or "colluded" in the preparation of their notes. While "conferring" or "collaborating" suggests a relatively innocuous process involving the discussion and comparison of information, "colluding" suggests a more sinister course of action involving some sort of deceitful, conspiratorial purpose.

Regardless of the term used, and regardless of the fact that such collaboration in the preparation of officers' notes was at one time legally acceptable and, in fact, encouraged (Salhany, 2006, p. 131), producing notes in this way today is detrimental to an officer's credibility as a witness. While the courts have acknowledged that it is understandable that police officers who have witnessed the same event would want to discuss it (*R. v. Charest*, 1978), they have stated firmly that what a court "expects and is entitled to hear is [the officer's] own independent recollection of the event, not a recorded recollection which has been agreed to between them" (pp. 326–327). Where an officer may want to refer later to notes as a memory aid for the purpose of giving evidence regarding an event, the officer, and all officers who witness the event, should take "contemporaneous, independent notes" (*R. v. Barrett*, 1993, section (iii), para. 2).

There are important reasons for requiring officers to prepare their notes independently. An officer's notes serve as a record of that officer's observations, and if they are the product of a joint effort, it is likely that an officer relying on his notes in a trial will be refreshing his or her memory with the observations of others: "In effect, the officer will be giving hearsay evidence as if it was his or her own recollection, rather than the observations of somebody else written into the notes without attribution" (*R. v. Green*, 1998, cited in Levy, 2004, p. 403).

The circumstances in which officers prepare their notes is important to determine both (1) the reliability of the officer's notes, and (2) officers' credibility as witnesses (*R. v. Graham*, 2011, para. 21). In *Graham*, the court was troubled by the fact that a number of officers had discussed their observations regarding an arrest at a debriefing before preparing their individual notes. The court held that, to the extent the officers relied on their notes, such a discussion seriously undermined the reliability of their evidence (para. 43). In addition, the fact that the officers likely realized this, but were reluctant to admit that such a discussion had taken place, seriously undermined their credibility as witnesses (para. 44).

To determine whether officers may have collaborated in the preparation of their notes, defence counsel look for consistencies between the notes that cannot be explained merely by coincidence. If these are present, defence may suggest that collaboration took place. In the event that an officer admits during cross-examination to having conferred with another officer when preparing his notes, but claims that his independent recollection was not compromised by this practice, defence counsel may engage in a series of questions designed to show that, despite the fact that the officer understands the dangers associated with the contamination of any witness's evidence, the officer failed to take precautions to avoid such dangers in preparing his or her own notes (Salhany, 2006, p. 132). The following is an example of how such an exchange might unfold (Salhany, p. 133):

> Q: When you interview two persons who have witnessed an event you always interview them separately, isn't that correct?
>
> A: Yes.
>
> Q: You do so because you do not want one witness's recollection to influence the other witness?
>
> A: Yes, that's correct.
>
> Q: That is standard practice for police to follow?
>
> A: Yes, it is.
>
> Q: And you usually follow that practice, don't you?
>
> A: Usually.
>
> Q: Here, you and Constable Brown didn't follow that practice. You conferred with each other when making your notes?
>
> A: Yes.
>
> Q: Here, you failed to follow your own practice to ensure that your thoughts and recollections would not be influenced by him or vice versa?
>
> A: Well, they were not.
>
> Q: The truth is that you and he failed to take the same precautions that you routinely take with any other witness. Isn't that true?
>
> A: Yes.

Where officers are shown to have collaborated in the preparation of their notes, the court will carefully consider the reliability of the evidence given by those officers. The ultimate effect of the collaboration on the officers' credibility will depend on the circumstances of the case and on the explanations given by the officers (as observed by Levy (2004)—for example, where officers confer only about the times at which certain events occurred, little damage may be done. Still, whenever officers collaborate, defence counsel is almost certain to suggest a number of possible explanations for such collaboration, including (Levy, 2004, pp. 402–403):

- the individual officers have a poor recollection of the event and, in cooperation with one another, cobbled together an inaccurate picture of what they believe took place;
- there were significant differences in what each officer recalled about the event that needed to be discussed; or
- the officers collaborated for the purpose of concocting an account of what happened.

Needless to say, none of these suggested explanations is likely to have a positive impact on an officer's credibility.

Omissions

Officers should expect to be carefully cross-examined not only about what is in their notes but also about what is *not*. This is especially the case where an officer testifies to a particular matter, but has no notes about it (Salhany, 2006, p. 133).

Defence counsel will typically lay the groundwork for this line of attack by establishing with the officer, through a question-and-answer sequence, why police take notes. They will seek to have the officer acknowledge that the purpose of notes, and their own personal practice, is to record anything that is relevant so that they can accurately refresh their memory before giving evidence in court. Once the officer agrees to this proposition, defence counsel will typically go on to another area of questioning to keep the witness off balance, before continuing their attack.

The next stage of the attack typically involves a second question-and-answer sequence in which counsel attempts to get the officer to agree to the following: they have testified to what they believe was an important piece of evidence; they have told the court, during the first questioning sequence, that it is their practice to record everything that is important; and, finally, that they have no record of the important piece of evidence they have testified to in their notes. The attack may end with counsel posing a rhetorical question to the witness for the benefit of the court, such as: "Is it reasonable to expect that, after all this time has passed, you remember this important piece of evidence even though you made no notes about it?" The question highlights the limitations of human memory and the importance of creating a timely record of important observations (Salhany, 2006, p. 134).

In light of the above, officers are encouraged to make "late entries" in their notes, concerns about delay notwithstanding, where necessary. For example, an officer who made observations about a traffic collision might remember additional information two days later. Rather than omit the observation, the officer should include the information, *clearly marked as a late entry*, including the date and time. Some officers are reluctant to make late entries for fear they will be criticized, but it is better to include the information than not. Your notes are a memory aid—they are not a statement.

HOW TO BE A MORE EFFECTIVE WITNESS

Giving your evidence truthfully, fairly, and with confidence is the best way to be an effective witness. Novice police officers who have never been on the witness stand or who have testified only occasionally would be wise to draw on the experience, both good and bad, of those who have gone before them. This section (derived from Kebbell & O'Kelly, 2007, pp. 8–20; Sherriff, 2003, chap. 13) describes some common challenges faced by police witnesses and suggests strategies for dealing with them when you encounter them in the courtroom. A chart with a dozen "do's and don'ts" follows, to help less-experienced officers perform more effectively in their role as professional witnesses.

As mentioned above, relatively little research has been conducted into how police officers experience the process of giving evidence. The research that does exist suggests that the most difficult stage is cross-examination for a number of reasons, including the form in which defence lawyers pose their questions (Kebbell &

O'Kelly, 2007). Police officers appear to experience particular difficulty responding to questions that contain negatives (for example, "Did he not tell you that he wasn't there?"), questions that can only be answered with a "yes" or a "no," ambiguous questions, and complex questions.

As a general rule, the best way to handle questions whose form is confusing, vague, or complicated is to ask counsel to clarify, rephrase, or repeat the question. It is perfectly acceptable to ask for clarification if you do not clearly understand what is being asked of you, and there is no need to feel hesitant about doing so.

Police officers report experiencing a number of other difficulties while giving evidence. On occasion, defence counsel might pose questions using a certain rhythm that makes witnesses feel that they must respond immediately to the questions being asked. Police witnesses must remember that it is the witness, not defence counsel, who decides when and how to answer a question. As a witness you may, and should, take your time; listen to the question; ensure that you clearly understand what is being asked; give your answer some thought; and only then respond.

Officers also report that, at times, they have found it difficult to say everything they want to say while giving evidence; said things they did not mean to say; and felt that if they responded to certain questions it would look like they were lying. A number of approaches can help you deal with such issues, beginning with learning how to properly elaborate on your answers during cross-examination. When responding to a question, an officer might feel that to give an accurate response they must refer to other evidence in their answer, instead of addressing only the issue contained in defence counsel's question. The way an officer chooses to phrase his or her answer plays an important role in determining whether the officer will be able to give a full response or whether defence counsel will be able to easily interrupt. Two ways that an officer might respond to the same question follow:

Example 1

Lawyer: Did you see my client strike Mrs. Smith?
Officer: No, I did not see him hit Mrs. Smith, but I saw him standing next to her.

In this example, the officer responds immediately to the question, including a reference to other evidence in the second half of his answer. This form of response makes it easy for defence counsel to interrupt before the officer is able to complete his or her answer.

Example 2

Lawyer: Did you see my client strike Mrs. Smith?
Officer: I saw your client standing next to Mrs. Smith, but I did not see him hit her.

In the second example, the officer referred to other evidence in the first half of his response, before completing his answer to the question; this form of response makes it more difficult for defence counsel to interrupt the officer before he completes his answer. This is an example of why you should take your time and think about your answer before responding; not only the content of your answer but also its form can have an impact on your ability to give evidence effectively.

BEING AN EFFECTIVE WITNESS: A DOZEN DO'S AND DON'TS

DO'S:

- Tell the truth.

- Review your notes and all other relevant materials long before you take the witness stand; while on the stand, use your notes to refresh your memory and help you testify accurately about details.

- Make a positive first impression with your dress and demeanour; part of being a professional is looking and acting like a professional.

- Use proper decorum in the courtroom; address the judge as "Your Honour" and all legal counsel as either "Sir" or "Ma'am."

- Make appropriate eye contact with the people you are talking to, such as the Crown attorney, defence counsel, and the judge and jury; failing to look at people when answering questions detracts from your ability to communicate effectively and can make you appear tentative.

- Listen to the question asked; make sure you understand it before you answer.

- Ask for a question to be repeated, rephrased, or clarified if you don't understand it; this will show that you are taking your duty as a witness seriously and are trying to do a good job.

- Take time to think about your response before you answer a question—there is no time limit; you will generally be given as much time as you reasonably require to answer questions.

- Speak loudly, clearly, and at a moderate pace (police witnesses often speak too quickly) when giving your evidence; everyone in the courtroom needs to hear you and understand what you are saying, especially the court reporter who will be forced to ask you to slow down if you speak too quickly.

- Answer the question that you are asked; it is part of your job as a witness and part of the process of establishing your credibility.

- Use plain language when answering a question; police jargon is often incomprehensible to laypersons and will not help you to communicate effectively.

- Be definitive when answering a question; if you are certain of your answer, say so by responding with either a "yes" or "no"; repeatedly qualifying your answers with terms such as "I believe so," "I think so," or "As far as I can recall," makes you appear to be uncertain, or unwilling to commit to your answer.

DON'TS:

- Never attempt to shade, evade, or obscure the truth for any reason; in its milder forms, such behaviour can destroy your credibility and, in its more severe form, such behaviour is called perjury and will destroy your career.

- Never be arrogant or combative on the witness stand; such behaviour is not the same thing as being firm and decisive when giving your evidence.

- Don't be intimidated by defence counsel; if defence counsel cuts you off before you have finished answering a question, firmly, but politely, indicate that you have not finished answering, then complete your answer.

- Never try to cover up if you make a mistake while testifying; admit your mistake promptly and correct it openly.

- Never guess at what you think a question means; if you are uncertain, ask for clarification.

- Don't give a speech in response to a question—such behaviour is inappropriate and unprofessional; answer the question that you were asked.

- Don't hesitate to admit that you don't know the answer to a question; guessing will only undermine your credibility.

- Don't let your emotions influence your behaviour on the witness stand; it is not uncommon to experience strong emotion as a result of things that you have observed or the evidence that you have to give, but managing your emotions is part of being a professional.

- Never refuse or hesitate to concede the obvious; such behaviour only makes you look petty and foolish.

- Never argue with defence counsel; it is not your job.

- Don't try to "defeat" defence counsel during cross-examination; it is not your job.

- Don't treat defence counsel as your adversary—they are not.

Source: Adapted from Van Brocklin (2009); Miller (2006); Stutler (1997); Henley (2011).

Another strategy for giving a full response to a question is to state that your answer consists of a number of points, then proceed to address each point. Remember, however, that you are not trying to avoid answering the questions, nor are you attempting to carve out an opportunity to give a speech; such behaviour is inappropriate. Rather, the strategies described above, are intended to address the frustration and anxiety that some police witnesses report experiencing while giving evidence, by providing them with examples of how they might structure their responses to optimize their chances of being able to answer questions fully and accurately without interruption.

The only one way to address the issue that some officers report of being afraid to answer some questions because they will appear to be lying is to tell the truth, even if you feel foolish as a result. Officers may, on occasion, be tempted to skirt the truth because they have made an error of some kind during their investigation and do not want to appear incompetent. Although having defence counsel expose flaws in your investigation—sometimes in a sarcastic and dismissive manner—can be a painful experience, trying to avoid such pain by evading the truth can be fatal. If you have made a mistake and you are confronted with it, admit it. If there is something that you could have done better and you are confronted with it, concede the point. No one has conducted or ever will conduct a perfect investigation; there will always be a weakness of one kind or another; there will always be something that you could have done differently or could improve on next time around. Such shortcomings normally go to the strength of one or a few pieces of evidence; however, a loss of credibility as a result of being untruthful will have an impact on an entire case, and, probably, your career.

Although reported cases of police officers engaging in outright perjury or giving testimony that is rejected by a court as non-credible are not commonplace, neither are they rare. See, for example, Fraser (2011), reporting that a retired Mountie pleaded guilty to perjury; *R. v. Harrison* (2009, para. 12), where the trial judge found the police officer's testimony to have been "contrived and defy credibility"; *R. v. Graham* (2011), where Justice Spies said, "I have concerns about the truthfulness of the evidence of [five] Officers" (para. 44) and "Unfortunately, it cannot be said that [out of fear of being charged with perjury and losing their jobs] police officers are always truthful" (para. 49); the Canadian Press (2011), where four RCMP officers in British Columbia were charged with perjury arising out of testimony given at the inquiry into the death of Robert Dziekanski; and Bruser and McLean (2012), who identified "100 plus" cases across Canada since 2005 in which judges found that officers had "misled" the court.

KEY TERMS

Browne v. Dunn rule
criminal information
cross-examination
examination-in-chief
leading question
open-ended question
re-examination

FURTHER READING

Brauti, P.M. (1997). Improper cross-examination. *Criminal Law Quarterly, 40,* 69–105.

Kebbell, M., & O'Kelly, C. (2007). Police detectives perceptions of giving evidence in court. *Policing: An International Journal of Police Strategies and Management, 30*(1), 8–20.

Levy, E. (2004). *Examination of witnesses in criminal cases* (5th ed.). Toronto: Thomson Carswell. (See, especially, chap. 17, Cross-examination of police officers, pp. 396–411.)

Salhany, R. (2006). *Cross examination: The art of the advocate* (3rd ed.). Markham, ON: LexisNexis. (See, especially, chap. 6, Witnesses: The police officer, pp. 108–112, and chap. 7, Particular problems: 1(a) notes prepared by the witness, pp. 127–143.)

REVIEW QUESTIONS

True or False?

1. The overall objective of cross-examination for the defence is to create reasonable doubt regarding the Crown's case.

2. Much of the evidence adduced at trial "speaks for itself."

3. The calling of witnesses forms the basis of our trial system.

4. A police witness's role differs significantly from that of any other witness.

5. A police witness's role includes trying to help the Crown convict the accused.

6. The Crown attorney's role as an officer of the court is to obtain a conviction in criminal proceedings.

7. The most important rule for defence counsel when cross-examining a witness is to maintain control of that witness.

8. According to the *Browne v. Dunn* rule, counsel who intend to discredit a witness on a specific matter must cross-examine that witness on that specific point.

9. Defence counsel automatically cross-examine all prosecution witnesses.

10. Defence counsel are given a great deal of latitude when cross-examining witnesses. Essentially, any question that is relevant to the issues at trial or to a witness's credibility is fair game.

Multiple Choice

1. A second general rule of cross-examination is that counsel must not ask questions:

   a. that the witness is unable to answer.

   b. whose prejudicial effect is greater than their probative value.

   c. which cause the witness to become uncomfortable.

   d. composed of multiple parts.

2. The purpose of re-examination is:

   a. to give counsel an opportunity to explore issues that they did not cover during examination-in-chief.

   b. to allow a witness to address significant issues raised during cross-examination that may have become confused or made less clear during that process.

   c. to give opposing counsel the opportunity to explore new areas of evidence not previously covered.

   d. to allow the judge an opportunity to question the witness on matters of interest to the court.

3. The reason police officers need to prepare their notes in a timely manner is because:

   a. once their notes are complete they are available to attend the next call for service.

   b. the law requires them to complete their notes as soon as possible after being involved in or observing an event during their tour of duty.

   c. the more time that elapses between an event and the time it is recorded in an officer's notes, the greater the probability that the notes will contain inaccuracies.

   d. the failure to complete their notes in a timely manner will result in disciplinary action being taken against them.

4. Although the use of leading questions is generally forbidden during evidence-in-chief, it is permissible during _____; as a result, police witnesses can reasonably expect that the majority of questions they will be asked during a typical _____ will be leading.

   a. re-examination

   b. evidence-in-chief

   c. cross-examination

   d. a *voir dire*

5. As "officers of the court," counsel are bound by a code of professional conduct that prohibits them from being unnecessarily abusive toward a witness. It is improper for counsel to:

   a. point out a witness's limitations.

   b. insist that a witness answer the question that was put to them.

   c. repeatedly remind a witness while they are testifying that they are still under oath.

   d. suggest that a witness is being evasive.

6. Witnesses might reasonably respond to leading questions by:

   a. focusing on the facts as they know and understand them, rather than on the premises inherent in the question.

   b. pointing out that the use of leading questions can, in fact, be misleading to the court.

   c. ignoring the questions and addressing the issues in a way that they feel is more appropriate.

   d. raising an objection to the use of the questions and asking that they be rephrased.

Short Answer

1. Discuss the purpose of cross-examination.

2. Discuss some of the things a police officer can do to be most effective as a witness.

Evidence, Error, and Justice

20

LEARNING OUTCOMES

After completing this chapter, you should be able to:

- Identify a number of key reports released in Canada, the United States, and elsewhere in the past decade, covering various investigative errors and challenges and their key findings.

- Define the term "cognitive bias" and understand the role that cognitive biases can play in investigative error.

- List several attitudes that can contribute to investigative errors and the persistence of errors in an investigation.

- Identify strategies and practices that investigators can adopt to manage the risk of error in their work.

- Explain changes that can be made to investigative culture and, more broadly, forensic practices that can reduce the risk of error and the effect of errors that do happen.

We learn, as we say, by "trial and error." Why do we always say that? Why not "trial and rightness" or "trial and triumph"? The old phrase puts it that way because that is, in real life, the way it is done.

—Lewis Thomas, U.S. physician, educator;
from the 1974 essay "Trial and Error"

INTRODUCTION

If one were to ask a group of criminal or forensic investigators who Alexander Pope was, it is likely that few, if any, would know. If one were to tell that same group of investigators that Pope was a 16th-century English poet, it is equally probable that few, if any, could say why he might be relevant to a discussion of evidence, error, and justice. Yet most of them would be familiar with Pope's well-known dictum: "To err is human; to forgive, divine." Our capacity to err, or to be mistaken about something that we believe to be true, is a basic human quality. And it is inevitable that in any human enterprise—including the criminal justice system—errors will be made. The intimate relationship that exists between evidence, error, and justice forms the focus of this final chapter.

In their work, investigators must use imperfect tools (minds subject to bias) and limited knowledge (an incomplete understanding of the world) to reconstruct historical events (typically, under significant time pressure) from artifacts—the things left behind, such as physical evidence, electronic records, and eyewitness memories—and, on the basis of that reconstruction, to gain knowledge about and an understanding of those events. What happened? How did it happen? Why did it happen? Was a criminal act committed and, if so, by whom? An investigator must use the knowledge and understanding generated from the evidence to answer these and other questions. And, in the event that a person has been charged with a crime, the investigator must pass his or her understanding of the circumstances and the evidence on which that understanding is based to a court of law for further scrutiny.

Given that investigators have not witnessed the events they are called on to investigate, they are dependent for their knowledge about and understanding of those events on evidence—those "bits and pieces" of information and material that are gathered together and interpreted during an investigation—to make "sense" of historical events—events that may have happened hours, days, or even years ago. It is in this very process of gathering and interpreting evidence that the greatest danger lies, because it is here that errors can be made that may have a profound effect on an investigator's ability to formulate a valid account of the events.

Errors can be made at any one or many points in the process of identifying, collecting, preserving, analyzing, and interpreting evidence, and can affect the validity of what is believed to be "known" about the events under investigation. When those errors lead to the construction of a flawed understanding of what happened, and when that understanding is acted on by others in the criminal justice system (such as Crown attorneys, defence lawyers, judges, and juries), it can lead—and has led—to injustices, including wrongful convictions.

For this reason, investigators' greatest challenge is *managing the risk of error* in their work. One way to help accomplish this is by gaining an awareness of the fundamental relationship that exists between evidence, error, and justice. One of the most important findings to emerge from the many reviews of criminal justice failures in Canada and elsewhere over the past three decades is that such cases involved errors. These errors were made, for the most part, by well-meaning, hard-working, criminal justice professionals (police investigators, forensic scientists, lawyers, and judges), who get it right most of the time, but who, on occasion, have gone horribly astray, with disastrous consequences.

ERRORS AND INSIGHTS: LEARNING FROM THE MISTAKES OF OTHERS

From 1989 to 2011 in Canada, there were numerous inquiries into and reports on investigative and forensic failures resulting in wrongful convictions, including the Marshall (Hickman, 1989), Kaufman (1998), Sophonow (Cory, 2001), Lamer (2006), Driskell (Lesage, 2007), Goudge (MacFarlane, 2008), and Milgaard (MacCallum, 2006) Inquiries, and the 2005 and 2011 FPT Reports (FPT Heads of Prosecutions Committee Working Group, 2005; Federal/Provincial/Territorial Heads of Prosecutions Subcommittee on the Prevention of Wrongful Convictions, 2011). All of these shed light on the Canadian criminal justice system's capacity for error and suggest how future investigations might better manage the risk. The United States and the United Kingdom have produced similar reports examining errors or shortcomings in investigative and forensic practices in their countries.

In this section we review some of the major findings of official inquiries into investigative and forensic failures to see what types of errors were made, by whom, and why. Because a detailed examination of the findings and recommendations of each report or inquiry is beyond the scope of this text, a number of common themes identified in these publications have been chosen to guide the discussion in this chapter.

Some of the most notable wrongful convictions and exonerations in the history of the Canadian justice system are highlighted in short boxes throughout the chapter. For information on these cases and others, interested readers are referred to the website of the Association in Defence of the Wrongfully Convicted (see the entry under Further Reading). Inquiries into what went wrong in these particular cases and others have shed invaluable light on some of the ways in which similar errors, and the associated consequences, might be avoided in the future. The inquiries are recommended reading for current and prospective criminal investigators. To read about wrongful conviction cases in the United States, consult the Innocence Project website (also listed under Further Reading).

DAVID MILGAARD

Sentenced to life imprisonment for the 1969 murder of a Saskatoon nursing aide, Mr. Milgaard spent 23 years in prison. At the time of the murder, he had been travelling throughout Canada with friends, who later gave evidence against him, both to police interviewers and at trial. They eventually recanted their testimony, and Mr. Milgaard was released in 1992. In 1997, he was exonerated by DNA evidence and awarded $10 million in compensation by the Saskatchewan and federal governments. That year, convicted rapist Larry Fisher was found guilty of the murder. The provincial inquiry into Milgaard's conviction found that police had failed to follow up on a lead from 1980, which might have led them to consider Fisher a serious suspect and might have led to a much earlier release for Milgaard. A "critical failure" of police in their questioning of key witnesses, a mistake by the trial judge, and an incorrect finding by the Saskatchewan Court of Appeal also played key roles in the case. In the words of the Alberta judge who headed the inquiry: "[T]he criminal justice system failed David Milgaard."

The FPT Reports, 2005 and 2011

In Canada, in 2002, a Federal/Provincial/Territorial (FPT) working group on the prevention of miscarriages of justice was struck to identify best practices to assist police and prosecutors in avoiding future wrongful convictions. The group reviewed international and Canadian studies on wrongful convictions since the early 1900s and issued their first report in 2005. Their suggestion that the recommendations be fully reviewed at least every five years led to the publication of the FPT Report of 2011.

The tremendously influential Reports, which have been cited at all levels of Canadian courts and should be required reading for anyone either currently working in or contemplating a career in forensic science or criminal investigation, offer a valuable overview of what has been learned about error in the Canadian criminal justice system and how the risk of committing similar errors in the future can be minimized. The major theme of the Reports is vigilance. Every professional involved in the criminal justice system must be aware of, and work to counteract, the factors that contribute to miscarriages of justice. These include the potential weaknesses of certain types of forensic evidence and the personal and professional limitations of those who work with and rely on evidence in the course of their daily activities as participants in the criminal justice system.

The 2011 Report states that one of the "most direct routes to proactively preventing miscarriages of justice in this country" is the education of criminal justice professionals (FPT Report, 2011, Chapter 10). A number of recommendations have been made regarding educational approaches and topics—namely, looking to the lessons that can be learned from wrongful convictions; learning about the limitations of certain types of evidence; seeking the insights of "outsiders," such as psychologists, law professors, and criminologists; and exploring topics such as cognitive bias (discussed below) that have the potential to significantly affect the way in which practitioners gather, analyze, and interpret evidence.

The NAS Report, 2009

The National Academy of Sciences (NAS) Report (National Research Council of the National Academies, 2009) is a significant, expansive, and highly detailed discussion of the state of forensic science in the United States that, like the FPT Reports, should be required reading for current and prospective forensic scientists and criminal investigators. The NAS Report addresses issues related to a wide variety of forensic evidence, including pattern and impression, digital, and biological evidence, and the ways in which professionals think about that evidence. Chapter 6 of the NAS Report (2009), "Improving Methods, Practice, and Performance in Forensic Science," alludes to the tension between critics, who point out the flaws and limitations of forensic science (when many disciplines may, within appropriate limits, provide reliable evidence), and certain overconfident practitioners, who believe that they know something with a high degree of certainty in the absence of evidence to support their conclusions.

Between these two extremes lies significant room for suggestions about how to improve forensic investigations in the United States and elsewhere. These include:

- making forensic labs independent of police agencies, to increase their objectivity;

- continuing research to develop accurate measures of the certainty with which forensic experts can express their opinions (relatively few forensic disciplines have done so—recall the earlier discussions of fingerprint evidence); and

- pursuing more research on the dangers of cognitive biases (discussed below), including how these can affect forensic analyses and how they may be counteracted.

The Scottish Fingerprint Inquiry, 2011

In January 1997, following a murder in Scotland, police discovered a mark on a doorframe in the victim's house that was "identified" as the thumbprint of police officer Shirley McKie. McKie, who denied ever having been inside the victim's residence and maintained that the fingerprint could not be hers, was subsequently charged with perjury. With the help of independent experts, the accuracy of the fingerprint identification process that "matched" McKie's print to the one found inside the victim's residence was called into question, and McKie was found not guilty of perjury; however, the accusation took a heavy toll on her life and her career. McKie was not the only one plagued by faulty fingerprint "evidence" in the case. The man convicted in the murder, David Asbury, was ultimately acquitted, also as a result of errors involving fingerprints—in this case, prints believed to belong to the victim that were found on an item in his home.

The Inquiry (Campbell, 2011), which was called, in part, to examine the process through which the "McKie" print was incorrectly identified and verified and, in general, to look at the subject of fingerprint identification to make recommendations to help avoid similar errors in the future, released its report in 2011. Among its 86 key findings and recommendations (Campbell, 2011, Pt. 8, chap. 43) were that fingerprint evidence is subjective, opinion evidence; the opinions of fingerprint examiners can be influenced by a number of factors; fingerprint examiners cannot (as they once did) claim absolute, 100 percent certainty in the correctness of their findings; and fingerprint examiners must be made aware of factors, such as context bias (discussed below), that have the potential to negatively affect their work.

The Inquiry attributed the misidentification of McKie's thumbprint and the print found in Asbury's residence, determined to belong to the murder victim, to human error. Among the contributing factors were fingerprint examiners, who:

- were taught that they could have absolute certainty in their findings;

- paid little attention to the opinions of less-experienced practitioners, especially when those opinions varied from their own;

- did not recognize the potential dangers of context bias in their work; and

- made varying assumptions about how "close" details in one print had to be to another in order to make an identification—that is, to say that the prints

---

DONALD MARSHALL JR.

In 1971, Mr. Marshall was convicted in the murder of his friend and sentenced to life imprisonment. After spending 12 years in jail, Mr. Marshall was released in light of new evidence, including eyewitness testimony that identified another individual as the murderer, and was acquitted by the Nova Scotia Court of Appeal. The 1989 Marshall Inquiry into Mr. Marshall's wrongful conviction was the first such inquiry in Canada. It identified police misconduct, mistakes, and racism (Marshall was of Mi'kmaq heritage), including pervasive systemic racism, as the primary causes of the wrongful conviction.

"matched"—and concentrated on certain groups of characteristics as opposed to the entire print.

The Inquiry found that the officers who originally identified and verified the fingerprints in the *McKie* (1999) case had followed their normal procedures, and there was no evidence to suggest that those procedures had caused them to make misidentifications in the past. Instead, the main reason for their errors was likely *an excess of confidence* on the part of investigators in their skills and abilities (Campbell, 2011, para. 28.87). The final paragraph of the Inquiry (para. 28.101) looked at why the original fingerprint examiners had refused to acknowledge their errors when confronted with the contradictory opinions of other experts, and concluded that the officers' genuine yet mistaken belief that they could make evidentiary findings with certainty served as a significant obstacle to considering alternative viewpoints (Campbell, 2011, Pt. 5, The Inquiry's Findings as to How the Errors Arose, Chapter 28, Factors Contributing to the SCRO Decisions).

The Office of the Inspector General (OIG) Report, 2006

In 2006, the U.S. Department of Justice, Office of the Inspector General (OIG) was called on to review the process that led to three FBI fingerprint examiners misidentifying a fingerprint in a terrorist investigation; a court-appointed expert also came to the same, erroneous conclusion. The factors included technical issues, such as an unusual degree of similarity between the known and unknown fingerprints, as well as the significant weight given by examiners to extremely small, variable details, which led them to interpret distortions as real print features; examiners were also found to have "explained away" discrepancies between the prints that would otherwise have prevented them from making an identification.

The same issue, identified five years later in the Scottish Fingerprint Inquiry, was identified here—namely, the examiners were *unwilling to consider the possibility that they had made an error*, even after another law enforcement agency had analyzed the fingerprints and concluded that they did not match. Instead, the examiners reiterated their absolute confidence in the correctness of their initial (erroneous) identification.

The OIG concluded that the FBI's sense of superiority and overconfidence in the skills of its examiners prevented investigators from seriously considering alternative interpretations of the evidence and discovering their error. The OIG Report (U.S. Department of Justice, Office of the Inspector General, 2006) characterized the misidentification as a "watershed event" for the FBI, which had previously characterized fingerprint identification as "the gold standard for forensic science," with many fingerprint examiners until that time claiming "absolute certainty for their identifications and a zero error rate for their discipline" p. 269). The FBI responded by admitting that they had made an identification using a substandard image of the print, initiating a review of their fingerprint identification practices, adopting new guidelines for examiners, asking an international panel of fingerprint experts to review the process that led to the misidentification, and issuing an apology to the person whose life was affected by the error (Federal Bureau of Investigation, 2004).

FACTORS THAT CONTRIBUTE TO ERROR

Given our human tendency to make mistakes, and the length and complexity of many investigations, all manner of little things may be expected to go wrong, and investigators must remain aware of this possibility. Among the factors that contribute to errors over the course of an investigation are natural human tendencies to process information in particular ways and various attitudes that investigators may possess or may come to possess. We explore these in the following sections and then turn to a discussion of some ways in which they can be minimized.

Cognitive Biases

Cognitive biases must be distinguished from "bias" as the term is commonly understood—that is, in the sense of cultural, racial, or religious bias. A **cognitive bias** is *not* the result of an emotional or intellectual choice for or against something; rather, it is a natural tendency to make systematic "thinking errors" (Heuer, 1999, p. 111). The term "cognition" refers to various thinking processes, such as perception, memory, judgment, and reasoning; "cognitive bias" refers to the tendency of humans to make consistent, and predictable, errors in the way they perceive, recall, interpret, and act on information.

Cognitive biases are a function of the way we think; we all use them without being aware of doing so (Findley & Scott, 2006). They are perhaps best thought of as automatic filtering mechanisms that help us cope with and efficiently process the mass of information that bombards us on a daily basis. Our need to use such mechanisms to categorize, interpret, and selectively attend to information can, however, lead us to make serious errors of which we are often totally unaware. But just because cognitive biases are natural inclinations does not mean that those who participate in the justice system bear no responsibility for trying to mitigate their effects: they do. When such errors occur among actors in the criminal justice system, the consequences can be devastating. As Findley and Scott (2006) stress, investigators and others must make themselves aware of the existence and effect of these tendencies and adopt strategies to counter their negative effects.

Although science has identified a number of cognitive biases (such as anchoring, availability, and hindsight bias, to name only a few), our discussion focuses on two: confirmation bias and context bias.

Confirmation Bias

Confirmation bias is "the tendency to seek or interpret evidence in ways that support existing beliefs, expectations or hypotheses" (Findley & Scott, 2006, p. 309). In addition to seeking information that confirms their hypotheses, people naturally tend to avoid information that would disprove them, or at least they often don't know where to look for such information.

THOMAS SOPHONOW

Sentenced to life imprisonment for a 1981 murder he did not commit, Mr. Sophonow was convicted on the basis of perjury by a jailhouse informant. He underwent three trials and was convicted twice; the Manitoba Court of Appeal overturned both convictions and, after the second conviction, ordered his acquittal. Sophonow had spent 45 months in jail. In 1998, the Winnipeg Police Service reopened the investigation and, two years later, announced that evidence had cleared Sophonow of the crime and identified a suspect. An inquiry into Sophonow's conviction criticized the actions of police in interrogating Sophonow, including techniques used in an attempt to break his will and obtain a confession, and unreasonably conducting a strip search.

cognitive bias
a natural tendency to make consistent and predictable errors in the way we think, perceive, recall, interpret, and act on information

confirmation bias
the tendency to seek information or interpret evidence that confirms our hypotheses and to avoid information that would disprove them

As illustrated in the experiment described in the box, "The Exception Proves the Rule," below and as shown consistently in subsequent studies, people tend to seek information in ways that increase their confidence in prior beliefs or hypotheses, even when they have "no vested interest" in the hypotheses (Findley & Scott, 2006, p. 311). This tendency is illogical for two reasons:

1. It prevents people from discovering that a particular hypothesis is wrong.

2. It does not provide as strong a confirmation of the truth of the hypothesis as the failure of a deliberate attempt to disprove the hypothesis would provide.

Findley and Scott (2006) point out that not only are people inclined to seek confirming information, they also have a tendency to *recall* information in a biased way—namely, in a way that favours information that is consistent with a presented hypothesis or belief. People also tend to give greater weight to information that supports existing beliefs than to information that is contrary to those beliefs. As a result, people tend to require *less* information that is *consistent* with their hypothesis to accept it as true, but *more* information that is *inconsistent* with their hypothesis to reject it as false. Moreover, people don't just ignore information that is inconsistent with their previously held belief—they often scrutinize it in order to undermine it; thus, there is a tendency to regard contradictory information as flawed or irrelevant.

Again, these are common human tendencies that have been identified and studied for many decades. The significance of such tendencies in the criminal

"THE EXCEPTION PROVES THE RULE"

Psychologist Peter Wason (1960) coined the term "confirmation bias" to describe a phenomenon he observed among participants in studies first conducted some 50 years ago. In one study, participants were given a series of three numbers {2, 4, 6} and told that they conformed to a rule. The participants were then asked to determine what the rule was by generating their own three-number series and submitting these to the experimenter, who would tell them whether each series fit the rule as they submitted it. The participants were told that when they believed they had discovered the rule, they should announce it to the experimenter. Most participants came up with a theory almost immediately—for example, "add two to the previous number"—but, for the most part, *they only submitted series of numbers that fit their theory*—for example, the series {8, 10, 12}. They tended *not* to submit series that could have potentially *disproved* their theory—for example, the series {2, 3, 4}. Had they done so, they would have realized that their theory was not correct—that is, they would have discovered that *any* series of ascending numbers was acceptable (Russo & Meloy, 2008).

Proposing examples that fit with a hypothesized rule may seem to be a perfectly logical way for a person to prove that their hypothesis is true, especially when their examples are shown to be *consistent* with the truth. But it *isn't* the most logical strategy, because it actually prevents one from discovering that one's hypothesis is *wrong*. This is the logic behind the common phrase "the exception proves the rule," where to "prove" means "to test" the rule, just as in the context of evaluating automobiles, a "proving ground" is another term for a "test track."

justice system, where a person is being judged (whether by police, prosecutors, defence counsel, judge, or jury) and where the initial working hypothesis that is presented to each "judge" is that the accused is guilty—notwithstanding the theoretical presumption of innocence—is clear (Findley & Scott, 2006, p. 314).

In light of the above, it should not be surprising that experiments conducted with police detectives, prosecutors, and judges have shown that their initial hypothesis regarding a crime affects how they interpret subsequent crime-related information. For example, in one experiment, a group of students and a group of criminal investigators were read a set of facts based on a preliminary homicide investigation. Their initial hypotheses regarding the crime were then manipulated by providing them with background information that suggested the prime suspect had a jealousy motive or that there might be an alternative suspect. Whereas the students ascribed guilt to the prime suspect only when a potential motive was presented, the investigators ascribed guilt to the prime suspect regardless of the hypothesis—suggesting that they were less sensitive to alternative explanations of the evidence (Ask & Granhag, 2005). A later study used the same experimental scenario on a group of police officers, prosecutors, and judges and obtained similar results: the participants' evaluations of the various investigative findings were equally incriminating for the prime suspect whether they were given information regarding a possible alternative suspect or not (Rassin, 2010).

One researcher has described the effect of confirmation bias on the investigative process by saying that investigators will search, not for the ideal solution to a problem, but for a "satisfactory conclusion" (Rossmo, 2009). They will look for and process information until a certain threshold of "proof" is reached, and will then seize on the understanding of the case that exists at that point with finality, adopting it as the "truth." From that point forward, the investigative process becomes one in which additional evidence is sought to confirm the "truth," and evidence that may disconfirm the investigator's belief (and which may prove the suspect is innocent) is often ignored or rationalized. The investigator's theory, which may be wrong, is merely corroborated by a search for confirmatory evidence and is never meaningfully challenged. As a result, the investigator's conclusions about who is responsible for a particular crime may be "questionable, if not altogether unreliable" (Rossmo, 2009, p. 59).

Confirmation bias has been a constant theme in several Canadian judicial inquiries, including the Kaufman (1998), Sophonow (Cory, 2001), Lamer (2006), and Goudge (MacFarlane, 2008) inquiries. In the Lamer Inquiry, retired Chief Justice Antonio Lamer made an observation that goes to the heart of the confirmation bias issue when he remarked, regarding one of the investigative theories held by the police, that "the theory must derive from an objective assessment of the evidence. Here the evidence was assessed with a view to supporting an unsupportable theory" (Lamer, 2006, p. 257). Interestingly, Justice Lamer's remarks are strikingly similar

RONALD DALTON

Sentenced in 1989 to life imprisonment in the second-degree murder of his wife, Mr. Dalton spent over eight years in prison, partly on the basis of an inexperienced pathologist, who testified that the cause of Mr. Dalton's wife's death was strangulation. Mr. Dalton was released pending a new trial; he was acquitted after a retrial in which new evidence was presented, including evidence from qualified pathologists that Mr. Dalton's wife had choked to death on her food rather than been strangled. Since his acquittal, Mr. Dalton has dedicated himself to cases of wrongful conviction and was instrumental in Newfoundland's decision to conduct a public inquiry (the Lamer Inquiry) into his own conviction and those of Randy Druken and Gregory Parsons.

BIAS AT WORK: R. v. PARISIEN

In *R. v. Parisien* (2011), the court had to decide whether a police officer could serve as an expert witness in a child pornography case. The judge ruled that the officer could do so (although the accused pleaded guilty before the officer gave any evidence), but indicated in his ruling that he had come very close to deciding against the officer because of concerns about the possible effects of confirmation bias on the officer's work.

During a *voir dire*, the officer admitted that he had already formed an opinion about the accused's guilt when he analyzed the contents of his computer; that his analytical method was to locate and present evidence in support of the charge (which he acknowledged was the opposite of the scientific method); that he had to make a number of decisions about what electronic data to extract from the accused's computer; and, in what the court characterized as the most "remarkable" admission of all, he stated that he believed he was working for the Crown as part of the prosecution team. Despite these concerns the judge was prepared to allow the officer to testify because he had been candid and transparent during cross-examination, his role in the investigation was restricted, and any opinions he offered could be tested against any alternative theories and the totality of the evidence to determine what role bias may have played in the development of his opinions (*Parisien*, para. 13).

Confirmation bias is not merely an "academic" issue; it is an ongoing concern in the courts. Officers who are unaware of its potential practical and legal consequences may find themselves poorly equipped to conduct objective investigations and, ultimately, to give credible evidence about what they find.

to comments made by Sir Arthur Conan Doyle's fictional detective Sherlock Holmes more than a century earlier. Holmes, in cautioning his sidekick Dr. Watson about the dangers of drawing premature conclusions during an investigation, said: "It is a capital mistake to theorize before one has data. Insensibly one begins to twist facts to suit theories, instead of theories to suit facts" (Doyle, "A Scandal in Bohemia," 1891). It is clear that while Doyle (a medical doctor who had received training in the scientific method) recognized the utility of a "theory of the crime" as a tool for helping make sense of the evidence gathered during an investigation, he also understood the danger of an investigator being blinded by his or her own theory. Once an investigator has formed a theory of the crime, the tendency is to consider only that evidence which *confirms* the theory; ironically, the more evidence an investigator considers that is consistent with his or her theory, the more confident the investigator may become that his or her theory is correct, even if it is not. This can lead to a corollary danger of confirmation bias, overconfidence, which is discussed below.

Context Bias

context bias
bias that arises from exposure to extraneous information, which can affect the judgment of forensic investigators

Studies suggest that **context bias**, or bias that arises from exposure to extraneous information, can affect the judgment of forensic investigators. Research on fingerprint identification, for example, indicates that it is possible to alter the identification decisions of forensic experts with respect to the same fingerprint, simply by changing the context in which the prints are presented (Dror, Charlton, & Perón,

2006). This effect has been demonstrated not only in scientific research but also in the larger context of criminal investigations.

For example, in the U.K. case of *R. v. Smith* (2011), a Nottinghamshire police fingerprint expert examined a print from a murder scene and concluded that it did not contain sufficient detail to allow him to make an identification. However, after the officer learned that a suspect (who had first been considered as a witness) had been charged with the murder, he reexamined the fingerprint and concluded that it belonged to the accused. The original fingerprint examiner's work was later verified by two other officers in the same police department. At trial, however, a fingerprint expert called by the defence testified that the fingerprint was of such poor quality that it could not be used for identification purposes. Because this was the conclusion that the original examiner had made before learning that the accused had been charged with murder, it is reasonable to assume that the context in which the fingerprint was reexamined—specifically, after a witness was recast as the suspect—was a factor in the examiner's conclusion. What an examiner expects to see may sometimes affect what he or she *does* see. Here, in the presence of irrelevant contextual information, in looking at the evidence a second time the officer did not "see" what he saw the first time—that is, insufficient information to permit an analysis; rather, he "saw" what he expected to see—that is, evidence that linked the newly accused individual to the crime. At the trial, two retired fingerprint officers also testified, saying that the original examining officers had confused different aspects of the print and ignored a part of the print that would have excluded the accused as the source.

The Court of Appeal ultimately rejected the fingerprint evidence and quashed the accused's original murder conviction. It also severely criticized the original fingerprint examiners for failing to adequately document their work and conclusions, questioned the standards used during the identification process, and censured the original fingerprint examiner for offering an after-the-fact explanation to account for the differences between his interpretation of the fingerprint and the interpretations of the other experts. Researchers have concluded that because fingerprint experts can be influenced by contextual information, procedures governing the fingerprint examination and verification process should attempt to limit the amount of extraneous contextual information available to examiners (Langenburg, Champod, & Wertheim, 2009).

In summary, investigators' decisions about what a particular piece of evidence "means" are malleable and subject to influence—for example, the influence of context. If the context is relevant, this is perfectly fine; however, the influence of unrelated contextual information is highly problematic.

Attitudes

In addition to the challenges presented by cognitive biases, the following attitudes identified by the studies described at the beginning of this chapter can (1) *contribute to* investigative errors, and (2) *prevent* errors from being discovered before they can cause damage:

JAMES DRISKELL

Convicted in 1991 of the first-degree murder of his friend and sentenced to life in prison, largely on the testimony of two witnesses and an expert who stated that microscopic examination of hairs in Mr. Driskell's vehicle belonged to the victim, Mr. Driskell spent 13 years in prison. An internal Winnipeg Police Service report later revealed that, unbeknownst to the jury, police had offered the witnesses various incentives, including the prospect of charges being dropped in another case. In addition, in 2003, the forensic evidence involving the hairs was discredited when DNA analysis excluded the victim as the donor. The inquiry into Driskell's conviction found that the jury had been "seriously misled."

1. *Overconfidence:* Believing that one knows more about something than one actually does. A related belief is that the tools one uses—that is, forensic or investigative techniques—to gain the knowledge one possesses are highly effective, objective, and accurate, either on the basis of limited empirical research supporting such a belief or in the absence of any such research.

2. *Certainty:* Believing that one has the ability to make determinations about the evidence one examines with an exceptionally high degree of accuracy, approaching, and sometimes reaching, certainty—that is, 100 percent.

3. *Reluctance:* A propensity to avoid considering the possibility that one has made an error in one's interpretation of evidence or a tendency to avoid considering other viewpoints that suggest alternative interpretations of that evidence.

4. *Cultural superiority:* A belief that one's professional culture is better than others; in particular, that practical experience (in contrast to scientific research) is a superior and a sufficient method for learning about the world.

The first attitude, overconfidence, is related to confirmation bias, and has been identified in a number of reports and inquiries as a significant—if not the primary—factor contributing to investigative error. Many, if not most, people have difficulty evaluating their abilities objectively. A bigger problem is that most people—including criminal justice professionals—see little reason to improve their decision-making processes, believing that they have the ability to reason objectively; if anyone's analytical skills are in need of improvement, it is assumed to be those of "other" people (Fitch, 2010). In addition, research suggests that overconfidence is at its highest in our own areas of expertise, and in relation to challenging, rather than routine, tasks—namely, where it can be most damaging.

Overconfidence has been called one of the "seven deadly sins," supporting our belief that we know something, when, in fact, we do not (Piatelli-Palmarini, 1994, p. 115). It has a negative effect on our ability to accurately assess information and causes us to overvalue our abilities or to value them more highly than the abilities of others. This can cause us to overlook or discredit facts, information, and alternative opinions that we should reasonably consider, which leads to errors in judgment. Overconfidence has been identified as a dangerous factor in criminal investigations and in many other aspects of law enforcement work (Fitch, 2010).

We have seen how confirmation bias can lead investigators to become overly confident in their understanding of things—for example, the relevance of certain evidence to an alleged crime; however, several other factors contribute to overconfidence. One is the value that society places on *certainty*. Kahneman (2011, p. 263) has pointed out that, although "[a]n unbiased appreciation of uncertainty is a cornerstone of rationality [and of a scientific approach to the interpretation of evidence] ... it is not what people and organizations want." Bold expressions of confidence are often valued more highly (even if based largely on pretense) than are honest admissions of uncertainty. In fact, confidence is frequently rewarded—especially in police environments—while uncertainty is often perceived as a sign of weakness, even though it may more accurately characterize our true understanding of a particular phenomenon. On the topic of certainty, the French philosopher Charles Renouvier suggested that, "[p]roperly speaking, there is no certainty; there are only people who are certain." Nevertheless, it is not difficult to see how an investigator might succumb to pressure to express a greater degree of confidence in his or her understanding of an event than may be warranted by the evidence (Kahneman, 2011, p. 263).

Another factor that may contribute to investigator over-confidence is the fact that a person's confidence in a theory is determined not so much by the quality and amount of evidence that supports it, but by the *coherence* of the theory—that is, if a theory is consistent with other beliefs that a person holds about the world, he or she is more likely to be confident that the theory is correct regardless of the evidence, which may or may not support it. For example, an investigator may believe (rightly or wrongly) that criminals who sexually assault and murder their victims do not begin their criminal activities by committing these extreme acts, but rather commit a series of less violent crimes and work their way up to murder. If the same investigator were called on to investigate a crime in which the victim was sexually assaulted and murdered, he or she would likely have more confidence in an investigative theory that was consistent with the belief that the offender had progressed through a series of lesser crimes before committing a murder than in a theory that suggested the killer had no criminal history and a sex-killing was the first crime he had ever committed. The fact that many sexual killers may in fact progress from less serious to more serious crimes is not the point; the point is that a theory's coherence with an investigator's beliefs may cause an investigator to have confidence in that theory quite apart from whether or not the theory is supported by the evidence (Kahneman, 2011, pp. 264, 431). In practice, this theory might lead an investigator to focus the investigation more narrowly on a certain pool of suspects (known sexual offenders) than on others (persons with no previous criminal history).

GUY PAUL MORIN
In 1992, at his second trial for the first-degree murder of his nine-year-old neighbour Christine Jessop, Guy Paul Morin was sentenced to life imprisonment. During the trials, among the Crown's most significant evidence was hair and fibre presented by scientists from the Centre of Forensic Sciences, later revealed to have been contaminated. In 1995, previously unavailable DNA testing excluded Mr. Morin as the donor of semen found on the victim, and he was acquitted by the Ontario Court of Appeal. Mr. Morin had spent ten years in prison. The Kaufman Inquiry into Morin's wrongful conviction concluded that the conviction resulted from errors both in the investigation and at trial—including mistakes made by police, prosecutors, and forensic scientists—and that key individuals involved had lacked objectivity.

MANAGING THE RISK OF ERROR: POSITIVE STRATEGIES FOR NEGATIVE TENDENCIES

Half a century's worth of research on human judgment and decision making indicates that people are not the rational, objective decision makers they were often thought to be, but are, in fact, subject to a number of influences that can negatively affect their ability to reliably and effectively evaluate and act on information. Poor decisions by investigators can lead to errors that result in miscarriages of justice, legal action, and a public loss of confidence in criminal justice and forensic authorities. Yet few investigators receive training in how to make sound decisions.

It is clear that, although we may not be able to eliminate bias and other reasoning errors, criminal justice professionals could benefit from an increased awareness of the factors that affect the quality of the decisions they make. Similarly, investigators could benefit from learning about some simple, effective strategies to help them counter the effects of bias (Fitch, 2010).

Prepare to Err

Errors are inevitable (though admittedly, for the most part, undesirable), and a critical first step in managing error is expecting errors to happen. Errors are not some rare aberration, committed only by those who fail to take proper care in their work (although that may, of course, increase the probability of making an error). In looking at the phenomenon of error in the field of medicine, human error expert Professor James Reason concluded that "great doctors are not the ones who never make errors, rather they are people who expect errors to happen and have strategies in place to cope with them" (Reason, 2008).

One strategy that investigators can use to manage the risk of error while observing, collecting, analyzing, and interpreting evidence is an approach known as the "scientific method." While the method has its limitations, and scientists themselves sometimes stray from its basic precepts, it is the best method developed so far for producing valid knowledge about our world. One of its core precepts is discussed in the next section.

Try to Prove Yourself Wrong

One of the basic tenets of the scientific method is that we can get closest to the truth, or to the best available explanation about how the world really works, not just by gathering observations that are *consistent with* and that *confirm* our beliefs, but by formulating an idea—sometimes called a "theory," a "working theory," or a "hypothesis"—about how the world works and then trying to prove that it is *wrong*. If we fail in our honest efforts to do so, then we can have a reasonable amount of confidence that our idea is correct. Because this approach toward acquiring knowledge may seem counterintuitive, it is worth briefly exploring the logic behind it.

The basic idea underlying this approach to gaining knowledge about our world is that, although we can never prove with certainty that our understanding of a particular phenomenon is correct, we *can* prove with certainty that it is *wrong* (at least theoretically; practically speaking, we may encounter obstacles that limit our ability to do so). To use a classic example, if Mary were to formulate the hypothesis "all swans are white" and subsequently make a thousand separate observations of swans, each of which was white, she would have gathered a considerable amount of evidence that was consistent with her hypothesis and would likely be quite confident that her hypothesis was correct. Yet she would still not be able to conclude with *certainty* that her theory was correct, because a black swan may exist somewhere that she had not yet observed. All it would take to disprove her theory would be for her, or anyone else, to observe a single black swan. As Einstein said, "the *truth* of a theory can never be proven, for one never knows if future experience will contradict its conclusions" (Calaprice, 2000, p. 237).

Although it is the way we often go about attempting to establish truth, trying to establish the truth of a theory—about how a crime occurred or what a piece of evidence really means—by considering only evidence that supports that theory:

1. prevents us from discovering that the theory may be wrong; and

2. does not generate as strong a degree of proof of the correctness of the theory as would a deliberate and unsuccessful attempt to prove it wrong—for example, by looking for evidence of black swans and not finding any.

As Taleb (2007, p. 56) observed in Chapter 5 (playfully titled "Confirmation Shmonfirmation!") of *The Black Swan*:

> We can get closer to the truth by negative instances, not by verification! It is misleading to build a general rule (such as, all swans are white) from observed facts. Contrary to conventional wisdom, our body of knowledge does not increase from a series of confirmatory observations.

Those who may be tempted to ask, "what does all this academic gibberish about swans have to do with real-life criminal investigation?" would do well to consider any one of the well-documented cases of wrongful conviction in which innocent persons were convicted of a crime on the basis of multiple pieces of evidence ("white swans") that were consistent with the theory of the crime (that is, "Johnny did it"), but where the theory of the crime was subsequently proven to be wrong by a single piece of disconfirming evidence ("black swan"), such as DNA. People have spent decades of their lives in prison for crimes they did not commit, and in some cases for crimes that never happened, on the basis of evidence that was consistent with, but did not conclusively prove, the theory of the crime. For criminal investigators, therefore, there can be no more important *practical* reason for understanding the importance of trying to prove oneself wrong before believing that one is right. The best explanations are not those that we grasp onto and believe to be correct simply because we have observed evidence that is consistent with them, but those that survive our attempts to disprove them.

> **GREGORY PARSONS**
>
> In 1994, Mr. Parsons was wrongfully convicted in the first-degree murder of his mother and sentenced to life imprisonment. Key to his conviction was hearsay evidence that Parsons's mother was afraid of her son. Mr. Parsons appealed, and was released on bail after 68 days in prison until his appeal could be resolved. Before the appeal, DNA testing excluded Mr. Parsons as the killer and, in 1998, he was acquitted by the Newfoundland Superior Court. A childhood friend of Mr. Parsons pled guilty to the second-degree murder of Parsons's mother in 2002.

Suspend Your Judgment, Consider Alternatives, and Counterargue

Investigators must consciously attempt to suspend their judgment about a case and resist the impulse to draw conclusions too quickly. They must try to keep an "open mind" as the facts come out and allow their understanding of a case to be formed and reformed as the evidence emerges. Investigators' initial judgments about the evidence in a case can have a significant influence on their final analysis of that evidence, and summarizing what each piece of evidence does or does not tell as it is gathered can help investigators avoid hasty judgments. During complex investigations, it has the added benefit of helping those involved maintain focus on the "big picture."

As part of their efforts to keep an open mind, investigators should put forth an alternative theory or theories of the crime and offer evidence and arguments to reject the alternatives. If the alternatives are fairly and successfully rejected, then confidence in the original theory may legitimately increase (as illustrated in the black swan example above). If, however, the evidence supports an alternative theory, that theory must be explored fully until it can either be rejected or replace the original theory. This is an important strategy because research indicates that investigators facing time pressures—a reality in virtually all significant investigations—generate fewer alternative explanations for the crimes they are investigating than those not facing such pressures (Doran, Long, & Allison, 2009).

As we have seen, one of the products of confirmation bias is overconfidence in the accuracy of one's own interpretations and conclusions; research suggests that this can be mitigated to some degree by requiring people to articulate the reasons why the *opposite* of their own position might be true. Investigators should therefore consider the opposite of their currently held position and articulate how the available evidence might support it—a technique known as "counterarguing." Counterarguing also has potential to offset the effects of belief perseverance (people's reluctance to give up their initial conclusions about something even when the foundation for their initial conclusion has been completely undermined). It has been suggested that, in order to be really effective, counterarguing should become an established part of every investigative process (Findley & Scott, 2006).

Check Your Key Assumptions

Cognitive biases can be rendered less harmful by making them explicit. Visualization has been suggested as one way to help maintain a realistic picture of the level of uncertainty in a situation (Kebbel, Muller, & Martin, 2010). Using visualization programs such as IBM i2 Analyst's Notebook, or simple charts, an investigator or analyst can keep all relevant information—both confirming and disconfirming—visible, and thus cognitively accessible. Making visual their assumptions, chains of inference, and areas of uncertainty forces investigators to confront them and consider on exactly what basis they know what they think they know. In doing so, they break their theories down into key parts and test the validity of each part. This is referred to as a "key assumptions check" (Central Intelligence Agency [CIA], 2009, p. 7). The act of making explicit assumptions and judgments of evidence will help investigators clarify the strengths and weaknesses of their case and identify errors or unwarranted assumptions that may not have been obvious previously.

Related to this is the role of the devil's advocate, or "contrarian." The devil's advocate identifies the key assumptions behind a strongly held belief of the investigator or investigative team and assesses the nature of the evidence that supports those assumptions. The devil's advocate then selects the assumptions that appear weakest and challenges them, pointing out the flaws and describing how the evidence could support an alternative hypothesis. The knowledge and insight gained through this process can be used to amend and improve the original idea, or it might reveal that the original idea is fundamentally flawed and should be abandoned in favour of a new one (CIA, 2009).

The value of having someone assigned to a devil's advocate role in an investigation has been recognized by Canadian police services and it forms part of the Major Case Management (MCM) methodology for managing major cases. The role can be assigned to an individual, or it can be encouraged among the investigative team as a whole.

Conduct a "Pre-mortem" Examination

Kahneman (2011) proposes a "pre-mortem" approach to addressing the problem of overconfidence. This process involves meeting with a group of individuals who are knowledgeable about the decision to be made—for example, adopting a particular theory to guide an investigation—and asking them to imagine that the decision was taken, the theory was adopted, and disaster resulted. The individuals are then asked to take 5 to 10 minutes to write a short "history" of that disaster. This process has two strengths:

1. It helps overcome "groupthink" (the negative tendency for people in a group to consider few alternative viewpoints and avoid giving their fellow team members critical feedback on their ideas throughout the process, but especially once a decision appears to have been made).

2. It encourages knowledgeable individuals to turn their imaginations toward the issue.

The primary virtues of the pre-mortem approach are that it gives those who may doubt the validity of the decision an "approved"—that is, an organizationally "safe"—forum in which to voice those doubts, and it encourages those who may support the decision to look for possible weaknesses they may not have considered. Although a pre-mortem examination is not necessarily a solution to the problem of cognitive biases and the overconfidence that may result, the process at least encourages decision makers (such as criminal investigators) to take a critical look at their thought processes and consider evidence that may suggest their understanding of the issues may not be as sound as first thought (Kahneman, 2011, pp. 264–265).

CULTURAL DIMENSIONS OF ERROR MANAGEMENT

In addition to the human tendencies discussed above, another factor that has contributed to miscarriages of justice in Canada is a criminal justice culture with certain ingrained attitudes and practices. In order to reduce the risk of similar failures in the future, these must change (FPT Report, 2011, pp. 186–187). The following have been suggested as key steps toward achieving this end.

The Importance of Error Barriers

Police and forensic organizations must view error as an inevitable (albeit, undesirable) part of human activity, which is most effectively managed on an organizational, as opposed to an individual, level. Organizations must continue to develop and employ organizational strategies for managing error by implementing procedures and protocols to make it more difficult for individuals to make errors and for errors that *are* made to persist uncorrected.

Today, many error experts have adopted the perspective that most errors are committed by capable individuals who operate within systems that were not designed to account for human fallibility. This perspective differs from the historical one, in which the actions of the person closest to the error (for example, the pilot

RANDY DRUKEN

Wrongfully convicted of the first-degree murder of his girlfriend and sentenced to life imprisonment in 1995, Mr. Druken spent six years in prison. The centrepiece of the Crown's case was the testimony of a jailhouse informant who said that Mr. Druken had confessed his crime to him. In 2000, DNA testing revealed that Mr. Druken was not the donor of DNA found on a cigarette believed to belong to the killer, and the informant admitted that his statement about the confession had been false, prompted by bullying by police. The Lamer Inquiry found that Mr. Druken had been a victim of tunnel vision within the justice system.

who was flying the plane at the time of the accident) were given the most attention and the root causes of the error (those systemic factors that allowed it to happen, such as understaffing leading to fatigue) were rarely considered. Doyle (2010) makes an important point—one that runs through this entire chapter—when he says, "All humans err frequently. Systems that rely on error-free performance are doomed to fail" (p. 122). There is a need to shift away from simply looking at individual practitioners (and their presumed carelessness or ineptitude) as "the cause" of error and consider the interplay between practitioners and the larger context in which they work and how that interaction contributes to errors (Wilkins & Shields, 2008).

Doyle (2010) suggests looking at wrongful convictions and other criminal justice system errors as "organizational accidents" in which a number of small errors (no one of which would be sufficient to cause the event) "combine with each other and with latent defects in the criminal justice system to create disasters." This approach can help create a "culture of safety" (Doyle, 2010, p. 109). Managing error effectively in criminal justice organizations requires that protocols be put in place that anticipate error and seek to minimize the risk of it going undetected. One simple example is the contrarian role, discussed above and currently used by the Vancouver Police Department. During the course of an investigation, an investigator is assigned the specific task of attempting to disprove the evidence pointing to the suspect.

The Benefits of Sharing Errors

One of the problems identified in the field of health care (which suffers from a significant number of practitioner errors that adversely affect patient well-being) is the absence of a system for practitioners to learn from the mistakes made by others in their field. It is primarily left to individual practitioners to learn those lessons, and this is simply not an effective way for a profession to improve (Leape, 2008). A similar situation exists in the criminal justice field and, as a result, there has been a call for professionals within the system to create a professional culture in which learning from error is an integral, systematic, and sustained practice (see, for example, Doyle, 2010; Sangha, Roach, & Moles, 2010). Errors should be regarded as "sentinel events" (events which signal the need for attention and action); when detected, errors should be corrected and treated as "important opportunities to illuminate hidden flaws" (Doyle, 2010, p. 128).

Existing and proposed mechanisms for sharing errors include:

- mandatory major-case debriefings, in which investigators are required to discuss all aspects of the case, especially anything that went wrong, and how those errors might be avoided in the future;
- the establishment of a national, investigative error clearinghouse, in which information on investigative failures is gathered, maintained, analyzed, and made available online; and
- ongoing professional development courses and conferences, where criminal justice participants from a variety of professions present case studies that highlight the lessons to be learned from various criminal justice failures.

For any of these mechanisms to be truly effective, however, a cultural shift is required from viewing error as the result of a personal or professional deficiency to seeing error as common and, typically, the result of a complex interaction between professionals and the environment in which they work. We learn far more from our errors than we do from our successes, and errors are simply too valuable not to be rigorously and regularly examined for the lessons they have to offer.

The Need for More Research

Forensic and investigative practitioners need to learn more about the limits of various forensic disciplines, in terms of both their methods and the type of knowledge that those methods can reliably produce—including the limits of such knowledge.

The FPT Report (2011), NAS Report (2009), and other publications that have examined the issue of error in the criminal justice field (for example, Mnookin et al., 2011) have all identified a need for more research in the field of forensic science. The NAS Report (2009) raises the possibility that courts may begin to question some forensic evidence because of the shortage of empirical research supporting much of it: in other words, premises and techniques in many fields have not been sufficiently validated through systematic research (NAS Report, 2009, p. 187). Multidisciplinary groups composed of forensic practitioners and academics have also agreed that "the traditional forensic sciences in general, and the pattern identification disciplines, such as fingerprint, firearm, toolmark, and handwriting identification evidence, in particular, do not currently possess—and absolutely must develop—a well-established scientific foundation" (Mnookin et al., 2011, pp. 725–726).

On the basis of its extensive review of the state of forensic science in the United States, the NAS Report (2009) states that, in relation to the ability of the various forensic disciplines to "individualize" a piece of evidence, "[w]ith the exception of DNA analysis … , no forensic method has been rigorously shown to have the capacity to consistently, and with a high degree of certainty, demonstrate a connection between evidence and a specific individual or source" (quoted in Mnookin et al., 2011, p. 729). This is an important point, and one that should cause forensic practitioners to reflect on the nature of the opinions they are capable of offering to a court. The inability of most forensic disciplines to demonstrate uniqueness, however, does not mean that experts cannot reasonably give testimony about having determined the source of an object. It *does* mean that such testimony must be measured and expressed in terms of probability, not certainty (Kaye, 2010).

The NAS Report also found a "wide variability" across different forensic science disciplines with respect to issues such as techniques and methodologies, reliability, error rates, reporting of results, research foundations, general acceptability of fundamental premises, and published research. Although some forensic disciplines involve the analysis of evidence in rigorous laboratory environments, drawing on well-established bodies of scientific research—for example, DNA and toxicological analysis—others rely primarily on an expert's subjective analysis of the patterns they observe—for example, fingerprints, handwriting, and toolmarks; in a field such as fingerprint identification, for example, little research has been conducted to determine such fundamental issues as what constitutes a sufficient basis for

SHARING ERRORS, SAVING LIVES

Although traditionally the sharing of information regarding errors has been, and continues to be, a problem in the health-care field, the situation is beginning to change. Recently, Quebec (the only province to make such numbers public) released data about errors in its health-care system. Quebec's register of errors and accidents indicates that during a six-month period, 179,000 "events" were recorded in approximately 270 facilities. The events were classified as either incidents or accidents. Incidents are events that could have had negative consequences, but were corrected before they did so—for example, a nurse noticing that he or she is about to give a patient the wrong medication in time to avoid doing so. An accident is an event that did have a negative effect on a patient's health—for example, the wrong medication actually being given to a patient. Quebec's minister of health emphasized that one of the benefits of the registry is the transparency it provides. Transparency has been identified as an important factor in an organization's ability to learn from and prevent errors (CBC News, 2011; Fidelman, 2011). This is especially important given that research suggests as many as 23,000 Canadians die each year from preventable medical errors (Baker et al., 2004).

The criminal justice field currently lacks—and would benefit from having—a similar, formal, error-sharing mechanism. Although judicial inquiries into wrongful convictions and official reports designed to address the causes of catastrophic failures (such as the Goudge Inquiry or the FPT Report) serve to educate criminal justice practitioners about error and, by so doing, help reduce the risk of similar errors being made in the future, they represent an irregular response to the everyday challenge of managing the risk of error in the criminal justice system.

making an identification or the potential error rate for fingerprint identification in practice (NAS Report, 2009; Mnookin, 2003).

The limited empirical foundation on which many of the traditional forensic disciplines rest is problematic, because it limits the ability of a court to guarantee the reliability of the forensic evidence that practitioners gather, interpret, and present in the form of expert testimony. The FPT Report (2011) cites Canadian common-law decisions, which, while acknowledging the cumulative, evolving nature of scientific knowledge, have stressed the need for such knowledge to be reliably grounded in research if it is to continue to be accepted. In *R. v. Trochym* (2007), the Supreme Court said that "the admissibility of scientific evidence is not frozen in time" (para. 31), and "even if it has received judicial recognition in the past, a technique or science whose underlying assumptions are challenged should not be admitted in evidence without first confirming the validity of those assumptions" (para. 32). In other words, the fact that a forensic discipline has been in use for nearly a century and is commonly accepted by the courts does not mean that the continued acceptance of that type of expert evidence is a given.

Justice Stephen Goudge, Commissioner of the Goudge Inquiry (MacFarlane, 2008), emphasized that a premium should be placed on the reliability of expert evidence by the criminal justice system "if it is to maximize the contribution of that evidence to the truth-seeking function and be faithful to the fundamental fairness required of the criminal process" (MacFarlane, 2008, p. 484). It is clear that the amount of "science"—that is, an accepted body of knowledge based on empirical research and well-defined analytical methods—that stands behind different forensic disciplines varies substantially and the claims that experts in most forensic disciplines can reasonably make fall far short of absolute. The real-world picture of the field of forensic science that has emerged from decades of inquiries stands in stark contrast not only to the idealized—and vastly more certain—"CSI-like" versions portrayed in popular culture, but also to the more idealized versions believed to exist in real life by some forensic practitioners. Ensuring the value and reliability of expert evidence will require the implementation of a comprehensive and ongoing research agenda (NAS Report, 2009, p. 188).

Establishing a Research Culture

A multidisciplinary group of forensic scientists and academics has pointed to the need for the development of a "research culture" in the forensic sciences (Mnookin et al., 2011), stating that the traditional forensic sciences, in general, and the pattern identification disciplines, in particular, do not currently possess—and must develop—a well-established scientific foundation. It is not that courts have necessarily begun to reject these types of evidence, but that forensic practitioners are now being forced to articulate and justify professional practices that had previously been accepted with little examination. Contributing factors to this shift include legal challenges; widely publicized forensic errors; skeptical scholarship; and a number of high-profile studies in the United States, United Kingdom, and Canada that indicate both that misleading, overstated, or erroneous forensic evidence has been a factor in a substantial number of wrongful convictions and that the scientific foundations for some long-accepted forms of forensic evidence are far less substantial than has been assumed.

The above studies have called for the development of a research culture in which the relationship between research-based knowledge and forensic practice is central, a culture in which the questions "What do we know?" and "How do we know it?" are answered on the basis of research data, published studies, and other publicly accessible materials and not primarily on the basis of experience, craft knowledge, or assumptions that because a particular type of knowledge or practice has been accepted for years, it must be valid.

The studies are not suggesting that a practitioner's experience-based knowledge is of no value, but that it cannot serve as the knowledge on which a forensic discipline rests and allow the discipline to produce claims of, for example, individualization in the case of fingerprints or handwriting. Personal experience *alone* is not a sufficient basis for making such claims; instead, claims must be based on rigorous scientific research. A research culture in the forensic sciences should emphasize the core values of empiricism, transparency, and critical perspective. While many of those working within the criminal justice field already embrace such values, their acceptance by some practitioners is lagging.

Empiricism stresses the importance of evidence (data), as discovered and tested by scientific research. Claims made about the overall capabilities of a forensic discipline or knowledge claims made by individual practitioners must be assessed with reference to the degree to which those claims are supported by the body of

THE MOVE TOWARD AN EVIDENCE-BASED CULTURE IN CANADA

Over the past ten years, the global movement toward a research, or evidence-based, culture in the forensic sciences has begun to be reflected in Canada. It is no longer sufficient for an expert providing evidence to offer an opinion based solely on the expert's claim to experience and expertise, as was commonly the case in the past. Instead, experts are increasingly required to identify both the empirical evidence on which their opinions are based (and any evidence that might contradict it) and the reasoning process used to arrive at their conclusions.

This approach helps reveal flawed assumptions and other types of error by requiring experts to articulate how and on what basis they arrived at their conclusions. This process also assists an expert to identify and clarify the level of confidence that they have in their opinion—which ultimately helps the courts protect the legal system from the harmful effects of flawed or improper evidence (FPT Report, 2011).

available data. Practitioners' hunches or beliefs (whether based on personal experience or anecdotal evidence) should not be given the same weight as knowledge based on scientific research, and practitioners should not make knowledge claims that extend beyond what is reasonably supported by existing research. Practitioners should expect that their claims to "know something" will only be accepted by a court to the extent that those claims rest on a firm empirical foundation.

Transparency is the sharing of knowledge and an openness regarding forensic practices and procedures. A culture that embraces transparency recognizes error as an inevitable part of the process through which people perceive and attempt to understand their world, and acknowledges errors as valuable learning opportunities, rather than shameful aberrations to be hidden from view.

Critical perspective is something that investigators and forensic specialists must maintain while carrying out their work. They must remember that their claims of knowledge about the evidence they analyze are provisional, and subject to revision if and as new information emerges. They must also acknowledge that research is an ongoing enterprise in which knowledge is gained incrementally and that a particular forensic discipline cannot simply rest on the results of several studies, but must continue to test and build on its knowledge base. Regardless of whether courts have accepted a particular type of forensic evidence in the past, ongoing research testing current forensic practices and knowledge is necessary.

CONCLUSION

Good investigative work involves more than simply gathering evidence that supports one's theory of the crime—that is relatively easy. Good investigative work requires an investigator to manage the risk of error while constructing his or her understanding of the event under investigation—and that is much more difficult. While some poets may consider it "divine" to forgive errors, there is little reason to forgive the investigator who, having made little or no effort to manage the risk of error, goes horribly astray. There is simply too much at stake.

An investigator's understanding of the events reconstructed during a criminal investigation is based on what is left behind. Each piece of evidence provides a partial glimpse of a past event and, to the extent that those glimpses are clear and accurate, our understanding of the event may improve. To the extent that they are unclear or misapprehended, our understanding may suffer. Given that, as humans, we grapple with the ever-present risk of committing errors of perception and comprehension, an investigator's most powerful tool for constructing a valid understanding of past events is *humility*: humility that comes from an appreciation of the provisional nature of the investigative enterprise and the knowledge it produces; humility that helps us counteract our tendency toward overconfidence; humility that recognizes that, no matter how much time and effort we put into an investigation, some degree of uncertainty will always remain in our knowledge and understanding of particular events.

Mnookin et al. (2011) discuss the need for knowledge claims (the claims a person makes to "know" something) to be put forward with "appropriate epistemic modesty" (p. 778), which is another way of saying that criminal justice practitioners need to take a measured position toward what they believe they know and the opinions they offer and allow for the possibility that, although they may believe they are right, they could be wrong.

Although an investigation may be described as "a search for the truth," the closest an investigator can hope to come to the truth is to identify the "best" explanation for a particular event given the available evidence. By "best," we mean the one explanation among the possible alternatives that is most probable based on an objective analysis of the available evidence, and which will have to be revisited if new evidence emerges. This distinction between the "truth" and the "best" explanation goes to the heart of the investigative process. Investigators who are certain that they have discovered the "truth" will be reluctant to modify their beliefs in response to new evidence or analysis, while those who understand that their explanation of a past event is provisional will remain open to better explanations, should they emerge.

Although determinations of "truth" and "guilt" are properly made by courts of law, the evidence on which they are made is typically informed by the work of forensic and criminal investigators. Justice requires, therefore, that this work be performed to the highest possible standards, which can only be attained when investigators recognize the intimate relationship that exists between evidence, error, and justice, and make knowledge claims with an appropriate degree of humility.

KEY TERMS

cognitive bias
confirmation bias
context bias

FURTHER READING

Association in Defence of the Wrongfully Convicted. http://www.aidwyc.org/index.html.

Federal/Provincial/Territorial Heads of Prosecutions Subcommittee on the Prevention of Wrongful Convictions. (2011). *The path to justice: Preventing wrongful convictions—Report of the federal/provincial/territorial heads of prosecutions subcommittee on the prevention of wrongful convictions.* Ottawa: Public Prosecution Service of Canada. http://www.ppsc-sppc.gc.ca/eng/pub/ptj-spj/ptj-spj-eng.pdf ("FPT Report").

Innocence Project. http://www.innocenceproject.org.

Kahneman, D. (2011). *Thinking, fast and slow.* Toronto: Doubleday Canada.

Konnikova, M. (2011, September 6). Lessons from Sherlock Holmes: Confidence is good; overconfidence, not so much. *Scientific American.* http://blogs.scientificamerican.com/guest-blog/2011/09/06/lessons-from-sherlock-holmes-confidence-is-good-overconfidence-not-so-much.

National Academy of Sciences (NAS). (2009). *Strengthening forensic science in the United States: A path forward.* Washington, DC: The National Academies Press. http://www.nap.edu/openbook.php?record_id=12589.

Rossmo, D.K. (2009). *Criminal investigative failures.* Boca Raton, FL: CRC Press.

Sangha, B., Roach, K., & Moles, R. (2010). *Forensic investigations and miscarriages of justice.* Toronto: Irwin Law.

Glossary

A

accelerant a substance that burns rapidly and will start and encourage a fire

accidental death death caused by unexpected or unintentional injury

accused a suspect who has been charged with a crime

admissibility process governing which materials (testimony, documents, and physical objects) offered as proof in a legal proceeding can be considered evidence by the trier of fact

admissions acts or words of an accused offered as evidence against the accused

adverse witness a witness called in support of one's own side, but whose evidence turns out to be unfavourable

affiant a person who makes and swears an affidavit

affidavit a written and witnessed statement of evidence that the maker swears and signs as proof of its truth

alibi an excuse, which typically takes the form of a claim that a person was somewhere else when the crime was committed

arrest the actual seizure or touching of an individual by an officer with the intent of taking physical control of that person for the purpose of detention; or an announcement by an officer of his or her intent to arrest a person accompanied by an attempt to take physical control of that person

arson the deliberate setting of a fire

authorization to intercept private communications authorizes tapping someone's phone by use of a wire and using a "bug"

B

ballistics the study of the path or trajectory of ordnance

best evidence rule a legal rule requiring that wherever possible, the original document (the best evidence), rather than a reproduction, should be introduced in evidence

***Browne v. Dunn* rule** a rule of fairness stating that if counsel is going to challenge the credibility of a witness by calling contradictory evidence, the witness must be given an opportunity to address the contradictory evidence

buccal swab sample of tissue taken from the inside of the mouth to obtain skin cells; less invasive than taking blood, with the advantage of obtaining tissue cells rather than blood

burden of proof also called "onus" of proof; the requirement of proving a particular fact or argument

C

calibre the diameter of the barrel of a gun, before rifling is added, measured from lands to lands, and providing class characteristics

Canadian Police Information Centre (CPIC) a national law enforcement computer database maintained by the RCMP, containing data on aspects of police investigations, such as stolen property, people in conflict with the law, surveillance, and missing persons

charging the jury the judge's instructions to the jury, usually at the end of a trial, in preparation for the jury's deliberations

chief medical examiner *see* coroner

circumstantial evidence evidence that logically supports a fact, but that is at least partly dependent on speculation

class characteristics characteristics that link an object to a group of objects, eliminating all other groups

clean evidence physical evidence that is free of taint related to mishandling by investigators or prosecutors

coerced–compliant false confession the most common type of false confession identified in *R. v. Oickle* (2000), it is given knowingly by an individual in response to threats or promises

coerced–persuaded false confession a false confession that shares the same characteristics as the non-coerced–persuaded false confession, but in which threats and promises have also been used

cognitive bias a natural tendency to make consistent and predictable errors in the way we think, perceive, recall, interpret, and act on information

common warrant to search and seize authorizes search for and seizure of anything that will afford evidence of the specific offence being investigated

compellability being without legal excuse (such as status as the accused's spouse) for not testifying

competence being legally permitted to testify (based on the absence of factors such as being a "spouse" or mental handicap)

computer forensic examination the analysis of information contained within and created with computer systems, typically for the purpose of determining who accessed the information, how they accessed it, and when they accessed it

confession an admission to all of the elements of an offence, including the mental element

confession rule a long-established doctrine of common law that holds that no statement made by an accused person to a person in authority is admissible against them unless the Crown can show beyond a reasonable doubt that the statement was given voluntarily

confirmation bias the tendency to seek information or interpret evidence that confirms our hypotheses and to avoid information that would disprove them

contamination the introduction of material, unrelated to the commission of the crime, into a crime scene after the crime has occurred

context bias bias that arises from exposure to extraneous information, which can affect the judgment of forensic investigators

continuity in the context of physical evidence, an ability to account for the whereabouts of the evidence (and the identity of those who have had access to it) from the time of its collection to the time it is entered as an exhibit in the trial record

conventional warrant *see* common warrant to search and seize

coroner a provincial medical authority responsible for determining the cause of sudden, unnatural deaths

coroner's inquest typically conducted after an accident or unnatural death, provides recommendations in an attempt to prevent further deaths in similar, future circumstances

corroborative evidence independently sourced evidence that supports another piece of evidence

crime scene any place in which a crime occurred or in which evidence relating to a possible crime has been located

criminal information a sworn document in which the charges against an individual are set out

criminal investigator *see* detective

cross-contamination the transfer of material from one piece of evidence to another

cross-examination the questioning of a witness by opposing counsel

Crown or public-interest privilege a class of privilege protecting information the disclosure of which would threaten the public interest, such as, in some cases, the identity of undercover investigators

CSI (crime scene investigator) *see* forensic identification specialist

CSI effect the alleged influence of popular television crime investigation programs on juror behaviour and the broader public's understanding of the criminal investigation process

D

declarant a person who makes a statement in testimony

declarations against interest statements made by a person that seem to acknowledge, for example, guilt or a debt—that is, the opposite of self-serving statements

demonstrative evidence evidentiary "tools" produced by a party to help explain a case, such as maps or photographs of the crime scene

detective also referred to as criminal investigator, investigator, or investigative officer; typically, the officer in charge of a criminal investigation

digital evidence information stored or transmitted in binary form that may be relied on in court—for example, email, pictures, videos, or text messages

direct evidence evidence that proves an important fact without the need to speculate

direct examination *see* examination-in-chief

disclosure duty requiring the Crown to provide the accused with access to all information in its possession or control that relates to the investigation, provided that there are no legal restrictions on doing so

DNA deoxyribonucleic acid, the genetic material found in the nucleus of cells, unique to every human except identical twins and used to individualize biological samples in an investigation

DNA fingerprinting *see* DNA typing

DNA profiling *see* DNA typing

DNA typing also called DNA fingerprinting and DNA profiling, a technique used by forensic biologists to individualize a person using their genetic profile

documentary evidence a class of physical/real evidence that consists of documents of any kind, handwritten or mechanically produced

E

enhanced cognitive interview (ECI) an interview that uses the four original CI techniques, but attempts to maximize their effectiveness by placing them in an appropriate structure and providing interviewers with instructions on how best to use them to minimize the tendency of police interviewers to engage in counterproductive behaviours such as interrupting or using short-answer questions

essential elements the particular acts and intentions required to prove a specified offence

evidence any information or physical material relied on in legal proceedings to prove or disprove a fact or legal argument

evidence-in-chief *see* examination-in-chief

examination-in-chief a party's questioning of its own witnesses

exculpatory that which clears or tends to clear a person of guilt

exemplar a sample of someone's handwriting, which can be either collected or requested, for comparison with a questioned document

exhibit any piece of evidence (physical or documentary) other than oral testimony that is "entered" in the trial record

expert witness a witness with specialized knowledge in a particular subject that is beyond that of the average lay person

F

Feeney warrant *see* warrant to enter a dwelling house

FIS officer *see* forensic identification specialist

forensic anthropologist an expert who specializes in human identification using the human skeleton in a medico-legal context

forensic identification specialist also referred to as an identification (or "ident") officer, an "FIS officer," a "SOCO" (scenes of crime officer), or a "CSI" (crime scene investigator); the person responsible for the physical investigation of the crime scene, including identifying, documenting, collecting, preserving, and analyzing or submitting for analysis the physical evidence obtained from a crime scene

forensic pathologist a medical doctor with specialized training in forensic pathology who conducts autopsies and determines the manner and cause of death in suspicious circumstances

forensic pathology the application of pathology in law through autopsies to determine manner and cause of death

forensic science the application of science to law

forensic scientist a civilian, laboratory scientist with analytical expertise in, for example, chemistry, biology, firearms, or questioned documents who analyzes and reports on evidence

G

gauge the width of the barrel in an unrifled shotgun

general warrant authorizes a peace officer to use any device, investigative technique, or procedure to do anything described in the warrant with the exception of interfering with a person's bodily integrity

H

having a view (look-see) an excursion by the judge or jury to a site outside the courtroom to view evidence that cannot reasonably be presented in court

hearsay evidence that is indirect because it is given by a witness who has heard it from another source; second-hand evidence

homicide death, directly or indirectly, of one person at the hands of another

I

identification (or "ident") officer *see* forensic identification specialist

impression evidence created when two objects come into contact with sufficient force to cause an impression or a mark

impression prints recognizable fingerprints left behind in any soft materials—for example, plasticine, tar, or caulking

inculpatory that which establishes or tends to establish a person's guilt

indictment a form, often prepared after a fuller investigation, that sets out the offence(s) for which the accused person will be tried at trial

individual characteristics characteristics that can be linked to a single source, belonging to a particular object and no other

inducement a promise, favour, threat, or representation made to an accused that can be perceived as an effort to coerce the accused into making a confession

information a form, prepared after the accused person has been arrested, that describes the offence(s) with which the accused is charged

information to obtain (ITO) a document used to apply for judicial authorization, setting out, for example, name of individual applying for authorization; offence being investigated; building, receptacle, or place to be searched and things to be searched for; and informant's grounds for believing that the application meets the test for issuance by a justice

innate characteristic a characteristic common to a group that does not apply to all objects in the group

intent also called *mens rea*; the mental element of an offence that must be proved to secure a conviction

interrogation an accusatory process, the primary purpose of which is to elicit a confession from a suspect who is believed to be responsible for the offence under investigation

interview a structured conversation between a witness, victim, or suspect and an investigator, in which the investigator asks a series of questions in order to elicit information from the witness, victim, or suspect about something that they observed, experienced, did, or have knowledge about

investigative detention brief detention by police of a person who is not a suspect in a crime, involving significant physical or psychological restraint, where police have reasonable grounds to suspect that the person is connected to the crime; activates a person's Charter rights related to detention or arrest

investigative interaction interaction between the police and a member of the public who may be kept waiting by police conducting a general investigative inquiry; as long as it does not involve significant physical or psychological restraint, it does not activate a person's Charter rights related to detention or arrest

investigative officer *see* detective

investigator *see* detective

J

judicial pre-authorization process in which a police officer obtains permission from a judicial authority to conduct a search or seizure

K

KGB caution a prepared statement read to an interviewee by the police before an interview, informing the interviewee that the interview will be electronically recorded and that the interviewee will be swearing an oath to tell the truth and will face potential criminal consequences if he or she lies to or deliberately misleads police during the interview

L

latent prints fingerprints that are not readily apparent, and require further processing to make them visible for comparison with file or reference prints

lay witness any witness testifying about a subject matter in which he or she is not an expert

leading question a question that suggests an answer to the person to whom it is directed, and limits their opportunity to respond to either a "yes" or "no" response, or to a short response—for example, "Was Mr. Smith a nice man?"

like with like the comparison of two objects, side by side—for example, a tool mark with a cast of the suspect tool

Locard's exchange principle formulation by one of the founding fathers of modern forensic science, Edmond Locard, stating that "every contact leaves a trace"

look-see *see* having a view (look-see)

M

master evidence log a record of all the individual pieces of physical evidence collected from a particular crime scene and what has been done with them

material witness a witness who has observed "material" facts, or facts that are relevant to proving the elements of the offence with which an accused is charged

materiality the degree to which a piece of evidence is necessary in proving a proposition

***Mills* regime** supersedes *O'Connor* as the procedure that governs the production of third-party records in sexual assault cases only

mitochondrial DNA genetic material found in the mitochondria of cells, shared by all individuals in a particular maternal line and thus of more limited use in an investigation than (nuclear) DNA

N

natural death caused by disease and not attributable to injury or abnormal environmental factors

natural variation differences in an individual's normal writing

non-coerced–persuaded false confession a false confession given as a result of certain police interrogation tactics that have confused a person or caused them to doubt their own memory, and which have temporarily persuaded them of their own guilt

number recorder warrant authorizes a peace officer to install, maintain, monitor, and remove any device used to record or identify the telephone number or location from which a telephone call originates or is received

O

oath a promise to tell the truth that is "sworn" with a hand on the Bible

oath helping when one witness (improperly) expresses an opinion about the credibility of another witness

objection a formal verbal declaration made in a courtroom for the purpose of notifying the judge and opposing counsel of counsel's belief that improper evidence is being adduced (such as hearsay) that should be excluded or that an improper procedure is being employed (such as leading the witness) that should be corrected

***O'Connor* application** procedure through which an accused can gain access to third-party records outside the first-party disclosure duty of the Crown as set out in *Stinchcombe*

open-ended question a question that gives the person to whom it is directed the opportunity to give a full and detailed response—for example, "Tell me about Mr. Smith."

opinion evidence evidence of what a witness thinks or believes, generally held to be inadmissible

oral (*viva voce*) evidence spoken (verbal) evidence of a witness as given under oath or affirmation in a legal proceeding

order of detention period of time required for judicial supervision of things seized under s. 490 of the *Criminal Code*

P

past recollection recorded a witness may adopt the events as recorded in a document for which he or she has no present recollection

patent prints fingerprints readily visible to the naked eye, which may be photographed and compared with other prints without further processing

pattern evidence additional evidence typically contained within the mark or impression evidence

PEACE model a best practice approach to interviewing victims, witnesses, and suspects developed by police, academics, and lawyers in the United Kingdom during the 1990s that focuses on eliciting the maximum amount of information from a subject and, in the case of a suspect, using that information to challenge inconsistencies between the suspect's account of events and the totality of the evidence

perjury lying while under oath or affirmation

person in authority typically refers to persons who are formally engaged in the arrest, detention, examination, or prosecution of the accused—for example, police officers, prison guards, and Crown attorneys

physical evidence evidence that takes the form of actual objects, as opposed to testimony; includes real, demonstrative, and view evidence

plain view doctrine a legal principle stating that when a police officer is executing a search warrant in respect of one crime and evidence of another crime comes into "plain view," such evidence may be lawfully seized

police informer privilege a privilege that attaches, in some situations, to the identity of a police informer, such as the provider of a "Crime Stoppers" tip

prejudicial effect the undesirable "side effects" of a piece of evidence that may be deemed unfair to the accused

preliminary hearing a hearing held before the real trial to determine preliminary issues, such as whether there is enough evidence to proceed to trial

present memory refreshed a witness may use a document to refresh his or her memory of past events

***prima facie* evidence** evidence that is reliable on first impression, and that is accepted in the absence of any challenge to its validity

primary caution a warning given by an investigator to a suspect informing him or her that an officer is conducting an investigation into a criminal allegation; that they are a suspect in that investigation; that they do not have to speak to the police, but if they choose to do so the police will make a record of it that may be used against them in court if they are charged with a criminal offence

prior consistent statement generally not admissible in court, but, in limited circumstances, an examiner may use such a statement made by the witness to bolster his or her credibility

prior inconsistent statement not immediately admissible in court, but an examiner may use such a statement to impeach a witness's credibility

privacy the condition of being free from the unsanctioned intrusion by others

privilege a kind of protection (exemption from admissibility) that attaches to evidence produced in special circumstances, such as in the course of certain classes of relationships

privilege against self-incrimination a privilege exempting the accused from the obligation to give self-incriminating evidence (or any evidence at all)

probative value evidence that logically helps prove a fact or issue

production the process by which an accused gains the right, through an *O'Connor* application, to third-party records—for example, medical or psychiatric records

production order an order by a judge or justice compelling a person or financial institution to produce documents, data, or information for a peace officer

proof beyond a reasonable doubt proof that is convincing and allows a reasonable person to be "sure" that the accused is guilty

proof on a balance of probabilities proof that leaves the trier of fact at least 51 percent certain of the truth of a fact

propensity evidence evidence that demonstrates that the accused is the type of person who tends to act in a particular manner

Q

questioned document anything that contains letters, numbers, or any type of symbol that could express a meaning to another person and whose authorship is in doubt

questioned document examination the scientific comparison and analysis of a document

R

real evidence physical objects (including documents in some cases) with a direct link to the crime that are introduced as evidence

rebuttal evidence *see* reply evidence

re-examination a party's questioning of its own witness after cross-examination has been completed

Reid technique an approach to questioning criminal suspects that consists of three principal elements: a non-accusatory fact-finding interview; a behavioural analysis interview designed to detect deception; and an accusatory, persuasive interrogation designed to obtain a confession

relevance the tendency of a piece of evidence to prove or disprove a proposition

reply (rebuttal) evidence a party who called the witness may ask him or her further questions relating to new matters brought out in cross-examination of the witness; also called rebuttal evidence

report to a justice *see* return

requested exemplar a sample of someone's handwriting requested by warrant and written under observation so that authorship is not in doubt

return a document describing things seized and identifying the place where they are being held

reverse onus clause sections of the *Criminal Code* that shift the burden from the prosecution to the defence to disprove a presumption—for example, in the case of possession of counterfeit money

rifling a series of spiral grooves made in the barrel of a gun to ensure that the bullet flies in a straight line and providing class characteristics

right to counsel the right of a person to consult with a lawyer upon arrest or detention, as guaranteed by s. 10(b) of the Charter

right to silence the right of an individual not to be compelled to be a witness against himself or herself and to freely choose whether or not to speak to agents of the state, such as police officers

rule against narrative rule stating that informants may offer conclusions, opinions, and facts in their information to obtain, but must also provide the court with the source or origin for those beliefs

S

search anything done by the state or its agents that infringes one's reasonable expectation of privacy

search incident to arrest (also search incidental to arrest) search of an arrested person permitted without a warrant

secondary caution a warning given by an investigator to a suspect where the investigator is not the first police officer to have contact with the suspect, advising the suspect that if he or she has had any previous contact with the police regarding the matter under investigation the suspect should not be influenced by anything said or done during that contact, and that he or she remains free to decide whether to speak to the investigator

secondary documentary evidence a piece of documentary evidence that is other than an original, such as a photocopy

seizure involves taking something belonging to or in the care and control of someone by a public authority

similar-fact evidence evidence that suggests that the accused has acted in the past in a way that is similar to the acts alleged as part of the offence being tried

SOCO (scenes of crime officer) *see* forensic identification specialist

solemn affirmation a promise to tell the truth without a hand on the Bible—for the non-religious—as provided for in s. 14 of the *Canada Evidence Act*

solicitor–client privilege an exemption from disclosure requirements for certain communications between a lawyer and client

spousal privilege an exemption from disclosure and compellability for the spouse of an accused

standard of proof the degree of certainty of the truth of a fact required before that fact can be relied on in support of a particular verdict or legal decision

stress–compliant false confession a false confession given knowingly in order to escape from what the person perceives to be an intolerably intense, punishing interrogation, and/or a situation in which someone has been convinced that it is futile to protest his or her innocence

strip search search in which a person's clothing is removed or rearranged to allow visual inspection of the genitals, buttocks, breasts, or undergarments

submissions arguments made in court by the parties, either orally or in writing

subpoena a written notice, usually hand-delivered, summoning a named person to court on a certain day for the purpose of giving testimony, and stating that if the person refuses to appear, penal consequences may follow

suicide the intentional taking of one's own life

suspect a person of interest (under arrest or not) suspected by the police on the basis of evidence of having committed a crime

T

taphonomy the study of everything that happens to a body from the moment of death to the time the body is discovered

technological crime investigations where digital evidence is paramount, whether in the investigation of a crime or in the commission of the crime itself

telewarrant an alternative method of applying for a warrant, whether by telephone or by other means of telecommunication

third-party records records not created as a result of a police investigation, but that contain information about "third parties" to a criminal proceeding—for example, a witness or a complainant

tool any hard object that can make a mark on a softer object

tool mark the impression made by any tool

trace evidence physical evidence left behind at a crime scene or exchanged between an offender and victim

tracking warrant authorizes a peace officer to install, maintain, and remove a tracking device to determine someone's or something's location

trial record the official written transcript of a legal proceeding

trier of fact the decision-maker(s) charged with determining whether the necessary facts of a case have been proved—the jury in a jury trial, or the judge in a trial by judge alone

tunnel vision the single-minded and overly narrow focus on a particular investigative or prosecutorial theory that unreasonably colours the evaluation of information received and one's conduct in response to that information

U

undetermined death death that cannot be determined to be natural, accidental, suicide, or homicide

uniformed police constable an officer who primarily patrols defined areas to which he or she is assigned and responds to emergency calls for service

uniformed police supervisor typically, a sergeant responsible for the supervision of uniformed patrol constables who ensures the quality of the uniformed response to calls for service

V

voir dire a hearing in the absence of the jury to consider the admissibility of a piece of evidence

voluntary false confession a false confession given voluntarily for a variety of reasons, including mental illness or a desire for attention, and not as a result of the use of police interrogation techniques

W

waiver a decision, communicated clearly by words or actions, to decline the exercise of a particular right

warrant a legal order authorizing a police officer or other official to enter and search premises

warrant to enter a dwelling house to carry out arrests authorizes a peace officer, under certain conditions specified in each section, to enter a dwelling house to arrest a person identified by the warrant

warrant to obtain blood samples authorizes a peace officer to require a qualified medical practitioner or technician to take samples of a person's blood to test for alcohol or drugs

warrant to obtain bodily impressions authorizes a peace officer to do anything described in the warrant to obtain, for example, a handprint, fingerprint, footprint, foot impression, or teeth impression

warrant to obtain bodily substances authorizes the taking of one or more bodily substances for the purpose of forensic DNA analysis from someone believed to be a party to the offence

warrant to search and seize authorizes search for and seizure of weapons, ammunition, and explosives

warrant to search, seize, and detain proceeds of crime authorizes the searching of a building, receptacle, or place for the seizure of any property under which a proceeds of crime forfeiture order may be made

Waterfield test a legal test that prescribes a way for a court to determine whether the exercise of a power *not* specified in a statute was justifiable

weight the probative value/importance assigned to a piece of evidence, based on an assessment of its reliability

Wigmore test a case-by-case model for establishing privilege

witness in a court case, any person who is called before the court to give evidence under oath or affirmation

References

A

Ahmed, R. v. (2002). 2002 CanLII 695 (Ont. C.A.).

Amat, R. v. (2003). 2003 ABPC 38 (CanLII).

Amos, R. v. (2009). 2009 CanLII 63592 (Ont. S.C.).

Anderson, G.S. (2005). Effects of arson on forensic entomology evidence. *Canadian Society of Forensic Science Journal, 38*(2), 49–67.

Anderson, G.S., & Cervenka, V.J. (2001). Insects associated with the body: Their use and analyses. In W. Haglund & M. Sorg (Eds.), *Advances in forensic taphonomy: Methods, theory and archeological perspectives.* Boca Raton, FL: CRC Press.

Anderson, J., Mangels, N., & Langsam, A. (2009). The challenges of teaching criminological theory: Can academia deliver what the media promises? *Criminal Justice Studies, 22*(2), 223–236.

Andrade, R. v. (1985). [1985] O.J. No. 968 (C.A.).

Araujo, R. v. (2000). 2000 SCC 65, [2000] 2 S.C.R. 992.

Asante-Mensah, R. v. (2003). 2003 SCC 38, [2003] 2 S.C.R. 3.

Ask, K., & Granhag, P. (2005). Motivational sources of confirmation bias in criminal investigations: The need for cognitive closure. *Journal of Investigative Psychology and Offender Profiling, 2*(1), 43–63.

Association of Chief Police Officers (ACPO). (n.d.). *Good practice guide for computer-based electronic evidence.* 7Safe Information Security. http://www.7safe.com/electronic_evidence/ACPO_guidelines_computer_evidence.pdf.

B

B. (F.C.), R. v. (2000). 182 N.S.R. (2d) 215, 142 C.C.C. (3d) 540.

B. (K.G.), R. v. (1993). [1993] 1 S.C.R. 740, 79 C.C.C. (3d) 257.

B.(M.), R. v. (2006). 2006 ONCJ 526 (CanLII).

Bachrach, B., Jain, A., Jung, S., & Koons, R.D. (2010). A statistical validation of the individuality and repeatability of striated tool marks: Screwdrivers and tongue and groove pliers. *Journal of Forensic Sciences, 55*(2), 348–357.

Baker, G.R., Norton, P.G., Flintoft, V., Blais, R., Brown, A., Cox, J., Etchells, E., Ghali, W., Jebert, P., Majumdar, S., O'Beirne, Palacios-Derflingher, L., Reid, R., Sheps, S., & Tamblyn, R. (2004). The Canadian adverse events study: The incidence of adverse events among hospital patients in Canada. *Canadian Medical Association Journal, 170*(11), 1678–1686.

Baldridge, R.S., Wallace, S.G., & Kirkpatrick, R. (2006). Investigation of nocturnal oviposition by necrophilous flies in central Texas. *Journal of Forensic Sciences, 51*(1), 125–126.

Banford, R. v. (2010). 2010 SKPC 110 (CanLII).

Barges, R. v. (2005). 2005 CanLII 47766 (Ont. S.C.).

Barrett, R. v. (1993). 13 O.R. (3d) 587 (C.A.), 1993 CanLII 3426.

Bartle, R. v. (1994). [1994] 3 S.C.R. 173, 92 C.C.C. (3d) 289, 33 C.R. (4th) 1.

Basarke, S., Stanley, D., & Turtle, J. (2011, March 2). You have the right to remain silent, so why are you talking? Paper presented at the annual meeting of the American Psychology–Law Society/4th International Congress of Psychology and Law, Hyatt Regency Miami, Miami, FL.

Bass, W.M. (1987). *Human osteology: A laboratory and field manual* (3rd ed.). Springfield, MO: Missouri Archaeological Society.

Baxter, R. v. (2009). 2009 ONCJ 16 (CanLII).

Beattie, O., & Geiger, J. (1998). *Frozen in time: The fate of the Franklin expedition.* Vancouver: Greystone Books.

Beaudry, R. v. (2007). 2007 SCC 5, [2007] 1 S.C.R. 190.

Bero, R. v. (2000). 2000 CanLII 16956 (Ont. C.A.).

Bevel, T., & Gardner, R.M. (2001). *Bloodstain pattern analysis: With an introduction to crime scene reconstruction* (2nd ed.). Boca Raton, FL: CRC Press.

Bill C-46, *An Act to amend the Criminal Code.* (1997). 2d Sess., 35th Parl., S.C. 1997, c. 30.

Biondo, R. v. (2009). 2009 ONCJ 171 (CanLII).

Bjelland, R. v. (2009). 2009 SCC 38, [2009] 2 S.C.R. 651.

Black, R. v. (1989). [1989] 2 S.C.R. 138, 50 C.C.C. (3d) 1.

Blackwood, R. v. (2009). 2009 CanLII 70996 (Ont. S.C.).

Blair, J., & McCamey, W. (2002). Detection of deception: An analysis of the behavioural analysis interview technique. *Illinois Law Enforcement Executive Forum, 2,* 165–170.

Bogoroch, R. (2005, May 27). Cross-examination: Emerge intact. Paper presented before the Ontario Trial Lawyers Association. Bogoroch & Associates. http://www.bogoroch.com/articles/crossexamination.php.

Borden, R. v. (1994). [1994] 3 S.C.R. 145, 92 C.C.C. (3d) 404, 33 C.R. (4th) 147.

Boucher v. The Queen. (1954). [1955] S.C.R. 16, 110 C.C.C. 263.

Boucher, S., & Landa, K. (2005). *Understanding section 8: Search and seizure and the Canadian Constitution.* Toronto: Irwin Law.

Brander, R. v. (2003). 2003 ABQB 756 (CanLII).

Brauti, P.M. (1997). Improper cross-examination, 1997–1998. *Criminal Law Quarterly, 40,* 69–105.

Brinsmead, R. v. (2006). 2006 NBPC 4 (CanLII).

Bryant, A.W., Lederman, S.N., & Fuerst, M. (2009). *The law of evidence in Canada* (3rd ed.). Markham, ON: Lexis-Nexis Canada.

Brydges, R. v. (1990). [1990] 1 S.C.R. 190, 53 C.C.C. (3d) 330.

Buckingham v. Daily News Ltd. (1956). [1956] 2 Q.B. 534, 2 All E.R. 904.

Buckley, J. (2006). The Reid technique of interviewing and interrogation. In T. Williamson (Ed.), *Investigative interviewing: Rights, research and regulation* (pp. 190–206). Cullompton, UK: Willan Publishing.

Burlingham, R. v. (1995). [1995] 2 S.C.R. 206, 97 C.C.C. (3d) 385, 38 C.R. (4th) 265.

Buyck, R. v. (2007). 2007 YKCA 11 (CanLII).

C

Calaprice, A. (Ed.). (2000). *The expanded quotable Einstein.* Princeton, NJ: Princeton University Press.

Calgary Police Service, Sections and Units. Investigative Support Section, Court and Disclosure Unit. http://www.calgarypolice.ca/sectionsandunits.html.

Campbell, A. (2011, 14 December). *Inquiry into fingerprints in Scotland.* Sir Anthony Campbell, Chairman. The Fingerprint Inquiry, Scotland. http://www.thefingerprintinquiryscotland.org.uk/inquiry/21.html ("Scottish Fingerprint Inquiry").

Canada Evidence Act. (1985). R.S.C. 1985, c. C-5.

Canadian Charter of Rights and Freedoms. (1982). Part I of the *Constitution Act, 1982,* being Schedule B to the *Canada Act 1982* (U.K.), 1982, c. 11.

Canadian Charter of Rights decisions digest. (Updated November 2004). http://www.canlii.org/en/ca/charter_digest/s-8.html.

Canadian Integrated Ballistics Identification Network (CIBIN). Royal Canadian Mounted Police. http://www.rcmp-grc.gc.ca.

Caslake, R. v. (1998). [1998] 1 S.C.R. 51.

CBC News. (2003, January 28). Widely used police interrogation technique can result in false confession: Disclosure. http://www.cbc.ca/news/canada/story/2003/01/27/interrogation030127.html.

CBC News. (2011, December 6). Quebec makes medical errors public. http://www.cbc.ca/news/health/story/2011/12/06/quebec-medical-errors-public-falls-medication.html.

CBC News. (2012, April 11). Stafford's blood almost certainly found in Rafferty's car. http://www.cbc.ca/news/canada/story/2012/04/11/rafferty-stafford-dna-evidence.html.

CBS. (2005). A bullet runs through it [Television series episode]. *CSI: Crime scene investigation* (Season 6, Part 2, Episode 125). New York: CBS Broadcasting.

Central Intelligence Agency (CIA). (2009, March). *A tradecraft primer: Structured analytic techniques for improving intelligence analysis.* United States Government. https://www.cia.gov/library/center-for-the-study-of-intelligence/csi-publications/books-and-monographs/Tradecraft%20Primer-apr09.pdf.

Champod, C., & Chamberlain, P. (2009). Fingerprints. In J. Fraser & R. Williams (Eds.), *Handbook of forensic science* (pp. 57–83). Devon, UK: Willan Publishing.

Charest, R. v. (1978). 42 C.C.C. (2d) 313 (Ont. Prov. Ct.).

Cheves, M. (2004). Forensic artist: Evidence technician uses robotic total station to map crime scene. *The American Surveyor.* http://www.amerisurv.com/PDF/TheAmericanSurveyor_ForensicArtist_Fall2004.pdf.

Child and Family Services Act. (1990). R.S.O. 1990, c. C.11.

Chisum, W.J., & Turvey, B.E. (2007). *Crime reconstruction.* Burlington, MA: Elsevier.

Cloutier v. Langlois. (1990). [1990] 1 S.C.R. 158.

Colangelo, R. v. (2007). 2007 ONCJ 489 (CanLII).

Collins, R. v. (1987). [1987] 1 S.C.R. 265.

Controlled Drugs and Substances Act. (1996). S.C. 1996, c. 19.

Cook, R. v. (2010). 2010 ONSC 1188 (CanLII).

Corbett, R. v. (1988). [1988] 1 S.C.R. 670.

Coroners Act. (1990). R.S.O. 1990, c. C.37.

Cory, P. (2001). *The inquiry regarding Thomas Sophonow.* The Honourable Peter de C. Cory, Commissioner. See, in particular, the recommendations for photo pack line-ups. http://www.gov.mb.ca/justice/publications/sophonow/recommendations/english.html#photo ("Sophonow Inquiry").

Côté, R. v. (2008). 2008 QCCS 3749; rev'd. 2010 QCCA 303; rev'd. 2011 SCC 46.

Criminal Code, Re. (1997). [1997] O.J. No. 4393 (Ont. Ct. Gen. Div.).

Criminal Code. (1985). R.S.C. 1985, c. C-46.

D

Dando, C., Wilcock, R., & Milne, R. (2009). The modified cognitive interview procedure for frontline police investigators. *Applied Cognitive Psychology, 23,* 138–147.

Daubert v. Merrell Dow Pharmaceutical Inc. (1993). 113 S. Ct. 2786 (1993).

Department of Justice Canada. (n.d.). YCJA explained. Department of Justice Canada. http://www.collectionscanada.gc.ca/webarchives/20071115073145/http://www.justice.gc.ca/en/ps/yj/repository/index.html.

Dinardo, R. v. (2008). 231 C.C.C. (3d) 177 (S.C.C.).

Dixon, R. v. (1998). [1998] 1 S.C.R. 244.

Doran, B., Long, M., & Allison, L. (2009, June). Working against the clock: An analysis of decisions in rape investigations under time pressure. Proceedings of NDM9, the 9th International Conference on Naturalistic Decision Making. London: British Computer Society. http://www.bcs.org/upload/pdf/ewic_ndm09_s2paper7.pdf.

Doyle, A.C. (1891, July). A scandal in Bohemia. *The Strand Magazine.*

Doyle, J.M. (2010). Learning from error in American criminal justice. *The Journal of Criminal Law and Criminology, 100*(1), 109–147.

Drizin, S., & Leo, R. (2004). The problem of false confessions in the post-DNA world. *North Carolina Law Review, 82,* 891–1007.

Dror, I. (2009). Video interview. Dr. Itel Dror on forensic decision-making, bias, and fingerprint identification. YouTube. http://www.youtube.com/watch?v=uo_atxdsffe.

Dror, I.E., & Charlton, D. (2006). Why experts make errors. *Journal of Forensic Identification, 56*(4), 600–616.

Dror, I.E., Charlton, D., & Perón, A.E. (2006). Contextual information renders experts vulnerable to making erroneous identifications. *Forensic Science International, 156*(1), 74–78.

Dulude, R. v. (2004). 2004 CanLII 30967 (Ont. C.A.).

Durnal, E.W. (2010). Crime scene investigation (as seen on TV). *Forensic Science International, 199,* 1–5.

Dyment, R. v. (1988). [1988] 2 S.C.R. 417.

E

Eakin, R. v. (2000). [2000] 132 O.A.C. 164, 74 C.R.R. (2d) 307, [2000] O.J. No. 1670.

Eastwood, J., & Snook, B. (2010). Comprehending Canadian police cautions: Are the rights to silence and counsel understandable? *Behavioral Sciences and the Law, 28,* 507–524.

Eastwood, J., Snook, B., & Chaulk, S.J. (2010). Measuring reading complexity and listening comprehension of Canadian police cautions. *Criminal Justice and Behavior, 37*(4), 453–471.

Eck, J. (2009). Investigators, information and interpretation: A summary of criminal investigation research. In D.K. Rossmo (Ed.), *Criminal investigative failures* (pp. ix–xii). Boca Raton, FL: CRC Press.

Edgar, R. v. (2010). 2010 ONCA 529.

Edwards, R. v. (1996). [1996] 1 S.C.R. 128.

F

Fanjoy v. The Queen. (1985). [1985] 2 S.C.R. 233.

Federal Bureau of Investigation (FBI). (2004, May 24). Statement on Brandon Mayfield case. FBI National Press Office. Washington, DC. http://www.fbi.gov/news/pressrel/press-releases/statement-on-brandon-mayfield-case.

Federal/Provincial/Territorial Heads of Prosecutions Subcommittee on the Prevention of Wrongful Convictions. (2011). *The path to justice: Preventing wrongful convictions—Report of the federal/provincial/territorial heads of prosecutions subcommittee on the prevention of wrongful convictions.* Ottawa: Public Prosecution Service of Canada. http://www.ppsc-sppc.gc.ca/eng/pub/ptj-spj/ptj-spj-eng.pdf ("FPT Report").

Feeney, R. v. (1997). [1997] 2 S.C.R. 13.

Ferguson, G. (2003). *Review and recommendations concerning various aspects of police misconduct* (Vols. 1 & 2). Toronto Police Service. http://www.torontopolice.on.ca/publications/files/reports/ferguson1.pdf and http://www.torontopolice.on.ca/publications/files/reports/ferguson2.pdf.

Fidelman, C. (2011, December 6). Quebec launches public registry of medical errors. *The Montreal Gazette.*

Findley, K., & Scott, M. (2006). The multiple dimensions of tunnel vision in criminal cases. *Wisconsin Law Review, 2.* http://hosted.law.wisc.edu/lawreview/issues/2006-2/findley-scott.pdf.

Fisher, R.P., & Geiselman, R.E. (1992). Memory-enhancing techniques for investigative interviewing: The cognitive interview. Springfield, IL: Charles C. Thomas.

Fisher, R.P., Geiselman, R.E., & Raymond, D.S. (1987). Critical analysis of police interview techniques. *Journal of Police Science and Administration, 15,* 177–185.

Fisher, R.P., Geiselman, R.E., Raymond, D.S., Jurkevich, L., & Warhaftig, M.L. (1987). Enhancing enhanced eyewitness memory: Refining the cognitive interview. *Journal of Police Science and Administration, 15,* 291–297.

Fitch, B. (2010, June). Good decisions: Tips and strategies for avoiding psychological traps. *FBI Law Enforcement Bulletin.* FBI Federal Bureau of Investigation. http://www.fbi.gov/stats-services/publications/law-enforcement-bulletin/june-2010/good-decisions.

Fliss, R. v. (2002). 16 C.C.C. (3d) 225 (S.C.C.).

Fontana, J., & Keeshan, D. (2007). *The law of search and seizure in Canada* (7th ed.). Markham, ON: LexisNexis Canada.

Fontana, J., & Keeshan, D. (2010). *The law of search and seizure in Canada* (8th ed.). Markham, ON: LexisNexis Canada.

FPT Heads of Prosecutions Committee Working Group. (2005). *Report on the prevention of miscarriages of justice.* Ottawa: Department of Justice Canada. http://www.justice.gc.ca/eng/dept-min/pub/pmj-pej/pmj-pej.pdf ("FPT Report").

Fraser, J., & Williams, R. (2009). *Handbook of forensic science.* Devon, UK: Willan Publishing.

Fraser, K. (2011, July 26). Former blood expert pleads guilty to perjury. *The StarPhoenix* (Saskatoon). http://www2.canada.com/saskatoonstarphoenix/news/story.html?id=61450e56-2fc7-4b0b-9753-56e3cc859673.

Frumkin, D., Wasserstrom, A., Davidson, A., & Grafit, A. (2010). Authentication of forensic DNA samples. *Forensic Science International: Genetics, 4*(2), 95–103. FSI: Genetics. http://www.fsigenetics.com/article/S1872-4973(09)00099-4/abstract.

G

G. (S.G.), R. v. (1997). [1997] 2 S.C.R. 716.

Gaensslen, R., & Young, K. (2003). Fingerprints. In S. James & J. Nordby (Eds.), *Forensic science: An introduction to scientific and investigative techniques* (pp. 277–296). Boca Raton, FL: CRC Press.

Geiselman, R.E., Fisher, R.P., MacKinnon, D.P., & Holland, H.L. (1985). Eyewitness memory enhancement in the police interview: Cognitive retrieval mnemonics versus hypnosis. *Journal of Applied Psychology, 70,* 401–412.

Genest, R. v. (1989). [1989] 1 S.C.R. 59.

Giles, R. v. (2007). 2007 BCSC 1147.

Golden, R. v. (2001). 2001 SCC 83, [2001] 3 S.C.R. 679.

Goudge, S.T. (2008). *Inquiry into pediatric forensic pathology in Ontario.* The Honourable Stephen T. Goudge, Commissioner. Ontario Ministry of the Attorney General. http://www.attorneygeneral.jus.gov.on.ca/inquiries/goudge/report/index.html ("Goudge Inquiry").

Graat v. The Queen. (1982). [1982] 2 S.C.R. 819.

Graham, R. v. (2011). 2011 ONSC 906 (CanLII).

Grandinetti, R. v. (2005). 2005 SCC 5, [2005] 1 S.C.R. 27.

Grant, R. v. (2009). 2009 SCC 32, [2009] 2 S.C.R. 353.

Green, R. v. (1998). [1998] O.J. No. 3598, 1998 CarswellOnt 3820 (Gen. Div.).

Gross, A.M., Harris, K.A., & Kaldun, G.L. (1999). The effect of luminol on presumptive tests and DNA analysis using the polymerase chain reaction. *Journal of Forensic Sciences, 44*(4), 837–840.

Grunwald, R. v. (2008). 2008 BCSC 1738.

Gudjonsson, G. (2007). Investigative interviewing. In T. Newburn, T. Williamson, & A. Wright (Eds.), *Handbook of criminal investigation* (pp. 466–492). Cullompton, UK: Willan Publishing.

Guiboche, R. v. (2004). 2004 MBCA 16 (CanLII), 183 C.C.C. (3d) 361.

H

Ha, R. v. (2009). 2009 ONCA 340 (CanLII).

Handy, R. v. (2002). [2002] 2 S.C.R. 908, 2002 SCC 56.

Harris, R. v. (2010). 2010 PESC 32 (CanLII).

Harrison, R. v. (2009). 2009 SCC 34, [2009] 2 S.C.R. 494.

Hatcher, R. v. (2005). 2005 CanLII 16614 (Ont. S.C.).

Hebert, R. v. (1990). [1990] 2 S.C.R. 151, 57 C.C.C. (3d) 1, 77 C.R. (3d) 145.

Henley, A. (2011, March). In the dock. *Police Magazine,* pp. 16–19. Police Federation of England & Wales. http://www.polfed.org/07_In_the_dock_PoliceMarch11.pdf.

Heuer, R. (1999). *Psychology of intelligence analysis.* Central Intelligence Agency. https://www.cia.gov.

Hickman, A. (1989, December). *Royal commission on the Donald Marshall Jr. prosecution: Digest of findings and recommendations.* Chief Justice T. Alexander Hickman, Chairman. http://www.gov.ns.ca/just/marshall_inquiry/_docs/Royal%20Commission%20on%20the%20Donald%20Marshall%20Jr%20Prosecution_findings.pdf.

Hodgson, R. v. (1998). [1998] 2 S.C.R. 449.

Home Office. (2008, July). The Research, Development and Statistics Directorate. *Crime in England and Wales 2007/08: A summary of the main findings.* http://rds.homeoffice.gov.uk/rds/pdfs08/hosb0708.pdf.

Horan, R. v. (2008). 2008 ONCA 589 (CanLII).

Horvath, F., & Jayne, B. (1994). Differentiation of truthful and deceptive criminal suspects in behavioural analysis interviews. *Journal of Forensic Sciences, 39,* 793–807.

Houck, M. (2009). Trace evidence. In J. Fraser & R. Williams (Eds.), *Handbook of forensic science* (pp. 166–195). Devon, UK: Willan Publishing.

Huber, R.A., & Headrick, A.M. (1999). *Handwriting identification: Facts and fundamentals.* Boca Raton, FL: CRC Press.

Hunter et al. v. Southam Inc. (1984). [1984] 2 S.C.R. 145.

Hutchison, S. (2003). *Canadian search warrant manual 2003.* Toronto: Thomson Canada.

Hutchison, S. (2004). *Hutchison's Canadian search warrant manual 2005.* Toronto: Thomson Canada.

Huxford, R. v. (2010). 2010 ONCJ 33 (CanLII).

I

IBM i2 Analyst's Notebook. http://www.i2group.com/uk/products/analysis-product-line/ibm-i2-analysts-notebook.

Identification of Criminals Act. (1985). R.S.C. 1985, c. I-1.

Inbau, F.E., Reid, J., & Buckley, J. (1986). *Criminal interrogation and confessions* (3rd ed.). Baltimore, MD: Williams and Wilkins.

Inbau, F.E., Reid, J., Buckley, J., & Jayne, B. (2001). *Criminal interrogation and confessions* (4th ed.). Gaithersburg, MD: Aspen Publishers.

Innisfil Township v. Vespra Township. (1981). [1981] 2 S.C.R. 145.

Innocence Project. (2010). Understand the causes: False confessions. http://www.innocenceproject.org/ understand/False-Confessions.php.

Ives, D.E. (2009). R. v. McNeil: Narrowing the gap between disclosure and production. *International Journal of Evidence and Proof, 13*(3), 225–231.

J

J.-L.J., R. v. (2000). 2000 SCC 51, [2000] 2 S.C.R. 600.

James, S., & Nordby, J. (Eds.). (2003). *Forensic science: An introduction to scientific and investigative techniques.* Boca Raton, FL: CRC Press.

James, S.H., & Nordby, J.J. (Eds.). (2005). *Forensic science: An introduction to scientific and investigative techniques* (2nd ed.). Boca Raton, FL: CRC Press.

Jeffreys, A.J., Wilson, V., & Thein, S.L. (1985). Individual-specific "fingerprints" of human DNA. *Nature, 316*(6023), 76–79.

Jobin, R.M., & De Gouffe, M. (2003). The persistence of seminal constituents on panties after laundering: Significance to investigations of sexual assault. *Canadian Society of Forensic Science Journal, 36*(1), 1–10.

Jones, D.E., & Ledingham, K.W.D. (1982). Arsenic in Napoleon's wallpaper. *Nature, 299*(5884), 626–627.

Jones, R. v. (2011). 2011 ONCA 632 (CanLII).

K

Kafarowski, E., Lyon, A.M., & Sloan, M.M. (1996). The retention and transfer of spermatozoa in clothing by machine washing. *Canadian Society of Forensic Science Journal, 29*(1), 7–11.

Kahneman, D. (2011). *Thinking, fast and slow.* Toronto: Doubleday Canada.

Kaiser, H.A. (2009). *McNeil*: A welcome clarification and extension of the disclosure principles—"The adversary system has lingered on." *Criminal Reports, 62* (6th ed.).

Kassin, S.M. (2005). On the psychology of confessions: Does innocence put innocents at risk? *American Psychologist, 60*, 215–228.

Kassin, S.M. (2008). False confessions: Causes, consequences and implications for reform. *Current Directions in Psychological Science, 17*(4), 249–255.

Kassin, S.M., & Fong, C. (1999). "I'm innocent!": Effects of training on judgments of truth and deception in the interrogation room. *Law and Human Behavior, 23*(5), 499–516.

Kassin, S.M., & McNall, K. (1991). Police interrogations and confessions: Communicating promises and threats by pragmatic implication. *Law and Human Behavior, 15*, 233–251.

Kassin, S.M., & Neumann, K. (1997). On the power of confession evidence: An experimental test of the fundamental difference hypothesis. *Law and Human Behavior, 21*(5), 469–484.

Kaufman, F. (1998). *Report of the Kaufman commission on proceedings involving Guy Paul Morin.* The Honourable Fred Kaufman, Commissioner. Ontario Ministry of the Attorney General. http://www.attorneygeneral.jus.gov .on.ca/english/about/pubs/morin.

Kaye, D. (2010). Probability, individualization, and uniqueness in forensic science evidence. *Brooklyn Law Review, 75*(4), 1163–1185.

Kebbel, M., Muller, D., & Martin, K. (2010). Understanding and managing bias. In G. Bammer (Ed.), *Dealing with uncertainties in policing serious crime* (pp. 87–97). Canberra, Australia: The Australian National University, ANU E Press. http://epress.anu.edu.au/titles/ dealing_citation.

Kebbell, M., & O'Kelly, C. (2007). Police detectives' perceptions of giving evidence in court. *Policing: An International Journal of Police Strategies and Management, 30*(1), 8–20.

Kelleher, R. v. (2009). 2009 ONCJ 54 (CanLII).

Khan, R. v. (1990). [1990] 2 S.C.R. 531.

Khan, R. v. (2010). 2010 ONSC 3818 (CanLII).

Khelawon, R. v. (2006). 2006 SCC 57, [2006] 2 S.C.R. 787.

King, L., & Snook, B. (2009). Peering inside a Canadian interrogation room: An examination of the Reid model of interrogation, influence tactics, and coercive strategies. *Criminal Justice and Behavior, 36*(7), 674–694.

Kirk, P. (1953). *Crime scene investigation: Physical evidence and the police laboratory.* New York: Interscience.

Klinger, L. (2005). *The new annotated Sherlock Holmes.* New York: W.W. Norton and Company.

Kotanen, P. (2010). To have and have not: Disclosure, duty and discretion post-McNeil. *Crown's Newsletter, 6*. Ontario Crown Attorneys' Association.

L

L.F., R. v. (2006). 2006 CanLII 4903 (Ont. S.C.).

L.T.H., R. v. (2008). 2008 SCC 49, [2008] 2 S.C.R. 739.

Lamer, A. (2006). *The Lamer commission of inquiry pertaining to the cases of Ronald Dalton, Gregory Parson, Randy Druken.* The Right Honourable Antonio Lamer. St. John's: Office of the Queen's Printer. http://www.justice.gov.nl.ca/just/ publications/lamerpart1.pdf.

Langenburg, G., Champod, C., & Wertheim, P. (2009). Testing for potential contextual bias effects during the verification stage of the ACE-V methodology when conducting fingerprint comparisons. *Journal of Forensic Sciences, 54*(3), 571–582.

Law, R. v. (2002). 2002 SCC 10, [2002] 1 S.C.R. 227.

Layson, G. (2011, March 4). Guelph police chief issues apologies over "not dead" case. *Guelph Mercury.* GuelphMercury.com. http://www.guelphmercury.com.

Leape, L. (2008). Why do errors happen? How can we prevent them? Institute for Healthcare Improvement, Open School for Health Professionals. Lecture by Lucian Leape, M.D., Professor of Health Policy, Harvard School of Public Health. YouTube. http://www.youtube.com/watch?v=JL5GTxDzApk&feature=related.

Leblanc, D. (2011, January 6). RCMP wants easier disclosure rules. *The Globe and Mail,* p. A4.

Leipert, R. v. (1997). [1997] 1 S.C.R. 281.

Leo, R. (2008). *Police interrogation and American justice.* Cambridge, MA: Harvard University Press.

Leo, R., Drizin, S., Neufeld, P., Hall, B., & Vatner, A. (2006). Bringing reliability back in: False confessions and legal safeguards in the twenty-first century. *Wisconsin Law Review, 26*(2), 479–538.

Lesage Code Report. (2008). See Lesage, P., & Code, M. (2008).

Lesage, P. (2007, January). *Report of the commission of inquiry into certain aspects of the trial and conviction of James Driskell.* The Honourable Patrick J. LeSage, QC, Commissioner, Manitoba Justice. http://www.driskellinquiry.ca.

Lesage, P., & Code, M. (2008). *Report of the review of large and complex criminal case procedures.* Queen's Printer for Ontario: Ontario Ministry of the Attorney General. http://www.attorneygeneral.jus.gov.on.ca.

Leslie, A.C.D., & Smith, H. (1978). Napoleon Bonaparte's exposure to arsenic during 1816. *Archives of Toxicology, 41,* 163–167.

Levy, E. (2004). *Examination of witnesses in criminal cases* (5th ed.). (See, especially, Chapter 17, Cross-examination of police officers, pp. 396–411). Toronto: Thomson Carswell.

Levy, E.J. (2011). *Examination of witnesses in criminal cases* (6th ed.). Toronto: Carswell.

Liew, R. v. (1999). [1999] 3 S.C.R. 227.

Lifchus, R. v. (1997). [1997] 3 S.C.R. 320.

Liquor Licence Act. (1990). R.S.O. 1990, c. L.19.

Little, R. v. (2009). 2009 CanLII 41212 (Ont. S.C.).

Lohidici, R. v. (2005). 2005 ABPC 171.

Lucas, R. v. (2009). 2009 CanLII 43418 (Ont. S.C.).

Lyttle, R. v. (2004). 2004 SCC 5, [2004] 1 S.C.R. 193.

M

M.J.S., R. v. (2000). [2000] A.J. No. 391 (Prov. Ct.).

MacCallum, E. (2006). *Report of the commission of inquiry into the wrongful conviction of David Milgaard: Final report.* The Honourable Mr. Justice Edward P. MacCallum, Commissioner. http://www.justice.gov.sk.ca/milgaard/DMfinal.shtml.

MacFarlane, B. (2008). *Wrongful convictions: The effect of tunnel vision and predisposing circumstances in the criminal justice system.* Prepared for the Inquiry into Pediatric Forensic Pathology in Ontario. The Honourable Stephen Goudge. http://canadiancriminallaw.com/articles/articles%20pdf/Wrongful-Convictions.pdf ("Goudge Inquiry").

Manley, R. v. (2011). 2011 ONCA 128.

Mann, R. v. (2004). 2004 SCC 52, [2004] 3 S.C.R. 59.

Manninen, R. v. (1987). [1987] 1 S.C.R. 1233, 34 C.C.C. (3d) 385.

Mapara, R. v. (2005). [2005] 1 S.C.R. 358, 2005 SCC 23.

Marshall c. R. (2005). 2005 QCCA 852.

McClure, R. v. (2001). 2001 SCC 14, [2001] 1 S.C.R. 445.

McCrimmon, R. v. (2010). 2010 SCC 36, [2010] 2 S.C.R. 402.

McEwen, T. (2009, July). *Evaluation of the Phoenix homicide clearance project: Vol. 1. Final report.* Prepared for the National Institute of Justice, Office of Justice Programs, U.S. Department of Justice. Institute for Law and Justice. http://www.ilj.org/publications/docs/EvalReport_Volume_I.pdf.

McKie, HM Advocate v. (1999). 1999 S.L.T. 123 (H.C.J.T.).

McKiernan, M. (2011, September 5). Police embracing e-disclosure: Pilot project has officers handing over materials more quickly. *Law Times.* http://www.lawtimesnews.com/201109058636/Headline-News/Police-embracing-e-disclosure.

McNeil, R. v. (2009). 2009 SCC 3, [2009] 1 S.C.R. 66.

Meigen, J.W. (1826). *Systematische Beschreibung der bekannten europäischen zweiflugeligen Insekten.*

Mendel, A. (2008). A Cypress Bowl homicide investigation. Unpublished case study presentation.

Mental Health Act. (1990). R.S.O. 1990, c. M.7.

Miller, L. (2006, October). On the spot: Testifying in court for law enforcement officers. *FBI Law Enforcement Bulletin,* pp. 1–7.

Mills, R. v. (1999). [1999] 3 S.C.R. 668.

Milne, R., & Bull, R. (1999). *Investigative interviewing: Psychology and practice.* New York: Wiley.

Minde, R. v. (2003). 2003 ABQB 797 (CanLII).

Mita, R. v. (2005). 2005 ONCJ 315 (CanLII).

Mnookin, J. (2003, September 22). Fingerprints: Not a gold standard. *Issues in Science and Technology.* http://www.issues.org/20.1/mnookin.html.

Mnookin, J., Cole, S., Dror, I., Fisher, B., Houck, M., Inman, K., Kaye, D., Koehler, J., Langenburg, G., Risinger, D., Rudin, N., Siegel, J., & Stoney, D. (2011). The need for a research culture in the forensic sciences. *UCLA Law Review, 58,* 725–779.

Mohan, R. v. (1994). [1994] 2 S.C.R. 9.

Moore, T.E., & Gagnier, K. (2008). "You can talk if you want to": Is the police caution on the "right to silence" understandable? *Criminal Reports, 51*, 233–249.

Moore-McFarlane, R. v. (2001). [2001] O.J. No. 4646, 56 O.R. (3d) 737 (C.A.).

Morelli, R. v. (2010). 2010 SCC 8, [2010] 1 S.C.R. 253.

N

Nafte, M., & Dalrymple, B. (2011). *Crime and measurement: Methods in forensic investigation.* Durham, NC: Carolina Academic Press.

Nairn, R. v. (2011). 2011 ABPC 5 (CanLII).

National Research Council of the National Academies. (2009). *Strengthening forensic science in the United States: A path forward.* Washington, DC. The National Academies Press. http://www.nap.edu ("NAS Report").

National Post, R. v. (2010). 2010 SCC 16, [2010] 1 S.C.R. 477.

Needleman, H., Riess, J., Tobin, M., Biesecker, G., & Greenhouse, J. (1996). Bone lead levels and delinquent behavior. *Journal of the American Medical Association, 275*(5), 363–369.

O

O'Connor, R. v. (1995). [1995] 4 S.C.R. 411, 103 C.C.C. (3d) 1.

Oakes, R. v. (1986). [1986] 1 S.C.R. 103.

Odgers, R. v. (2009). 2009 ONCJ 287 (CanLII).

Oickle, R. v. (2000). 2000 SCC 38, [2000] 2 S.C.R. 3.

Ontario Ministry of Community Safety and Correctional Services. (2004). Major case management. http://www.mcscs.jus.gov.on.ca/english/police_serv/MajorCaseManagement/mcm.html and MCM manual http://www.attorneygeneral.jus.gov.on.ca/inquiries/cornwall/en/hearings/exhibits/OPC/pdf/56_MCM_Manual.pdf.

Ontario Ministry of Health and Long-Term Care. (2010, December). Deceased patient standard. *Training Bulletin, 111*: version 1.0. http://www.ambulance-transition.com/pdf_documents/training_bulletin_111_deceased_patient_standard.pdf.

Osolin, R. v. (1993). [1993] 4 S.C.R. 595.

P

Paciocco, D. (2007). Filling the seam between Stinchcombe and O'Connor: The "McNeil" disclosure application. *Criminal Law Quarterly, 53*, 161–205.

Paciocco, D. (2009). Stinchcombe on steroids: The surprising legacy of *McNeil. Criminal Reports, 62* (6th ed.), 26–35.

Paciocco, D.M., & Stuesser, L. (2005). *The law of evidence* (4th ed.). Toronto: Irwin Law.

Paciocco, D.M., & Stuesser, L. (2008). *The law of evidence* (5th ed.). Toronto: Irwin Law.

Parisien, R. v. (2011). 2011 ONCJ 354 (CanLII).

Patrick, R. v. (2009). 2009 SCC 17, [2009] 1 S.C.R. 579.

Peglar, R. v. (2006). 2006 ONCJ 207 (CanLII).

Pelchat, A. (2006). A monstrous plot. *Beaver, 86*(3), 39–41. For a discussion of the case, see Jacques Trempe Collection. http://1000aircraftphotos.com/Contributions/Trempe/2469.htm.

Personal Information Protection and Electronic Documents Act. (2000). S.C. 2000, c. 5.

Piatelli-Palmarini, M. (1994). *Inevitable illusions: How mistakes of reason rule our minds.* New York: John Wiley & Sons.

Plant, R. v. (1993). [1993] 3 S.C.R. 281.

Polius, R. v. (2009). 196 C.R.R. (2d) 288, [2009] O.J. No. 3074 (S.C.J.).

Pollack, A. (2009). DNA evidence can be fabricated, scientists show. *The New York Times.* http://www.nytimes.com.

Polyviou, P.G. (1982). *Search and seizure: Constitutional and common law.* London: Duckworth.

Proceedings of the American Academy of Forensic Sciences. http://www.aafs.org/proceedings.

Procunier, M. (2011). Investigating with innovation: Breaking forensic boundaries at the Pickton pig farm. *RCMP Gazette, 73*(1), 7–10.

Prosper, R. v. (1994). [1994] 3 S.C.R. 236, 92 C.C.C. (3d) 353, 33 C.R. (4th) 85.

R

Ramsum, R. v. (2003). 2003 ABQB 45.

Ranger, R. v. (2010). 2010 ONSC 2061 (CanLII).

Rassin, E. (2010). Blindness to alternative scenarios in evidence evaluation. *Journal of Investigative Psychology and Offender Profiling, 7*(2), 153–163.

Reason, J. (2008). Delivering patient safety [From the DVD series *Delivering patient safety*]. London: TVC Films Ltd. YouTube. http://www.youtube.com/watch?v=2H4vs-KbZEA.

Richfield, R. v. (2003). 178 C.C.C. (3d) 23, 14 C.R. (6th) 77 (Ont. C.A.).

Ringler, R. v. (2004). 2004 ONCJ 104 (CanLII).

Rogers, R., Harrison, K.S., Hazelwood, L.L., & Sewell, K.W. (2007). Knowing and intelligent: A study of Miranda warnings in mentally disordered defendants. *Law and Human Behavior, 31*, 401–418.

Rogers, R., Hazelwood, L.L., Sewell, K.W., Harrison, K.S., & Shuman, D.W. (2008). The language of Miranda warnings in American jurisdictions: A replication and vocabulary analysis. *Law and Human Behavior, 32*(2), 124–136.

Roks, R. v. (2007). 2007 CanLII 13368 (Ont. S.C.).

Ross, R. v. (1989). [1989] 1 S.C.R. 3.

Rossmo, K. (2009). *Criminal investigative failures.* Boca Raton, FL: CRC Press.

Rothman v. The Queen. (1981). [1981] 1 S.C.R. 640.

Royal Canadian Mounted Police. (2011). Bloodstain pattern analysis (BPA). http://www.rcmp-grc.gc.ca/fsis-ssji/fis-sij/bpa-ats-eng.htm.

Ruble, R. (2009). *Round up the usual suspects: Criminal investigation in Law & Order, Cold Case, and CSI.* Westport, CT: Praeger.

Russano, M., Meissner, C., Narchet, F., & Kassin, S. (2005). Investigating true and false confessions within a novel experimental paradigm. *Psychological Science, 16*(6), 481–486.

Russell Williams confession, Pts. 1–3. YouTube. http://www.youtube.com/watch?v=hzh3adTWZOg, http://www.youtube.com/watch?v=Ah51vPzcVEM, http://www.youtube.com/watch?v=2mQA2yQFZ8o &feature=relmfu.

Russo, J., & Meloy, M. (2008). Hypothesis generation and testing in Wason's 2-4-6 task. Working Paper, Cornell University. http://forum.johnson.cornell.edu/faculty/russo/Rule%20Discovery%2022%20May%2008.pdf.

S

Saferstein, R. (2011). *Criminalistics: An introduction to forensic science* (10th ed.). Upper Saddle River, NJ: Prentice Hall.

Salhany, R. (2006). *Cross-examination: The art of the advocate* (3rd ed.). Markham, ON: LexisNexis.

Sangha, B., Roach, K., & Moles, R. (2010). *Forensic investigations and miscarriages of justice.* Toronto: Irwin Law.

Sankoff, P. (2006). *The portable guide to witnesses.* Toronto: Carswell.

Schertzer, R. v. (2007). 2007 CanLII 38577 (Ont. S.C.).

Schollum, M. (2005). *Investigative interviewing: The literature.* Wellington, NZ: Police National Headquarters. New Zealand Police. http://www.police.govt.nz/resources/2005/investigative-interviewing/index.html.

Schuster v. Royal & Sun Alliance Insurance Co. of Canada. (2009). [2009] O.J. No. 4518, 2009 CanLII 58971 (Ont. S.C.).

Schwartz, R. v. (1988). [1988] 2 S.C.R. 443.

Scott, R. v. (2002). 2002 CanLII 44950 (Ont. C.A.).

Seaboyer, R. v.; Gayme, R. v. (1991). [1991] 2 S.C.R. 577.

Seguin, R. (2006, December 22). Mentally handicapped Quebec man receives millions for injustice. *The Globe and Mail.* http://www.theglobeandmail.com/news/national/mentally-handicapped-quebec-man-receives-millions-for-injustice/article862837.

Shepherd, E. (2007). *Investigative interviewing: The conversation management approach.* Oxford: Oxford University Press.

Sherriff, S. (2003). *Convicting the guilty: A strategy manual of law and technique for dedicated investigators and prosecutors combating major crime* (10th ed.). Toronto: Steve Sherriff. (Restricted publication available from Steve Sherriff, Office of the Crown Counsel, Peel Region, Ontario.)

Silveira, R. v. (1995). [1995] 2 S.C.R. 297.

Sinclair, R. v. (2010). 2010 SCC 35, [2010] 2 S.C.R. 310.

Singh, R. v. (2007). 2007 SCC 48, [2007] 3 S.C.R. 405.

Singh, R. v. (2008). 2008 ONCJ 306 (CanLII).

Singh, R. v. (2010). 2010 ONSC 1945 (CanLII).

Skinnider, E. (2005). *The art of confessions: A comparative look at the law of confessions—Canada, England, the United States and Australia.* Vancouver: International Centre for Criminal Justice Reform and Criminal Justice Policy. http://www.icclr.law.ubc.ca/publications/reports/es%20paper%20confessions%20revised.pdf.

Small, P. (2009, January 6). The art of cross-examination. *Toronto Star.* thestar.com. http://www.thestar.com/article/562179.

Smith, R. v. (1989). [1989] 2 S.C.R. 368, 50 C.C.C. (3d) 308, 71 C.R. (3d) 129.

Smith, R. v. (1991). [1991] 1 S.C.R. 714, 63 C.C.C. (3d) 313, 4 C.R. (4th) 125.

Smith, R. v. (1992). [1992] 2 S.C.R. 915.

Smith, R. v. (2009). 2009 SKCA 38 (CanLII).

Smith, R. v. (2011). [2011] E.W.C.A. Crim. 1296.

Smyth, R. v. (2006). 2006 CanLII 52358 (Ont. S.C.).

Snook, B., Eastwood, J., Stinson, M., Tedeschini, J., & House, J. (2010, April). Reforming investigative interviewing in Canada. *Canadian Journal of Criminology and Criminal Justice, 52*(2), 215–229.

Sophonow, Thomas, inquiry regarding. (2001). See Cory, P. (2001).

Sorg, M.H. (2005). Forensic anthropology. In S.H. James & J.J. Nordby (Eds.), *Forensic science: An introduction to scientific and investigative techniques* (2nd ed.). Boca Raton, FL: CRC Press.

Sossin, L. (2008). Accountability and oversight for death investigations in Ontario. Sossin PFP inquiry paper: Oversight & accountability. http://www.attorneygeneral.jus.gov.on.ca/inquiries/goudge/policy_research/pdf/Sossin_Accountability-and-Oversight.pdf.

Spencer, R. v. (2007). 2007 SCC 11, [2007] 1 S.C.R. 500.

Starr, R. v. (2000). 147 C.C.C. (3d) 449.

Starrs, J.E. (2005). Foreword. In S.H. James & J.J. Nordby (Eds.), *Forensic science: An introduction to scientific and investigative techniques* (2nd ed., pp. v–xi). Boca Raton, FL: CRC Press.

Statistics Canada. (2007). Canadian Centre of Justice Studies. *Police resources in Canada, 2007.* Catalogue no. 85-225-XIE. http://dsp-psd.pwgsc.gc.ca/collection_2007/statcan/85-225-X/85-225-XIE2007000.pdf.

Statistics Canada. (2011a). Deaths and age-standardized mortality rate, by province and territory (deaths, 2003 to 2007). http://www40.statcan.ca/l01/cst01/HLTH86A-eng.htm.

Statistics Canada. (2011b). Homicide in Canada, 2009. http://www.statcan.gc.ca/daily-quotidien/101026/dq101026a-eng.htm.

Stein, L.M., & Memon, A. (2006). Testing the efficacy of the cognitive interview in a developing country. *Applied Cognitive Psychology, 20,* 597–605.

Stillman, R. v. (1997). [1997] 1 S.C.R. 607.

Stinchcombe, R. v. (1991). [1991] 3 S.C.R. 326.

Stirling, R. v. (2008). 2008 SCC 10, [2008] 1 S.C.R. 272.

Strachan, R. v. (1988). [1988] 2 S.C.R. 980, 46 C.C.C. (3d) 479, 67 C.R. (3d) 87.

Stuesser, L. (2005). *An advocacy primer* (3rd ed.). Toronto: Thomson Carswell.

Stutler, T. (1997, September). Cross-examination strategies for law enforcement. *FBI Law Enforcement Bulletin,* pp. 1–5.

St-Yves, M. (2006). The psychology of rapport: Five basic rules. In T. Williamson (Ed.), *Investigative interviewing: Rights, research, regulation* (pp. 87–106). Cullompton, UK: Willan Publishing.

Suberu, R. v. (2009). 2009 SCC 33, [2009] 2 S.C.R. 460.

Sweet, D., & Hildebrand, D. (1999). Saliva from cheese bite yields DNA profile of burglar: A case report. *International Journal of Legal Medicine, 112*(3), 201–203.

Sweet, D., & Shutler, G.G. (1999). Analysis of salivary DNA evidence from a bite mark on a body submerged in water. *Journal of Forensic Sciences, 44*(5), 1069–1072.

Sweet, D., Hildebrand, D., & Phillips, D. (1999). Identification of a skeleton using DNA from teeth and a PAP smear. *Journal of Forensic Sciences, 44*(3), 630–633.

Sweet, D., Lorente, M., Lorente, J.A., Valenzuela, A., & Villanueva, E. (1997). An improved method to recover saliva from human skin: The double swab technique. *Journal of Forensic Sciences, 42*(2), 320–322.

Sweet, D.J., & Sweet, C.H. (1995). DNA analysis of dental pulp to link incinerated remains of homicide victim to crime scene. *Journal of Forensic Sciences, 40*(2), 310—314.

Szibor, R., Schubert, C., Schoning, R., Krause, D., & Wendt, U. (1998). Pollen analysis reveals murder season. *Nature, 395*(6701), 449–450.

T

Taillefer, R. v.; Duguay, R. v. (2003). 2003 SCC 70, [2003] 3 S.C.R. 307.

Taleb, N. (2007). *The black swan: The impact of the highly improbable.* New York: Random House.

Technical Working Group on Crime Scene Investigation. (2000). *Crime scene investigation: A guide for law enforcement.* Washington, DC: U.S. Department of Justice.

Teerhuis-Moar, R. v. (2011). 263 C.C.C. (3d) 100 (Man. C.A.).

Tessling, R. v. (2004). 2004 SCC 67, [2004] 3 S.C.R. 432.

The Canadian Press. (2011, May 13). Four Mounties charged with perjury in Dziekanski case. *The Globe and Mail.* http://www.theglobeandmail.com/news/national/british-columbia/four-mounties-charged-with-perjury-in-dziekanski-case/article2020699.

Thomas, L. (1974). Trial and error. In *The Medusa and the snail* (pp. 36–40). Middlesex, UK: Penguin Books.

Tillman, W.L. (1987). Automated gunshot residue particle search and characterization. *Journal of Forensic Sciences, 32,* 62–71.

Transport Canada. (2011). Canadian motor vehicle traffic collision statistics: 2009. Transport Canada. http://www.tc.gc.ca/eng/roadsafety/tp-tp3322-2009-1173.htm.

Tremblay, R. v. (1987). [1987] 2 S.C.R. 435, 37 C.C.C. (3d) 565.

Trochym, R. v. (2007). 2007 SCC 6, [2007] 1 S.C.R. 239.

Tumram, N.K., Bardale, R.V., & Dongre, A.P. (2011). Post-mortem analysis of synovial fluid and vitreous humour for determination of death interval: A comparative study. *Forensic Science International, 204*(1–3), 186–190.

Turtle, J.W., & Yuille, J.C. (1994). Lost but not forgotten details: Repeated eyewitness recall leads to reminiscence but not hypermnesia. *Journal of Applied Psychology, 79,* 260–271.

U

Underwood, R.H. (1997). The limits of cross-examination, 1997-1998. *American Journal of Trial Advocacy, 21,* 113–129.

Uphoff, R. (2006). Convicting the innocent: Aberration or systemic problem? *Wisconsin Law Review, 26*(2), 739–842.

U.S. Department of Justice. (2004). NIJ Special Report, *Forensic examination of digital evidence: A guide for law enforcement.* Washington, DC: Office of Justice Programs, National Institute of Justice. https://www.ncjrs.gov/pdffiles1/nij/199408.pdf.

U.S. Department of Justice. (2006). Federal Bureau of Investigation, Criminal Justice Information Services Division. *Crime in the United States.* http://www2.fbi.gov/ucr/cius2006/offenses/clearances/index.html.

U.S. Department of Justice, Office of the Inspector General. (2006). *A review of the FBI's handling of the Brandon Mayfield case.* Washington, DC: U.S. Department of Justice. http://www.justice.gov/oig/special/s0601/final.pdf ("OIG Report").

V

Van Allen, B. (2012). *Criminal investigation: In search of the truth* (2nd ed.). Toronto: Pearson Canada.

Van Brocklin, V. (2009). Ten tips for winning courtroom confrontations. *RCMP Gazette, 40,* 69–105.

Vital Statistics Act. (1990). R.R.O. 1990, Reg. 1094.

Vrij, A. (2008). *Detecting lies and deceit: Pitfalls and opportunities* (2nd ed.). Chichester, UK: Wiley.

Vrij, A., Mann, S., Kristin, S., & Fisher, R. (2007). Cues to deception and ability to detect lies as a function of police interview styles. *Law and Human Behavior, 31,* 499–518.

Vu, R. v. (2010). 2010 BCSC 1260.

W

Wain, A., & Linacre, A. (2009). Bloodstain pattern analysis. In J. Fraser & R. Williams (Eds.), *Handbook of forensic science* (pp. 229–253). Devon, UK: Willan Publishing.

Walsh, D., & Bull, R. (2010). What really is effective in interviews with suspects? A study comparing interviewing skills against interviewing outcomes. *Legal and Criminological Psychology, 15*(2), 305–321.

Wason, P.C. (1960). On the failure to eliminate hypotheses in a conceptual task. *The Quarterly Journal of Experimental Psychology, 12*(3), 129–140.

Waterfield, R. v. (1963). [1964] 1 Q.B. 164, [1963] 3 All E.R. 659.

Watts, D. (2007). *Watts manual of criminal evidence.* Toronto: Thomson Carswell.

Weider, B., & Harry, J. (1999). Activation analyses of authenticated hairs of Napoleon Bonaparte confirm arsenic poisoning. *American Journal of Forensic Medicine and Pathology, 20*(4), 378–382.

Wellford, C., & Cronin, J. (2000, April). Clearing up homicide clearance rates. *National Institute of Justice Journal.* National Criminal Justice Reference Service (NCJRS). http://www.ncjrs.gov/pdffiles1/jr000243b.pdf.

Wellman, F. (1997). *The art of cross-examination* (4th ed.). New York: Touchstone.

"We're not the experts": Police call doctor to certify headless corpse is dead. (2011, April 26). *London Evening Standard.* http://www.thisislondon.co.uk/news/were-not-the-experts-police-call-doctor-to-certify-headless-corpse-is-dead-6395659.html.

Wigmore on evidence. (1990). As adopted in *R. v. Meddoui* (1990), 61 C.C.C. (3d) 345 (Alta. C.A.).

Wigmore, J. (1904). *Treatise on the Anglo-American system of evidence in trials at common law* (Chadbourne, Rev. ed., 1974) (Vol. 5, p. 32, para. 1367).

Wigmore, J.H. (1961). *Evidence in trials at common law* (Vol. 8, Rev. ed., J.T. McNaughton, Ed.). Boston: Little, Brown.

Wilkins, K., & Shields, M. (2008, June). Correlates of medication error in hospitals. *Health Reports, 19*(2), 7–18. Statistics Canada, Catalogue no. 82-003-XPE. Statistics Canada. http://www.statcan.gc.ca/pub/82-003-x/82-003-x2008002-eng.pdf.

Willier, R. v. (2010). 2010 SCC 37, [2010] 2 S.C.R. 429.

Wills, R. v. (1992). 1992 CanLII 2780, 70 C.C.C. (3d) 529 (Ont. C.A.).

Winchester, R. v. (2010). 2010 ONSC 652 (CanLII).

Woolmington v. Director of Public Prosecutions. (1935). [1935] A.C. 462 H.L.(E).

Wray, The Queen v. (1970). [1971] S.C.R. 272, 4 C.C.C. 1.

Y

Younger, I. (1975, Summer). The ten commandments of cross-examination. Lecture delivered to the National Institute for Trial Advocacy's National Session, Boulder, CO. National Institute for Trial Advocacy. http://thenitablog.blogspot.com/2008/05/ten-commandments-of-cross-examination.html.

Index

W